PRIMARY SOURCEBOOK SERIES

THE
COLD
WAR

PRIMARY SOURCEBOOK SERIES

THE
COLD
WAR

Kevin Hillstrom

Foreword by
Christian Ostermann
Director, Cold War International History Project

Omnigraphics

615 Griswold, Detroit MI 48226

Omnigraphics, Inc.

Kevin Hillstrom, *Series Editor*
Cherie D. Abbey, *Managing Editor*

Peter E. Ruffner, *Publisher*
Frederick G. Ruffner, Jr., *Chairman*
Matthew P. Barbour, *Senior Vice President*

Kay Gill, *Vice President – Directories*
Elizabeth Barbour, *Research and Permissions Coordinator*
David P. Bianco, *Marketing Director*
Leif Gruenberg, *Development Manager*
Kevin Hayes, *Operations Manager*

Barry Puckett, *Librarian*
Cherry Stockdale, *Permissions Assistant*
Shirley Amore, Kevin Glover, Martha Johns, Kirk Kauffman, Angelesia Thorington, *Administrative Staff*

The Cold War / Kevin Hillstrom, editor.
    p. cm. -- (Primary sourcebook series)
    Summary: "Examines the Cold War and its impact on America, the Soviet Union, and the world. Features include narrative overviews of key events and trends, 100+ primary source documents, chronology, glossary, bibliography, and subject index""--Provided by publisher.
    Includes bibliographical references and index.
    ISBN 0-7808-0934-3 (hardcover : alk. paper) 1. Cold War--Sources 2. World politics--1945-1989--Sources 3. World politics--1985-1995--Sources. I. Hillstrom, Kevin. II. Series.
    D839.3.C55 2006
    909.82'5--dc22

    2006015330

TABLE OF CONTENTS

FOREWORD

The military and political-ideological confrontation between the United States and the Soviet Union that came to be called the "Cold War" shaped the history of the second half of the 20ᵗʰ century. Global in its reach, often violent in its near fifty-year career, and with profound impact on societies from northeast Asia to central America to southern Africa, it came to a sudden and surprisingly peaceful end in 1989/1991. Though in the post-September 11, 2001, world it increasingly seems a distant, curiously artificial historical construct, its legacy lingers on today in "hot spots" from Afghanistan to North Korea.

No wonder then that there has been no end to the debate over what the Cold War was all about, how and why it came about, and why it lasted as long as it did. The end of the conflict has meant that the scholarly debate over the Cold War has become less politicized: While it was going on, the scholarly debate in the United States often reflected the larger political debate over American foreign policy at the time. Now the history of the Cold War can be told as "history," and with the knowledge about its outcome in mind—though that has not necessarily made getting the story right any easier.

What has made perhaps the most dramatic difference in how we think about the Cold War are the new sources that have become accessible in the wake of the conflict's end. Until 1989/91, almost all serious historical writing on the Cold War was based on Western—in particular American—documents, which were being declassified in the U.S. and Western European archives since the 1970s by the thousands. Even more have become available since the end of the conflict. When it came to analyzing Soviet or Communist views or behavior—the perspective and actions of what we used to call "the other side"—scholars at the time had to rely on newspapers and public statements, the occasional smuggled-out document, and Western intelligence estimates (of uncertain accuracy). Archives under the Communist regimes of the Soviet bloc were tightly closed to researchers—Soviet bloc citizens and Western researchers alike. We hence looked at the dynamics of the Cold War only through the eyes of Western observers at the time, through the documents they left behind, and this inevitably resulted in an incomplete, one-sided view of what actually occurred.

With the fall of the Communist regimes in Eastern Europe, and the disintegration of the Soviet Union and these countries' transition to democracy, the archives of the former Communist world started to become available. Documents from the government and Communist party archives of the former Communist "camp," some of which are contained in this document reader, now allow us to be a "fly on the wall" in the discussions in Stalin's Kremlin or in Warsaw Pact embassies from East Berlin to Pyongyang, and to understand better how Communist leaders looked at the world—and at us in the West. As a result, a new *international* history of the "Cold War" is emerging, a history that takes into account the perspectives of all sides of the conflict. Such a new history can not only show us more accurately the motives, perceptions, and choices behind U.S. foreign policy, but also its impact and consequences, many of which continue to shape the world we face today.

Christian Friedrich Ostermann
Director, Cold War International History Project

PREFACE

The *Primary Sourcebook Series* has been created to provide students and other users with an overview of the most important and influential eras, events, and movements of the modern world. The *Series* seeks to meet this goal by assembling a wide cross-section of the most historic and illuminating primary documents on these subjects. Primary source materials featured in each volume of the *Series* include treaties, speeches, legislation, diplomatic dispatches, journalism, editorials, personal correspondence, government reports, memoirs, and oral histories.

The documents featured in each volume of *Primary Sourcebook* Series are supplemented by narrative features—chapter overviews and document-specific introductory pieces—that place each document within its historical context. This context is essential for readers to understand the full significance of these documents and competently interpret for themselves the meaning of the eras and events that shaped the world they live in today.

Arrangement of the Work

Primary Sourcebook Series: The Cold War assembles more than 100 primary documents to help users gain a greater understanding of this pivotal era in world history. These primary source materials are distributed among fourteen chapters, arranged roughly in chronological order. Each of these chapters, beginning with "The End of World War II and the Descent of the Iron Curtain" and concluding with "Russia and the World in the Post-Cold War Era," focuses on a specific topic or event within the larger historical period under discussion.

Each of these chapters begins with an introductory overview that provides readers with the background information they need to understand the significance of the documents selected for inclusion. In essence, these chapter overviews introduce the main players, events, and themes that will be illuminated in the documents to come.

Each chapter then moves on to the documents themselves. Every document featured in *The Cold War* is preceded by a brief introduction that provides additional background on the origins and significance of that particular document. The documents themselves include source materials that are universally recognized as essential to any meaningful study of the Cold War. But they also include works that were chosen for inclusion because they provide readers with glimpses into the perspectives of both national leaders and ordinary citizens in the East and West. Chapter Five, for example, entitled "Behind the Curtain," examines events in the Soviet empire during the 1950s; its featured documents include both an excerpt from Nikita Khrushchev's famous 1956 speech denouncing Stalinism and an excerpt from a 1950s-era prison memoir penned by a survivor of Romania's totalitarian regime.

Since each of the enclosed chapters focuses on a significant topic in its own right, the chapters have a user-friendly, stand-alone quality to them. Taken together, however, the chapters tell a much larger, but thoroughly coherent story. Strung together like historical beads, they can guide readers through the world's most momentous historical events.

Other valuable features included in *Primary Sourcebook Series: The Cold War* include:

- Glossary of important Cold War figures and terms.
- Detailed Chronology of events with a *see reference* feature. Under this arrangement, events listed in the chronology include page references to relevant primary documents featured in the book.
- Extensive bibliography of works consulted in the creation of this book, including books, periodicals, Internet sites, and videotape materials.
- A Subject Index.

Document Selection

In approaching historical subjects of great size and scope, it is impossible to assemble a truly comprehensive selection of primary documents in a single book. Inevitably, some worthwhile material is left out due to space constraints. What we set out to do, then, was to bring together a representative sampling of primary source materials that provides a framework for understanding the major political, social, and economic currents that shaped the era being studied. These source materials run the gamut from what might be termed "official views"—treaties, speeches, legislation, diplomatic dispatches, newspaper coverage, and doctrinal pronouncements—to documents that bring the "human" side of history to life, such as personal correspondence, memoirs, and oral histories. Blended together, these disparate materials form a fascinating narrative that can provide the basis for both lively, informed debate and somber reflection.

Similarly, excerpting a document is a delicate undertaking, for one never wishes to alter the meaning of the original source. In instances where we have chosen to publish excerpts instead of the full text of documents, we have taken care to excerpt representative sections of the featured document and to focus on the portions of text that are most relevant to Cold War studies. All excerpts are clearly labeled as such.

In closing, we believe that the *Primary Sourcebook Series* will give readers a greater appreciation for the importance of history and its impact on their lives. It will also sharpen their capacity to analyze and interpret materials that often provide conflicting perspectives on major historical events, causes, and individuals. Finally, we hope that the series will motivate users to seek out even more information on the rich and fascinating tapestry of people, places, and events that have brought us to this point in our collective history.

Editor's Note: This volume includes quoted material containing offensive language and epithets. We regret any pain or discomfort created by the inclusion of this material. We feel, however, that the inclusion of this material will help users more fully understand the views and emotions of the people who lived through and shaped the Cold War era.

Acknowledgements

The series editors would like to thank Cold War scholar Christian F. Ostermann for providing the foreword for this volume. Mr. Ostermann is director of the Woodrow Wilson Center's Cold War International History Project and editor of *Uprising in East Germany, 1953* (2001).

This series was developed in consultation with a distinguished Advisory Board comprised of public librarians, school librarians, and educators. The editors would like to extend their appreciation to the following Board members:

Melissa C. Bergin, L.M.S., NBCT
Library Media Specialist
Niskayuna High School
Niskayuna, NY

Linda Garrett, M.L.I.S.
Librarian
Crestwood High School
Dearborn Heights, MI

Nancy Larsen, M.L.S., M.S. Ed.
Library Media Specialist
Clarkston High School
Clarkston, MI

Rosemary Orlando, M.L.I.S.
Library Director
St. Clair Shores Public Library
St. Clair Shores, MI

Comments and Suggestions

We welcome your comments on the *Primary Sourcebook Series*, including suggestions for topics that you would like to see covered in future volumes. Correspondence should be addressed to:

Editor, *Primary Sourcebook Series*
Omnigraphics, Inc.
615 Griswold
Detroit, MI 48226
E-mail: editorial@omnigraphics.com

THE COLD WAR

There are at the present time two great nations in the world, which started from different points, but seem to tend towards the same end: I allude to the Russians and the Americans…. The Anglo-American relies upon personal interest to accomplish his ends and gives free scope to the unguided strength and common sense of the people. The Russian centers all the authority of society in a single arm. The principle instrument of the former is freedom; of the latter, servitude. Their starting point is different and their courses are not the same, yet each of them seems marked out by the will of Heaven to sway the destinies of half the globe.

—Alexis de Tocqueville, Democracy in America, 1835

During the second half of the twentieth century, world events were shaped in large measure by the "Cold War," a grim competition that pitted the United States and its allies against the Soviet Union and its satellites in a struggle for global dominance. This battle was waged between nations that were armed not only with massive armies and weapons of apocalyptic power, but also with economic and political systems that they saw as morally superior to those of the other side. Leaders in both the White House and the Kremlin were convinced that the future of the planet hinged on their capacity to advance their own blueprint for world development and stop their adversary from doing the same. As far as these policymakers, diplomats, and generals were concerned, the stakes of the Cold War could not have been higher.

Not surprisingly, then, the Cold War conflict shaped the economic, cultural, and political fabric of both the West and the Soviet bloc for the better part of five decades. In addition, the Cold War left its mark on virtually every other corner of the globe. Europe was divided into two hostile camps by the conflict. Even regions of the world that lay thousands of miles from Moscow and Washington, D.C., such as Southeast Asia, sub-Saharan Africa, and Latin America, were left forever changed by the long shadow of the Cold War.

This state of affairs endured for half a century, ending only with the sudden and spectacular collapse of the Soviet empire in 1991. Today, Communist governments hold power in only a handful of nations around the globe. And even in Communist strongholds like China, experiments with capitalism and democratic reforms are on the rise. But the Cold War lingers in the hearts and minds of millions of people around the globe. And looking back on those years of fear and suspicion, more than a few observers openly marvel at the number of times American and Soviet leaders marched to the brink of nuclear war before turning away.

1

THE END OF WORLD WAR II AND THE DESCENT OF THE IRON CURTAIN

British Prime Minister Winston Churchill (left), U.S. President Franklin D. Roosevelt (center), and Soviet Premier Joseph Stalin (right) at the 1945 Yalta Summit, where they struggled to hammer out a postwar blueprint for the world.

INTRODUCTION

The roots of the Cold War can be traced to the final months of World War II. At that time, the Allied powers began negotiating the postwar future of Germany, Poland, and other European nations left battered by the war. By the time Germany surrendered on May 7, 1945, many of the continent's major cities had been bombed into smoking ruins, and millions of desperate Europeans had been uprooted from their homes.

The Yalta Summit

The first major gathering of Allied leaders took place in February 1945 in the Soviet city of Yalta on the shores of the Black Sea. Soviet leader Joseph Stalin, British Prime Minister Winston Churchill, and American President Franklin D. Roosevelt entered the Yalta Summit in good spirits, cheered and relieved by the prospect of an imminent German defeat.

Over the next several days, Churchill and Roosevelt made a special effort to establish a tone of good will and cooperation with Stalin. This attitude stemmed in large part from American and British sympathy for the horrifying losses suffered by the Soviet Union in the war—25 million dead, another 25 million left homeless, and enormous devastation to its agricultural and industrial capacity. These Soviet losses were so great that the United States and Great Britain temporarily set aside their deep hostility to the Soviet political system. At that time, the Soviet Union was governed by a Communist system that had been wrenched into violent life by Vladimir Lenin and the Bolshevik Revolution of 1917. Under Stalin's leadership, the Communist government had grown into a brutal, totalitarian regime. But in the war against Nazi Germany, the Soviets had carried the heaviest burden of fighting of all the Allied powers, and this sacrifice could not be ignored.

The Allied leaders emerged from the Yalta Summit with tentative agreements on a range of diplomatic issues. Roosevelt advisor Harry Hopkins later admitted that the atmosphere there was so conciliatory that "we really believed in our hearts that this was the dawn of the new day we had all been praying for." Within months of Yalta, however, the spirit of compromise and mutual respect that seemed so strong there had all but disappeared.

On April 12, 1945, Franklin D. Roosevelt died and Vice President Harry S. Truman was sworn in as the nation's thirty-third president. Germany formally surrendered one month later, triggering euphoric celebrations across America and Western Europe and rampant looting and raping by Red Army troops in eastern Berlin. During this same period, Stalin moved quickly to install Communist governments in other areas of Eastern Europe that had fallen under Soviet control during the final months of the war.

The Potsdam Conference

On July 17 the new American president met with Churchill and Stalin at Potsdam, a war-battered suburb of Berlin. They planned to discuss their remaining differences and establish a postwar blueprint for the world. Over the course of this historic two-week conference (during which Churchill was replaced by new British Prime Minister Clement Attlee), U.S. and British negotiators reluctantly agreed to recognize a Soviet-sponsored regime in Poland. The Allied leaders also unveiled the Potsdam Declaration, which warned a defiant Japan to surrender to the Allies or face total destruction.

Negotiators at Potsdam also hammered out a compromise on Germany's political and economic future. Under this plan, Germany and its capital, Berlin, were divided into four occupation zones to be administered by France, Great Britain, the United States, and the Soviet Union. This fateful decision paved the way for Germany's eventual partition into two parts: West Germany, which was administered by France, Great Britain, and the United States and developed a democratic form of government; and East Germany, which was administered by the Soviet Union and developed a Communist form of government. Similarly, the capital city of Berlin was divided into western and eastern sectors. These developments made Berlin a focus of Cold War tensions for the next four decades.

Despite these diplomatic agreements, though, American and British suspicion of Stalin intensified after the Potsdam Summit. Even before the conference, American and British analysts had voiced deep uneasiness about the Soviet Union's aggressive actions in Eastern Europe. Soviet behavior during and after Potsdam did nothing to calm their fears. By the end of the year many Western diplomats were convinced that Stalin was intent on a course of relentless Communist expansion.

On August 6, 1945, the United States dropped an atomic bomb on the Japanese city of Hiroshima. Two days later Stalin hurriedly declared war on the Japanese; he hoped to position the USSR to lay claim to some of the territory that would come with Japan's defeat. But the Soviet move came too late for Stalin to make meaningful territorial gains anywhere but in Manchuria. On August 9 the Americans detonated a second atomic bomb on the city of Nagasaki. The Japanese surrendered five days later, bringing World War II to a sudden and decisive end.

The conclusion of the war ushered in a new era of global history. After all, the European nations that had long taken the lead in directing world affairs had all been devastated by World War II. "There is complete economic, social, and political collapse going on in central Europe, the extent of which is unparalleled in history unless one goes back to the collapse of the Roman Empire," wrote one aide to U.S. Secretary of War Henry Stimson in 1945. Both the United States and the Soviet Union rushed to fill this void.

The Cold War Begins

Each nation had been wounded by World War II, but each had emerged from the conflict with greater confidence than before. And each was now certain that it was best equipped to lead the world forward into the second half of the twentieth century. This budding rivalry for world leadership—combined with their very different political and economic systems—made it virtually inevitable that the two nations would come to regard each other with undisguised distrust and suspicion.

Soviet-American relations continued to worsen in late 1945 and early 1946. By the end of 1945 much of eastern Europe was under the control of repressive Communist regimes that were loyal to the Kremlin. Pro-Soviet forces had even carved a new nation, Azerbaijan, out of northern Iran. Meanwhile, the deepening divide between the United States and the Soviet Union assumed ever-deeper philosophical overtones. In February 1946, Stalin delivered a widely publicized speech in which he described the capitalist philosophy of the West as morally bankrupt. "The development of world capitalism proceeds not in the path of smooth and even progress but through crisis and the catastrophes of war," he proclaimed. To many listeners in Washington and London, these words seemed to breathe new life into Lenin's famous prediction that "as long as capitalism and socialism exist, we cannot live in peace; in the end, one or the other will triumph. A funeral dirge will be sung either over the Soviet Republic or over Capitalism."

By 1946 the leading architects of foreign policy in both the United States and Great Britain believed that stopping Soviet expansion was the West's top priority. One of the State Department's leading Soviet experts, George F. Kennan, outlined this doctrine of "Communist containment" in a famous February 1946 memorandum known as the "Long Telegram." Kennan's report characterized Communist leaders as "committed fanatically to the belief that … it is desirable and necessary that the internal harmony of our [American] society be disrupted, our traditional way of life be destroyed, the international authority of our state be broken, if Soviet power is to be secure." Kennan also claimed that an epic struggle between democracy and communism was fast approaching. He asserted that the only way for the United States to prevail in this conflict was to firmly oppose all Soviet efforts to expand their global reach. This telegram took Washington by storm, and its "containment" message became the cornerstone of American policy toward the Soviet Union for the duration of the Cold War.

Others soon echoed Kennan's sentiments, but more publicly. In March 1946, for example, Winston Churchill delivered his "Sinews of Peace" speech at Westminster College in Fulton, Missouri. In this address, Churchill simultaneously urged the United States to focus on Europe's many wounds and warned that the Soviet Union was building an "iron curtain" of Communist, totalitarian governments across the heart of Europe. Churchill's blunt words met with disapproval from some war-weary Americans, but in Washington, London, and Moscow they confirmed the widespread feeling that a showdown was looming.

DOCUMENTS

1.1
The Yalta Summit – 1945
Protocol of the Proceedings of the Crimea Conference

*As World War II entered its final stages, Soviet leader Joseph Stalin, British
Prime Minister Winston Churchill, and American President Franklin D.
Roosevelt held a summit in Yalta, a Soviet city perched on the Crimean
Peninsula on the shores of the Black Sea. During this summit, which was
held from February 4-11, 1945, the "Big Three" Allied leaders hammered
out an agreement on Europe's postwar reorganization. The Yalta agreement
was initially hailed as a symbol of postwar cooperation, but many scholars
and lawmakers have since described it as a flawed document that contained
too many concessions to the Soviet Union. These experts are especially critical of American and British concessions to the Soviets on the issue of
Poland, which the Kremlin was determined to bring under the Communist
umbrella. Excerpts of the Yalta Agreement follow below.*

Protocol of Proceedings of Crimea Conference

The Crimea Conference of the heads of the Governments of the United States of
America, the United Kingdom, and the Union of Soviet Socialist Republics, which
took place from Feb. 4 to 11, came to the following conclusions:

I. WORLD ORGANIZATION

It was decided:

1. That a United Nations conference on the proposed world organization
should be summoned for Wednesday, 25 April, 1945, and should be held in the
United States of America.

2. The nations to be invited to this conference should be: (a) the United
Nations as they existed on 8 Feb., 1945; and (b) Such of the Associated Nations as
have declared war on the common enemy by 1 March, 1945. (For this purpose, by
the term "Associated Nations" was meant the eight Associated Nations and Turkey.)
When the conference on world organization is held, the delegates of the United
Kingdom and United States of America will support a proposal to admit to original
membership two Soviet Socialist Republics, i.e., the Ukraine and White Russia.

3. That the United States Government, on behalf of the three powers, should consult the Government of China and the French Provisional Government in regard to decisions taken at the present conference concerning the proposed world organization.

4. That the text of the invitation to be issued to all the nations which would take part in the United Nations conference should be as follows:

"The Government of the United States of America, on behalf of itself and of the Governments of the United Kingdom, the Union of Soviet Socialistic Republics and the Republic of China and of the Provisional Government of the French Republic invite the Government of —————— to send representatives to a conference to be held on 25 April, 1945, or soon thereafter, at San Francisco, in the United States of America, to prepare a charter for a general international organization for the maintenance of international peace and security.

"The above-named Governments suggest that the conference consider as affording a basis for such a Charter the proposals for the establishment of a general international organization which were made public last October as a result of the Dumbarton Oaks conference and which have now been supplemented by the following provisions for Section C of Chapter VI:

C. Voting

1. Each member of the Security Council should have one vote.

2. Decisions of the Security Council on procedural matters should be made by an affirmative vote of seven members.

3. Decisions of the Security Council on all matters should be made by an affirmative vote of seven members, including the concurring votes of the permanent members; provided that, in decisions under Chapter VIII, Section A and under the second sentence of Paragraph 1 of Chapter VIII, Section C, a party to a dispute should abstain from voting.

Territorial trusteeship:

It was agreed that the five nations which will have permanent seats on the Security Council should consult each other prior to the United Nations conference on the question of territorial trusteeship.

The acceptance of this recommendation is subject to its being made clear that territorial trusteeship will only apply to:

(a) existing mandates of the League of Nations; (b) territories detached from the enemy as a result of the present war; (c) any other territory which might voluntarily be placed under trusteeship; and (d) no discussion of actual territories is contemplated at the forthcoming United Nations conference or in the preliminary consultations, and it will be a matter for subsequent agreement which territories within the above categories will be place under trusteeship.

II. DECLARATION OF LIBERATED EUROPE

The following declaration has been approved:

The Premier of the Union of Soviet Socialist Republics, the Prime Minister of the United Kingdom and the President of the United States of America have consulted with each other in the common interests of the people of their countries and those of liberated Europe. They jointly declare their mutual agreement to concert during the temporary period of instability in liberated Europe the policies of their three Governments in assisting the peoples liberated from the domination of Nazi Germany and the peoples of the former Axis satellite states of Europe to solve by democratic means their pressing political and economic problems.

The establishment of order in Europe and the rebuilding of national economic life must be achieved by processes which will enable the liberated peoples to destroy the last vestiges of nazism and fascism and to create democratic institutions of their own choice. This is a principle of the Atlantic Charter—the right of all people to choose the form of government under which they will live—the restoration of sovereign rights and self-government to those peoples who have been forcibly deprived to them by the aggressor nations.

To foster the conditions in which the liberated people may exercise these rights, the three governments will jointly assist the people in any European liberated state or former Axis state in Europe where, in their judgment conditions require,

(a) to establish conditions of internal peace; (b) to carry out emergency relief measures for the relief of distressed peoples; (c) to form interim governmental authorities broadly representative of all democratic elements in the population and pledged to the earliest possible establishment through free elections of Governments responsive to the will of the people; and (d) to facilitate where necessary the holding of such elections.

The three Governments will consult the other United Nations and provisional authorities or other Governments in Europe when matters of direct interest to them are under consideration.

When, in the opinion of the three Governments, conditions in any European liberated state or former Axis satellite in Europe make such action necessary, they will immediately consult together on the measure necessary to discharge the joint responsibilities set forth in this declaration.

By this declaration we reaffirm our faith in the principles of the Atlantic Charter, our pledge in the Declaration by the United Nations and our determination to build in cooperation with other peace-loving nations world order, under law, dedicated to peace, security, freedom and general well-being of all mankind.

In issuing this declaration, the three powers express the hope that the Provisional Government of the French Republic may be associated with them in the procedure suggested.

III. DISMEMBERMENT OF GERMANY

It was agreed that Article 12 (a) of the Surrender terms for Germany should be amended to read as follows:

"The United Kingdom, the United States of America and the Union of Soviet Socialist Republics shall possess supreme authority with respect to Germany. In the exercise of such authority they will take such steps, including the complete dismemberment of Germany as they deem requisite for future peace and security."

The study of the procedure of the dismemberment of Germany was referred to a committee consisting of Mr. Anthony Eden, Mr. John Winant, and Mr. Fedor T. Gusev. This body would consider the desirability of associating with it a French representative.

IV. ZONE OF OCCUPATION FOR THE FRENCH AND CONTROL COUNCIL FOR GERMANY

It was agreed that a zone in Germany, to be occupied by the French forces, should be allocated France. This zone would be formed out of the British and American zones and its extent would be settled by the British and Americans in consultation with the French Provisional Government.

It was also agreed that the French Provisional Government should be invited to become a member of the Allied Control Council for Germany.

V. REPARATION

The following protocol has been approved:

On the Talks Between the Heads of Three Governments at the Crimean Conference on the Question of the German Reparations in Kind

1. Germany must pay in kind for the losses caused by her to the Allied nations in the course of the war. Reparations are to be received in the first instance by those countries which have borne the main burden of the war, have suffered the heaviest losses and have organized victory over the enemy.

2. Reparation in kind is to be exacted from Germany in three following forms:

(a) Removals within two years from the surrender of Germany or the cessation of organized resistance from the national wealth of Germany located on the territory of Germany herself as well as outside her territory (equipment, machine tools, ships, rolling stock, German investments abroad, shares of industrial, transport and other enterprises in Germany, etc.), these removals to be carried out chiefly for the purpose of destroying the war potential of Germany. (b) Annual deliveries of goods from current production for a period to be fixed. (c) Use of German labor.

3. For the working out on the above principles of a detailed plan for exaction of reparation from Germany an Allied reparation commission will be set up in Moscow. It will consist of three representatives - one from the Union of Soviet Socialist Republics, one from the United Kingdom and one from the United States of America.

4. With regard to the fixing of the total sum of the reparation as well as the distribution of it among the countries which suffered from the German aggression, the Soviet and American delegations agreed as follows: "The Moscow reparation commission should take in its initial studies as a basis for discussion the suggestion of the Soviet Government that the total sum of the reparation in accordance with the points (a) and (b) of the Paragraph 2 should be 22 billion dollars and that 50 per cent should go to the Union of Soviet Socialist Republics." The British delegation was of the opinion that, pending consideration of the reparation question by the Moscow reparation commission, no figures of reparation should be mentioned. The above Soviet-American proposal has been passed to the Moscow reparation commission as one of the proposals to be considered by the commission.

VI. MAJOR WAR CRIMINALS

The conference agreed that the question of the major war criminals should be the subject of inquiry by the three Foreign Secretaries for report in due course after the close of the conference.

VII. POLAND

The following declaration on Poland was agreed by the conference:

"A new situation has been created in Poland as a result of her complete liberation by the Red Army. This calls for the establishment of a Polish Provisional Government which can be more broadly based than was possible before the recent liberation of the western part of Poland. The Provisional Government which is now functioning in Poland should therefore be reorganized on a broader democratic basis with the inclusion of democratic leaders from Poland itself and from Poles abroad. This new Government should then be called the Polish Provisional Government of National Unity.

"M. Molotov, Mr. Harriman and Sir A. Clark Kerr are authorized as a commission to consult in the first instance in Moscow with members of the present Provisional Government and with other Polish democratic leaders from within Poland and from abroad, with a view to the reorganization of the present Government along the above lines. This Polish Provisional Government of National Unity shall be pledged to the holding of free and unfettered elections as soon as possible on the basis of universal suffrage and secret ballot. In these elections all democratic and anti-Nazi parties shall have the right to take part and to put forward candidates.

"When a Polish Provisional of Government National Unity has been properly formed in conformity with the above, the Government of the U.S.S.R., which now maintains diplomatic relations with the present Provisional Government of Poland, and the Government of the United Kingdom and the Government of the United States of America will establish diplomatic relations with the new Polish Provisional Government National Unity, and will exchange Ambassadors by whose reports the respective Governments will be kept informed about the situation in Poland.

"The three heads of Government consider that the eastern frontier of Poland should follow the Curzon Line with digressions from it in some regions of five to eight kilometers in favor of Poland. They recognize that Poland must receive substantial accessions in territory in the north and west. They feel that the opinion of the new Polish Provisional Government of National Unity should be sought in due course of the extent of these accessions and that the final delimitation of the western frontier of Poland should thereafter await the peace conference."

VIII. YUGOSLAVIA

It was agreed to recommend to Marshal Tito and to Dr. Ivan Subasitch:

(a) That the Tito-Subasitch agreement should immediately be put into effect and a new government formed on the basis of the agreement. (b) That as soon as the new Government has been formed it should declare: (I) That the Anti-Fascist Assembly of the National Liberation (AVNOJ) will be extended to include members of the last Yugoslav Skupstina who have not compromised themselves by collaboration with the enemy, thus forming a body to be known as a temporary Parliament and (II) That legislative acts passed by the Anti-Fascist Assembly of the National Liberation (AVNOJ) will be subject to subsequent ratification by a Constituent Assembly; and that this statement should be published in the communiques of the conference.

IX. ITALO-YUGOSLAV FRONTIER - ITALO-AUSTRIAN FRONTIER

Notes on these subjects were put in by the British delegation and the American and Soviet delegations agreed to consider them and give their views later.

X. YUGOSLAV-BULGARIAN RELATIONS

There was an exchange of views between the Foreign Secretaries on the question of the desirability of a Yugoslav-Bulgarian pact of alliance. The question at issue was whether a state still under an armistice regime could be allowed to enter into a treaty with another state. Mr. Eden suggested that the Bulgarian and Yugoslav Governments should be informed that this could not be approved. Mr. Stettinius suggested that the British and American Ambassadors should discuss the matter further with Mr. Molotov in Moscow. Mr. Molotov agreed with the proposal of Mr. Stettinius.

XI. SOUTHEASTERN EUROPE

The British delegation put in notes for the consideration of their colleagues on the following subjects:

(a) The Control Commission in Bulgaria. (b) Greek claims upon Bulgaria, more particularly with reference to reparations. (c) Oil equipment in Rumania.

XII. IRAN

Mr. Eden, Mr. Stettinius and Mr. Molotov exchanged views on the situation in Iran. It was agreed that this matter should be pursued through the diplomatic channel.

XIII. MEETINGS OF THE THREE FOREIGN SECRETARIES

The conference agreed that permanent machinery should be set up for consultation between the three Foreign Secretaries; they should meet as often as necessary, probably about every three or four months.

These meetings will be held in rotation in the three capitals, the first meeting being held in London.

XIV. THE MONTREAUX CONVENTION AND THE STRAITS

It was agreed that at the next meeting of the three Foreign Secretaries to be held in London, they should consider proposals which it was understood the Soviet Government would put forward in relation to the Montreaux Convention, and report to their Governments. The Turkish Government should be informed at the appropriate moment. The forgoing protocol was approved and signed by the three Foreign Secretaries at the Crimean Conference February 11, 1945.

AGREEMENT REGARDING JAPAN

The leaders of the three great powers - the Soviet Union, the United States of America and Great Britain - have agreed that in two or three months after Germany has surrendered and the war in Europe is terminated, the Soviet Union shall enter into war against Japan on the side of the Allies on condition that:

1. The status quo in Outer Mongolia (the Mongolian People's Republic) shall be preserved.

2. The former rights of Russia violated by the treacherous attack of Japan in 1904 shall be restored, viz.: (a) The southern part of Sakhalin as well as the islands adjacent to it shall be returned to the Soviet Union; (b) The commercial port of Dairen shall be internationalized, the pre-eminent interests of the Soviet Union in this port being safeguarded, and the lease of Port Arthur as a naval base of the U.S.S.R. restored; (c) The Chinese-Eastern Railroad and the South Manchurian

Railroad, which provide an outlet to Dairen, shall be jointly operated by the establishment of a joint Soviet-Chinese company, it being understood that the pre-eminent interests of the Soviet Union shall be safeguarded and that China shall retain sovereignty in Manchuria;

3. The Kurile Islands shall be handed over to the Soviet Union.

It is understood that the agreement concerning Outer Mongolia and the ports and railroads referred to above will require concurrence of Generalissimo Chiang Kai-shek. The President will take measures in order to maintain this concurrence on advice from Marshal Stalin.

The heads of the three great powers have agreed that these claims of the Soviet Union shall be unquestionably fulfilled after Japan has been defeated. For its part, the Soviet Union expresses it readiness to conclude with the National Government of China a pact of friendship and alliance between the U.S.S.R. and China in order to render assistance to China with its armed forces for the purpose of liberating China from the Japanese yoke.

Source: "The Yalta Conference," February 1945. *A Decade of American Foreign Policy: Basic Documents, 1941-49.* Prepared at the Request of the Senate Committee on Foreign Relations By the Staff of the Committee and the Department of State. Washington, DC: Government Printing Office, 1950. Available online at the Avalon Project, Yale Law School, http://www.yale.edu/lawweb/avalon/wwii/yalta.htm.

1.2
The Potsdam Agreement – 1945
Protocol of the Proceedings of the Potsdam Conference

> *From July 17 to August 2, 1945, the leaders of the "Big Three" Allied powers—the United States, Great Britain, and the Soviet Union—held a summit at Potsdam, a suburb of Berlin, to build on the agreements reached at Yalta earlier that year. This summit reorganized Germany's institutions and economy and also produced a scheme to divide postwar Germany into four occupation zones, administered by Britain, France, the United States, and the Soviet Union. In addition, it included a stark warning to the Japanese to surrender to the Allies or risk total destruction.*

Protocol of the Proceedings, August l, 1945

The Berlin Conference of the Three Heads of Government of the U.S.S.R., U.S.A., and U.K., which took place from July 17 to August 2, 1945, came to the following conclusions…:

II. THE PRINCIPLES TO GOVERN THE TREATMENT OF GERMANY IN THE INITIAL CONTROL PERIOD.

16

A. POLITICAL PRINCIPLES.

1. In accordance with the Agreement on Control Machinery in Germany, supreme authority in Germany is exercised, on instructions from their respective Governments, by the Commanders-in-Chief of the armed forces of the United States of America, the United Kingdom, the Union of Soviet Socialist Republics, and the French Republic, each in his own zone of occupation, and also jointly, in matters affecting Germany as a whole, in their capacity as members of the Control Council.

2. So far as is practicable, there shall be uniformity of treatment of the German population throughout Germany.

3. The purposes of the occupation of Germany by which the Control Council shall be guided are:

(i) The complete disarmament and demilitarization of Germany and the elimination or control of all German industry that could be used for military production. To these ends:

(a) All German land, naval and air forces, the SS., SA., SD., and Gestapo, with all their organizations, staffs and institutions, including the General Staff, the Officers' Corps, Reserve Corps, military schools, war veterans' organizations and all other military and semi-military organizations, together with all clubs and associations which serve to keep alive the military tradition in Germany, shall be completely and finally abolished in such manner as permanently to prevent the revival or reorganization of German militarism and Nazism; (b) All arms, ammunition and implements of war and all specialized facilities for their production shall be held at the disposal of the Allies or destroyed. The maintenance and production of all aircraft and all arms, ammunition and implements of war shall be prevented.

(ii) To convince the German people that they have suffered a total military defeat and that they cannot escape responsibility for what they have brought upon themselves, since their own ruthless warfare and the fanatical Nazi resistance have destroyed [the] German economy and made chaos and suffering inevitable.

(iii) To destroy the National Socialist Party and its affiliated and supervised organizations, to dissolve all Nazi institutions, to ensure that they are not revived in any form, and to prevent all Nazi and militarist activity or propaganda.

(iv) To prepare for the eventual reconstruction of German political life on a democratic basis and for eventual peaceful cooperation in international life by Germany.

4. All Nazi laws which provided the basis of the Hitler regime or established discriminations on grounds of race, creed, or political opinion shall be abolished. No such discriminations, whether legal, administrative or otherwise, shall be tolerated.

5. War criminals and those who have participated in planning or carrying out Nazi enterprises involving or resulting in atrocities or war crimes shall be arrested

and brought to judgment. Nazi leaders, influential Nazi supporters and high officials of Nazi organizations and institutions and any other persons dangerous to the occupation or its objectives shall be arrested and interned.

6. All members of the Nazi Party who have been more than nominal participants in its activities and all other persons hostile to Allied purposes shall be removed from public and semi-public office, and from positions of responsibility in important private undertakings. Such persons shall be replaced by persons who, by their political and moral qualities, are deemed capable of assisting in developing genuine democratic institutions in Germany.

7. German education shall be so controlled as completely to eliminate Nazi and militarist doctrines and to make possible the successful development of democratic ideas.

8. The judicial system will be reorganized in accordance with the principles of democracy, of justice under law, and of equal rights for all citizens without distinction of race, nationality or religion.

9. The administration in Germany should be directed towards the decentralization of the political structure and the development of local responsibility. To this end:

(i) local self-government shall be restored throughout Germany on democratic principles and in particular through elective councils as rapidly as is consistent with military security and the purposes of military occupation; (ii) all democratic political parties with rights of assembly and of public discussion shall be allowed and encouraged throughout Germany; (iii) representative and elective principles shall be introduced into regional, provincial and state (Land) administration as rapidly as may be justified by the successful application of these principles in local self- government; (iv) for the time being, no central German Government shall be established. Notwithstanding this, however, certain essential central German administrative departments, headed by State Secretaries, shall be established, particularly in the fields of finance, transport, communications, foreign trade and industry. Such departments will act under the direction of the Control Council.

10. Subject to the necessity for maintaining military security, freedom of speech, press and religion shall be permitted, and religious institutions shall be respected. Subject likewise to the maintenance of military security, the formation of free trade unions shall be permitted.

B. ECONOMIC PRINCIPLES.

11. In order to eliminate Germany's war potential, the production of arms, ammunition and implements of war as well as all types of aircraft and sea-going ships shall be prohibited and prevented. Production of metals, chemicals, machinery and other items that are directly necessary to a war economy shall be rigidly controlled and restricted to Germany's approved post-war peacetime needs to meet the objectives stated in Paragraph 15. Productive capacity not needed for permit-

ted production shall be removed in accordance with the reparations plan recommended by the Allied Commission on Reparations and approved by the Governments concerned or if not removed shall be destroyed.

12. At the earliest practicable date, the German economy shall be decentralized for the purpose of eliminating the present excessive concentration of economic power as exemplified in particular by cartels, syndicates, trusts and other monopolistic arrangements.

13. In organizing the German Economy, primary emphasis shall be given to the development of agriculture and peaceful domestic industries.

14. During the period of occupation Germany shall be treated as a single economic unit. To this end common policies shall be established in regard to:

(a) mining and industrial production and its allocation;

(b) agriculture, forestry and fishing;

(c) wages, prices and rationing;

(d) import and export programs for Germany as a whole;

(e) currency and banking, central taxation and customs;

(f) reparation and removal of industrial war potential;

(g) transportation and communications.

In applying these policies account shall be taken, where appropriate, of varying local conditions.

15. Allied controls shall be imposed upon the German economy but only to the extent necessary:

(a) to carry out programs of industrial disarmament, demilitarization, of reparations, and of approved exports and imports.

(b) to assure the production and maintenance of goods and services required to meet the needs of the occupying forces and displaced persons in Germany and essential to maintain in Germany average living standards not exceeding the average of the standards of living of European countries. (European countries means all European countries excluding the United Kingdom and the U.S.S.R.).

(c) to ensure in the manner determined by the Control Council the equitable distribution of essential commodities between the several zones so as to produce a balanced economy throughout Germany and reduce the need for imports.

(d) to control German industry and all economic and financial international transactions including exports and imports, with the aim of preventing Germany from developing a war potential and of achieving the other objectives named herein.

(e) to control all German public or private scientific bodies, research and experimental institutions, laboratories, et cetera connected with economic activities.

16. In the imposition and maintenance of economic controls established by the Control Council, German administrative machinery shall be created and the German authorities shall be required to the fullest extent practicable to proclaim and assume administration of such controls. Thus it should be brought home to the German people that the responsibility for the administration of such controls and any break-down in these controls will rest with themselves. Any German controls which may run counter to the objectives of occupation will be prohibited.

17. Measures shall be promptly taken:

(a) to effect essential repair of transport;

(b) to enlarge coal production;

(c) to maximize agricultural output; and

(d) to erect emergency repair of housing and essential utilities.

18. Appropriate steps shall be taken by the Control Council to exercise control and the power of disposition over German-owned external assets not already under the control of United Nations which have taken part in the war against Germany.

19. Payment of Reparations should leave enough resources to enable the German people to subsist without external assistance. In working out the economic balance of Germany the necessary means must be provided to pay for imports approved by the Control Council in Germany. The proceeds of exports from current production and stocks shall be available in the first place for payment for such imports.

The above clause will not apply to the equipment and products referred to in paragraphs 4 (a) and 4 (b) of the Reparations Agreement.

III. REPARATIONS FROM GERMANY.

1. Reparation claims of the U.S.S.R. shall be met by removals from the zone of Germany occupied by the U.S.S.R., and from appropriate German external assets.

2. The U.S.S.R. undertakes to settle the reparation claims of Poland from its own share of reparations.

3. The reparation claims of the United States, the United Kingdom and other countries entitled to reparations shall be met from the Western Zones and from appropriate German external assets.

4. In addition to the reparations to be taken by the U.S.S.R. from its own zone of occupation, the U.S.S.R. shall receive additionally from the Western Zones:

(a) 15 per cent of such usable and complete industrial capital equipment, in the first place from the metallurgical, chemical and machine manufacturing industries as is unnecessary for the German peace economy and should be removed from the Western Zones of Germany, in exchange for an equivalent value of food, coal, potash, zinc, timber, clay products, petroleum products, and such other commodities as may be agreed upon.

(b) 10 per cent of such industrial capital equipment as is unnecessary for the German peace economy and should be removed from the Western Zones, to be transferred to the Soviet Government on reparations account without payment or exchange of any kind in return.

Removals of equipment as provided in (a) and (b) above shall be made simultaneously.

5. The amount of equipment to be removed from the Western Zones on account of reparations must be determined within six months from now at the latest.

6. Removals of industrial capital equipment shall begin as soon as possible and shall be completed within two years from the determination specified in paragraph 5. The delivery of products covered by 4 (a) above shall begin as soon as possible and shall be made by the U.S.S.R. in agreed installments within five years of the date hereof. The determination of the amount and character of the industrial capital equipment unnecessary for the German peace economy and therefore available for reparation shall be made by the Control Council under policies fixed by the Allied Commission on Reparations, with the participation of France, subject to the final approval of the Zone Commander in the Zone from which the equipment is to be removed.

7. Prior to the fixing of the total amount of equipment subject to removal, advance deliveries shall be made in respect to such equipment as will be determined to be eligible for delivery in accordance with the procedure set forth in the last sentence of paragraph 6.

8. The Soviet Government renounces all claims in respect of reparations to shares of German enterprises which are located in the Western Zones of Germany as well as to German foreign assets in all countries except those specified in paragraph 9 below.

9. The Governments of the U. K. and U.S. A. renounce all claims in respect of reparations to shares of German enterprises which are located in the Eastern Zone of occupation in Germany, as well as to German foreign assets in Bulgaria, Finland, Hungary, Rumania and Eastern Austria.

10. The Soviet Government makes no claims to gold captured by the Allied troops in Germany....

Source: "Potsdam Conference," July-August 1945. *A Decade of American Foreign Policy: Basic Documents, 1941-1949.* Prepared at the Request of the Senate Committee on Foreign Relations by the Staff of the Committee and the Department of State. Washington, DC: Government Printing Office, 1950. Available online at the Avalon Project, Yale Law School, http://www.yale.edu/lawweb/avalon/decade/decade17.htm.

1.3
America's Policy of Soviet "Containment" – 1946
Excerpts from "The Long Telegram" of George F. Kennan

In February 1946 a U.S. State Department analyst and diplomat named George F. Kennan wrote a landmark document known as "the Long Telegram." This document advocated a firm policy of "containment" against Soviet ambitions to expand Communism. This telegram described the Communist leadership of the Soviet regime as a "political force committed fanatically to the belief that with US there can be no permanent modus vivendi, that it is desirable and necessary that the internal harmony of our society be disrupted, our traditional way of life be destroyed, the international authority of our state be broken, if Soviet power is to be secure." Kennan's grim assessment of Soviet aims and his conviction that the Kremlin would only yield to superior military force quickly became accepted fact in Washington. Today, his telegram is universally acknowledged to be a major factor in America's military build-up during the early years of the Cold War.

... I apologize in advance for this burdening of telegraphic channel; but questions involved are of such urgent importance, particularly in view of recent events, that our answers to them, if they deserve attention at all, seem to me to deserve it at once....

Basic Features of Post War Soviet Outlook, as Put Forward by Official Propaganda Machine, Are as Follows:

a. USSR still lives in antagonistic "capitalist encirclement" with which in the long run there can be no permanent peaceful coexistence.... Capitalist world is beset with internal conflict, inherent in nature of capitalist society.... Internal conflicts in capitalism inevitably generate wars ... intra-capitalist wars between two capitalist states, and wars of intervention against socialist world.... Intervention against USSR, while it would be disastrous to those who undertook it, would cause renewed delay in progress of Soviet socialism and must therefore be forestalled at all costs.... Conflicts between capitalist states, though likewise fraught with danger for USSR, nevertheless hold out great possibilities for advancement of socialist cause....

On official plane we must look for following:

(a) Internal policy devoted to increasing in every way strength and prestige of Soviet state: ... great displays to impress outsiders; continued secretiveness about internal matters, designed to conceal weakness and to keep opponents in dark.

(b) Wherever it is considered timely and promising, efforts will be made to advance official limits of Soviet power. For the moment, these efforts are restricted to certain neighboring points conceived of here as being of immediate strategic necessity.... However, other points may at any time come into question....

(c) Russians will participate officially in international organizations where they see opportunity of extending Soviet power or of inhibiting or diluting power of others. Moscow sees in UNO [United Nations Organization] not the mechanism for a permanent and stable world society founded on mutual interest and aims of all, but an arena in which aims just mentioned can be favorably pursued. As long as UNO is considered here to serve this purpose, Soviets will remain with it. But if at any time they come to conclusion that it is serving to embarrass or frustrate their aims for power expansion and if they see better prospects for pursuit of these aims along other lines, they will not hesitate to abandon UNO.... Its attitude to that organization will remain essentially pragmatic and tactical.

(d) Toward colonial areas and backward or dependent peoples, Soviet policy, even on official plane, will be directed toward weakening of power and influence and contacts of advanced Western nations, on theory that insofar as this policy is successful, there will be created a vacuum which will favor Communist-Soviet penetration....

(e) Russians will strive energetically to develop Soviet representation in, and official ties with, countries in which they sense strong possibilities of opposition to Western centers of power. This applies to such widely separated points as Germany, Argentina, Middle Eastern countries, etc.

"The Soviet regime is a police regime par excellence, reared in the dim half-world of Tsarist police intrigue, accustomed to think primarily in terms of police power. This should never be lost sight of in gauging Soviet motives."

(f) In international economic matters, Soviet policy will really be dominated by pursuit of autarchy for Soviet Union and Soviet-dominated adjacent areas taken together. That, however, will be underlying policy. As far as official line is concerned, position is not yet clear. Soviet Government has shown strange reticence since termination hostilities on subject foreign trade. If large scale long term credits should be forthcoming, I believe Soviet Government may eventually again do lip service, as it did in 1930's to desirability of building up international economic exchanges in general. Otherwise I think it possible Soviet foreign trade may be restricted largely to Soviet's own security sphere, including occupied areas in Germany, and that a cold official shoulder may be turned to principle of general economic collaboration among nations.

(g) With respect to cultural collaboration, lip service will likewise be rendered to desirability of deepening cultural contacts between peoples, but this will not in practice be interpreted in any way which could weaken security position of

Soviet peoples. Actual manifestations of Soviet policy in this respect will be restricted to arid channels of closely shepherded official visits and functions, with superabundance of vodka and speeches and dearth of permanent effects.

(h) Beyond this, Soviet official relations will take what might be called "correct" course with individual foreign governments, with great stress being laid on prestige of Soviet Union and its representatives and with punctilious attention to protocol as distinct from good manners....

It may be expected that the component parts of this far-flung [Soviet] apparatus will be utilized, in accordance with their individual suitability as follows:

1. To undermine general political and strategic potential of major Western powers. Efforts will be made in such countries to disrupt national self-confidence, to hamstring measures of national defense, to increase social and industrial unrest, to stimulate all forms of disunity. All persons with grievances, whether economic or racial, will be urged to seek redress not in mediation and compromise, but in defiant violent struggle for destruction of other elements of society. Here poor will be set against rich, black against white, young against old, newcomers against established residents, etc.

2. On unofficial plane particularly violent efforts will be made to weaken power and influence of Western powers over colonial, backward, or dependent peoples. On this level, no holds will be barred. Mistakes and weaknesses of Western colonial administration will be mercilessly exposed and exploited. Liberal opinion in Western countries will be mobilized to weaken colonial policies. Resentment among dependent peoples will be stimulated. And while latter are being encouraged to seek independence of Western powers, Soviet-dominated puppet political machines will be undergoing preparation to take over domestic power in respective colonial areas when independence is achieved.

3. Where individual governments stand in path of Soviet purposes pressure will be brought for their removal from office. This can happen where governments directly oppose Soviet foreign policy aims (Turkey, Iran), where they seal their territories off against Communist penetration (Switzerland, Portugal), or where they compete too strongly, like Labor government in England, for moral domination among elements which it is important for Communists to dominate....

4. In foreign countries Communists will, as a rule, work toward destruction of all forms of personal independence, economic, political, or moral....

5. Everything possible will be done to set major Western powers against each other. Anti-British talk will be plugged among Americans, anti-American talk among British. Continentals, including Germans, will be taught to abhor both Anglo-Saxon powers. Where suspicions exist, they will be fanned; where not, ignited. No effort will be spared to discredit and combat all efforts which threaten to lead to any sort of unity or cohesion among others from which Russia might be

excluded. Thus, all forms of international organization not amenable to Communist penetration and control, whether it be the Catholic Church, international economic concerns, or the international fraternity of royalty and aristocracy, must expect to find themselves under fire.

6. In general, all Soviet efforts on unofficial international plane will be negative and destructive in character, designed to tear down sources of strength beyond reach of Soviet control…. The Soviet regime is a police regime par excellence, reared in the dim half-world of Tsarist police intrigue, accustomed to think primarily in terms of police power. This should never be lost sight of in gauging Soviet motives.

Practical Deductions from Standpoint of US Policy

In summary, we have here a political force committed fanatically to the belief that with US there can be no permanent modus vivendi, that it is desirable and necessary that the internal harmony of our society be disrupted, our traditional way of life be destroyed, the international authority of our state be broken, if Soviet power is to be secure. This political force has complete power of disposition over energies of one of the world's greatest peoples and resources of the world's richest national territory, and is borne along by deep and powerful currents of Russian nationalism. In addition, it has an elaborate and far-flung apparatus for exertion of its influence in other countries, an apparatus of amazing flexibility and versatility, managed by people whose experience and skill in underground methods are presumably without parallel in history. Finally, it is seemingly inaccessible to considerations of reality in its basic reactions. For it, the vast fund of objective fact about human society is not, as with us, the measure against which outlook is constantly being tested and reformed, but a grab bag from which individual items are selected arbitrarily and tendentiously to bolster an outlook already preconceived. This is admittedly not a pleasant picture. Problem of how to cope with this force is undoubtedly greatest task our diplomacy has ever faced and probably the greatest it will ever have to face…. But I would like to record my conviction that the problem is within our power to solve—and that without recourse to any general military conflict. And in support of this conviction there are certain observations of a more encouraging nature I should like to make:

(1) Soviet power, unlike that of Hitlerite Germany, is neither schematic nor adventuristic. It does not work by fixed plans. It does not take unnecessary risks. Impervious to logic of reason, and it is highly sensitive to logic of force. For this reason it can easily withdraw—and usually does—when strong resistance is encountered at any point. Thus, if the adversary has sufficient force and makes clear his readiness to use it, he rarely has to do so. If situations are properly handled there need be no prestige-engaging showdowns.

(2) Gauged against Western world as a whole, Soviets are still by far the weaker force. Thus, their success will really depend on degree of cohesion, firmness and vigor which Western world can muster….

(3) Success of Soviet system, as form of internal power, is not yet finally proven.... We here are convinced that never since termination of the civil war have the mass of Russian people been emotionally farther removed from doctrines of Communist Party than they are today. In Russia, party has now become a great and—for the moment—highly successful apparatus of dictatorial administration, but it has ceased to be a source of emotional inspiration. Thus, internal soundness and permanence of movement need not yet be regarded as assured.

(4) All Soviet propaganda beyond Soviet security sphere is basically negative and destructive. It should therefore be relatively easy to combat it by any intelligent and really constructive program.

For these reasons I think we may approach calmly and with good heart the problem of how to deal with Russia. As to how this approach should be made, I only wish to advance, by way of conclusion, the following comments:

1. Our first step must be to apprehend, and recognize for what it is, the nature of the movement with which we are dealing ....

2. We must see that our public is educated to realities of Russian situation. I cannot overemphasize the importance of this. Press cannot do this alone. It must be done mainly by government, which is necessarily more experienced and better informed on practical problems involved. In this we need not be deterred by ugliness of the picture. I am convinced that there would be far less hysterical anti-Sovietism in our country today if the realities of this situation were better understood by our people. There is nothing as dangerous or as terrifying as the unknown ... Our stake in this country, even coming on the heels of tremendous demonstrations of our friendship for Russian people, is remarkably small. We have here no investments to guard, no actual trade to lose, virtually no citizens to protect, few cultural contacts to preserve. Our only stake lies in what we hope rather than what we have; and I am convinced we have a better chance of realizing those hopes if our public is enlightened and if our dealings with Russians are placed entirely on realistic and matter of fact basis.

3. Much depends on health and vigor of our own society. World Communism is like malignant parasite which feeds only on diseased tissue. This is the point at which domestic and foreign policies meet. Every courageous and incisive measure to solve internal problems of our own society, to improve self-confidence, discipline, morale, and community spirit of our own people, is a diplomatic victory over Moscow....

4. We must formulate and put forward for other nations a much more positive and constructive picture of the sort of world we would like to see than we have put forward in the past. It is not enough to urge the people to develop political processes similar to our own. Many foreign peoples, in Europe at least, are tired and frightened by experiences of the past, and are less interested in abstract freedom than in securi-

ty. They are seeking guidance rather than responsibilities. We should be better able than the Russians to give them this. And unless we do, the Russians certainly will.

5. Finally, we must have courage and self-confidence to cling to our own methods and conceptions of human society. After all, the greatest danger that can befall us in coping with this problem of Soviet Communism is that we shall allow ourselves to become like those with whom we are coping.

Source: Kennan, George. Telegram to the Secretary of State, February 22, 1946. *Foreign Relations of the United States 1946*, Vol. 6. Washington, DC: Government Printing Office, 1969.

1.4
Churchill's "Iron Curtain" Speech – 1946
Excerpt from a Speech Delivered at Westminster College in Fulton, Missouri

> *In March 1946 former British Prime Minister Winston Churchill delivered a famous speech at Westminster College in Fulton, Missouri, in which he warned that the Soviets were drawing an "iron curtain" of repressive, totalitarian governments across the heart of Europe. The speech received mixed reviews when it was given. Many observers thought it was too alarmist and combative. But today it is widely regarded as one of the most insightful and influential speeches of the early Cold War era.*

The Sinews of Peace

.... A shadow has fallen upon the scenes so lately lighted by the Allied victory. Nobody knows what Soviet Russia and its communist international organization intends to do in the immediate future, or what are the limits, if any, to their expansive and proselytizing tendencies. I have a strong admiration and regard for the valiant Russian people and for my wartime comrade, Marshal Stalin. There is deep sympathy and goodwill in Britain—and I doubt not here also—towards the peoples of all the Russias and a resolve to persevere through many differences and rebuffs in establishing lasting friendships. We understand the Russian need to be secure on her western frontiers by the removal of all possibility of German aggression. We welcome Russia to her rightful place among the leading nations of the world. We welcome her flag upon the seas. Above all, we welcome constant, frequent and growing contacts between the Russian people and our own people on both sides of the Atlantic. It is my duty however, for I am sure you would wish me to state the facts as I see them to you, to place before you certain facts about the present position in Europe.

"The Sinews of Peace," Address delivered at Westminster College, Fulton, Missouri, March 5, 1946. Reproduced with permission of Curtis Brown Ltd, London on behalf of The Estate of Winston Churchill. © Winston Churchill.

From Stettin in the Baltic to Trieste in the Adriatic, an iron curtain has descended across the Continent. Behind that line lie all the capitals of the ancient states of Central and Eastern Europe. Warsaw, Berlin, Prague, Vienna, Budapest, Belgrade, Bucharest and Sofia, all these famous cities and the populations around them lie in what I must call the Soviet sphere, and all are subject in one form or another, not only to Soviet influence but to a very high and, in many cases, increasing measure of control from Moscow. Athens alone—Greece with its immortal glories—is free to decide its future at an election under British, American and French observation. The Russian-dominated Polish government has been encouraged to make enormous and wrongful inroads upon Germany, and mass expulsions of millions of Germans on a scale grievous and undreamed of are now taking place. The

> *"From Stettin in the Baltic to Trieste in the Adriatic, an iron curtain has descended across the Continent."*

communist parties, which were very small in all these eastern states of Europe, have been raised to pre-eminence and power far beyond their numbers and are seeking everywhere to obtain totalitarian control. Police governments are prevailing in nearly every case, and so far, except in Czechoslovakia, there is no true democracy....

I have felt bound to portray the shadow which, alike in the West and in the East, falls upon the world. I was a high minister at the time of the Versailles Treaty and a close friend of Mr. Lloyd-George, who was the head of the British delegation at Versailles. I did not myself agree with many things that were done, but I have a very strong impression in my mind of that situation, and I find it painful to contrast it with that which prevails now. In those days there were high hopes and unbounded confidence that the wars were over, and that the League of Nations would become all-powerful. I do not see or feel that same confidence or even the same hopes in the haggard world at the present time.

On the other hand I repulse the idea that a new war is inevitable; still more that it is imminent. It is because I am sure that our fortunes are still in our own hands and that we hold the power to save the future, that I feel the duty to speak out now that I have the occasion and the opportunity to do so. I do not believe that Soviet Russia desires war. What they desire is the fruits of war and the indefinite expansion of their power and doctrines. But what we have to consider here today while time remains is the permanent prevention of war and the establishment of conditions of freedom and democracy as rapidly as possible in all countries. Our difficulties and dangers will not be removed by closing our eyes to them. They will not be removed by mere waiting to see what happens; nor will they be removed by a policy of appeasement. What is needed is a settlement, and the longer this is delayed, the more difficult it will be and the greater our dangers will become.

From what I have seen of our Russian friends and Allies during the war, I am convinced that there is nothing they admire so much as strength, and there is nothing for which they have less respect than for weakness, especially military weakness. For that reason the old doctrine of a balance of power is unsound. We cannot afford, if we can help it, to work on narrow margins, offering temptations to a trial of strength. If the Western democracies stand together in strict adherence to the principles of the United Nations Charter, their influence for furthering those principles will be immense and no one is likely to molest them. If however they become divided or falter in their duty and if these all-important years are allowed to slip away then indeed catastrophe may overwhelm us all.

Last time I saw it all coming and cried aloud to my own fellow-countrymen and to the world, but no one paid any attention. Up till the year 1933 or even 1935, Germany might have been saved from the awful fate which has overtaken her and we might all have been spared the miseries Hitler let loose upon mankind. There never was a war in all history easier to prevent by timely action than the one which has just desolated such great areas of the globe. It could have been prevented in my belief without the firing of a single shot, and Germany might be powerful, prosperous and honored today; but no one would listen and one by one we were all sucked into the awful whirlpool. We surely must not let that happen again. This can only be achieved by reaching now, in 1946, a good understanding on all points with Russia under the general authority of the United Nations Organization and by the maintenance of that good understanding through many peaceful years, by the world instrument, supported by the whole strength of the English-speaking world and all its connections. There is the solution which I respectfully offer to you in this address to which I have given the title "The Sinews of Peace." …

Source: Churchill, Winston S. Speech at Westminster College in Fulton, Missouri, March 1946. Reprinted in *Never Give In: The Best of Winston Churchill's Speeches*. New York: Hyperion, 2003.

1.5
Soviet Ambassador Novikov Assesses the Americans – 1946
An Excerpt from a Telegram from the Soviet Embassy in Washington, DC, to the Kremlin in Moscow

In September 1946 the Soviet ambassador to Washington, Nikolai Novikov, sent a long and somber telegram to the Kremlin. In this message, the diplomat warned that the United States and its allies in Western Europe seemed intent on achieving "world supremacy." Novikov's telegram was in many ways a Soviet version of Kennan's Long Telegram: an effort to interpret the postwar goals of a wartime ally that, almost in the blink of an eye, had become a potentially deadly foe.

The foreign policy of the United States, which reflects the imperialist tendencies of American monopolistic capital, is characterized in the postwar period by a striving for *world supremacy*. This is the real meaning of the many statements by President Truman and other representatives of American ruling circles; that the United States has the right to lead the world. All the forces of American diplomacy—the army, the air force, the navy, industry, and science—are enlisted in the service of this foreign policy. For this purpose broad plans for expansion have been developed and are being implemented through diplomacy and the establishment of a system of naval and air bases stretching far beyond the boundaries of the United States, through the arms race, and through the creation of ever newer types of weapons.

1a) The foreign policy of the United States is conducted now *in a situation that differs greatly* from the one that existed in the prewar period. This situation does not fully conform to the calculations of those reactionary circles which hoped that during the Second World War they would succeed in avoiding, at least for a long time, the main battles in Europe and Asia. They calculated that the United States of America, if it was unsuccessful in completely avoiding direct participation in the war, would enter it only at the last minute, when it could easily affect the outcome of the war, completely ensuring its interests.

In this regard, it was thought that the main competitors of the United States would be crushed or greatly weakened in the war, and the United States by virtue of this circumstance would assume *the role of the most powerful factor* in resolving the fundamental questions of the postwar world. These calculations were also based on the assumption, which was very widespread in the United States in the initial stages of the war, that the Soviet Union, which had been subjected to the attack of German Fascism in June 1941, would also be exhausted or even completely destroyed as a result of the war.

Reality did not bear out the calculations of the American imperialists.

b) The two main aggressive powers, fascist Germany and militarist Japan, which were at the same time the main competitors of the United States in both the economic and foreign policy fields, were thoroughly defeated. The third great power, Great Britain, which had taken heavy blows during the war, now faces enormous economic and political difficulties. The political foundations of the British Empire were appreciably shaken, and crises arose, for example, in India, Palestine, and Egypt.

Europe has come out of the war with a completely dislocated economy, and the economic devastation that occurred in the course of the war cannot be overcome in a short time. All of the countries of Europe and Asia are experiencing a

Telegram from N. Novikov, Soviet Ambassador to the US, to the Soviet Leadership, September 27, 1946. Reprinted with permission from the Cold War International History Project Virtual Archive (http://www.cwihp.org).

colossal need for consumer goods, industrial and transportation equipment, etc. Such a situation provides American monopolistic capital with *prospects for enormous shipments of goods and the importation of capital* into these countries—a circumstance that would permit it to infiltrate their national economies.

Such a development would mean a serious strengthening of the economic position of the United States in the whole world and would be a stage on the road to world domination by the United States.

c) On the other hand, we have seen a failure of calculations on the part of U.S. circles which assumed that the Soviet Union would be destroyed in the war or would come out of it so weakened that it would be forced to go begging to the United States for economic assistance. Had that happened, they would have been able to dictate conditions permitting the United States to carry out its expansion in Europe and Asia without hindrance from the USSR.

In actuality, despite all of the economic difficulties of the postwar period connected with the enormous losses inflicted by the war and the German fascist occupation, the Soviet Union continues to remain economically independent of the outside world and is rebuilding its national economy with its own forces.

At the same time *the USSR's international position is currently stronger than it was in the prewar period*. Thanks to the historical victories of Soviet weapons, the Soviet armed forces are located on the territory of Germany and other formerly hostile countries, thus guaranteeing that these countries will not be used again for an attack on the USSR. In formerly hostile countries, such as *Bulgaria, Finland, Hungary, and Romania*, democratic reconstruction has established regimes that have undertaken to strengthen and maintain friendly relations with the Soviet Union. In the Slavic countries that were liberated by the Red Army or with its assistance—Poland, Czechoslovakia, and Yugoslavia—democratic regimes have also been established that maintain relations with the Soviet Union on the basis of agreements on friendship and mutual assistance.

> *"Obvious indications of the U.S. effort to establish world dominance are also to be found in the increase in military potential in peacetime."*

The enormous relative weight of the USSR in international affairs in general and in the European countries in particular, the independence of its foreign policy, and the economic and political assistance that it provides to neighboring countries, both allies and former enemies, has led to the growth of the political influence of the Soviet Union in these countries and to the further strengthening of democratic tendencies in them. Such a situation in Eastern and Southeastern Europe cannot help but be regarded by the American imperialists as an obstacle in the path of the expansionist policy of the United States.

2a) The foreign policy of the United States is not determined at present by the circles in the Democratic Party that (as was the case during Roosevelt's lifetime) strive to strengthen the cooperation of the three great powers that constituted the basis of the anti-Hitler coalition during the war. The ascendance to power of President Truman, a politically unstable person but with certain conservative tendencies, and the subsequent appointment of (James) Byrnes as Secretary of State meant a *strengthening of the influence of U.S. foreign policy of the most reactionary circles of the Democratic party.*

The constantly increasing reactionary nature of the foreign policy course of the United States, which consequently approached the policy advocated by the Republican party, laid the groundwork for close cooperation in this field between the far right wing of the Democratic party and the Republican party. This cooperation of the two parties, which took shape in both houses of Congress in the form of an unofficial *bloc of reactionary Southern Democrats and the old guard of the Republicans* headed by (Senator Arthur) Vandenberg and (Senator Robert) Taft, was especially clearly manifested in the essentially identical foreign policy statements issued by figures of both parties. In Congress and at international conferences, where as a rule leading Republicans are represented in the delegations of the United States, the Republicans actively support the foreign policy of the government. This is the source of what is called, even in official statements, "bipartisan" foreign policy.

b) At the same time, there has been *a decline in the influence on foreign policy of those who follow Roosevelt's course for cooperation among peace-loving countries.* Such persons in the government, in Congress, and in the leadership of the Democratic party are being pushed farther and farther into the background. The contradictions in the field of foreign policy and existing between the followers of (Henry) Wallace and (Claude) Pepper, on the one hand, and the adherents of the reactionary "bipartisan" policy, on the other, were manifested with great clarity recently in the speech by Wallace that led to his resignation from the post as Secretary of Commerce. *Wallace's resignation means the victory of the reactionary course* that Byrnes is conducting in cooperation with Vandenberg and Taft.

3. Obvious indications of the U.S. effort to establish world dominance are also to be found in the increase in military potential in peacetime and in the establishment of a large number of naval and air bases both in the United States and beyond its borders.

In the summer of 1946, for the first time in the history of the country, Congress passed a law on the establishment of a peacetime army, not on a volunteer basis but on the basis of universal military service. The size of the army, which is supposed to amount to about one million persons as of July 1, 1947, was also increased significantly. The size of the navy at the conclusion of the war decreased quite insignificantly in comparison with wartime. At the present time, the American navy occupies first place in the world, leaving England's navy far behind, to say nothing of those of other countries.

Expenditures on the army and navy have risen colossally, amounting to $13 billion according to the budget for 1946-47 (about 40 percent of the total budget of $36 billion). This is more than 10 times greater than corresponding expenditures in the budget for 1938, which did not amount to even $1 billion.

Along with maintaining a large army, navy, and air force, the budget provides that these enormous amounts also will be spent on establishing a very extensive system of naval and air bases in the Atlantic and Pacific oceans. According to existing official plans, in the course of the next few years *228 bases*, points of support, and radio stations are to be constructed *in the Atlantic Ocean and 258 in the Pacific*. A large number of these bases and points of support are located outside the boundaries of the United States. In the Atlantic Ocean bases exist or are under construction in the following foreign island territories: Newfoundland, Iceland, Cuba, Trinidad, Bermuda, the Bahamas, the Azores, and many others; in the Pacific Ocean: former Japanese mandated territories—the Marianas, Caroline and Marshall Islands, Bonin, Ryukyu, Philippines, and the Galapagos Islands (they belong to Ecuador).

The establishment of American bases on islands that are often 10,000 to 12,000 kilometers from the territory of the United States and are on the other side of the Atlantic and Pacific oceans clearly indicates *the offensive nature of the strategic concepts* of the commands of the U.S. army and navy. This interpretation is also confirmed by the fact that the American navy is intensively studying the naval approaches to the boundaries of Europe. For this purpose American naval vessels in the course of 1946 visited the ports of Norway, Denmark, Sweden, Turkey, and Greece. In addition, the American navy is constantly operating in the Mediterranean Sea.

All of these facts show clearly that a decisive role in the realization of plans for world dominance by the United States is played by its armed forces.

4a) One of the stages in the achievement of dominance over the world by the United States is its understanding with England concerning the partial division of the world on the basis of mutual concessions. The basic lines of the secret agreement between the United States and England regarding the division of the world consist, as shown by facts, in their agreement on the inclusion of Japan and China in the sphere of influence of the United States in the Far East, while the United States, for its part, has agreed not to hinder England either in resolving the Indian problem or in strengthening its influence in Siam and Indonesia.

b) In connection with this division, the United States at the present time is in control of China and Japan without any interference from England. The American policy in China is striving for the complete economic and political submission of China to the control of American monopolistic capital. Following this policy, the

American government does not shrink even from interference in the internal affairs of China. At the present time in China, there are more than 50,000 American soldiers. In a number of cases, American Marines participated directly in military operations against the people's liberation forces. The so-called "mediation" mission of General (George) Marshall is only a cover for interference in the internal affairs of China.

How far the policy of the American government has gone with regard to China is indicated by the fact that at present it is striving to effect control over China's army. Recently, the U.S. administration submitted to Congress a bill on military assistance to China that provided for the complete reorganization of the Chinese army, its training with the aid of U.S. military instructors and its supply with American weapons and equipment. For the purpose of carrying out this program in China, an American consultative mission including army and naval officers would be sent to China.

China is gradually being transformed into a bridgehead for the American armed forces. American air bases are located all over its territory. The main ones are found in Peking, Tsingtao, Tientsin, Nanking, Shanghai, Chendu, Chungking, and Kunming. The main American naval base in China is located in Tsingtao. The headquarters of the 7th Fleet is also there. In addition more than 30,000 U.S. Marines are concentrated in Tsingtao and its environs. The measures carried out in northern China by the American army show that it intends to stay there for a long time.

In Japan, despite the presence there of only a small contingent of American troops, control is in the hands of the Americans. Although English capital has substantial interests in the Japanese economy, English foreign policy toward Japan is conducted in such a way as not to hinder the Americans from carrying out their penetration of the Japanese national economy and subordinating it to their influence. In the Far Eastern Commission in Washington and in the Allied Council in Tokyo, the English representatives as a rule make common cause with the U.S. representatives conducting this policy.

Measures taken by the American occupational authorities in the area of domestic policy and intended to support reactionary classes and groups, which the United States plans to use in the struggle against the Soviet Union, also meet with a sympathetic attitude on the part of England.

c) The United States follows a similar line with regard to the English sphere of influence in the Far East. Recently, the United States has ceased the attempts it has made over the past year to influence the resolution of *Indian* questions. Lately there have been frequent instances in which the reputable American press more or less faithfully reflecting the official policy of the U.S. government, has made positive statements with regard to the English policy *in India*. American foreign policy also did not hinder British troops in joint action with the Dutch army from suppressing the national liberation movement in Indonesia. Moreover, there have even been instances in which the United States facilitated this British imperialist policy, handing over American weapons and equipment to the English and Dutch troops in *Indonesia*, sending Dutch naval personnel from the United States to Indonesia, etc.

5a) If the division of the world in the Far East between the United States and England may be considered an accomplished fact, it cannot be said that an analogous situation exists in the basin of the Mediterranean Sea and in the countries adjacent to it. Rather, the facts indicate that an agreement of this sort has not yet been reached in the region of the Near East and the Mediterranean Sea. The difficulty experienced by the United States and England in reaching an agreement over this region derives from the fact that concessions on the part of England to the United States in the Mediterranean basin would be fraught with serious consequences for the whole future of the British Empire, for which the basin has exceptional strategic and economic significance. England would have nothing against using American armed forces and influence in this region, directing them northward against the Soviet Union. The United States, however, is not interested in providing assistance and support to the British Empire in this vulnerable point, but rather in its own more thorough penetration of the Mediterranean basin and Near East, to which the United States is attracted by the area's natural resources, primarily *oil*.

b) In recent years American capital has penetrated very intensively into the economy of the Near Eastern countries, in particular into the oil industry. At present there are American oil concessions in all of the Near Eastern countries that have oil deposits (Iraq, Bahrain, Kuwait, Egypt, and Saudi Arabia). American capital, which made its first appearance in the oil industry of the Near East, only in 1927, now controls 42 percent of all proven reserves in the Near East, excluding Iran. Of the total proven reserves of 26.8 billion barrels, over 11 billion barrels are owned by U.S. concessions. Striving to ensure further development of their concessions in different countries (which are often very large—Saudi Arabia, for example), the American oil companies plan to build a trans-Arabian pipeline to transport oil from the American concession in Saudi Arabia and in other countries on the southeastern shore of the Mediterranean Sea to ports in Palestine and Egypt.

In expanding in the Near East, American capital has English capital as its greatest and most stubborn competitor. The fierce competition between them is the chief factor preventing England and the United States from reaching an understanding on the division of spheres of influence in the Near East, a division of that can occur only at the expense of direct British interests in this region.

Palestine is an example of the very acute contradictions in the policy of the United States and England in the Near East. The United States has been displaying great initiative there of late, creating many difficulties for England, as in the case of the U.S. demand that 100,000 Jews from Europe be permitted to enter *Palestine*. The American interest in Palestine, outwardly expressed as sympathy for the Zionist cause, actually only signifies that American capital wishes to interfere in Palestinian affairs and thus penetrate the economy. The selection of a port in Palestine as one of the terminal points of the American oil pipeline explains a great deal regarding the foreign policy of the United States on the Palestine question.

c) The irregular nature of relations between England and the United States in the Near East is manifested in part also in the great *activity of the American naval fleet in the eastern part of the Mediterranean Sea*. Such activity cannot help but be in conflict with the basic interests of the British Empire. These actions on the part of the U.S. fleet undoubtedly are also linked with American oil and other economic interests in the Near East.

It must be kept in mind, however, that incidents such as the visit by the American battleship Missouri to the Black Sea straits, the visit of the American fleet to Greece, and the great interest that U.S. diplomacy displays in the problem of the straits have a double meaning. On the one hand, they indicate that the United States has decided to consolidate its position in the Mediterranean basin to support its interests in the countries of the Near East and that it has selected the navy as the tool for this policy. On the other hand, these incidents constitute a political and military demonstration against the Soviet Union. The strengthening of U.S. positions in the Near East and the establishment of conditions for basing the American navy at one or more points on the Mediterranean Sea (Trieste, Palestine, Greece, Turkey) will therefore signify the emergence of a new threat to the security of the southern regions of the Soviet Union.

6a) Relations between the United States and England are determined by two basic circumstances. On the one hand, *the United States regards England as its greatest potential competitor*; on the other hand, *England constitutes a possible ally for the United States*. Division of certain regions of the globe into *spheres of influence* of the United States and England would create the opportunity, if not for preventing competition between them, which is impossible, then at least of reducing it. At the same time, such a division facilitates the achievement of economic and political cooperation between them.

b) England needs American credits for reorganizing its economy, which was disrupted by the war. To obtain such credits England is compelled to make significant concessions. This is the *significance of the loan* that the United States recently granted England. With the aid of the loan, England can strengthen its economy. At the same time this loan opens the door for American capital to penetrate the British Empire. The narrow bounds in which the trade of the so-called Sterling Bloc has found itself in the recent past have expanded at the present time and provide an opportunity for the Americans to trade with British dominions, India, and other countries of the Sterling Bloc (Egypt, Iraq, and Palestine).

c) The political *support that the United States provides for England* is very often manifested in the international events of the postwar period. At recent international conferences the United States and England have closely coordinated their policies, especially in cases when they had to oppose the policy of the Soviet Union. The United States provided moral and political assistance to England in the latter's reactionary policy in Greece, India and Indonesia. American and English policy is fully coordinated with regard to the Slavic and other countries adjoining the Soviet Union. The most important demarches of the United States and England in these countries after the end of the war were quite similar and parallel in nature. The policy of the United States and England in the Security Council of the United Nations (particularly in questions concerning Iran, Spain, Greece, the withdrawal of foreign troops from Syria and Lebanon, etc.) has the same features of coordination.

d) The ruling circles of the United States obviously have a sympathetic attitude toward *the idea of a military alliance with England*, but at the present time the matter has not yet culminated in an official alliance. Churchill's speech in Fulton calling for the conclusion of an Anglo-American military alliance for the purpose of establishing joint domination over the world was therefore not supported officially by Truman or Byrnes, although Truman by his presence (during the "Iron Curtain" speech) did indirectly sanction Churchill's appeal.

Even if the United States does not go so far as to conclude a military alliance with England just now, in practice they still maintain very close contact on military questions. The combined Anglo-American headquarters in Washington continues to exist, despite the fact that over a year has passed since the end of the war. Frequent personal contact continues among leading military figures of England and the United States. The recent trip of Field Marshal Montgomery to America is evidence of this contact. It is characteristic that as a result of his meetings with leading military figures of the United States, Montgomery announced that *the English army would be structured on the American model*. Cooperation is also carried out *between the navies of the two countries*. In this connection it is sufficient to note the participation of the English navy in recent maneuvers by the American navy in the North Sea in autumn of this year.

e) The current relations between England and the United States, despite the temporary attainment of agreements on very important questions, are plagued with *great* internal *contradictions* and can not be lasting.

The economic assistance from the United States conceals within itself a danger for England in many respects. First of all, in accepting the loan, England finds herself in a certain financial dependence on the United States from which it will not be easy to free herself. Second, it should be kept in mind that the conditions created by the loan for the penetration by American capital of the British Empire can entail serious political consequences. The countries included in the British Empire or dependent on it may—under economic pressure from powerful American capital—reorient themselves toward the United States, following in this respect the example of Canada, which more and more is moving away from the influence of England and orienting itself toward the United States. The strengthening of American positions in the Far East could stimulate a similar process in Australia and New Zealand. In the Arabic countries of the Near East, which are striving to emancipate themselves from the British Empire, there are groups within the ruling circles that would not be averse to working out a deal with the United States. It is quite possible that the Near East will become a *center of Anglo-American contradictions* that will explode the agreements now reached between the United States and England.

7a) The *"hard-line"* policy with regard to the USSR announced by Byrnes after the rapprochement of the reactionary Democrats with the Republicans is at present the main obstacle on the road to cooperation of the Great Powers. It consists mainly of the fact that in the postwar period the United States no longer follows a policy of strengthening cooperation among the Big Three (or four) but rather has striven to undermine the unity of these countries. The *objective* has been to *impose* the will of other countries on the Soviet Union. This is precisely the tenor of the policy of certain countries, which is being carried out with the blessing of the United States, to undermine or completely *abolish the principle of the veto* in the Security Council of the United Nations. This would give the United States opportunities to form among the Great Powers narrow groupings and blocs directed primarily against the Soviet Union, and thus to split the United Nations. Rejection of the veto by the Great Powers would transform the United Nations into an Anglo-Saxon domain in which the United States would play the leading role.

b) The present policy of the American government with regard to the USSR is also directed at limiting or dislodging the influence of the Soviet Union from neighboring countries. In implementing this policy in former enemy or Allied countries adjacent to the USSR, the United States attempts, at various international conferences or directly in these countries themselves, to support reactionary forces with *the purpose of creating obstacles to the process of democratization of these countries. In so doing, it also attempts to secure positions for the penetration of American capital into their economies.* Such a policy is intended to weaken and overthrow the democratic governments in power there, which are friendly toward the USSR, and replace them in the future with new governments that would obediently carry out a policy dictated from the United States. In this policy, the United States receives full support from English diplomacy.

c) One of the most important elements in the general policy of the United States, which is directed toward limiting the international role of the USSR in the post war world, is the *policy with regard to Germany.* In Germany, the United States is taking measures to strengthen reactionary forces for the purpose of opposing democratic reconstruction. Furthermore, it displays special insistence on accompanying this policy with completely inadequate measures for the demilitarization of Germany.

The American occupation policy does not have the objective of eliminating the remnants of *German Fascism* and rebuilding German political life *on a democratic basis*, so that Germany might cease to exist as an aggressive force. The United States is not taking measures *to eliminate the monopolistic associations* of German industrialists on which German Fascism depended in preparing aggression and waging war. Neither is any *agrarian* reform being conducted to eliminate large landholders, who were also a reliable support for the Hitlerites. Instead, the United States is considering the possibility *of terminating the Allied occupation* of German territory before the main tasks of the occupation—the demilitarization and democratization of Germany—have been [missing text] … an imperialist Germany, which the United States plans to use in a future war on its side. One cannot help seeing that such a policy has a clearly outlined *anti-Soviet edge* and constitutes a serious danger to the cause of peace.

d) The numerous and extremely hostile statements by American government, political, and military figures with regard to the Soviet Union and its foreign policy are very characteristic of the current relationship between the ruling circles of the United States and the USSR. These statements are echoed in an even more unrestrained tone by the overwhelming majority of the American press organs. *Talk about a "third war,"* meaning a war against the Soviet Union, even a direct call for this war—with the threat of using the atomic bomb—such is the content of the statements on relations with the Soviet Union by reactionaries at public meetings and in the press. At the present time, preaching war against he Soviet Union is not a monopoly of the far-right, yellow American press represented by the newspaper associations of Hearst and McCormick. This anti-Soviet campaign also has been joined by the "reputable" and "respectable" organs of the conservative press, such as the *New York Times* and *New York Herald Tribune*. Indicative in this respect are the numerous articles by Walter Lippmann in which he almost undisguisedly calls on the United States to launch a strike against the Soviet Union in the most vulnerable areas of the south and southeast of the USSR.

The basic goal of this anti-Soviet campaign of American "public opinion" is to exert political pressure on the Soviet Union and compel it to make concessions. Another, no less important goal of the campaign is the attempt *to create an atmosphere of war psychosis* among the masses, who are weary of war, thus making it easier for the U.S. government to carry out measure for the maintenance of high military potential. It was in this very atmosphere that the law on universal military service in peacetime was passed by congress, that the huge military budget was adopted, and that plans are being worked out for the construction of an extensive system of naval and air bases.

e) Of course, all of these measures for maintaining a highly military potential are not goals in themselves. They are only intended *to prepare the conditions for winning world supremacy* in a new war, the date for which, to be sure, cannot be determined now by anyone, but which is contemplated by the most bellicose circles of American imperialism.

Careful note should be taken of the fact that the preparation by the United State for a future is being conducted with the prospect of *war against the Soviet Union*, which in the eyes of the American imperialists is the main obstacle in the path of the United States to world domination. This is indicated by facts such as the tactical training of the American army for war with the Soviet Union as the future opponent, the siting of American strategic bases in regions from which it is possible to launch strikes on Soviet territory, intensified training and strengthening of Arctic regions as close approaches to the USSR, and attempts to prepare Germany and Japan to use those countries in a war against the USSR.

Source: Novikov, N. Telegram to the Soviet Leadership, September 27, 1946. Available online at the Cold War International History Project Virtual Archive, http://www.wilsoncenter.org.

2

THE MARSHALL PLAN
AND THE BERLIN AIRLIFT

A U.S. cargo plane loaded with food and other relief supplies
flies into beleaguered Berlin during the 1948-49 Berlin Airlift.

INTRODUCTION

I n July 1946 representatives of twenty-one nations gathered in Paris for a
peace conference intended to settle lingering issues from World War II. But
the Paris Peace Conference foundered due to the growing tensions between
the West and the Soviet Union. The disappointing outcome in Paris reinforced the belief among leaders in Washington that Moscow and its Communist
allies were America's most dangerous postwar foes. "The Soviet Union constitutes
a real menace to freedom in this world," Special Counsel Clark Clifford charged in
one report. "So we must prepare for it."

To that end, President Harry Truman went before a joint session of Congress
on March 12, 1947, and asserted his determination to counter Communist aggression wherever it appeared. He vowed to actively "support free peoples who are
resisting attempted subjugation by armed minorities or by outside pressures." This
philosophy, which immediately became known as the Truman Doctrine, guided
American foreign policy for the next three decades.

In the meantime, the Truman administration had become convinced that
rebuilding Europe's economy was vital in preventing further Soviet expansion. As
Secretary of State George C. Marshall declared in April 1947, "disintegrating forces
are becoming evident. The patient is sinking whilst the doctors deliberate." Over
the next several weeks, Marshall and his staff worked tirelessly on an economic
recovery program for Europe. He unveiled this plan at commencement ceremonies
at Harvard University on June 5, 1947.

Western European leaders responded enthusiastically to the so-called Marshall Plan, which eventually provided $13 billion in economic assistance to Euro-
pean nations to rebuild after the war. The Marshall Plan addressed the terrible

poverty, hunger, and insecurity that gripped Europe in the immediate postwar era. In addition, it solidified America's new status as leader of the free world.

The need for the economic aid contained in the Marshall Plan was made clear by events in Czechoslovakia. In the months immediately following the end of the war, Czech leaders had sought to avoid becoming too dependent on either the Soviets or the West. But when Stalin forced Czechoslovakia to forsake all claims to Marshall Plan aid, the nation became completely dependent on the Soviets. As Czech Foreign Minister Jan Masaryk lamented in the summer of 1947, "I went to Moscow as the foreign minister of an independent sovereign state; I returned as a Soviet slave." By February 1948, the Communist takeover of Czechoslovakia was complete.

Crisis in Berlin

In Germany, meanwhile, the simmering hostility between East and West dramatically escalated. From September 1945 to mid-1948, there had been free movement around the capital of Berlin, even though the Soviets controlled the easternmost of the four zones of military occupation in the city. But the East and West had vastly different ideas about how to treat postwar Germany. The United States and its Western allies believed that a unified and economically vibrant Germany was essential to the future vitality of Europe as a whole. The Soviets, however, were determined to keep their grip on this strategically important piece of Europe—and to prevent Germany from regaining the power that had enabled it to cause such enormous devastation in the USSR during World War II.

Negotiations between Soviet and Western diplomats to unify Germany broke down, and France, Great Britain, and the United States began making plans to establish an independent West German state. Stalin reacted decisively. In September 1947 the Kremlin established the Communist Information Bureau, or Cominform, for the express purpose of tightening its control over its Eastern European satellite states. Then, on June 24, 1948, Stalin abruptly imposed the so-called Berlin Blockade—a complete halt to all ground access to West Berlin.

The blockade isolated West Berlin, which was located more than 100 miles inside Soviet-controlled eastern Germany. Concerns were immediately raised that trapped West Berliners might be forced to endure a nightmarish winter without food, heating fuel, or other necessities. But Stalin underestimated Western resolve in this case. "If we mean that we are to hold Europe against Communism, we must not budge [in the case of Berlin]," declared U.S. General Lucius D. Clay. "I believe the future of democracy requires us to stay here until forced out."

Truman shared this conviction. He and other Western leaders approved a continuous airlift of supplies into the embattled city. This airlift, conducted under the direction of Clay, was a spectacular success. Despite continual harassment from Soviet fighter planes, Western planes carried in as much as 4,000 tons of supplies on a daily basis, including food, clothing, coal, and other necessities. By the spring of 1949 the Berlin airlift had become a major symbolic victory for the Americans and their Western allies. The episode cast the Soviet leaders as monsters willing to starve thousands of people to achieve their political goals. Western governments, meanwhile, claimed that the airlift showed that they would be resolute in defending democratic causes around the world. On May 12, 1949, Stalin quietly called an end to the Berlin Blockade.

DOCUMENTS

2.1
The Truman Doctrine – 1947
Excerpts from President Truman's Address before a Joint Session of Congress

In 1947 Great Britain informed the United States that it could no longer provide financial assistance to Greece and Turkey, two nations mired in economic and political turmoil. Great Britain's announcement prompted growing fears in Washington that both nations might fall to Communism. On March 12, 1947, President Truman addressed a joint session of Congress and requested $400 million in economic aid for Greece and Turkey. During this address, which was broadcast across the nation on radio, he argued that "It must be the policy of the United States to support free peoples who are resisting attempted subjugation by armed minorities or by outside pressures." This policy, which became known as the Truman Doctrine, guided U.S. foreign policy for the next forty years.

Mr. President, Mr. Speaker, Members of the Congress of the United States:

The gravity of the situation which confronts the world today necessitates my appearance before a joint session of the Congress. The foreign policy and the national security of this country are involved.

One aspect of the present situation, which I wish to present to you at this time for your consideration and decision, concerns Greece and Turkey.

The United States has received from the Greek Government an urgent appeal for financial and economic assistance. Preliminary reports from the American Economic Mission now in Greece and reports from the American Ambassador in Greece corroborate the statement of the Greek Government that assistance is imperative if Greece is to survive as a free nation.

I do not believe that the American people and the Congress wish to turn a deaf ear to the appeal of the Greek Government.

Greece is not a rich country. Lack of sufficient natural resources has always forced the Greek people to work hard to make both ends meet. Since 1940, this industrious and peace loving country has suffered invasion, four years of cruel enemy occupation, and bitter internal strife.

When forces of liberation entered Greece they found that the retreating Germans had destroyed virtually all the railways, roads, port facilities, communications, and merchant marine. More than a thousand villages had been burned. Eighty-five per cent of the children were tubercular. Livestock, poultry, and draft animals had almost disappeared. Inflation had wiped out practically all savings.

As a result of these tragic conditions, a militant minority, exploiting human want and misery, was able to create political chaos which, until now, has made economic recovery impossible.

Greece is today without funds to finance the importation of those goods which are essential to bare subsistence. Under these circumstances the people of Greece cannot make progress in solving their problems of reconstruction. Greece is in desperate need of financial and economic assistance to enable it to resume purchases of food, clothing, fuel, and seeds. These are indispensable for the subsistence of its people and are obtainable only from abroad. Greece must have help to import the goods necessary to restore internal order and security, so essential for economic and political recovery.

The Greek Government has also asked for the assistance of experienced American administrators, economists and technicians to insure that the financial and other aid given to Greece shall be used effectively in creating a stable and self-sustaining economy and in improving its public administration.

The very existence of the Greek state is today threatened by the terrorist activities of several thousand armed men, led by Communists, who defy the government's authority at a number of points, particularly along the northern boundaries. A Commission appointed by the United Nations Security Council is at present investigating disturbed conditions in northern Greece and alleged border violations along the frontier between Greece on the one hand and Albania, Bulgaria, and Yugoslavia on the other.

Meanwhile, the Greek Government is unable to cope with the situation. The Greek army is small and poorly equipped. It needs supplies and equipment if it is to restore the authority of the government throughout Greek territory. Greece must have assistance if it is to become a self-supporting and self-respecting democracy.

The United States must supply that assistance. We have already extended to Greece certain types of relief and economic aid but these are inadequate.

There is no other country to which democratic Greece can turn.

No other nation is willing and able to provide the necessary support for a democratic Greek government.

The British Government, which has been helping Greece, can give no further financial or economic aid after March 31. Great Britain finds itself under the necessity of reducing or liquidating its commitments in several parts of the world, including Greece.

We have considered how the United Nations might assist in this crisis. But the situation is an urgent one requiring immediate action and the United Nations and its related organizations are not in a position to extend help of the kind that is required.

It is important to note that the Greek Government has asked for our aid in utilizing effectively the financial and other assistance we may give to Greece, and in improving its public administration. It is of the utmost importance that we supervise the use of any funds made available to Greece; in such a manner that each dollar spent will count toward making Greece self-supporting, and will help to build an economy in which a healthy democracy can flourish.

No government is perfect. One of the chief virtues of a democracy, however, is that its defects are always visible and under democratic processes can be pointed out and corrected. The Government of Greece is not perfect. Nevertheless it represents 85 per cent of the members of the Greek Parliament who were chosen in an election last year. Foreign observers, including 692 Americans, considered this election to be a fair expression of the views of the Greek people.

The Greek Government has been operating in an atmosphere of chaos and extremism. It has made mistakes. The extension of aid by this country does not mean that the United States condones everything that the Greek Government has done or will do. We have condemned in the past, and we condemn now, extremist measures of the right or the left. We have in the past advised tolerance, and we advise tolerance now.

Greece's neighbor, Turkey, also deserves our attention.

The future of Turkey as an independent and economically sound state is clearly no less important to the freedom-loving peoples of the world than the future of Greece. The circumstances in which Turkey finds itself today are considerably different from those of Greece. Turkey has been spared the disasters that have beset Greece. And during the war, the United States and Great Britain furnished Turkey with material aid.

Nevertheless, Turkey now needs our support.

Since the war Turkey has sought financial assistance from Great Britain and the United States for the purpose of effecting that modernization necessary for the maintenance of its national integrity.

That integrity is essential to the preservation of order in the Middle East.

The British government has informed us that, owing to its own difficulties, it can no longer extend financial or economic aid to Turkey.

As in the case of Greece, if Turkey is to have the assistance it needs, the United States must supply it. We are the only country able to provide that help.

I am fully aware of the broad implications involved if the United States extends assistance to Greece and Turkey, and I shall discuss these implications with you at this time.

One of the primary objectives of the foreign policy of the United States is the creation of conditions in which we and other nations will be able to work out a way of life free from coercion. This was a fundamental issue in the war with Germany and Japan. Our victory was won over countries which sought to impose their will, and their way of life, upon other nations.

To ensure the peaceful development of nations, free from coercion, the United States has taken a leading part in establishing the United Nations. The United Nations is designed to make possible lasting freedom and independence for all its members. We shall not realize our objectives, however, unless we are willing to help free peoples to maintain their free institutions and their national integrity against aggressive movements that seek to impose upon them totalitarian regimes. This is no more than a frank recognition that totalitarian regimes imposed on free peoples, by direct or indirect aggression, undermine the foundations of international peace and hence the security of the United States.

The peoples of a number of countries of the world have recently had totalitarian regimes forced upon them against their will. The Government of the United States has made frequent protests against coercion and intimidation, in violation of the Yalta agreement, in Poland, Rumania, and Bulgaria. I must also state that in a number of other countries there have been similar developments.

At the present moment in world history nearly every nation must choose between alternative ways of life. The choice is too often not a free one.

One way of life is based upon the will of the majority, and is distinguished by free institutions, representative government, free elections, guarantees of individual liberty, freedom of speech and religion, and freedom from political oppression.

The second way of life is based upon the will of a minority forcibly imposed upon the majority. It relies upon terror and oppression, a controlled press and radio, fixed elections, and the suppression of personal freedoms.

I believe that it must be the policy of the United States to support free peoples who are resisting attempted subjugation by armed minorities or by outside pressures.

I believe that we must assist free peoples to work out their own destinies in their own way.

I believe that our help should be primarily through economic and financial aid which is essential to economic stability and orderly political processes.

The world is not static, and the status quo is not sacred. But we cannot allow changes in the status quo in violation of the Charter of the United Nations by such methods as coercion, or by such subterfuges as political infiltration. In helping free and independent nations to maintain their freedom, the United States will be giving effect to the principles of the Charter of the United Nations.

It is necessary only to glance at a map to realize that the survival and integrity of the Greek nation are of grave importance in a much wider situation. If Greece should fall under the control of an armed minority, the effect upon its neighbor, Turkey, would be immediate and serious. Confusion and disorder might well spread throughout the entire Middle East.

Moreover, the disappearance of Greece as an independent state would have a profound effect upon those countries in Europe whose peoples are struggling against great difficulties to maintain their freedoms and their independence while they repair the damages of war.

It would be an unspeakable tragedy if these countries, which have struggled so long against overwhelming odds, should lose that victory for which they sacrificed so much. Collapse of free institutions and loss of independence would be disastrous not only for them but for the world. Discouragement and possibly failure would quickly be the lot of neighboring peoples striving to maintain their freedom and independence.

Should we fail to aid Greece and Turkey in this fateful hour, the effect will be far reaching to the West as well as to the East.

We must take immediate and resolute action.

I therefore ask the Congress to provide authority for assistance to Greece and Turkey in the amount of $400 million for the period ending June 30, 1948. In requesting these funds, I have taken into consideration the maximum amount of relief assistance which would be furnished to Greece out of the $350 million which I recently requested that the Congress authorize for the prevention of starvation and suffering in countries devastated by the war.

In addition to funds, I ask the Congress to authorize the detail of American civilian and military personnel to Greece and Turkey, at the request of those countries, to assist in the tasks of reconstruction, and for the purpose of supervising the use of such financial and material assistance as may be furnished. I recommend that authority also be provided for the instruction and training of selected Greek and Turkish personnel.

Finally, I ask that the Congress provide authority which will permit the speediest and most effective use, in terms of needed commodities, supplies, and equipment, of such funds as may be authorized.

If further funds, or further authority, should be needed for purposes indicated in this message, I shall not hesitate to bring the situation before the Congress. On this subject the Executive and Legislative branches of the Government must work together.

This is a serious course upon which we embark.

I would not recommend it except that the alternative is much more serious. The United States contributed $341 billion toward winning World War II. This is an investment in world freedom and world peace.

The assistance that I am recommending for Greece and Turkey amounts to little more than 1 tenth of 1 per cent of this investment. It is only common sense that we should safeguard this investment and make sure that it was not in vain.

The seeds of totalitarian regimes are nurtured by misery and want. They spread and grow in the evil soil of poverty and strife. They reach their full growth when the hope of a people for a better life has died. We must keep that hope alive.

The free peoples of the world look to us for support in maintaining their freedoms.

If we falter in our leadership, we may endanger the peace of the world—and we shall surely endanger the welfare of our own nation.

Great responsibilities have been placed upon us by the swift movement of events.

I am confident that the Congress will face these responsibilities squarely.

Source: Truman, Harry S. "Special Message to the Congress on Greece and Turkey: The Truman Doctrine," March 12, 1947. Truman Public Papers, Truman Library. Available online at http://trumanlibrary.org/ publicpapers/index.php?pid=2189&st=truman+doctrine&st1=1.

2.2
The Marshall Plan – 1947
Excerpts from George C. Marshall's Harvard University Commencement Address

On July 5, 1947, U.S. Secretary of State George C. Marshall gave a speech at the commencement ceremony at Harvard University. He used this occasion to unveil an ambitious American financial aid program to rebuild war-ravaged Europe. Eligibility for the program was even extended to the Soviet Union. This initiative, quickly dubbed the "Marshall Plan," ultimately provided $13 billion in aid to Europe. This initiative was vital to Europe's postwar economic recovery. The Kremlin, however, saw the Marshall Plan as a threat to its influence on the continent. Joseph Stalin turned down the offer of assistance, and he forbade any of the Soviet Union's satellite states in Eastern Europe from participating.

I need not tell you gentlemen that the world situation is very serious. That must be apparent to all intelligent people. I think one difficulty is that the problem is one of such enormous complexity that the very mass of facts presented to the public by press and radio make it exceedingly difficult for the man in the street to reach a clear appraisement of the situation. Furthermore, the people of this country are distant from the troubled areas of the earth, and it is hard for them to comprehend the plight and consequent reactions of the long-suffering peoples, and the effect of those reactions on their governments in connection with our efforts to promote peace in the world.

"Our policy is directed not against any country or doctrine but against hunger, poverty, desperation, and chaos."

In considering the requirements for the rehabilitation of Europe, the physical loss of life, the visible destruction of cities, factories, mines, and railroads was correctly estimated, but it has become obvious during recent months that this visible destruction was probably less serious than the dislocation of the entire fabric of European economy. For the past 10 years conditions have been highly abnormal. The feverish preparation for war and the more feverish maintenance of the war effort engulfed all aspects of national economies. Machinery has fallen into disrepair or is entirely obsolete. Under the arbitrary and destructive Nazi rule, virtually every possible enterprise was geared into the German war machine. Long-standing commercial ties, private institutions, banks, insurance companies, and shipping companies disappeared, through loss of capital, absorption through nationalization, or by simple destruction. In many countries, confidence in the local currency has been severely shaken. The breakdown of the business structure of Europe during the war was complete. Recovery has been seriously retarded by the fact that two years after the close of hostilities, a peace settlement with Germany and Austria has not been agreed upon. But even given a more prompt solution of these difficult problems, the rehabilitation of the economic structure of Europe quite evidently will require a much longer time and greater effort than has been foreseen.

There is a phase of this matter which is both interesting and serious. The farmer has always produced the foodstuffs to exchange with the city dweller for the other necessities of life. This division of labor is the basis of modern civilization. At the present time it is threatened with breakdown. The town and city industries are not producing adequate goods to exchange with the food-producing farmer. Raw materials and fuel are in short supply. Machinery is lacking or worn out. The farmer or the peasant cannot find the goods for sale which he desires to purchase. So the sale of his farm produce for money which he cannot use seems to him an unprofitable transaction. He, therefore, has withdrawn many fields from crop cultivation and is using them for grazing. He feeds more grain to stock and finds for himself and his family an ample supply of food, however short he may be on clothing and the other ordinary gadgets of civilization.

Meanwhile people in the cities are short of food and fuel, and in some places approaching the starvation levels. So the governments are forced to use their foreign money and credits to procure these necessities abroad. This process exhausts funds which are urgently needed for reconstruction. Thus, a very serious situation is rapidly developing which bodes no good for the world. The modern system of the division of labor upon which the exchange of products is based is in danger of breaking down.

The truth of the matter is that Europe's requirements for the next three or four years of foreign food and other essential products—principally from America—are so much greater than her present ability to pay that she must have substantial additional help or face economic, social, and political deterioration of a very grave character.

The remedy lies in breaking the vicious circle and restoring the confidence of the European people in the economic future of their own countries and of Europe as a whole. The manufacturer and the farmer throughout wide areas must be able and willing to exchange their products for currencies, the continuing value of which is not open to question.

Aside from the demoralizing effect on the world at large and the possibilities of disturbances arising as a result of the desperation of the people concerned, the consequences to the economy of the United States should be apparent to all. It is logical that the United States should do whatever it is able to do to assist in the return of normal economic health in the world, without which there can be no political stability and no assured peace. Our policy is directed not against any country or doctrine but against hunger, poverty, desperation, and chaos. Its purpose should be the revival of a working economy in the world so as to permit the emergence of political and social conditions in which free institutions can exist. Such assistance, I am convinced, must not be on a piecemeal basis as various crises develop. Any assistance that this government may render in the future should provide a cure rather than a mere palliative. Any government that is willing to assist in the task of recovery will find full cooperation, I am sure, on the part of the United States government. Any government which maneuvers to block the recovery of other countries cannot expect help from us. Furthermore, governments, political parties, or groups which seek to perpetuate human misery in order to profit therefrom politically or otherwise will encounter the opposition of the United States.

It is already evident that, before the United States government can proceed much further in its efforts to alleviate the situation and help start the European world on its way to recovery, there must be some agreement among the countries of Europe as to the requirements of the situation and the part those countries themselves will take in order to give proper effect to whatever action might be undertaken by this government. It would be neither fitting nor efficacious for this government to undertake to draw up unilaterally a program designed to place Europe on its feet economically. This is the business of the Europeans. The initiative, I think, must come from Europe. The role of this country should consist of friendly aid in the drafting of a European program and of later support of such a program so far as it may be practical for us to do so. The program should be a joint one, agreed to by a number, if not all, European nations.

An essential part of any successful action on the part of the United States is an understanding on the part of the people of America of the character of the problem and the remedies to be applied. Political passion and prejudice should have no part. With foresight, and a willingness on the part of our people to face up to the vast responsibility which history has clearly placed upon our country, the difficulties I have outlined can and will be overcome.

Source: Marshall, George C. "The Marshall Plan," June 5, 1947. *Congressional Record*, 80th Congress, 1st Session, 1947. Available online at the U.S. Department of State, http://www.usinfo.state.gov/usa/infousa/facts/democrac/57.htm.

2.3
Soviet Reaction to the Marshall Plan – 1947
Andrei Vyshinsky's Speech to the United Nations General Assembly

> *The Marshall Plan had a tremendous effect on post-World War II Europe. It lifted Western Europe out of postwar impoverishment and restored it to a position of global economic and political prominence. The Soviet Union and its satellite nations rejected the aid, however. This decision accelerated the economic and political division of Europe into Eastern and Western blocs. In this September 1947 speech to the United Nations General Assembly, Soviet Deputy Foreign Minister Andrei Vyshinsky explained the Kremlin's opposition to the Marshall Plan.*

…. The so-called Truman Doctrine and the Marshall Plan are particularly glaring examples of the manner in which the principles of the United Nation are violated, of the way in which the organization is ignored.

As the experience of the past few months has shown, the proclamation of this doctrine meant that the United States government has moved towards a direct renunciation of the principles of international collaboration and concerted action

---

Andrei Vyshinsky, Address to the United Nations General Assembly, September 18, 1947. Reprinted with permission from the United Nations.

by the great powers and towards attempts to impose its will on other independent states, while at the same time obviously using the economic resources distributed as relief to individual needy nations as an instrument of political pressure. This is clearly proved by the measures taken by the United States government with regard to Greece and Turkey which ignore and bypass the United Nations as well as by the measures proposed under the so-called Marshall Plan in Europe. This policy conflicts sharply with the principle expressed by the General Assembly in its resolution of 11 December 1946, which declares that relief supplies to other countries "should ... at no time be used as a political weapon."

As is now clear, the Marshall Plan constitutes in essence merely a variant of the Truman Doctrine adapted to the conditions of postwar Europe. In bringing forward this plan, the United States government apparently counted on the cooperation of governments of the United Kingdom and France to confront the European countries in need of relief with the necessity of renouncing their inalienable right to dispose of their economic resources and to plan their national economy in their own way. The United States also counted on making all these countries directly dependent on the interests of American monopolies, which are striving to avert the approaching depression by an accelerated export of commodities and capital to Europe....

It is becoming more and more evident to everyone that the implementation of the Marshall Plan will mean placing European countries under the economic and political control of the United States and direct interference by the latter in the internal affairs of those countries.

Moreover, this plan is an attempt to split Europe into two camps and, with the help of the United Kingdom and France, to complete the formation of a bloc of several European countries hostile to the interests of the democratic countries of Eastern Europe and most particularly to the interests of the Soviet Union.

An important feature of this plan is the attempt to confront the countries of Eastern Europe with a bloc of Western European states including Western Germany. The intention is to make use of Western Germany and German heavy industry (the Ruhr) as one of the most important economic bases for American expansion in Europe, in disregard of the national interests of the countries which suffered from German aggression.

I need only recall these facts to show the utter incompatibility of this policy of the United States, and of the British and French governments which support it, with the fundamental principles of the United Nations.

Source: Vyshinsky, Andrei. Address to the United Nations General Assembly, September 18, 1947. *Official Records of the General Assembly*, Second Session, Verbatim Record, Vol. I, September 16-November 29, 1947. Geneva: United Nations, 1947.

2.4

An American Commander Recalls the Berlin Airlift – 1948-49
"Inside the Berlin Airlift" by T. Ross Milton

In June 1948 the Soviet Union blocked road access to all Western sectors within West Berlin, which was located deep within the Soviet administrative zone of postwar Germany. On June 25, 1948, the United States and Great Britain launched the Berlin Airlift in response. This massive effort delivered vital food, clothing, fuel, and other supplies to trapped West Berliners. The airlift lasted from June 25, 1948, to September 30, 1949. The Soviets actually lifted the blockade on May 11, 1949; by then, the blockade had not only failed but become a public relations nightmare for the Kremlin. But the West continued with the airlift until the end of September because it wanted to provide extra supplies to West Berlin in case the Soviets reimposed a blockade at a later time. The following recollection of the airlift was written by retired U.S. Air Force General T. Ross Milton, a World War II fighter pilot who served as chief of staff for the Combined Berlin Airlift Task Force in 1948-49.

The spring of 1948 began quietly enough. New cars were once again in the showrooms, a chaotic demobilization had ended, and the main excitement ahead, it appeared, would be the presidential election. On June 24, the Republican Party confidently nominated Thomas E. Dewey for the White House. The Democrats, having failed to attract Dwight D. Eisenhower, resigned themselves to Harry S. Truman and defeat.

That same day, Soviet forces had halted all surface traffic into Berlin, citing "technical difficulties." They also shut down electricity for the Allied sectors in the German city. Allied currency reform provided the proximate cause for this new Soviet provocation, but it was plain that dictator Joseph Stalin intended to end the curious status of Berlin, which had become a Western outpost deep inside Soviet-controlled territory.

Gen. Lucius D. Clay, commander of US forces in occupied Germany and Europe and a steadfast figure if there ever was one, announced that no Soviet action short of war would force the Americans out of Berlin. The question was how to make good on that promise, for the Western sectors of the city had a total of less than two weeks of critical supplies, and the small American force in Germany could not have put down the mighty Red Army.

Some farsighted fellow at the Potsdam Conference had inserted a provision for three air corridors into Berlin, and Clay now asked Lt. Gen. Curtis E. LeMay,

Gen. T. Ross Milton, USAF (Ret.), "Inside the Berlin Airlift," Air Force Magazine, October 1998. © 1998 Air Force Association. Reprinted with permission.

the commander of US forces in Europe, to exploit them with an emergency airlift. Looking around for someone to do just that, LeMay tagged Brig. Gen. Joseph Smith, Wiesbaden (Germany) Military Post commander. As he assembled this ad hoc operation with about 100 C-47 "Gooney Birds" left over from Sicily and Arnhem and pilots pulled away from their desks and other duties, a distinct chill settled over occupied Germany.

Life up to that point had been relatively pleasant for the Western occupying forces, with nice old houses requisitioned as family quarters and cheap cigarettes, coffee, and other items widely, if unofficially, used as currency. A few cigarettes could get your laundry done, a carton or so might fetch a hunting rifle or even a piano…. Cigarettes were far too valuable for the occupied, the Germans, to smoke until, that is, they reached the farmers. They, having life's necessities, smoked them.

No Compromise

British officials agreed with Clay's uncompromising stand and had, in fact, been a little ahead on preparations for an airlift. The other concerned ally, France, initially distanced itself from this challenge but only briefly. France, preoccupied with its struggle in Indochina, had almost nothing in the way of air transport available in Europe. They would make a significant contribution later on, however.

The West's improbable answer to the hostile Soviet action got under way June 26. On July 4, with a maximum effort, US airlifters delivered 675 tons. It was clearly an all-out performance, one that could not be continued for long. An assortment of Dakotas (British C-47s) and converted bombers were delivering a similar amount. Since Berlin required a minimum of 2,500 tons of food per day to sustain the lives of the two million inhabitants in the Allied sectors, any serious long-term effort would require some major commitments.

"The Berlin Airlift was the first real event of the Cold War. Many people in high places thought it was the first event in World War III."

One of the few persons on earth who truly believed air transport could solve this problem was Maj. Gen. William H. Tunner, and he was chafing to get involved. There was no similar enthusiasm to be found within the Air Staff. Any major diversion of air transport to Berlin would have a serious effect on combat capabilities, and there was a general view that this blockade might very well lead to war.

Tunner left on an inspection swing around Military Air Transport Service bases, leaving me with instructions to haunt the Pentagon and find out what was going on. He called each night, and he was not happy with the news, for there appeared to be no sentiment for a major effort and no mention of Tunner going over to run it.

Tunner had commanded "the Hump" operation from India into China during the last year of World War II. Army Lt. Gen. Albert C. Wedemeyer, Defense Department director of plans and operations, remembered this as he surveyed the situation in Europe. He, seconded by the undersecretary of the Army, William H. Draper, Jr., urged that Tunner be sent without delay to take over the airlift to Berlin.

It was a persuasive recommendation. Tunner was ordered to proceed to Wiesbaden, along with whomever he needed, and assume command of the airlift under the overall command of CINCUSAFE. He left almost immediately in a C-54 with his longtime pilot and friend, Col. Red Forman, at the controls. I was to follow with the people Tunner decided were needed. We left a few days later with a few secretaries and various staff officers. Our orders called for 30 days of temporary duty. No room for us was available in the existing USAFE headquarters building, a rambling structure in downtown Wiesbaden, so we located some apartments on Taunusstrasse, facing a small park featuring hot sulfur baths. The Schwartzerbach Hotel, where Tunner and I lived, was just a block away. The Rose, home for most of the staff, was even closer. And so, barely adjusted to the local time, we set out to survey the situation.

Edge of Exhaustion

Wiesbaden AB, undamaged and with fine permanent structures, was one of two bases that Smith was using for the Berlin run. The sight that greeted us there was not encouraging. It was evident that everyone—pilots, supervisors, everyone—was on the edge of exhaustion. The same was true at RheinMain AB, near Frankfort. Operation Vittles, as Smith had dubbed his operation, had been a heroic effort, but the end was clearly in sight, barring major reinforcements.

Some of these reinforcements, in the form of C-54 troop carrier wings, were already on the way. However, US authorities had registered no specific requirement. We had made only tentative calculations.

At about this time, a call came from LeMay's office, and Tunner sent me over to see what the general wanted. He wanted to know how many C-54s we would need for the mission. I told LeMay I would hustle back to airlift headquarters and get right on it. He had a different idea. LeMay, direct as always, motioned to a chair and table in the corner of his office and told me to do it there. Maj. Gen. August Kissner, LeMay's chief of staff, came in with pencils, paper, and a slide rule, and I was left to my thoughts while LeMay entertained some foreign visitors.

I scratched away and came up with a total of 225 C-54s, using some planning figures that I knew to be in Tunner's mind. Clay was waiting for the answer. LeMay took my work sheet and placed a call to Berlin, meanwhile giving me a wave of dismissal. I lingered in the outer office long enough to hear LeMay give Clay not my total, but my subtotal. I didn't dare barge back in. Instead, I hurried back to Tunner and told him what had gone on. He approved the figure of 225 and ordered me back on the run to correct the inaccurate statement that I had overheard. LeMay then placed a second call to Clay, said something to the effect that we had made some corrections, and gave Clay the right number. Hanging up, he said: "Thanks, Milton"—a rare encomium from that taciturn man.

That summer, the C-47s were retired in favor of the augmented force of C-54s, and Tunner began to eye bases in the British zone, where the distance was a third shorter and the flat terrain allowed for shorter climbs. British authorities readily agreed to make room for the more productive C-54s and chose Fassberg, an old Luftwaffe training base on the Lueneburg Heath. Our initial reactions were favorable. The base had fine permanent buildings, a gymnasium with an indoor swimming pool, and a visiting officers' quarters, complete with a huge armchair, rumored to have been reserved for Hermann Goering, the Luftwaffe chief and No. 2 Nazi official in Hitler's Germany.

Fassberg in Danger

The initial results at Fassburg more than justified the move. However, as initial enthusiasm ran down, real difficulties began to develop. The combination of depressing surroundings, divided authority, and an impersonal functional organization patterned after the airlines—one that worked against any sense of unit esprit—proved too much. The operation at Fassberg began to come apart.

The cure was simple and the results dramatic. The Air Force reorganized the pilots and mechanics into squadrons and started to make recreational runs to Hamburg and Copenhagen. The Royal Air Force turned Fassberg over to the US Air Force, with Col. Theron "Jack" Coulter assuming command. His wife, movie star Constance Bennett, showed herself as one of the most formidable scroungers in any service. The mess halls and the barracks were spruced up with new furniture and the latest movies shipped by USAFE supply services. Fassberg, very nearly a Berlin Airlift disaster, became a showpiece.

Britain followed up its gift of Fassberg with an offer of another base at Celle, an attractive town near Hanover. An old fighter base, Celle was without runways or, it seemed, room for a runway, but the facilities were excellent. The British said not to worry and, dragooning the locals, gave an insight into how the British Empire came about.

As the summer went on, the airlift began to lose the happy informality of its early days. One horrendous foul-up over Berlin put an end to the sleepy air traffic control system that had served Berlin well enough before the blockade. The weather was bad that Friday, Aug. 13, and Tunner was due in Berlin. He was, in fact, overdue, as his airplane milled about in the stack with an undetermined number of others. Meanwhile, new arrivals were en route along the corridors, generating a chaotic condition that infuriated Tunner.

As it turned out, the day was a blessing. Given such an unmistakable warning, the Air Force moved when it still had time to straighten out the procedures before the bad weather set in around Berlin. The job was splendidly done by Maj. Sterling Bettinger, who got some professional air traffic controllers back in uniform before the weather turned really sour.

Tunner's Rules

Admittedly, the new procedures instituted after that infamous Friday were calculated to make any air traffic controller's job easier. Exact airspeeds were specified for climb, cruise, and letdown. Tunner declared a new rule forbidding second tries at a Berlin landing. This made for a smooth and continuous circuit, eliminating the need for holding patterns. These factors, plus the arrival of the new CPS-5 radar, made it in all likelihood the best ordered air traffic situation in history.

Another edict required all pilots to make their approaches under instrument conditions, regardless of the weather. The Ground Control Approach teams, given this continual exercise, became wonderfully proficient. There was a particular final approach controller, a Sergeant McNulty as I remember, who could make you believe, by gentle corrections interspersed with compliments, that your rotten job of flying into Templehof was one of aviation's milestones.

Across town, at Gatow, things were no different except for the accents. There the RAF [England's Royal Air Force] was in charge and thus host to the C-54s from Fassberg and Celle. Sometimes the long nights in the Gatow tower were lightened by some irreverent American radio calls. There was the anonymous poet who gladdened the British traffic controllers with his inbound report:

Here comes a Yankee
With a blackened soul
Heading for Gatow
With a load of coal.

With the exception of December's battles against a heavy fog, one that brought back memories of the Great Fog of 1944 and the Battle of the Ardennes, the airlift became almost routine. Visitors who came for a look at this famous defiance of Stalin were slightly disappointed by the orderly and measured way the airplanes came and went through Berlin.

There was, however, one bit of excitement, and it was provided by the French. The Allies had constructed a third airfield, located on a former panzer drill ground in the French sector. The labor force which carried out this project was recruited from the local populace, and it was made up of a most unlikely mix of women and men, young and old, most of whom gave no indication of having ever before done manual labor. However, no group had ever worked harder and with such goodwill. Aggregate for the runways came from the rubble of air raids, and the heavy machinery, too large for our aircraft, had been sliced up by acetylene torch at RheinMain, carefully marked, and welded back together at Tegel. At last, everything was ready for the start of operations, except for one thing. In the midst of the traffic pattern stood a 200-foot-tall radio tower, one that belonged to Soviet controlled East Berlin.

British and American diplomats proposed a diplomatic solution to the problem. It called for the Soviets, in return for compensation, to dismantle the obstructing tower. French forces thought this notion preposterous. And so, one morning, soon after Tegel opened for business, Brig. Gen. Jean Ganeval had a platoon of engineers march to the tower, lay some charges, and blow it flat. Direct action, the French said, is what the Russians understand. Tegel made a substantial contribution to the airlift and is today, in its modern form, Berlin's principal airport.

Early in the airlift, Britain agreed to the concept of a unified command structure with Tunner commanding and Air Commodore J.W.F. Merer as his deputy. One RAF officer, Group Capt. Noel Hyde, an unforgettable fellow who had spent four years of the war engineering escapes from Axis POW camps, came down to represent RAF interests and act as chief of plans. The rest of our staff remained as before, and there was never a time when there was any friction between the two Allies. Relations between the temporary duty Airlift Task Force and USAFE were not quite as congenial after the arrival of LeMay's successor, Lt. Gen. John K. Cannon, but it wasn't important. It was just one of those things.

Still Vivid

Even after the passage of 50 years, it is easy to remember the tension of that period. Scarcely three years had passed since we had thought of Germany as enemy territory. It still caused a flinch to lumber across, at vulnerable altitudes, those dangerous places we remembered so well. Now we had a new adversary with 300,000 troops within a day's march of the border separating East and West Germany and nothing to stop them if they invaded.

Well, almost nothing. The United States did have a monopoly on the atomic bomb and the means—B-29s—to deliver it. Indeed, early in the crisis, Washington had deployed a squadron of B-29s to the UK, without fanfare. Even so, it was evident that Moscow got the message. Our strategy, as it would be for many years to come, was one of all or nothing if it came to war.

For reasons that have never been made clear, the Soviet Union made no serious attempt to sabotage the airlift. Fighters occasionally made passes at the lumbering transports, but that was it. It would have been simple to jab the GCA frequencies and the navigational beacons, but it was never done. For want of a better answer, we have to credit the presence of those American B-29 bombers in the UK.

The Berlin Airlift was the first real event of the Cold War. Many people in high places thought it was the first event in World War III. It gave credence to the need for the NATO Alliance and it was reassuring evidence that the United States had a firm ally in Britain. Berlin, a shattered city in 1948, was an island under siege. Now, it is once more the elegant capital of a unified Germany. And while there are many things that contributed to the present happy state in Berlin, the airlift, 50 years ago, was a vivid show of Allied resolution and competence at a very dangerous time.

Source: Milton, T. Ross. "Inside the Berlin Airlift." *Air Force Magazine*, October 1998.

2.5

The Formation of the North Atlantic Treaty Organization (NATO) – 1949
The Text of the NATO Treaty

In January 1949 U.S. President Harry S. Truman announced his intention to provide military aid to Western Europe. Four months later, the North Atlantic Treaty was signed by representatives of the United States, Canada, and ten West European governments. Under the terms of this mutual defense pact, all signatories agreed to come to the aid of each other if attacked. Historians agree that this momentous pact was a direct response to the perceived threat of Soviet aggression. Today, NATO has twenty-six members from North America and Europe.

Washington DC, 4th April 1949

The Parties to this Treaty reaffirm their faith in the purposes and principles of the Charter of the United Nations and their desire to live in peace with all peoples and all governments.

They are determined to safeguard the freedom, common heritage and civilisation of their peoples, founded on the principles of democracy, individual liberty and the rule of law.

They seek to promote stability and well-being in the North Atlantic area.

They are resolved to unite their efforts for collective defence and for the preservation of peace and security.

They therefore agree to this North Atlantic Treaty:

ARTICLE 1

The Parties undertake, as set forth in the Charter of the United Nations, to settle any international dispute in which they may be involved by peaceful means in such a manner that international peace and security and justice are not endangered, and to refrain in their international relations from the threat or use of force in any manner inconsistent with the purposes of the United Nations.

ARTICLE 2

The Parties will contribute toward the further development of peaceful and friendly international relations by strengthening their free institutions, by bringing about a better understanding of the principles upon which these institutions are founded, and by promoting conditions of stability and well-being. They will seek to eliminate conflict in their international economic policies and will encourage economic collaboration between any or all of them.

ARTICLE 3

In order more effectively to achieve the objectives of this Treaty, the Parties, separately and jointly, by means of continuous and effective self-help and mutual aid, will maintain and develop their individual and collective capacity to resist armed attack.

ARTICLE 4

The Parties will consult together whenever, in the opinion of any of them, the territorial integrity, political independence or security of any of the Parties is threatened.

ARTICLE 5

The Parties agree that an armed attack against one or more of them in Europe or North America shall be considered an attack against them all, and consequently they agree that, if such an armed attack occurs, each of them, in exercise of the right of individual or collective self defence recognised by Article 51 of the Charter of the United Nations, will assist the Party or Parties so attacked by taking forthwith, individually, and in concert with the other Parties, such action as it deems necessary, including the use of armed force, to restore and maintain the security of the North Atlantic area.

Any such armed attack and all measures taken as a result thereof shall immediately be reported to the Security Council. Such measures shall be terminated when the Security Council has taken the measures necessary to restore and maintain international peace and security.

ARTICLE 6

For the purpose of Article 5, an armed attack on one or more of the Parties is deemed to include an armed attack:

- on the territory of any of the Parties in Europe or North America, on the Algerian Departments of France (2), on the territory of Turkey or on the islands under the jurisdiction of any of the Parties in the North Atlantic area north of the Tropic of Cancer;

- on the forces, vessels, or aircraft of any of the Parties, when in or over these territories or any area in Europe in which occupation forces of any of the Parties were stationed on the date when the Treaty entered into force or the Mediterranean Sea or the North Atlantic area north of the Tropic of Cancer.

ARTICLE 7

The Treaty does not affect, and shall not be interpreted as affecting, in any way the rights and obligations under the Charter of the Parties which are members of the United Nations, or the primary responsibility of the Security Council for the maintenance of international peace and security.

ARTICLE 8

Each Party declares that none of the international engagements now in force between it and any other of the Parties or any third State is in conflict with the provisions of this Treaty, and undertakes not to enter into any international engagement in conflict with this Treaty.

ARTICLE 9

The Parties hereby establish a Council, on which each of them shall be represented to consider matters concerning the implementation of this Treaty. The Council shall be so organised as to be able to meet promptly at any time. The Council shall set up such subsidiary bodies as may be necessary; in particular it shall establish immediately a defence committee which shall recommend measures for the implementation of Articles 3 and 5.

ARTICLE 10

The Parties may, by unanimous agreement, invite any other European State in a position to further the principles of this Treaty and to contribute to the security of the North Atlantic area to accede to this Treaty. Any State so invited may become a party to the Treaty by depositing its instrument of accession with the Government of the United States of America. The Government of the United States of America will inform each of the Parties of the deposit of each such instrument of accession.

ARTICLE 11

This Treaty shall be ratified and its provisions carried out by the Parties in accordance with their respective constitutional processes. The instruments of ratification shall be deposited as soon as possible with the Government of the United States of America, which will notify all the other signatories of each deposit. The Treaty shall enter into force between the States which have ratified it as soon as the ratification of the majority of the signatories, including the ratifications of Belgium, Canada, France, Luxembourg, the Netherlands, the United Kingdom and the United States, have been deposited and shall come into effect with respect to other States on the date of the deposit of their ratifications.

ARTICLE 12

After the Treaty has been in force for ten years, or at any time thereafter, the Parties shall, if any of them so requests, consult together for the purpose of reviewing the Treaty, having regard for the factors then affecting peace and security in the North Atlantic area including the development of universal as well as regional arrangements under the Charter of the United Nations for the maintenance of international peace and security.

ARTICLE 13

After the Treaty has been in force for twenty years, any Party may cease to be a Party one year after its notice of denunciation has been given to the Government of the United States of America, which will inform the Governments of the other Parties of the deposit of each notice of denunciation.

ARTICLE 14

This Treaty, of which the English and French texts are equally authentic, shall be deposited in the archives of the Government of the United States of America. Duly certified copies will be transmitted by that government to the governments of the other signatories.

Source: North Atlantic Treaty Organization. "The North Atlantic Treaty, 4 April 1949." *American Foreign Policy 1950-1955: Basic Documents*. Vol. 1, Department of State Publication 6446, General Foreign Policy Series 117. Washington, DC: Government Printing Office, 1957. Available online at http://www.nato.int/docu/basictxt/treaty.htm.

3

THE KOREAN WAR

A grief-stricken American infantryman comforts another soldier who has lost a friend to enemy
fire in Korea, site of a long and bloody war between U.S. and Communist forces.

INTRODUCTION

During the late 1940s, the Cold War between the Americans and the Soviets seemed to become more menacing with each passing month. In September 1949, for example, the Soviets successfully exploded their first atomic bomb. This was an alarming development for American scientists and lawmakers who had believed that the USSR was several years away from possessing "the Bomb." One month later, Communist forces led by Mao Zedong formally took control of China after a two-decade-long civil war with the government of Nationalist leader Chiang Kai-shek. Mao announced that the "liberated" nation would henceforth be known as the People's Republic of China. Chiang and his inner circle fled into exile on the island of Taiwan and set up a government in exile, the Republic of China.

The Communist victory in China was a tremendous psychological blow to the United States. It had given millions of dollars in aid to the corrupt Chiang government to help it fend off the Communists. Some analysts feared that Mao's rise to power could jeopardize Western efforts to remake postwar Japan as a reliable ally of the West.

These worries soon intensified. Both Mao and Soviet leader Joseph Stalin were uneasy about their counterpart's ambitions and political designs, yet the two Communist leaders managed to negotiate a Sino-Soviet Treaty of Friendship in February 1950. This announcement marked the opening of the Asian theatre as a major battleground in the Cold War and intensified an already fiery partisan debate in Washington about who was most responsible for "losing China" to the Communists. It also convinced President Harry Truman to order the development of a hydrogen bomb, a weapon much more powerful than the atomic bombs that had decimated the Japanese cities of Hiroshima and Nagasaki.

A few months later, Communist North Korean forces staged a surprise invasion of South Korea. This attack—which was encouraged by both the Soviets and the Chinese—was led by Kim Il Sung, a veteran North Korean guerrilla leader who had directed the fight against Japan's long occupation of the Korean Peninsula.

Japan had controlled the country since 1910, but it had been forced to relinquish its grip on Korea at the end of World War II. In the weeks following the war, however, the Allies had partitioned the peninsula. They divided the country along the 38th parallel into a northern half under Communist rule and a southern region protected by the West. Subsequent efforts to unify the country under a single government had failed, wrecked by nonstop American and Soviet maneuvering for advantage.

By 1950 the United States had withdrawn virtually all of its armed forces from the Korean peninsula. This departure left North Korea with overwhelming military superiority over South Korea. Both Mao and Stalin became convinced that the Americans would never risk a third world war over the peninsula. On June 25, 1950, North Korean troops invaded South Korea with the intention to unify the country under Communist rule.

American Forces in Korea

But the Communists miscalculated the U.S. response. As North Koreans flooded into the South, Truman declared that "the attack upon Korea makes it plain beyond all doubt that Communism has passed beyond the use of subversion to conquer independent nations and will now use armed invasion and war." The United States recognized that events in Korea posed a direct challenge to its stated vow of containing Communist aggression around the world. The United States thus mobilized all its armed forces to come to the aid of South Korean President Syngman Rhee and his government.

The U.S. military suffered a series of jarring defeats after its arrival on the Korean peninsula. General Douglas MacArthur's bold landing at Inchon on September 15, 1950, temporarily turned the tide in favor of the American and South Korean forces. But MacArthur then made a tragic blunder. Armed with a United Nations resolution stating that the "essential objective" of the UN troops "was the establishment of a unified, independent and democratic Government of Korea," he charged deep into North Korea. Ignoring warnings that Chinese leaders might be aroused by the presence of American troops on their border, MacArthur instead suggested that the war might be over by that very Christmas.

70

As it turned out, MacArthur's offensive to the Chinese border provoked a fearsome response from Mao and Chinese military leaders. In mid-October, tens of thousands of Chinese "volunteers" flooded into North Korea in an unrelenting assault on the UN forces (composed primarily of U.S. and South Korean troops). "The oncoming waves of massed manpower were astonishing, terrifying, and to those Americans who believed the war was over, utterly demoralizing," wrote historian Clay Blair in *The Forgotten War*.

Over the next few months, Chinese and North Korean forces pushed the Americans and their South Korean allies back behind the 38th parallel. In December 1950 U.S. General Matthew B. Ridgway assumed command of the Eighth Army, the cornerstone of the American military presence in Korea. In his own words, he inherited "a bewildered army, not sure of itself or its leaders, not sure what they were doing there, wondering when they would hear the whistle of that homebound transport."

Ridgway did a remarkable job of reversing the morale and performance of the Eighth Army in the opening months of 1951. When Truman stripped MacArthur of his command in April 1951 for insubordination, Ridgway was given the reins as commander of U.S. armed forces in the Far East. But the best he could do was to turn the war into a bloody stalemate for the next two years. In July 1953 the warring parties finally signed an armistice that brought the fighting to a close, but failed to unify the country. Instead, both the Communist North Korean government and pro-Western South Korean government were left intact, presiding over territories that were virtually the same as before the war.

DOCUMENTS

3.1
Truman Sends American Troops into Korea – 1950
The Text of a Public Statement by President Truman

In the wake of North Korea's surprise invasion of South Korea, U.S. President Harry S. Truman publicly condemned the invasion in strong terms. He also declared his belief that events on the Korean Peninsula showed that "Communism has passed beyond the use of subversion to conquer independent nations and will now use armed invasion and war." Following is the complete text of Truman's statement of June 27, 1950.

In Korea the Government forces, which were armed to prevent border raids and to preserve internal security, were attacked by invading forces from North Korea. The Security Council of the United Nations called upon the invading troops to cease hostilities and to withdraw to the 38th parallel. This they have not done, but on the contrary, have pressed the attack. The Security Council called upon all members of the United Nations to render every assistance to the United Nations in the execution of this resolution. In these circumstances, I have ordered United States air and sea forces to give the Korean Government troops cover and support.

The attack upon Korea makes it plain beyond all doubt that Communism has passed beyond the use of subversion to conquer independent nations and will now use armed invasion and war. It has defied the orders of the Security Council of the United Nations issued to preserve international peace and security. In these circumstances, the occupation of Formosa [now called Taiwan] by Communist forces would be a direct threat to the security of the Pacific area and to United States forces performing their lawful and necessary functions in that area.

Accordingly, I have ordered the Seventh Fleet to prevent any attack on Formosa. As a corollary of this action I am calling upon the Chinese Government on Formosa to cease all air and sea operations against the mainland. The Seventh Fleet will see that this is done. The determination of the future status of Formosa must await the restoration of security in the Pacific, a peace settlement with Japan, or consideration by the United Nations.

I have also directed that United States Forces in the Philippines be strengthened and that military assistance to the Philippine Government be accelerated.

I have similarly directed acceleration in the furnishing of military assistance to the forces of France and the Associated States in Indo China and the dispatch of a military mission to provide close working relations with those forces.

I know that all members of the United Nations will consider carefully the consequences of this latest aggression in Korea in defiance of the Charter of the United Nations. A return to the rule of force in international affairs would have far reaching effects. The United States will continue to uphold the rule of law.

I have instructed Ambassador Austin, as the representative of the United States to the Security Council, to report these steps to the Council.

Source: Truman, Harry S. "Statement by the President on the Situation in Korea." June 27, 1950. Truman Public Papers, Truman Library. Available online at http://trumanlibrary.org/publicpapers/index.php?pid=800&st=&st1=.

3.2

Herbert Hoover's "Fortress America" Speech – 1950
Excerpts from a National Radio Broadcast

> *In the years immediately following the end of World War II, factions within the United States waged a struggle to shape the nation's foreign policy philosophy. After World War II, many Americans believed that the country had a responsibility to encourage democracy abroad and defend vulnerable nations from Communist aggression. But many other Americans continued to adhere to an "isolationist" philosophy that had been widespread prior to World War II. According to this view, the United States should refrain from becoming entangled in any foreign struggles that did not pose a direct threat to its welfare. This belief system also became known as the "fortress America" program. The following speech by former president Herbert Hoover, given to a nationwide radio audience only weeks after China had entered the Korean War, illustrates many of the fundamental tenets of American isolationist thought during that era.*

I speak with a deep sense of responsibility. And I speak tonight under the anxieties of every American for the nation's sons who are fighting and dying on a mission of peace and the honor of our country.

No appraisal of the world situation can be final in an unstable world. However, to find our national path we must constantly reexamine where we have arrived

---

Herbert Hoover, "Our National Policies in This Crisis" (Address, December 20, 1950). Reprinted with permission from the Herbert Hoover Presidential Library and Museum.

and at times revise our direction. I do not propose to traverse the disastrous road by which we reached this point.

We may first survey the global military situation. There is today only one center of aggression on the earth. That is the Communist-controlled Asian-European land mass of 800 million people. They have probably over 300 trained and equipped combat divisions with over 30,000 tanks, 10,000 tactical planes, and further large reserves they can put in action in ninety days. But they are not a great sea power. Their long-range power is limited. This congeries of over thirty different races will some day go to pieces. But in the meantime they furnish unlimited cannon fodder.

Facing this menace on the Eastern front there are about 100 million non-Communist island people in Japan, Formosa, the Philippines, and Korea. Aside from Korea... they have probably only twelve effective combat divisions with practically no tanks, air, or navy.

Facing this land mass on the south are the Indies and the Middle East of about 600 million non-Communist people. There are about 150 million further non-Communist people in North Africa and Latin America. Except Turkey and Formosa, these 850 million non-Communist people have little military force which they would or could spare. But they could contribute vital economic and moral strength.

> *"Americans have no reason for hysteria or loss of confidence in our security or our future. And in American security rests the future security of all mankind."*

Facing this menace on the Continental European front there are about 160 million further non-Communist people who, excluding Spain, have less than twenty combat divisions now available, few tanks, and little air or naval force. And their will to defend themselves is feeble and their disunities are manifest.

Of importance in military weight at this moment there is the British Commonwealth of 150 million people, with probably thirty combat divisions under arms, a superior Navy, considerable Air Force, and a few tanks.

And there are 150 million people in the United States preparing 3.5 million men into a gigantic Air Force and Navy, with about thirty equipped combat divisions. Thus there are 1,310,000,000 non-Communist people in the world, of whom today only about 320 million have any military potency.

If we weigh these military forces as they stand today, we must arrive at certain basic conclusions:

1. We must face the fact that to commit the sparse ground forces of the non-Communist nations into a land war against this Communist land mass would be a war without victory, a war without a successful political terminal. The Ger-

mans failed with a magnificent army of 240 combat divisions and with powerful air and tank forces. That compares with only 60 divisions proposed today for the North Atlantic Pact nations. Even were Western Europe armed far beyond any contemplated program, we could never reach Moscow. Therefore, any attempt to make war on the Communist mass by land invasion, through the quicksands of China, India, or Western Europe, is sheer folly. That would be the graveyard of millions of American boys and would end in the exhaustion of this Gibraltar of Western civilization.

2. Equally, we Americans alone, with sea and air power, can so control the Atlantic and Pacific Oceans that there can be no possible invasion of the Western Hemisphere by Communist armies. They can no more reach Washington in force than we can reach Moscow.

3. In this military connection we must realize the fact that the atomic bomb is a far less dominant weapon that it was once thought to be.

4. It is obvious that the United Nations have been defeated in Korea by the aggression of Communist China. There are no available forces in the world to repel them. Even if we sacrifice more American boys to hold a bridgehead, we know we shall not succeed at the present time in the mission given to us by the fifty members of the United Nations.

We may explore our American situation still further. The 150 million American people are already economically strained by government expenditures. It must not be forgotten that we are carrying huge burdens from previous wars, including obligations to veterans and $260 billion of bond and currency issues from those wars. In the fiscal year 1952, federal and local expenditures are likely to exceed $90 billion. That is more than our total savings. We must finance huge deficits by further government issues. Inflation is already moving. The dollar has in six months fallen 15 or 20 percent in purchasing power. But we might with stern measures avoid the economic disintegration of such a load for a very few years. If we continued long on this road, the one center of resistance in the world will collapse in economic disaster.

We may also appraise the diplomatic front. Our great hope was in the United Nations. We have witnessed the sabotage of its primary purpose of preserving peace. It has been down to last week, a forum for continuous smear on our honor, our ideals, and our purposes. It did stiffen up against raw aggression last July in Korea. But in its call for that military action, America had to furnish over 90 percent of the foreign forces and suffer over 90 percent of their dead and injured. That effort now comes at least to a measurable military defeat by the aggression of Communist hordes.

Whether or not the United Nations is to have a moral defeat and suffer the collapse of its whole moral stature now depends on whether it has the courage to:

1. Declare Communist China an aggressor.

2. Refuse admission of this aggressor to its membership.

3. Demand that each member of the United Nations cease to furnish or transport supplies of any kind to Communist China that can aid in their military operations. Such a course honestly carried out by the non-Communist nations is not economic sanctions nor does it require military actions. But it would constitute a great pressure for rectitude.

4. For once, pass a resolution condemning the infamous lies about the United States.

Any course short of such action is appeasement.

And now I come to where we should go from here…. First, the foundation of our national policies must be to preserve the world this Western Hemisphere Gibraltar of Western civilization.

Second, we can, without any measure of doubt, with our own air and naval forces, hold the Atlantic and Pacific Oceans with one frontier on Britain (if she wishes to cooperate); the other, on Japan, Formosa, and the Philippines. We can hold open the sea lanes for our supplies. And I devoutly hope that a maximum of cooperation can be established between the British Commonwealth and ourselves.

Third, to do this we should arm our air and naval forces to the teeth. We have little need for large armies unless we are going to Europe or China. We should give Japan her independence and aid her in arms to defend herself. We should stiffen the defenses of our Pacific frontier in Formosa and the Philippines. We can protect this island chain by our sea and air power.

Fourth, we could, after initial outlays for more air and navy equipment, greatly reduce our expenditures, balance our budget, and free ourselves from the dangers of inflation and economic degeneration.

Fifth, if we toil and sacrifice as the President has so well asked, we can continue aid to the hungry of the world. Out of our productivity, we can give aid to other nations when they have already displayed spirit and strength in defense against Communism. We have the stern duty to work and sacrifice to do it.

Sixth, we should have none of appeasement. Morally there is no appeasement of Communism. Appeasement contains more dangers than Dunkirks. We want no more Teherans and no more Yaltas. We can retrieve a battle but we cannot retrieve an appeasement. We are grateful that President Truman has denounced such a course.

Seventh, we are not blind to the need to preserve Western civilization on the continent of Europe or to our cultural and religious ties to it. But the prime obligation of defense of Western Continental Europe rests upon the nations of Europe. The test is whether they have the spiritual force, the will, and acceptance of unity among them by their own volition. America cannot create their spiritual forces; we cannot buy them with money.

You can search all the history of mankind and there is no parallel to the effort and sacrifice we have made to elevate their spirit and to achieve their unity. To this date it has failed. Their minds are confused with fears and disunities. They exclude Spain, although she has the will and means to fight. They higgle with Germany, although she is their frontier. They vacillate in the belief that they are in little danger and they hope to avoid again being a theater of war. And Karl Marx had added to their confusions. They still suffer from battle shock. Their highly organized Communist parties are a menace that we must not ignore.

In both World War I and World War II (including West Germany) those nations placed more than 250 trained and equipped combat divisions in the field within sixty days, with strong air and naval forces. They have more manpower and more productive capacity today than in either one of those wars. To warrant our further aid they should show they have spiritual strength and unity to avail themselves of their own resources. But it must be far more than pacts, conferences, paper promises, and declarations. Today it must express itself in organized and equipped combat divisions of such huge numbers as would erect a sure dam against the red flood. And that before we land another man or another dollar on their shores. Otherwise we shall be inviting another Korea. That would be a calamity to Europe as well as to us. Our policy in this quarter of the world should be confined to a period of watchful waiting before we take on any commitments.

There is a proper urge in all Americans for unity in troubled times. But unless unity is based on right principles and right action it is a vain and dangerous thing. Honest difference of views and honest debate are not disunity. They are the vital process of policymaking among free men.

A right, a specific, an open foreign policy must be formulated which gives confidence in our own security before we can get behind it.

American eyes should now be opened to these hordes in Asia.

These policies I have suggested would be no isolationism. Indeed, they are the opposite. They would avoid rash involvement of our military forces in hopeless campaigns. They do not relieve us of working to our utmost. They would preserve a stronghold of Christian civilization in the world against any peradventure.

With the policies I have outlined, even without Europe, Americans have no reason for hysteria or loss of confidence in our security or our future. And in American security rests the future security of all mankind.

It would be an uneasy peace, but we could carry it on with these policies indefinitely even if the Communist should attack our lines on the seas.

We can hope that in time the more than a billion of other non-Communist peoples of the world will rise to their dangers. We can hope that sometime the evils of Communism and the crumbling of their racial controls will bring their own disintegration. It is a remote consolation, but twice before in world history Asiatic hordes have swept over a large part of the world and their racial dissensions dissolved their empires.

Our people have braved difficult and distressing situations in these three centuries we have been on this continent. We have faced our troubles without fear and we have not failed. We shall not fail in this, even if we have to stand alone. But we need to realize the whole truth and gird ourselves for troubled times. The truth is ugly. We face it with prayer and courage. The Almighty is on our side.

Source: Hoover, Herbert. *Addresses Upon the American Road, 1950-1955*. Stanford, CA: Stanford University Press, 1955.

3.3
Stalin Praises North Korea for Challenging the "Imperialist Yoke" – 1950
Telegram from Joseph Stalin to Kim Il Sung

> *In the opening months of the Korean War, Soviet leader Joseph Stalin stayed in regular contact with Kim Il Sung, who was both prime minister of North Korea and the general secretary of the nation's Communist Party. In this August 27, 1950, telegram, Stalin offers praise and encouragement to the North Korean leader, as well as strategic advice on how best to use his air force against the American "imperialists."*

8th Department of the General Staff of the Armed Forces of the USSR

CIPHERED TELEGRAM No.75021

Pyongyang Soviet Ambassador.

Verbally transmit the following to Kim Il Sung. If he demands it in written form—give it to him in written form, but without my signature.

1. The CC VKP(b) [Central Committee, All-Union Communist Party (Bolshevik)] salutes Comrade Kim Il Sung and his friends for the great liberational struggle of the Korean people which comrade Kim Il Sung is leading with brilliant success. CC VKP(b) has no doubt that in the soonest time the interventionists will be driven out of Korea with ignominy.

Telegram from Joseph Stalin to Kim Il Sung, August 27, 1950. Reprinted with permission from the Cold War International History Project Virtual Archive (http://www.cwihp.org).

2. Comrade Kim Il Sung should not be embarrassed by the fact that he does not have solid successes in the war against the interventionists, that the successes are sometimes interrupted by delays in the advance or even by some local set-backs. In such a war continuous successes do not occur. The Russians also did not have continuous successes during the civil war and even more during the war with Germany. The greatest success of the Korean people is that Korea has now become the most popular country in the world and has turned into the banner of the movement in Asia for liberation from the imperialist yoke. The armies of all enslaved peoples will now learn from the Korean People's Army the art of bringing decisive blows to the Americans and to any imperialists. Moreover, Comrade Kim Il Sung should not forget that Korea is not alone now, that it has allies, who are rendering and will render it aid. The position of the Russians during the Anglo-French-American intervention in 1919 was several times worse than the position of the Korean comrades at the present time.

3. Advise Comrade Kim Il Sung not to scatter the air force, but to concentrate it at the front. It is necessary that each attack by the People's Army on any portion of the front begin with a number of decisive blows by attack planes on the troops of the enemy, that the fighter planes defend the troops of the People's Army from the blows of the enemy planes as much as possible. If it is necessary, we can throw in additional assault aircraft and fighter aircraft for the Korean air force.

FYN-SI [Stalin]

Source: Stalin, Joseph. Telegram to Kim Il Sung. Obtained and translated by the Cold War International History Project. Available online at the Cold War International History Project Virtual Archive, http://www.wilsoncenter.org.

3.4
A Crushing Blow at Inchon – 1950
Telegram from Kim Il Sung and Pak Hon-Yong to Joseph Stalin

In the opening weeks of the Korean War, American forces and their South Korean allies suffered a series of demoralizing defeats. On September 15, 1950, though, U.S. General Douglas MacArthur staged a bold landing of American forces at Inchon, a port city far behind enemy lines. This smashing victory stunned the Communists and triggered a series of military triumphs for American and South Korean forces. The following somber telegram from North Korean leader Kim Il Sung and South Korean Communist leader Pak Hon-Yong to Soviet Premier Joseph Stalin, written just two weeks after the Battle of Inchon, contains an urgent appeal for direct military assistance.

Telegram from Kim Il Sung and Pak Hon-Yong to Joseph Stalin, September 29, 1950. Reprinted with permission from the Cold War International History Project Virtual Archive (http://www.cwihp.org).

Moscow, Kremlin

DEEPLY RESPECTED Iosif Vissarionovich STALIN.

On behalf of the Workers' Party of Korea, we express to You, the liberator of the Korean people and the leader of the working peoples of the entire world, our profound gratitude for compassion and assistance which You constantly provide to our people struggling for the freedom and independence of its Motherland.

In this letter, we would like to brief You on the current situation at the fronts of the liberation war of our people against the American aggressors. Prior to the assault lanching at Inch'on (Chemulp'o) one could not judge the situation at the fronts as unfavorable to us. The adversary, suffering one defeat after another, was cornered into a tiny piece of land at the southern-most tip of South Korea and we had a great chance of winning a victory in the last decisive battles.

Such a situation considerably damaged the military authority of the United States. Therefore, in those conditions, in order to restore its prestige and to implement by any means its long-held plans of conquering Korea and transforming it into its military-strategic bridgehead, on 16.9.50, the U.S. performed an assault landing operation and landed a considerable number of troops and armaments in the vicinity of Inch'on after having mobilized almost all its land, naval, and air troops deployed in the Pacific ocean. The enemy took over Inch'on and is engaged in street combats in the city of Seoul itself. The military situation became perilous.

The units of our People's Army heroically fight against advancing assault landing units of the enemy. However, we consider it necessary to report to You about the emergence of very unfavorable conditions for us.

The enemy's air force numbering about a thousand airplanes of various types, facing no rebuff from our side, totally dominate the air space and perform air raids at the fronts and in the rear day and night. At the fronts, under the air cover of hundreds of airplanes the motorized units of the enemy engage us in combat at their free will and inflict great losses to our manpower and destroy our armaments. Moreover, by freely destroying railroads and highways, telegraph and telephone communications lines, means of transportation and other facilities, the enemy's air force impedes the provision of supplies to our combat units and bars maneuvers by our troops, thereby making their timely redeployments impossible. We experience this difficulty on all fronts.

Having cut off all the communications lines of our troops and joined the assault force that landed in Inch'on with the units of their southern front that broke through our frontline, the adversary has a real opportunity to take over the city of Seoul completely. As a result, the units of the People's Army that are still fighting in the southern part of Korea have been cut off from the northern part of Korea, they are torn into pieces and cannot receive munitions, armaments, and food rations. Moreover, some units do not have any communication with each other, while some of them are surrounded by enemy troops.

After taking over Seoul completely, the enemy is likely to launch a further offensive into North Korea. Therefore, we believe that if in future the above-mentioned conditions unfavorable to us continue, then the American aggression ultimately will be successful.

In order to provide troops with all the necessary supplies and to feed the frontline without any interruption, first of all, we need to have an appropriate air force. But we do not possess well-trained pilots.

Dear Comrade STALIN, we are determined to overcome all the difficulties facing us so that Korea will not be a colony and a military springboard of the U.S. imperialists. We will fight for the independence, democracy and happiness of our people to the last drop of blood. Therefore, with all our energy we are taking decisive measures for the formation and training of many new divisions with the aim of using more than 100,000 troops mobilized in South Korea … in the most advantageous operational areas, as well as arming the entire people so as to be prepared to fight a protracted war.

This notwithstanding, if the enemy does not give us time to implement the measures which we plan, and, making use of our extremely grave situation, steps up its offensive operations into North Korea, then we will not be able to stop the enemy troops solely with our own forces.

Therefore, dear Iosif Vissarionovich, we cannot help asking You to provide us with special assistance. In other words, at the moment when the enemy troops cross over the 38th parallel we will badly need direct military assistance from the Soviet Union.

If for any reason this is impossible, please assist us by forming international volunteer units in China and other countries of people's democracy for rendering military assistance to our struggle.

We request Your directive regarding the aforementioned proposal.

Respectfully, The CC of the Workers' Party of Korea

KIM IL SUNG, PAK HÒN-YÒNG

Source: Kim Il Sung and Pak Hon-Yong. Telegram to Joseph Stalin. Obtained and translated by the Cold War International History Project. Available online at the Cold War International History Project Virtual Archive, http://www.wilsoncenter.org.

3.5
China Enters the Korean War – 1950
An Interview from No Bugles, No Drums: An Oral History of the Korean War

In November 1950 United Nations forces led by the United States appeared to be on the cusp of total victory on the Korean Peninsula. General Douglas MacArthur's brilliant landing at Inchon on September 15 had decisively turned the war's momentum in favor of the Americans. Over the ensuing weeks the U.S.-led UN forces continued to push the Communist North Korean troops north, pushing far past the 38th parallel. In fact, American troops pushed all the way to the southern banks of the Yalu River, which served as the border between China and North Korea. When American troops approached that border, however, alarmed Chinese leaders ordered a massive invasion across the Yalu. China's entry into the Korean War demoralized the U.S. troops and transformed the conflict into a bloody stalemate. Following is an excerpt from an interview with Sherman Pratt, a captain with the U.S. 2nd Infantry Division of the Eighth Army, who witnessed the Chinese incursion firsthand.

A New Enemy

When I got to Korea in early September I was given command of a rifle company. Baker Company of the 23rd Regiment. I hadn't been with my company for more than a few days when we went on the attack along the Naktong River. At the same time MacArthur landed at Inchon in the north, and within a week the enemy broke.

All through September and into October we pressed forward with great speed, and almost before we knew it we were at the 38th parallel. The North Korean resistance had collapsed. Our main problem in those days was trying to keep up with them.

We crossed the parallel and raced up to Pyongyang, the North Korean capital. The city was hardly being defended. When we cleared Pyongyang and moved into the high ground to the north I looked back and saw the sky filled with hundreds of paratroopers. I was puzzled. Everybody who saw it was puzzled. Why were they dropping in our rear, in an area that had already been captured? It turned out that the front was moving so rapidly that the drop zone was captured while these guys were still loading and getting airborne, and they never got the word. We stopped

Rudy Tomedi, No Bugles, No Drums: An Oral History of the Korean War. Copyright © 1993 Rudy Tomedi. Reprinted with permission of John Wiley & Sons, Inc.

finally when we were almost at the Yalu River. As I recall, we were about forty miles away. And it was here that we had our first brushes with Chinese troops.

Our intelligence reports had been telling us they were in the area. We were well aware that the border was only fifty miles away. But the intentions of these Chinese were by no means clear to us. In fact their actions were rather puzzling. They did things that led us to think they wouldn't fight unless we advanced too far. They even showed signs of friendliness. I remember taking a patrol out one day and having Chinese appear on the hilltops all around us. We were surrounded. I put out the word that under no circumstances were we to fire the first shot. They had us, and it would have been a massacre. Then a couple of my men waved, and lo and behold the Chinese starting waving back. We turned around very slowly and went back the way we came, and nobody fired a shot. Colonel [Paul] Freeman was at the battalion CP and he grilled me over and over for details. He just couldn't believe it.

"We began to see American troops pouring back through our positions, some at a dead run. They were pathetic, scared-looking men. The panic began to spread contagiously among my own men."

The next day I saw the Colonel again, and he had more strange news. He'd sent out a follow-up patrol, with instructions to push farther north to see what the Chinese would do. They got as far as we had without any problems, but when they tried to go farther the Chinese opened fire.

In the confusion the patrol left some wounded behind, and that was the most bizarre aspect of the whole matter. When a third patrol returned to the area they found the wounded men all bandaged up and warmly covered with blankets, lying comfortably on litters by the side of the road where they'd fallen.

We just couldn't figure it out. What were they up to? And just how many were out there? Of course, at the time we had no inkling they were out there in the hundreds and hundreds of thousands.

Around Thanksgiving word came that the Eighth Army was going to launch a general attack all along the front. We were told that theater intelligence believed the Chinese in the area would fall back into Manchuria. My own attitude was optimistic. We understood that the UN objective was to push on to the Manchurian border. Over on the eastern side of Korea General Almond's X Corps had landed and they had in fact already reached the Yalu River at certain points. It looked like this would be the final stage of the war, and that we'd all be home by Christmas.

That same night, the night the UN offensive was supposed to be in full swing, all hell broke loose. My company was in reserve just behind the lines, and there was heavy fighting to our front, to our right, to our left. And then we began to see American troops pouring back through our positions, some at a dead run. They were pathetic, scared-looking men. The panic began to spread contagiously among my own men, and it took close supervision to keep them under control.

We grabbed some of these guys who were running back through our positions and asked them what was happening, and they said the Chinese were attacking, that they're all around us, and that they were going to overrun us. Then A Company to our left got into a big fight, and shortly after that my own company was hit.

During the rest of the night we were engaged in almost continuous firefights. It was total confusion. We'd fire at the Chinese, and they would withdraw. They were trying to avoid a direct confrontation with American units, we found out later. Trying to avoid our heavier firepower, and instead hit South Korean units, or work around American units and hit them from behind.

All during this time stragglers from the front continued to filter back through our positions. Pitiful guys. Dazed, bewildered, most with no weapons, many of them with their clothes frozen stiff from splashing through rice paddies and across rivers, some with no shoes and their feet already turning black from frostbite.

At dawn the Chinese broke contact, and later that same day we were ordered to take a hill called Chinaman's Hat, but that was called off when casualties got too heavy.

Finally we got orders to withdraw. So the division and the regiment and our battalion started leapfrogging back out of the area. Because by then the only word we were hearing was, "Boy, all hell's broken loose. The Chinese have hit us with an ocean of manpower all along the front."

This was the great bugout. In ten days I believe the Eighth Army retreated one hundred thirty miles. It was not an orderly retreat. I hesitate to call it a complete rout, because some units did hold their ground under the most appalling conditions. But just about everybody had only one thing in mind, and that was to get out of the trap the Chinese had sprung on us....

The withdrawing columns finally thinned out, and we received our orders to pull out ourselves, as soon as the last of the retreating units had passed us. By now we had collected about fifty Chinese prisoners. We were keeping them in a rice paddy near the company CP. I wanted to get rid of them, because by the time we moved out there would be nothing between us and the Chinese army except empty space, and the prisoners would slow us down. So I tried to persuade one of the units passing through us to take them to the rear.

Nobody would take them. No one wanted to be slowed down. I remember one infantry officer in the column saying, "Just shoot the bastards," tossing the comment back over his shoulder as he walked away.

I'm thankful today I didn't follow his advice, although I must have been tempted.

Shortly after moving out of the first blocking position we were ordered into another one. We were told to hold the pass on the south bank of the Chongchon River, just outside of Kunu-ri, until the rest of the 2nd Division could get out. We were still the rear guard....

That same day we finally got our orders to pull out. All day we could see the Chinese moving around our flanks. By then we must have been the northernmost unit in the entries Eighth Army. Everybody was to the south of us, including a lot of Chinese. It seemed they had just about blanketed the countryside. But they also seemed disorganized. Sometimes we could see small knots of them just milling around. I had the feeling they were as confused as we were.

During that retreat the cold was our enemy as much as the Chinese. That should be kept in mind by anyone trying to understand the Korean War. We suffered constantly from the cold. Painfully. It dulled our senses. It made us move slow. It made us *think* slow.

Wounded men who otherwise might have survived died because they couldn't be kept warm. Our vehicles wouldn't start. Batteries gave out. The grease on our rifles turned to glue and they wouldn't fire. Our rations would freeze solid. Men would carry cans of food around inside their clothes, under their armpits, trying to thaw them a little so they could be eaten. When the wind blew over those Korean hilltops the chill factor must have been twenty or thirty degrees below zero.

We retreated from Kunu-ri in a motorized column, got through the Chinese, and by the third of December we were in bivouac around Munsan, just below the Imjin River.

We were south of the parallel again. But now we faced a new enemy. We had an entirely new war on our hands.

Source: Pratt, Sherman. Interview in *No Bugles, No Drums: An Oral History of the Korean War*. By Rudy Tomedi. New York: Wiley, 1993.

3.6
Eisenhower's "I Shall Go to Korea" Speech – 1952
A Speech from the Presidential Campaign of Dwight Eisenhower

By the time of the 1952 presidential campaign in the United States, the Korean War had settled into a grim deadlock, with neither side able to gain a significant strategic advantage. During the campaign, Republican nominee Dwight D. Eisenhower, a famous World War II hero, promised to go to Korea and personally assess the situation if he was elected. The text of his "I

Shall Go to Korea" speech, which also included a blistering assessment of the Truman administration's response to Korea and a description of the fight against Communism as a noble "crusade," is reprinted here. In November 1952 Eisenhower defeated Democratic candidate Adlai Stevenson for the presidency. One month later, Eisenhower fulfilled his campaign promise and spent three days visiting with commanders and soldiers along the front. His time there convinced him that the United States should press for a negotiated settlement that would leave both South Korea and North Korea intact.

In this anxious autumn for America, one fact looms above all others in our people's mind. One tragedy challenges all men dedicated to the work of peace. One word shouts denial to those who foolishly pretend that ours is not a nation at war.

This fact, this tragedy, this word is: Korea.

A small country, Korea has been, for more than two years, the battleground for the costliest foreign war our nation has fought, excepting the two world wars. It has been the burial ground for 20,000 America dead. It has been another historic field of honor for the valor and skill and tenacity of American soldiers.

All these things it has been—and yet one thing more. It has been a symbol—a telling symbol—of the foreign policy of our nation. It has been a sign—a warning sign—of the way the Administration has conducted our world affairs. It has been a measure—a damning measure—of the quality of leadership we have been given.

Tonight I am going to talk about our foreign policy and of its supreme symbol—the Korean war. I am not going to give you elaborate generalizations—but hard, tough facts. I am going to state the unvarnished truth.

What, then, are the plain facts?

The biggest fact about the Korean war is this: It was never inevitable, it was never inescapable, no fantastic fiat of history decreed that little South Korea—in the summer of 1950—would fatally tempt Communist aggressors as their easiest victim. No demonic destiny decreed that America had to be bled this way in order to keep South Korea free and to keep freedom itself self-respecting.

We are not mute prisoners of history. That is a doctrine for totalitarians, it is no creed for free men.

There is a Korean war—and we are fighting it—for the simplest of reasons: Because free leadership failed to check and to turn back Communist ambition before it savagely attacked us. The Korean war—more perhaps than any other war in history—simply and swiftly followed the collapse of our political defenses. There is no other reason than this: We failed to read and to outwit the totalitarian mind.

I know something of this totalitarian mind. Through the years of World War II, I carried a heavy burden of decision in the free world's crusade against the tyranny then threatening us all. Month after month, year after year, I had to search out and to weigh the strengths and weaknesses of an enemy driven by the lust to rule the great globe itself.

World War II should have taught us all one lesson. The lesson is this: To vacillate, to hesitate—to appease even by merely betraying unsteady purpose—is to feed a dictator's appetite for conquest and to invite war itself.

That lesson—which should have firmly guided every great decision of our leadership through these later years—was ignored in the development of the Administration's policies for Asia since the end of World War II. Because it was ignored, the record of these policies is a record of appalling failure.

The record of failure dates back—with red-letter folly—at least to September of 1947. It was then that Gen. Albert Wedemeyer—returned from a Presidential mission to the Far East—submitted to the President this warning: "The withdrawal of American military forces from Korea would result in the occupation of South Korea by either Soviet troops or, as seems more likely, by the Korean military units trained under Soviet auspices in North Korea."

That warning and his entire report were disregarded and suppressed by the Administration.

The terrible record of these years reaches its dramatic climax in a series of unforgettable scenes on Capitol Hill in June of 1949. By then the decision to complete withdrawal of American forces from Korea—despite menacing signs from the North—had been drawn up by the Department of State. The decision included the intention to ask Congress for aid to Korea to compensate for the withdrawal of American forces.

This brought questions from Congress. The Administration parade of civilian and military witnesses before the House Foreign Affairs Committee was headed by the Secretary of State. He and his aides faced a group of Republican Congressmen both skeptical and fearful.

What followed was historic and decisive.

I beg you to listen carefully to the words that followed, for they shaped this nation's course from that date to this.

Listen, then:

First: Republican Congressman John Lodge of Connecticut asked "(do) you feel that the Korean Government is able to fill the vacuum caused by the withdrawal of the occupation forces?"

The Administration answered: "Definitely."

Second: A very different estimate of the risk involved came from Republican Congressman Walter Judd of Minnesota. He warned: "I think the thing necessary to give security to Korea at this stage of the game is the presence of a small American force and the knowledge (on the Soviet side) that attack upon it would bring trouble with us."

"I am convinced," Representative Judd continued, "that if we keep even a battalion there, they are not going to move. And if the battalion is not there"—listen now to his warning—"the chances are they will move within a year."

What a tragedy that the Administration shrugged off that accurate warning!

Third: The Secretary of State [Dean Acheson] was asked if he agreed that the South Koreans alone—and I quote—"will be able to defend themselves against any attack from the northern half of the country." To this the Secretary answered briskly: "We share the same view. Yes, sir."

Rarely in Congressional testimony has so much misinformation been compressed so efficiently into so few words.

Fourth: Republican Congressman Lodge had an incisive comment on all this. "That," he said, "'is wishful thinking … I am afraid it confesses a kind of fundamental isolationism that exists in certain branches of the Government, which I think is a very dangerous pattern. I think the presence of our troops there is a tremendous deterrent to the Russians."

Finally: This remarkable scene of the summer of 1949 ends with a memorable document. The minority report of five Republican members of the House Foreign Affairs Committee on July 26, 1949, submitted this solemn warning.

Listen to it:

"It is reliably reported that Soviet troops, attached to the North Korean puppet armies, are in position of command as well as acting as advisors … This development may well presage the launching of a full-scale military drive across the Thirty-eighth Parallel.

"Our forces … have been withdrawn from South Korea at the very instant when logic and common sense both demanded no retreat from the realities of the situation."

The report continues: "Already along the Thirty-eighth Parallel aggression is speaking with the too-familiar voices of howitzers and cannons. Our position is untenable and indefensible.

"The House should be aware of these facts."

These words of eloquent, reasoned warning were spoken eleven months before the Korean war broke.

Behind these words was a fervent, desperate appeal. That appeal was addressed to the Administration. It begged at least some firm statement of American intention that might deter the foreseen attack.

What was the Administration answer to that appeal? The first answer was silence—stubborn, sullen silence for six months.

Then, suddenly, came speech—a high Government official at long last speaking out on Asia. It was now January of 1950. What did he say? He said, "The United States Government will not provide military aid or advice to Chinese forces on Formosa."

Then, one week later, the Secretary of State announced his famous "defense perimeter"—publicly advising our enemies that, so far as nations outside this perimeter were concerned, "no person can guarantee these areas against military attack." Under these circumstances, it was cold comfort to the nations outside this perimeter to be reminded that they could appeal to the United Nations.

These nations, of course, included Korea. The armies of communism, thus informed, began their big build-up. Six months later they were ready to strike across the Thirty-eighth Parallel. They struck on June 25, 1950. On that day, the record of political and diplomatic failure of this Administration was completed and sealed.

The responsibility for this record cannot be dodged or evaded. Even if not a single Republican leader had warned so clearly against the coming disaster, the responsibility for the fateful political decisions would still rest wholly with the men charged with making those decisions—in the Department of State and in the White House. They cannot escape that responsibility now or ever.

When the enemy struck, on that June day of 1950, what did America do? It did what it always has done in all its times of peril. It appealed to the heroism of its youth. This appeal was utterly right and utterly inescapable. It was inescapable not only because this was the only way to defend the idea of collective freedom against savage aggression. That appeal was inescapable because there was now in the plight into which we had stumbled no other way to save honor and self-respect.

The answer to that appeal has been what any American knew it would be. It has been sheer valor on all the Korean mountainsides that, each day, bear fresh scars of new graves. Now—in this anxious autumn—from these heroic men there comes back an answering appeal. It is no whine, no whimpering plea. It is a question that addresses itself to simple reason. It asks: Where do we go from here? When comes the end? Is there an end?

These questions touch all of us. They demand truthful answers. Neither glib promises nor glib excuses will serve. They would be no better than the glib prophecies that brought us to this pass.

To these questions there are two false answers—both equally false. The first would be any answer that dishonestly pledged an end to war in Korea by any imminent, exact date. Such a pledge would brand its speaker as a deceiver.

The second and equally false answer declares that nothing can be done to speed a secure peace. It dares to tell us that we, the strongest nation in the history of freedom, can only wait—and wait—and wait. Such a statement brands its speaker as a defeatist.

My answer—candid and complete—is this:

The first task of a new Administration will be to review and re-examine every course of action open to us with one goal in view: To bring the Korean war to an early and honorable end. This is my pledge to the American people.

For this task a wholly new Administration is necessary. The reason for this is simple. The old Administration cannot be expected to repair what it failed to prevent.

Where will a new Administration begin?

It will begin with its President taking a simple, firm resolution. The resolution will be: To forego the diversions of politics and to concentrate on the job of ending the Korean war—until that job is honorably done.

That job requires a personal trip to Korea. I shall make that trip. Only in that way could I learn how best to serve the American people in the cause of peace. I shall go to Korea. That is my second pledge to the American people.

Carefully, then, this new Administration, unfettered by past decisions and inherited mistakes, can review every factor—military, political and psychological—to be mobilized in speeding a just peace.

Progress along at least two lines can instantly begin. We can first step up the program of training and arming the South Korean forces. Manifestly, under the circumstances of today, United Nations forces cannot abandon that unhappy land. But just as troops of the Republic of Korea covet and deserve the honor of defending their frontiers, so should we give them maximum assistance to insure their ability to do so. Then, United Nations forces in reserve positions and supporting roles would be assurance that disaster would not again strike. We can secondly shape our psychological warfare program into a weapon capable of cracking the Communist front.

Beyond all this we must carefully weigh all interrelated courses of action. We will, of course, constantly confer with associated free nations of Asia and with the cooperating members of the United Nations. Thus we could bring into being a practical plan for world peace.

That is my third pledge to you.

As the next Administration goes to work for peace, we must be guided at every instant by that lesson I spoke of earlier. The vital lesson is this: To vacillate, to appease, to placate is only to invite war—vaster war—bloodier war. In the words of the late Senator [Arthur H.] Vandenberg, appeasement is not the road to peace; it is only surrender on the installment plan. I will always reject appeasement.

And that is my fourth pledge to you.

A nation's foreign policy is a much graver matter than rustling papers and bustling conferences. It is much more than diplomatic decisions and trade treaties and military arrangements.

A foreign policy is the face and voice of a whole people. It is all that the world sees and hears and understands about a single nation. It expresses the character and the faith and the will of that nation. In this, a nation is like any individual of our personal acquaintance; the simplest gesture can betray hesitation or weakness, the merest inflection of voice can reveal doubt or fear.

It is in this deep sense that our foreign policy has faltered and failed.

For a democracy, a great election, such as this, signifies a most solemn trial. It is the time when—to the bewilderment of all tyrants—the people sit in judgment upon the leaders. It is the time when these leaders are summoned before the bar of public decision. There they must give evidence both to justify their actions and explain their intentions.

In the great trial of this election, the judges—the people—must not be deceived into believing that the choice is between isolationism and internationalism. That is a debate of the dead past. The vast majority of Americans of both parties know that to keep their own nation free, they bear a majestic responsibility for freedom through all the world. As practical people, Americans also know the critical necessity of unimpaired access to raw materials on other continents for our own economic and military strength.

Today the choice—the real choice—lies between policies that assume that responsibility awkwardly and fearfully—and policies that accept that responsibility with sure purpose and firm will. The choice is between foresight and blindness, between doing and apologizing, between planning and improvising.

In rendering their verdict, the people must judge with courage and with wisdom. For—at this date—any faltering in America's leadership is a capital offense against freedom.

In this trial, my testimony, of a personal kind, is quite simple. A soldier all my life, I have enlisted in the greatest cause of my life—the cause of peace.

I do not believe it a presumption for me to call the effort of all who have enlisted with me a crusade. I use that word only to signify two facts. First: We are united and devoted to a just cause of the purest meaning to all humankind. Second: We know that—for all the might of our effort—victory can come only with the gift of God's help.

In this spirit—humble servants of a proud ideal—we do soberly say: This is a crusade.

Source: Eisenhower, Dwight D. "Address of the Republican Nominee for President, Delivered at Detroit, Michigan, October 24, 1952." Presidential Papers of Dwight D. Eisenhower, Eisenhower Presidential Library and Museum. Available online at http://www.eisenhower.utexas.edu/Korea/documents/ishallgotokorea1.html.

4

MCCARTHYISM
AND THE "RED MENACE"

During the 1950s Republican Senator Joseph McCarthy (center) effectively exploited
American fears of Communist infiltration to make himself one of the most powerful politicians
in Washington. He is seen here at the 1954 Army-McCarthy hearings, flanked by Army Private
G. David Schine (left) and Roy Cohn, McCarthy's chief counsel.

INTRODUCTION

The perception that the United States and the Soviet Union were locked in a high-stakes battle to chart the future course of the world had an enormous impact on American culture and society. Fears that Communist agents were infiltrating American universities, government agencies, and other institutions became embedded in the public consciousness. This was especially true after the widely publicized Whittaker Chambers-Alger Hiss case of 1948. Whittaker Chambers was a writer who testified before Congress that he had been a Communist in the past, that he had given secret information to the Soviets, and that State Department official Alger Hiss had worked as a Soviet spy. Hiss always maintained his innocence, but he was eventually convicted of perjury, and historians generally believe that Hiss did pass classified information on to the Soviets.

The Alger Hiss case brought nationwide recognition to California congressman and anti-Communist crusader Richard Nixon. During the late 1940s he became one of the most prominent members of the House Un-American Activities Committee (HUAC). For over thirty years, HUAC conducted investigations into American citizens accused of subversive activities, particularly pro-Communist activities. Fears about "enemies within" were given legitimacy by these Congressional investigations into the issue.

FBI (Federal Bureau of Investigation) Director J. Edgar Hoover further fanned the flames of paranoia about the "Red Menace." He denounced Communism as "an evil and malignant way of life" that needed to be quarantined wherever found "to keep it from infecting the nation." During his long tenure with the FBI, Hoover approved a variety of legal and illegal domestic surveillance and intelligence techniques to root out this perceived threat.

Finally, concerns about the "Red Menace" were heightened by the fact that there *were* some Communist agents operating in the United States. Their impact and sheer numbers never approached the dimensions that some Americans feared. Nonetheless, high-profile cases such as that of Julius and Ethel Rosenberg, who were executed on June 19, 1953, for passing secrets about the construction of atomic weapons to the Soviets, were closely followed by the American public. The Hiss and Rosenberg cases, combined with ongoing Congressional investigations, convinced many Americans that there were traitors in their midst.

The McCarthy Witch Hunts

The most infamous of the American politicians to exploit the fear of Communism for political gain was Republican Senator Joseph R. McCarthy of Wisconsin. On February 9, 1950, McCarthy delivered a speech in which he declared that he had in his possession a list of more than fifty-seven "card-carrying" Communists who had infiltrated the State Department—the very department responsible for setting U.S. foreign policy. Over the ensuing months, McCarthy made progressively more outrageous claims against hundreds of men and women from the worlds of government, education, and entertainment. At one point he even attacked George C. Marshall, the distinguished World War II general and architect of the Marshall Plan, as "part of a [Communist] conspiracy so immense, an infamy so black, as to dwarf any in the history of man."

McCarthyism intensified during the 1950s. The fear of Communism that McCarthy so effectively exploited made many people reluctant to express any independent thoughts or controversial beliefs for fear of being labeled a "red." Indeed, the lives of many Americans were ruined by unsubstantiated charges that they harbored Communist sympathies or associated with Communist individuals or groups.

Some brave Americans spoke out against the Communist witch hunts and the many ruined lives left in McCarthy's wake. Supreme Court Justice William O. Douglas, for example, warned in 1952 that America's longstanding "philosophy of strength through free speech is being forsaken for the philosophy of fear through repression" commonly practiced by "the enemy we detest."

Ultimately, though, McCarthy was undone by his own irresponsible and unprincipled behavior. Early on, many fellow Republicans sensed political advantage in supporting McCarthy. But by 1954, these politicians had become embarrassed by his bullying attitude and his habit of aiming wild charges of disloyalty in all directions. McCarthy's nationally televised confrontation with U.S. Army counsel Joseph N. Welch in 1954 proved especially crippling to McCarthy's reputation. Welch's withering criticism of McCarthy seemed to break the spell that the senator had cast over both Washington and the country. Over the next several months he increasingly came to be seen as a liability for the Republican Party, and in December 1954 the U.S. Senate voted to condemn him for dishonorable and unethical conduct. McCarthy quickly faded from public view, and he died three years later.

4.1
J. Edgar Hoover Warns of Communist Infiltration in the United States – 1947
Excerpts from Hoover's Testimony before the House Un-American Activities Committee

> *J Edgar Hoover served as director of the Federal Bureau of Investigation (FBI) from May 10, 1924, until May 2, 1972, when he died. He served eight presidents during his 48-year tenure. He is credited with developing the FBI into an effective crime-fighting unit, but he also routinely abused his extraordinary power: he persecuted left-leaning groups and individuals and blackmailed political foes.*
>
> *In the 1930s and 1940s, Hoover devoted a lot of the FBI's resources to investigations of alleged Communist agents in America. In the following testimony before the House Un-American Activities Committee on March 26, 1947, Hoover detailed his thoughts on the threat that Communism posed to the future of the United States.*

My feelings concerning the Communist Party of the United States are well known. I have not hesitated over the years to express my concern and apprehension. As a consequence its professional smear brigades have conducted a relentless assault against the FBI. You who have been members of this committee also know the fury with which the party, its sympathizers and fellow travelers can launch an assault. I do not mind such attacks. What has been disillusioning is the manner in which they have been able to enlist support often from apparently well-meaning but thoroughly duped persons....

The communist movement in the United States began to manifest itself in 1919. Since then it has changed its name and its party line whenever expedient and tactical. But always it comes back to fundamentals and bills itself as the party of Marxism-Leninism. As such, it stands for the destruction of our American form of government; it stands for the destruction of American democracy; it stands for the destruction of free enterprise; and it stands for the creation of a "Soviet of the United States" and ultimate world revolution....

The communist, once he is fully trained and indoctrinated, realizes that he can create his order in the United States only by "bloody revolution." Their chief textbook, "The History of the Communist Party of the Soviet Union," is used as a basis for planning their revolution. Their tactics require that to be successful they must have:

1. The will and sympathy of the people.

2. Military aid and assistance.

3. Plenty of guns and ammunition.

4. A program for extermination of the police as they are the most important enemy and are termed "trained fascists."

5. Seizure of all communications, buses, railroads, radio stations, and other forms of communications and transportation....

One thing is certain. The American progress which all good citizens seek, such as old-age security, houses for veterans, child assistance, and a host of others, is being adopted as window dressing by the communists to conceal their true aims and entrap gullible followers....

The mad march of Red fascism is a cause for concern in America. But the deceit, the trickery, and the lies of the American communists are catching up with them. Whenever the spotlight of truth is focused upon them they cry, "Red-baiting." Now that their aims and objectives are being exposed, they are creating a Committee for the Constitutional Rights of Communists, and are feverishly working to build up what they term a quarter-million-dollar defense fund to place ads in papers, to publish pamphlets, to buy radio time. They know that their backs will soon be to the wall....

What is important is the claim of the communists themselves that for every party member there are 10 others ready, willing and able to do the party's work. Herein lies the greatest menace of communism. For these are the people who infiltrate and corrupt various spheres of American life. So rather than the size of the Communist Party, the way to weigh its true importance is by testing its influence, its ability to infiltrate....

The communists have developed one of the greatest propaganda machines the world has ever known. They have been able to penetrate and infiltrate many respectable public opinion mediums. They capitalize upon ill-founded charges associating known honest progressive liberals with left-wing causes. I have always entertained the view that there are few appellations more degrading than "communist" and hence it should be reserved for those justly deserving the degradation.

The communist propaganda technique is designed to promote emotional response with the hope that the victim will be attracted by what he is told the communist way of life holds in store for him. The objective, of course, is to develop discontent and hasten the day when the communists can gather sufficient support and following to overthrow the American way of life....

Communists and their followers are prolific letter writers, and some of the more energetic ones follow the practice of directing numerous letters of protest to editors but signing a different name to each. Members of Congress are well aware of communists starting their pressure campaigns by an avalanche of mail which follows the party line....

The American communists launched a furtive attack on Hollywood in 1935 by the issuance of a directive calling for a concentration in Hollywood. The orders called for action on two fronts: One, an effort to infiltrate the labor unions; two, infiltrate the so-called intellectual and creative fields.

In movie circles, communists developed an effective defense a few years ago in meeting criticism. They would counter with the question "After all, what is the matter with communism?" It was effective because many persons did not possess adequate knowledge of the subject to give an intelligent answer....

I feel that this committee could render a great service to the nation through its power of exposure in quickly spotlighting existing front organizations and those which will be created in the future. There are easy tests to establish the real character of such organizations:

1. Does the group espouse the cause of Americanism or the cause of Soviet Russia?

2. Does the organization feature as speakers at its meeting known communists, sympathizers, or fellow travelers?

3. Does the organization shift when the party line shifts?

4. Does the organization sponsor causes, campaigns, literature, petitions, or other activities sponsored by the party or other front organizations?

5. Is the organization used as a sounding board by or is it endorsed by communist-controlled labor unions?

6. Does its literature follow the communist line or is it printed by the communist press?

7. Does the organization receive consistent favorable mention in the communist publications?

8. Does the organization present itself to be nonpartisan yet engage in political activities and consistently advocate causes favored by the communists?

9. Does the organization denounce American and British foreign policy while always lauding Soviet policy?

10. Does the organization utilize communist "double-talk" by referring to Soviet dominated countries as democracies, complaining that the United States is imperialistic and constantly denouncing monopoly-capital?

11. Have outstanding leaders in public life openly renounced affiliation with the organization?

12. Does the organization, if espousing liberal progressive causes, attract well-known honest patriotic liberals or does it denounce well-known liberals?

13. Does the organization have a consistent record of supporting the American viewpoint over the years?...

The Communist Party of the United States is a fifth column if there ever was one. It is far better organized than were the Nazis in occupied countries prior to their capitulation. They are seeking to weaken America just as they did in their era of obstruction when they were aligned with the Nazis. Their goal is the overthrow of our government. There is no doubt as to where a real communist's loyalty rests. Their allegiance is to Russia, not the United States....

What can we do? And what should be our course of action? The best antidote to communism is vigorous, intelligent, old-fashioned Americanism, with eternal vigilance. I do not favor any course of action which would give the communists cause to portray and pity themselves as martyrs. I do favor unrelenting prosecution wherever they are found to be violating our country's laws.

As Americans, our most effective defense is a workable democracy that guarantees and preserves our cherished freedoms.

I would have no fears if more Americans possessed the zeal, the fervor, the persistence and the industry to learn about this menace of Red fascism. I do fear for the liberal and progressive who has been hoodwinked and duped into joining hands with the communists. I confess to a real apprehension so long as communists are able to secure ministers of the gospel to promote their evil work and espouse a cause that is alien to the religion of Christ and Judaism. I do fear so long as school boards and parents tolerate conditions whereby communists and fellow travelers, under the guise of academic freedom, can teach our youth a way of life that eventually will destroy the sanctity of the home, that undermines faith in God, that causes them to scorn respect for constituted authority and sabotage our revered Constitution.

I do fear so long as American labor groups are infiltrated, dominated or saturated with the virus of communism. I do fear the palliation and weasel-worded gestures against communism indulged in by some of our labor leaders who should know better, but who have become pawns in the hands of sinister but astute manipulations for the communist cause.

I fear for ignorance on the part of all our people who may take the poisonous pills of communist propaganda.

Source: U.S. Congress. House. Hoover, J. Edgar. Testimony before the House Un-American Activities Committee, March 26, 1947. Records of the U.S. House of Representatives. Available online at *CNN: Cold War*, http://www.cnn.com/specials/cold.war/episodes/06/documents/hoover.

4.2
Joseph McCarthy's Speech on Communists in the State Department – 1950
Excerpts from McCarthy's Famous Speech in Wheeling, West Virginia

On February 9, 1950, an obscure Republican senator from Wisconsin made his mark in Cold War history with a speech that warned that Communist agents were infiltrating the American government at every level. Senator Joseph McCarthy specifically charged that the U.S. State Department was filled with Communist operatives and sympathizers. (This version of the speech specifically says fifty-seven Communists, but other versions of the speech cite different numbers, and there is some controversy over exactly what McCarthy said.)

This speech launched McCarthy's meteoric political rise. It also ushered in the so-called "McCarthy Era," in which fear and suspicion cast a shadow over virtually all aspects of American politics and culture. During this period, many Americans saw their careers and lives ruined by false accusations that they were Communist. It also became commonplace for writers, union organizers, and lawmakers with liberal political beliefs to be branded as Communists by their political enemies.

McCarthy's speech includes references to Alger Hiss, a State Department official who was accused by journalist Whittaker Chambers of being a spy for the Soviets. Two weeks before McCarthy's speech, Hiss was convicted of perjury after a sensational trial. Many historians believe that he was guilty of spying on behalf of the Soviets, but Hiss always maintained his innocence. McCarthy's Wheeling speech also includes a vicious attack on Secretary of State Dean Acheson. In subsequent months, Acheson strongly defended State Department employees from McCarthy's charges—none of which were ever proven.

Ladies and Gentlemen:

Tonight as we celebrate the 141st birthday of one of the great men in American history, I would like to be able to talk about what a glorious day today is in the history of the world. As we celebrate the birth of this man, who with his whole heart and soul hated war, I would like to be able to speak of peace in our time, of war being outlawed, and of worldwide disarmament. These would be truly appropriate things to be able to mention as we celebrate the birthday of Abraham Lincoln.

Five years after a world war has been won, men's hearts should anticipate a long peace, and men's minds should be free from the heavy weight that comes with war. But this is not such a period—for this is not a period of peace. This is a time of the Cold War. This is a time when all the world is split into two vast, increasingly hostile armed camps—a time of a great armaments race. Today we can almost physically hear the mutterings and rumblings of an invigorated god of war. You can see it, feel it, and hear it all the way from the hills of Indochina, from the shores of Formosa right over into the very heart of Europe itself....

Today we are engaged in a final, all-out battle between communistic atheism and Christianity. The modern champions of communism have selected this as the time. And, ladies and gentlemen, the chips are down—they are truly down.

Lest there be any doubt that the time has been chosen, let us go directly to the leader of communism today—Joseph Stalin. Here is what he said—not back in 1928, not before the war, not during the war—but two years after the last war was ended: "To think that the communist revolution can be carried out peacefully, within the framework of a Christian democracy, means one has either gone out of one's mind and lost all normal understanding, or has grossly and openly repudiated the communist revolution."

> *"Ladies and gentlemen, can there be anyone here tonight who is so blind as to say that the war is not on?"*

And this is what was said by Lenin in 1919, which was also quoted with approval by Stalin in 1947: "We are living," said Lenin, "not merely in a state but in a system of states, and the existence of the Soviet Republic side by side with Christian states for a long time is unthinkable. One or the other must triumph in the end. And before that end supervenes, a series of frightful collisions between the Soviet Republic and the bourgeois states will be inevitable."

Ladies and gentlemen, can there be anyone here tonight who is so blind as to say that the war is not on? Can there be anyone who fails to realize that the communist world has said, "The time is now"—that this is the time for the showdown between the democratic Christian world and the communist atheistic world? Unless we face this fact, we shall pay the price that must be paid by those who wait too long.

Six years ago, at the time of the first conference to map out peace—Dumbarton Oaks—there was within the Soviet orbit 180 million people. Lined up on the anti-totalitarian side there were in the world at that time roughly 1.625 billion people. Today, only six years later, there are 800 million people under the absolute domination of Soviet Russia—an increase of over 400 percent. On our side, the figure has shrunk to around 500 million. In other words, in less than six years the odds have changed from 9 to 1 in our favor to 8 to 5 against us. This indicates the swiftness of the tempo of communist victories and American defeats in the Cold War. As one of our outstanding historical figures once said, "When a great democracy is destroyed, it will not be because of enemies from without but rather because of enemies from within." The truth of this statement is becoming terrifyingly clear as we see this country each day losing on every front.

At war's end we were physically the strongest nation on Earth and, at least potentially, the most powerful intellectually and morally. Ours could have been the honor of being a beacon in the desert of destruction, a shining, living proof that civilization was not yet ready to destroy itself. Unfortunately, we have failed miserably and tragically to arise to the opportunity.

The reason why we find ourselves in a position of impotency is not because our only powerful, potential enemy has sent men to invade our shores, but rather because of the traitorous actions of those who have been treated so well by this nation. It has not been the less fortunate or members of minority groups who have been selling this nation out, but rather those who have had all the benefits that the wealthiest nation on earth has had to offer—the finest homes, the finest college education, and the finest jobs in government we can give.

This is glaringly true in the State Department. There the bright young men who are born with silver spoons in their mouths are the ones who have been worst.

Now I know it is very easy for anyone to condemn a particular bureau or department in general terms. Therefore, I would like to cite one rather unusual case—the case of a man who has done much to shape our foreign policy.

When Chiang Kai-shek was fighting our war, the State Department had in China a young man named John S. Service. His task, obviously, was not to work for the communization of China. Strangely, however, he sent official reports back to the State Department urging that we torpedo our ally Chiang Kai-shek and stating, in effect, that communism was the best hope of China.

Later, this man—John Service—was picked up by the Federal Bureau of Investigation for turning over to the communists secret State Department information. Strangely, however, he was never prosecuted. However, Joseph Grew, the undersecretary of state, who insisted on his prosecution, was forced to resign. Two days after, Grew's successor, Dean Acheson, took over as undersecretary of state, this man—John Service—who had been picked up by the FBI and who had previously urged that communism was the best hope of China, was not only reinstated in the State Department but promoted; and finally, under Acheson, placed in charge of all placements and promotions. Today, ladies and gentlemen, this man Service is on his way to represent the State Department and Acheson in Calcutta—by far and away the most important listening post in the Far East.

Now, let's see what happens when individuals with communist connections are forced out of the State Department. Gustave Duran, who was labeled as, I quote, "a notorious international communist," was made assistant secretary of state in charge of Latin American affairs. He was taken into the State Department from his job as a lieutenant colonel in the Communist International Brigade. Finally, after intense congressional pressure and criticism, he resigned in 1946 from the State Department—and, ladies and gentlemen, where do you think he is now? He took over a high-salaried job as chief of Cultural Activities Section in the office of the assistant secretary-general of the United Nations....

This, ladies and gentlemen, gives you somewhat of a picture of the type of individuals who have been helping to shape our foreign policy. In my opinion the State Department, which is one of the most important government departments, is thoroughly infested with communists.

I have in my hand 57 cases of individuals who would appear to be either card-carrying members or certainly loyal to the Communist Party, but who nevertheless are still helping to shape our foreign policy.

One thing to remember in discussing the communists in our government is that we are not dealing with spies who get 30 pieces of silver to steal the blueprints of new weapons. We are dealing with a far more sinister type of activity because it permits the enemy to guide and shape our policy.

This brings us down to the case of one Alger Hiss, who is important not as an individual anymore but rather because he is so representative of a group in the State Department. It is unnecessary to go over the sordid events showing how he sold out the nation which had given him so much. Those are rather fresh in all of our minds. However, it should be remembered that the facts in regard to his connection with this international communist spy ring were made known to the then-Undersecretary of State Berle three days after Hitler and Stalin signed the Russo-German Alliance Pact. At that time one Whittaker Chambers—who was also part of the spy ring—apparently decided that with Russia on Hitler's side, he could no longer betray our nation to Russia. He gave Undersecretary of State Berle—and this is all a matter of record—practically all, if not more, of the facts upon which Hiss' conviction was based.

Undersecretary Berle promptly contacted Dean Acheson and received word in return that Acheson, and I quote, "could vouch for Hiss absolutely"—at which time the matter was dropped. And this, you understand, was at a time when Russia was an ally of Germany. This condition existed while Russia and Germany were invading and dismembering Poland, and while the communist groups here were screaming "warmonger" at the United States for their support of the Allied nations.

Again in 1943, the FBI had occasion to investigate the facts surrounding Hiss' contacts with the Russian spy ring. But even after that FBI report was submitted, nothing was done.

Then, late in 1948—on August 5—when the Un-American Activities Committee called Alger Hiss to give an accounting, President Truman at once issued a presidential directive ordering all government agencies to refuse to turn over any information whatsoever in regard to the communist activities of any government employee to a congressional committee.

Incidentally, even after Hiss was convicted, it is interesting to note that the president still labeled the expose of Hiss as a "red herring."

If time permitted, it might be well to go into detail about the fact that Hiss was Roosevelt's chief adviser at Yalta when Roosevelt was admittedly in ill health and tired physically and mentally ... and when, according to the secretary of state, Hiss and Gromyko drafted the report on the conference.

According to the then-Secretary of State Stettinius, here are some of the things that Hiss helped to decide at Yalta: (1) the establishment of a European High Commission; (2) the treatment of Germany—this you will recall was the conference at which it was decided that we would occupy Berlin with Russia occupying an area completely encircling the city, which as you know, resulted in the Berlin airlift which cost 31 American lives; (3) the Polish question; (4) the relationship between UNRRA and the Soviet; (5) the rights of Americans on control commissions of Rumania, Bulgaria and Hungary; (6) Iran; (7) China—here's where we gave away Manchuria; (8) Turkish Straits question; (9) international trusteeships; (10) Korea.

Of the results of this conference, Arthur Bliss Lane of the State Department had this to say: "As I glanced over the document, I could not believe my eyes. To me, almost every line spoke of a surrender to Stalin."

As you hear this story of high treason, I know that you are saying to yourself, "Well, why doesn't the Congress do something about it?" Actually, ladies and gentlemen, one of the important reasons for the graft, the corruption, the dishonesty, the disloyalty, the treason in high government positions—one of the most important reasons why this continues—is a lack of moral uprising on the part of the 140 million American people. In the light of history, however, this is not hard to explain.

It is the result of an emotional hangover and a temporary moral lapse which follows every war. It is the apathy to evil which people who have been subjected to the tremendous evils of war feel. As the people of the world see mass murder, the destruction of defenseless and innocent people, and all of the crime and lack of morals which go with war, they become numb and apathetic. It has always been thus after war. However, the morals of our people have not been destroyed. They still exist. This cloak of numbness and apathy has only needed a spark to rekindle them. Happily, this spark has finally been supplied.

As you know, very recently the secretary of state [Dean Acheson] proclaimed his loyalty to a man guilty of what has always been considered as the most abominable of all crimes—of being a traitor to the people who gave him a position of great trust. The secretary of state, in attempting to justify his continued devotion to the man who sold out the Christian world to the atheistic world, referred to

107

Christ's Sermon on the Mount as a justification and reason therefore, and the reaction of the American people to this would have made the heart of Abraham Lincoln happy. When this pompous diplomat in striped pants, with a phony British accent, proclaimed to the American people that Christ on the Mount endorsed communism, high treason, and betrayal of a sacred trust, the blasphemy was so great that it awakened the dormant indignation of the American people.

He has lighted the spark which is resulting in a moral uprising and will end only when the whole sorry mess of twisted warped thinkers are swept from the national scene so that we may have a new birth of national honesty and decency in government.

Source: McCarthy, Joseph. U.S. Senate. Speech on Communists in the State Department in Wheeling, West Virginia, February 9, 1950. State Department Loyalty Investigation Committee on Foreign Relations. *Congressional Record*, 81st Congress, 2nd session, 1950.

4.3
McCarthy Urges Truman to Help Root Out Communists – 1950
A Letter from Joseph McCarthy to President Harry S. Truman

As anti-Communism emerged as a major factor in American politics, Democratic President Harry S. Truman established a loyalty program for federal employees and instructed the Justice Department to compile a list of "subversive" organizations operating in the United States. But these steps failed to protect Truman from charges that he was soft on Communism.

One of Truman's harshest critics was Republican Senator Joseph McCarthy, who rose to national prominence after a February 1950 speech in Wheeling, West Virginia, in which he claimed to possess evidence of widespread Communist infiltration of Truman's State Department. Two days after his infamous speech, on February 11, 1950, McCarthy issued a public letter to Truman demanding that his administration pursue Communists more energetically. He also charged that if Truman failed to obey his demands, Truman's Democratic Party would become known as "the bedfellow of international communism." The following is the full text of McCarthy's letter. Truman, however, refused to knuckle under to McCarthy's demands. Instead, he repeatedly claimed that the McCarthy "witch hunts" were enormously destructive, both to U.S. foreign policy and national unity.

In the Lincoln Day speech at Wheeling Thursday night I stated that the State Department harbors a nest of Communists and Communist sympathizers who are helping to shape our foreign policy. I further stated that I have in my possession the names of 57 Communists who are in the State Department at present. A State Department spokesman promptly denied this, claiming that there is not a single Communist in the Department. You can convince yourself of the falsity of the State Department claim very easily. You will recall that you personally appointed a board to screen State Department employees for the purpose of weeding out fellow travelers—men whom the board considered dangerous to the security of this Nation. Your board did a painstaking job, and named hundreds which had been listed as dangerous to the security of the Nation, because of communistic connections.

While the records are not available to me, I know absolutely of one group of approximately 300 certified to the Secretary for discharge because of communism. He actually only discharged approximately 80. I understand that this was done after lengthy consultation with the now-convicted traitor, Alger Hiss. I would suggest, therefore, Mr. President, that you simply pick up your phone and ask Mr. Acheson how many of those whom your board had labeled as dangerous Communists he failed to discharge. The day the House Un-American Activities Committee exposed Alger Hiss as an important link in an international Communist spy ring you signed an order forbidding the State Department's giving any information in regard to the disloyalty or the communistic connections of anyone in that Department to the Congress.

Despite this State Department black-out, we have been able to compile a list of 57 Communists in the State Department. This list is available to you but you can get a much longer list by ordering Secretary Acheson to give you a list of those whom your own board listed as being disloyal and who are still working in the State Department. I believe the following is the minimum which can be expected of you in this case.

1. That you demand that Acheson give you and the proper congressional committee the names and a complete report on all of those who were placed in the Department by Alger Hiss, and all of those still working in the State Department who were listed by your board as bad security risks because of their communistic connections.

2. That you promptly revoke the order in which you provided under no circumstances could a congressional committee obtain any information or help in exposing Communists.

Failure on your part will label the Democratic Party of being the bedfellow of international communism. Certainly this label is not deserved by the hundreds of thousands of loyal American Democrats throughout the Nation, and by the sizable number of able loyal Democrats in both the Senate and the House.

Source: McCarthy, Joseph. Letter to President Harry S. Truman. February 11, 1950. *Congressional Record*, 81st Congress, 2nd session, 1950. Also available at the National Archives, http://www.archives.gov/education/lessons/mccarthy-telegram.

4.4

"The Greatest Asset the Kremlin Has Is Senator McCarthy" – 1950
Excerpts from President Truman's Comments Made During a Press Conference at Key West, Florida

President Harry S. Truman disliked Wisconsin Senator Joseph McCarthy and believed that the McCarthy-led search for Communist agents in America was enormously destructive both to U.S. foreign policy and national unity. Truman's beliefs about McCarthy are evident in the following transcript from a March 30, 1950, press conference in Florida.

Q. Mr. President, do you think Senator McCarthy is getting anywhere in his attempt to win the case against the State Department?

The President. What's that?

Q. Do you think that Senator McCarthy can show any disloyalty exists in the State Department?

The President. I think the greatest asset that the Kremlin has is Senator McCarthy.

Q. Would you care to elaborate on that?

The President. I don't think it needs any elaboration—I don't think it needs any elaboration.

Q. Brother, will that hit page one tomorrow!

Q. If you think we are going to bust down the fence on what you have got later, that's a pretty good starter. [*Laughter*]

Q. Mr. President, could we quote that one phrase, "I think the greatest asset the Kremlin has is Senator McCarthy"?

The President. Now let me give you a little preliminary, and then I will tell you what I think you ought to do. Let me tell you what the situation is.

We started out in 1945, when I became President, and the two wars were still going on, and the Russians were our allies, just the same as the British and the French and Brazil and the South American countries. And we won the war together.

We organized the United Nations in April 1945, and one of the first questions that was asked me, after I was sworn in at 7:09 o'clock on the 12th of April, was whether or not the San Francisco conference on the United Nations should go ahead. And I said it certainly will. It went ahead and we finally succeeded in getting a charter and getting it agreed to by I think 51 nations, if I remember correctly.

Then our objective was to—as quickly as possible—get peace in the world. We made certain agreements with the Russians and the British and the French and the Chinese. We kept those agreements to the letter. They have nearly all been—those agreements where the Russians were involved—been broken by the Russians. And it became perfectly evident that they had no intention of carrying out the fundamental principles of the United Nations Charter and the agreements which had been made at Teheran, Yalta, and Potsdam. And it became evident that there was an endeavor on the part of the Kremlin to control the world.

A procedure was instituted which came to be known as the cold war. The airlift to Berlin was only one phase of it. People became alarmed here in the United States then, that there might be people whose sympathies were with the Communist ideal of government—which is not communism under any circumstances, it is totalitarianism of the worst brand. There isn't any difference between the totalitarian Russian Government and the Hitler government and the Franco government in Spain. They are all alike. They are police state governments.

In 1947 I instituted a loyalty program for Government employees, and that loyalty procedure program was set up in such a way that the rights of individuals were respected.

In a survey of the 2,200,000 employees at that time, I think there were some 205—something like that—who left the service. I don't know—a great many of them left of their own accord.

Q. How many, Mr. President?

The President. Somewhere in the neighborhood of 205. Does anybody remember those figures exactly? It's a very small figure.

Q. Very small.

The President. An infinitesimal part of 1 percent. We will get the figures for you.

And then, for political background, the Republicans have been trying vainly to find an issue on which to make a bid for the control of the Congress for next year. They tried "statism." They tried "welfare state." They tried "socialism." And there are a certain number of members of the Republican Party who are trying to dig up that old malodorous dead horse called "isolationism." And in order to do that, they are perfectly willing to sabotage the bipartisan foreign policy of the United States. And this fiasco which has been going on in the Senate is the very best asset that the Kremlin could have in the operation of the cold war. And that is what I mean when I say that McCarthy's antics are the best asset that the Kremlin can have.

Now, if anybody really felt that there were disloyal people in the employ of the Government, the proper and the honorable way to handle the situation would be to come to the President of the United States and say, "This man is a disloyal person. He is in such and such a department." We will investigate him immediately, and if he were a disloyal person he would be immediately fired.

That is not what they want. They are trying to create an issue, and it is going to be just as big a fiasco as the campaign in New York and other places on these other false and fatuous issues.

With a little bit of intelligence they could find an issue at home without a bit of trouble!

Q. What would it be, Mr. President?

The President. Anything in the domestic line. I will meet them on any subject they want, but to try to sabotage the foreign policy of the United States, in the face of the situation with which we are faced, is just as bad as trying to cut the Army in time of war.

Q. On that question we were just kidding.

The President. And that gave me a chance to give you an answer. To try to sabotage the foreign policy of the United States is just as bad in this cold war as it would be to shoot our soldiers in the back in a hot war.

I am fed up with what is going on, and I am giving you the facts as I see them....

Source: Truman, Harry S., and others. "News Conference at Key West," March 30, 1950. *Public Papers of the Presidents of the United States: Harry S. Truman, 1950.* Washington, DC: Office of the Federal Register, 1965.

4.5

The Sentencing of Julius and Ethel Rosenberg – 1951
Judge Irving Kaufman's Comments Upon Imposing the Death Sentence on the Rosenbergs

America's deep fear of Communism in the 1940s and 1950s was fueled in part by several high-profile espionage cases that captivated the nation. One of these concerned Alger Hiss, a State Department official who was accused of spying for the Soviets. He was eventually convicted of perjury, but always maintained his innocence. Another was the case of Julius and Ethel Rosenberg, a couple accused of assisting Soviet efforts to obtain top-secret information on the U.S.'s atomic bomb program. Today, historians generally accept that Julius Rosenberg did in fact seek to pass atomic secrets on to Communist agents, but many disagree over the extent of Ethel Rosenberg's role. Some believe that she was deeply involved in the scheme, while others contend that she had little or no involvement.

The Rosenbergs were convicted of conspiracy to commit espionage. On April 5, 1951, Judge Irving Kaufman imposed the death sentence on both of them. The announcement of his decision is reprinted below. Kaufman's decision was appealed by the Rosenbergs' lawyers, but the conviction was upheld by the U.S. Circuit Court of Appeals on February 25, 1952. Julius and Ethel Rosenberg were executed on June 19, 1953.

April 5, 1951

Because of the seriousness of this case and the lack of precedence, I have refrained from asking the Government for a recommendation. The responsibility is so great that I believe that the Court alone should assume this responsibility....

The issue of punishment in this case is presented in a unique framework of history. It is so difficult to make people realize that this country is engaged in a life and death struggle with a completely different system. This struggle is not only manifested externally between these two forces but this case indicates quite clearly that it also involves the employment by the enemy of secret as well as overt outspoken forces among our own people. All of our democratic institutions are, therefore, directly involved in this great conflict. I believe that never at any time in our history were we ever confronted to the same degree that we are today with such a challenge to our very existence. The atom bomb was unknown when the espionage statute was drafted. I emphasize this because we must realize that we are dealing with a missile of destruction which can wipe out millions of Americans.

The competitive advantage held by the United States in super-weapons has put a premium on the services of a new school of spies—the homegrown variety that places allegiance to a foreign power before loyalty to the United States. The punishment to be meted out in this case must therefore serve the maximum interest for the preservation of our society against these traitors in our midst.

It is ironic that the very country which these defendants betrayed and sought to destroy placed every safeguard around them for obtaining a fair and impartial trial, a trial which consumed three weeks in this court. I recall the defendant Julius Rosenberg testifying that our American system of jurisprudence met with his approval and was preferred over Russian justice. Even the defendants realize—by this admission—that this type of trial would not have been afforded to them in Russia. Certainly, to a Russian national accused of a conspiracy to destroy Russia not one day would have been consumed in a trial. It is to America's credit that it took the pains and exerted the effort which it did in the trial of these defendants. Yet, they made a choice of devoting themselves to the Russian ideology of denial of God, denial of the sanctity of the individual, and aggression against free men everywhere instead of serving the cause of liberty and freedom.

I consider your crime worse than murder. Plain deliberate contemplated murder is dwarfed in magnitude by comparison with the crime you have committed. In committing the act of murder, the criminal kills only his victim. The immediate family is brought to grief and when justice is meted out the chapter is closed. But in your case, I believe your conduct in putting into the hands of the Russians the

A-bomb years before our best scientists predicted Russia would perfect the bomb has already caused, in my opinion, the Communist aggression in Korea, with the resultant casualties exceeding 50,000 and who knows but that millions more of innocent people may pay the price of your treason. Indeed, by your betrayal you undoubtedly have altered the course of history to the disadvantage of our country.

> *"They made a choice of devoting themselves to the Russian ideology of denial of God, denial of the sanctity of the individual, and aggression against free men everywhere instead of serving the cause of liberty and freedom."*

No one can say that we do not live in a constant state of tension. We have evidence of your treachery all around us every day—for the civilian defense activities throughout the nation are aimed at preparing us for an atom bomb attack.

Nor can it be said in mitigation of the offense that the power which set the conspiracy in motion and profited from it was not openly hostile to the United States at the time of the conspiracy. If this was your excuse the error of your ways in setting yourselves above our properly constituted authorities and the decision of those authorities not to share the information with Russia must now be obvious.

The evidence indicated quite clearly that Julius Rosenberg was the prime mover in this conspiracy. However, let no mistake be made about the role which his wife, Ethel Rosenberg, played in this conspiracy. Instead of deterring him from pursuing his ignoble cause, she encouraged and assisted the cause. She was a mature woman—almost three years older than her husband and almost seven years older than her younger brother. She was a full-fledged partner in this crime.

Indeed the defendants Julius and Ethel Rosenberg placed their devotion to their cause above their own personal safety and were conscious that they were sacrificing their own children, should their misdeeds be detected—all of which did not deter them from pursuing their course. Love for their cause dominated their lives—it was even greater than their love for their children.

What I am about to say is not easy for me. I have deliberated for hours, days and nights. I have carefully weighed the evidence. Every nerve, every fiber of my body has been taxed. I am just as human as are the people who have given me the power to impose sentence. I am convinced beyond any doubt of your guilt. I have searched the records—I have searched my conscience—to find some reason for mercy—for it is only human to be merciful and it is natural to try to spare lives. I am convinced, however, that I would violate the solemn and sacred trust that the people of this land have placed in my hands were I to show leniency to the defendants Rosenberg. It is not in my power, Julius and Ethel Rosenberg, to forgive you. Only the Lord can find mercy for what you have done.

The sentence of the Court upon Julius and Ethel Rosenberg is, for the crime for which you have been convicted, you are hereby sentenced to the punishment of death, and it is ordered upon some day within the week beginning with Monday, May 21st, you shall be executed according to law.

Source: Kaufman, Judge Irving. "Sentencing of Julius and Ethel Rosenberg," April 5, 1951. In transcript of Record, Supreme Court of the United States, *Julius Rosenberg and Ethel Rosenberg v. United States of America*, October Term, 1951.

4.6
"The Black Silence of Fear" – 1952
An Excerpt from an Article by Supreme Court Justice William O. Douglas

> *During the 1950s a number of prominent Americans publicly condemned the "McCarthy witch hunts" and asserted that anti-Communist hysteria was eroding basic American freedoms and values. One such critic was William O. Douglas, who served as a U.S. Supreme Court associate justice from 1939 until his retirement in 1975. The following opinion piece was written by Douglas and published in the* New York Times Magazine *on January 13, 1952, at the height of the McCarthy era.*

There is an ominous trend in this nation. We are developing tolerance only for the orthodox point of view on world affairs, intolerance for new or different approaches. We have over the years swung from tolerance to intolerance and back again. There have been years of intolerance when the views of minorities have been suppressed. But there probably has not been a period of greater intolerance than we witness today.

To understand this, I think one has to leave the country, go into the back regions of the world, lose himself there, and become absorbed in the problems of the peoples of different civilizations. When he returns to America after a few months he probably will be shocked. He will be shocked not at the intentions or purposes or ideals of the American people. He will be shocked at the arrogance and intolerance of great segments of the American press, at the arrogance and intolerance of many leaders in public office, at the arrogance and intolerance reflected in many of our attitudes toward Asia. He will find that thought is being standardized, that the permissible area for calm discussion is being narrowed, that the range of ideas is being limited, that many minds are closed....

This is alarming to one who loves his country. It means that the philosophy of strength through free speech is being forsaken for the philosophy of fear through repression.

William O. Douglas, "The Black Silence of Fear," New York Times Magazine, January 13, 1952. Reprinted with permission from the Estate of William O. Douglas.

That choice in Russia is conscious. Under Lenin the ministers and officials were encouraged to debate, to advance new ideas and criticisms. Once the debate was over, however, no dissension or disagreement was permitted. But even that small degree of tolerance for free discussion that Lenin permitted disappeared under Stalin. Stalin maintains a tight system of control, permitting no free speech, no real clash in ideas, even in the inner circle. We are, of course, not emulating either Lenin or Stalin. But we are drifting in the direction of repression, drifting dangerously fast.

The drift goes back, I think, to the fact that we carried over to days of peace the military approach to world affairs. Today in Asia we are identified not with ideas of freedom, but with guns. Today at home we are thinking less and less in terms of defeating communism with ideas, more and more in terms of defeating communism with military might.

"The philosophy of strength through free speech is being forsaken for the philosophy of fear through repression."

The concentration on military means has helped to breed fear. It has bred fear and insecurity partly because of the horror of atomic war. But the real reason strikes deeper. In spite of our enormous expenditures, we see that Soviet imperialism continues to expand and that the expansion proceeds without the Soviets firing a shot. The free world continues to contract without a battle for its survival having been fought. It becomes apparent, as country after country falls to Soviet imperialistic ambitions, that military policy alone is a weak one, that military policy alone will end in political bankruptcy and futility. Thus fear mounts.

Fear has many manifestations. The Communist threat inside the country has been magnified and exalted far beyond its realities. Irresponsible talk by irresponsible people has fanned the flames of fear. Accusations have been loosely made. Character assassinations have become common. Suspicion has taken the place of goodwill. Once we could debate with impunity along a wide range of inquiry. Once we could safely explore to the edges of a problem, challenge orthodoxy without qualms, and run the gamut of ideas in search of solutions to perplexing problems. Once we had confidence in each other. Now there is suspicion. Innocent acts become telltale marks of disloyalty. The coincidence that an idea parallels Soviet Russia's policy for a moment of time settles an aura of suspicion around a person.

Suspicion grows until only the orthodox idea is the safe one. Suspicion grows until only the person who loudly proclaims that orthodox view, or who, once having been a Communist, has been converted, is trustworthy. Competition for embracing the new orthodoxy increases. Those who are unorthodox are suspect. Everyone who does not follow the military policymakers is suspect. Everyone who voices opposition to the trend away from diplomacy and away from political tactics takes a chance. Some who are opposed are indeed "subversive." Therefore, the thundering edict commands that all who are opposed are "subversive." Fear is fanned to a fury. Good and honest men are pilloried. Character is assassinated. Fear runs rampant.

Fear has driven more and more men and women in all walks of life either to silence or to the folds of the orthodox. Fear has mounted: fear of losing one's job, fear of being investigated, fear of being pilloried. This fear has stereotyped our thinking, narrowed the range of free public discussion, and driven many thoughtful people to despair. This fear has even entered universities, great citadels of our spiritual strength, and corrupted them. We have the spectacle of university officials lending themselves to one of the worst witch-hunts we have seen since early days.

This fear has affected the youngsters. Youth, like the opposition party in a parliamentary system, has served a powerful role. It has cast doubts on our policies, challenged our inarticulate major premises, put the light on our prejudices, and exposed our inconsistencies. Youth has made each generation indulge in self-examination.

But a great change has taken place. Youth is still rebellious; but it is largely holding its tongue. There is the fear of being labeled a "subversive" if one departs from the orthodox party line. That charge, if leveled against a young man or young woman, may have profound effects. It may ruin a youngster's business or professional career. No one wants a Communist in his organization nor anyone who is suspect.

This pattern of orthodoxy that is shaping our thinking has dangerous implications. No one man, no one group can have the answer to the many perplexing problems that today confront the management of world affairs. The scene is a troubled and complicated one. The problems require the pooling of many ideas, the exposure of different points of view, the hammering out in public discussions of the pros and cons of this policy or of that.

The great danger of this period is not inflation, nor the national debt, nor atomic warfare. The great, the critical danger is that we will so limit or narrow the range of permissible discussion and permissible thought that we will become victims of the orthodox school. If we do, we will lose flexibility. We will lose the capacity for expert management. We will then become wedded to a few techniques, to a few devices. They will define our policy and at the same time limit our ability to alter or modify it. Once we narrow the range of thought and discussion, we will surrender a great deal of our power. We will become like the man on the toboggan who can ride it but who can neither steer it nor stop it.

The mind of man must always be free. The strong society is one that sanctions and encourages freedom of thought and expression. Our real power is our spiritual strength, and that spiritual strength stems from our civil liberties. If we are true to our traditions, if we are tolerant of a whole marketplace of ideas, we will

117

always be strong. Our weakness grows when we become intolerant of opposing ideas, depart from our standards of civil liberties, and borrow the policeman's philosophy from the enemy we detest.

Source: Douglas, William O. "The Black Silence of Fear." *The New York Times Magazine*, January 13, 1952.

4.7
Lillian Hellman Defies the House Un-American Activities Committee – 1952
The Text of Hellman's Letter to the HUAC

> *In 1952 playwright and screenwriter Lillian Hellman appeared before the House Un-American Activities Committee (HUAC), which had been holding hearings since 1947 on alleged Communist activity in the United States. The entertainment industry was a particular focus of the HUAC investigation, and the careers of a number of notable American writers and film directors were ruined when they refused to answer HUAC questions about the political beliefs that they and various colleagues held.*
>
> *On May 19, 1952, prior to her HUAC appearance, Hellman sent a letter to the committee (reprinted below). She offered to testify about her own activities, provided she was not asked to inform on friends and colleagues. The members of HUAC flatly refused this request, so when Hellman appeared, she repeatedly invoked the Fifth Amendment protection against self-incrimination. This decision made most members of the entertainment industry reluctant to hire or even associate with her for fear of attracting the attention of HUAC. Her status as a "blacklisted" writer and playwright endured for a decade before her plays once again began appearing on the American stage.*

Dear Mr. Wood:

As you know, I am under subpoena to appear before your committee on May 21, 1952.

I am most willing to answer all questions about myself. I have nothing to hide from your committee and there is nothing in my life of which I am ashamed. I have been advised by counsel that under the fifth amendment I have a constitutional privilege to decline to answer any questions about my political opinions, activities, and associations, on the grounds of self-incrimination. I do not wish to claim this privilege. I am ready and willing to testify before the representatives of our Government as to my own opinions and my own actions, regardless of any risks or consequences to myself.

But I am advised by counsel that if I answer the committee's questions about myself, I must also answer questions about other people and that if I refuse to do so, I can be cited for contempt. My counsel tells me that if I answer questions about myself, I will have waived my rights under the fifth amendment and could be forced legally to answer questions about others. This is very difficult for a layman to understand. But there is one principle that I do understand: I am not willing, now or in the future, to bring bad trouble to people who, in my past association with them, were completely innocent of any talk or any action that was disloyal or subversive. I do not like subversion or disloyalty in any form and if I had ever seen any I would have considered it my duty to have reported it to the proper authorities. But to hurt innocent people whom I knew many years ago in order to save myself is, to me, inhuman and indecent and dishonorable. I cannot and will not cut my conscience to fit this year's fashions, even though I long ago came to the conclusion that I was not a political person and could have no comfortable place in any political group.

I was raised in an old-fashioned American tradition and there were certain homely things that were taught to me: To try to tell the truth, not to bear false witness, not to harm my neighbor, to be loyal to my country, and so on. In general, I respected these ideals of Christian honor and did as well with them as I knew how. It is my belief that you will agree with these simple rules of human decency and will not expect me to violate the good American tradition from which they spring. I would, therefore, like to come before you and speak of myself.

I am prepared to waive the privilege against self-incrimination and to tell you everything you wish to know about my views or actions if your committee will agree to refrain from asking me to name other people. If the committee is unwilling to give me this assurance, I will be forced to plead the privilege of the fifth amendment at the hearing.

A reply to this letter would be appreciated.
Sincerely yours,
Lillian Hellman

Source: Hellman, Lillian. Letter to the U.S. Congress, House of Representatives, Committee on Un-American Activities, May 19, 1952. Published in *Communist Infiltration of the Hollywood Motion-Picture Industry—Part 8: Hearings Before the Committee on Un-American Activities*, 82nd Congress, 2nd session, May 21, 1952.

4.8

"Have You No Sense of Decency, Sir?" – 1954
An Excerpt from the Army-McCarthy Hearings

By 1952 Republican Senator Joseph McCarthy had risen to national prominence by exploiting anti-Communist fears. His appointment as chairman of the Senate Committee on Government Operations and its Subcommittee on Investigations gave him the authority to begin searching for "reds" in various government agencies, the defense industry, American universities, and the United Nations.

In November 1953, an advisor to McCarthy named G. David Schine was drafted and given an overseas assignment. This development infuriated McCarthy's closest political ally, Subcommittee Chief Counsel Roy Cohn. When Secretary of the Army Robert T. Stevens ignored their demand that Schine be allowed to continue his work with the committee, McCarthy and Cohn intensified an existing investigation of alleged Communist activity within the U.S. Army.

On March 16, 1954, the Senate Committee on Government Operations created a Permanent Subcommittee on Investigations led by Senator Karl Mundt of South Dakota. The Subcommittee reviewed the charge that McCarthy was trying "to punish the U.S. Army for drafting his former aide." These "Army-McCarthy hearings" were televised live from April 22 to June 17, 1954, and they featured a number of tense clashes between McCarthy, Cohn, Special Counsel for the Army Joseph N. Welch, and Counselor for the Army John G. Adams. Many historians believe that McCarthy's behavior during these televised hearings, combined with Edward R. Murrow's damning portrait of McCarthy on a March 9, 1954, broadcast of the CBS news show "See It Now," pierced the senator's aura of invincibility. They cite these events as pivotal in McCarthy's sudden and dramatic fall from power by the end of 1954.

The following famous exchange began with a heated confrontation between Joseph N. Welch, Special Counsel for the Army, and Roy Cohn (other participants in this part of the hearing include Senator Mundt and Secretary of the Army Stevens). Welch challenges Cohn to identify known Communists, implying that Cohn doesn't actually possess hard evidence of Communist infiltrators. That confrontation is followed by another heated exchange in which McCarthy retaliates against Welch for embarrassing Cohn. McCarthy does this by attacking one of Welch's protégés, Fred G. Fisher Jr., as a former member of a Communist organization. Welch's stunned response remains one of the most famous moments in the history of the McCarthy era.

.... **Mr. WELCH.** Mr. Cohn, what is the exact number of Communists or subversives that are loose today in these defense plants?

Mr. COHN. The exact number that is loose, sir?

Mr. WELCH. Yes, sir.

Mr. COHN. I don't know.

Mr. WELCH. Roughly how many?

Mr. COHN. I can only tell you, sir, what we know about it.

Mr. WELCH. That is 130, is that right?

Mr. COHN. Yes, sir. I am going to try to particularize for you, if I can.

Mr. WELCH. I am in a hurry. I don't want the sun to go down while they are still in there, if we can get them out.

Mr. COHN. I am afraid we won't be able to work that fast, sir.

Mr. WELCH. I have a suggestion about it, sir. How many are there?

Mr. COHN. I believe the figure is approximately 130.

Mr. WELCH. Approximately one-two-three?

Mr. COHN. Yes, sir. Those are people, Mr. Welch—

Mr. WELCH. I don't care. You told us who they are. In how many plants are they?

Mr. COHN. How many plants?

Mr. WELCH. How many plants.

Mr. COHN. Yes, sir; just I minute, sir. I see 16 offhand, sir.

Mr. WELCH. Sixteen plants?

Mr. COHN. Yes, sir.

Mr. WELCH. Where are they, sir?

Mr. COHN. Senator McCarthy—

Mr. WELCH. Reel off the cities.

Mr. COHN. Would you stop me if I am going too far?

Mr. WELCH. You can't go too far revealing Communists, Mr. Cohn. Reel off the cities for us.

Mr. COHN. Schenectady, N.Y.; Syracuse, N.Y.; Rome, N.Y.; Quincy, Mass.; Fitchburg, Mass.; Buffalo, N.Y.; Dunkirk, N.Y.; another at Buffalo, N.Y.; Cambridge, Mass.; New Bedford, Mass.; Boston, Mass.; Quincy, Mass.; Lynn, Mass.; Pittsfield Mass.; Boston, Mass.

Mr. WELCH. Mr. Cohn, you not only frighten me, you make me ashamed when there are so many in Massachusetts. [*Laughter.*] This is not a laughing matter, believe me. Are you alarmed at that situation, Mr. Cohn?

Mr. COHN. Yes, sir; I am.

Mr. WELCH. Nothing could be more alarming, could it?

Mr. COHN. It certainly is a very alarming thing.

Mr. WELCH. Will you not, before the sun goes down, give those names to the FBI and at least have those men put under surveillance.

Mr. COHN. Mr. Welch, the FBI—

Senator McCARTHY. Mr. Chairman.

Mr. WELCH. That is a fair question.

Senator McCARTHY. Mr. Chairman, let's not be ridiculous. Mr. Welch knows, as I have told him a dozen times, that the FBI has all of this information. The defense plants have the information. The only thing we can do is to try and publicly expose these individuals and hope that they will be gotten rid of. And you know that, Mr. Welch.

Mr. WELCH. I do not know that.... Cannot the FBI put these 130 men under surveillance before sundown tomorrow?

Mr. COHN. Sir, if there is need for surveillance in the case of espionage or anything like that, I can well assure you that Mr. John Edgar Hoover and his men know a lot better than I, and I quite respectfully suggest, sir, than probably a lot of us, just who should be put under surveillance. I do not propose to tell the FBI how to run its shop. It does it very well.

Mr. WELCH. And they do it, don't they, Mr. Cohn?

Mr. COHN. When the need arises, of course.

Mr. WELCH. And will you tell them tonight, Mr. Cohn, that here is a case where the need has arisen, so that it can be done by sundown tomorrow night?

Mr. COHN. No, sir; there is no need for my telling the FBI what to do about this or anything else....

Mr. WELCH. Mr. Cohn, tell me once more: Every time you learn of a Communist or a spy anywhere, is it your policy to get them out as fast as possible?

Mr. COHN. Surely, we want them out as fast as possible, sir.

Mr. WELCH. And whenever you learn of one from now on, Mr. Cohn, I beg of you, will you tell somebody about them quick?

Mr. COHN. Mr. Welch, with great respect, I work for the committee here. They know how we go about handling situations of Communist infiltration and failure to act on FBI information about Communist infiltration. If they are displeased with the speed with which I and the group of men who work with me proceed, if they are displeased with the order in which we move, I am sure they will give me appropriate instructions along those lines, and I will follow any which they give me.

Mr. WELCH. May I add my small voice, sir, and say whenever you know about a subversive or a Communist spy, please hurry. Will you remember those words?

Senator McCARTHY. Mr. Chairman.

Mr. COHN. Mr. Welch, I can assure you, sir, as far as I am concerned, and certainly as far as the chairman of this committee and the members, and the members of the staff, are concerned, we are a small group, but we proceed as expeditiously as is humanly possible to get out Communists and traitors and to bring to light the mechanism by which they have been permitted to remain where they were for so long a period of time.

Senator McCARTHY. Mr. Chairman, in view of that question—

Senator MUNDT. Have you a point of order?

Senator McCARTHY. Not exactly, Mr. Chairman, but in view of Mr. Welch's request that the information be given once we know of anyone who might be performing any work for the Communist Party, I think we should tell him that he has in his law firm a young man named Fisher whom he recommended, incidentally, to do work on this committee, who has been for a number of years a member of an organization which was named, oh, years and years ago, as the legal bulwark of the Communist Party, an organization which always swings to the defense of anyone who dares to expose Communists. I certainly assume that Mr. Welch did not know of this young man at the time he recommended him as the assistant counsel for this committee, but he has such terror and such a great desire to know where anyone is located who may be serving the Communist cause, Mr. Welch, that I thought we should just call to your attention the fact that your Mr. Fisher, who is still in your law firm today, whom you asked to have down here looking over the secret and classified material, is a member of an organization, not named by me but named by various committees, named by the Attorney General, as I recall, and I think I quote this verbatim, as "the legal bulwark of the Communist Party." He belonged to that for a sizable number of years, according to his own admission, and he belonged to it long after it had been exposed as the legal arm of the Communist Party.

Knowing that, Mr. Welch, I just felt that I had a duty to respond to your urgent request that before sundown, when we know of anyone serving the Communist cause, we let the agency know. We are now letting you know that your man did belong to this organization for, either 3 or 4 years, belonged to it long after he was out of law school.

I don't think you can find anyplace, anywhere, an organization which has done more to defend Communists—I am again quoting the report—to defend Communists, to defend espionage agents, and to aid the Communist cause, than the man whom you originally wanted down here at your right hand instead of Mr. St. Clair.

I have hesitated bringing that up, but I have been rather bored with your phony requests to Mr. Cohn here that he personally get every Communist out of government before sundown. Therefore, we will give you information about the young man in your own organization.

I am not asking you at this time to explain why you tried to foist him on this committee. Whether you knew he was a member of that Communist organization or not, I don't know. I assume you did not, Mr. Welch, because I get the impression that, while you are quite an actor, you play for a laugh, I don't think you have any conception of the danger of the Communist Party. I don't think you yourself would ever knowingly aid the Communist cause. I think you are unknowingly aiding it when you try to burlesque this hearing in which we are attempting to bring out the facts, however.

Mr. WELCH. Mr. Chairman.

Senator MUNDT. Mr. Welch, the Chair should say he has no recognition or no memory of Mr. Welch's recommending either Mr. Fisher or anybody else as counsel for this committee.

I will recognize Mr. Welch.

Senator McCARTHY. Mr. Chairman, I will give you the news story on that.

Mr. WELCH. Mr. Chairman, under these circumstances I must have something approaching a personal privilege.

Senator MUNDT. You may have it, sir. It will not be taken out of your time.

Mr. WELCH. Senator McCarthy, I did not know—Senator, sometimes you say "May I have your attention?"

Senator McCARTHY. I am listening to you. I can listen with one ear.

Mr. WELCH. This time I want you to listen with both.

Senator McCARTHY. Yes.

Mr. WELCH. Senator McCarthy, I think until this moment—

Senator McCARTHY. Jim, will you get the news story to the effect that this man belonged to this Communist-front organization? Will you get the citations showing that this was the legal arm of the Communist Party, and the length of time that he belonged, and the fact that he was recommended by Mr. Welch? I think that should be in the record.

Mr. WELCH. You won't need anything in the record when I have finished telling you this.

Until this moment, Senator, I think I never really gauged your cruelty or your recklessness. Fred Fisher is a young man who went to the Harvard Law School and came into my firm and is starting what looks to be a brilliant career with us.

When I decided to work for this committee I asked Jim St. Clair, who sits on my right, to be my first assistant. I said to Jim, "Pick somebody in the firm who works under you that you would like." He chose Fred Fisher and they came down on an afternoon plane. That night, when he had taken a little stab at trying to see what the case was about, Fred Fisher and Jim St. Clair and I went to dinner together. I then said to these two young men, "Boys, I don't know anything about you except I have always liked you, but if there is anything funny in the life of either one of you that would hurt anybody in this case you speak up quick."

Fred Fisher said, "Mr. Welch, when I was in law school and for a period of months after, I belonged to the Lawyers Guild," as you have suggested, Senator. He went on to say, "I am secretary of the Young Republicans League in Newton with the son of Massachusetts' Governor, and I have the respect and admiration of the 25 lawyers or so in Hale & Dorr."

I said, "Fred, I just don't think I am going to ask you to work on the case. If I do, one of these days that will come out and go over national television and it will just hurt like the dickens."

So, Senator, I asked him to go back to Boston.

Little did I dream you could be so reckless and cruel as to do an injury to that lad. It is true he is still with Hale & Dorr. It is true that he will continue to be with Hale & Dorr. It is, I regret to say, equally true that I fear he shall always bear a scar needlessly inflicted by you. If it were in my power to forgive you for your reckless cruelty, I will do so. I like to think I am a gentleman, but your forgiveness will have to come from someone other than me.

Senator McCARTHY. Mr. Chairman.

Senator MUNDT. Senator McCarthy?

Senator McCARTHY. May I say that Mr. Welch talks about this being cruel and reckless. He was just baiting; he has been baiting Mr. Cohn here for hours, requesting that Mr. Cohn, before sundown, get out of any department of Government anyone who is serving the Communist cause.

I just give this man's record, and I want to say, Mr. Welch, that it has been labeled long before he became a member, as early as 1944—

Mr. WELCH. Senator, may we not drop this? We know he belonged to the Lawyers Guild, and Mr. Cohn nods his head at me. I did you, I think, no personal injury, Mr. Cohn.

Mr. COHN. No, sir.

Mr. WELCH. I meant to do you no personal injury, and if I did, beg your pardon.

Let us not assassinate this lad further, Senator. You have done enough. Have you no sense of decency sir, at long last? Have you left no sense of decency?

Senator McCARTHY. I know this hurts you, Mr. Welch. But I may say, Mr. Chairman, on a point of personal privilege, and I would like to finish it—

Mr. WELCH. Senator, I think it hurts you, too, sir.

Senator McCARTHY. I would like to finish this.

Mr. Welch has been filibustering this hearing, he has been talking day after day about how he wants to get anyone tainted with communism out before sundown. I know Mr. Cohn would rather not have me go into this. I intend to, however, Mr. Welch talks about any sense of decency. If I say anything which is not the truth, then I would like to know about it....

I have heard you and every one else talk so much about laying the truth upon the table that when I hear—and it is completely phony, Mr. Welch, I have listened to you for a long time—when you say "Now, before sundown, you must get these people out of Government," I want to have it very clear, very clear that you were not so serious about that when you tried to recommend this man for this committee.

And may I say, Mr. Welch, in fairness to you, I have reason to believe that you did not know about his Communist-front record at the time you recommended him. I don't think you would have recommended him to the committee, if you knew that.

I think it is entirely possible you learned that after you recommended him.

Senator MUNDT. The Chair would like to say again that he does not believe that Mr. Welch recommended Mr. Fisher as counsel for this committee, because he has through his office all the recommendations that were made. He does not recall any that came from Mr. Welch, and that would include Mr. Fisher.

Senator McCARTHY. Let me ask Mr. Welch. You brought him down, did you not, to act as your assistant?

Mr. WELCH. Mr. McCarthy, I will not discuss this with you further. You have sat within 6 feet of me, and could have asked me about Fred Fisher. You have brought it out. If there is a God in heaven, it will do neither you nor your cause any good. I will not discuss it further. I will not ask Mr. Cohn any more questions. You, Mr. Chairman, may, if you will, call the next witness.

Senator MUNDT. Are there any questions?...

Mr. JENKINS. Senator McCarthy, how do you regard the communistic threat to our Government as compared with other threats with which it is confronted?

Senator McCARTHY. Mr. Jenkins, the thing that I think we must remember is that this is a war which a brutalitarian force has won to a greater extent than any brutalitarian force has won a war in the history of the world before.

For example, Christianity, which has been in existence for 2,000 years, has not converted, convinced nearly as many people as this Communist brutalitarianism has enslaved in 106 years, and they are not going to stop.

I know that many of my good friends seem to feel that this is a sort of a game you can play, that you can talk about communism as though it is something 10,000 miles away.

126

Mr. Jenkins, in answer to your question, let me say it is right here with us now. Unless we make sure that there is no infiltration of our Government, then just as certain as you sit there, in the period of our lives you will see a red world. There is no question about that, Mr. Jenkins....

Source: U.S. Congress. Senate. Permanent Subcommittee on Investigations of the Committee on Government Operations. *Executive Sessions of the Senate Permanent Subcommittee on Investigations of the Committee on Government Operations* – Vol. 5, 83rd Congress, 2nd Session, 1954. Washington, DC: U.S. Government Printing Office, 2003. Available online at the U.S. Senate Historical Office, http://www.senate.gov/artandhistory/history/common/generic/News_McCarthy_Hearings.htm.

4.9
The Censuring of Joseph McCarthy – 1954
The Text of the U.S. Senate Resolution of Condemnation of Senator McCarthy

By the fall of 1954 Senator Joseph R. McCarthy's meteoric career was falling back to earth. During this period, Senators Arthur V. Watkins of Utah, Ralph E. Flanders of Vermont, Wayne Morse of Oregon, and J. William Fulbright of Arkansas brought charges of official misconduct against McCarthy, and a resolution of censure was introduced. In December the Senate voted to "condemn" the senator for bringing the reputation of the entire Senate into "dishonor and disrepute" with his conduct. The resolution of censure specifically mentioned only a handful of events from 1954, but it was widely understood to be a commentary on McCarthy's behavior over the previous five years. The full text of the U.S. Senate resolution of condemnation from December 2, 1954, is reprinted below.

Resolved, that the senator from Wisconsin, Mr. McCarthy, failed to cooperate with the Subcommittee on Privileges and Elections of the Senate Committee on Rules and Administration in clearing up matters referred to that subcommittee which concerned his conduct as a senator and affected the honor of the Senate and, instead, repeatedly abused the subcommittee and its members who were trying to carry out assigned duties, thereby obstructing the constitutional processes of the Senate; and that this conduct of the senator from Wisconsin, Mr. McCarthy, is contrary to senatorial traditions and is hereby condemned.

Section 2. The senator from Wisconsin, Mr. McCarthy, in writing to the chairman of the Select Committee to Study Censure Charges (Mr. Watkins) after the Select Committee had issued its report and before the report was presented to the Senate charging three members of the Select Committee with "deliberate deception" and "fraud" for failure to disqualify themselves; in stating to the press on

Nov. 4, 1954, that the special Senate session that was to begin Nov. 8, 1954, was a "lynch party"; in repeatedly describing this special Senate session as a "lynch bee" in a nationwide television and radio show on Nov. 7, 1954; in stating to the public press on Nov. 13, 1954, that the chairman of the Select Committee (Mr. Watkins) was guilty of "the most unusual, most cowardly thing I've heard of," and stating further: "I expected he would be afraid to answer the questions, but didn't think he'd be stupid enough to make a public statement"; and in characterizing the said committee as the "unwitting handmaiden," involuntary agent," and "attorneys in fact" of the Communist Party, and in charging that the said committee in writing its report "imitated Communist methods—that it distorted, misrepresented, and omitted in its effort to manufacture a plausible rationalization" in support of its recommendations to the Senate, which characterizations and charges were contained in a statement released to the press and inserted in the *Congressional Record* of Nov. 10, 1954, acted contrary to senatorial ethics and tended to bring the Senate into dishonor and disrepute, to obstruct the constitutional processes of the Senate, and to impair its dignity; and such conduct is hereby condemned.

Source: U.S. Congress. Senate. "Senate Resolution 301: Censure of Senator Joseph McCarthy." 83rd Congress, 2nd Session, Senate Resolution 301, December 2, 1954. National Archives. Records of the U.S. Senate. Available online at the U.S. State Department, http://usinfo.state.gov/usa/infousa/facts/democrac/60.htm.

5

BEHIND THE CURTAIN

Soviet Premier Nikita Khrushchev (right) served as leader of the USSR
for eleven turbulent years after succeeding Joseph Stalin in 1953.

INTRODUCTION

The 1950s was a decade of internal turmoil for the Soviet Union and its satellite states. Cold War tensions led already repressive and ruthless leaders of these countries to exert even greater control over the lives of their citizens. "McCarthyism, and every other American hysteria, paled in comparison to the paranoia that permeated the Soviet system and Communist East Europe in the late 1940s and early 1950s," wrote Jeremy Isaacs and Taylor Downing in *The Cold War: An Illustrated History, 1945-1991*.

During this period, Soviet leader Joseph Stalin resurrected a reign of state-sponsored terror that had devastated thousands of Soviet families back in the 1930s. Driven by deep paranoia and complete disregard for life, the Soviet leader used the massive state bureaucracy at his disposal to steer an indiscriminate path of destruction through the heart of the nation he led. Acting on Stalin's orders, the state executed thousands of Soviet citizens, including countless loyal Communist party members.

One of Stalin's chief instruments in this reign of terror was Lavrenti Beria, the head of the Soviet secret police. The secret police, or KGB, seized millions of citizens, including a disproportionate percentage of doctors, teachers, and other educated people. They were arbitrarily spirited away to the "gulag," the vast system of squalid labor camps and prisons that dotted Siberia and other remote parts of the empire. As he waged this campaign of terror and intimidation, Stalin also used the state's resources to elevate himself to a position of God-like status in the hearts and minds of the Soviet people.

Meanwhile, the Communist Party bureaucracy controlled virtually all aspects of Soviet culture and economic development. "Society during the Stalin era left open no real opportunities for self-realization or self-expression except within this perverted system of the Communist Party," recalled *Moscow News* editor Len Karpinsky in David Remnick's *Lenin's Tomb*. "The system destroyed all the other channels: the artist's canvas, the farmer's land. All that was left was the gigantic hierarchic system of the Party, wide at the base and growing narrower as one climbed to the top."

Similarly grim circumstances prevailed in Eastern Europe, albeit on a smaller scale. In 1948 Yugoslavian leader Marshall Josip Tito defied the Soviet Communist Information Bureau, or Cominform, and staked out his own independent socialist path. That made Soviet leaders determined to strangle all other moves toward "Titoism," and they became even more involved in directing the affairs of nations in the Soviet orbit. All across Eastern Europe, Communist governments controlled by the Kremlin moved to stamp out independent thought and instill a culture of fear among their citizenry.

In addition, major initiatives in collectivization and industrialization were launched in Soviet-bloc nations. These programs had twin goals: to liquidate the natural resources of the Eastern bloc for use by the Soviet state, and to consolidate government control over every aspect of citizens' lives. Such initiatives were introduced in places like East Germany, led by Stalin favorite Walter Ulbricht, and Romania, which experienced a succession of Communist leaders until Nicolae Ceauşescu began his bloody twenty-two-year reign in 1967.

In March 1953, however, Stalin's sudden death from a stroke rocked the Communist world. Many Soviet citizens mourned his death, having been indoctrinated since birth to believe that Stalin was a virtual god on earth. Many Soviet families that had been touched by his cruel hand, however, were secretly gratified by the news. As Communist leaders in Eastern Europe waited anxiously for the identity of their new ruler to be revealed, unexpected displays of citizen unrest flared up in Czechoslovakia, Hungary, and Romania. After months of political infighting, a Soviet official named Nikita Khrushchev gained leadership of the Central Committee of the Communist Party in September 1953. When Beria, the head of the KGB, was executed in December 1953 on fabricated charges of being an agent for the West, Khrushchev's place as the new leader of the Soviet Union was assured.

The Khrushchev "Thaw"

When Khrushchev took the reins of the Soviet state, it marked a major turning point in the history of the USSR and the Eastern bloc nations under its control. He promptly set about repairing relations with China, which had been strained by animosity between Stalin and Mao Zedong. Khrushchev also extended conciliatory gestures and words to General Tito and launched new diplomatic efforts in the Third World. Countries in Southeast Asia and Africa were just beginning to emerge from years of colonial rule, primarily under England, France, Spain, and Portugal. These former colonies reacted warmly to the Soviet overtures, recognizing that Khrushchev's eagerness to enlist them as Cold War allies might bring them much-needed economic and military aid. More importantly, his descriptions of socialism sounded attractive to people that had been economically disenfranchised by Western powers during their colonial eras.

Finally, Khrushchev made important changes within Soviet society. He placed a greater emphasis on the production of consumer goods to make life easier and more comfortable for the average family. He also supported gradual but noticeable improvements to the state pension system and other social programs. In addition, Khrushchev approved the release of millions of prisoners from the gulags and loosened censorship of state media and the arts.

Meanwhile, Cold War maneuvering continued. In 1954 a defensive alliance called the Southeast Asia Treaty Organization (SEATO) was launched to thwart the spread of Communism in that region. It included the United States, United Kingdom, France, Australia, New Zealand, Pakistan, the Philippines, and Thailand. In May 1955 West Germany was admitted into NATO (North Atlantic Treaty Organization). The Soviet Union responded by forming a rival alliance called the Warsaw Pact with East Germany and other nations of Eastern Europe inside its sphere of influence. These developments completed the formal division of Europe into two rival camps.

Nevertheless, Khrushchev's rise to power led to a brief improvement in Soviet relations with the United States. In July 1955 the United States and the USSR held their first diplomatic summit since the end of World War II. Nothing of substance occurred at the summit, which was held in Geneva, Switzerland. But the mere fact that it took place encouraged hopes that it might be the first step toward improved relations between the two superpowers.

Khrushchev's performance at the Twentieth Congress of the Soviet Communist Party in February 1956 also heartened the Americans. Early in the Congress, which attracted Communist leaders from around the world, Khrushchev publicly dismissed the conventional Marxist-Leninist view that Communism and capitalism were destined to wage a fight to the death for world leadership. "War is not fatalistically inevitable," he insisted. Khrushchev instead claimed that Communism would triumph over time simply by virtue of its superiority.

Then, on the last night of the Congress, Khrushchev delivered a six-hour speech in closed session that harshly condemned the Stalin regime for its many crimes and abuses of power. Copies of the speech were widely distributed in both the West and East. In the West, the reaction was one of dazed, cautious delight. In the East, the repercussions were far greater. Mao's regime in China was angered by the speech, which it interpreted as an insult to its own authoritarian philosophy and a betrayal of Communism. In Eastern Europe, meanwhile, many Communist party leaders worried that Khrushchev's denunciation of Stalin—and the Kremlin's dismantling of Cominform two months later—might create instability within their own borders. As it turned out, their concerns were justified.

Rebellion in the Eastern Bloc

Khrushchev's reforms and his criticism of Stalin's "cult of personality" emboldened many in the Soviet sphere. In Poland, workers staged large demonstrations to protest the government's economic policies and its subordinate relationship with Moscow. After several weeks of violence and mounting tension, Khrushchev decided against a full-scale military intervention to crush the revolt. Instead the popular Wladyslaw Gomulka was left in control. Khrushchev grudgingly promised Gomulka a measure of independence in return for promises that Poland would remain a loyal member of the Warsaw Pact. Gomulka consented to the terms, and for the next fourteen years he pursued a "Polish way to socialism" while simultaneously remaining loyal to the Kremlin.

In Hungary, workers also carried out large demonstrations against their Soviet masters beginning on October 23, 1956. But in this case, the outcome was much different. Moscow hoped that new prime minister Imre Nagy could defuse the crisis. But the demonstrations grew into a genuine national uprising. On November 1, Nagy abruptly declared that Hungary intended to withdraw from the Warsaw Pact and adopt a neutral stance in the Cold War. "This went much further than the Poles had dared in their revolt," observed historians Jeremy Isaacs and Taylor Downing in *Cold War*. "It effectively faced the Kremlin with an ultimatum to get out."

Instead, on November 3, 1956, fifteen Soviet army divisions and more than four thousand tanks roared into Hungary. Over the next few days, the Soviet forces crushed the rebellion, killing thousands of Hungarians in the process. Nagy went into hiding, but he was later captured and executed. The nation of Hungary, meanwhile, was left in the hands of János Kádár, who imposed hard-line control in accordance with Soviet wishes. These grim events made it clear that the new Soviet leadership, despite its reformist rhetoric, remained willing to use brute force to maintain its grip on power.

5.1
The Warsaw Pact – 1955
The Text of the "Treaty of Friendship, Co-operation and Mutual Assistance"

In 1954 a defensive alliance called the Southeast Asia Treaty Organization (SEATO) was launched by the United States, United Kingdom, France, Australia, New Zealand, Pakistan, the Philippines, and Thailand to thwart the spread of Communism in that region. The following year, the North Atlantic Treaty Organization (NATO) formally welcomed West Germany into its ranks. The Soviet Union responded to these developments by forming a rival alliance called the Warsaw Pact with East Germany, Albania, Bulgaria, Hungary, Poland, Romania, and Czechoslovakia. The creation of the Warsaw Pact, signed on May 1, 1955, completed the formal division of Europe into two rival camps led by the Soviet Union and the United States.

The contracting parties,

Reaffirming their desire for the organisation of a system of collective security in Europe, with the participation of all the European states, irrespective of their social and state systems, which would make it possible to combine their efforts in the interests of securing peace in Europe,

Taking into consideration at the same time the situation obtaining in Europe as the result of ratification of the Paris agreements, which provide for the formation of a new military grouping in the shape of the "Western European Union" together with a remilitarised Western Germany, and for the integration of Western Germany in the North Atlantic bloc, which increases the threat of another war and creates a menace to the national security of the peaceloving states,

Convinced that, under these circumstances, the peaceloving states of Europe should take the necessary measures for safeguarding their security, and in the interests of maintaining peace in Europe,

Guided by the purposes and principles of the United Nations Charter,

In the interests of further strengthening and promoting friendship, co-operation and mutual assistance, in accordance with the principles of respect for the independence and sovereignty of states, and also with the principle of noninterference in their internal affairs,

Have resolved to conclude this Treaty of Friendship, Co-operation and Mutual Assistance,...

Article 1. The contracting parties undertake, in accordance with the Charter of the United Nations Organisation, to refrain in their international relations from the threat or use of force, and to settle their international disputes by peaceful means so as not to endanger international peace and security.

Article 2. The contracting parties declare their readiness to take part, in the spirit of sincere co-operation, in all international undertakings intended to safeguard international peace and security and they shall use all their energies for the realisation of these aims.

Moreover, the contracting parties shall work for the adoption, in agreement with other states desiring to co-operate in this matter, of effective measures towards a general reduction of armaments and prohibition of atomic, hydrogen and other weapons of mass destruction.

Article 3. The contracting parties shall take council among themselves on all important international questions relating to their common interests, guided by the interests of strengthening international peace and security.

They shall take council among themselves immediately, whenever, in the opinion of any of them, there has arisen the threat of an armed attack on one or several states that are signatories of the treaty, in the interests of organising their joint defence and of upholding peace and security.

Article 4. In the event of an armed attack in Europe on one or several states that are signatories of the treaty by any state or group of states, each state that is a party to this treaty shall, in the exercise of the right to individual or collective self-defence in accordance with Article 51 of the Charter of the United Nations Organisation, render the state or states so attacked immediate assistance, individually and in agreement with other states that are parties to this treaty, by all the means it may consider necessary, including the use of armed force. The states that are parties to this treaty shall immediately take council among themselves concerning the necessary joint measures to be adopted for the purpose of restoring and upholding international peace and security.

In accordance with the principles of the Charter of the United Nations Organisation, the Security Council shall be advised of the measures taken on the basis of the present article. These measures shall be stopped as soon as the Security Council has taken the necessary measures for restoring and upholding international peace and security.

Article 5. The contracting parties have agreed on the establishment of a joint command for their armed forces, which shall be placed, by agreement among these parties, under this command, which shall function on the basis of jointly defined principles. They shall also take other concerted measures necessary for strengthening their defence capacity, in order to safeguard the peaceful labour of their peoples, to guarantee the inviolability of their frontiers and territories and to provide safeguards against possible aggression.

Article 6. For the purpose of holding the consultations provided for in the present treaty among the states that are parties to the treaty, and for the purpose of considering problems arising in connection with the implementation of this treaty, a political consultative committee shall be formed in which each state that is a party to this treaty shall be represented by a member of the government, or any other specially appointed representative.

The committee may form the auxiliary organs for which the need may arise.

Article 7. The contracting parties undertake not to participate in any coalitions and alliances, and not to conclude any agreements the purposes of which would be at variance with those of the present treaty.

The contracting parties declare that their obligations under existing international treaties are not at variance with the provisions of this treaty.

Article 8. The contracting parties declare that they will act in the spirit of friendship and co-operation with the object of furthering the development of, and strengthening the economic and cultural relations between them, adhering to the principles of mutual respect for their independence and sovereignty, and of non-interference in their internal affairs.

Article 9. The present treaty is open to be acceded to by other states—irrespective of their social and state systems—which may express their readiness to assist, through participation in the present treaty, in combining the efforts of the peaceloving states for the purpose of safeguarding the peace and security of nations. This act of acceding to the treaty shall become effective, with the consent of the states that are parties to this treaty, after the instrument of accedence has been deposited with the government of the Polish People's Republic.

Article 10. The present treaty is subject to ratification, and the instruments of ratification shall be deposited with the government of the Polish People's Republic.

The treaty shall take effect on the date on which the last ratification instrument is deposited. The government of the Polish People's Republic shall advise the other states that are parties to the treaty of each ratification instrument deposited with it.

Article 11. The present treaty shall remain in force for 20 years. For the contracting parties which will not have submitted to the government of the Polish People's Republic a statement denouncing the treaty a year before the expiration of its term, it shall remain in force throughout the following ten years.

In the event of the organisation of a system of collective security in Europe and the conclusion of a general European treaty of collective security to that end, which the contracting parties shall unceasingly seek to bring about, the present treaty shall cease to be effective on the date the general European treaty comes into force.

Done in Warsaw, on May 1, 1955, in one copy each in the Russian, Polish, Czech, and German languages, all the texts being equally authentic. Certified copies of the present treaty shall be transmitted by the government of the Polish People's Republic to all the parties to this treaty.

Source: "Treaty of Friendship, Cooperation, and Mutual Assistance," May 14, 1955. *American Foreign Policy 1950-1955*. Basic Documents, Volume 1. Department of State Publication 6446. Washington, DC : Government Printing Office, 1957. Available online at the Avalon Project, Yale Law School, http://www.yale.edu/lawweb/avalon/ intdip/soviet/warsaw.

5.2
Life in a Romanian Prison – 1955
An Excerpt from The Silent Escape: Three Thousand Days in Romanian Prisons, *by Lena Constante*

For most citizens living behind the "iron curtain" of totalitarian regimes in Eastern Europe, daily existence was marked by economic austerity and political repression. Fear of shadowy state police existed in all of these East bloc countries, but it was particularly acute in nations like East Germany, where the secret police—known as "Stasi"—were an omnipotent presence, and Romania, where government agents terrorized the populace.

One Romanian victim of this era was Lena Constante, an artist who became ensnared in one of the many Communist "show trials" of the late 1940s and early 1950s. These trials were developed by Soviet leader Joseph Stalin and exported to the USSR's satellite states. Show trials were nominally meant to purge nations of enemies of the state, but their primary purpose was to keep the general populace in a state of cowering fear. Constante served a twelve-year sentence in the Romanian prison system on fabricated charges—including eight consecutive years of solitary confinement, where two sparrows were her only companions. After gaining her release in 1961, she wrote an account of her long years of isolation in Romanian prison cells. Following is an excerpt from her memoir.

… In the very thick wall of this very old prison, in an upper corner of the window, on the outside, of course, a couple of sparrows had come to make their home. Finding a chink in the masonry, they had warmly lined it with down, dry grass, bits of wool, and they had made it their nest. With silky rustlings, they soared out and returned. Each day, I sacrificed a few crumbs of bread or polenta on the windowsill for them. The sparrows pecked away, hopping and peeping. I was sometimes tempted to deny them this beakful of my bread. But each time, I was moved by their tiny birds' bellies. I very much wanted to touch them. Caress their plumage with my fingertips. I never managed this, but it was a joy and a consolation to feel them close by and to be able—I the destitute one—to provide for them and, in my ugliness, to admire their beauty. They gave me the blessing of my tenderness for them.

So many days and nothing else to say about them. I must have lived these days in some way or other since I reached this day, May 18, 1955, a crucial day of all my days of prison, past and future....

On May 17, a new political officer rushed into my cell. The Duce [another guard] had gone elsewhere. The officer entered with a wild look. He made a few steps, paused, and began looking around. He appeared so totally absorbed in eyeing the bed, the bench, and the coat rack that I couldn't keep from asking if he was looking for anything in particular and I even offered to help him with his search. He turned his back on me and went up to the window. It was a luminous spring day. On the windowsill, the striking yellow of the sunlit polenta stood out sharply against the blue of the sky. Finally ungluing his thin lips, he asked if my ration of food was excessive. On the contrary. Quite insufficient. Then how was it that I threw some of it out? I don't throw any of it away. I do without these crumbs for the sake of two sparrows. Since I am forced to be alone, they are my only companions.

Should I have answered otherwise?

An hour later, a militiaman escorted me to the walk. It lasted longer than usual. Upon my return to the cell, the sparrows appeared panic-stricken. They went round and round, hurried to the nest, banged up against the wall, left again, came back, began again, and I couldn't understand the cause of their confusion. I saw some sticks coming from the nest, but it seemed impossible that they had put them there to destroy the nest. How could I believe that a political officer had gone to the trouble of ordering that a ladder be brought up, that someone climb up it and destroy a nest of sparrows by plugging it up with twigs only for the sake of depriving a woman in solitary confinement the company of two tiny little birds?

With tears in my eyes, unable to come to their aid, for the nest was beyond my reach, I watched the two birds struggle, their beaks and talons clutching the twigs, beating their wings feverishly to keep themselves at nest level. After an hour, however, I was delighted to see them settle in anew. Piece by piece, they had succeeded in taking everything away.

Day 2137 of detention—May 21, 1955

The next day, a new outing, a new devastation. But this time the sparrows had to give up. The hole with the nest had been filled with cement. The two birds flew away forever.

Source: Constante, Lena. *The Silent Escape: Three Thousand Days in Romanian Prisons.* Translated by Franklin Philip. Berkeley: University of California Press, 1995.

5.3
Khrushchev Denounces Stalin – 1956
Excerpts from Premier Nikita Khruschev's Address to the Twentieth Party Congress of the USSR

On February 25, 1956, Khrushchev addressed the 20th Party Congress of the USSR. During the course of his long speech, he openly condemned the paranoia and brutality that characterized the reign of Joseph Stalin. He also denounced Stalin's creation of a "personality cult" across Soviet society. He specifically refers to mass terror created by the NKVD, also known as the People's Commisariat for Internal Affairs, a state department with a variety of internal security and secret police functions during Stalin's reign. This speech came as a shock to his listening audience, which was liberally sprinkled with leading Communist officials from around the world.

Khrushchev's speech was one of the true turning points in Soviet history. It marked the nation's first tentative efforts to confront its bloody history, sparked unrest and calls for increased independence in previously docile Eastern Bloc nations such as Hungary and Poland, and set the stage for reforms in various areas of Soviet society. Following are excerpts from Khrushchev's historic address.

… Comrades! In the Party Central Committee report to the 20th Congress, in a number of speeches by delegates to the Congress, and earlier at plenary sessions of the Party Central Committee, quite a lot has been said about the cult of the individual and about its harmful consequences.

After Stalin's death the Party Central Committee began to implement a policy of explaining concisely and consistently that it is impermissible and foreign to the spirit of Marxism-Leninism to elevate one person, to transform him into a superman possessing supernatural characteristics akin to those of a god. Such a man supposedly knows everything, sees everything, thinks for everyone, can do anything, is infallible in his behavior.

Such a belief about a man—specifically about Stalin—was cultivated among us for many years…. Stalin's role in the preparation and execution of the socialist revolution, in the Civil War, and in the fight for the construction of socialism in our country is universally known.... At present we are concerned with a question which has immense importance for the Party now and in the future—with how the Stalin cult gradually grew, the cult which became at a certain specific stage the source of a whole series of exceedingly serious and grave perversions of Party principles, of Party democracy, of revolutionary legality....

When we analyze Stalin's practice in directing the Party and the country, when we pause to consider everything Stalin perpetrated, we must be convinced that Lenin's fears [of Stalin's unsuitability for leadership, expressed repeatedly in correspondence] were justified. Stalin's negative characteristics, which in Lenin's time were only incipient, turned during the last years into grave abuse of power by Stalin, which caused untold harm to our party....

Stalin acted not through persuasion, explanation and patient cooperation with people, but by imposing his concepts and demanding absolute submission to his opinion. Whoever opposed this concept or tried to prove his viewpoint and the correctness of his position was doomed to removal from the leading collective and to subsequent moral and physical annihilation. This was especially true during the period following the 17th Party Congress, when many prominent Party leaders and rank-and-file Party workers, honest and dedicated to the cause of communism, fell victim to Stalin's despotism....

> *"[Stalin] abandoned the method of ideological struggle for that of administrative violence, mass repressions and terror."*

Stalin originated the concept "enemy of the people." This term automatically rendered it unnecessary that the ideological errors of a man or men engaged in a controversy be proved; this term made possible the use of the most cruel repression, violating all norms of revolutionary legality, against anyone who in any way disagreed with Stalin, against those who were only suspected of hostile intention, against those who had bad reputations. This concept, "enemy of the people," actually eliminated the possibility of any kind of ideological fight or the making of one's views known on this or that issue, even issues of a practical nature. In the main, and in actuality, the only proof of guilt used, contrary to all norms of current law, was the "confession" of the accused himself; and, as subsequent investigation has proved, "confessions" were obtained through physical pressures against the accused....

It is a fact that many persons who were later annihilated as enemies of the Party and people had worked with Lenin during his life. Some of these persons had made mistakes during Lenin's life, but, despite this, Lenin benefited by their work, he corrected them and he did everything possible to retain them in the ranks of the Party; he induced them to follow him....

An entirely different relationship with people characterized Stalin. Lenin's traits—patient work with people; stubborn and painstaking education of them; the ability to induce people to follow him without using compulsion, but rather through the ideological influence on them of the whole collective—were entirely foreign to Stalin. He discarded the Leninist method of persuading and educating; he abandoned the method of ideological struggle for that of administrative violence, mass repressions and terror. He acted on an increasingly larger scale and more stubbornly through punitive organs, at the same time often violating all existing standards of morality and of Soviet law…. Arbitrary behavior by one person encouraged and permitted arbitrariness in others. Mass arrests and deportations of many thousands of people, execution without trial and without normal investigation created conditions of insecurity, fear and even desperation….

Stalin showed in a whole series of cases his intolerance, his brutality and his abuse of power…. He often chose the path of repression and annihilation, not only against actual enemies, but also against individuals who had not committed any crimes against the party and the Soviet government….

Many party, Soviet and economic activists who were branded in 1937-38 as "enemies" were actually never enemies, spies, wreckers and so on, but were always honest communists; they were only so stigmatized, and often, no longer able to bear barbaric tortures, they charged themselves (at the order of the investigative judges-falsifiers) with all kinds of grave and unlikely crimes.

This was the result of the abuse of power by Stalin, who began to use mass terror against the party cadres…. Stalin put the party and the NKVD [the People's Commisariat for Internal Affairs] up to the use of mass terror when the exploiting classes had been liquidated in our country and when there were no serious reasons for the use of extraordinary mass terror. The terror was directed … against the honest workers of the party and the Soviet state….

Facts prove that many abuses were committed on Stalin's orders without reckoning with any norms of Party and Soviet legality. Stalin was a very distrustful man, sickly suspicious; we knew this from our work with him. He could look at a man and say: "Why are your eyes so shifty today?" or "Why are you turning so much today and avoiding looking me directly in the eyes?" The sickly suspicion created in him a general distrust even toward eminent Party workers whom he had known for years. Everywhere and in everything he saw "enemies," "two-facers" and "spies."

Possessing unlimited power, he indulged in great willfulness and strangled a person morally and physically. A situation was created where one could not express one's own will. When Stalin said that one or another would be arrested, it was necessary to accept on faith that he was an "enemy of the people." What proofs were offered? The confession of the arrested…. How is it possible that a person confesses to crimes that he had not committed? Only in one way—because of application of physical methods of pressuring him, tortures, bringing him to a state of unconsciousness, deprivation of his judgment, taking away his human dignity. In this manner were "confessions" acquired....

We must state that after the war [World War II]... Stalin became even more capricious, irritable and brutal; in particular, his suspicion grew. His persecution mania reached unbelievable dimensions. Many workers were becoming enemies before his very eyes. After the war Stalin separated himself from the collective even more. He decided everything alone, without any consideration for anyone or anything.... If we are to consider this matter as Marxists and as Leninists, then we must state unequivocally that the leadership practice which came into being during the last years of Stalin's life became a serious obstacle in the path of the development of Soviet society....

Source: Khrushchev, Nikita. Address to 20th Party Congress, February 25, 1956. English translation published as "Address by First Party Secretary N.S. Khrushchev at 20th Party Congress of the Communist Party of the Soviet Union" in *Congressional Record*, 84th Congress, 2nd session, June 4, 1956.

5.4
The Last Message of Imre Nagy – 1956
The Text of Prime Minister Nagy's Final Radio Broadcast to the Hungarian People

In 1956 Hungarians desperate for greater political freedom from Moscow staged major demonstrations in Bucharest and other cities. On November 1, 1956, Hungarian Prime Minister Imre Nagy abruptly declared that Hungary intended to become a neutral country in the Cold War. Nagy's government announced its intention to withdraw from the Warsaw Pact, and it asked for the removal of Soviet troops from its lands. Angered and alarmed by this insurrection, the Kremlin ordered a massive invasion. The United States and other Western powers were sympathetic to the Hungarians, but feared that intervening would spark a larger war involving the Soviets and their allies. These fears kept them on the sidelines.

As fighting raged throughout the city on November 4, Nagy broadcast the following message only hours before he was arrested by the Soviets, who eventually executed him. In his message, Nagy offers a grim view of the future if Western countries failed to come to Hungary's aid.

This fight is the fight for freedom by the Hungarian people against the Russian intervention, and it is possible that I shall only be able to stay at my post for one or two hours. The whole world will see how the Russian armed forces, contrary to all treaties and conventions, are crushing the resistance of the Hungarian people. They will also see how they are kidnapping the prime minister of a country which is a member of the United Nations, taking him from the capital, and therefore it cannot be doubted at all that this is the most brutal form of intervention. I should like in these last moments to ask the leaders of the revolution, if they can, to leave the country. I ask that all that I have said in my broadcast, and what we have agreed on with the revolutionary leaders during meetings in Parliament, should be put in a memorandum, and the leaders should turn to all the peoples of the world for help and explain that today it is Hungary and tomorrow, or the day after tomorrow, it will be the turn of other countries, because the imperialism of Moscow does not know borders and is only trying to play for time.

Source: Nagy, Imre. Radio broadcast, November 4, 1956. Available online at CNN: The Cold War. http://edition.cnn.com/SPECIALS/cold.war/episodes/07/documents/nagy.

5.5
A Russian Journalist Recalls the U.S.-Soviet Propaganda Wars
Excerpts from an Interview for the PBS Series "Red Files"

Throughout the Cold War, propaganda was an important tool used by both the United States and the Soviet Union. Assisted by their respective allies, both nations used propaganda to advance their cause and to undermine the position of their foe. Some propaganda campaigns were targeted to reach the other side's citizenry, while others were shaped to sway leaders and peoples of Third World countries. Finally, both the Soviet Union and the United States developed propaganda intended for their own populations. This latter type of propaganda typically extolled the moral and strategic superiority of their own political and economic systems—and condemned the systems of the other side as morally corrupt and destined for failure. In the following excerpt, Russian journalist Vladimir Pozner reflects on Soviet and American propaganda efforts.

Pozner: I would say that basically everyone working knew what the restrictions were. There were certain things you could not write about. That could be seen as being anti-Soviet or detrimental to the interests of the Soviet Union, seen by the powers that were. You couldn't criticize the Communist Party, you couldn't criticize a member of the central committee, you certain couldn't criticize the General Secretary, you could not criticize Soviet foreign policy—at least you couldn't do it openly. You could write an article where, if someone could read between the lines, it would be clear that you were saying that this kind of policy was not going to produce good

---

Interview with Vladimir Pozner, © 1999 Abamedia. Reprinted with permission.

results. But, you had to be very careful how you did that. It was a rather narrow, very narrow street that you had to walk. And you knew what the confines were.

Interviewer: You didn't actually have to tell lies, I think this is the thing that people don't understand, but it's more what you were not allowed to put in.

Pozner: Well, I think that that's pretty much what propaganda's always about. Intelligent propaganda is not a propaganda that tells blatant lies. It's something where you try to show the good side of what you're supporting and you don't tell about the negatives, you only tell about the positive. So, there were many positive things to talk about in the Soviet Union, you know, guaranteed work and free this and free that and free education and free medical help and all true. What you didn't talk about was the negatives that could be in fact connected to those same things. Because free health meant endless lines, meant doctors who were not adequately prepared, meant lack of medication, because too many people applied including people who were not ill. You didn't talk about those things as much. You talked about the positives only, which is true, but it's a half-truth, and then it makes it a half lie if you will.

Interviewer: Did you feel very uncomfortable about some of the things?

Pozner: Yes and no. There were some things I definitely felt uncomfortable about. Probably the most uncomfortable was in 1968 with the invasion of Prague and Czechoslovakia, and attempting in some way to justify that. On the other hand I was very dedicated, I was very much a pro-Soviet, pro-Socialist slash 'Communist ideal' was something I believed in. I realized that the West I was addressing really didn't care about how we lived. All this business about oh, the poor dissidents and all that, that was just the same kind of propaganda. In fact they couldn't give a tinker's damn about the fact that we've stood in line. They exploited that for a political purpose. So I always thought if I'm going to criticize my country, I'm not going to criticize it to the West. Or they're gonna applaud and say—oh what a wonderful guy Vladimir Pozner is, because in fact they're using me. If I want to improve my country, I'd better do it from the inside and not expect the United States or anyone else out there to come to help the Soviet Union. That's not going to happen. I felt that I was between a rock and a hard place in many senses, because what do you do, I mean, how? What I did want to show people in America, because that's where I addressed most of my commentary, was that we're human beings here. We don't have horns or tails, many of us support this system, many of us have in fact given life and limb for the system, and don't think that we're all waiting for you to liberate us. Yes there are dissidents and maybe they consist of one percent or two percent of the population. But you've had your dissidents and you don't treat them all that well, Paul Robeson being just one case in point....

Interviewer: Can you just talk about Czechoslovakia and Hungary? Did that not ring alarm bells for you?

Pozner: When the Soviet tanks invaded Budapest in 1956, I was a student of Moscow University. I was one of 300 who was kicked out because we protested against that. But let's not forget that in 1956 Khrushchev made his famous de-Stalinization speech. For many of us that ushered in what we thought would be a new dawn. This would finally mean that yes we admitted our sins that we'd done some pretty terrible things in our own country basically, and that now we had publicly admitted them which not many countries do. Things would now be much better and the ideal for which this country had suffered so much would finally be realized. So in that sense, 1956 was a combination of things.

> "The Cold War was really a propaganda war; it was not a hot war, in which all sides participated very, very actively. It was a struggle for people's minds."

Interviewer: Can you talk about foreign radio, short wave broadcasts? How much influence did they have in the Soviet Union?

Pozner: You mean coming in?

Interviewer: Yes coming in, Voice of America, Radio Free Europe?

Pozner: I think the radio broadcasts that came in from the Voice of America, the BBC World Service, the Deutsche Welle, and then, of course, Radio Liberty, had a great impact. According to different statistics, but approximately 40 million people, 40 to 50 million people, listened regularly to those broadcasts for information. Some listened for some other things like jazz music that you have. But I think they had a very big impact especially on younger people, and especially, of course, on the intellectual community. It's hard to measure but I remember that people listened and listened a lot. And it wasn't easy because jamming was going on. You had to find the spot and the time when you could actually tune in. People did listen very, very much. This was Western propaganda as countering Soviet propaganda, and I feel it was done in a much more sophisticated way. Clearly the West, in particular the US and the UK, have a much greater experience in that type of activity.

Interviewer: How was it and why was it more sophisticated?

Pozner: I believe that there was much more of, well not everything is perfect in our country, a much more presentable way of saying we don't have this and that. They were admitting certain faults so as to really make the point. That was never part of the way the Soviets worked. As a matter of fact when I began to do my regular piece for the Western audiences, for American audiences, I did just that. Because the West knew that you have to admit certain things to be plausible. So I would admit certain things that at first created certain problems for me. I mean, when I said that yes we had anti-Semitism, I mean how could you say that? Whereas in an American broadcast they would obviously say that Blacks have a difficult time, but "we've progressed a lot." Then you get all the positive stuff. You begin by admitting that not all is perfect. In that sense it was a much more sophisticated broadcast.

Interviewer: Do you think that the jamming backfired? In that it created more curiosity?

Pozner: Don't know. I really don't know. I think that the jamming backfired in that it was extremely expensive. It's economically absolutely beyond the means of the country. There was jamming all over the place and it wasn't effective in the sense of, in Moscow itself say, the jamming worked. If you went to the outskirts of Moscow it no longer did. There was huge money invested in this and it really didn't block it all out. So I think it was ineffective.

Interviewer: What about the Voice of Russia or is it the Voice of Moscow? Did it work?

Pozner: It's called Moscow Radio. That was officially.

Interviewer: How did that compare? Did it have much influence at all in the West?

Pozner: I think that Moscow radio probably had more influence in third world countries than it did in the United States. Let's begin with the fact that Americans don't listen to anything except their own radio anyway. They're not very interested in the outside world. How many Americans listen to short wave to begin with? And I don't think that in Western Europe a whole lot of people tune in to short wave for information. Let's not forget that the whole point was in the West, if you wanted to get information that was not establishment, left wing, you could get it, not so much in America but you could read Communist newspapers. It was out there for you if you wanted to make the effort. So, the broadcasts from Moscow weren't such a big deal, as differing from say Africa or the Middle East, where there were more repressive regimes. Therefore you wouldn't get the information. If you have a little short-wave set, you listened. Now people listened to the Voice of America, they listened to the BBC, but they also listened to Moscow Radio. And I think in that sense Moscow radio was not without certain effect in third world countries.

Interviewer: What you're saying really is that America is very insular and not interested in the outside World. And that's what everybody says about the Soviet Union. I just wonder if you could make that parallel that people say the Soviet Union knew nothing about the outside world?

Pozner: Well, that's a whole different story. If we compare the United States and the Soviet Union, the fact of the matter is that the average Russian had a tremendous interest in the outside world that was blocked. He couldn't get that access, but he wanted it. He read everything he could get his hands on; he tried to get through that jamming and listen. If there was a foreign movie, you had a line of people standing just to get to see it no matter what it was. There was tremendous interest. That information wasn't blocked, at least not in the Soviet way. But people were not encouraged in the United States to go look for information outside of what they can get in their own little town. Forget about the United States, people are not encouraged to go read other things or go to other sources. They are very insular. There's a long explanation probably to that, but there is no comparison in the actual interest inside that abides each of these representatives, if you will....

Interviewer: Can you explain how you belong to a system that withheld information from people? Can you explain why? In America a lot of people think that the Soviet people were just blinded, and that they were not getting information. They were totally starved of information. But it's a lot more complex than that, isn't it?

Pozner: The Soviet people were not getting certain kinds of information. The Soviet people were getting information that had been processed. That's not to say that they had no information. The Soviet people were well-educated, knowledgeable people; I would say more so than your average American by a long shot. They knew much more about America than Americans knew about Russia or the Soviet Union. In fact most Americans didn't even know the difference between Russia and the Soviet Union. They used the words without even knowing. But the fact of the matter is that there were certain kinds of information that were simply taboo. Even to this day there are areas of so-called closed information. For instance, if you want to go read what Lenin had to write in the last years of his life, you still need permission, which I find absurd, because the things that he wrote are explosive. This'll be the old system, and this'll be who Lenin actually was. I think that in Russia, traditionally, there has been a mistrust of the population's ability to deal with information. Information has to be doctored; it has to be packaged; now, I don't think this is only a Russian phenomenon. I don't think there is anything such as "All right, here's all the information." Except maybe now with the Internet, there is this possibility of having information that is not really processed at all. Because in the West it is processed anyway. There are certain things that people in the West never ever knew. They came here and they said, "Oh well, we didn't know that." Well, why didn't you? And you know there are people who have said, "Oh the sun shines." Good lord, because all they saw on television were gray skies, which is also a way of handling information. All they saw were old people limping around on crutches....

Interviewer: Vladimir can you talk about the fact that Americans were producing propaganda? It wasn't that propaganda is just a Soviet thing in this Cold War exchange. Both sides were doing pretty much the same things.

Pozner: Well, I would say that from the minute the revolution occurred in this country back in 1917, the West actively began churning out propaganda about the Bolsheviks, about the Reds, about the sharing lives, about all these things. The Cold War was really a propaganda war; it was not a hot war, in which all sides participated very, very actively. It was a struggle for people's minds. That's what propaganda is about. It was propaganda in both sides with all the vestiges of propaganda. I would not say that there was an aggressor and someone who defended. They were all aggressors. They were all trying to prove to anyone and everyone that they were right, their ideology, their ideals. That's what they wanted to do, that was what humanity should want. Basically that's that. You know it takes two to tango. Well for propaganda it takes two, but there were many more than two.

Interviewer: Americans always think that the Soviet Union's propaganda was much worse. They always say, well, you know the Soviet system would hide the secrets of Stalin. And yet it would immediately eject somebody like McCarthy who was a little bit extreme by comparison. Do you think that the Soviet propaganda was more extreme in a way? ...

Pozner: To say it was more extreme than American or any other propaganda, I don't think so. I think that all propaganda is always extreme. It hides certain things. I mean, you know you did not go out there. Today we find out that there were many things that were never told about experiments conducted on convicts, and sterilization projects and the atomic projects in the United States, and actually there were soldiers who were subject to radiation without their even knowing this was going on. This was never stated. So I think that in that sense, propaganda is always evil, it's always extreme and its goal is get the thing done and who cares about all of these ethical questions. Basically for me that is what propaganda is all about, which is why it is such a terrible thing to do....

Interviewer: Do you think that propaganda is something that actually backfires against the politicians in the end? Going back to the reason that if you hit someone loads of times, it stops hurting. In the sense that if politicians keep on churning out, using propaganda both domestically and as a foreign policy tool, that in the end the people would just stop listening to politicians and lose all faith in politics.

Pozner: I think that we have seen a worldwide phenomenon that reflects the disillusionment of people with their governments, with the people in government because of the propaganda, be it here in Russia, or be it anywhere else. There is a sense of cynicism with the politicians, because of the propaganda that they put out, and then it turns out to be untrue. People are led to believe in something and they sacrifice for that and they give their hearts and minds for it, then they wake up one day and they find out that they have been used. I think that it's a common phenomenon now; it's all over the place.

Interviewer: Is it more extreme here because the people have suffered a bit more?

Pozner: Oh, I think that this loss of ideals is as extreme as it gets in Russia. Because, let's not forget, that for decades the majority of the people in this country deeply believed in the ideals that were announced. Few countries in the world have sacrificed the way this country has for those ideals. Then there was a kind of epoxy glue with two things, it was the belief and, of course, the fear as well. These two things mixed together really held the country. Then, as gradually it began to dissipate, as the ideals began to disappear, as the fear also began to disappear what with a certain democratization of the Soviet system, especially when Gorbachev came up, but even under Brezhnev, it was no longer like Stalin. The whole thing began to crumble, precisely because there was no more belief and no more fear. So I think that now this is a country that has been taught a terribly, terribly, painful lesson. It's not soon that you're going to find people with any real political ideals in Russia.... They've been lied to so terribly that they no longer have this desire to believe in anything except okay, one day at a time, and the devil take the hindmost....

Source: Interview with Vladimir Pozner. "Episode 4: Soviet Propoganda," *Red Files*, PBS, 1999. Available online at http://www.pbs.org/redfiles/prop/deep/interv/p_int_vladimir_pozner.htm.

6

THE COLD WAR HEATS UP

As Cold War tensions rose, air-raid drills became a familiar childhood
experience for a generation of American schoolchildren.

INTRODUCTION

The 1956 Soviet invasion of Hungary ensured that Cold War tensions would remain high for the remainder of the decade. During this time, in fact, "the two sides became locked into the roles of hero and villain in one another's morality play," wrote Martin Walker in *The Cold War: A History*. "Two distinct theories of social and political organization believed they were grappling for nothing less than the inheritance of the planet."

Much of the maneuvering for advantage was carried out in the developing countries of Africa, the Middle East, Latin America, and Southeast Asia. Western and Soviet diplomats courted the leaders of these countries with offers of economic assistance and military aid. But the superpowers also reserved the right to resort to other methods to get what they wanted. In 1954, for example, the U.S. Central Intelligence Agency (CIA) helped overthrow unfriendly regimes in both Iran and Guatemala and install more dependable governments in their place.

Khrushchev's reformist agenda, though, gave the Soviets a clear edge in building support for Communism in the Third World. Millions of poor people in these struggling nations supported the socialist ideal of sharing national wealth equally among all citizens. At the same time, the long history of colonialism in Western Europe and the United States' ugly and ongoing struggles with segregation aroused suspicion and disapproval.

The Suez Canal Crisis

The West's behavior during the 1956 Suez Canal crisis also angered many developing nations. The Suez Canal is a vital waterway in northeastern Egypt that connects the Mediterranean Sea and the Red Sea. It allows ships to avoid traveling around the southern tip of Africa and instead pass between the Mediterranean, the Red Sea, and the Indian Ocean. In particular, it provides key shipping routes for the countries in Eastern Europe, northern Africa, and the Middle East. A series of international treaties had declared the Suez Canal neutral territory. But when the United States withdrew earlier pledges of financial support for Egypt's massive Aswan Dam project, Egypt's socialist president, Gamal Abdel Nasser, abruptly decided to claim the canal for Egypt. In October 1956, British, French, and Israeli forces invaded Egypt and seized the Suez Canal. This military action caught the administration of U.S. President Dwight Eisenhower completely off guard and attracted furious criticism from around the world. Even the United States, which was desperate to keep the Middle East from drifting into the Soviet camp, condemned the invasion as a blatant violation of international law.

In November 1956 the Soviet Union darkly suggested that it was weighing military retaliation against France and Britain for its seizure of the Suez Canal. This was almost certainly a bluff, but it underscored the importance of the region in the Cold War struggle. The United States managed to negotiate a cease-fire, and the canal reopened in April 1957 under the authority of the United Nations.

The Suez Canal crisis spurred President Eisenhower to unveil the so-called Eisenhower Doctrine in 1957. The main goal of this set of policy proposals, which included increased assistance to pro-Western regimes in the Middle East, was to halt "overt armed aggression from any nation controlled by International Communism."

Other Cold War Flash Points

Another chapter in the Cold War—the so-called "Space Race"—began on October 4, 1957, when the Soviet Union launched the *Sputnik* satellite into orbit. This first launch into space stunned the United States, which had long believed that its technology was far superior to that of its rival. Roused to action by visions of nuclear-armed Soviet missiles raining down on American soil, the United States allocated massive amounts of money for space technology and missile research and development. Much of this funding was funneled to the National Aeronautics and Space Administration (NASA), which was founded in 1958 in direct response to *Sputnik*.

Relations between the United States and China also heated up during this period. After the Chinese civil war, Chairman Mao Zedong and the Communists controlled the People's Republic of China on the mainland, while Chiang Kai-shek and the Chinese Nationalists had set up a government in exile, the Republic of China, on the island of Taiwan. On August 23, 1958, Mao Zedong's Communist forces began shelling two islands in the Taiwan Strait that had been controlled by Chiang and the Nationalists ever since they had fled to Taiwan a decade earlier. Determined to honor a U.S. pledge to defend Taiwan, Eisenhower sent nuclear-equipped warships and submarines to the region in a massive show of military force. Khrushchev added to the mounting tension by firing off a September 19 letter to Eisenhower. In this letter Khrushchev warned the American president that if the United States used nuclear weapons against China, it "would spark off a conflagration of a world war" and thus "doom to certain death sons of the American people." The crisis subsided only after the Chinese agreed to end the shelling, which in turn enabled the United States to suspend its naval maneuvers in Taiwan Strait.

In addition, Western and Eastern forces continued to compete fiercely for power and influence in Africa, where numerous newly independent nations were still shaking off years of colonial rule. Events in the Congo, a former Belgian colony, showed the lengths to which U.S. leaders would go in their fight against Communism. When nationalist leader Patrice Lumumba received Soviet military equipment and aid in 1960, the CIA actually dispatched an assassination team to murder him. When this effort failed, the United States began directing the activities of power-hungry and pro-Western forces in the country against Lumumba. They murdered him in 1961, and Joseph Mobuto soon took his place. Over the next three decades, Mobuto would prove to be a staunch U.S. ally in central Africa—and one of the most corrupt and ruthless despots on the entire continent.

The Berlin Wall

Another front was opened in the Cold War in late 1958, when Berlin once again erupted as a flashpoint of East-West tensions. On November 10, 1958, Khrushchev unexpectedly demanded the withdrawal of all foreign troops from divided Berlin. He also called on the West to formally recognize the existence of two Germanys. Two weeks later, Moscow gave the Western powers a six-month deadline to withdraw troops from Berlin or face forcible eviction from the capital— which was, after all, located deep inside Communist East Germany. "Berlin is the testicles of the West," boasted Khrushchev. "Every time I want to make the West scream, I squeeze on Berlin."

These provocative Soviet moves constituted another test of U.S. resolve in Europe. But the administrations of both Eisenhower and his successor, John F. Kennedy, refused to knuckle under to Khrushchev's demands. Instead, they pledged continued protection for democratic West Berlin. "We cannot and will not permit the Communists to drive us out of Berlin," declared Kennedy in 1961. "The endangered frontier of freedom runs through divided Berlin."

On the morning of August 13, 1961, East Germans awoke to find that East German leader Walter Ulbricht had begun erecting a barbed-wire fence along the boundaries of the military sectors controlled by the Americans, British, and French. Four days later, construction of the Berlin Wall—one of the most recognizable symbols of the entire Cold War era—began under the watchful eye of Soviet tank commanders. West Berlin Mayor Willy Brandt and others angrily appealed to the United States to intervene, but Kennedy decided that "a wall is a hell of a lot better than a war."

6.1
Gamal Abdel Nasser Comments on the Suez Crisis – 1956
A Speech by Egyptian President Nasser

> *During the mid-1950s, American officials became increasingly unhappy with Egyptian President Gamal Abdel Nasser and his cordial relations with Communist leaders in Moscow and Beijing. When Nasser purchased weapons from the Soviets and extended formal recognition to the Communist government of the People's Republic of China, Washington decided to withdraw earlier pledges of financial support for construction of Egypt's massive Aswan Dam project. This decision enraged Nasser, who responded by claiming the strategically and commercially vital Suez Canal for Egypt. The following is an excerpt from a speech Nasser made on September 15, 1956, in which he warned Western powers not to challenge Egypt's sovereignty over the canal.*

In these decisive days in the history of mankind, these days in which truth struggles to have itself recognized in international chaos where powers of evil domination and imperialism have prevailed, Egypt stands firmly to preserve her sovereignty. Your country stands solidly and staunchly to preserve her dignity against imperialistic schemes of a number of nations who have uncovered their desires for domination and supremacy.

In these days and in such circumstances Egypt has resolved to show the world that when small nations decide to preserve their sovereignty, they will do that all right and that when these small nations are fully determined to defend their rights and maintain their dignity, they will undoubtedly succeed in achieving their ends….

I am speaking in the name of every Egyptian Arab and in the name of all free countries and of all those who believe in liberty and are ready to defend it. I am speaking in the name of principles proclaimed by these countries in the Atlantic Charter. But they are now violating these principles and it has become our lot to shoulder the responsibility of reaffirming and establishing them anew….

We have tried by all possible means to cooperate with those countries which claim to assist smaller nations and which promised to collaborate with us but they demanded their fees in advance. This we refused so they started to fight with us.

They said they will pay toward building the High Dam and then they withdrew their offer and cast doubts on the Egyptian economy. Are we to disclaim our sovereign right? Egypt insists her sovereignty must remain intact and refuses to give up any part of that sovereignty for the sake of money.

Egypt nationalized the Egyptian Suez Canal company. When Egypt granted the concession to de Lesseps it was stated in the concession between the Egyptian Government and the Egyptian company that the company of the Suez Canal is an Egyptian company subject to Egyptian authority. Egypt nationalized this Egyptian company and declared freedom of navigation will be preserved.

But the imperialists became angry. Britain and France said Egypt grabbed the Suez Canal as if it were part of France or Britain. The British Foreign Secretary forgot that only two years ago he signed an agreement stating the Suez Canal is an integral part of Egypt.

Egypt declared she was ready to negotiate. But as soon as negotiations began threats and intimidations started....

[British Prime Minister Anthony Eden] stated in the House of Commons there shall be no discrimination between states using the canal. We on our part reaffirm that and declare there is no discrimination between canal users. He also said Egypt shall not be allowed to succeed because that would spell success for Arab nationalism and would be against their policy, which aims at the protection of Israel.

Today they are speaking of a new association whose main objective would be to rob Egypt of the canal and deprive her of rightful canal dues. Suggestions made by Eden in the House of Commons which have been backed by France and the United States are a clear violation of the 1888 convention, since it is impossible to have two bodies organizing navigation in the canal....

By stating that by succeeding, Abdel Nasser would weaken Britain's stand against Arab nationalism, Eden is in fact admitting his real objective is not Abdel Nasser as such but rather to defeat Arab nationalism and crush its cause. Eden speaks and finds his own answer. A month ago he let out the cry that he was after Abdel Nasser. Today the Egyptian people are fully conscious of their sovereign rights and Arab nationalism is fully awakened to its new destiny....

Those who attack Egypt will never leave Egypt alive. We shall fight a regular war, a total war, a guerrilla war. Those who attack Egypt will soon realize they brought disaster upon themselves. He who attacks Egypt attacks the whole Arab world. They say in their papers the whole thing will be over in forty-eight hours. They do not know how strong we really are.

We believe in international law. But we will never submit. We shall show the world how a small country can stand in the face of great powers threatening with armed might. Egypt might be a small power but she is great inasmuch as she has faith in her power and convictions. I feel quite certain every Egyptian shares the same convictions as I do and believes in everything I am stressing now.

We shall defend our freedom and independence to the last drop of our blood. This is the staunch feeling of every Egyptian. The whole Arab nation will stand by us in our common fight against aggression and domination. Free peoples, too, people who are really free will stand by us and support us against the forces of tyranny....

Source: Nasser, Gamal Abdel. Speech given on September 15, 1956. *The Suez Canal Problem, 26 July-22 September 1956.* U.S. Department of State Publication No. 6392. Washington, DC: Government Printing Office, 1956.

6.2
The Eisenhower Doctrine – 1957
The Text of President Dwight Eisenhower's Address on the Middle East to a Joint Session of Congress

The 1956 Suez Canal crisis threatened all of the painstaking efforts that had been made by the United States to forge a Middle East that was politically stable and friendly to the West. Determined to keep the politically volatile region from sliding into the Communist orbit, President Dwight D. Eisenhower rolled out the so-called Eisenhower Doctrine. This vague doctrine combined new financial aid programs for pro-Western governments in the Middle East with explicit warnings that the United States would not hesitate to use its military to stop "overt armed aggression from any nation controlled by International Communism." It portrayed the U.S. as the protector of Middle East nations and the USSR as an aggressor trying to dominate the region. The following is Eisenhower's first public explanation of this doctrine, delivered in an address to Congress on January 5, 1957.

…. The Middle East has abruptly reached a new and critical stage in its long and important history. In past decades many of the countries in that area were not fully self-governing. Other nations exercised considerable authority in the area and the security of the region was largely built around their power. But since the First World War there has been a steady evolution toward self-government and independence. This development the United States has welcomed and has encouraged. Our country supports without reservation the full sovereignty and independence of each and every nation of the Middle East.

The evolution to independence has in the main been a peaceful process. But the area has been often troubled. Persistent crosscurrents of distrust and fear with raids back and forth across national boundaries have brought about a high degree of instability in much of the Mid East. Just recently there have been hostilities

159

involving Western European nations that once exercised much influence in the area. Also the relatively large attack by Israel in October has intensified the basic differences between that nation and its Arab neighbors. All this instability has been heightened and, at times, manipulated by International Communism.

Russia's rulers have long sought to dominate the Middle East. That was true of the Czars and it is true of the Bolsheviks. The reasons are not hard to find. They do not affect Russia's security, for no one plans to use the Middle East as a base for aggression against Russia. Never for a moment has the United States entertained such a thought. The Soviet Union has nothing whatsoever to fear from the United States in the Middle East, or anywhere else in the world, so long as its rulers do not themselves first resort to aggression.

That statement I make solemnly and emphatically.

Neither does Russia's desire to dominate the Middle East spring from its own economic interest in the area. Russia does not appreciably use or depend upon the Suez Canal. In 1955 Soviet traffic through the Canal represented only about three fourths of 1% of the total. The Soviets have no need for, and could provide no market for, the petroleum resources which constitute the principal natural wealth of the area. Indeed, the Soviet Union is a substantial exporter of petroleum products.

The reason for Russia's interest in the Middle East is solely that of power politics. Considering her announced purpose of Communizing the world, it is easy to understand her hope of dominating the Middle East. This region has always been the crossroads of the continents of the Eastern Hemisphere. The Suez Canal enables the nations of Asia and Europe to carry on the commerce that is essential if these countries are to maintain well-rounded and prosperous economies. The Middle East provides a gateway between Eurasia and Africa.

It contains about two thirds of the presently known oil deposits of the world and it normally supplies the petroleum needs of many nations of Europe, Asia and Africa. The nations of Europe are peculiarly dependent upon this supply, and this dependency relates to transportation as well as to production! This has been vividly demonstrated since the closing of the Suez Canal and some of the pipelines. Alternate ways of transportation and, indeed, alternate sources of power can, if necessary, be developed. But these cannot be considered as early prospects.

These things stress the immense importance of the Middle East. If the nations of that area should lose their independence, if they were dominated by alien forces hostile to freedom, that would be both a tragedy for the area and for many other free nations whose economic life would be subject to near strangulation. Western Europe would be endangered just as though there had been no Marshall Plan, no North Atlantic Treaty Organization. The free nations of Asia and

Africa, too, would be placed in serious jeopardy. And the countries of the Middle East would lose the markets upon which their economies depend. All this would have the most adverse, if not disastrous, effect upon our own nation's economic life and political prospects.

Then there are other factors which transcend the material. The Middle East is the birthplace of three great religions—Moslem, Christian and Hebrew. Mecca and Jerusalem are more than places on the map. They symbolize religions which teach that the spirit has supremacy over matter and that the individual has a dignity and rights of which no despotic government can rightfully deprive him. It would be intolerable if the holy places of the Middle East should be subjected to a rule that glorifies atheistic materialism.

"International Communism…seeks to mask its purposes of domination by expressions of good will and by superficially attractive offers of political, economic and military aid."

International Communism, of course, seeks to mask its purposes of domination by expressions of good will and by superficially attractive offers of political, economic and military aid. But any free nation, which is the subject of Soviet enticement, ought, in elementary wisdom, to look behind the mask.

Remember Estonia, Latvia and Lithuania! In 1939 the Soviet Union entered into mutual assistance pacts with these then dependent countries; and the Soviet Foreign Minister, addressing the Extraordinary Fifth Session of the Supreme Soviet in October 1939, solemnly and publicly declared that "we stand for the scrupulous and punctilious observance of the pacts on the basis of complete reciprocity, and we declare that all the nonsensical talk about the Sovietization of the Baltic countries is only to the interest of our common enemies and of all anti-Soviet provocateurs." Yet in 1940, Estonia, Latvia and Lithuania were forcibly incorporated into the Soviet Union.

Soviet control of the satellite nations of Eastern Europe has been forcibly maintained in spite of solemn promises of a contrary intent, made during World War II. Stalin's death brought hope that this pattern would change. And we read the pledge of the Warsaw Treaty of 1955 that the Soviet Union would follow in satellite countries "the principles of mutual respect for their independence and sovereignty and noninterference in domestic affairs." But we have just seen the subjugation of Hungary by naked armed force. In the aftermath of this Hungarian tragedy, world respect for and belief in Soviet promises have sunk to a new low. International Communism needs and seeks a recognizable success.

Thus, we have these simple and indisputable facts:

1. The Middle East, which has always been coveted by Russia, would today be prized more than ever by International Communism.

2. The Soviet rulers continue to show that they do not scruple to use any means to gain their ends.

3. The free nations of the Mid East need, and for the most part want, added strength to assure their continued independence.

Our thoughts naturally turn to the United Nations as a protector of small nations. Its charter gives it primary responsibility for the maintenance of international peace and security. Our country has given the United Nations its full support in relation to the hostilities in Hungary and in Egypt. The United Nations was able to bring about a cease-fire and withdrawal of hostile forces from Egypt because it was dealing with governments and peoples who had a decent respect for the opinions of mankind as reflected in the United Nations General Assembly. But in the case of Hungary, the situation was different. The Soviet Union vetoed action by the Security Council to require the withdrawal of Soviet armed forces from Hungary. And it has shown callous indifference to the recommendations, even the censure, of the General Assembly. The United Nations can always be helpful, but it cannot be a wholly dependable protector of freedom when the ambitions of the Soviet Union are involved.

Under all the circumstances I have laid before you, a greater responsibility now devolves upon the United States. We have shown, so that none can doubt, our dedication to the principle that force shall not be used internationally for any aggressive purpose and that the integrity and independence of the nations of the Middle East should be inviolate. Seldom in history has a nation's dedication to principle been tested as severely as ours during recent weeks.

There is general recognition in the Middle East, as elsewhere, that the United States does not seek either political or economic domination over any other people. Our desire is a world environment of freedom, not servitude. On the other hand many, if not all, of the nations of the Middle East are aware of the danger that stems from International Communism and welcome closer cooperation with the United States to realize for themselves the United Nations' goals of independence, economic well-being and spiritual growth.

If the Middle East is to continue its geographic role of uniting rather than separating East and West; if its vast economic resources are to serve the well-being of the peoples there, as well as that of others; and if its cultures and religions and their shrines are to be preserved for the uplifting of the spirits of the peoples, then the United States must make more evident its willingness to support the independence of the freedom-loving nations of the area.

.... It is nothing new for the President and the Congress to join to recognize that the national integrity of other free nations is directly related to our own security. We have joined to create and support the security system of the United Nations. We have reinforced the collective security system of the United Nations by a series of collective defense arrangements. Today we have security treaties with 42 other nations which recognize that our peace and security are intertwined. We have joined to take decisive action in relation to Greece and Turkey and in relation to Taiwan.

Thus, the United States through the joint action of the President and the Congress, or, in the case of treaties, the Senate, has manifested in many endangered areas its purpose to support free and independent governments—and peace—against external menace, notably the menace of International Communism. Thereby we have helped to maintain peace and security during a period of great danger. It is now essential that the United States should manifest through joint action of the President and the Congress our determination to assist those nations of the Mid East area, which desire that assistance.

The action which I propose would have the following features.

It would, first of all, authorize the United States to cooperate with and assist any nation or group of nations in the general area of the Middle East in the development of economic strength dedicated to the maintenance of national independence.

It would, in the second place, authorize the Executive to undertake in the same region programs of military assistance and cooperation with any nation or group of nations which desires such aid.

It would, in the third place, authorize such assistance and cooperation to include the employment of the armed forces of the United States to secure and protect the territorial integrity and political independence of such nations, requesting such aid, against overt armed aggression from any nation controlled by International Communism.

These measures would have to be consonant with the treaty obligations of the United States, including the Charter of the United Nations and with any action or recommendations of the United Nations. They would also, if armed attack occurs, be subject to the overriding authority of the United Nations Security Council in accordance with the Charter.

The present proposal would, in the fourth place, authorize the President to employ, for economic and defensive military purposes, sums available under the Mutual Security Act of 1954, as amended, without regard to existing limitations.

The legislation now requested should not include the authorization or appropriation of funds because I believe that, under the conditions I suggest, presently appropriated funds will be adequate for the balance of the present fiscal year ending June 30. I shall, however, seek in subsequent legislation the authorization of $200,000,000 to be available during each of the fiscal years 1958 and 1959 for discretionary use in the area, in addition to the other mutual security programs for the area hereafter provided for by the Congress.

This program will not solve all the problems of the Middle East. Neither does it represent the totality of our policies for the area. There are the problems of Palestine and relations between Israel and the Arab States, and the future of the Arab refugees. There is the problem of the future status of the Suez Canal. These difficulties are aggravated by International Communism, but they would exist quite apart from that threat. It is not the purpose of the legislation I propose to deal directly with these problems. The United Nations is actively concerning itself with all these matters, and we are supporting the United Nations. The United States has made clear, notably by Secretary Dulles' address of August 26, 1955, that we are willing to do much to assist the United Nations in solving the basic problems of Palestine.

The proposed legislation is primarily designed to deal with the possibility of Communist aggression, direct and indirect. There is imperative need that any lack of power in the area should be made good, not by external or alien force, but by the increased vigor and security of the independent nations of the area.

Experience shows that indirect aggression rarely if ever succeeds where there is reasonable security against direct aggression; where the government disposes of loyal security forces, and where economic conditions are such as not to make Communism seem an attractive alternative. The program I suggest deals with all three aspects of this matter and thus with the problem of indirect aggression.

It is my hope and belief that if our purpose be proclaimed, as proposed by the requested legislation, that very fact will serve to halt any contemplated aggression. We shall have heartened the patriots who are dedicated to the independence of their nations. They will not feel that they stand alone, under the menace of great power. And I should add that patriotism is, throughout this area, a powerful sentiment. It is true that fear sometimes perverts true patriotism into fanaticism and to the acceptance of dangerous enticements from without. But if that fear can be allayed, then the climate will be more favorable to the attainment of worthy national ambitions.

And as I have indicated, it will also be necessary for us to contribute economically to strengthen those countries, or groups of countries, which have governments manifestly dedicated to the preservation of independence and resistance to subversion. Such measures will provide the greatest insurance against Communist inroads. Words alone are not enough.

.... The policy which I outline involves certain burdens and indeed risks for the United States. Those who covet the area will not like what is proposed. Already, they are grossly distorting our purpose. However, before this Americans have seen our nation's vital interests and human freedom in jeopardy, and their fortitude and resolution have been equal to the crisis, regardless of hostile distortion of our words, motives and actions.

Indeed, the sacrifices of the American people in the cause of freedom have, even since the close of World War II, been measured in many billions of dollars and in thousands of the precious lives of our youth. These sacrifices, by which great areas of the world have been preserved to freedom, must not be thrown away.

In those momentous periods of the past, the President and the Congress have united, without partisanship, to serve the vital interests of the United States and of the free world.

The occasion has come for us to manifest again our national unity in support of freedom and to show our deep respect for the rights and independence of every nation—however great, however small. We seek not violence, but peace. To this purpose we must now devote our energies, our determination, ourselves.

Source: Eisenhower, Dwight D. Address to Congress on January 5, 1957. *Public Papers of the Presidents of the United States: Dwight D. Eisenhower, January 1-December 31, 1957*. Washington, DC: Office of the Federal Register, 1958.

6.3

America Reacts to the Soviet Sputnik Launch – 1957
Excerpts from a News Conference Held by U.S. Secretary of State John Foster Dulles

On October 4, 1957, the Soviet Union successfully launched the world's first man-made satellite into space. The triumphant launch of Sputnik greatly alarmed the West, which feared that had it had fallen dangerously behind the USSR in terms of technological capability. "America has lost a battle more important and greater than Pearl Harbor," declared Dr. Edward Teller, the father of the hydrogen bomb.

Twelve days after the successful launch of Sputnik by the Soviets, U.S. Secretary of State John Foster Dulles held a news conference in which he strongly asserted the need for America to increase its investment in scientific education and research. He also proclaimed U.S. determination to triumph in the developing space race. Following are excerpts from that news conference held on October 16, 1957.

Secretary Dulles: I am sorry there has been an interval longer than usual between my press conferences, due to the United Nations and various incidents of the United Nations including the visitations here of foreign ministers. I suspect that the interval has allowed a number of questions to accumulate; if so, I will be glad to hear them.

Q. Mr. Secretary, relating to one of the things that happened in this interval, would you evaluate the relative power of Russia and the United States in the light of the ICBM and satellite successes they have had?

A. I can give you a rough approximation, although that, of course, is a question that perhaps should be directed primarily to the Department of Defense. But also, of course, it is very vital from the standpoint of the conduct of foreign relations. I would say this: The Soviet Union started back in 1945 to work intensively on this guided-missile program. It took over the assets of the Germans at Peenemunde. I recall that when I was in Moscow in 1947 with Secretary Marshall, we were impressed at the time with the intensity of effort along those lines and the VIP treatment being given to the Germans who had been taken in from the Peenemunde experiment. They have been pushing very actively along that line and I would think probably have some advance over us in respect to that particular area of potential military activity.

On the other hand, I think that we have in terms of actual military power, and potential military power for some years to come, a very marked superiority over them, particularly in terms of heavy bombers, which are for now and for some years to come will be the preferred and most effective means for the delivery of missiles.

I think that this satellite coming along as it did is a very useful thing to have happened, so as to avoid any possible complacency on our part with our present superiority. It arouses the whole country, I think, and the Congress, to the importance of pushing forward actively in this field, which may be the field where superiority will be militarily decisive perhaps 5 or 10 years from now.

Q. Mr. Secretary, as a historical note, there has been some confusion in Washington as to whether or not the administration anticipated the kind of worldwide reaction which has taken place in light of the launching of the satellite. Can you tell us whether at the time in 1955 the Vanguard project was decided upon—whether you were consulted and considered the problem of what might happen and its effect upon our foreign relations if the Russians were the first to launch this satellite? And did that play any part in the decisions on how we handle that program?

A. I cannot recall that there was any particular discussion about the satellite project as such. There was considerable discussion about the missile program and the importance of not allowing the Soviet Union to gain any decisive superiority in the use of outer space for its missiles. But I do not recall a particular discussion about the launching of the satellite, although I believe there was some discussion at one of the National Security Council meetings that I was not present at.

Q. Mr. Secretary, Mr. Lloyd and Mr. Sandys of Britain have called for a great deal closer cooperation between the United States and Britain and a lowering of the barriers to the exchange of scientific information, especially in view of Sputnik. Do you now favor eliminating all of these present barriers to a complete exchange of cooperation between the two countries on this problem?

A. I have always favored a very large degree of cooperation, a larger degree perhaps than has actually taken place. We are under certain legal restrictions, as you know which were put on by Congress some years ago—I think back in '48 or '49—at a time when it was believed we had a monopoly of knowledge with respect to atomic weapons—and, indeed, we did have, I think, at the time that original position was taken. It was hoped to preserve that monopoly in the interests of world peace and so that we could carry out our offer at that time to internationalize all use of atomic energy. That was the so-called Baruch Plan. I think that that legislative point of view has become somewhat obsolete with the passage of time and that there is a basis for a closer cooperation than has existed.

Some of it can be done, perhaps, under the present law, but I think it would be useful to give a fresh look at that law at this time because I think it may have become obsolete.

Q. Mr. Secretary, from a foreign policy point of view, do you believe that recent developments have called for a new look in our defense policies?

A. In our defense policies?

Q. That is right; and I am thinking particularly of reductions in our military establishment and some cutbacks in scientific programs.

A. Well, I would say that that defense policy is constantly getting a new look. Every year the budget is very closely examined from the standpoint of striking an appropriate balance between security on the one hand and budgetary burdens on the other hand and the problem of balancing the budget. I do not think that any recent developments call for any different kind of "new look" than occurs every year.

Q. Mr. Secretary, on that point of possible closer scientific cooperation, how do you regard this? Do you regard this as urgent, or do you regard this as a desirable thing that might be worked out in time? And could you say whether basically you think that the United States, unaided, as it is now progressing, can catch up in the missile field and indeed move ahead in all the defense fields where it is important?

A. I feel absolutely confident that there is no doubt whatsoever of our ability to move ahead and, I believe, keep ahead in this field. As I said before, I think that perhaps it is a good thing that this satellite was put up in good time, so that there would not be an undue complacency anywhere. I do not think that there has been complacency within the administration, but there has been a certain complacency, I think, felt generally that we were almost ahead of the Russians in every respect. Well, that is not so, and those of us who have been close to the situation have, I think, realized that for some time. You cannot take a nation of the size of the Soviet Union, under the kind of despotic government they have, and have it concentrate for now 40 years upon almost a single objective without getting some results. Now, the Russians have always had good minds. That has been shown by the fact that the Russians have over the years produced great chess players, champion chess players quite frequently, and their artillery in the past has been extremely good. Now when you take a despotic form of government and you provide scientific training—and

167

scientific training is almost the only training that is provided—and you pick out all the best brains you have and funnel them into this scientific course of training, you are going to get outstanding results. So it is no surprise, I think, to any of us who followed the situation closely to know that that is going to happen.

I recall a Cabinet meeting some two or three years ago where this was fully discussed. The question was raised whether we should try to get our people to concentrate more upon scientific work. I think we all felt at the time that there was need, not only for scientists, but, for our form of society, you had to have ministers and historians, teachers, and people interested in the humanities, and that we did not want to become a lopsided society. If you are going to have this great force in a democratic form of society, you have to have not only the power to use it but you have got to have the power to exercise self-restraint and self-control. That is inherent in our form of society.

But I still think that, even though we have a balanced society, with balanced teaching and balanced training, there is still the capacity to do that and at the same time, if we handle ourselves properly, to keep ahead of the Russians in this particular field.

Q. Mr. Secretary, I am confused. Is Sputnik a good thing because it taught the administration something or because it taught the American people something?

A. I think it has created a unity of purpose and thinking between the administration, the Congress, and the people which is very desirable at this stage.

Source: Dulles, John Foster. News conference on October 16, 1957. *Department of State Bulletin*, November 4, 1957.

6.4
Deterrence and Survival in the Nuclear Age – 1957
Excerpts from the Gaither Report

In 1957 President Dwight Eisenhower approved the formation of a panel to study whether the United States should develop a nationwide system of fallout shelters in case of a Soviet nuclear attack. A prominent attorney named Rowan Gaither was appointed to head the panel, which expanded its mandate to examine the larger issue of changing trends in the U.S.-Soviet balance of power. The most prominent and influential member of this panel was Paul Nitze, a hawkish analyst who played a key role in shaping the final draft of the report for the president's consideration (Nitze also had an important hand in the landmark NSC-68 report of 1950).

This report, technically called "Deterrence and Survival in the Nuclear Age" but often known simply as the Gaither Report, was presented to Eisenhower on

November 7, 1957. It proved to be deeply influential in shaping American security policy for the next decade. Its predictions about robust Soviet economic growth proved erroneous, but it accurately noted that the USSR was determined to expand its missile program. It also offered grim interpretations of Soviet political and military goals, describing the USSR as an already deadly foe that was becoming more powerful by the hour.

When the contents of the Gaither Report became publicly known because of press leaks, it fueled widespread American fears of a growing missile gap between the two nations. Eisenhower, however, knew from his review of top-secret surveillance data that the so-called "missile gap" was nonexistent.

...We have found no evidence in Russian foreign and military policy since 1945 to refute the conclusion that USSR intentions are expansionist, and that her great efforts to build military power go beyond any concepts of Soviet defense. We have, therefore, weighed the relative military and economic capabilities of the United States and the USSR in formulating our broad-brush opinions, basing our findings on estimates of present and future Russian capabilities furnished by the Intelligence community.

The evidence clearly indicates an increasing threat which may become critical in 1959 or early 1960. The evidence further suggests the urgency of proper time-phasing of needed improvements in our military position vis-à-vis Russia....

II. NATURE OF THE THREAT

A. Economic

The Gross National Product (GNP) of the USSR is now more than one-third that of the United States and is increasing half again as fast. Even if the Russian rate of growth should decline, because of increasing difficulties in management and shortage of raw materials, and should drop by 1980 to half its present rate, its GNP would be more than half of ours as of that date. This growing Russian economic strength is concentrated on the armed forces and on investment in heavy industry, which this year account for the equivalent of roughly $40 billion and $17 billion, respectively, in 1955 dollars. Adding these two figures, we get an allocation of $57 billion per annum, which is roughly equal to the combined figures for these two items in our country's current effort. If the USSR continues to expand its military expenditures throughout the next decade, as it has during the 1950's, and ours remains constant, its annual military expenditures may be double ours, even allowing for a gradual improvement of the low living standards of the Russian peoples.

This extraordinary concentration of the Soviet economy on military power and heavy industry, which is permitted, or perhaps forced, by their peculiar political structure, makes available economic resources sufficient to finance both the rapid expansion of their impressive military capability and their politico-economic offensive by which, through diplomacy, propaganda and subversion, they seek to extend the Soviet orbit.

B. Military

The Soviet military threat lies not only in their present military capabilities—formidable as they are—but also in the dynamic development and exploitation of their military technology. Our demobilization after World War II left them with a great superiority in ground forces, but they had no counter in 1946 for our Strategic Air Force nor for our Navy. They had no atomic bombs, no productive capacity for fissionable materials, no jet engine production, and only an infant electronics industry. This situation was compatible with a then-backward country, so much of whose most productive areas had suffered military attack and occupation. Their industrial base was then perhaps one-seventh that of the United States.

The singleness of purpose with which they have pressed their military-centered industrial development has led to spectacular progress. They have developed a spectrum of A- and H-bombs and produced fissionable material sufficient for at least 1500 nuclear weapons. They created from scratch a long-range air force with 1500 B-29 type bombers; they then substantially re-equipped it with jet aircraft, while developing a short-range air force of 3000 jet bombers. In the field of ballistic missiles they have weapons of 700 n.m. range, in production for at least a year; successfully tested a number of 950 n.m. missiles; and probably surpassed us in ICBM development. They have developed air-to-surface and probably submarine-launched cruise missiles; built 250 to 300 new long-range submarines and partially modernized 200 others. They have created an air defense system composed of 1500 all-weather and 8500 day jet fighters; equipped at least 60 sites, each with 60 launchers, for a total of over 3600 launching pads for surface-to-air missiles provided with a sophisticated and original guidance system and a ground environment of 4000 radars. At the same time, they have maintained and largely re-equipped their army of 175 line divisions, while furnishing large quantities of military equipment to their satellites and Red China....

III. BROAD-BRUSH OPINIONS

The Panel has arrived at the following broad-brush opinions as to the present situation:

A. In case of a nuclear attack against the continental United States:

1. Active defense programs now in being and programmed for the future will not give adequate assurance of protection to the civil population. If the attack were at low altitude, or at high altitude with electronic countermeasures (jamming), little protection would be afforded. If the attack should come at moderately high altitude and without electronic countermeasures, some considerable protection will be afforded the civil population.

2. Passive defense programs now in being and programmed for the future will afford no significant protection to the civil population.

B. The protection of the United States and its population rests, therefore, primarily upon the deterrence provided by SAC [Strategic Air Command]. The current vulnerability of SAC to surprise attack during a period of lessened world tension (i.e., a time when SAC is not on a SAC "alert" status), and the threat posed to SAC by the prospects of an early Russian ICBM capability, call for prompt remedial action.

The Panel has arrived at the following conclusions as to the value, relative to cost, of various measures for protecting the civil population.

A. Measures to Secure and Augment Our Deterrent Power

Since the prevention of war would best protect our urban population, we assign the highest relative value to the following measures to secure and augment our deterrent power. These would protect our manned bombers from surprise attack, increase our forces available for limited military operations, and give us an earlier and stronger initial operational capability (IOC) with intermediate-range and intercontinental ballistic missiles. [The committee then sets forth a series of recommendations to protect and bolster the readiness of the U.S. Strategic Air Command] …

B. Measures to Reduce Vulnerability of Our People and Cities

The main protection of our civil population against a Soviet nuclear attack has been and will continue to be the deterrent power of our armed forces, to whose strengthening and securing we have accorded the highest relative value. But this is not sufficient unless it is coupled with measures to reduce the extreme vulnerability of our people and our cities. As long as the U.S. population is wide open to Soviet attack, both the Russians and our allies may believe that we shall feel increasing reluctance to employ SAC in any circumstance other than when the United States is directly attacked. To prevent such an impairment of our deterrent power and to ensure our survival if nuclear war occurs through miscalculation or design, we assign a somewhat lower than higher value, in relation to cost, to a mixed program of active and passive defenses to protect our civil population. [The committee then issues several recommendations for strengthening of U.S. defenses, including "a nationwide fallout shelter program to protect the civil population. This seems the only feasible protection for millions of people who will be increasingly exposed to the hazards of radiation."] …

VI. PUBLIC EDUCATION AND POLITICAL CONSEQUENCES

The Panel urges an improved and expanded program for educating the public in current national defense problems, in the belief that the future security of the United States depends heavily upon an informed and supporting public opinion. We have been heartened by the recent announcement that positive steps will be taken to initiate what we hope will be a broad and sustained program of such education. We must act now to protect, for this and succeeding generations not only our human and material resources, but our free institutions as well. We have no doubt of the will and capacity of the American people to do so if they are informed of the nature and probable duration of the threat and if they understand what is required of them. Only through such enlightenment and understanding can we avoid the danger of complacency and the enervation of our inherent strengths.

VII. DETERRENCE AND SURVIVAL

The measures advocated by the Panel will help to unite, to strengthen and to defend the Free World, and to deter general war which would expose our cities and bases to thermonuclear attack. They would improve our posture to deter or promptly to suppress subversion or limited war, which may be more likely in the years immediately ahead. No one of these lesser enemy moves might directly threaten our survival. Yet, if continued, they might nibble away the security of the Free World as Germany undermined the superior military power of Great Britain and France between 1936 and 1939.

If deterrence should fail, and nuclear war should come through miscalculation or design, the programs outlined above would, in our opinion, go far to ensure our survival as a nation.

To illustrate the urgency of prompt decision and rapid action, we submit in Appendix A a time table of relative strengths under our present programs and the assumed Russian programs. As this appendix indicates, the United States is now capable of making a decisive air nuclear attack on the USSR. The USSR could make a very destructive attack on this country, and SAC is still vulnerable to a surprise attack in a period of lessened world tension. As soon as SAC acquires an effective "alert" status, the United States will be able to carry out a decisive attack even if surprised. This could be the best time to negotiate from strength, since the U.S. military position vis-à-vis Russia might never be so strong again.

By 1959, the USSR may be able to launch an attack with ICBMs carrying megaton warheads, against which SAC will be almost completely vulnerable under present programs. By 1961-1962, at our present pace, or considerably earlier if we accelerate, the United States could have a reliable early-warning capability against a missile attack, and SAC forces should be on a 7 to 22 minute operational "alert." The next two years seem to us critical. If we fail to act at once, the risk, in our opinion, will be unacceptable.

Source: President's Science Advisory Committee, Security Resources Panel. *Deterrence and Survival in the Nuclear Age (the "Gaither Report" of 1957)*. Printed for the use of the Joint Committee on Defense Production, Congress of the United States, 94th Congress, 2nd session. Washington, DC: U.S. Government Printing Office, 1976. Available online at the National Security Archive, George Washington University, http://www.gwu.edu/~nsarchiv/NSAEBB/NSAEBB139/nitze02.pdf.

6.5

Eisenhower Warns the Soviets About Militarization of Space – 1958

An Excerpt from a Letter from President Dwight Eisenhower

> *As the American-Soviet "space race" intensified, U.S. leaders expressed increasing anxiety that the Kremlin might attempt to extend its military resources into space via satellite and missile technology. U.S. President Dwight D. Eisenhower sought to discourage any such plans in the following diplomatic correspondence, dated February 15, 1958, to Nikolai Bulganin, Chairman of the USSR Council of Ministers.*

…Another new idea was that outer space should be perpetually dedicated to peaceful purposes. You belittle this proposal as one made to gain strategic advantages for the United States. Mr. Khrushchev in his Minsk speech said, "This means they want to prohibit that which they do not possess."

Since the record completely disproves that uncalled for statement, may we now hope between us to consider and devise cooperative international procedures to give reality to the idea of use of outer space for peace only.

When the United States alone possessed atomic weapons and the Soviet Union possessed none, the United States proposed to forego its monopoly in the interest of world peace and security. We are prepared to take the same attitude now in relation to outer space. If this peaceful purpose is not realized, and the worse than useless race of weapons goes on, the world will have only the Soviet Union to blame, just as it has only the Soviet Union to blame for the fact that atomic and nuclear power are now used increasingly for weapons purposes instead of being dedicated wholly to peaceful uses as the United States proposed a decade ago.

The Soviet Union refused to cooperate in tackling the problem of international control of atomic energy when that problem was in its infancy. Consequently, it has now become too late to achieve totally effective control although there can be, as we propose, a controlled cessation of further weapons testing and of the manufacture of fissionable material for weapons purposes. But, as your Government said on May 10, 1955, a total "ban" on atomic and hydrogen weapons could not now be enforced because "the possibility would be open to a potential aggressor to accumulate stocks of atomic and hydrogen weapons for a surprise attack on peace-loving states."

A terrible new menace can be seen to be in the making. That menace is to be found in the use of outer space for war purposes. The time to deal with that menace is now. It would be tragic if the Soviet leaders were blind or indifferent toward this menace as they were apparently blind or indifferent to the atomic and nuclear menace at its inception a decade ago.

If there is a genuine desire on the part of the Soviet leaders to do something more than merely talk about the menace resulting from what you described as "the production of ever newer types of weapons," let us actually do what even now would importantly reduce the scope of nuclear warfare, both in terms of checking the use of fissionable material for weapons purposes and in wholly eliminating the newest types of weapons which use outer space for human destruction.

Source: Eisenhower, Dwight D. Letter to Nikolai Aleksandrovich Bulganin, February 15, 1958. *The Papers of Dwight David Eisenhower: The Presidency*, edited by L. Galambos and D. van Ee. Baltimore, MD: Johns Hopkins University Press, 1996. Available online at the Presidential Papers of Dwight D. Eisenhower, the Dwight D. Eisenhower Memorial Commission, http://www.eisenhowermemorial. org/presidential-papers/second-term/documents/574.cfm.

6.6

Premier Khrushchev Comments on the U.S.-Soviet Rivalry in Space – 1958

An Excerpt from a Letter from Nikita Khrushchev to President Eisenhower

During the Space Race of the late 1950s and early 1960s, both the East and West maneuvered for political and military advantage on the issue. The following excerpt is taken from a letter from Soviet leader Nikita Khrushchev to American President Dwight Eisenhower dated April 22, 1958. Khrushchev insists that the USSR is dedicated to peaceful use of outer space—and pointedly questions whether the United States shares the same perspective.

… I should like to touch upon a matter of the use of outer space for peaceful purposes.

In the course of the exchange of views in connection with the preparations for convening a summit conference, you proposed that the question of the prohibition of the use of outer space for military purposes be discussed at that meeting. We seriously considered this proposal of yours, and we stated that we were prepared to consider at a summit meeting the question of the prohibition of the use of outer space for military purposes and the liquidation of military bases in foreign territories. In this connection we proceed from the premise that any solution of this problem must take into account the security of the Soviet Union, the United States of America, and other countries. The proposal of the Soviet Government for the prohibition of the use of outer space for military purposes, the liquidation of bases in foreign territories, and international cooperation in the field of study of outer space meets this objective. We are prepared to conclude an agreement which would provide for the

174

prohibition of the use of outer space for military purposes and would permit the launching of rockets into outer space only in accordance with an agreed international program of scientific research. At the same time, we cannot ignore the fact that atomic and hydrogen weapons can be delivered to the target not only by means of intercontinental rockets but also by means of conventional bombers stationed at the numerous American military bases located in areas adjacent to the Soviet Union.

Your proposal for the use of outer space for peaceful purposes provides, in fact, for the prohibition of intercontinental ballistic missiles alone, leaving aside the other important aspects of this problem. It is easy to see that you propose such a solution of the question as would correspond to the interests of the security of the United States alone, but would not provide any measures that would remove the threat to the security of the Soviet Union or to that of many other states created by the existence of numerous American military bases in foreign territories. The essence of your proposal is to prevent, through the prohibition of intercontinental ballistic missiles, a nuclear counterblow through outer space from being delivered against yourselves. Of course, it is impossible to agree to such an inequitable solution, which would put one side in a privileged position with regard to the other. Therefore we stated that an agreement on the prohibition of the use of outer space for military purposes must also provide for the liquidation of military bases located in foreign territories, and primarily in Europe, in the Near and Middle East, and in North Africa.

Such a solution of the problem, in our opinion, is equitable because it fully meets the interests of security of the United States, of the Soviet Union, and of other countries, and offers no advantage to any of them. As for the states on the territories of which American military bases are located, it may be said with assurance that they would only profit from such a solution of the problem, in as much as a liquidation of bases would fully meet the interests of the national security of these states by averting the deadly peril which could threaten their populations in case of war.

In your message, Mr. President, you pass over our proposal in complete silence and state that you await the acceptance of your proposal by the Soviet Government. An impression is created that it is desired to impose upon us a solution of the problem of the use of outer space such as would correspond to the interests of the United States alone and would completely ignore the interests of the Soviet Union. Such a one-sided approach is absolutely inadmissible in negotiations between independent states and, of course, cannot lead to the achievement of an agreement.

Source: Khrushchev, Nikita. Letter to President Dwight Eisenhower, April 22, 1958. Reprinted in *Department of State Bulletin*, May 19, 1958.

6.7

Premier Khrushchev Assesses the State of the World – 1960
Excerpts from Nikita Khrushchev's Address to the United Nations General Assembly

> *In the fall of 1960, Democratic nominee John F. Kennedy and Republican nominee (and Eisenhower administration vice president) Richard M. Nixon dueled to succeed Dwight Eisenhower as president. One of the major campaign issues of this battle was U.S. foreign policy toward the USSR. The importance of this issue was underscored on September 23, 1960, when Soviet Premier Nikita Khrushchev delivered an address to the United Nations General Assembly. His speech, which assessed the state of the world from the Communist perspective, included repeated denunciations of U.S. foreign policy. It also claimed that the Soviet Union had established itself as the champion of working people around the world.*

Our century is the century of the struggle for freedom, the century in which nations are liberating themselves from foreign domination. The peoples desire a worthwhile life and are fighting to secure it.

Victory has already been won in many countries and lands. But we cannot rest on our laurels, for we know that tens of millions of human beings are still languishing in colonial slavery and are suffering grave hardships....

Every intelligent individual gives some thought to what scientific progress, what this great twentieth century, is bringing mankind. Some rightly say that the world has been given new horizons, unlimited opportunities for the creation of abundant material wealth and for the ample satisfaction of human needs. With no less justification, others point to the great danger of scientific and technical achievements being used, not for these beneficial purposes, but primarily for the production of appalling means of destruction. These means of destruction are not being used at the present time. But, in the last analysis, they are produced to be used.

This argument between optimists and pessimists reflects the facts of our times. The most important of these facts is the conflict between two trends or lines of policy in international relations. I am not, of course, referring here to differences in social systems, since this is a domestic issue, which can and must be settled only by nations and states themselves....

These two lines of policy in international relations have long been in opposition. Although parallel lines never meet in elementary geometry they may come

Nikita Khrushchev, Address to the United Nations General Assembly, September 23, 1960. Reprinted with permission from the United Nations.

into collision in international affairs. That would be a fearful moment indeed. Only ten or fifteen years ago, few could predict the outcome of the struggle between these two lines of international policy. In the year 1960, however, only the blind can fail to see how the majority of peoples are becoming more and more positively and plainly convinced of the need to maintain peace.

The peoples of all countries—workers, peasants, intellectuals and the bourgeoisie, excluding a small handful of militarists and monopolists—want not war but peace, and peace alone. And if, therefore, the peoples actively fight to tie the hands of the militarist and monopolist circles, peace can be ensured....

No one can dispute the fact that the Soviet Union has been unsparing in its efforts to ensure the continuation of this welcome trend in the development of international relations. But the sinister forces which profit from the maintenance of international tension are clinging tenaciously to their positions. Though only a handful of individuals is involved, they are quite powerful and exert a strong influence on the policy of their respective States. A major effort is therefore required to break their resistance. As soon as the policy of easing international tension begins to yield tangible results, they immediately resort to extreme measures in order to ensure that the people should feel no relief; they strain every nerve to plunge the world back again and again into an atmosphere of gloom and to exacerbate international tension.

We saw a dangerous manifestation of the work of these forces last spring when the aircraft of one of the largest States Members of the United Nations, the United States of America, treacherously invaded the air space of the Soviet Union and that of other States. What is more, the United States has elevated such violations of international law into a principle of deliberate State policy.

The aggressive intrusion into our country by a United States aircraft and the whole course of the United States Government's subsequent behaviour showed the peoples that they were dealing with a calculated policy on the part of the United States Government, which was trying to substitute brigandage for international law and treachery for honest negotiations between sovereign and equal States....

The flights by the United States spy aircraft are also instructive in another respect. They have shown up the danger to peace presented by the network of United States bases in which dozens of States in Europe, Asia, Africa and Latin America are enmeshed.

Like a deep-seated form of acute infection in a living organism, these bases disrupt the normal political and economic life of the States upon which they have been foisted. They hinder the establishment of normal relations between those States and their neighbours. How, indeed, can there be any question of normal relations if the people of these neighbouring countries cannot sleep peacefully, if they have to live with the threat of being subjected to an annihilating blow whenever the United States militarists take it into their heads to embark on fresh acts of provocation? …

United States relations with Cuba are illuminating. As you know, before the victory of the popular revolution, all branches of the Cuban economy were wholly dominated by United States monopolies which earned vast profits from exploiting the working people of Cuba and the wealth of their fertile soil.

Some people in the United States occasionally like to boast that the standard of living in their country is higher than that in other countries. There is no gainsaying the fact that the standard of living in the United States is now higher than in Cuba, but why is that so? Is it because the Cuban people are less industrious or because the Cuban soil is less fertile? No, this of course is not the reason. The Cuban people are well known for their industry and for their attachment to their country and to their soil. The explanation is entirely different. For many years the fruits of the Cuban people's toil were enjoyed not by the Cuban people but by United States monopolies. Is it therefore surprising that in 1958, for example, the per capita income in Cuba was 6.5 times lower than in the United States? This telling fact speaks for itself.…

We are all witnesses to the fact that many peoples are being continually subjected to hostile acts and crude pressure by a certain group of States which seek to set at naught the legitimate interests and rights of other countries. This is why the international situation is fraught with acute conflicts, the danger of which is intensified by the mounting arms race.

It is quite evident that international relations cannot continue on such a basis, as that would mean a headlong descent to the abyss. It is the sacred duty of the United Nations to uphold the sovereign rights of States, and to press for the reestablishment of international relations on a sound legal basis and for the ending of the arms race.

Unfortunately, the policy of violating the inalienable rights of peoples is still in evidence in the United Nations itself.

Take, for instance, the question of the representation in the United Nations of the Chinese people. To impede the reinstatement of the People's Republic of China in its legitimate rights in the United Nations, simply because the socialist regime of that State is not to the taste of the leading circles of certain Western countries, and in particular of the United States, is to disregard the facts; it betokens the absence of any desire for a relaxation of international tension; it means that the interests of strengthening world peace and of developing international cooperation are being sacrificed to the narrow political calculations of a small group of States. This situation is inimical to peace and is degrading to the United Nations.…

Is the solution of major international problems really conceivable today without the participation of the People's Republic of China? Is it possible to solve these problems without the participation of India, Indonesia, Burma, Ceylon, the United Arab Republic, Iraq, Ghana, Guinea and the other States? If anyone has this idea, let him try to disregard the opinion and the votes of the representatives of the Asian, African and Latin American States here in the United Nations. It is true that the appearance of the new Asian and African States in the United Nations is giving rise to apprehension in certain Western countries. More than that, people are beginning to discuss ways of limiting the further influx of newly-emerging States into the United Nations.

As regards the Soviet Union, I can say frankly that we are glad to see a great number of new States making their appearance in the United Nations. We have always opposed and we shall continue to oppose any curtailment of the rights of peoples who have won their national independence. We share with these States the desire to preserve and strengthen peace, to create on our planet conditions for the peaceful coexistence and co-operation of countries regardless of their political and social structure, in accordance with the peaceful principles proclaimed at the Conference of African and Asian States at Bandung. The facts show that the liberation of nations and peoples under colonial domination leads to an improvement in international relations, an increase in international co-operation and the reinforcement of world peace....

It would be difficult to exaggerate the vast significance which the abolition of the colonial system would have for the entire world. Everyone knows that the economics of the colonies and the Trust Territories are at present subordinated to the mercenary interests of foreign monopolies, and the industrialization of these countries is being deliberately impeded. Imagine that the situation has changed and that these countries and territories, having become independent, are in a position to make ample use of their rich natural resources and to proceed with their industrialization, and that a better life has begun for their peoples. This would lead to a tremendous growth in the capacity of the world market, which would no doubt have a beneficial effect, not only on the economic development of the countries of the East but also on the economies of the industrially developed countries of the West....

A year has elapsed since the General Assembly adopted the resolution on general and complete disarmament. Having regard to the present pace of life, that is a comparatively long period of time and we need have no doubt that those engaged in the production of weapons and in the perfection and invention of new lethal means have not let it go to waste.

But in the sphere of disarmament not the slightest progress has been made in the past year. What are the reasons for this state of affairs to which we are forced to refer with great regret and serious concern? Who is preventing the implementation of the General Assembly resolution on general and complete disarmament, perhaps the most important and outstanding decision in the history of the United

Nations? Who is making it impossible to break the deadlock on the problem of disarmament?

The facts show that the absence of any progress towards the solution of the disarmament problem is the consequence of the position taken by the United States and by certain other States linked with it through NATO.

Throughout the work of the Ten-Nation Committee on Disarmament, the Western Powers refused to start working out a treaty on general and complete disarmament and in every way avoided discussion of the substance of the Soviet programme of general and complete disarmament [A/4219] which the General Assembly had referred to the Committee for detailed consideration. For their part, they made proposals which provided for neither general nor complete disarmament, nor any disarmament at all, but only for measures of control over armaments, i.e. control without disarmament. However, one cannot but see that the establishment of control without disarmament would be tantamount to setting up an international espionage system which, far from contributing to the consolidation of peace, could, on the contrary, make it easier for a potential aggressor to realize his plans which pose a threat to the peoples....

The Soviet Government, together with the Governments of a number of other States, was compelled to suspend its participation in the work of the Ten-Nation Committee which the Western Powers had turned into a screen for concealing the arms race. It was not easy for the Soviet Government to make this decision, because it was precisely our country that had first raised the issue of general and complete disarmament, and had been doing its utmost to achieve in the Committee a constructive solution to the problem, in strict conformity with the General Assembly resolution. In the circumstances, however, staying on the Committee would only have meant helping the opponents of disarmament. It was impossible to tolerate attempts to make the great cause of disarmament an object of speculation for purposes inimical to the interests of universal peace.

That is why the Soviet Government has placed the question of disarmament before the United Nations General Assembly, a considerable majority of whose members have no interest whatever in the arms race and sincerely wish to see it brought to an end....

The new Soviet proposal on the question of general and complete disarmament, which is based on the provisions of the proposal dated 2 June 1960 [A/4374], submitted by the Soviet Government to all the Governments of the world for consideration, has been drafted with due regard for all the useful ideas expressed in the past year in the course of the discussions on this question in political and public circles in various countries. This proposal goes a long way towards meeting the position of the Western Powers and this we hope will make for early agreement on disarmament.

We now provide, in particular, that all means of delivering nuclear weapons to their targets should be eliminated in the very first stage of general and complete disarmament; we have worked out detailed measures for effective international control at all stages; and we have taken into account the wish of certain Western Powers that, from the outset, there should be provision for reduction in the strength of armed forces and in conventional armaments. We have also introduced quite a number of other amendments to and modifications of our programme. In our view all these amendments render the programme of general and complete disarmament more concrete and even more realistic and practicable....

The Soviet Government is deeply convinced that only a radical solution of the problem of disarmament, providing for the complete prohibition of nuclear weapons together with the cessation of their manufacture and testing and the destruction of all accumulated stockpiles of these weapons, can accomplish the task of delivering mankind from the threat of nuclear war which hangs over it. This is precisely the aim which the Soviet Union is pursuing in consistently and resolutely advocating general and complete disarmament.

"I am revealing no secret when I say that we have no liking for capitalism. But we do not want to impose our system on other peoples by force."

All this, in our view, leads to one important conclusion. In order finally to break the deadlock on the disarmament problem, the General Assembly should call to order those who are hindering its solution and are trying to replace business-like negotiations on disarmament by empty beating about the bush....

The peoples of the Soviet Union and the Soviet Government are striving unremittingly to have the principles of peaceful coexistence firmly established in relations between States, and to ensure that these principles become the fundamental law of life for the whole of modern society. There is no communist-devised "trick" behind these principles, but simple truths dictated by life itself, such as that relations between all States should develop peacefully, without the use of force, without war and without interference in each other's internal affairs.

I am revealing no secret when I say that we have no liking for capitalism. But we do not want to impose our system on other peoples by force. Let those, then, who determine the policy of States with a different social system from ours, renounce their fruitless and dangerous attempts to dictate their will. It is time they also recognized that the choice of a particular way of life is the domestic concern of every people. Let us build up our relations having regard to actual realities. That is true peaceful coexistence....

The policy of peaceful coexistence assumes a readiness to solve all outstanding issues without resort to force, by means of negotiations and reasonable compromises. We all know that during the cold war years such questions for the most part did not find a solution, and that led to the creation of dangerous foci of tension in Europe, Asia and other parts of the world.

The Soviet Union considers that, in order to strengthen peace in the Far East and throughout the world, it is most essential to settle the Korean question.

Only madmen could think of settling the Korean question by armed force. The only correct proposal, namely to leave the solution of the question of the peaceful reunification of Korea to the Koreans themselves with no interference from outside, is finding ever wider acceptance. An essential condition for this is the immediate and complete withdrawal of all United States troops from South Korea, for their presence poisons the atmosphere not only in Korea but throughout the Far East and has made possible such shameful facts as the rigging of elections in South Korea. The proposal of the Government of the Democratic People's Republic of Korea to establish a confederation of North and South Korea is just as reasonable as the proposal of the Government of the German Democratic Republic to set up a confederation of the two German States. It is the only way to lay a sound foundation for the reunification of these States....

We are now firmly convinced that the time has come to take steps to create conditions for an improved functioning both of the United Nations as a whole and of the Organization's executive, working organ. I repeat, the matter relates primarily to the Secretary-General and his staff. We must particularly bear in mind the necessity for certain changes and improvements, with a view to the immediate future....

We consider it reasonable and just for the executive organ of the United Nations to consist not of a single person—the Secretary-General—but of three persons invested with the highest trust of the United Nations, persons representing the States belonging to the three basic groups I have mentioned. The point at issue is not the title of the organ but that this executive organ should represent the States belonging to the military block of the Western Powers, the socialist States and the neutralist States. This composition of the United Nations executive organ would create conditions for a more correct implementation of the decisions taken....

The Soviet Government hopes that the proposals it has raised for questions to be considered at the present session of the General Assembly will meet with support and understanding, since they are prompted by a sincere desire to secure a better life and tranquility on our planet....

The Soviet Government is ready to do its utmost in order that colonial servitude may be destroyed here and now, that here and now the problems of disarmament may find their concrete and effective solution.

The Soviet Government is ready to do its utmost in order that the testing of nuclear weapons may be prohibited here and now, that this means of mass destruction may be prohibited and destroyed.

It could be said that these are complicated problems and that they cannot be solved at one stroke. But these are problems posed by life itself and they must be solved before it is too late. Their solution cannot be evaded.

In concluding my statement I wish to emphasize once again that the Soviet Government, guided by the interests of the Soviet people, by the interests of the citizens of a free socialist State, once again proposes to all: let us talk, let us argue, but let us settle the questions of general and complete disarmament and let us bury colonialism that is accursed of all mankind.

Source: Khrushchev, Nikita. Address to the United Nations General Assembly, September 23, 1960. *Official Records of the General Assembly*, Fifteenth Session, Verbatim Records of Meetings September 20–October 17, 1960. Geneva: United Nations, 1960.

6.8
Patrice Lumumba's Last Statement – 1960
An Excerpt from a Message Smuggled Out of Prison before His Execution

In 1960 the African nation of Congo received its independence from Belgium after years of colonial rule. From the outset, though, the new country grappled with political instability, interference from Western corporations with business interests in the region, and rebels in the southern part of the country. The government put together by Prime Minister Patrice Lumumba was also threatened by the United States, which mistakenly interpreted his proud nationalism and socialist leanings as clear evidence that he was a Soviet puppet. A 1960 U.S. plot to assassinate Lumumba failed, but a year later Congolese military forces backed by the United States took him prisoner and executed him. Before his murder, however, Lumumba managed to smuggle a last message to his countrymen out of his prison cell. Following is an excerpt from that message.

My dear compatriots! Citizens of the Republic! Greetings!

I am certain that you will rejoice today to hear the voice of a man who has vowed never to betray his people.

In good fortune as in bad, I will always be at your side. It is with you that I have fought to liberate this country from foreign domination. It is with you that I am fighting to consolidate our national independence. It is with you that I will fight to safeguard the integrity and the national unity of the Republic of the Congo.

We have made a choice, that of serving our country loyally and faithfully. We shall never depart from this path. Freedom is the ideal for which, in all times down through the centuries, men have fought and died. The Congo could not fail to experience this truth, and it is thanks to our heroic and glorious struggle that we have valiantly won our independence and our dignity as free men.

We were born to live in freedom, not in slavery as we did for eighty years. Eighty years of oppression, humiliation, and exploitation. Eighty years during which the inhabitants of this country were arbitrarily robbed of the enjoyment of their most sacred rights. It was in order to put an end to this disgrace of the twentieth century that colonialism represents and in order to allow the Congolese people to govern themselves and manage the affairs of their country themselves that we fought a decisive battle against the usurpers of our rights.

> *"The powers that are fighting us or fighting my government, under the false pretense that they are fighting communism, are in fact concealing their real intentions."*

History has proved that independence is never handed a people on a silver platter. It must be wrested away. But in order to wrest away our independence, we were obliged to organize and mobilize all the living forces of the country. The Congolese answered our appeal and it was thanks to this pooling of our energies that we were able to deal decadent colonialism a mortal blow.

Since the forces of liberation always win out over that of oppression, we emerged victorious. All peoples have had to fight for their freedom. This was the case for the nationalists who headed the French, Belgian, Russian, and other revolutions….

The former colonies of America were liberated in this way. I remind you here of the Declaration of Independence adopted by the Congress of the United States in 1766 [sic], which proclaimed the overthrow of the colonial regime, the united colonies' liberation from the British yoke, and their transformation into a free and independent state. The Congolese nationalists have thus merely followed in the footsteps of the French, Belgian, American, Russian, and other nationalists. We have chosen only one weapon for our struggle: nonviolence. The only weapon that would bring victory in dignity and honor. Our watchword during the liberation campaign was always the immediate and total independence of the Congo….

The powers that are fighting us or fighting my government, under the false pretense that they are fighting communism, are in fact concealing their real intentions. These European powers favor only those African leaders who are tied to their apron strings and deceive their people. Certain of these powers conceive of their presence in the Congo or Africa only as a chance to exploit their rich resources to the maximum by conniving with certain corrupted leaders.

This policy of corruption whereby every incorruptible leader is called pro-communist and every leader who is a traitor to his country pro-Western must be fought.

We don't want to tag along with any bloc....

That is why, dear compatriots and comrades in the struggle, I call upon you in a spirit of brotherhood to put an end to fratricidal wars, internal and intertribal quarrels, the rivalries between individuals and between brothers. Our children will judge us harshly if out of blind heedlessness we do not thwart the maneuvers to profit from this dissension and sabotage our national independence and slow down the economic and social development of our state....

Such is the message of a man who has fought at your side so that this country may go ever forward and effectively play its role as the standard-bearer of African liberation.

Onward, men and women citizens, to the building of a united, proud, and prosperous Congo.

A radiant future is dawning on our horizon.

Long live the independent and sovereign Republic of the Congo!

Source: Lumumba, Patrice. *Lumumba Speaks: The Speeches and Writings of Patrice Lumumba, 1958-1961.* Edited by Jean Van Lierde. Translated by Helen R. Lane. Boston: Little, Brown, 1972.

6.9
Kennedy Pledges to Defend World Liberty – 1961
Excerpts from President John F. Kennedy's Inaugural Address

John F. Kennedy won the presidential election in 1960 by the narrowest of margins, but he entered the White House promising dramatic changes in U.S. foreign policy. His inaugural address, delivered on January 20, 1961, was devoted almost exclusively to that subject. He pledged that the United States would "pay any price, bear any burden, meet any hardship, support any friend, oppose any foe ... to assure the survival and success of liberty."

Vice President Johnson, Mr. Speaker, Mr. Chief Justice, President Eisenhower, Vice President Nixon, President Truman, reverend clergy, fellow citizens, we observe today not a victory of party, but a celebration of freedom—symbolizing an end, as well as a beginning—signifying renewal, as well as change.

For I have sworn before you and Almighty God the same solemn oath our forebears prescribed nearly a century and three quarters ago. The world is very different now. For man holds in his mortal hands the power to abolish all forms of human poverty and all forms of human life. And yet the same revolutionary beliefs for which our forebears fought are still at issue around the globe—the belief that the rights of man come not from the generosity of the state, but from the hand of God.

We dare not forget today that we are the heirs of that first revolution. Let the word go forth from this time and place, to friend and foe alike, that the torch has been passed to a new generation of Americans—born in this century, tempered by war, disciplined by a hard and bitter peace, proud of our ancient heritage—and unwilling to witness or permit the slow undoing of those human rights to which this nation has always been committed, and to which we are committed today at home and around the world.

Let every nation know, whether it wishes us well or ill, that we shall pay any price, bear any burden, meet any hardship, support any friend, oppose any foe, in order to assure the survival and the success of liberty. This much we pledge—and more.

To those old allies whose cultural and spiritual origins we share, we pledge the loyalty of faithful friends. United, there is little we cannot do in a host of cooperative ventures. Divided, there is little we can do—for we dare not meet a powerful challenge at odds and split asunder.

To those new states whom we welcome to the ranks of the free, we pledge our word that one form of colonial control shall not have passed away merely to be replaced by a far more iron tyranny. We shall not always expect to find them supporting our view. But we shall always hope to find them strongly supporting their own freedom—and to remember that, in the past, those who foolishly sought power by riding the back of the tiger ended up inside. To those peoples in the huts and villages across the globe struggling to break the bonds of mass misery, we pledge our best efforts to help them help themselves, for whatever period is required—not because the communists may be doing it, not because we seek their votes, but because it is right. If a free society cannot help the many who are poor, it cannot save the few who are rich. To our sister republics south of our border, we offer a special pledge—to convert our good words into good deeds—in a new alliance for progress—to assist free men and free governments in casting off the chains of poverty. But this peaceful revolution of hope cannot become the prey of hostile powers.

Let all our neighbors know that we shall join with them to oppose aggression or subversion anywhere in the Americas. And let every other power know that this hemisphere intends to remain the master of its own house. To that world assembly of sovereign states, the United Nations, our last best hope in an age where the instruments of war have far outpaced the instruments of peace, we renew our pledge of support—to prevent it from becoming merely a forum for invective—to strengthen its shield of the new and the weak—and to enlarge the area in which its writ may run.

Finally, to those nations who would make themselves our adversary, we offer not a pledge but a request: that both sides begin anew the quest for peace, before the dark powers of destruction unleashed by science engulf all humanity in planned or accidental self-destruction.

We dare not tempt them with weakness. For only when our arms are sufficient beyond doubt can we be certain beyond doubt that they will never be employed. But neither can two great and powerful groups of nations take comfort from our present course—both sides overburdened by the cost of modern weapons, both rightly alarmed by the steady spread of the deadly atom, yet both racing to alter that uncertain balance of terror that stays the hand of mankind's final war.

So let us begin anew—remembering on both sides that civility is not a sign of weakness, and sincerity is always subject to proof. Let us never negotiate out of fear. But let us never fear to negotiate.

Let both sides explore what problems unite us instead of belaboring those problems which divide us.

Let both sides, for the first time, formulate serious and precise proposals for the inspection and control of arms—and bring the absolute power to destroy other nations under the absolute control of all nations.

Let both sides seek to invoke the wonders of science instead of its terrors. Together let us explore the stars, conquer the deserts, eradicate disease, tap the ocean depths, and encourage the arts and commerce.

Let both sides unite to heed in all corners of the Earth the command of Isaiah—to "undo the heavy burdens ... and to let the oppressed go free." And if a beachhead of cooperation may push back the jungle of suspicion, let both sides join in creating a new endeavor, not a new balance of power, but a new world of law, where the strong are just and the weak secure and the peace preserved.

All this will not be finished in the first 100 days. Nor will it be finished in the first 1,000 days, nor in the life of this administration, nor even perhaps in our lifetime on this planet. But let us begin. In your hands, my fellow citizens, more than in mine, will rest the final success or failure of our course. Since this country was founded, each generation of Americans has been summoned to give testimony to its national loyalty. The graves of young Americans who answered the call to service surround the globe.

Now the trumpet summons us again—not as a call to bear arms, though arms we need; not as a call to battle, though embattled we are—but a call to bear the burden of a long twilight struggle, year in and year out, "rejoicing in hope, patient in tribulation"—a struggle against the common enemies of man: tyranny, poverty, disease, and war itself.

Can we forge against these enemies a grand and global alliance, North and South, East and West, that can assure a more fruitful life for all mankind? Will you join in that historic effort?

In the long history of the world, only a few generations have been granted the role of defending freedom in its hour of maximum danger. I do not shrink from this responsibility—I welcome it. I do not believe that any of us would exchange places with any other people or any other generation. The energy, the faith, the devotion which we bring to this endeavor will light our country and all who serve it—and the glow from that fire can truly light the world. And so, my fellow Americans: Ask not what your country can do for you—ask what you can do for your country.

My fellow citizens of the world: Ask not what America will do for you, but what together we can do for the freedom of man.

Finally, whether you are citizens of America or citizens of the world, ask of us the same high standards of strength and sacrifice which we ask of you. With a good conscience our only sure reward, with history the final judge of our deeds, let us go forth to lead the land we love, asking His blessing and His help, but knowing that here on Earth God's work must truly be our own.

Source: Kennedy, John F. "Inaugural Address, January 20, 1961." John F. Kennedy Library and Museum. Available online at http://www.jfklibrary.org.

6.10

President Kennedy Speaks on the "Berlin Crisis" – 1961
Excerpt from John F. Kennedy's Televised Speech to the Nation

During the late 1950s East German and Soviet authorities became increasingly distraught about the steady exodus of skilled and educated East Germans into the West. In 1961 Communist officials announced plans to build a wall that would close down all travel routes between East and West Berlin. This provocative move had two purposes: to choke off the sole passageway that East Germans had to the West, and to increase pressure on the United States and its allies to abandon West Berlin.

But the Kennedy administration stood firm and pledged continued protection for democratic West Berlin. President John F. Kennedy gave a nationally televised speech months after Khrushchev had begun planning to build the Berlin Wall and just days before the border was permanently closed between East and West Berlin. In his address of July 25, 1961, Kennedy stressed the need for NATO countries to protect West Berlin and declared that any Soviet attack on Berlin would be treated as an attack on NATO.

188

Good Evening.

Seven weeks ago tonight I returned from Europe to report on my meeting with Premier Khrushchev and the others. His grim warnings about the future of the world, his aide mémoire on Berlin, his subsequent speeches and threats which he and his agents have launched, and the increase in the Soviet military budget that he has announced, have all prompted a series of decisions by the administration and a series of consultations with the members of the NATO organization. In Berlin, as you recall, he intends to bring to an end, through a stroke of the pen, first our legal rights to be in West Berlin and secondly our ability to make good on our commitment to the 2 million free people of that city. That we cannot permit.

We are clear about what must be done—and we intend to do it. I want to talk frankly with you tonight about the first steps that we shall take. These actions will require sacrifice on the part of many of our citizens. More will be required in the future. They will require, from all of us, courage and perseverance in the years to come. But if we and our allies act out of strength and unity of purpose—with calm determination and steady nerves—using restraint in our words as well as our weapons—I am hopeful that both peace and freedom will be sustained.

> *"The source of world trouble and tension is Moscow, not Berlin. And if war begins, it will have begun in Moscow and not Berlin."*

The immediate threat to free men is in West Berlin. But that isolated outpost is not an isolated problem. The threat is worldwide. Our effort must be equally wide and strong and not be obsessed by any single manufactured crisis. We face a challenge in Berlin, but there is also a challenge in Southeast Asia, where the borders are less guarded, the enemy harder to find, and the dangers of communism less apparent to those who have so little. We face a challenge in our own hemisphere, and indeed wherever else the freedom of human beings is at stake.

Let me remind you that the fortunes of war and diplomacy left the free people of West Berlin, in 1945, 110 miles behind the Iron Curtain.

This map makes very clear the problem that we face. The white is West Germany—the East is the area controlled by the Soviet Union, and as you can see from the chart, West Berlin is 110 miles within the area which the Soviets now dominate—which is immediately controlled by the so-called East German regime.

We are there as a result of our victory over Nazi Germany—and our basic rights to be there, deriving from that victory, include both our presence in West Berlin and the enjoyment of access across East Germany. These rights have been repeatedly confirmed and recognized in special agreements with the Soviet Union. Berlin is not a part of East Germany, but a separate territory under the control of the Allied powers. Thus our rights there are clear and deep-rooted. But in addition to those rights is our commitment to sustain and defend, if need be, the opportunity for more than 2 million people to determine their own future and choose their own way of life.

Thus, our presence in West Berlin, and our access thereto, cannot be ended by any act of the Soviet government. The NATO shield was long ago extended to cover West Berlin—and we have given our word that an attack upon that city will be regarded as an attack upon us all.

For West Berlin—lying exposed 110 miles inside East Germany, surrounded by Soviet troops and close to Soviet supply lines—has many roles. It is more than a showcase of liberty, a symbol, an island of freedom in a communist sea. It is even more than a link with the free world, a beacon of hope behind the Iron Curtain, an escape hatch for refugees.

West Berlin is all of that. But above all it has now become—as never before—the great testing place of Western courage and will, a focal point where our solemn commitments, stretching back over the years since 1945, and Soviet ambitions now meet in basic confrontation....

We cannot and will not permit the communists to drive us out of Berlin, either gradually or by force. For the fulfillment of our pledge to that city is essential to the morale and security of Western Germany, to the unity of Western Europe, and to the faith of the entire free world.

Soviet strategy has long been aimed, not merely at Berlin, but at dividing and neutralizing all of Europe, forcing us back on our own shores. We must meet our oft-stated pledge to the free peoples of West Berlin—and maintain our rights and their safety, even in the face of force—in order to maintain the confidence of other free peoples in our word and our resolve. The strength of the alliance on which our security depends is dependent in turn on our willingness to meet our commitments to them.

So long as the communists insist that they are preparing to end by themselves unilaterally our rights in West Berlin and our commitments to its people, we must be prepared to defend those rights and those commitments. We will at all times be ready to talk, if talk will help. But we must also be ready to resist with force, if force is used upon us. Either alone would fail. Together, they can serve the cause of freedom and peace.

[*Kennedy then detailed several planned measures to quickly increase U.S. military defenses and capabilities.*]

.... I am well aware of the fact that many American families will bear the burden of these requests. Studies or careers will be interrupted; husbands and sons will be called away; incomes in some cases will be reduced. But these are burdens which must be borne if freedom is to be defended. Americans have willingly borne them before—and they will not flinch from the task now.

We have another sober responsibility. To recognize the possibilities of nuclear war in the missile age, without our citizens knowing what they should do and where they should go if bombs begin to fall, would be a failure of responsibility. In May, I pledged a new start on Civil Defense. Last week, I assigned, on the recommendation of the Civil Defense director, basic responsibility for this program to the Secretary of Defense, to make certain it is administered and coordinated with our continental defense efforts at the highest civilian level. Tomorrow, I am requesting of the Congress new funds for the following immediate objectives: to identify and mark space in existing structures public and private that could be used for fallout shelters in case of attack; to stock those shelters with food, water, first-aid kits and other minimum essentials for survival; to increase their capacity; to improve our air-raid warning and fallout detection systems, including a new household warning system which is now under development; and to take other measures that will be effective at an early date to save millions of lives if needed. In the event of an attack, the lives of those families which are not hit in a nuclear blast and fire can still be saved—if they can be warned to take shelter and if that shelter is available. We owe that kind of insurance to our families—and to our country. In contrast to our friends in Europe, the need for this kind of protection is new to our shores. But the time to start is now. In the coming months, I hope to let every citizen know what steps he can take without delay to protect his family in case of attack. I know that you will want to do no less.

.... But I must emphasize again that the choice is not merely between resistance and retreat, between atomic holocaust and surrender. Our peacetime military posture is traditionally defensive; but our diplomatic posture need not be. Our response to the Berlin crisis will not be merely military or negative. It will be more than merely standing firm. For we do not intend to leave it to others to choose and monopolize the forum and the framework of discussion. We do not intend to abandon our duty to mankind to seek a peaceful solution.

As signers of the U.N. Charter, we shall always be prepared to discuss international problems with any and all nations that are willing to talk—and listen—with reason. If they have proposals—not demands—we shall hear them. If they seek genuine understanding—not concessions of our rights—we shall meet with them. We have previously indicated our readiness to remove any actual irritants in West Berlin, but the freedom of that city is not negotiable. We cannot negotiate with those who say, "What's mine is mine and what's yours is negotiable." But we are willing to consider any arrangement or treaty in Germany consistent with the maintenance of peace and freedom, and with the legitimate security interests of all nations.

We recognize the Soviet Union's historical concern about their security in Central and Eastern Europe, after a series of ravaging invasions, and we believe arrangements can be worked out which will help to meet those concerns, and make it possible for both security and freedom to exist in this troubled area.

For it is not the freedom of West Berlin which is "abnormal" in Germany today, but the situation in that entire divided country. If anyone doubts the legality of our rights in Berlin, we are ready to have it submitted to international adjudication. If anyone doubts the extent to which our presence is desired by the people of West Berlin, compared to East German feelings about their regime, we are ready to have that question submitted to a free vote in Berlin and, if possible, among all the German people. And let us hear at that time from the two and one-half million refugees who have fled the communist regime in East Germany—voting for Western-type freedom with their feet.

The world is not deceived by the communist attempt to label Berlin as a hotbed of war. There is peace in Berlin today. The source of world trouble and tension is Moscow, not Berlin. And if war begins, it will have begun in Moscow and not Berlin.

For the choice of peace or war is largely theirs, not ours. It is the Soviets who have stirred up this crisis. It is they who are trying to force a change. It is they who have opposed free elections. It is they who have rejected an all-German peace treaty, and the rulings of international law. And as Americans know from our history on our own old frontier, gun battles are caused by outlaws, and not by officers of the peace.

In short, while we are ready to defend our interests, we shall also be ready to search for peace—in quiet exploratory talks in formal or informal meetings. We do not want military considerations to dominate the thinking of either East or West.

And Mr. Khrushchev may find that his invitation to other nations to join in a meaningless treaty may lead to their inviting him to join in the community of peaceful men, in abandoning the use of force, and in respecting the sanctity of agreements.

While all of these efforts go on, we must not be diverted from our total responsibilities, from other dangers, from other tasks. If new threats in Berlin or elsewhere should cause us to weaken our program of assistance to the developing nations who are also under heavy pressure from the same source, or to halt our efforts for realistic disarmament, or to disrupt or slow down our economy, or to neglect the education of our children, then those threats will surely be the most successful and least costly maneuver in communist history. For we can afford all these efforts, and more—but we cannot afford not to meet this challenge. And the challenge is not to us alone. It is a challenge to every nation which asserts its sovereignty under a system of liberty. It is a challenge to all those who want a world of free choice. It is a special challenge to the Atlantic Community—the heartland of human freedom....

The solemn vow each of us gave to West Berlin in time of peace will not be broken in time of danger. If we do not meet our commitments to Berlin, where will we later stand? If we are not true to our word there, all that we have achieved in collective security, which relies on these words, will mean nothing. And if there is one path above all others to war, it is the path of weakness and disunity.

Today, the endangered frontier of freedom runs through divided Berlin. We want it to remain a frontier of peace. This is the hope of every citizen of the Atlantic Community; every citizen of Eastern Europe; and, I am confident, every citizen of the Soviet Union. For I cannot believe that the Russian people who bravely suffered enormous losses in the Second World War would now wish to see the peace upset once more in Germany. The Soviet government alone can convert Berlin's frontier of peace into a pretext for war.

The steps I have indicated tonight are aimed at avoiding that war....

I would like to close with a personal word. When I ran for the presidency of the United States, I knew that this country faced serious challenges, but I could not realize—nor could any man realize who does not bear the burdens of this office— how heavy and constant would be those burdens.

Three times in my lifetime our country and Europe have been involved in major wars. In each case serious misjudgments were made on both sides of the intentions of others, which brought about great devastation. Now, in the thermonuclear age, any misjudgment on either side about the intentions of the other could rain more devastation in several hours than has been wrought in all the wars of human history.

Therefore I, as president and commander in chief, and all of us as Americans, are moving through serious days. I shall bear this responsibility under our Constitution for the next three and one-half years, but I am sure that we all, regardless of our occupations, will do our very best for our country, and for our cause. For all of us want to see our children grow up in a country at peace, and in a world where freedom endures.

I know that sometimes we get impatient, we wish for some immediate action that would end our perils. But I must tell you that there is no quick and easy solution. The communists control over a billion people, and they recognize that if we should falter, their success would be imminent.

We must look to long days ahead, which if we are courageous and persevering can bring us what we all desire. In these days and weeks I ask for your help, and your advice. I ask for your suggestions when you think we could do better. All of us, I know, love our country, and we shall all do our best to serve it. In meeting my responsibilities in these coming months as president, I need your good will, and your support—and above all, your prayers.

Thank you, and good night.

Source: Kennedy, John F. "Radio and Television Report to the American People on the Berlin Crisis, July 25, 1961." John F. Kennedy Library and Museum. Available online at http://www.jfklibrary.org.

7

MUTUAL ASSURED DESTRUCTION

A Czech demonstrator clings to a Soviet tank rolling through the streets of Prague in August 1968, when Warsaw Pact troops crushed Czechoslovakia's reformist "Prague Spring."

INTRODUCTION

One of the most terrifying elements of the Cold War was the escalating nuclear arms race between the two superpowers. This deadly race began in August 1949, when the Soviet Union detonated its first atomic bomb. From that point forward, achieving and keeping "nuclear supremacy" was a major policy goal in both countries. Each side spent the next few decades building and stockpiling enormous numbers of nuclear weapons that it hoped that it would never use. "Their strategic value lay in deterring the other side," wrote Jeremy Isaacs and Taylor Downing in *The Cold War: An Illustrated History, 1945-1991*. "The superpowers would refrain from attacking each other because of the certainty of mutual assured destruction, better known by its apt acronym, MAD."

Following the Soviet Union's first successful atomic test, President Harry Truman had ordered his National Security Council (NSC) to conduct a comprehensive review of Soviet and American military, economic, and political capabilities. The NSC returned in April 1950 with a document known as "NSC-68." This report described the Soviet Union as an extremely dangerous rival that was determined to expand its power and influence. NSC-68 argued that the only way the United States could curb Soviet expansion was to show steely resolve and dramatically increase military spending.

The Arms Race

During the 1950s both the Americans and Soviets carried out major build-ups of both conventional and nuclear arms. Between 1950 and 1953 alone, the United States increased its armed forces by over one million troops, and in October 1952 it successfully tested a thermonuclear device—an "H-bomb"—that was far more powerful than the bombs that had devastated Hiroshima and Nagasaki. Two years later, the United States unveiled an even more powerful hydrogen bomb. Meanwhile, President Dwight Eisenhower took office in 1953. His administration invested heavily in a variety of sophisticated delivery systems, including intercontinental ballistic missiles (ICBMs)—rocket-propelled missiles capable of striking targets in the Soviet Union after being launched from American soil. By the time Eisenhower left office in January 1961, the United States had 18,000 nuclear warheads at its disposal.

The Soviet Union tried hard to keep up. The size of the Red Army soon eclipsed that of the American military, and by the end of 1955 the Soviets also had the hydrogen bomb in its arsenal. But the quality of their other armaments—especially their missile delivery systems—was markedly inferior to that of the United States. Soviet missiles could only reach Western Europe, so both sides knew that the Soviets were at a significant strategic disadvantage. After Eisenhower emerged from one 1953 meeting concerning the comparative strike capabilities of the two nations, he commented that the Soviets "must be scared as hell."

Regular U-2 reconnaissance flights over Soviet airspace and other U.S. intelligence-gathering operations enabled Eisenhower to remain confident of continued U.S. military superiority throughout the late 1950s. He knew that widespread claims that the Soviets had opened up a significant "missile gap" advantage over the United States were false. Concerns about this nonexistent gap were fed not only by the 1957 *Sputnik* launch, but also by Soviet leader Nikita Khrushchev's boastful promises to produce missiles "like sausages."

On January 17, 1961, outgoing President Dwight Eisenhower gave a farewell address to the nation in which he bluntly warned about the unhealthy influence of America's "military-industrial complex" on the nation's economy and culture. But incoming President John F. Kennedy continued to see "Massive Retaliation," first articulated by Eisenhower's Secretary of State John Foster Dulles in the mid-1950s, as a cornerstone of the U.S. stance toward the Soviets. Under this doctrine, the United States reserved the right to use its nuclear arsenal if Communist aggression or use of conventional military forces became too threatening. The Soviets reciprocated with equally threatening language.

Mutual Assured Destruction

This Cold War deadlock based on the concept of "Mutual Assured Destruction" endured throughout the 1960s. Occasionally the dark clouds of mutual hatred and suspicion thinned or parted, such as with the 1963 ratification of the Nuclear Test

Ban Treaty, in which the United States, Great Britain, and the Soviet Union agreed to a ban on all nuclear test explosions in the atmosphere, outer space, and under water. As the decade unfolded, however, a series of cataclysmic and historic events—the 1962 Cuban Missile Crisis, the 1963 assassination of Kennedy, the 1967 Six-Day War, the civil rights movement, and protests against the Vietnam War—contributed to a deepening sense of instability and dislocation in American society.

Many Americans came to feel that nuclear war with the Soviet empire was inevitable. Certainly, some American military leaders were prepared to engage in such a struggle. "The whole idea is to kill the bastards," declared General Thomas Power, a commander of U.S. Strategic Air Command (SAC) in the 1960s. "At the end of the war if there are two Americans and one Russian left alive, we win."

The fear of nuclear attack kept both sides on edge for years at a time. Various high-tech early warning systems were adopted, upgraded, and discarded in favor of ever more sophisticated technology in both the East and West. As early as 1961, SAC kept at least a dozen nuclear-armed B-52 bombers airborne and ready to strike at all times; in addition, ICBMs housed in remote missile silos across America were kept ready to fire at a moment's notice. The Soviets, meanwhile, displayed a single-minded zeal to catch up with their rival's nuclear stockpile. They took an early lead in developing anti-ballistic missiles (ABMs), which are theoretically capable of intercepting enemy missiles before they reach their target. This technology threatened to destabilize the whole concept of mutual deterrence upon which the Cold War balanced.

Another development that elicited dread in the West was China's successful detonation of an atomic bomb on October 16, 1964. China's arrival as a nuclear power had been widely anticipated, but the news was still a blow to Western leaders. Even the Soviets were uneasy about China's nuclear capabilities. In fact, Moscow took pains to educate Mao Zedong about the size and capabilities of America's nuclear arsenal. But Mao voiced unnerving indifference to the idea of a nuclear Armageddon. "We may lose more than 300 million people," he acknowledged. "So what? War is war. The years will pass and we'll get to work producing more babies than before." This rhetoric, combined with China's disastrous "Great Leap Forward" and its brutal Cultural Revolution, led many American analysts to conclude that the unpredictable Mao regime posed a greater threat to world survival than the Soviets.

The Brezhnev Era Begins

Meanwhile, Cold War tensions between the United States and the Soviet Union remained high throughout the 1960s, despite changes in leadership. President Lyndon B. Johnson, who took office following Kennedy's death, adhered to the basic belief that Communist aggression had to be checked forcefully wherever it raised its head. Meanwhile, Nikita Khrushchev's rule came to an end after years of halting domestic reform and international brinkmanship. In October 1964 he was ousted by conservative Kremlin forces that opposed his reformist policies, his anti-Stalin rhetoric, and his 1961 retreat from Cuba. He was replaced by a trio of hard-line officials: Leonid Brezhnev, Nikolai Podgorny, and Aleksei Kosygin.

Under this new leadership, the Soviet empire lurched back toward its pre-Khrushchev orientation. Modest initiatives to modernize and reform the Soviet economy were set aside, even though it was groaning under the strain of huge military expenditures and poor productivity levels. The Kremlin also took a harder line in dealing with political dissidents and the leadership of satellite states. These moves sparked unrest in various parts of the Eastern bloc, where Khrushchev's liberal reforms had been embraced.

The most spectacular example of Eastern European unhappiness with Soviet attempts to roll back Khrushchev's "thaw" was the Prague Spring of 1968. This event began in January 1968, when Communist leader Alexander Dubček rose to power in Czechoslovakia. Over the next several months, he worked hard to meet growing public demands for greater political freedom and economic reform without arousing the anger of the Soviet Union. Czech citizens reveled in these changes, and a celebratory spirit took hold in the streets of Prague and other major cities.

Officials in the Kremlin and the leaders of other hard-line Eastern bloc states watched events unfold in Czechoslovakia with growing concern. They feared that the Prague Spring might breed unrest in other parts of Communist-controlled Eastern Europe. With this in mind, Brezhnev and his colleagues decided to send a stern message. On the evening of August 20, Soviet tanks and Warsaw Pact troops rolled into Czechoslovakia and crushed the nation's reformist movement. Dubček was arrested and later expelled from the Communist Party, and a hard-line regime loyal to Moscow was put in place.

Over the next several months, the Soviet leadership described the invasion as a reasonable response to unacceptable behavior. They explained that countries within the Soviet sphere of influence were free to chart independent paths of development—as long as they remained loyal to the tenets of Communism as defined by the Kremlin. In practical terms, this philosophy, which came to be known as the Brezhnev Doctrine, meant that Moscow intended to keep the people of the Eastern bloc shackled to the Soviet empire forever.

DOCUMENTS

7.1
"NSC-68" – 1950
Excerpts from a Secret National Security Council Report on Soviet and American Military Capabilities

In the fall of 1949, Western powers were shaken by the Communist takeover of China and the Soviet Union's successful test of an atomic bomb. President Truman subsequently requested a comprehensive analysis of Soviet and American capabilities. The National Security Council responded with a document that examined the U.S.-Soviet relationship from military, economic, political, and psychological standpoints. The paper painted a grim picture of Soviet military capabilities and international aims, and it recommended a massive increase in U.S. military spending so that the United States could effectively contain Soviet ambitions down the line.

Writing in Inside the Cold War: An Oral History, *author John Sharnik asserted that "NSC-68 is to the secret history of the Cold War what Churchill's Iron Curtain speech is to its public literature—a landmark document.... This policy was an extraordinary development—on one hand, generous and courageous; on the other, risky and officious—an astonishing undertaking for a nation traditionally antimilitarist and also isolationist as far as Europe is concerned. Yet this would be the basic policy of the United States during the next four decades. Presidents during that time would pursue it, expand it, redefine it, or try to reverse it. But in the end the policy stood fast."*

April 14, 1950

I. Backgrounds of the Present World Crisis

Within the past thirty-five years the world has experienced two global wars of tremendous violence. It has witnessed two revolutions—the Russian and the Chinese—of extreme scopes and intensity. It has also seen the collapse of five empires—the Ottoman, the Austro-Hungarian, German, Italian and Japanese—and the drastic decline of two major imperial systems, the British and the French. During the span of one generation, the international distribution of power has been fundamentally alerted. For several centuries it had proved impossible for any one nation to gain such preponderant strength that a coalition of other nations could not in time face it with greater strength. The international scene was marked by recurring periods of violence and war, but a system of sovereign and independent states was maintained, over which no state was able to achieve hegemony.

Two complex sets of factors have now basically altered this historical distribution of power. First, the defeat of Germany and Japan and the decline of the British and French Empires have interacted with the development of the United States and the Soviet Union in such a way that power has increasingly gravitated to these two centers. Second, the Soviet Union, unlike previous aspirants to hegemony, is animated by a new fanatic faith, antithetical to our own, and seeks to impose its absolute authority over the rest of the world. Conflict has, therefore, become endemic and is waged, on the part of the Soviet Union, by violent or non-violent methods in accordance with the dictates of expediency.

> *"The Soviet Union is developing the military capacity to support its design for world domination."*

With the development of increasingly terrifying weapons of mass destruction, every individual faces the ever-present possibility of annihilation should the conflict enter the phase of total war.

On the one hand, the people of the world yearn for relief from the anxiety arising from the risk of atomic war. On the other hand, any substantial further extension of the area under the domination of the Kremlin would raise the possibility that no coalition adequate to confront the Kremlin with greater strength could be assembled. It is in this context that this Republic and its citizens in the ascendancy of their strength stand in their deepest peril.

The issues that face us are momentous, involving the fulfillment or destruction not only of this Republic but of civilization itself. They are issues which will not await our deliberation. With conscience and resolution this Government and the people it represents must now take new and fateful decisions....

III. Fundamental Design of the Kremlin

The fundamental design of those who control the Soviet Union and the international communist movement is to retain and solidify their absolute power, first in the Soviet Union and second in the areas now under their control. In the mind of the Soviet leaders, however, achievement of this design requires the dynamic extension of their authority and the ultimate elimination of any effective opposition to their authority.

The design, therefore, calls for the complete subversion or forcible destruction of the machinery of government and structure of society in the countries of the non-Soviet world and their replacement by an apparatus and structure subservient to and controlled from the Kremlin. To that end Soviet efforts are now directed toward the domination of the Eurasian land mass. The United States, as the principal center of power in the non-Soviet world and the bulwark of opposition to Soviet expansion, is the principal enemy whose integrity and vitality must be subverted or destroyed by one means or another if the Kremlin is to achieve its fundamental design....

C. Military

The Soviet Union is developing the military capacity to support its design for world domination. The Soviet Union actually possesses armed forces far in excess of those necessary to defend its national territory. These armed forces are probably not yet considered by the Soviet Union to be sufficient to initiate a war which would involve the United States. This excessive strength, coupled now with an atomic capability, provides the Soviet Union with great coercive power for use in time of peace in furtherance of its objectives and serves as a deterrent to the victims of its aggression from taking any action in opposition to its tactics which would risk war.

Should a major war occur in 1950 the Soviet Union and its satellites are considered by the Joint Chiefs of Staff to be in a sufficiently advanced state of preparation immediately to undertake and carry out the following campaigns.

a. To overrun Western Europe, with the possible exception of the Iberian and Scandinavian Peninsulas; to drive toward the oil-bearing areas of the Near and Middle East; and to consolidate Communist gains in the Far East;

b. To launch air attacks against the British Isles and air and sea attacks against the lines of communications of the Western Powers in the Atlantic and Pacific;

c. To attack selected targets with atomic weapons, now including the likelihood of such attacks against targets in Alaska, Canada, and the United States. Alternatively, this capability, coupled with other actions open to the Soviet Union, might deny the United Kingdom as an effective base of operations for allied forces. It also should be possible for the Soviet Union to prevent any allied "Normandy" type amphibious operations intended to force a re-entry into the continent of Europe.

After the Soviet Union completed its initial campaigns and consolidated its positions in the Western European area, it could simultaneously conduct:

a. Full-scale air and limited sea operations against the British Isles;

b. Invasions of the Iberian and Scandinavian Peninsulas;

c. Further operations in the Near and Middle East, continued air operations against the North American continent, and air and sea operations against Atlantic and Pacific lines of communication; and

d. Diversionary attacks in other areas....

It is not possible at this time to assess accurately the finite disadvantages to the Soviet Union which may accrue through the implementation of the Economic

Cooperation Act of 1948, as amended, and the Mutual Defense Assistance Act of 1949. It should be expected that, as this implementation progressed, the internal security situation of the recipient nations should improve concurrently. In addition, a strong United States military position, plus increases in the armaments of the nations of Western Europe, should strengthen the determination of the recipient nations to counter Soviet moves and in the event of war could be considered as likely to delay operations and increase the time required for the Soviet Union to overrun Western Europe. In all probability, although United States backing will stiffen their determination, the armaments increase under the present aid programs will not be of any major consequence prior to 1952. Unless the military strength of the Western European nations is increased on a much larger scale than the current programs and at an accelerated rate, it is even more likely that those nations will not be able to oppose even by 1960 the Soviet armed forces in war with any degree of effectiveness. Considering the Soviet Union military capability, the long-range allied military objective in Western Europe must envisage an increased military strength in that area sufficient possibly to deter the Soviet Union from a major war, or, in any event, to delay materially the overrunning of Western Europe and, if feasible, to hold a bridgehead on the continent against Soviet Union offensives.

We do not know accurately what the Soviet atomic capability is but the Central Intelligence Agency intelligence estimates, concurred in by State, Army, Navy, Air Force, and Atomic Energy Commission, assign to the Soviet Union a production capability giving it a fission bomb stockpile within the following ranges:

By mid-1950 10-20

By mid-1951 25-45

By mid-1952 45-90

By mid-1953 70-135

By mid-1954 200

This estimate is admittedly based on incomplete coverage of Soviet activities and represents the production capabilities of known or deducible Soviet plants. If others exist, as is possible, this estimate could lead us into a feeling of superiority in our atomic stockpile that might be dangerously misleading, particularly with regard to the timing of a possible Soviet offensive. On the other hand, if the Soviet Union experiences operating difficulties, this estimate would be reduced. There is some evidence that the Soviet Union is acquiring certain materials essential to research on and development of thermonuclear weapons.

The Soviet Union now has aircraft able to deliver the atomic bomb. Our intelligence estimates assign to the Soviet Union an atomic bomber capability already in excess of that needed to deliver available bombs. We have at present no evaluated estimate regarding the Soviet accuracy of delivery on target. It is believed that the Soviets cannot deliver their bombs on target with a degree of accuracy comparable to ours, but a planning estimate might well place it at 40-60 percent of bombs sortied. For planning purposes, therefore, the date the Soviets possess an atomic stockpile of 200 bombs would be a critical date for the United States for the delivery of 100 atomic bombs on targets in the United States would seriously damage this country.

At the time the Soviet Union has a substantial atomic stockpile and if it is assumed that it will strike a strong surprise blow and if it is assumed further that its atomic attacks will be met with no more effective defense opposition than the United States and its allies have programmed, results of those attacks could include:

a. Laying waste to the British Isles and thus depriving the Western Powers of their use as a base;

b. Destruction of the vital centers and of the communications of Western Europe, thus precluding effective defense by the Western Powers; and

c. Delivering devastating attacks on certain vital centers of the United States and Canada.

The possession by the Soviet Union of a thermonuclear capability in addition to this substantial atomic stockpile would result in tremendously increased damage....

VI. U.S. Intentions and Capabilities—Actual and Potential

C. Military

The United States now possesses the greatest military potential of any single nation in the world. The military weaknesses of the United States vis-à-vis the Soviet Union, however, include its numerical inferiority in forces in being and in total manpower. Coupled with the inferiority of forces in being, the United States also lacks tenable positions from which to employ its forces in event of war and munitions power in being and readily available.

It is true that the United States armed forces are now stronger than ever before in other times of apparent peace; it is also true that there exists a sharp disparity between our actual military strength and our commitments. The relationship of our strength to our present commitments, however, is not alone the governing factor. The world situation, as well as commitments, should govern; hence, our military strength more properly should be related to the world situation confronting us. When our military strength is related to the world situation and balanced against the likely exigencies of such a situation, it is clear that our military strength is becoming dangerously inadequate.

If war should begin in 1950, the United States and its allies will have the military capability of conducting defensive operations to provide a reasonable measure of protection to the Western Hemisphere, bases in the Western Pacific, and essential military lines of communication; and an inadequate measure of protection to vital military bases in the United Kingdom and in the Near and Middle East. We will have the capability of conducting powerful offensive air operations against vital elements of the Soviet war-making capacity.

If the potential military capabilities of the United States and its allies were rapidly and effectively developed, sufficient forces could be produced to deter war, or if the Soviet Union chooses war, to withstand the initial Soviet attacks, to stabilize supporting attacks, and to retaliate in turn with even greater impact on the Soviet capabilities. From the military point of view alone, however, this would require not only the generation of the necessary military forces but also the development and stockpiling of improved weapons of all types.

Under existing peacetime conditions, a period of from two to three years is required to produce a material increase in military power. Such increased power could be provided in a somewhat shorter period in a declared period of emergency or in wartime through a full-out national effort. Any increase in military power in peacetime, however, should be related both to its probable military role in war, to the implementation of immediate and long-term United States foreign policy vis-à-vis the Soviet Union and to the realities of the existing situation. If such a course of increasing our military power is adopted now, the United States would have the capability of eliminating the disparity between its military strength and the exigencies of the situation we face; eventually of gaining the initiative in the "cold" war and of materially delaying if not stopping the Soviet offensive in war itself.

VIII. Atomic Armaments

A. Military Evaluation of U.S. and U.S.S.R. Atomic Capabilities

1. The United States now has an atomic capability, including both numbers and deliverability, estimated to be adequate, if effectively utilized, to deliver a serious blow against the war-making capacity of the U.S.S.R. It is doubted whether such a blow, even if it resulted in the complete destruction of the contemplated target systems, would cause the U.S.S.R. to sue for terms or prevent Soviet forces from occupying Western Europe against such ground resistance as could presently be mobilized. A very serious initial blow could, however, so reduce the capabilities of the U.S.S.R. to supply and equip its military organization and its civilian population as to give the United States the prospect of developing a general military superiority in a war of long duration.

2. As the atomic capability of the U.S.S.R. increases, it will have an increased ability to hit at our atomic bases and installations and thus seriously hamper the ability of the United States to carry out an attack such as that outlined above. It is quite possible that in the near future the U.S.S.R. will have a sufficient number of atomic bombs and a sufficient deliverability to raise a question whether Britain

with its present inadequate air defense could be relied upon as an advance base from which a major portion of the U.S. attack could be launched.

It is estimated that, within the next four years, the U.S.S.R. will attain the capability of seriously damaging vital centers of the United States, provided it strikes a surprise blow and provided further that the blow is opposed by no more effective opposition than we now have programmed. Such a blow could so seriously damage the United States as to greatly reduce its superiority in economic potential.

Effective opposition to this Soviet capability will require among other measures greatly increased air warning systems, air defenses, and vigorous development and implementation of a civilian defense program which has been thoroughly integrated with the military defense systems.

In time the atomic capability of the U.S.S.R. can be expected to grow to a point where, given surprise and no more effective opposition than we now have programmed, the possibility of a decisive initial attack cannot be excluded.

3. In the initial phases of an atomic war, the advantages of initiative and surprise would be very great. A police state living behind an iron curtain has an enormous advantage in maintaining the necessary security and centralization of decision required to capitalize on this advantage.

4. For the moment our atomic retaliatory capability is probably adequate to deter the Kremlin from a deliberate direct military attack against ourselves or other free peoples. However, when it calculates that it has a sufficient atomic capability to make a surprise attack on us, nullifying our atomic superiority and creating a military situation decisively in its favor, the Kremlin might be tempted to strike swiftly and with stealth. The existence of two large atomic capabilities in such a relationship might well act, therefore, not as a deterrent, but as an incitement to war.

5. A further increase in the number and power of our atomic weapons is necessary in order to assure the effectiveness of any U.S. retaliatory blow, but would not of itself seem to change the basic logic of the above points. Greatly increased general air, ground and sea strength, and increased air defense and civilian defense programs would also be necessary to provide reasonable assurance that the free world could survive an initial surprise atomic attack of the weight which it is estimated the U.S.S.R. will be capable of delivering by 1954 and still permit the free world to go on to the eventual attainment of its objectives. Furthermore, such a build-up of strength could safeguard and increase our retaliatory power, and thus might put off for some time the date when the Soviet Union could calculate that a surprise blow would be advantageous. This would provide additional time for the effects of our policies to produce a modification of the Soviet system.

6. If the U.S.S.R. develops a thermonuclear weapon ahead of the U.S., the risks of greatly increased Soviet pressure against all the free world, or an attack against the U.S., will be greatly increased.

7. If the U.S. develops a thermonuclear weapon ahead of the U.S.S.R., the U.S. should for the time being be able to bring increased pressure on the U.S.S.R.

B. Stockpiling and Use of Atomic Weapons

1. From the foregoing analysis it appears that it would be to the long-term advantage of the United States if atomic weapons were to be effectively eliminated from national peacetime armaments;... In the absence of such elimination and the securing of these objectives, it would appear that we have no alternative but to increase our atomic capability as rapidly as other considerations make appropriate. In either case, it appears to be imperative to increase as rapidly as possible our general air, ground and sea strength and that of our allies to a point where we are militarily not so heavily dependent on atomic weapons....

Conclusions

The foregoing analysis indicates that the probable fission bomb capability of the Soviet Union has greatly intensified the Soviet threat to the security of the United States. This threat is of the same character as the threat described in NSC 20/4 (approved by the President on November 24, 1948) but is more immediate than had previously been estimated. In particular, the United States now faces the contingency that within the next four or five years the Soviet Union will possess the military capability of delivering a surprise atomic attack of such weight that the United States must have substantially increased general air, ground, and sea strength, atomic capabilities, and air and civilian defenses to deter war and to provide reasonable assurance, in the event of war, that it could survive the initial blow and go on to the eventual attainment of its objectives. In turn, this contingency requires the intensification of our efforts in the fields of intelligence and research and development....

In the light of present and prospective Soviet atomic capabilities, the action which can be taken under present programs and plans, however, becomes dangerously inadequate, in both timing and scope, to accomplish the rapid progress towards the attainment of the United States political, economic, and military objectives which is now imperative.

A continuation of present trends would result in a serious decline in the strength of the free world relative to the Soviet Union and its satellites. This unfavorable trend arises from the inadequacy of current programs and plans rather than from any error in our objectives and aims. These trends lead in the direction of isolation not by deliberate decision but by lack of the necessary basis for a vigorous initiative in the conflict with the Soviet Union.

Our position as the center of power in the free world places a heavy responsibility upon the United States for leadership. We must organize and enlist the energies and resources of the free world in a positive program for peace which will frustrate the Kremlin design for world domination by creating a situation in the free world to which the Kremlin will be compelled to adjust. Without such a cooperative effort, led by the United States, we will have to make gradual withdrawals under pressure until we discover one day that we have sacrificed positions of vital interest.

It is imperative that this trend be reversed by a much more rapid and concerted build-up of the actual strength of both the United States and the other nations of the free world. The analysis shows that this will be costly and will involve significant domestic financial and economic adjustments.

The execution of such a build-up, however, requires that the United States have an affirmative program beyond the solely defensive one of countering the threat posed by the Soviet Union. This program must light the path to peace and order among nations in a system based on freedom and justice, as contemplated in the Charter of the United Nations. Further, it must envisage the political and economic measure with which and the military shield behind which the free world can work to frustrate the Kremlin design by the strategy of the cold war; for every consideration of devotion to our fundamental values and to our national security demands that we achieve our objectives by the strategy of the cold war, building up our military strength in order that it may not have to be used. The only sure victory lies in the frustration of the Kremlin design by the steady development of the moral and material strength by the free world and its projection into the Soviet world in such a way as to bring about an internal change in the Soviet system. Such a positive program—harmonious with our fundamental national purpose and our objectives—is necessary if we are to regain and retain the initiative and to win and hold the necessary popular support and cooperation in the United States and the rest of the free world.

This program should include a plan for negotiation with the Soviet Union, developed and agreed with our allies and which is consonant with our objectives. The United States and its allies, particularly the United Kingdom and France, should always be ready to negotiate with the Soviet Union on terms consistent with our objectives. The present world situation, however, is one which militates against successful negotiations with the Kremlin—for the terms of agreements on important pending issues would reflect present realities and would therefore be unacceptable, if not disastrous, to the United States and the rest of the free world. After a decision and a start on building up the strength of the free world has been made, it might then be desirable for the United States to take an initiative in seeking negotiations in the hope that it might facilitate the process of accommodation by the Kremlin to the new situation. Failing that, the unwillingness of the Kremlin to accept equitable terms or its bad faith in observing them would assist in consolidating popular opinion in the free world in support of the measures necessary to sustain the build-up.

In summary, we must, by means of a rapid and sustained build-up of the political, economic, and military strength of the free world, and by means of an affirmative program intended to wrest the initiative from the Soviet Union, confront it with convincing evidence of the determination and ability of the free world to frustrate the Kremlin design of a world dominated by its will. Such evidence is the only means short of war which eventually may force the Kremlin to abandon its present course of action and to negotiate acceptable agreements on issues of major importance.

The whole success of the proposed program hangs ultimately on recognition by this Government, the American people, and all free peoples, that the cold war is in fact a real war in which the survival of the free world is at stake. Essential prerequisites to success are consultations with Congressional leaders designed to make the program the object of non-partisan legislative support, and a presentation to the public of a full explanation of the facts and implications of the present international situation. The prosecution of the program will require of us all the ingenuity of the issue and the tenacity to persevere until our national objectives have been attained.

Source: National Security Council. "NSC-68: U.S. Objectives and Programs for National Security," April 14, 1950. *Foreign Relations of the United States 1950*, Vol. 4. Washington, DC: Government Printing Office, 1981.

7.2
The U-2 Spy Plane Affair – 1960
The Text of a Soviet Telegram Detailing the Capture of an American U-2 Reconnaissance Plane

In the fall of 1959 Soviet Premier Nikita Khrushchev accepted an invitation from President Dwight Eisenhower to visit the United States. During the Soviet leader's visit, the two men agreed to hold a summit meeting in Paris in 1960. Shortly before the Paris summit was scheduled to begin, however, Soviet forces shot down an American U-2 spy plane flown by U. S. pilot Gary Francis Powers. U-2 military reconnaissance flights had provided American officials with valuable intelligence over the previous few years, but the capture of Powers was enormously embarrassing to the Eisenhower White House—especially after its initial claim that the pilot had not been on a spy mission was exposed as a blatant falsehood. The U-2 incident also prompted the cancellation of the Paris summit, and it ushered in an era of renewed hostility in the Cold War. Following is the text of a telegram from the Kremlin to Washington, D.C., detailing the events surrounding the U-2 incident.

From: Moscow

To: Secretary of State

No: 2780, MAY 10, 3 PM (SECTION ONE OF THREE)

FOLLOWING EMB TRANSLATION SOVIET NOTE 39/OSA, DATED MAY 10 WITH UNESSENTIAL WORDS DELETED:

GOVT USSR CONSIDERS NECESSARY STATE FOLLOWING TO GOVT USA:

ON MAY 1 OF THIS YEAR AT 5 HOURS 36 MINUTES MOSCOW TIME A MILITARY AIRCRAFT VIOLATED BOUNDARY USSR AND INTRUDED ACROSS BORDERS OF SOVIET UNION FOR DISTANCE OF MORE THAN 2,000 KILO-METERS. GOVT USSR NATURALLY COULD NOT LEAVE UNPUNISHED SUCH A FLAGRANT VIOLATION OF SOVIET STATE BOUNDARIES. WHEN INTEN-TIONS OF VIOLATING AIRCRAFT BECAME APPARENT, IT WAS SHOT DOWN BY SOVIET ROCKET TROOPS IN AREA OF SVERDLOVSK.

UPON EXAMINATION BY EXPERTS OF ALL DATA AT DISPOSAL OF SOVIET SIDE, IT WAS INCONTROVERTIBLY ESTABLISHED THAT INTRUDER AIRCRAFT BELONGED TO USA, WAS PERMANENTLY BASED IN TURKEY AND WAS SENT THROUGH PAKISTAN INTO SOV UNION WITH HOSTILE PURPOSES.

AS CHAIRMAN OF USSR COUNCIL MINISTERS N. S. KHRUSHCHEV MADE PUBLIC ON MAY 7 AT FINAL SESSION OF USSR SUPREME SOVIET, EXACT DATA FROM INVESTIGATION LEAVE NO DOUBTS WITH RESPECT TO PURPOSE OF FLIGHT OF AMERICAN AIRCRAFT WHICH VIOLATED THE USSR BORDER ON MAY 1. THIS AIRCRAFT WAS SPECIALLY EQUIPPED FOR RECONNAISSANCE AND DIVERSIONARY FLIGHT OVER TERRITORY OF SOVIET UNION. IT HAD ON BOARD APPARATUS FOR AERIAL PHOTOGRA-PHY FOR DETECTING SOVIET RADAR NETWORK AND OTHER SPECIAL RADIO-TECHNICAL EQUIPMENT WHICH FORM PART OF USSR ANTI-AIR-CRAFT DEFENSES. AT DISPOSAL OF SOVIET EXPERT COMMISSION WHICH CARRIED OUT INVESTIGATION, THERE IS INDISPUTABLE PROOF OF ESPI-ONAGE-RECONNAISANCE MISSION OF THE AMERICAN AIRCRAFT: FILMS OF SOVIET DEFENSE AND INDUSTRIAL ESTABLISHMENTS, A TAPE RECORDING OF SIGNALS OF SOVIET RADAR STATIONS AND OTHER DATA.

PILOT POWERS, ABOUT WHOSE FATE EMB OF USA INQUIRED IN ITS NOTE OF MAY 6, IS ALIVE AND, AS INDICATED IN AFOREMENTIONED SPEECH OF CHAIRMAN OF USSR COUNCIL OF MINISTERS N. S. KHRUSHCHEV, WILL BE BROUGHT TO ACCOUNT UNDER LAWS OF SOV STATE. PILOT HAS INDICATED THAT HE DID EVERYTHING IN FULL ACCOR-DANCE WITH ASSIGNMENT GIVEN HIM. ON FLIGHT MAP TAKEN FROM HIM THERE WAS CLEARLY AND ACCURATELY MARKED ENTIRE ROUTE HE

WAS ASSIGNED AFTER TAKE OFF FROM CITY OF ADADN (TURKEY): PESHAWAR (PAKISTAN)-THE URAL SEA-SVERDLOVSK-ARCHANGEL-MURMANSK, FOLLOWED BY A LANDING AT NORWEGIAN AIRFIELD AT BUDE. PILOT HAS ALSO STATED THAT HE SERVED IN SUBUNIT NUMBER 10-10 WHICH UNDER COVER OF NATIONAL AERONAUTICS AND SPACE AGENCY IS ENGAGED IN HIGH ALTITUDE MILITARY RECONNAISANCE.

THIS AND OTHER INFO REVEALED IN SPEECHES OF HEAD OF SOVIET GOVT COMPLETELY REFUTED US STATE DEPT'S CONCOCTED AND HURRIEDLY FABRICATED VERSION, RELEASED MAY 5 IN OFFICIAL ANNOUNCEMENT FOR PRESS, TO EFFECT THAT AIRCRAFT WAS ALLEGEDLY CARRYING OUT METEOROLOGICAL OBSERVATIONS IN UPPER STRATA OF ATMOSPHERE ALONG TURKISH-SOVIET BORDER.

AFTER COMPLETE ABSURDITY OF AFOREMENTIONED VERSION HAD BEEN SHOWN AND IT HAD BEEN INCONTROVERTIBLY PROVEN THAT AMERICAN AIRCRAFT INTRUDED ACROSS BORDERS OF SOVIET UNION FOR AGGRESSIVE RECONNAISSANCE PURPOSES, A NEW ANNOUNCEMENT WAS MADE BY US STATE DEPT ON MAY 8 WHICH CONTAINED THE FORCED ADMISSION THAT AIRCRAFT WAS SENT INTO SOV UNION FOR MILITARY RECONNAISSANCE PURPOSES AND, BY THAT VERY FACT, IT WAS ADMITTED THAT FLIGHT WAS PURSUINIG AGGRESSIVE PURPOSES.

IN THIS WAY, AFTER THREE DAYS, THE STATE DEPT ALREADY HAD TO DENY VERSION WHICH OBVIOUSLY HAD BEEN INTENDED TO MISLEAD WORLD PUBLIC OPINION AS WELL AS PUBLIC OPINION OF AMERICAN [sic] ITSELF.

STATE DEPT CONSIDERED IT INAPPROPRIATE TO REFER IN ITS ANNOUNCEMENT TO "OPEN SKIES" PROPOSAL MADE BY GOVT OF USA IN 1955 AND TO REFUSAL OF SOV GOVT TO ACCEPT THIS PROPOSAL. YES, SOV GOVT, LIKE GOVTS OF MANY OTHER STATES, REFUSED TO ACCEPT THIS PROPOSAL WHICH WAS INTENDED TO THROW OPEN DOORS OF OTHER NATIONS TO AMERICAN RECONNAISSANCE. ACTIVITIES OF AMERICAN AVIATION ONLY CONFIRM CORRECTNESS OF EVALUATION GIVEN TO THIS PROPOSAL AT TIME BY SOV GOVT.

(SECTION TWO OF THREE)

DOES THIS NOT RPT NOT MEAN THAT, WITH REFUSAL OF NUMBER OF STATES TO ACCEPT THIS PROPOSAL FOR "OPEN SKIES," USA IS ATTEMPTING ARBITRARILY TO TAKE UPON ITSELF RIGHT "TO OPEN" A FOREIGN SKY? IT IS ENOUGH TO PUT QUESTION THIS WAY, FOR THE COMPLETE GROUNDLESSNESS OF AFOREMENTIONED REFERENCE TO THE USA "OPEN SKIES" PROPOSAL TO BECOME CLEAR.

IT FOLLOWS FROM AFOREMENTIONED MAY 8 ANNOUNCEMENT OF USA STATE DEPARTMENT THAT HOSTILE ACTS OF AMERICAN AVIATION, WHICH HAVE TAKEN PLACE NUMEROUS TIMES IN RELATION TO SOVIET UNION, ARE NOT SIMPLY RESULT OF ACTIVITY OF MILITARY COMMANDS OF USA IN VARIOUS AREAS BUT ARE EXPRESSION OF A CALCULATED USA POLICY. THAT WHICH SOV GOVT HAS REPEATEDLY DECLARED IN ITS REPRESENTATIONS TO GOVT OF USA IN CONNECTION WITH VIOLATIONS OF USSR NATIONAL BOUNDARIES BY AMERICAN AIRPLANES HAS BEEN CONFIRMED, NAMELY, THAT THESE VIOLATIONS ARE PREMEDITATED. ALL THIS TESTIFIES THAT GOVT OF USA, INSTEAD OF TAKING MEASURES TO STOP SUCH ACTIONS BY AMERICAN AVIATION, DANGER OF WHICH HAS MORE THAN ONCE BEEN POINTED OUT BY SOV GOVT, OFFICIALLY ANNOUNCES SUCH ACTIONS AS ITS NATIONAL POLICY.

THUS, THE GOVT OF THE USA, IN FIRST PLACE, TESTIFIES TO FACT THAT ITS ANSWERS TO REPRESENTATIONS OF SOV GOVT WERE ONLY FOR SAKE OF FORM, BEHIND WHICH WAS CONCEALED EFFORT TO AVOID SUBSTANCE OF ISSUE, AND THAT ALL VIOLATIONS BY AMERICAN AIRCRAFT OF NATIONAL BOUNDARIES OF USSR REPRESENTED ACTIONS CONFORMING TO USA POLICY.

IN SECOND PLACE, AND THIS IS MAIN POINT, BY SANCTIONING SUCH ACTIONS OF AMERICAN AVIATION, GOVT OF USA AGGRAVATES SITUATION EVEN MORE.

ONE MUST ASK, HOW IS IT POSSIBLE TO RECONCILE THIS WITH DECLARATIONS ON PART OF LEADING FIGURES OF USA, THAT GOVT OF USA LIKE SOV GOVT, ALSO STRIVES FOR IMPROVEMENT OF RELATIONS BETWEEN USSR AND USA, FOR RELAXATION INTERNATIONAL TENSION, AND STENGTHENING [sic] OF TRUST BETWEEN STATES. MILITARY INTELLIGENCE ACTIVITIES OF ONE NATION BY MEANS OF INTRUSION OF ITS AIRCRAFT INTO AREA OF ANOTHER COUNTRY CAN HARDLY BE CALLED METHOD FOR IMPROVING RELATIONS AND STRENGTHENING TRUST.

IT IS SELF-EVIDENT THAT SOV GOVT IS COMPELLED, UNDER SUCH CIRCUMSTANCES, GIVE STRICT ORDERS TO ITS ARMED FORCES TO TAKE ALL NECESSARY MEASURES AGAINST VIOLATION OF SOV BOUNDARIES BY FOREIGN AVIATION. GOVT OF USA REGRETFULLY STATES THAT, WHILE IT UNDERTAKES EVERYTHING POSSIBLE FOR NORMALIZATION AND IMPROVEMENT OF INTERNATIONAL SITUATION, GOVT OF USA FOLLOWS DIFFERENT PATH. IT IS IMPOSSIBLE TO EXCLUDE THOUGHT THAT, APPARENTLY, TWO GOVTS VIEW DIFFERENTLY NECESSITY FOR IMPROVING RELATIONS BETWEEN OUR COUNTRIES AND FOR CREATION OF FAVORABLE GROUND FOR SUCCESS OF FORTHCOMING SUMMIT MEETING.

THE SOV GOVT, AS WELL AS ALL OF SOV PEOPLE, CONSIDERED THAT PERSONAL MEETINGS AND DISCUSSIONS WITH PRESIDENT OF USA AND OTHER AMERICAN OFFICIAL FIGURES WHICH CHAIRMAN OR COUNCIL MINISTERS OF USSR HAD DURING HIS VISIT IN USA, MADE GOOD BEGINNING IN CAUSE OF NORMALIZING SOVIET-AMERICAN RELATIONS AND THEREFORE IMPROVEMENT OF ENTIRE INTERNATIONAL SITUATION AS WELL. HOWEVER, LATEST ACTIONS OF AMERICAN AUTHORITIES APPARENTLY SEEK TO RETURN STATE OF AMERICAN-SOVIET RELATIONS TO WORST TIMES OF "COLD WAR" AND TO POISON INTERNATIONAL SITUATION BEFORE SUMMIT MEETING.

GOVT OF USSR CANNOT AVOID POINTING OUT THAT, STATE DEPARTMENT'S STATEMENT, WHICH IS UNPRECEDENTED IN ITS CYNICISM, NOT ONLY JUSTIFIES PROVOCATIVE FLIGHTS OF AIRCRAFT OF ARMED FORCES OF USA BUT ALSO ACKNOWLEDGES THAT SUCH ACTIONS ARE "A NORMAL PHENOMENON" AND THUS IN FACT STATES THAT IN FUTURE US INTENDS TO CONTINUE PROVOCATIVE INVASIONS INTO CONFINES OF AIRSPACE OF SOVIET UNION FOR PURPOSE OF INTELLIGENCE.

(SECTION THREE OF THREE)

THUS GOVT OF USSR CONCLUDES THAT ANNOUNCEMENT OF STATE DEPT THAT FLIGHT WAS CARRIED OUT WITHOUT KNOWLEDGE AND PERMISSION OF GOVT OF USA DOES NOT CORRESPOND TO REALITY, SINCE IN VERY SAME ANNOUNCEMENT NECESSITY FOR CARRYING ON INTELLIGENCE ACTIVITIES AGAINST SOVIET UNION IS JUSTIFIED. THIS MEANS THAT ESPIONAGE ACTIVITIES OF AMERICAN AIRCRAFT ARE CARRIED ON WITH SANCTION OF GOVT OF USA.

GOVT OF SOV UNION MADE AN EMPHATIC PROTEST TO GOVT OF USA IN CONNECTION WITH AGGRESSIVE ACTS OF AMERICAN AVIATION AND WARNS THAT, IF SIMILAR PROVOCATIONS ARE REPEATED, IT WILL BE OBLIGED TO TAKE RETALIATORY MEASURES, RESPONSIBILITY FOR CONSEQUENCES OF WHICH WILL REST ON GOVTS OF STATES COMMITTING AGGRESSION AGAINST OTHER COUNTRIES.

THE SOV GOVT WOULD SINCERELY LIKE TO HOPE THAT GOVT OF USA RECOGNIZES IN FINAL ANALYSIS THAT INTERESTS OF PRESERVING AND STRENGTHENING PEACE AMONG PEOPLES INCLUDING INTERESTS OF AMERICAN PEOPLE ITSELF, WHOSE STRIVING FOR PEACE WAS WELL DEMONSTRATED DURING VISIT OF HEAD OF SOVIET GOVT N. S. KHRUSHCHEV TO USA, WOULD BE SERVED BY CESSATION OF AFOREMENTIONED DANGEROUS PROVOCATIVE ACTIVITIES WITH REGARD TO USSR, BY CESSATION OF "COLD WAR," AND BY A SEARCH THROUGH JOINT EFFORTS WITH SOV UNION AND WITH OTHER INTERESTED STATES FOR

SOLUTION OF UNSETTLED INTERNATIONAL PROBLEMS, ON MUTUALLY ACCEPTABLE BASIS, WHICH IS AWAITED BY ALL PEOPLES.

Source: "Telegram from American Embassy in Moscow to Secretary of State Transmitting Ttranslation of Soviet Note Concerning U-2 Spy Plane" May 10, 1960. Dwight Eisenhower Presidential Library. Available online at http://www.eisenhower.utexas.edu/dl/U2Incident/U2documents.html.

7.3
The Strategy of "Massive Retaliation" – 1954
Excerpts from a Speech by U.S. Secretary of State John Foster Dulles

Longtime U.S. Secretary of State John Foster Dulles's foreign policy views rested upon two main philosophical pillars: "massive retaliation" against Communist aggression wherever it cropped up around the world, and bold assistance to democratic movements in regions already under Communist control. Dulles explained his thoughts on the first of these two bedrock principles in the following excerpt from a speech to the Council on Foreign Relations on January 12, 1954.

We live in a world where emergencies are always possible, and our survival may depend upon our capacity to meet emergencies. Let us pray that we shall always have that capacity. But, having said that, it is necessary also to say that emergency measures—however good for the emergency—do not necessarily make good permanent policies. Emergency measures are costly; they are superficial; and they imply that the enemy has the initiative. They cannot be depended on to serve our long-time interests. This "long-time" factor is of critical importance.

The Soviet Communists are planning for what they call "an entire historical era," and we should do the same. They seek through many types of maneuvers, gradually to divide and weaken the free nations by overextending them in efforts which, as Lenin put it, are "beyond their strength, so that they come to practical bankruptcy." Then, said Lenin, "our victory is assured." Then, said Stalin, will be "the moment for the decisive blow."

In the face of this strategy, measures cannot be judged adequate merely because they ward off an immediate danger. It is essential to do this, but it is also essential to do so without exhausting ourselves.

When the Eisenhower administration applied this test, we felt that some transformations were needed.

It is not sound military strategy permanently to commit U.S. land forces to Asia to a degree that leaves us no strategic reserves. It is not sound economics or

215

good foreign policy to support permanently other countries; for, in the long run, that creates as much ill will as goodwill. Also, it is not sound to become permanently committed to military expenditures so vast that they lead to "practical bankruptcy."

Change was imperative to assure the stamina needed for permanent security. But it was equally imperative that change should be accompanied by understanding of our true purposes. Sudden and spectacular change had to be avoided. Otherwise, there might have been a panic among our friends and miscalculated aggression by our enemies. We can, I believe, make a good report in these respects.

We need allies and collective security. Our purpose is to make these relations more effective, less costly. This can be done by placing more reliance on deterrent power and less dependence on local defensive power. This is accepted practice so far as local communities are concerned. We keep locks on our doors, but we do not have an armed guard in every home. We rely principally on a community security system so well equipped to punish any who break in and steal that, in fact, would-be aggressors are generally deterred. That is the modern way of getting maximum protection at a bearable cost.

What the Eisenhower administration seeks is a similar international security system. We want, for ourselves and the other free nations, a maximum deterrent at a bearable cost.

Local defense will always be important. But there is no local defense which alone will contain the mighty landpower of the Communist world. Local defenses must be reinforced by the further deterrent of massive retaliatory power. A potential aggressor must know that he cannot always prescribe battle conditions that suit him. Otherwise, for example, a potential aggressor, who is glutted with manpower, might be tempted to attack in places where his superiority was decisive.

The way to deter aggression is for the free community to be willing and able to respond vigorously at places and with means of its own choosing.

So long as our basic policy concepts were unclear, our military leaders could not be selective in building our military power. If an enemy could pick his time and place and method of warfare—and if our policy was to remain the traditional one of meeting aggression by direct and local opposition—then we needed to be ready to fight in the Arctic and in the Tropics; in Asia, the Near East, and in Europe; by sea, by land, and by air; with old weapons and with new weapons.

The total cost of our security efforts, at home and abroad, was over $50 billion per annum, and involved, for 1953, a projected budgetary deficit of $9 billion; and $11 billion for 1954. This was on top of taxes comparable to wartime taxes; and the dollar was depreciating in effective value. Our allies were similarly weighed down. This could not be continued for long without grave budgetary, economic, and social consequences.

But before military planning could be changed, the President and his advisers, as represented by the National Security Council, had to make some basic policy decisions. This has been done. The basic decision was to depend primarily upon a great capacity to retaliate, instantly by means and at places of our choosing. Now the Department of Defense and the Joint Chiefs of Staff can shape our military establishment to fit what is *our* policy instead of having to try to be ready to meet the enemy's many choices....

We do not, of course, claim to have found some magic formula that insures against all forms of Communist successes. It is normal that at some times and at some places there may be setbacks to the cause of freedom. What we do expect to insure is that any setbacks will have only temporary and local significance, because they will leave unimpaired those free-world assets which in the long run will prevail.

If we can deter such aggression as would mean general war, and that is our confident resolve, then we can let time and fundamentals work for us. We do not need self-imposed policies which sap our strength.

The fundamental, on our side, is the richness—spiritual, intellectual, and material—that freedom can produce and the irresistible attraction it then sets up. That is why we do not plan ourselves to shackle freedom to preserve freedom. We intend that our conduct and example shall continue, as in the past, to show all men how good can be the fruits of freedom.

If we rely on freedom, then it follows that we must abstain from diplomatic moves which would seem to endorse captivity. That would, in effect, be a conspiracy against freedom. I can assure you that we shall never seek illusory security for ourselves by such a "deal." We do not negotiate about specific matters but only to advance the cause of human welfare.

President Eisenhower electrified the world with his proposal to lift a great weight of fear by turning atomic energy from a means of death into a source of life. Yesterday, I started procedural talks with the Soviet government on that topic.

We have persisted, with our allies, in seeking the unification of Germany and the liberation of Austria. Now the Soviet rulers have agreed to discuss these questions. We expect to meet them soon in Berlin. I hope they will come with a sincerity which will equal our own.

We have sought a conference to unify Korea and relieve it of foreign troops. So far, our persistence is unrewarded; but we have not given up.

These efforts at negotiation are normal initiatives that breathe the spirit of freedom. They involve no plan for a partnership division of world power with those who suppress freedom.

If we persist in the courses I outline, we shall confront dictatorship with a task that is, in the long run, beyond its strength. For unless it changes, it must suppress the human desires that freedom satisfies—as we shall be demonstrating. If the dicta-

217

tors persist in their present course, then it is they who will be limited to superficial successes, while their foundation crumbles under the tread of their iron boots.

Source: Dulles, John Foster. Speech to the Council on Foreign Relations, January 12, 1954. *Department of State Bulletin,* January 25, 1954.

7.4

Eisenhower Decries the Military-Industrial Complex – 1961
Excerpts from Dwight Eisenhower's Farewell Address

> *At the end of his tenure as president, Dwight Eisenhower—a former World War II military hero—gave a remarkable speech in which he explicitly warned of the unhealthy influence of the "military-industrial complex" on American politics and society. Noting that the defense industry was a major factor in America's economic boom of the 1950s—by 1960 defense spending accounted for more than half of all federal expenditure—he warned that if this state of affairs continued, it could warp the nation's foreign and domestic policies for years to come. Following are excerpts from Eisenhower's speech.*

Throughout America's adventure in free government, our basic purposes have been to keep the peace; to foster progress in human achievement, and to enhance liberty, dignity and integrity among people and among nations. To strive for less would be unworthy of a free and religious people. Any failure traceable to arrogance, or our lack of comprehension or readiness to sacrifice would inflict upon us grievous hurt both at home and abroad.

Progress toward these noble goals is persistently threatened by the conflict now engulfing the world. It commands our whole attention, absorbs our very beings. We face a hostile ideology — global in scope, atheistic in character, ruthless in purpose, and insidious in method. Unhappily the danger it poses promises to be of indefinite duration. To meet it successfully, there is called for, not so much the emotional and transitory sacrifices of crisis, but rather those which enable us to carry forward steadily, surely, and without complaint the burdens of a prolonged and complex struggle — with liberty the stake. Only thus shall we remain, despite every provocation, on our charted course toward permanent peace and human betterment.

Crises there will continue to be. In meeting them, whether foreign or domestic, great or small, there is a recurring temptation to feel that some spectacular and costly action could become the miraculous solution to all current difficulties. A huge increase in newer elements of our defense; development of unrealistic programs to cure every ill in agriculture; a dramatic expansion in basic and applied research — these and many other possibilities, each possibly promising in itself, may be suggested as the only way to the road we wish to travel.

But each proposal must be weighed in the light of a broader consideration: the need to maintain balance in and among national programs — balance between the private and the public economy, balance between cost and hoped for advantage — balance between the clearly necessary and the comfortably desirable; balance between our essential requirements as a nation and the duties imposed by the nation upon the individual; balance between actions of the moment and the national welfare of the future.

Good judgment seeks balance and progress; lack of it eventually finds imbalance and frustration.

The record of many decades stands as proof that our people and their government have, in the main, understood these truths and have responded to them well, in the face of stress and threat. But threats, new in kind or degree, constantly arise. I mention two only.

A vital element in keeping the peace is our military establishment. Our arms must be mighty, ready for instant action, so that no potential aggressor may be tempted to risk his own destruction. Our military organization today bears little relation to that known by any of my predecessors in peacetime, or indeed by the fighting men of World War II or Korea.

Until the latest of our world conflicts, the United States had no armaments industry. American makers of plowshares could, with time and as required, make swords as well. But now we can no longer risk emergency improvisation of national defense; we have been compelled to create a permanent armaments industry of vast proportions. Added to this, three and a half million men and women are directly engaged in the defense establishment. We annually spend on military security more than the net income of all United States corporations. This conjunction of an immense military establishment and a large arms industry is new in the American experience. The total influence — economic, political, even spiritual — is felt in every city, every State house, every office of the Federal government.

We recognize the imperative need for this development. Yet we must not fail to comprehend its grave implications. Our toil, resources and livelihood are all involved; so is the very structure of our society.

In the councils of government, we must guard against the acquisition of unwarranted influence, whether sought or unsought, by the military industrial complex. The potential for the disastrous rise of misplaced power exists and will persist.

We must never let the weight of this combination endanger our liberties or democratic processes. We should take nothing for granted. Only an alert and knowledgeable citizenry can compel the proper meshing of the huge industrial and military machinery of defense with our peaceful methods and goals, so that security and liberty may prosper together....

Source: Eisenhower, Dwight D. Farewell speech given on January 17, 1961. *Public Papers of the Presidents of the United States: Dwight D. Eisenhower, 1960-1961.* Washington, DC: Office of the Federal Register, 1961.

7.5
A Call to Victory in the Cold War – 1961
Excerpts from a Speech by U.S. Senator Barry Goldwater

One of the fiercest anti-Communist voices in the United States during the 1950s and 1960s was conservative Senator Barry Goldwater of Arizona. Goldwater—who went on to become the Republican candidate for President in 1964—was at the vanguard of an influential group of policymakers and analysts who believed that "peaceful coexistence" between the United States and the Soviet Union was impossible. Instead, they asserted that the Cold War was essentially a struggle to the death. With that in mind, they called for major new investments in the U.S. military and dismissed efforts to improve relations with the Soviets through diplomacy. In the following excerpt from a July 14, 1961, speech he made on the floor of the Senate, Goldwater urges President Kennedy and his colleagues to pursue a strategy of "total victory" over the Communists.

.... Mr. President, it is really astounding that our government has never stated its purpose to be that of complete victory over the tyrannical forces of international communism. I am sure that the American people cannot understand why we spend billions upon billions of dollars to engage in a struggle of worldwide proportions unless we have a clearly defined purpose to achieve victory. Anything less than victory, over the long run, can only be defeat, degradation, and slavery. Are these stakes not high enough for us? Is not this reason enough for us to fight to win?

I suggest that our failure to declare total victory as our fundamental purpose is a measure of an official timidity that refuses to recognize the all-embracing determination of communism to capture the world and destroy the United States. This timidity has sold us short, time and time again. It denied us victory in the Korean War, when victory was there for the taking. It refused General MacArthur the right to prosecute a war for the purpose of winning, and caused him to utter these prophetic words:

The best that might be said for the policy makers responsible for these monumental blunders is that they did not comprehend the truism, as old as history itself, that a great nation which voluntarily enters upon war and does not fight it through to victory must ultimately accept all of the consequences of defeat—that in war, there is no substitute for victory.

Mr. President, we would do well to heed those words of General MacArthur, and apply them to the present—apply them to our position in the cold war, for if we engage in this cold war, and we do not fight it through to victory, we must be prepared to accept the consequences of defeat. And the consequences of such a defeat, I can assure you, Mr. President, will be slavery for all the peoples of the world....

Source: Goldwater, Barry. Remarks of July 14, 1961. *Congressional Record*, 87th Congress, 1st session, 1961.

7.6
"The Strategy of Peace" – 1963
Excerpts from President Kennedy's Address at The American University

In October 1962, the Soviet Union placed nuclear missiles in Cuba, about 100 miles from the coast of Florida. President John F. Kennedy insisted on their removal. The Cuban Missile Crisis brought the United States and the Soviet Union to the brink of nuclear war. That showdown clearly had an impact on Kennedy's view of the Cold War, for eight months later, he delivered a commencement address at American University, excerpted below. In this speech, titled "The Strategy of Peace," Kennedy defied the hawkish atmosphere in the United States by calling for new efforts to establish civil relations with Communist powers and defuse the Cold War. One centerpiece of Kennedy's speech, for example, explicitly called for the adoption of a nuclear test ban to slow down the arms race. Conservative critics in America and Europe decried the speech's tone as naïve and soft. But the Kremlin released most—but not all—of the speech in Russian, and the British newspaper the Manchester Guardian *described it as "one of the great state papers of American history." Following are excerpts from Kennedy's address on June 10, 1963.*

I have ... chosen this time and this place to discuss a topic on which ignorance too often abounds and the truth is too rarely perceived—yet it is the most important topic on earth: world peace.

What kind of peace do I mean? What kind of peace do we seek? Not a *Pax Americana* enforced on the world by American weapons of war. Not the peace of the grave or the security of the slave. I am talking about genuine peace, the kind of

221

peace that makes life on earth worth living, the kind that enables men and nations to grow and to hope and to build a better life for their children—not merely peace for Americans but peace for all men and women, not merely peace in our time but peace for all time.

First: Let us examine our attitude toward peace itself. Too many of us think it is impossible. Too many think it unreal. But that is a dangerous, defeatist belief. It leads to the conclusion that war is inevitable, that mankind is doomed, that we are gripped by forces we cannot control.

We need not accept that view. Our problems are manmade; therefore they can be solved by man. And man can be as big as he wants. No problem of human destiny is beyond human beings. Man's reason and spirit have often solved the seemingly unsolvable, and we believe they can do it again.

I am not referring to the absolute, infinite concept of universal peace and good will of which some fantasies and fanatics dream. I do not deny the values of hopes and dreams, but we merely invite discouragement and incredulity by making that our only and immediate goal.

Let us focus instead on a more practical, more attainable peace, based not on a sudden revolution in human nature but on a gradual evolution in human institutions—on a series of concrete actions and effective agreements which are in the interest of all concerned.

There is no single, simple key to this peace, no grand or magic formula to be adopted by one or two powers. Genuine peace must be the product of many nations, the sum of many acts. It must be dynamic, not static, changing to meet the challenge of each new generation. For peace is a process, a way of solving problems.

With such a peace there will still be quarrels and conflicting interests, as there are within families and nations. World peace, like community peace, does not require that each man love his neighbor; it requires only that they live together in mutual tolerance, submitting their disputes to a just and peaceful settlement....

Second: Let us reexamine our attitude toward the Soviet Union.

No government or social system is so evil that its people must be considered as lacking in virtue. As Americans we find communism profoundly repugnant as a negation of personal freedom and dignity. But we can still hail the Russian people for their many achievements—in science and space, in economic and industrial growth, in culture and in acts of courage.

Among the many traits the peoples of our two countries have in common, none is stronger than our mutual abhorrence of war. Almost unique among the major world powers, we have never been at war with each other. And no nation in the history of battle ever suffered more than the Soviet Union suffered in the course of the Second World War....

Today, should total war ever break out again—no matter how—our two countries would become the primary targets. It is an ironic but accurate fact that the two strongest powers are the two in the most danger of devastation. All we have built, all we have worked for, would be destroyed in the first 24 hours. And even in the cold war, which brings burdens and dangers to so many countries—including this nation's closest allies—our two countries bear the heaviest burdens. For we are both devoting massive sums of money to weapons that could be better devoted to combating ignorance, poverty, and disease. We are both caught up in a vicious and dangerous cycle in which suspicion on one side breeds suspicion on the other and new weapons beget counter-weapons.

> *"Let us reexamine our attitude toward the Soviet Union. No government or social system is so evil that its people must be considered as lacking in virtue."*

In short, both the United States and its allies, and the Soviet Union and its allies, have a mutually deep interest in a just and genuine peace and in halting the arms race. Agreements to this end are in the interests of the Soviet Union as well as ours, and even the most hostile nations can be relied upon to accept and keep those treaty obligations, and only those treaty obligations, which are in their own interest....

Third: Let us reexamine our attitude toward the cold war, remembering that we are not engaged in a debate, seeking to pile up debating points. We are not here distributing blame or pointing the finger of judgment. We must deal with the world as it is and not as it might have been had the history of the last 18 years been different....

Speaking of other nations, I wish to make one point clear. We are bound to many nations by alliances. Those alliances exist because our concern and theirs substantially overlap. Our commitment to defend Western Europe and West Berlin, for example, stands undiminished because of the identity of our vital interests. The United States will make no deal with the Soviet Union at the expense of other nations and other peoples, not merely because they are our partners but also because their interests and ours converge.

Our interests converge, however, not only in defending the frontiers of freedom but in pursuing the paths of peace. It is our hope—and the purpose of Allied policies—to convince the Soviet Union that she, too, should let each nation choose its own future, so long as that choice does not interfere with the choices of others. The Communist drive to impose their political and economic system on others is the primary cause of world tension today. For there can be no doubt that, if all nations could refrain from interfering in the self-determination of others, the peace would be much more assured....

I am taking this opportunity … to announce two important decisions …

First: Chairman Khrushchev, Prime Minister Macmillan, and I have agreed that high-level discussions will shortly begin in Moscow looking toward early agreement on a comprehensive test ban treaty. Our hopes must be tempered with the caution of history, but with our hopes go the hopes of all mankind.

Second: To make clear our good faith and solemn convictions on the matter, I now declare that the United States does not propose to conduct nuclear tests in the atmosphere so long as other states do not do so. We will not be the first to resume. Such a declaration is no substitute for a formal binding treaty, but I hope it will help us achieve one. Nor would such a treaty be a substitute for disarmament, but I hope it will help us achieve it.

Finally, my fellow Americans, let us examine our attitude toward peace and freedom here at home. The quality and spirit of our own society must justify and support our efforts abroad....

It is the responsibility of the executive branch at all levels of government—local, state, and national—to provide and protect that freedom for all of our citizens by all means within their authority. It is the responsibility of the legislative branch at all levels, wherever that authority is not now adequate, to make it adequate. And it is the responsibility of all citizens in all sections of this country to respect the rights of all others and to respect the law of the land....

While we proceed to safeguard our national interests, let us also safeguard human interests. And the elimination of war and arms is clearly in the interest of both. No treaty, however much it may be to the advantage of all, however tightly it may be worded, can provide absolute security against the risks of deception and evasion. But it can, if it is sufficiently effective in its enforcement and if it is sufficiently in the interests of its signers, offer far more security and far fewer risks than an unabated, uncontrolled, unpredictable arms race.

The United States, as the world knows, will never start a war. We do not want a war. We do not now expect a war. This generation of Americans has already had enough—more than enough—of war and hate and oppression. We shall be prepared if others wish it. We shall be alert to try to stop it. But we shall also do our part to build a world of peace where the weak are safe and the strong are just. We are not helpless before that task or hopeless of its success. Confident and unafraid, we labor on—not toward a strategy of annihilation but toward a strategy of peace.

Source: Kennedy, John F. "Commencement Address at American University, June 10, 1963." *Department of State Bulletin*, No. 1253, July 1, 1963. Available online at the John F. Kennedy Library and Museum, http://www.jfklibrary.org.

7.7
"Mutual Deterrence" Explained – 1967
Excerpts from a Speech by U.S. Secretary of Defense Robert McNamara

In the following speech, given on September 18, 1967, U.S. Secretary of Defense Robert McNamara explained America's increasing Cold War emphasis on the concept of "mutual deterrence." Boiled down to its essence, mutual deterrence relied on the idea of mutual assured destruction. It meant that the United States intended to continue its military buildup until the nation possessed the capability to retaliate against any Soviet attack—even a nuclear one—with equal force. McNamara and other advocates of this policy reasoned that the Soviets would be less likely to launch an attack on American soil or institutions if they knew the U.S. would retaliate by reducing their empire to rubble. This philosophy became integral to Cold War strategy in both the United States and the Soviet Union until the late 1980s, when the USSR began to crumble.

In a complex and uncertain world, the gravest problem that an American Secretary of Defense must face is that of planning, preparation and policy against the possibility of thermonuclear war. It is a prospect that most of mankind understandably would prefer not to contemplate. For technology has now circumscribed us all with a horizon of horror that could dwarf any catastrophe that has befallen man in his more than a million years on earth.

Man has lived now for more than twenty years in what we have come to call the Atomic Age. What we sometimes overlook is that every future age of man will be an atomic age, and if man is to have a future at all, it will have to be one overshadowed with the permanent possibility of thermonuclear holocaust. About that fact there is no longer any doubt. Our freedom in this question consists only in facing the matter rationally and realistically and discussing actions to minimize the danger.

No sane citizen, political leader or nation wants thermonuclear war. But merely not wanting it is not enough. We must understand the differences among actions which increase its risks, those which reduce them and those which, while costly, have little influence one way or another. But there is a great difficulty in the way of constructive and profitable debate over the issues, and that is the exceptional complexity of nuclear strategy. Unless these complexities are well understood rational discussion and decision-making are impossible.

One must begin with precise definitions. The cornerstone of our strategic policy continues to be to deter nuclear attack upon the United States or its allies. We do this by maintaining a highly reliable ability to inflict unacceptable damage upon any single aggressor or combination of aggressors at any time during the course of a strategic nuclear exchange, even after absorbing a surprise first strike. This can be defined as our assured-destruction capability.

It is important to understand that assured destruction is the very essence of the whole deterrence concept. We must possess an actual assured-destruction capability, and that capability also must be credible. The point is that a potential aggressor must believe that our assured-destruction capability is in fact actual, and that our will to use it in retaliation to an attack is in fact unwavering. The conclusion, then, is clear: if the United States is to deter a nuclear attack in itself or its allies, it must possess an actual and a credible assured-destruction capability.

When calculating the force required, we must be conservative in all our estimates of both a potential aggressor's capabilities and his intentions. Security depends upon assuming a worst plausible case, and having the ability to cope with it. In that eventuality we must be able to absorb the total weight of nuclear attack on our country—on our retaliatory forces, on our command and control apparatus, on our industrial capacity, on our cities, and on our population—and still be capable of damaging the aggressor to the point that his society would be simply no longer viable in twentieth-century terms. That is what deterrence of nuclear aggression means. It means the certainty of suicide to the aggressor, not merely to his military forces, but to his society as a whole.

Let us consider another term: first-strike capability. This is a somewhat ambiguous term, since it could mean simply the ability of one nation to attack another nation with nuclear forces first. But as it is normally used, it connotes much more: the elimination of the attacked nation's retaliatory second-strike forces. This is the sense in which it should be understood.

Clearly, first-strike capability is an important strategic concept. The United States must not and will not permit itself ever to get into a position in which another nation, or combination of nations, would possess a first-strike capability against it. Such a position not only would constitute an intolerable threat to our security, but it obviously would remove our ability to deter nuclear aggression.

We are not in that position today, and there is no foreseeable danger of our ever getting into that position. Our strategic offensive forces are immense: 1,000 Minuteman missile launchers, carefully protected below ground; 41 Polaris submarines carrying 656 missile launchers, with the majority hidden beneath the seas at all times; and about 600 long-range bombers, approximately 40 percent of which are kept always in a high state of alert.

Our alert forces alone carry more than 2,200 weapons, each averaging more than the explosive equivalent of one megaton of TNT. Four hundred of these delivered on the Soviet Union would be sufficient to destroy over one-third of her population and one-half of her industry. All these flexible and highly reliable forces are equipped with devices that ensure their penetration of Soviet defenses.

Now what about the Soviet Union? Does it today possess a powerful nuclear arsenal? The answer is that it does. Does it possess a first-strike capability against the United States? The answer is that it does not. Can the Soviet Union in the foreseeable future acquire such a first-strike capability against the United States? The answer is that it cannot. It cannot because we are determined to remain fully alert and we will never permit our own assured-destruction capability to drop to a point at which a Soviet first-strike capability is even remotely feasible.

Is the Soviet Union seriously attempting to acquire a first-strike capability against the United States? Although this is a question we cannot answer with absolute certainty, we believe the answer is no. In any event, the question itself is—in a sense—irrelevant: for the United States will maintain and, where necessary strengthen its retaliatory forces so that, whatever the Soviet Union's intentions or actions, we will continue to have an assured-destruction capability vis a vis their society.

Source: McNamara, Robert. Public Address, September 18, 1967. *Foreign Relations of the United States 1967.* Vol. 14. Washington, DC: U.S. Government Printing Office, 2001.

7.8
The Soviets Justify the Invasion of Czechoslovakia – 1968
Excerpt from Pravda's *"Sovereignty and International Duties of Socialist Countries"*

On August 20, 1968, the Soviet Union launched a major military invasion of Czechoslovakia in order to crush a widening rebellion against Communist rule. One month later, on September 25, an ideological justification for the invasion of Czechoslovakia was unveiled in Pravda, *the official newspaper of the Soviet Communist Party. This article, titled "Sovereignty and International Duties of Socialist Countries," was written by Sergei Kovalev, a Pravda staff specialist on propaganda. Remarkably, it declared that the Soviet intervention was actually a valiant move to lend "help to the working people of Czechoslovakia" against agitators determined to undermine "the very foundations of the country's independence and sovereignty." It also asserted that although citizens of socialist nations have the right to chart their own course, "none of their decisions should damage either socialism in their own country or the fundamental interests of other socialist countries." Following are excerpts from this article.*

Two months later, Soviet leader Leonid Brezhnev echoed many of the Pravda *article's points in a November 13 speech at the Fifth Congress of the Polish United Workers' Party. "When a threat arises to the cause of socialism in [a] country—a threat to the security of the socialist commonwealth as a whole— this is no longer merely a problem for that country's people, but a common problem, the concern of all socialist countries," Brezhnev stated to enthusiastic applause. This justification for the invasion became known in the West as the "Brezhnev Doctrine." It remained standard policy in the Kremlin for the next two decades as Moscow sought to "protect" Communist regimes from outside influences and consolidate its control over satellite states.*

In connection with the events in Czechoslovakia, the question of the correlation and interdependence of the national interests of the socialist countries and their international duties acquire particular topical and acute importance.

The measures taken by the Soviet Union, jointly with other socialist countries, in defending the socialist gains of the Czechoslovak people are of great significance for strengthening the socialist community, which is the main achievement of the international working class.

We cannot ignore the assertions, made in some places, that the actions of the five socialist countries run counter to the Marxist-Leninist principle of sovereignty and the rights of nations to self-determination.

The groundlessness of such reasoning consists primarily in that it is based on an abstract, nonclass approach to the question of sovereignty and the rights of nations to self-determination.

The peoples of the socialist countries and Communist parties certainly do have and should have freedom for determining the ways of advance of their respective countries. However, none of their decisions should damage either socialism in their country or the fundamental interests of other socialist countries, and the whole working class movement, which is working for socialism.

This means that each Communist party is responsible not only to its own people, but also to all the socialist countries, to the entire Communist movement. Whoever forgets this, in stressing only the independence of the Communist party, becomes one-sided. He deviates from his international duty.

Marxist dialectics are opposed to one-sidedness. They demand that each phenomenon be examined concretely, in general connection with other phenomena, with other processes. Just as, in Lenin's words, a man living in a society cannot be free from the society, a particular socialist state, staying in a system of other states composing the socialist community, cannot be free from the common interests of that community.

The sovereignty of each socialist country cannot be opposed to the interests of the world of socialism, of the world revolutionary movement. Lenin demanded that all Communists fight against small-nation narrowmindedness, seclusion, and isolation, consider the whole and the general, subordinate the particular to the general interest.

The socialist states respect the democratic norms of international law. They have proved this more than once in practice, by coming out resolutely against the attempts of imperialism to violate the sovereignty and independence of nations. It is from these same positions that they reject the leftist, adventurist conception of "exporting revolution," of "bringing happiness" to other peoples....

Each Communist party is free to apply the basic principles of Marxism-Leninism and of socialism in its country, but it cannot depart from these principles (assuming, naturally, that it remains a Communist party). Concretely, this means, first of all, that, in its activity, each Communist party cannot but take into account such a decisive fact of our time as the struggle between two opposing social systems—capitalism and socialism.

> "Each Communist party is free to apply the basic principles of Marxism-Leninism and of socialism in its country, but it cannot depart from these principles."

This is an objective struggle, a fact not depending on the will of the people, and stipulated by the world's being split into two opposite social systems. Lenin said: "Each man must choose between joining our side or the other side. Any attempt to avoid taking sides in this issue must end in fiasco."

It has got to be emphasized that when a socialist country seems to adopt a "non-affiliated" stand, it retains its national independence, in effect, precisely because of the might of the socialist community, and above all the Soviet Union as a central force, which also includes the might of its armed forces. The weakening of any of the links in the world system of socialism directly affects all the socialist countries, which cannot look indifferently upon this.

The antisocial elements in Czechoslovakia actually covered up the demand for so-called neutrality and Czechoslovakia's withdrawal from the socialist community with talk about the right of nations to self-determination. However, the implementation of such "self-determination," in other words, Czechoslovakia's withdrawal from the socialist community, would have come into conflict with its own vital interests and would have been detrimental to the other socialist states.

Such "self-determination," as a result of which NATO troops would have been able to come up to the Soviet border, while the community of European socialist countries would have been split, in effect encroaches upon the vital interests of the peoples of these countries and conflicts, as the very root of it, with the right of these people to socialist self-determination.

Discharging their internationalist duty toward the fraternal peoples of Czechoslovakia and defending their own socialist gains, the U.S.S.R. and the other socialist states had to act decisively and they did act against the antisocialist forces in Czechoslovakia....

People who "disapprove" of the actions of the allied socialist states are ignoring the decisive fact that these countries are defending the interests of all of world socialism, of the entire revolutionary movement.

The system of socialism exists in concrete form in some countries, which have their own definite state boundaries; this system is developed according to the specific conditions of each country. Furthermore, nobody interferes in the concrete measures taken to improve the socialist system in the different socialist countries.

However, the picture changes fundamentally when a danger arises to socialism itself in a particular country. As a social system, world socialism is the common gain of the working people of all lands; it is indivisible and its defense is the common cause of all Communists and all progressives in the world, in the first place, the working folk of the socialist countries....

What the right-wing anti-socialist forces set out to achieve in recent months in Czechoslovakia did not refer to the specific features of socialist development or the application of the principles of Marxism-Leninism to the concrete conditions obtaining in that country, but constituted encroachment on the foundations of socialism, on the basic principles of Marxism-Leninism.

This is the nuance that people who have fallen for the hypocritical nonsense of the antisocialist and revisionist elements still cannot understand. Under the guise of "democratization," these elements were little by little shaking the socialist state, seeking to demoralize the Communist party and befog the minds of the masses, stealthily hatching a counter-revolutionary coup, and they were not duly rebuffed inside the country.

Naturally the Communists of the fraternal countries could not allow the socialist states to be inactive in the name of an abstractly understood sovereignty, when they saw that the country stood in peril of antisocial degeneration....

Source: Kovalev, Sergei. "Sovereignty and International Duties of Socialist Countries." *Pravda*, September 25, 1968.

8

THE BAY OF PIGS AND THE
CUBAN MISSILE CRISIS

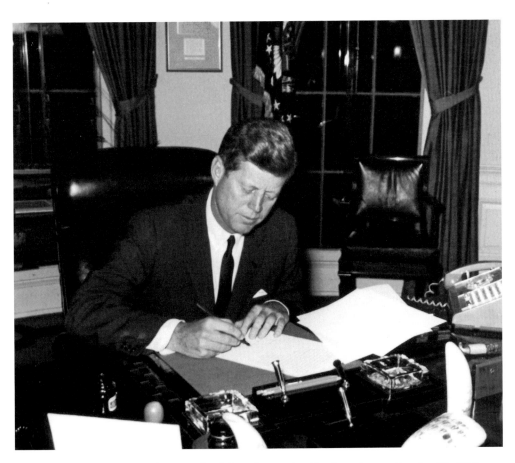

President John F. Kennedy signs the Cuban Quarantine Proclamation on October 23, 1962, at the height of the Cuban Missile Crisis.

INTRODUCTION

During the 1950s and 1960s, when the nuclear arms race was at its most feverish, both the Soviet Union and the United States engaged in frequent political and military posturing. On a few occasions, however, the simmering tensions between the world superpowers truly threatened to erupt into a nuclear war. Of these events, the one that brought the United States and the USSR closest to the nuclear abyss was the Cuban Missile Crisis of 1962.

Cuba is an island nation in the northern Caribbean Sea, just 90 miles from the southern tip of Florida. In 1959 guerrilla leader Fidel Castro and his followers overthrew dictator Fulgencio Batista, who had been a corrupt but reliable ally of the United States. Castro moved decisively to reshape Cuba as a Communist nation. He seized the factories and assets of American companies that had long thrived on the island, and he nationalized the country's oil and sugar industries. He also publicly condemned the United States for its years of interference in Cuban politics and business.

The sudden appearance of a Communist stronghold on America's doorstep sent ripples of apprehension throughout the administrations of both Dwight Eisenhower and John F. Kennedy, who became president in January 1961. "They feared, as much as we hoped, that a socialist Cuba might become a magnet that would attract other Latin American countries to socialism," Soviet leader Nikita Khrushchev observed in *Khrushchev Remembers: The Last Testament*.

The Bay of Pigs

After Castro became the leader of Cuba, the United States imposed a trade embargo on the country and began exploring options for removing Castro from

233

power. By the time Kennedy was inaugurated, the United States had broken off all diplomatic relations with Castro's government. Meanwhile, Soviet aid to Cuba was steadily increasing. In the early spring of 1961 Kennedy approved a CIA plan to send an invasion force into Cuba of 1,400 Cuban exiles (native Cubans who were living in the U.S.). Their mission was to trigger a popular uprising that would remove Castro from power and replace him with a pro-American leader. The U.S.-sponsored invasion force landed on Zapata Beach in Cuba's Bay of Pigs under cover of darkness on April 17, 1961. But the popular uprising against the Castro regime never materialized. Instead, Cuba's army and militia forces routed the landing force over the course of a single weekend.

The failed Bay of Pigs invasion aroused indignation and even fury in many other parts of the world. Large anti-American demonstrations erupted in several Latin American cities, and the Kremlin denounced the attempted coup. But even though the Bay of Pigs fiasco was a humiliating early setback for Kennedy, it did not shake his conviction that Latin America loomed as a major battleground in the Cold War. Over the next few months, in fact, he proposed major aid packages to developing countries in Latin America and elsewhere. Kennedy saw this aid as an essential element in his self-proclaimed Freedom Doctrine, which defined the Cold War struggle between West and East as "a contest of will and purpose as well as force and violence—a battle for minds and souls as well as lives and territory. And in that contest, we cannot stand aside."

Over the next year, relations between the United States and Cuba continued to deteriorate. American relations with the Soviets, meanwhile, remained deeply troubled. In June 1962, for example, Kennedy and Khrushchev held a summit in Vienna, Austria, to discuss Berlin, nuclear proliferation, and many other issues. The summit proved to be a diplomatic disaster. Their conversations were littered with bitter and ominous exchanges, and both leaders departed for home with heightened distrust for the other.

The Cuban Missile Crisis

Then, on October 14, 1962, an American U-2 reconnaissance spy plane returned from a flight over Cuba with frightening information. Footage taken by the plane made it clear that the Soviets were secretly building intermediate-range missiles sites on the island. Two days later, the CIA confirmed that dozens of Soviet missiles with nuclear warheads were being deployed in Cuba. They estimated that some of the missiles would be fully operational—and capable of reaching most major American cities and strategic military locations—within a week.

Alarmed by this news, Kennedy put together an Executive Committee (Ex Comm) of his National Security Council to take stock of the crisis. Over the next several days, Kennedy and his Ex Comm group debated a number of response options, including launching air strikes against the missile sites, mounting a full-scale invasion of Cuba, imposing a naval blockade around the island, or trying to negotiate an end to the crisis.

Ultimately, Kennedy and his advisors settled on a course of action that, in the president's own judgment, had a one-in-three likelihood of triggering nuclear war. Temporarily setting aside the idea of a full-scale invasion of the island, the United States organized a blanket naval "quarantine" around Cuba and put all its armed forces on high alert. (Years later, the United States learned that Soviet forces in Cuba had been outfitted with short-range nuclear weapons that they were authorized to use in the case of a U.S. invasion; when Kennedy administration Secretary of Defense Robert McNamara heard this news, he estimated that if the United States had invaded Cuba, there was a 99 percent probability that the Cuban Missile Crisis would have triggered a full-scale nuclear war.)

Kennedy Explains the Stakes

Within days, American planes armed with atomic weapons patrolled the sky and U.S. nuclear submarines prowled the ocean depths waiting for orders to fire. On the evening of October 22, 1962, Kennedy went on national television to inform the American people about the missile crisis. He also used this speech to urge Khrushchev to remove the missiles and thus "move the world back from the abyss of destruction." Later that evening, Secretary of State Dean Rusk reportedly told several foreign diplomats that "I would not be candid and I would not be fair with you if I did not say that we are in as grave a crisis as mankind has been in."

Khrushchev and his lieutenants were surprised by the fierce American reaction to the missile placement. Indeed, Soviet records indicate that they placed the missiles in Cuba to defend the country from possible U.S. invasion, as well as to give the United States a taste of what it felt like living in Moscow. "The Americans had surrounded our country with military bases and threatened us with nuclear weapons, and now they would learn just what it feels like to have enemy missiles pointing at you," Khrushchev later explained. "We'd be doing nothing but giving them a little of their own medicine."

Unwilling to back down on the world stage, the Kremlin ordered Red Army and Warsaw Pact forces to prepare for war. It also issued a grim warning to the United

States that any naval blockade could lead to "catastrophic consequences." On October 24, however, Soviet ships heading for Cuba stopped short of the blockade line, averting a showdown. "Eyeball to eyeball, they blinked first," Rusk later declared.

On October 25, worldwide anxiety over the missile showdown reached even greater heights. That day, at a meeting of the United Nations Security Council in New York, Soviet Ambassador to the UN Valerian Zorin and U.S. ambassador Adlai Stevenson heatedly confronted one another in front of a spellbound assembly of UN delegates. At one point in the exchange, Stevenson bluntly asked, "Do you, Ambassador Zorin, deny that the USSR has placed and is placing missile sites in Cuba? Yes or no?" When Zorin responded that "You will have your answer in due course," Stevenson declared that "I am prepared to wait for my answer until hell freezes over."

Searching for a Way Out

Meanwhile, U.S. Attorney General Robert Kennedy and Soviet Ambassador Anatoly Dobrynin held several secret meetings to try to find a way out of the crisis. A possible compromise emerged in which the Soviets might consent to remove the missiles from Cuba in exchange for guarantees that the United States would not invade Cuba. On October 26 Khrushchev sent Kennedy a letter laying out this very scenario as a way to end the crisis. But as the president and Ex Comm pondered this offer, Khrushchev issued a second letter that was much more defiant in tone. In this second letter, the Soviet leader said that he would not remove the missiles unless the Americans issued a no-invasion pledge *and* removed NATO nuclear missiles in Turkey that were aimed at the Kremlin.

Kennedy and the Ex Comm membership eventually decided to respond to Khrushchev's first letter, essentially pretending that the second one never arrived. On the evening of October 27, Kennedy signed a letter addressed to the Soviet leader that pledged not to invade Cuba and to end the blockade if the Soviets removed their nuclear missiles from Cuba. Robert Kennedy then met with Dobrynin once again, and the two of them agreed to a secret side-deal: the United States would remove the NATO missiles in Turkey four or five months down the line if the Kremlin removed the missiles from Cuba.

Khrushchev agreed to the deal, and on the morning of October 28, Radio Moscow announced that the Soviet Union was dismantling and removing the missiles from Cuba. Afterward, both sides claimed victory. But the biggest victors were ordinary citizens in America, the USSR, and around the world who had spent the previous week wondering if each day would be their last.

8.1
Assessing the Bay of Pigs Catastrophe – 1961
Excerpts From the CIA "Inspector General's Survey of the Cuban Operation"

In 1961 the Central Intelligence Agency (CIA) received approval from President John F. Kennedy to launch a plan to remove Cuba's Fidel Castro from power and replace his Communist regime with a pro-Western government. On the weekend of April 17-19, the CIA plan was put into motion. An invasion force of 1,400 Cuban exiles trained by the CIA landed in Cuba's Bay of Pigs. Officials from the CIA and other U.S. government agencies expected that the invasion would spark a popular uprising against Castro and that Cuban citizens would overthrow their government. But the planned popular uprising never materialized, and the so-called "Bay of Pigs" operation fell apart in spectacular and embarrassing fashion.

Following are excerpts from a highly critical internal inquiry conducted by the CIA into the agency's Bay of Pigs invasion. The 150-page report was one of the most secret documents of the Cold War. In 1997, it was released under the Freedom of Information Act to the National Security Archive, a nonprofit, nongovernmental organization that collects and publishes declassified government reports.

Views of Joint Chiefs

30. Agency participants in the project have sought to defend the invasion plan by citing the approval given to the plan by the Joint Chiefs of Staff, (JCS). To this argument, members of the JCS have replied, in the course of another inquiry, (1) that the final plan was presented to them only orally, which prevented normal staffing, (2) that they regarded the operation as being solely CIA's, with the military called on to furnish various types of support and the chief interest of the JCS being to see to it that every kind of support requested was furnished, (3) that they went on the assumption that full air support would be furnished and control of the air secured and on the Agency's assurances that a great number of insurgents would immediately join forces with the invasion forces; and (4) that, in the event the battle went against them, the brigade would at once "go guerrilla" and take to the hills.

31. The Agency committed at least four extremely serious mistakes in planning:

a. Failure to subject the project, especially in its latter frenzied stages, to a cold and objective appraisal by the best operating talent available, particularly by those not involved in the operation, such as the Chief of Operations and the chiefs of the Senior Staffs. Had this been done, the two following mistakes (b and c, below) might have been avoided.

b. Failure to advise the President, at an appropriate time, that success had become dubious and to recommend that the operation be therefore canceled and that the problem of unseating Castro be restudied.

c. Failure to recognize that the project had become overt and that the military effort had become too large to be handled by the Agency alone.

d. Failure to reduce successive project plans to formal papers and to leave copies of them with the president and his advisers and to request specific written approval and confirmation thereof.

32. Timely and objective scrutiny of the operation in the months before the invasion, including study of all available intelligence, would have demonstrated to Agency officials that the clandestine paramilitary operations had almost totally failed, that there was no controlled and responsive underground movement ready to rally to the invasion force, and that Castro's ability both to fight back and to roll up the internal opposition must be very considerably upgraded.

33. It would also have raised the question of why the United States should contemplate pitting 1,500 soldiers, however well trained and armed, against an enemy vastly superior in number and armament on a terrain which offered nothing but vague hope of significant local support. It might also have suggested that the agency's responsibility in the operation should be drastically revised and would certainly have revealed that there was no real plan for the post-invasion period, whether for success or failure.

Existence of Warnings

34. The latest United States Intelligence Board, Office of National Estimates, and Office of Current Intelligence studies on Cuba available at the time provided clear warning that a calm reappraisal was necessary.

35. But the atmosphere was not conducive to it. The chief of the project and his subordinates had been subjected to such grueling pressures of haste and overwork for so long that their impetus and drive would have been difficult to curb for such a purpose. The strike preparations, under the powerful influence of the project's paramilitary chief, to which there was no effective counterbalance, had gained such momentum that the operation had surged far ahead of policy. The Cuban volunteers were getting seriously restive and threatening to get out of hand before they could be committed. The Guatemalan Government was urging the Agency to take away its Cubans. The rainy season was hard upon the Caribbean.

The reappraisal never happened, though these very factors which helped prevent it should have warned the Agency of its necessity.

36. These adverse factors were compounded and exacerbated by policy restrictions that kept coming one upon another throughout a period of weeks and right up until the point of no return. These caused successive planning changes and piled up more confusion. Rapidly accumulating stresses, in our opinion, caused the Agency operators to lose sight of the fact that the margin of error was swiftly narrowing and had even vanished before the force was committed. At some point in this degenerative cycle they should have gone to the President and said frankly: "Here are the facts. The operation should be halted. We request further instructions."

Consequences of Cancellation

37. Cancellation would have been embarrassing. The brigade could not have been held any longer in a ready status, probably could not have been held at all. Its members would have spread their disappointment far and wide. Because of multiple security leaks in this huge operation, the world already knew about the preparations, and the Government's and the Agency's embarrassment would have been public.

38. However, cancellation would have averted failure, which brought even more embarrassment, carried death and misery to hundreds, destroyed millions of dollars' worth of U.S. property, and seriously damaged U.S. prestige.

39. The other possible outcome—the one the project strove to achieve—was a successful brigade lodgment housing the Revolutionary Council but isolated from the rest of Cuba by swamps and Castro's forces. Arms were held in readiness for 30,000 Cubans who were expected to make their way unarmed through the Castro army and wade the swamps to rally to the liberators. Except for this, we are unaware of any planning by the Agency or by the U.S. Government for this success.

40. It is beyond the scope of this report to suggest what U.S. action might have been taken to consolidate victory, but we can confidently assert that the Agency had no intelligence evidence that Cubans in significant numbers could or would join the invaders or that there was any kind of an effective and cohesive resistance movement under anybody's control, let alone the Agency's, that could have furnished internal leadership for an uprising in support of the invasion. The consequences of a successful lodgment, unless overtly supported by U.S. armed forces, were dubious.

The Choice

41. The choice was between retreat without honor and a gamble between ignominious defeat and dubious victory. The Agency chose to gamble, at rapidly decreasing odds.

42. The project had lost its covert nature by November 1960. As it continued to grow, operational security became more and more diluted. For more than three months before the invasion the American press was reporting, often with some accuracy, on the recruiting and training of Cubans. Such massive preparations could only be laid to the U.S. The agency's name was freely linked with these activities. Plausible denial was a pathetic illusion....

Source: *Inspector General's Survey of the Cuban Operation and Associated Documents.* February 16, 1962. Washington, DC: Central Intelligence Agency, 1997. Available online at the CIA, http://www.foia.cia. gov/bay_of_pigs.asp.

8.2
Khrushchev Scolds Kennedy on Cuba – 1961
Excerpts from Correspondence from Premier Nikita Khrushchev to President John F. Kennedy

> *On April 22, 1961, Soviet Premier Nikita Khrushchev sent a letter to American President John F. Kennedy in which he rebuked the United States for its ill-fated Bay of Pigs campaign in Cuba. He described the operation as a criminal act and he warned that the USSR was ready to help defend Cuba from future aggression. Khrushchev also addressed American fears that Soviet "rockets and other weapons could be installed on Cuban territory for possible use against the United States," assuring Kennedy that "we have no bases in Cuba, and we do not intend to establish any." Six months later, American spy planes discovered that the Soviets were constructing secret missile sites in Cuba—a discovery that precipitated the Cuban Missile Crisis.*

MR. PRESIDENT, I have received your reply of April 18. You write that the United States intends no military intervention in Cuba. But numerous facts known to the whole world—and to the Government of the United States, of course, better than to any one else—speak differently. Despite all assurances to the contrary, it has now been proved beyond doubt that it was precisely the United States which prepared the intervention, financed its arming and transported the gangs of mercenaries that invaded the territory of Cuba.

United States armed forces also took a direct part in the accomplishment of the gangster attack upon Cuba. American bombers and fighters supported the operations of the mercenaries who landed on Cuban territory, and participated in the military operations against the armed forces of the lawful Government and people of Cuba.

Such are the facts. They bear witness to direct United States participation in the armed aggression against Cuba.

In your message you took the course of justifying, and even lauding, the attack on Cuba—this crime which has revolted the entire world. You try to justify the organization of a military attack on Cuba, committed for the sole reason that the way of life chosen by its people is not to the taste of the ruling circles of the United States and the North American monopolies operating in Latin America, by talk about the United States Government's adherence to the ideals of "freedom." But, one may ask, of what freedom are you speaking?

Of freedom to strangle the Cuban people with the bony hand of hunger through the establishment of an economic blockade? Is that freedom?

Of freedom to send military planes over the territory of Cuba, to subject peaceful Cuban cities to barbarous bombing, to set fire to sugar-cane plantations? Is that freedom?

History records many cases in which, on the pretext of defending freedom, peoples have been drowned in blood, colonial wars waged, and one small nation after another taken by the throat.

In the present case, apparently, the United States Government is seeking to restore to Cuba that "freedom" under which Cuba would dance to the tune of her more powerful neighbour and foreign monopolies would again be able to plunder the country's national wealth, to wax rich on the sweat and blood of the Cuban people. But it is precisely against such "freedom" that the Cuban people accomplished their revolution when they threw out Batista, who may have loyally served the interests of his foreign masters but who was a foreign element in the body of the Cuban nation.

You, Mr. President, display concern for a handful of enemies who were expelled by their people and found refuge under the wing of those who want to keep the guns of their cruisers and destroyers trained on Cuba. But why are you not concerned about the fate of the six million Cuban people, why do you not wish to pay regard to their inalienable right to a free and independent life, their right to arrange their domestic affairs as they see fit? Where are the standards of international law, or even of simple human morality, that would justify such a position? They simply do not exist.

The Cuban people have once again expressed their will with a clarity which should have left no room for doubt, even in the minds of those who prefer to close their eyes to reality. They have shown that they not only know their interests, but can stand up for them. Cuba today is not, of course, the Cuba you identify with the handful of traitors who have come out against their people. It is the Cuba of workers, peasants and intellectuals, it is a people which has rallied round its revolutionary Government headed by the national hero, Fidel Castro. And, judging from everything, this people received the interventionists in a fitting way. Is not this convincing proof of the real will of the Cuban people?

I think it is. And since this is so, is it not time for all to draw from it the right conclusions?

As for the Soviet Union, we have stated on many occasions, and I now state again, that our Government does not seek any advantages or privileges in Cuba. We have no bases in Cuba, and we do not intend to establish any. And this is well known to you, to your generals and your admirals. If, despite this, they still try to frighten the people by fabrications about "Soviet bases" on Cuba, that is obviously designed for consumption by simpletons. But there are fewer and fewer such simpletons, and that applies also, I hope, to the United States.

By the way, Mr. President, I would like to express my opinion concerning the statements made by you and by certain other United States politicians to the effect that rockets and other weapons could be installed on Cuban territory for possible use against the United States.

> "A powerful State can of course always find a pretext for attacking a weaker country, and then justify its attack by claiming that that country was a potential menace."

The inference from this is that the United States has some alleged right to attack Cuba, either directly or through the traitors to the Cuban people whom you arm with your weapons, train on your territory, maintain with the money of United States taxpayers and transport with the resources of your armed forces, covering them from the air and the sea while they fight against the Cuban people and their lawful government.

You also refer to some United States obligations to protect the Western hemisphere against external aggression. But what obligations can possibly apply in the present case? No one can have any obligations to defend rebels against the lawful government of a sovereign State, such as Cuba is.

Mr. President, you are setting out on a very dangerous road. Think of it. You speak of your rights and obligations, and, of course, anyone can claim this or that right. But then you will have to admit that other States, too, can base their actions in similar circumstances on similar arguments and considerations.

You allege that Cuba cannot lend her territory for actions against the United States. That is your supposition, but it is based on no facts. We, on the other hand, can already refer to concrete facts, not suppositions: in some countries, bordering on the Soviet Union by land and sea, there are at present Governments following a policy that is far from reasonable, Governments which have concluded military agreements with the United States and have made their territory available for the establishment of American military bases. And your military say openly that these bases are spearheaded against the Soviet Union, as if this were not already sufficiently clear. So, if you consider yourself entitled to take such measures against

Cuba as the United States Government has been resorting to lately, you must admit that other countries have no lesser grounds for acting in the same way with regard to States whose territories are the scene of actual preparations constituting a threat to the security of the Soviet Union. If you do not want to sin against elementary logic, you must obviously concede this right to other States. We, for our part, do not hold such views. We consider that the arguments advanced on this score in the United States constitute, not merely an extremely free interpretation of international law, but, to put it plainly, open advocacy of a treacherous policy.

A powerful State can of course always find a pretext for attacking a weaker country, and then justify its attack by claiming that that country was a potential menace. But is this twentieth-century morality? This is the morality of the colonialists, of the brigands who once pursued precisely such a policy. Today, in the second half of the twentieth century, it is no longer possible to take the pirate morality of the colonialists as a guide. We all see, today, how the colonial system is crumbling and becoming a thing of the past. The Soviet Union, for its part, is doing everything to promote this process, and we are proud of it.

Or take the United States actions with regard to China. What standards of law can be invoked to justify these actions? Everyone knows that Taiwan is an inalienable part of China. This has been admitted even by the Government of the United States, whose signature appears on the Cairo Declaration of 1943. But later the United States seized Taiwan — took, in fact, the road to brigandage. The People's Republic of China announced its natural aspiration to reunite the territory of Taiwan with the rest of Chinese territory. But how did the United States react to this? It declared that it would use armed force to prevent reunification of this Chinese territory, seized by it, with the rest of China. It threatens war if China takes any steps towards the recovery of Taiwan. And this is being done by a country which has officially recognized that Taiwan belongs to China! Is not this perfidy in international relations? If such methods were to become the rule in relations between States, there would be no place left for law. Its place would be taken by lawlessness and arbitrariness.

So, Mr. President, your sympathies are one thing; but actions against the security and independence of other peoples, taken on the basis of such sympathies, are very much another. You may, of course, express your sympathy with the imperialist and colonialist countries; that does not surprise anyone. For example, you vote with them in the United Nations. This is a matter of your morality. But what has been done against Cuba is no longer morality. It is gangsterism.

I should like to stress that if the United Nations is really to become strong and fulfil the functions for which it was established — and at present this Organization, unfortunately, is a body already infected by the bacilli of colonialism and imperialism — the United Nations must resolutely condemn the banditry undertaken against Cuba. And the point here is not merely to condemn the United

States. The important thing is that the condemnation of aggression should be seen to be a precedent, a lesson which other countries, too, might learn, so that aggression should never again be repeated. For if we were to take the course of approving or even, simply, condoning the morality of the aggressors, it could be adopted by other States as well, and this would inevitably lead to military conflicts, any of which might result in a third world war.

What you said in your last statement to the Press must fill the entire world with great alarm. For you simply claim, in fact, some right of yours to employ military force whenever you find it necessary, and to suppress other peoples each time you decide that their expression of their will constitutes "communism." But what right have you, what right has anyone in general, to deprive a people of the possibility of choosing their social and political system of their own free will? Have you never considered that other countries, too, might perhaps advance a demand similar to yours and might declare that you, in the United States, have a system which breeds wars and espouses an imperialist policy, the policy of threats and attacks against other countries? There is every ground for such accusations. And, proceeding from the principles which you now proclaim, one could, apparently, demand a change in the internal system of the United States. We, as you know, do not follow that road. We favour the peaceful coexistence of all States, and non-interference in the internal affairs of other countries.

You allude to Budapest. But we can tell you openly, without any allusions: it is you, the United States, that crushed the independence of Guatemala by sending your mercenaries there, as you are now trying to do with regard to Cuba. It is the United States, and no other country, that still mercilessly exploits and keeps in economic bondage the countries of Latin America and many other countries of the world. This is known to all. And if, Mr. President, your logic is to be followed, actions from without could apparently be organized against your country too, to put an end forever to this imperialist policy, the policy of threats, the policy of suppressing the freedom-loving peoples.

As for your concern for the emigres expelled by the Cuban people, I should like to add the following. You are of course well aware that there are, in many countries, emigres who are dissatisfied with the situation and the system existing in the countries from which they fled. And if the abnormal practice were introduced, in relations between States, of using these emigres, especially with arms in their hand, against the countries they had fled from, it can be openly said that this would inevitably lead to conflicts and wars. It would therefore be well to refrain from such ill-advised actions. This is a slippery and dangerous road which can lead to a new world war.

In your reply, you saw fit to touch upon certain questions unrelated to the subject of my message to you, including the question—as interpreted by you—of the historic inevitability of a communist revolution. I can only regard this as an attempt to evade the main question—that of aggression against Cuba. We are prepared, in appropriate circumstances, to exchange opinions on the question of the ways in which human society develops, although this question cannot be settled by debates between groups or individuals, however high their position may be. The question of whose system is the better will be decided by history, by the peoples themselves.

You, Mr. President, speak often and much of your desire that Cuba should be free. But that attitude is flatly contradicted by all United States actions with regard to this small country, let alone the latest armed attack upon Cuba organized with a view to changing Cuba's internal system by force. It was the United States which nearly 60 years ago imposed on Cuba the enslaving terms of the Havana Treaty and established its Guantanamo naval base on Cuban territory. Yet the United States is the most powerful country in the Western hemisphere, and no one in that hemisphere can threaten you with a military invasion. Consequently, if you continue to retain your naval base on Cuban territory against the clearly expressed will of the Cuban people and its Government, it is because this base is designed, not to serve as a defense against an attack by any external forces, but to suppress the will of the Latin American peoples. It was established to fulfill the functions of a gendarme, to keep the peoples of Latin America politically and economically dependent.

The Government of the United States is now fulminating against Cuba. But this indicates only one thing—your lack of trust in your own system, in the policy pursued by the United States. And this is understandable, as it is a policy of exploitation, a policy for the economic enslavement of under-developed countries. You have no confidence in your own system, and therefore fear that Cuba's example may prove contagious for other countries. But aggressive, bandit actions cannot save your system. In the historic process of the development of human society, each people decides, and will decide, its own destiny.

As for the Soviet Union, the peoples of our country settled this question finally and irrevocably over 43 years ago. We constitute a socialist state. Our social system is the most equitable of all that have so far existed, because in our country all the means of production are owned by those who work. That is indeed a contagious example, and the sooner the need to go over to this system is realized, the sooner will the whole of mankind achieve a really just society. By this very development, an end will be put, once and for all, to war.

You, Mr. President, did not like it when I said, in my previous message, that there can be no stable place in the world if anywhere war is aflame. But this is really so. The world is a single whole, whether we like it or not. And I can only repeat what I said: it is impossible to proceed by adjusting the situation and putting out the flames in one area, and kindling a new conflagration in another.

The Soviet State has always been a consistent defender of the freedom and independence of all peoples. We naturally, therefore, cannot concede to the United

States any right to control the destinies of other countries, including the countries of Latin America. We consider that any interference by one State in the affairs of another — especially armed interference — is a violation of all international laws and of the principles of peaceful coexistence which the Soviet Union has invariably upheld since the first days of its existence.

If it is now, more than ever before, the duty of every State and its leaders not to permit actions which are capable of jeopardizing universal peace, that applies with all the more force to the leaders of the great Powers. It is this that I urge upon you, Mr. President.

The Soviet Government's position in international affairs remains unchanged. We wish to build our relations with the United States in such a way that neither the Soviet Union nor the United States, as the two most powerful countries in the world, shall engage in sabre-rattling or push their military or economic superiority to the forefront, since that would lead to an aggravation of the international situation, not to its improvement. We are sincerely desirous of reaching agreement, both with you and with other countries of the world, on disarmament and all the other questions whose solution would promote peaceful coexistence, the recognition of every people's right to the social and political systems established by it, genuine respect for the will of the peoples and non-interference in their internal affairs. Only under these conditions can one really speak of coexistence, for coexistence is possible only if States with different social systems obey international laws and recognize the maintenance of world peace as their highest aim. Only in that event will peace be based on firm foundations.

Source: Khrushchev, Nikita. Letter to President John F. Kennedy, April 22, 1961. Kennedy-Khruschev Exchanges, *Foreign Relations of the United States, 1961-1963,* Vol. 6. Washington, DC: U.S. Government Printing Office, 1996. Available online at U.S. Department of State, http://www.state.gov/www/about_state/history/volume_vi/exchanges.html.

8.3

President Kennedy Describes the Cuban Missile Crisis – 1962
The Text of John F. Kennedy's Nationally Televised Address to the American People

On October 14, 1962, an American spy plane shot film footage over Cuba that showed that the Soviets were secretly building intermediate-range missile sites on the island. Two days later, the CIA confirmed that the Soviets were deploying dozens of missiles with nuclear warheads. The CIA estimated that some of the missiles would be capable of reaching most major American cities and strategic military locations within a week.

The following speech, delivered on TV by President John F. Kennedy on October 22, 1962, marked the first public revelation to the American people of what became known as the Cuban Missile Crisis. President Kennedy informed the American public that the Soviet Union was attempting to establish nuclear missile sites in Cuba, a mere 90 miles from the American mainland. The grim tone and content of the President's speech convinced many Americans that nuclear war with the USSR was imminent.

Good evening, my fellow citizens:

This government, as promised, has maintained the closest surveillance of the Soviet military build-up on the island of Cuba. Within the past week, unmistakable evidence has established the fact that a series of offensive missile sites is now in preparation on that imprisoned island. The purpose of these bases can be none other than to provide a nuclear strike capability against the Western Hemisphere.

Upon receiving the first preliminary hard information of this nature last Tuesday morning at 9:00 a.m., I directed that our surveillance be stepped up. And having now confirmed and completed our evaluation of the evidence and our decision on a course of action, this government feels obliged to report this new crisis to you in fullest detail.

The characteristics of these new missile sites indicate two distinct types of installations. Several of them include Medium Range Ballistic Missiles, capable of carrying a nuclear warhead for a distance of more than 1000 nautical miles. Each of these missiles, in short, is capable of striking Washington DC, the Panama Canal, Cape Canaveral, Mexico City, or any other city in the Southeastern part of the United States, in Central America, or in the Caribbean area.

Additional sites not yet completed appear to be designed for intermediate range ballistic missiles—capable of traveling more than twice as far—and thus capable of striking most of the major cities of the Western Hemisphere, ranging as far North as Hudson's Bay, Canada, and as far South as Lima, Peru. In addition, jet bombers, capable of carrying nuclear weapons, are now being uncrated and assembled in Cuba, while the necessary air bases are being prepared.

This urgent transformation of Cuba into an important strategic base—by the presence of these large, long-range, and clearly offensive weapons of sudden mass destruction—constitutes an explicit threat to the peace and security of all the Americas, in flagrant and deliberate defiance of the Rio Pact of 1947, the traditions of this Nation and Hemisphere, the Joint Resolution of the 87th Congress, the Charter of the United Nations, and my own public warnings to the Soviets on September 4 and 13. This action also contradicts the repeated assurances of Soviet spokesmen, both publicly and privately delivered, that the arms build in Cuba would retain its original defensive character, and that the Soviet Union had no need or desire to station strategic missiles on the territory of any other nation.

The size of this undertaking makes clear that it has been planned for some months. Yet only last month, after I had made clear the distinctions between any introduction of ground-to-ground missiles, the Soviet Government publicly stated on September 11 that, and I quote, "The armaments and military equipment sent to Cuba are designed exclusively for defensive purposes," and, and I quote the Soviet Government, "There is no need for the Soviet Government to shift its weapons for a retaliatory blow to any other country, for instance, Cuba" and that, and I quote the government, "The Soviet Union has so powerful rockets to carry these nuclear warheads that there is no need to search for sites for them beyond the boundaries of the Soviet Union." That statement was false.

Only last Thursday, as evidence of this rapid offensive build-up was already in my hand, Soviet Foreign Minister Gromyko told me in my office that he was instructed to make it clear once again, as he said his government had already done, that Soviet assistance to Cuba, and I quote, "pursued solely the purpose of contributing to the defense capabilities of Cuba," that, and I quote him, "training by Soviet specialists of Cuban nationals in handling defensive armaments was by no means offensive," and that "if it were otherwise," Mr. Gromyko went on, "the Soviet Government would never become involved in rendering such assistance." That statement was false.

Neither the United States of America nor the world community of nations can tolerate deliberate deception and offensive threats on the part of any nation, large or small. We no longer live in a world where only the actual firing of weapons represents a sufficient challenge to a nation's security to constitute maximum peril. Nuclear weapons are so destructive and ballistic missiles are so swift, that any substantially increased possibility of their use or any sudden change in their deployment may well be regarded as a definite threat to peace.

For many years, both the Soviet Union and the United States, recognizing this fact, have deployed strategic nuclear weapons with great care, never upsetting the precarious status quo which insured that these weapons would not be used in the absence of some vital challenge. Our own strategic missiles have never been transferred to the territory of any other nation, under a cloak of secrecy and deception; and our history, unlike that of the Soviets since the end of World War II, demonstrates that we have no desire to dominate or conquer any other nation or impose our system upon its people. Nevertheless, American citizens have become adjusted to living daily on the bull's eye of Soviet missiles located inside the USSR or in submarines.

In that sense, missiles in Cuba add to an already clear and present danger—although it should be noted the nations of Latin America have never previously been subjected to a potential nuclear threat.

But this secret, swift and extraordinary build-up of Communist missiles—in an area well known to have a special and historical relationship to the United States and the nations of the Western Hemisphere, in violation of Soviet assurances, and in defiance of American and Hemispheric policy—this sudden, clandestine decision to station strategic weapons for the first time outside of Soviet soil—is a deliberately provocative and unjustified change in the status quo which cannot be accepted by this country, if our courage and our commitments are ever to be trusted again by either friend or foe.

The 1930s taught us a clear lesson: aggressive conduct, if allowed to grow unchecked and unchallenged, ultimately leads to war. This nation is opposed to war. We are also true to our word. Our unswerving objective, therefore, must be to prevent the use of these missiles against this or any other country, and to secure their withdrawal or elimination from the Western Hemisphere.

> *"[Khrushchev] has an opportunity now to move the world back from the abyss of destruction."*

Our policy has been one of patience and restraint, as befits a peaceful and powerful nation, which leads a worldwide alliance. We have been determined not to be diverted from our central concerns by mere irritants and fanatics. But now further action is required—and it is underway; and these actions may only be the beginning. We will not prematurely or unnecessarily risk the costs of worldwide nuclear war in which even the fruits of victory would be ashes in our mouth—but neither will we shrink from that risk at any time it must be faced.

Acting, therefore, in the defense of our own security and of the entire Western Hemisphere, and under the authority entrusted to me by the Constitution as endorsed by the Resolution of the Congress, I have directed that the following *initial* steps be taken immediately:

First: To halt this offensive build-up, a strict quarantine on all offensive military equipment under shipment to Cuba is being initiated. All ships of any kind bound for Cuba from whatever nation or port will, if found to contain cargoes of offensive weapons, be turned back. This quarantine will be extended, if needed, to other types of cargo and carriers. We are not at this time, however, denying the necessities of life as the Soviets attempted to do in their Berlin blockade of 1948.

Second: I have directed the continued and increased close surveillance of Cuba and its military build-up. The Foreign ministers of the OAS, in their communiqué of October 6, rejected secrecy on such matters in this Hemisphere. Should these offensive military preparations continue, thus increasing the threat to the Hemisphere, further action will be justified. I have directed the Armed Forces to prepare for any eventualities; and I trust that in the interest of both the Cuban people and the Soviet technicians at the sites, the hazards to all concerned of continuing this threat will be recognized.

Third: It shall be the policy of this Nation to regard any nuclear missile launched from Cuba against any nation in the Western Hemisphere as an attack by the Soviet Union on the United States, requiring a full retaliatory response upon the Soviet Union.

Fourth: As a necessary military precaution, I have reinforced our base at Guantanamo, evacuated today the dependents of our personnel there, and ordered additional military units to be on a standby alert basis.

Fifth: We are calling tonight for an immediate meeting of the Organ of Consultation under the Organization of American States, to consider this threat to hemispheric security and to invoke Articles 6 and 8 of the Rio Treaty in support of all necessary action. The United Nations Charter allows for regional security arrangements—and the nations of this Hemisphere decided long ago against the military presence of outside powers. Our other allies around the world have also been alerted.

Sixth: Under the Charter of the United Nations, we are asking tonight that an emergency meeting of the Security Council be convoked without delay to take action against this latest Soviet threat to world peace. Our resolution will call for the prompt dismantling and withdrawal of all offensive weapons in Cuba, under the supervision of UN observers, before the quarantine can be lifted.

Seventh and finally: I call upon Chairman Khrushchev to halt and eliminate this clandestine, reckless, and provocative threat to world peace and to stable relations between our two nations. I call upon him further to abandon this course of world domination, and to join in an historic effort to end the perilous arms race and transform the history of man. He has an opportunity now to move the world back from the abyss of destruction—by returning to his government's own words that it had no need to station missiles outside its own territory, and withdrawing these weapons from Cuba—by refraining from any action which will widen or deepen the present crisis—and then by participating in a search for peaceful and permanent solutions.

This Nation is prepared to present its case against the Soviet threat to peace, and our own proposals for a peaceful world, at any time and in any forum—in the OAS, in the United Nations, or in any other meeting that could be useful—without limiting our freedom of action. We have in the past made strenuous efforts to limit the spread of nuclear weapons. We have proposed the elimination of all arms and military bases in a fair and effective disarmament treaty. We are prepared to discuss new proposals for the removal of tensions on both sides—including the possibilities of a genuinely independent Cuba, free to determine its own destiny. We have no wish to war with the Soviet Union—for we are a peaceful people who desire to live in peace with all other peoples.

But it is difficult to settle or even discuss these problems in an atmosphere of intimidation. That is why this latest Soviet threat—or any other threat which is made either independently or in response to our actions this week—must and will be met with determination. Any hostile move anywhere in the world against the safety and freedom of peoples to whom we are committed—including in particular the brave people of West Berlin—will be met by whatever action is needed.

Finally, I want to say a few words to the captive people of Cuba, to whom this speech is being directly carried by special radio facilities. I speak to you as a friend, as one who knows of your deep attachment to your fatherland, as one who shares your aspirations for liberty and justice for all. And I have watched and the American people have watched with deep sorrow how your nationalist revolution was betrayed—and how your fatherland fell under foreign domination. Now your leaders are no longer Cuban leaders inspired by Cuban ideals. They are puppets and agents of an international conspiracy which has turned Cuba against your friends and neighbors in the Americas—and turned it into the first Latin American country to have these weapons on its soil.

These new weapons are not in your interest. They contribute nothing to your peace and well being. They can only undermine it. But this country has no wish to cause you to suffer or to impose any system upon you. We know that your lives and land are being used as pawns by those who deny you freedom.

Many times in the past, the Cuban people have risen to throw out tyrants who destroyed their liberty. And I have no doubt that most Cubans today look forward to the time when they will be truly free—free from foreign domination, free to choose their own leaders, free to select their own system, free to own their own land, free to speak, and write, and worship without fear or degradation. And then shall Cuba be welcomed back to society of free nations and to the associations of this Hemisphere.

My fellow citizens: Let no one doubt that this is a difficult and dangerous effort on which we have set out. No one can foresee precisely what course it will take or what costs or casualties will be incurred. Many months of sacrifice and self-discipline lie ahead—months in which both our patience and our will will be tested—months in which many threats and denunciations will keep us aware of our dangers. But the greatest danger of all would be to do nothing.

The path we have chosen for the present is full of hazards, as all paths are—but it is the one most consistent with our character and courage as a nation and our commitments around the world. The cost of freedom is always high—but Americans have always paid it. And one path we shall never choose, and that is the path of surrender or sublimation.

Our goal is not the victory of might, but the vindication of right—not peace at the expense of freedom, but both peace *and* freedom, here in this Hemisphere, and, we hope, around the world. God willing, that goal will be achieved.

Thank you and good night.

Source: Kennedy, John F. "Radio and Television Report to the American People on the Soviet Arms Buildup in Cuba." October 22, 1962. John F. Kennedy Library and Museum. Available online at www.jfk library.org.

8.4
Fidel Castro Decries the American "Imperialists" – 1962
The Text of Correspondence from Castro to Soviet Premier Khrushchev

> *This message from Cuban dictator Fidel Castro to Soviet Premier Nikita Khrushchev was composed and delivered at the height of the Cuban Missile Crisis, on October 26, 1962. It clearly illustrates that many leaders on both sides of the conflict believed that a nuclear exchange between the two powers was likely. U.S. Secretary of Defense Robert McNamara later recalled that he took a break from the White House situation room on October 27—a few hours after this letter from Castro was delivered—and went outside. "I went up into the open air to look and to smell it," McNamara recalled, "because I thought it was the last Saturday I would ever see."*

October 26, 1962

Dear Comrade Khrushchev:

Given the analysis of the situation and the reports which have reached us, [I] consider an attack to be almost imminent—within the next 24 to 72 hours. There are two possible variants: the first and most probable one is an air attack against certain objectives with the limited aim of destroying them; the second, and though less probable, still possible, is a full invasion. This would require a large force and is the most repugnant form of aggression, which might restrain them.

You can be sure that we will resist with determination, whatever the case. The Cuban people's morale is extremely high and the people will confront aggression heroically.

I would like to briefly express my own personal opinion.

If the second variant takes place and the imperialists invade Cuba with the aim of occupying it, the dangers of their aggressive policy are so great that after such an invasion the Soviet Union must never allow circumstances in which the imperialists could carry out a nuclear first strike against it.

I tell you this because I believe that the imperialists' aggressiveness makes them extremely dangerous, and that if they manage to carry out an invasion of Cuba—a brutal act in violation of universal and moral law—then that would be the moment to eliminate this danger forever, in an act of the most legitimate self-defense. However harsh and terrible the solution, there would be no other.

This opinion is shaped by observing the development of their aggressive policy. The imperialists, without regard for world opinion and against laws and principles, have blockaded the seas, violated our air-space, and are preparing to invade, while at the same time blocking any possibility of negotiation, even though they understand the gravity of the problem.

You have been, and are, a tireless defender of peace, and I understand that these moments, when the results of your superhuman efforts are so seriously threatened, must be bitter for you. We will maintain our hopes for saving the peace until the last moment, and we are ready to contribute to this in any way we can. But, at the same time, we are serene and ready to confront a situation which we see as very real and imminent.

I convey to you the infinite gratitude and recognition of the Cuban people to the Soviet people, who have been so generous and fraternal, along with our profound gratitude and admiration to you personally. We wish you success with the enormous task and great responsibilities which are in your hands.

Fraternally,
Fidel Castro

Source: Castro, Fidel. "Letter to Nikita Khrushchev from Fidel Castro Regarding Defending Cuban Air Space." October 26, 1962. John F. Kennedy Library and Museum. Available online at www.jfk library.org.

8.5
The Kennedy-Khrushchev Letters – 1962
The Text of Correspondence between President John F. Kennedy and Premier Nikita Khrushchev at the Height of the Cuban Missile Crisis

On October 26, 1962, Soviet Premier Nikita Khrushchev sent a secret message to President John F. Kennedy about the Cuban Missile Crisis. Conciliatory in tone, it offered the framework for a diplomatic deal that would defuse the crisis: "You would declare that the US will not invade Cuba with its forces, and will not support any sort of forces which might intend to carry out an invasion of Cuba. Then the necessity for the presence of our military specialists in Cuba would disappear." As Kennedy and his advisors mulled this message, they received a far more combative letter from Khrushchev. This letter strongly defended the Soviet right to keep missiles in Cuba as long as American missiles stationed in Turkey were aimed at Soviet cities.

After much discussion, Kennedy opted to respond to Khrushchev's first letter and in effect pretend that the second one did not exist. Kennedy accepted the compromise laid out in Khrushchev's first correspondence. When the Soviets signaled their acceptance of Kennedy's overture, the confrontation over the missiles in Cuba was finally defused— though both sides issued rumbling warnings over the ensuing weeks.

The first letter below is the text of Khrushchev's first, secret message. The second letter is Khrushchev's more defiant second message. The third letter is Kennedy's response to Khrushchev's first message; it makes no acknowledgement of the second message and instead embraces the deal contained in Khrushchev's first letter.

Correspondence from Chairman Khrushchev to President Kennedy, October 26, 1962

Dear Mr. President:

I have received your letter of October 25.

From your letter, I got the feeling that you have some understanding of the situation which has developed and (some) sense of responsibility. I value this.

Now we have already publicly exchanged our evaluations of the events around Cuba and each of us has set forth his explanation and his understanding of these events. Consequently, I would judge that, apparently, a continuation of an exchange of opinions at such a distance, even in the form of secret letters, will hardly add anything to that which one side has already said to the other.

I think you will understand me correctly if you are really concerned about the welfare of the world. Everyone needs peace: both capitalists, if they have not lost their reason, and, still more, Communists, people who know how to value not only their own lives but, more than anything, the lives of the peoples. We, Communists, are against all wars between states in general and have been defending the cause of peace since we came into the world. We have always regarded war as a calamity, and not as a game nor as a means for the attainment of definite goals, nor, all the more, as a goal in itself. Our goals are clear, and the means to attain them is labor. War is our enemy and a calamity for all the peoples.

It is thus that we, Soviet people, and, together with US, other peoples as well, understand the questions of war and peace. I can, in any case, firmly say this for the peoples of the Socialist countries, as well as for all progressive people who want peace, happiness, and friendship among peoples.

I see, Mr. President, that you too are not devoid of a sense of anxiety for the fate of the world ... and of what war entails. What would a war give you? You are threatening us with war. But you well know that the very least which you would receive in reply would be that you would experience the same consequences as those which you sent us. And that must be clear to us, people invested with authority, trust, and responsibility. We must not succumb to intoxication and petty passions, regardless of whether elections are impending in this or that country, or not impending. These are all transient things, but if indeed war should break out, then it would not be in our power to stop it, for such is the logic of war. I have participated in two wars and know that war ends when it has rolled through cities and villages, everywhere sowing death and destruction....

In the name of the Soviet Government and the Soviet people, I assure you that your conclusions regarding offensive weapons on Cuba are groundless. It is apparent from what you have written me that our conceptions are different on this score, or rather, we have different estimates of these or those military means. Indeed, in reality, the same forms of weapons can have different interpretations.

You are a military man and, I hope, will understand me. Let us take for example a simple cannon. What sort of means is this: offensive or defensive? A cannon is a defensive means if it is set up to defend boundaries or a fortified area. But if one concentrates artillery, and adds to it the necessary number of troops, then the same cannons do become an offensive means, because they prepare and clear the way for infantry to attack. The same happens with missile-nuclear weapons as well, with any type of this weapon.

You are mistaken if you think that any of our means on Cuba are offensive. However, let us not quarrel now. It is apparent that I will not be able to convince you of this. But I say to you: You, Mr. President, are a military man and should understand: Can one attack, if one has on one's territory even an enormous quantity of missiles of various effective radiuses and various power, but using only these means. These missiles are a means of extermination and destruction. But one cannot attack with these missiles, even nuclear missiles of a power of 100 megatons because only people, troops, can attack. Without people, any means however powerful cannot be offensive.

How can one, consequently, give such a completely incorrect interpretation as you are now giving, to the effect that some sort of means on Cuba are offensive. All the means located there, and I assure you of this, have a defensive character, are on Cuba solely for the purposes of defense, and we have sent them to Cuba at the request of the Cuban Government. You, however, say that these are offensive means.

But, Mr. President, do you really seriously think that Cuba can attack the United States and that even we together with Cuba can attack you from the territory of Cuba? Can you really think that way? How is it possible? We do not understand this. Has something so new appeared in military strategy that one can think that it is possible to attack thus. I say precisely attack, and not destroy, since barbarians, people who have lost their sense, destroy.

I believe that you have no basis to think this way. You can regard us with distrust, but, in any case, you can be calm in this regard, that we are of sound mind and understand perfectly well that if we attack you, you will respond the same way. But you too will receive the same that you hurl against us. And I think that you also understand this. My conversation with you in Vienna gives me the right to talk to you this way.

255

This indicates that we are normal people, that we correctly understand and correctly evaluate the situation. Consequently, how can we permit the incorrect actions which you ascribe to us? Only lunatics or suicides, who themselves want to perish and to destroy the whole world before they die, could do this. We, however, want to live and do not at all want to destroy your country. We want something quite different: To compete with your country on a peaceful basis. We quarrel with you, we have differences on ideological questions. But our view of the world consists in this, that ideological questions, as well as economic problems, should be solved not by military means, they must be solved on the basis of peaceful competition, i.e., as this is understood in capitalist society, on the basis of competition. We have proceeded and are proceeding from the fact that the peaceful co-existence of the two different social-political systems, now existing in the world, is necessary, that it is necessary to assure a stable peace. That is the sort of principle we hold.

You have now proclaimed piratical measures, which were employed in the Middle Ages, when ships proceeding in international waters were attacked, and you have called this "a quarantine" around Cuba. Our vessels, apparently, will soon enter the zone which your Navy is patrolling. I assure you that these vessels, now bound for Cuba, are carrying the most innocent peaceful cargoes. Do you really think that we only occupy ourselves with the carriage of so-called offensive weapons, atomic and hydrogen bombs? Although perhaps your military people imagine that these (cargoes) are some sort of special type of weapon, I assure you that they are the most ordinary peaceful products.

Consequently, Mr. President, let us show good sense. I assure you that on those ships, which are bound for Cuba, there are no weapons at all. The weapons which were necessary for the defense of Cuba are already there. I do not want to say that there were not any shipments of weapons at all. No, there were such shipments. But now Cuba has already received the necessary means of defense.

I don't know whether you can understand me and believe me. But I should like to have you believe in yourself and to agree that one cannot give way to passions; it is necessary to control them. And in what direction are events now developing? If you stop the vessels, then, as you yourself know, that would be piracy. If we started to do that with regard to your ships, then you would also be as indignant as we and the whole world now are. One cannot give another interpretation to such actions, because one cannot legalize lawlessness. If this were permitted, then there would be no peace, there would also be no peaceful coexistence. We should then be forced to put into effect the necessary measures of a defensive character to protect our interests in accordance with international law. Why should this be done? To what would all this lead?

Let us normalize relations. We have received an appeal from the Acting Secretary General of the UN, U Thant, with his proposals. I have already answered him.

His proposals come to this, that our side should not transport armaments of any kind to Cuba during a certain period of time, while negotiations are being conducted—and we are ready to enter such negotiations—and the other side should not undertake any sort of piratical actions against vessels engaged in navigation on the high seas. I consider these proposals reasonable. This would be a way out of the situation which has been created, which would give the peoples the possibility of breathing calmly. You have asked what happened, what evoked the delivery of weapons to Cuba? You have spoken about this to our Minister of Foreign Affairs. I will tell you frankly, Mr. President, what evoked it.

We were very grieved by the fact—I spoke about it in Vienna—that a landing took place, that an attack on Cuba was committed, as a result of which many Cubans perished. You yourself told me then that this had been a mistake. I respected that explanation. You repeated it to me several times, pointing out that not everybody occupying a high position would acknowledge his mistakes as you had done. I value such frankness. For my part, I told you that we too possess no less courage; we also acknowledged those mistakes which had been committed during the history of our state, and not only acknowledged, but sharply condemned them.

If you are really concerned about the peace and welfare of your people, and this is your responsibility as President, then I, as the Chairman of the Council of Ministers, am concerned for my people. Moreover, the preservation of world peace should be our joint concern, since if, under contemporary conditions, war should break out, it would be a war not only between the reciprocal claims, but a worldwide cruel and destructive war.

Why have we proceeded to assist Cuba with military and economic aid? The answer is: We have proceeded to do so only for reasons of humanitarianism. At one time, our people itself had a revolution, when Russia was still a backward country. We were attacked then. We were the target of attack by many countries. The USA participated in that adventure. This has been recorded by participants in the aggression against our country. A whole book has been written about this by General Graves, who, at that time, commanded the US Expeditionary Corps. Graves called it "The American Adventure in Siberia."

We know how difficult it is to accomplish a revolution and how difficult it is to reconstruct a country on new foundations. We sincerely sympathize with Cuba and the Cuban people, but we are not interfering in questions of domestic structure, we are not interfering in their affairs. The Soviet Union desires to help the Cubans build their life as they themselves wish and that others should not hinder them.

You once said that the United States was not preparing an invasion. But you also declared that you sympathized with the Cuban counter-revolutionary emigrants, that you support them and would help them to realize their plans against the present Government of Cuba. It is also not a secret to anyone that the threat of armed attack, aggression, has constantly hung, and continues to hang over Cuba. It was only this which impelled us to respond to the request of the Cuban Government to furnish it aid for the strengthening of the defensive capacity of this country.

If assurances were given by the President and the Government of the United States that the USA itself would not participate in an attack on Cuba and would restrain others from actions of this sort, if you would recall your fleet, this would immediately change everything. I am not speaking for Fidel Castro, but I think that he and the Government of Cuba, evidently, would declare demobilization and would appeal to the people to get down to peaceful labor. Then, too, the question of armaments would disappear, since, if there is no threat, then armaments are a burden for every people. Then too, the question of the destruction, not only of the armaments which you call offensive, but of all other armaments as well, would look different.

I spoke in the name of the Soviet Government in the United Nations and introduced a proposal for the disbandment of all armies and for the destruction of all armaments. How then can I now count on those armaments?

Armaments bring only disasters. When one accumulates them, this damages the economy, and if one puts them to use, then they destroy people on both sides. Consequently, only a madman can believe that armaments are the principal means in the life of society. No, they are an enforced loss of human energy, and what is more are for the destruction of man himself. If people do not show wisdom, then in the final analysis they will come to a clash, like blind moles, and then reciprocal extermination will begin.

Let us therefore show statesmanlike wisdom. I propose: We, for our part, will declare that our ships, bound for Cuba, will not carry any kind of armaments. You would declare that the United States will not invade Cuba with its forces and will not support any sort of forces which might intend to carry out an invasion of Cuba. Then the necessity for the presence of our military specialists in Cuba would disappear.

Mr. President, I appeal to you to weigh well what the aggressive, piratical actions, which you have declared the USA intends to carry out in international waters, would lead to. You yourself know that any sensible man simply cannot agree with this, cannot recognize your right to such actions.

If you did this as the first step towards the unleashing of war, well then, it is evident that nothing else is left to us but to accept this challenge of yours. If, however, you have not lost your self-control and sensibly conceive what this might lead to, then, Mr. President, we and you ought not now to pull on the ends of the rope in which you have tied the knot of war, because the more the two of us pull, the tighter that knot will be tied. And a moment may come when that knot will be tied so tight that even he who tied it will not have the strength to untie it, and then it will be necessary to cut that knot, and what that would mean is not for me to explain to you, because you yourself understand perfectly of what terrible forces our countries dispose.

Consequently, if there is no intention to tighten that knot and thereby to doom the world to the catastrophe of thermonuclear war, then let us not only relax the forces pulling on the ends of the rope, let us take measures to untie that knot. We are ready for this.

We welcome all forces which stand on positions of peace. Consequently, I expressed gratitude to Mr. Bertrand Russell, too, who manifests alarm and concern for the fate of the world, and I readily responded to the appeal of the Acting Secretary General of the UN, U Thant.

There, Mr. President, are my thoughts, which, if you agreed with them, could put an end to that tense situation which is disturbing all peoples.

These thoughts are dictated by a sincere desire to relieve the situation, to remove the threat of war.

Respectfully yours,
N. Khrushchev
October 26, 1962.

Correspondence from Chairman Khrushchev to President Kennedy, October 27, 1962

DEAR MR. PRESIDENT, I have studied with great satisfaction your reply to Mr. Thant concerning measures that should be taken to avoid contact between our vessels and thereby avoid irreparable and fatal consequences. This reasonable step on your part strengthens my belief that you are showing concern for the preservation of peace, which I note with satisfaction.

I have already said that our people, our Government, and I personally, as Chairman of the Council of Ministers, are concerned solely with having our country develop and occupy a worthy place among all peoples of the world in economic competition, in the development of culture and the arts, and in raising the living standard of the people. This is the most noble and necessary field for competition, and both the victor and the vanquished will derive only benefit from it, because it means peace and an increase in the means by which man lives and finds enjoyment.

In your statement you expressed the opinion that the main aim was not simply to come to an agreement and take measures to prevent contact between our vessels and consequently a deepening of the crisis which could, as a result of such contacts spark a military conflict, after which all negotiations would be superfluous because other forces and other laws would then come into play—the laws of war. I agree with you that this is only the first step. The main thing that must be done is to normalize and stabilize the state of peace among states and among peoples.

I understand your concern for the security of the United States, Mr. President, because this is the primary duty of a President. But we too are disturbed about these same questions; I bear these same obligations as Chairman of the Council of Ministers of the U.S.S.R. You have been alarmed by the fact that we have aided Cuba with weapons, in order to strengthen its defense capability—precisely defense capability—because whatever weapons it may possess, Cuba cannot be equated with you since the difference in magnitude is so great, particularly in view of modern means of destruction. Our aim has been and is to help Cuba, and no one can dispute the humanity of our motives, which are oriented toward enabling Cuba to live peacefully and develop in the way its people desire.

You wish to ensure the security of your country, and this is understandable. But Cuba, too, wants the same thing; all countries want to maintain their security. But how are we, the Soviet Union, our Government, to assess your actions which are expressed in the fact that you have surrounded the Soviet Union with military bases; surrounded our allies with military bases; placed military bases literally around our country; and stationed your missile armaments there? This is no secret. Responsible American personages openly declare that it is so. Your missiles are located in Britain, are located in Italy, and are aimed against us. Your missiles are located in Turkey.

You are disturbed over Cuba. You say that this disturbs you because it is 90 miles by sea from the coast of the United States of America. But Turkey adjoins us; our sentries patrol back and forth and see each other. Do you consider, then, that you have the right to demand security for your own country and the removal of the weapons you call offensive, but do not accord the same right to us? You have placed destructive missile weapons, which you call offensive, in Turkey, literally next to us. How then can recognition of our equal military capacities be reconciled with such unequal relations between our great states? This is irreconcilable.

It is good, Mr. President, that you have agreed to have our representatives meet and begin talks, apparently through the mediation of U Thant, Acting Secretary General of the United Nations. Consequently, he to some degree has assumed the role of a mediator and we consider that he will be able to cope with this responsible mission, provided, of course, that each party drawn into this controversy displays good will.

I think it would be possible to end the controversy quickly and normalize the situation, and then the people could breathe more easily, considering that statesmen charged with responsibility are of sober mind and have an awareness of their responsibility combined with the ability to solve complex questions and not bring things to a military catastrophe.

I therefore make this proposal: We are willing to remove from Cuba the means which you regard as offensive. We are willing to carry this out and to make this pledge in the United Nations. Your representatives will make a declaration to the effect that the United States, for its part, considering the uneasiness and anxiety of the Soviet State, will remove its analogous means from Turkey. Let us reach agreement as to the period of time needed by you and by us to bring this about. And, after that, persons entrusted by the United Nations Security Council could inspect on the spot the fulfillment of the pledges made. Of course, the permission of the Governments of Cuba and Turkey is necessary for the entry into those countries of these representatives and for the inspection of the fulfillment of the pledge made by each side. Of course it would be best if these representatives enjoyed the confidence of the Security Council as well as yours and mine—both the United States and the Soviet Union—and also that of Turkey and Cuba. I do not think it would be difficult to select people who would enjoy the trust and respect of all parties concerned.

We, in making this pledge, in order to give satisfaction and hope of the peoples of Cuba and Turkey and to strengthen their confidences in their security, will make a statement within the framework of the Security Council to the effect that the Soviet Government gives a solemn promise to respect the inviolability of the borders and sovereignty of Turkey, not to interfere in its internal affairs, not to invade Turkey, not to make available our territory as a bridgehead for such an invasion, and that it would also restrain those who contemplate committing aggression against Turkey, either from the territory of the Soviet Union or from the territory of Turkey's other neighboring states.

The United States Government will make a similar statement within the framework of the Security Council regarding Cuba. It will declare that the United States will respect the inviolability of Cuba's borders and its sovereignty, will pledge not to interfere in its internal affairs, not to invade Cuba itself or make its territory available as a bridgehead for such an invasion, and will also restrain those who might contemplate committing aggression against Cuba, either from the territory of the United States or from the territory of Cuba's other neighboring states.

Of course, for this we would have to come to an agreement with you and specify a certain time limit. Let us agree to some period of time, but without unnecessary delay—say within two or three weeks, not longer than a month.

The means situated in Cuba, of which you speak and which disturb you, as you have stated, are in the hands of Soviet officers. Therefore, any accidental use of them to the detriment of the United States is excluded. These means are situated in Cuba at the request of the Cuban Government and are only for defense purposes. Therefore, if there is no invasion of Cuba, or attack on the Soviet Union or any of our other allies, then of course these means are not and will not be a threat to anyone. For they are not for purposes of attack.

If you are agreeable to my proposal, Mr. President, then we would send our representatives to New York, to the United Nations, and would give them comprehensive instructions in order that an agreement may be reached more quickly. If you also select your people and give them the corresponding instructions, then this question can be quickly resolved.

Why would I like to do this? Because the whole world is now apprehensive and expects sensible actions of us. The greatest joy for all peoples would be the announcement of our agreement and of the eradication of the controversy that has arisen. I attach great importance to this agreement in so far as it could serve as a good beginning and could in particular make it easier to reach agreement on banning nuclear weapons tests. The question of the tests could be solved in parallel fashion, without connecting one with the other, because these are different issues. However, it is important that agreement be reached on both these issues so as to present humanity with a fine gift, and also to gladden it with the news that agreement has been reached on the cessation of nuclear tests and that consequently the atmosphere will no longer be poisoned. Our position and yours on this issue are very close together.

All of this could possibly serve as a good impetus toward the finding of mutually acceptable agreements on other controversial issues on which you and I have been exchanging views. These issues have so far not been resolved, but they are awaiting urgent solution, which would clear up the international atmosphere. We are prepared for this.

These are my proposals, Mr. President.

Respectfully yours,
N. Khrushchev

Correspondence from President Kennedy to Chairman Khruschev, October 27, 1962

Dear Mr. Chairman:

I have read your letter of October 26th with great care and welcomed the statement of your desire to seek a prompt solution to the problem. The first thing that needs to be done, however, is for work to cease on offensive missile bases in Cuba and for all weapons systems in Cuba capable of offensive use to be rendered inoperable, under effective United Nations arrangements.

Assuming this is done promptly, I have given my representatives in New York instructions that will permit them to work out this weekend—in cooperation with the Acting Secretary General and your representative—an arrangement for a permanent solution to the Cuban problem along the lines suggested in your letter of October 26th. As I read your letter, the key elements of your proposals—which seem generally acceptable as I understand them—are as follows:

1) You would agree to remove these weapons systems from Cuba under appropriate United Nations observation and supervision; and undertake, with suitable safeguards, to halt the further introduction of such weapons systems into Cuba.

2) We, on our part, would agree—upon the establishment of adequate arrangements through the United Nations to ensure the carrying out and continuation of these commitments—(a) to remove promptly the quarantine measures now in effect and (b) to give assurances against an invasion of Cuba. I am confident that other nations of the Western Hemisphere would be prepared to do likewise.

If you will give your representative similar instructions, there is no reason why we should not be able to complete these arrangements and announce them to the world within a couple of days. The effect of such a settlement on easing world tensions would enable us to work toward a more general arrangement regarding 'other armaments', as proposed in your second letter which you made public. I would like to say again that the United States is very much interested in reducing tensions and halting the arms race; and if your letter signifies that you are prepared to discuss a detente affecting NATO and the Warsaw Pact, we are quite prepared to consider with our allies any useful proposals.

But the first ingredient, let me emphasize, is the cessation of work on missile sites in Cuba and measures to render such weapons inoperable, under effective international guarantees. The continuation of this threat, or a prolonging of this discussion concerning Cuba by linking these problems to the broader questions of European and world security, would surely lead to an intensification of the Cuban crisis and a grave risk to the peace of the world. For this reason I hope we can quickly agree along the lines in this letter and in your letter of October 26th.

John F. Kennedy

Source: Correspondence between Nikita Khrushchev and John F. Kennedy, October 26-27, 1962. Kennedy-Khrushchev Exchanges, *Foreign Relations of the United States, 1961-1963*, Vol. 6. Washington, DC: U.S. Government Printing Office, 1996. Available online at U.S. Department of State, http://www.state.gov/www/about_state/history/volume_vi/exchanges.html.

8.6
Backdoor Diplomacy during the Cuban Missile Crisis – 1962
The Text of a Memorandum from Attorney General Robert F. Kennedy to Secretary of State Dean Rusk

In this memorandum dated October 30, 1962, U.S. Attorney General Robert F. Kennedy—the brother of President John F. Kennedy—recounts a secret meeting he held with Soviet Ambassador Anatoly Dobrynin during the Cuban Missile Crisis. One of the major topics of this meeting between Kennedy and Dobrynin concerned the continued existence of NATO nuclear missiles in Turkey—and whether those missiles might be removed in exchange for the removal of Soviet missiles from Cuba. A sentence on this subject is actually crossed out in the original text; the sentence is reprinted below in italics and within brackets.

October 30, 1962

MEMORANDUM FOR THE SECRETARY OF STATE
FROM THE ATTORNEY GENERAL

At the request of Secretary Rusk, I telephoned Ambassador Dobrynin at approximately 7:15 p.m. on Saturday, October 27th. I asked him if he would come to the Justice Department at a quarter of eight.

We met in my office. I told him first that we understood that the work was continuing on the Soviet missile bases in Cuba. Further, I explained to him that in the last two hours we had found that our planes flying over Cuba had been fired upon and that one of our U-2's had been shot down and the pilot killed. I said these men were flying unarmed planes.

I told him that this was an extremely serious turn in events. We would have to make certain decisions within the next 12 or possibly 24 hours. There was a very little time left. If the Cubans were shooting at our planes, then we were going to shoot back. This could not help but bring on further incidents and that he had better understand the full implications of this matter.

He raised the point that the argument the Cubans were making was that we were violating Cuban air space. I replied that if we had not been violating Cuban air space then we would still be, believing what he and Khrushchev had said … that there were no long-range missiles in Cuba. In any case I said that this matter was far more serious than the air space over Cuba and involved peoples all over the world.

I said that he had better understand the situation and he had better communicate that understanding to Mr. Khrushchev. Mr. Khrushchev and he had misled us. The Soviet Union had secretly established missile bases in Cuba while at the same time proclaiming, privately and publicly, that this would never be done. I said those missile bases had to go and they had to go right away. We had to have a commitment by at least tomorrow that those bases would be removed. This was not an ultimatum, I said, but just a statement of fact. He should understand that if they did not remove those bases then we would remove them. His country might take retaliatory action but he should understand that before this was over, while there might be dead Americans there would also be dead Russians.

He asked me then what offer we were making. I said a letter had just been transmitted to the Soviet Embassy, which stated in substance that the missile bases should be dismantled and all offensive weapons should be removed from Cuba. In return, if Cuba and Castro and the Communists ended their subversive activities in other Central and Latin-American countries, we would agree to keep peace in the Caribbean and not permit an invasion from American soil.

He then asked me about Khrushchev's other proposal dealing with the removal of the missiles from Turkey. I replied that there could be no quid pro quo — no deal of this kind could be made. This was a matter that had to be considered by NATO and that it was up to NATO to make the decision. I said it was completely impossible for NATO to take such a step under the present threatening position of the Soviet Union. [*If some time elapsed—and per your instructions, I mentioned four or five months—I said I was sure that these matters could be resolved satisfactorily.*]

Per your instructions I repeated that there could be no deal of any kind and that any steps toward easing tensions in other parts of the world largely depended on the Soviet Union and Mr. Khrushchev taking action in Cuba and taking it immediately.

I repeated to him that this matter could not wait and that he had better contact Mr. Khrushchev and have a commitment from him by the next day to withdraw the missile bases under United Nations supervision for otherwise, I said, there would be drastic consequences.

Source: Kennedy, Robert F. "Memorandum for the Secretary of State from the Attorney General, October 30, 1962." John F. Kennedy Library and Museum. Available online at http://www.jfklibrary.org.

8.7

Premier Khrushchev Withdraws Soviet Missiles from Cuba – 1962
The Text of a Message from Nikita Khrushchev to President John F. Kennedy, Delivered over Radio Moscow

On October 28, 1962, Soviet Premier Nikita Khrushchev read the following message to U.S. President John F. Kennedy over Radio Moscow. He accepted Kennedy's promise that the United States would not invade Cuba and said that the USSR would remove all Soviet missiles from the island. Following is the full text of Khrushchev's broadcast message.

Dear Mr. President:

I have received your message of 27th October. I express my satisfaction and thank you for the sense of proportion you have displayed and for the realization of the responsibility which now devolves on you for the preservation of the peace of the world.

I regard with great understanding your concern and the concerns of the United States people in connection with the fact that the weapons you describe as offensive are formidable weapons indeed. Both you and we understand what kind of weapons these are.

In order to eliminate as rapidly as possible the conflict which endangers the cause of peace, to give an assurance to all the people who crave peace, and to reassure the American people, who, I am certain, also want peace, as do the people of the Soviet Union, the Soviet Government, in addition to earlier instructions on the discontinuation of further work on weapons constructions sites, has given a new order to dismantle the arms which you describe as offensive, and to crate and return them to the Soviet Union.

Mr. President, I should like to repeat what I had already written to you in my earlier messages—that the Soviet Government has given economic assistance to the Republic of Cuba, as well as arms, because Cuba and the Cuban people were under the continuous threat of an invasion of Cuba.

A piratic vessel had shelled Havana. They said that this shelling was done by irresponsible Cuban emigres. Perhaps so. However, the question is from where did they shoot. It is a fact that these Cubans have no territory, they are fugitives from their country, and they have no means to conduct military operations.

> *"Is it not a fact that an intruding American plane could be easily taken for a nuclear bomber, which might push us to a fateful step?"*

This means that someone put into their hands these weapons for shelling Havana and for piracy in the Caribbean in Cuban territorial waters. It is impossible in our time not to notice a piratic ship, considering the concentration in the Caribbean of American ships from which everything can be seen and observed.

In these conditions, pirate ships freely roam around and shell Cuba and make piratic attacks on peaceful ships. It is known that they even shelled a British cargo ship. In a word, Cuba was under serious threat of aggressive forces, which did not conceal their intention to invade its territory.

The Cuban people want to build their life in their own interest without the external interference. This is their right, and they cannot be blamed for wanting to be masters of their own country and disposing of the fruits of their own labor. The threat of invasion of Cuba and all other schemes for creating tension over China are designed to strike the Cuban people with a sense of insecurity, intimidate them, and prevent them from peacefully building their new life.

Mr. President, I should like to say clearly once more that we could not remain indifferent to this. The Soviet Government decided to render assistance to Cuba with means of defense against aggression—only with means for defense purposes. We have supplied the defense means which you describe as offensive means. We have supplied them to prevent an attack on Cuba—to prevent rash acts.

I regard with respect and trust the statement you made in your message of 27 October 1962 that there would be no attack, no invasion of Cuba, and not only on the part of the United States, but also on the part of other nations of the Western Hemisphere, as you said in your same message. Then the motives which induced us to render assistance of such a kind to Cuba disappear.

It is for this reason that we instructed our officers—these means as I had already informed you earlier are in the hands of the Soviet officers—to take appropriate measures to discontinue construction of the aforementioned facilities, to dismantle them, and to return them to the Soviet Union. As I had informed you in the letter of 27 October, we are prepared to reach agreement to enable the U.N. representatives to verify the dismantling of these means. Thus in view of the assurances you have given and our instructions on dismantling, there is every condition for eliminating the present conflict.

I note with satisfaction that you have responded to the desire I expressed with regard to elimination of aforementioned dangerous situation, as well as with regard to providing conditions for a more thoughtful appraisal of the international situation, fraught as it is with great dangers in our age of thermonuclear weapons, rocketry, spaceships, global rockets, and other deadly weapons. All people are interested in insuring peace.

Therefore, vested with trust and great responsibility, we must not allow the situation to become aggravated and must stamp out the centers where a dangerous situation fraught with grave consequences to the cause of peace has arisen. If we, together with you, and with assistance of other people of good will, succeed in eliminating this tense atmosphere, we should also make certain that no other dangerous conflicts, which could lead to a world nuclear catastrophe, would arise.

In conclusion, I should like to say something about a detente between NATO and the Warsaw Treaty countries that you have mentioned. We have spoken about this long since and are prepared to continue to exchange views on this question with you and to find a reasonable solution.

We should like to continue the exchange of views on the prohibition of atomic and thermonuclear weapons, general disarmament, and other problems relating to the relaxation of international tension.

Although I trust your statement, Mr. President, there are irresponsible people who would like to invade Cuba now and thus touch off a war. If we do take practical steps and proclaim the dismantling and evacuation of the means in question from Cuba, in so doing we, at the same time, want the Cuban people to be certain that we are with them and are not absolving ourselves of responsibility for rendering assistance to the Cuban people.

We are confident that the people of all countries, like you, Mr. President, will understand me correctly. We are not threatening. We want nothing but peace. Our country is now in upsurge. Our people are enjoying the fruits of peaceful labor. They have achieved tremendous success since the October Revolution, and created the greatest material, spiritual and cultural values. Our people are enjoying these values; they want to continue development on the way to peace and social progress by their persistent labor.

I should like to remind you, Mr. President, that military reconnaissance planes have violated the borders of the Soviet Union. In connection with this there have been conflicts between us and notes exchanged. In 1960 we shot down your U-2 plane, whose reconnaissance flight over the U.S.S.R. wrecked the summit meeting in Paris. At that time, you took a correct position and denounced that criminal act of the former U.S. administration.

But during your term in office as president another violation of our border has occurred, by an American U-2 plane in the Sakhalin area. We wrote you about that violation on 30 August. At that time you replied that that violation had occurred as a result of poor weather, and gave assurances that this would not be repeated. We trusted your assurance, because the weather was indeed poor in that area at that time.

But had not your plane been ordered to fly about our territory, even poor weather could not have brought an American plane into our airspace, hence, the conclusion that this is being done with the knowledge of the Pentagon, which tramples on international norms and violates the borders of other states.

A still more dangerous case occurred on 28 October, when one of your reconnaissance planes intruded over Soviet borders in the Chukotka Peninsula in the north and flew over our territory. The question is, Mr. President: How should we regard this? What is this, a provocation? One of your planes violates our frontier during this anxious time we are both experiencing, when everything has been put into combat readiness. Is it not a fact that an intruding American plane could be easily taken for a nuclear bomber, which might push us to a fateful step; and all the more so since the U.S. Government and Pentagon long ago declared that you are maintaining a continuous nuclear bomber patrol?

Therefore, you can imagine the responsibility you are assuming; especially now, when we are living through such anxious times.

I should also like to express the following wish; it concerns the Cuban people. You do not have diplomatic relations. But through my officers in Cuba, I have reports that American planes are making flights over Cuba.

We are interested that there should be no war in the world, and that the Cuban people should live in peace. And besides, Mr. President, it is no secret that we have our people in Cuba. Under a treaty with the Cuban Government we have sent them officers, instructors, mostly plain people: specialists, agronomists, zoo technicians, irrigators, land reclamation specialists, plain workers, tractor drivers, and others. We are concerned about them.

I should like you to consider, Mr. President, that violation of Cuban airspace by American planes could also lead to dangerous consequences. And if you do not want this to happen, it would be better if no cause is given for a dangerous situation to arise. We must be careful now and refrain from any steps which would not be useful to defense of the states involved in the conflict, which could only cause irritation and even serve as a provocation for a fateful step. Therefore, we must display sanity, reason, and refrain from such steps.

We value peace perhaps even more than other peoples because we went through a terrible war with Hitler. But our people will not falter in the face of any test. Our people trust their government, and we assure our people and world public opinion that the Soviet Government will not allow itself to be provoked. But if the provocateurs unleash a war, they will not evade responsibility and the grave consequences a war will bring them. But we are confident that reason will triumph, that war will not be unleashed, and peace and the security of the peoples will be insured.

In connection with the current negotiations between Acting Secretary General U Thant and representatives of the Soviet Union, the United States, and the Republic of Cuba, the Soviet Government has sent First Deputy Foreign Minister V.V. Kuznetsov to New York to help U Thant in his noble efforts aimed at eliminating the present dangerous situation.

Respectfully yours,

N. Khrushchev
28 October 1962

Source: Khrushchev, Nikita. Message to President John F. Kennedy, October 28, 1962. Kennedy-Khruschev Exchanges, *Foreign Relations of the United States, 1961-1963*, Vol. 6. Washington, DC: U.S. Government Printing Office, 1996. Available online at U.S. Department of State, http://www.state.gov/www/about_state/history/volume_vi/exchanges.html.

8.8
"Placing Ourselves in the Other Country's Shoes" – 1962
An Excerpt from Robert F. Kennedy's Thirteen Days: A Memoir of the Cuban Missile Crisis

Attorney General Robert F. Kennedy wrote the memoir Thirteen Days, one of the most famous books written about the Cuban Missile Crisis. In this passage from the memoir, Kennedy asserts that President John F. Kennedy's ability to empathize with the Soviet position was one of the keys to the peaceful defusing of the crisis.

The final lesson of the Cuban missile crisis is the importance of placing ourselves in the other country's shoes. During the crisis, President Kennedy spent more time trying to determine the effect of a particular course of action on Khrushchev or the Russians than on any other phase of what he was doing. What guided all his deliberations was an effort not to disgrace Khrushchev, not to humiliate the Soviet Union, not to have them feel they would have to escalate their response because their national security or national interests so committed them.

This was why he was so reluctant to stop and search a Russian ship; this was why he was so opposed to attacking the missile sites. The Russians, he felt, would have to react militarily to such actions on our part....

Miscalculation and misunderstanding and escalation on one side bring a counterresponse. No action is taken against a powerful adversary in a vacuum. A government or people will fail to understand this only at their great peril. For that is how wars begin—wars that no one wants, no one intends, and no one wins.

Each decision that President Kennedy made kept this in mind. Always he asked himself: Can we be sure that Khrushchev understands what we feel to be our vital national interest? Has the Soviet Union had sufficient time to react soberly to a particular step we have taken? All action was judged against that standard—stopping a particular ship, sending low-flying planes, making a public statement.

President Kennedy understood that the Soviet Union did not want war, and they understood that we wished to avoid armed conflict. Thus, if hostilities were to come, it would be either because our national interests collided—which, because of their limited interests and our purposely limited objectives, seemed unlikely— or because of our failure or their failure to understand the other's objectives.

President Kennedy dedicated himself to making it clear to Khrushchev by word and deed—for both are important—that the U.S. had limited objectives and that we had no interest in accomplishing those objectives by adversely affecting the national security of the Soviet Union or by humiliating her.

Later, he was to say in his speech at American University in June of 1963: "Above all, while defending our own vital interests, nuclear powers must avert those confrontations which bring an adversary to the choice of either a humiliating defeat or a nuclear war."

During our crisis talks, he kept stressing the fact that we would indeed have a war if we placed the Soviet Union in a position she believed would adversely affect her national security or such public humiliation that she lost the respect of her own people and countries around the globe. The missiles in Cuba, we felt, vitally concerned our national security, but not that of the Soviet Union.

The fact was ultimately recognized by Khrushchev, and this recognition, I believe, brought about his change in what, up to that time, had been a very adamant position. The President believed from the start that the Soviet Chairman was a rational, intelligent man who, if given sufficient time and shown our determination, would alter his position. But there was always the chance of error, of mistake, miscalculation, or misunderstanding, and President Kennedy was committed to doing everything possible to lessen that chance on our side.

The possibility of the destruction of mankind was always in his mind. Someone once said that World War Three would be fought with atomic weapons and the next war with sticks and stones....

After it was finished, he made no statement attempting to take credit for himself or for the Administration for what had occurred. He instructed all members of the Ex Comm and government that no interview should be given, no statement made, which would claim any kind of victory. He respected Khrushchev for properly determining what was in his own country's interest and what was in the interest of mankind. If it was a triumph, it was a triumph for the next generation and not for any particular government or people.

At the outbreak of the First World War the ex-Chancellor of Germany, Prince von Bülow, said to his successor, "How did it all happen?" "Ah, if only we knew," was the reply.

Source: Kennedy, Robert F. *Thirteen Days: A Memoir of the Cuban Missile Crisis.* New York: Norton, 1969.

9

THE VIETNAM WAR

American soldiers carry a wounded comrade through the swamps of Vietnam in 1969.

INTRODUCTION

Many observers hoped that the peaceful conclusion of the 1962 Cuban Missile Crisis might lead to a new era of understanding and reconciliation between the world's two superpowers. U.S.-Soviet relations did see modest improvement afterward. But during this same period, American relations with China plummeted to new lows. In fact, historian Robert J. McMahon contended in *The Cold War* that China "supplanted the Soviet Union as America's most feared adversary. Of the two communist giants, it appeared far more militant, hostile, and belligerent." These enduring fears of Communist aggression and expansionism—from China rather than the Soviet Union—ultimately led the United States into the Vietnam War, the most controversial war in its entire history.

Vietnam had a long history of foreign occupation and colonialism. Beginning in the late 1800s France became an important power in Southeast Asia and created French Indochina, which included much of Vietnam, Cambodia, and Laos. During World War II, Japan exerted control over much of this region. After the war, when France tried to reassert its claims to this region, Vietnamese guerrilla fighter Ho Chi Minh led nationalists fighting for independence from the French.

In 1954, after years of fighting between Vietnamese nationalists and French colonial rulers, the Geneva Peace Accords divided the nation of Vietnam in half at the seventeenth parallel. North Vietnam came under the control of a Communist government led by Ho Chi Minh, while South Vietnam came under the control of a U.S.-supported government led by Ngo Dinh Diem. North Vietnamese leaders, with support from nationalists in the South, immediately began formulating plans to unify Vietnam under Communist rule. They received both military arms and diplomatic support from China's Communist leaders in support of this goal.

China's posture further convinced American analysts that Beijing intended to carry the banner of Communism to all corners of Asia.

American involvement in Vietnam began in earnest in 1954, after the signing of the Geneva Peace Accords. The United States was determined to prevent the spread of Communism into South Vietnam. Many U.S. policymakers subscribed to the "domino theory"—the belief that if one nation in Southeast Asia fell to Communism, then all the others would soon follow. As a result, policymakers steadily increased American involvement in Vietnam during the late 1950s and early 1960s. The growing American presence in Vietnam failed to neutralize the Communists, however. Instead, U.S. military advisors watched in frustration as Southern nationalists—known as Viet Cong—took control of large swaths of the South Vietnamese countryside.

In November 1963 Diem was assassinated and a new pro-American government was installed in South Vietnam. But this failed to slow the insurgency, either, and Washington began to consider the notion of direct military intervention in Southeast Asia. Indeed, some leaders in Washington lobbied for a major U.S. offensive against North Vietnam and its Viet Cong allies. In May 1964, for example, Air Force Chief of Staff General Curtis E. LeMay declared that his solution to Vietnam was to "tell the Vietnamese they've got to draw in their horns or we're going to bomb them back to the Stone Age."

But direct U.S. involvement in Vietnam did not begin until August 1964, after a controversial and mysterious clash between American and North Vietnamese vessels in the Gulf of Tonkin, along the coast of North Vietnam. On August 2, the Navy destroyer *USS Maddox* fended off a surprise attack from three North Vietnamese patrol torpedo (PT) boats. Two nights later, U.S. vessels in the Gulf reported a second attack. But evidence now suggests that this second attack was a mirage conjured up by stormy weather and faulty radar and sonar readings. Nonetheless, President Lyndon Johnson seized on the reports of a second attack to order U.S. bombing runs against North Vietnamese targets. On August 5 he sent the Tonkin Gulf Resolution to Congress, requesting authority to "take all necessary measures to repel any armed attack against the forces of the United States and to prevent future aggression." The bill was easily approved by both houses of Congress.

Americanization of the War

Over the next several months, the "Americanization" of the Vietnamese conflict escalated rapidly. The U.S. military launched intensive aerial bombing campaigns such as Operation Rolling Thunder, and in March 1965 the first U.S. combat troops were sent to Vietnam. "Over this war—and all Asia—is another reality," President Lyndon B. Johnson declared in April 1965. "The deepening shadow of Communist China. The contest in Vietnam is part of a wider pattern of [Chinese] aggressive purposes."

By late 1967, the U.S. military force in Vietnam had escalated to 485,000 troops. Despite several significant military triumphs, the war bogged down into a bloody stalemate. Stymied by the weak South Vietnamese government and the deadly hit-and-run tactics of North Vietnamese and Viet Cong forces, American forces resorted to increasingly ruthless tactics to turn the tide. But they made little headway, and as U.S. and Vietnamese casualties soared, a strong antiwar movement emerged in the United States. These developments led some American strategists to conclude that victory was unlikely. "In essence, what [Secretary of Defense Robert] McNamara and a handful of others ... began to see was this: No matter how many men our side was willing to put in, the enemy would be willing to put in more," wrote Paul Hendrickson in *The Living and the Dead*. "They would match us, and up it. They would give a million dead over to their cause. And keep going."

Johnson, McNamara, and others kept these growing doubts to themselves, however. Instead, they continued to express public optimism about the war. Their positive assessments were dismissed by antiwar protestors but welcomed by millions of Americans who desperately wanted to believe that the war was going well. Then came the Tet Offensive, a major assault carried out by North Vietnamese and Viet Cong troops against targets across South Vietnam. Launched on January 30, 1968, the Tet Offensive sparked the most intensive and widespread fighting yet. In the end, U.S. forces and their South Vietnamese allies beat back the Communists to claim a significant military triumph. But the Tet Offensive shattered America's hopes that the war was close to being won. Stunned by the televised images of fierce fighting in cities and hamlets across South Vietnam, Americans voiced growing doubts about the Johnson administration and its handling of the war. In March 1968 President Johnson announced that he would not seek reelection.

In November 1968 Republican Richard M. Nixon narrowly defeated Democrat Hubert H. Humphrey, who had been Johnson's vice president, to win the presidency of the United States. In June 1969 the Nixon administration launched a program it called "Vietnamization," which was designed to gradually shift responsibility for fighting the war from American troops to South Vietnamese forces. American casualties dropped, as did the total number of troops committed to Vietnam. "Americans needed tangible evidence that we were winding down the war," Nixon

277

later explained in his book *No More Vietnams*. "As South Vietnamese forces became stronger, the rate of American withdrawal could become greater." In March 1970 Nixon announced his intention to bring 150,000 more American soldiers home by the end of the year. This was welcome news to antiwar protestors and also to the millions of Americans—Nixon's so-called "Silent Majority"—who still defended U.S. intervention in Vietnam.

One month later, however, Nixon abruptly extended the war into neighboring Cambodia to root out Communist camps there. This development brought the flagging antiwar movement back to life. College campuses and city streets erupted in furious demonstrations once again. At Kent State University in Ohio, clashes between antiwar demonstrators and National Guardsmen resulted in the shooting deaths of four unarmed students. News of the Kent State shootings stunned the nation and triggered even greater campus unrest across the country. An estimated 536 campuses were shut down completely in the days after Kent State, and 51 remained closed for the remainder of the school year.

America Withdraws from Vietnam

The Kent State shootings further polarized American society. The event was also a contributing factor in the Senate's decision to repeal the Tonkin Gulf Resolution on June 26, 1970. From that point forward, the Nixon administration steadily reduced the number of U.S. troops stationed in Vietnam while simultaneously conducting peace negotiations with North Vietnam. By many accounts, U.S. military performance declined alarmingly during this period as disillusioned soldiers became convinced that they had been abandoned to an unwinnable war. During this period, some American units suffered serious problems with alcohol and drug abuse, insubordination, and mistreatment of Vietnamese people.

In January 1973 the United States and North Vietnam signed a cease-fire agreement at the Paris Peace Accords. Two months later the last 24,000 American troops that had been stationed in Vietnam returned home, although some support personnel remained. In July 1973, the U.S. Congress passed the Case-Church Amendment, which prohibited further American military involvement in Southeast Asia. The Nixon administration continued to provide financial aid to the regime in Saigon, but with American troops no longer directly involved in the conflict, the war faded from public consciousness. The Vietnam War faded even deeper into the background with the Watergate scandal, which culminated with the resignation of President Nixon in August 1974. With his departure, Vice President Gerald R. Ford was sworn in as President.

In March 1975 the North Vietnamese launched a major offensive deep into South Vietnam. This was a blatant violation of the terms of the 1973 Paris Peace Accords, but the United States declined to come to the aid of South Vietnam. Pressing their advantage, North Vietnamese forces rolled deeper into the south, claiming city after city. By April 27 the South Vietnamese capital of Saigon was totally surrounded. Over the next few days U.S. helicopters buzzed over the city's skyline, frantically evacuating thousands of American and Vietnamese personnel. Ford finally ordered an end to the evacuation on the morning of April 30. Later that day North Vietnamese forces moved into the helpless capital, renaming it Ho Chi Minh City. Their conquest of the city marked the end of the Vietnam War and the birth of a single, unified Vietnamese nation under Communist rule.

9.1

Vietnam's Declaration of Independence – 1945
The Text of the Declaration of Independence of the Democratic Republic of Vietnam, Delivered by Ho Chi Minh

Before World War II, France was a colonial power in Southeast Asia. During the war, Japan exerted control over former French colonies in the region. After the defeat of Japan in 1945, France tried to reassert control over its longstanding colonies in Vietnam, Cambodia, and Laos. But this scheme was opposed by the Viet Minh (Vietnamese League for Independence), a nationalist Communist organization founded by Ho Chi Minh that had actually fought against Japan—on the side of the Allies—in World War II.

After Japan's defeat, the Viet Minh proclaimed the existence of a new post-colonial country called the Democratic Republic of Vietnam. This declaration of Vietnamese independence, delivered by Ho Chi Minh on September 2, 1945, was clearly patterned after the U.S. Declaration of Independence. It even opened by quoting the opening lines of that hallmark document of American history. But the United States was unswayed, and it voiced support for France's colonial claims on Vietnam.

From 1946 to 1954 the Viet Minh waged a bitter war against French forces for control of the country. In 1954 the country was partitioned into two sections—a northern half controlled by Ho Chi Minh and his Communist followers, and a southern half led by Ngo Dinh Diem and supported by the West. U.S. involvement would soon follow.

"All men are created equal. They are endowed by their Creator with certain inalienable rights; among these are Life, Liberty, and the pursuit of Happiness."

This immortal statement was made in the Declaration of Independence of the United States of America in 1776. In a broader sense, this means: All the peoples on the earth are equal from birth, all the peoples have a right to live, to be happy and free.

The Declaration of the French Revolution made in 1791 on the Rights of Man and the Citizen also states: "All men are born free and with equal rights, and must always remain free and have equal rights."

Those are undeniable truths.

Nevertheless, for more than eighty years, the French imperialists, abusing the standard of Liberty, Equality, and Fraternity, have violated our Fatherland and oppressed our fellow citizens. They have acted contrary to the ideals of humanity and justice.

In the field of politics, they have deprived our people of every democratic liberty.

They have enforced inhuman laws; they have set up three distinct political regimes in the North, the Center, and the South of Vietnam in order to wreck our national unity and prevent our people from being united.

They have built more prisons than schools. They have mercilessly slain our patriots; they have drowned our uprisings in rivers of blood.

They have fettered public opinion; they have practised obscurantism against our people.

To weaken our race they have forced us to use opium and alcohol.

In the field of economics, they have fleeced us to the backbone, impoverished our people, and devastated our land.

They have robbed us of our rice fields, our mines, our forests, and our raw materials. They have monopolized the issuing of banknotes and the export trade.

They have invented numerous unjustifiable taxes and reduced our people, especially our peasantry, to a state of extreme poverty.

They have hampered the prospering of our national bourgeoisie; they have mercilessly exploited our workers.

In the autumn of 1940, when the Japanese Fascists violated Indochina's territory to establish new bases in their fight against the Allies, the French imperialists went down on their bended knees and handed over our country to them.

Thus, from that date, our people were subjected to the double yoke of the French and the Japanese. Their sufferings and miseries increased. The result was that from the end of last year to the beginning of this year, from Quang Tri province to the North of Vietnam, more than two million of our fellow citizens died from starvation. On March 9, the French troops were disarmed by the Japanese. The French colonialists either fled or surrendered showing that not only were they incapable of "protecting" us, but that, in the span of five years, they had twice sold our country to the Japanese.

On several occasions before March 9, the Vietminh League urged the French to ally themselves with it against the Japanese. Instead of agreeing to this proposal, the French colonialists so intensified their terrorist activities against the Vietminh members that before fleeing they massacred a great number of our political prisoners detained at Yen Bay and Caobang.

Notwithstanding all this, our fellow citizens have always manifested toward the French a tolerant and humane attitude. Even after the Japanese putsch of March 1945, the Vietminh League helped many Frenchmen to cross the frontier, rescued some of them from Japanese jails, and protected French lives and property.

From the autumn of 1940, our country had in fact ceased to be a French colony and had become a Japanese possession.

After the Japanese had surrendered to the Allies, our whole people rose to regain our national sovereignty and to found the Democratic Republic of Vietnam.

The truth is that we have wrested our independence from the Japanese and not from the French.

The French have fled, the Japanese have capitulated, Emperor Bao Dai has abdicated. Our people have broken the chains which for nearly a century have fettered them and have won independence for the Fatherland. Our people at the same time have overthrown the monarchic regime that has reigned supreme for dozens of centuries. In its place has been established the present Democratic Republic.

For these reasons, we, members of the Provisional Government, representing the whole Vietnamese people, declare that from now on we break off all relations of a colonial character with France; we repeal all the international obligation that France has so far subscribed to on behalf of Vietnam and we abolish all the special rights the French have unlawfully acquired in our Fatherland.

The whole Vietnamese people, animated by a common purpose, are determined to fight to the bitter end against any attempt by the French colonialists to reconquer their country.

We are convinced that the Allied nations, which at Tehran and San Francisco have acknowledged the principles of self-determination and equality of nations, will not refuse to acknowledge the independence of Vietnam.

A people who have courageously opposed French domination for more than eight years, a people who have fought side by side with the Allies against the Fascists during these last years, such a people must be free and independent.

For these reasons, we, members of the Provisional Government of the Democratic Republic of Vietnam, solemnly declare to the world that Vietnam has the right to be a free and independent country—and in fact is so already. The entire Vietnamese people are determined to mobilize all their physical and mental strength, to sacrifice their lives and property in order to safeguard their independence and liberty.

Source: Ho Chi Minh. "Declaration of Independence of the Democratic Republic of Vietnam," September 2, 1945. Reprinted in *Selected Writings*. Hanoi: Foreign Languages Publishing House, 1977.

9.2
Gulf of Tonkin Resolution – 1964
The Text of the U.S. Congressional Resolution Authorizing U.S. Military Involvement in Vietnam

After the 1954 Geneva Peace Accords divided Vietnam in half at the seventeenth parallel, American involvement in Vietnam began in earnest. North Vietnam came under the control of a Communist government led by Ho Chi Minh, while South Vietnam was placed in the hands of a U.S.-supported government led by Ngo Dinh Diem. But North Vietnamese leaders, with support from nationalists in the South—called Viet Cong—began working to unify Vietnam under Communist rule. American officials were determined to keep South Vietnam out of Communist hands. So the U.S. steadily increased its involvement in the region in the form of economic aid and military advisors.

Direct U.S. military involvement in Vietnam began in August 1964, after American and North Vietnamese forces clashed in the Gulf of Tonkin, along the coast of North Vietnam. The exact events that took place in the Gulf of Tonkin during this time are shrouded in mystery and controversy, but on two separate nights U.S. vessels reported that the North Vietnamese had attacked them. Later evidence suggested that a second attack may never have occurred. Still, the administration of Lyndon B. Johnson characterized the reported clashes as unprovoked attacks on U.S. vessels. On August 5 he sent the Tonkin Gulf Resolution to Congress, requesting authority to "take all necessary measures to repel any armed attack against the forces of the United States and to prevent future aggression." Both houses of Congress passed the resolution by overwhelming majorities on August 7, 1964. Their approval gave Johnson the clearance he needed to dramatically escalate American military involvement in Vietnam, even without a formal declaration of war.

Joint Resolution of Congress

Resolved by the Senate and House of Representatives of the United States of America in Congress assembled,

That the Congress approves and supports the determination of the President, as Commander in Chief, to take all necessary measures to repel any armed attack against the forces of the United States and to prevent further aggression.

Section 2. The United States regards as vital to its national interest and to world peace the maintenance of international peace and security in southeast Asia. Consonant with the Constitution of the United States and the Charter of the United Nations and in accordance with its obligations under the Southeast Asia Collective Defense Treaty, the United States is, therefore, prepared, as the President determines, to take all necessary steps, including the use of armed force, to assist any member or protocol state of the Southeast Asia Collective Defense Treaty requesting assistance in defense of its freedom.

Section 3. This resolution shall expire when the President shall determine that the peace and security of the area is reasonably assured by international conditions created by action of the United Nations or otherwise, except that it may be terminated earlier by concurrent resolution of the Congress.

Source: "Joint Resolution of Congress H.J. RES 1145 August 7, 1964."*Department of State Bulletin*, August 24, 1964. Available online at the Avalon Project, Yale Law School, http://www.yale.edu/lawweb/avalon/tonkin-g.htm.

9.3
"Aggression from the North" – 1965
U.S. State Department "White Paper" on Vietnam

The following report from the State Department was written on February 27, 1965. At that time, the United States was preparing to step up its involvement in Vietnam with Operation Rolling Thunder, a large-scale bombing campaign against North Vietnamese military targets. The memorandum strongly defended the U.S. military presence in Vietnam, describing the struggle for the country as a crossroads in the Western fight to stop Communist expansionism. It also described the South Vietnamese government and people as willing and able allies in the struggle—an assessment that would be heavily criticized as the war progressed.

Aggression from the North
State Department White Paper on Vietnam
February 27, 1965

South Vietnam is fighting for its life against a brutal campaign of terror and armed attack inspired, directed, supplied, and controlled by the Communist regime in Hanoi. This flagrant aggression has been going on for years, but recently the pace has quickened and the threat has now become acute.

The war in Vietnam is a new kind of war, a fact as yet poorly understood in most parts of the world. Much of the confusion that prevails in the thinking of many people, and even governments, stems from this basic misunderstanding. For in Vietnam a totally new brand of aggression has been loosed against an independent people who want to make their way in peace and freedom.

Vietnam is not another Greece, where indigenous guerrilla forces used friendly neighboring territory as a sanctuary.

Vietnam is not another Malaya, where Communist guerrillas were, for the most part, physically distinguishable from the peaceful majority they sought to control.

Vietnam is not another Philippines, where Communist guerrillas were physically separated from the source of their moral and physical support.

Above all, the war in Vietnam is not a spontaneous and local rebellion against the established government.

There are elements in the Communist program of conquest directed against South Vietnam common to each of the previous areas of aggression and subversion. But there is one fundamental difference. In Vietnam a Communist government has set out deliberately to conquer a sovereign people in a neighboring state. And to achieve its end, it has used every resource of its own government to carry out its carefully planned program of concealed aggression. North Vietnam's commitment to seize control of the South is no less total than was the commitment of the regime in North Korea in 1950. But knowing the consequences of the latter's undisguised attack, the planners in Hanoi have tried desperately to conceal their hand. They have failed and their aggression is as real as that of an invading army.

This report is a summary of the massive evidence of North Vietnamese aggression obtained by the Government of South Vietnam. This evidence has been jointly analyzed by South Vietnamese and American experts.

The evidence shows that the hard core of the Communist forces attacking South Vietnam were trained in the North and ordered into the South by Hanoi. It shows that the key leadership of the Vietcong (VC), the officers and much of the cadre, many of the technicians, political organizers, and propagandists have come from the North and operate under Hanoi's direction. It shows that the training of essential military personnel and their infiltration into the South is directed by the Military High Command in Hanoi. In recent months new types of weapons have been introduced in the VC army, for which all ammunition must come from outside sources. Communist China and other Communist states have been the prime suppliers of these weapons and ammunition, and they have been channeled primarily through North Vietnam.

The directing force behind the effort to conquer South Vietnam is the Communist Party in the North, the Lao Dong (Workers) Party. As in every Communist state, the party is an integral part of the regime itself. North Vietnamese officials have expressed their firm determination to absorb South Vietnam into the Communist world.

Through its Central Committee, which controls the Government of the North, the Lao Dong Party directs the total political and military effort of the Vietcong. The Military High Command in the North trains the military men and sends them into South Vietnam. The Central Research Agency, North Vietnam's central intelligence organization, directs the elaborate espionage and subversion effort....

286

Under Hanoi's overall direction the Communists have established an extensive machine for carrying on the war within South Vietnam. The focal point is the Central Office for South Vietnam with its political and military subsections and other specialized agencies. A subordinate part of this Central Office is the liberation Front for South Vietnam. The front was formed at Hanoi's order in 1960. Its principle function is to influence opinion abroad and to create the false impression that the aggression in South Vietnam is an indigenous rebellion against the established Government.

For more than 10 years the people and the Government of South Vietnam, exercising the inherent right of self-defense, have fought back against these efforts to extend Communist power south across the 17th parallel. The United States has responded to the appeals of the Government of the Republic of Vietnam for help in this defense of the freedom and independence of its land and its people.

In 1961 the Department of State issued a report called A Threat to the Peace. It described North Vietnam's program to seize South Vietnam. The evidence in that report had been presented by the Government of the Republic of Vietnam to the International Control Commission (ICC). A special report by the ICC in June 1962 upheld the validity of that evidence. The Commission held that there was "sufficient evidence to show beyond reasonable doubt" that North Vietnam had sent arms and men into South Vietnam to carry out subversion with the aim of overthrowing the legal Government there. The ICC found the authorities in Hanoi in specific violation of four provisions of the Geneva Accords of 1954.

Since then, new and even more impressive evidence of Hanoi's aggression has accumulated. The Government of the United States believes that evidence should be presented to its own citizens and to the world. It is important for free men to know what has been happening in Vietnam, and how, and why. That is the purpose of this report....

The record is conclusive. It establishes beyond question that North Vietnam is carrying out a carefully conceived plan of aggression against the South. It shows that North Vietnam has intensified its efforts in the years since it was condemned by the International Control Commission. It proves that Hanoi continues to press its systematic program of armed aggression into South Vietnam. This aggression violates the United Nations Charter. It is directly contrary to the Geneva Accords of 1954 and of 1962 to which North Vietnam is a party. It is a fundamental threat to the freedom and security of South Vietnam.

The people of South Vietnam have chosen to resist this threat. At their request, the United States has taken its place beside them in their defensive struggle.

The United States seeks no territory, no military bases, no favored position. But we have learned the meaning of aggression elsewhere in the post-war world, and we have met it.

If peace can be restored in South Vietnam, the United States will be ready at once to reduce its military involvement. But it will not abandon friends who want to remain free. It will do what must be done to help them. The choice now between peace and continued and increasingly destructive conflict is one for the authorities in Hanoi to make.

Source: U.S. Department of State. "Aggression from the North," February 27, 1965. *Department of State Bulletin*, March 22, 1965.

9.4

Walter Cronkite Assesses the "Stalemate" in Vietnam – 1968
The Text of an Editorial Broadcast on CBS Television

By the beginning of 1968 antiwar demonstrations were a growing phenomenon in the United States, even as U.S. military officials and Johnson administration officials insisted that the war was turning in favor of the American troops and their South Vietnamese allies. In January 1968 the heated debate over the Vietnam War took a dramatic turn with the Tet Offensive, a massive campaign launched by North Vietnamese and Viet Cong forces against more than 150 cities, villages, and military installations across South Vietnam. The Tet Offensive, which began on the night of January 30, triggered weeks of fierce fighting across the South. American and South Vietnamese forces eventually beat back the Communist offensive, which did not succeed in triggering a general uprising against the South Vietnamese regime based in Saigon. In fact, many historians now count the Tet Offensive as an American victory in purely military terms. But the sheer scale of the offensive stunned the American people, who had been repeatedly assured by Washington that victory was near.

The strength of the Communist forces shocked the respected television journalist Walter Cronkite as well. America's best-known and most popular journalist of the era, Cronkite went to South Vietnam in February 1968 to get a firsthand look at the ongoing Tet Offensive. After touring war-ravaged sections of major cities like Saigon and Hue, he determined that the war had become a bloody "stalemate." He conveyed this view to a national television audience on February 27, 1968. After hearing Cronkite's commentary, President Lyndon B. Johnson reportedly lamented that "If I've lost Cronkite, I've lost middle America."

Tonight, back in more familiar surroundings in New York, we'd like to sum up our findings in Vietnam, an analysis that must be speculative, personal, subjective. Who won and who lost in the great Tet Offensive against the cities?

288

I'm not sure. The Viet Cong did not win by a knockout, but neither did we. The referees of history may make it a draw. Another stand-off may be coming in the big battles expected south of the Demilitarized Zone. Khe Sanh could well fall, with a terrible loss in American lives, prestige, and morale, and this is a tragedy of our stubbornness there; but the bastion no longer is a key to the rest of the northern regions, and it is doubtful that the American forces can be defeated across the breadth of the DMZ with any substantial loss of ground. Another stand-off. On the political front, past performance gives no confidence that the Vietnamese government can cope with its problems, now compounded by the attack on the cities. It may not fall, it may hold on, but it probably won't show the dynamic qualities demanded of this young nation. Another stand-off.

> "We have been too often disappointed by the optimism of the American leaders, both in Vietnam and Washington, to have faith any longer in the silver linings they find in the darkest clouds."

We have been too often disappointed by the optimism of the American leaders, both in Vietnam and Washington, to have faith any longer in the silver linings they find in the darkest clouds. They may be right, that Hanoi's winter-spring offensive had been forced by the Communist realization that they could not win the long war of attrition, and that the Communists hope that any success in the offensive will improve their position for eventual negotiations. It would improve their position, and it would also require our realization, that we should have had all along, that any negotiations must be that—negotiations, not the dictation of peace terms. For it seems now more certain than ever that the bloody experience of Vietnam is to end in a stalemate.

This summer's almost certain stand-off will either end in real give-and-take negotiations or terrible escalation; and for every means we have to escalate, the enemy can match us, and that applies to invasion of the North, the use of nuclear weapons, or the mere commitment of 100-, or 200-, or 300,000 more American troops to the battle. And with each escalation, the world comes closer to the brink of cosmic disaster.

To say that we are closer to victory today is to believe, in the face of the evidence, the optimists who have been wrong in the past. To suggest we are on the edge of defeat is to yield to unreasonable pessimism. To say that we are mired in stalemate seems the only realistic, yet unsatisfactory, conclusion. On the off chance that military and political analysts are right, in the next few months we must test the enemy's intentions, in case this is indeed his last gasp before negotiations. But

---

Walter Cronkite broadcast, February 27, 1968. © CBS Inc. Reprinted by permission.

it is increasingly clear to this reporter that the only rational way out then will be to negotiate, not as victors, but as an honorable people who lived up to their pledge to defend democracy, and did the best they could.

This is Walter Cronkite. Good night.

Source: Cronkite, Walter. Television broadcast on February 27, 1968. *Reporting Vietnam: Part One: American Journalism 1959-1969.* New York: Library of America, 1988.

9.5
Lyndon B. Johnson Announces His Decision Not to Seek Re-election – 1968
Excerpts from Johnson's Speech of March 31, 1968

The North Vietnamese Tet Offensive of early 1968 shattered fragile American beliefs that victory was near in the war in Vietnam. Tet also was enormously discouraging to President Lyndon B. Johnson, who had approved a major escalation of U.S. involvement in the war over the previous four years. Buffeted by the antiwar movement and the growing doubts of Americans who had previously supported the war, Johnson issued a nationally televised speech on March 31, 1968. This address sought to convey to the American public the importance of continued involvement in Vietnam, while simultaneously offering assurances that the U.S. government was working hard to limit American casualties and bring its troops home. But the most notable part of this address came at the very end, when he shocked critics and supporters alike with the news that he had no intention of running for re-election.

Good evening, my fellow Americans:

Tonight I want to speak to you of peace in Vietnam and Southeast Asia.

No other question so preoccupies our people. No other dream so absorbs the 250 million human beings who live in that part of the world. No other goal motivates American policy in Southeast Asia.

For years, representatives of our Government and others have traveled the world—seeking to find a basis for peace talks.

Since last September, they have carried the offer that I made public at San Antonio. That offer was this:

That the United States would stop its bombardment of North Vietnam when that would lead promptly to productive discussions—and that we would assume that North Vietnam would not take military advantage of our restraint.

Hanoi denounced this offer, both privately and publicly. Even while the search for peace was going on, North Vietnam rushed their preparations for a savage assault on the people, the government, and the allies of South Vietnam.

Their attack—during the Tet holidays—failed to achieve its principal objectives. It did not collapse the elected government of South Vietnam or shatter its army—as the Communists had hoped. It did not produce a "general uprising" among the people of the cities as they had predicted. The Communists were unable to maintain control of any of the more than 30 cities that they attacked. And they took very heavy casualties.

But they did compel the South Vietnamese and their allies to move certain forces from the countryside into the cities. They caused widespread disruption and suffering. Their attacks, and the battles that followed, made refugees of half a million human beings.

The Communists may renew their attack any day. They are, it appears, trying to make 1968 the year of decision in South Vietnam—the year that brings, if not final victory or defeat, at least a turning point in the struggle.

This much is clear:

If they do mount another round of heavy attacks, they will not succeed in destroying the fighting power of South Vietnam and its allies. But tragically, this is also clear: Many men—on both sides of the struggle—will be lost. A nation that has already suffered 20 years of warfare will suffer once again. Armies on both sides will take new casualties. And the war will go on.

There is no need for this to be so.

There is no need to delay the talks that could bring an end to this long and this bloody war.

Tonight, I renew the offer I made last August—to stop the bombardment of North Vietnam. We ask that talks begin promptly, that they be serious talks on the substance of peace. We assume that during those talks Hanoi will not take advantage of our restraint.

We are prepared to move immediately toward peace through negotiations.

So, tonight, in the hope that this action will lead to early talks, I am taking the first step to deescalate the conflict. We are reducing—substantially reducing—the present level of hostilities. And we are doing so unilaterally, and at once.

Tonight, I have ordered our aircraft and our naval vessels to make no attacks on North Vietnam, except in the area north of the demilitarized zone where the continuing enemy buildup directly threatens allied forward positions and where the movements of their troops and supplies are clearly related to that threat.

The area in which we are stopping our attacks includes almost 90 percent of North Vietnam's population, and most of its territory. Thus there will be no attacks around the principal populated areas, or in the food-producing areas of North Vietnam.

Even this very limited bombing of the North could come to an early end—if our restraint is matched by restraint in Hanoi. But I cannot in good conscience stop all bombing so long as to do so would immediately and directly endanger the lives of our men and our allies. Whether a complete bombing halt becomes possible in the future will be determined by events.

Our purpose in this action is to bring about a reduction in the level of violence that now exists. It is to save the lives of brave men—and to save the lives of innocent women and children. It is to permit the contending forces to move closer to a political settlement....

> "I have lived—daily and nightly—with the cost of this war. I know the pain that it has inflicted. I know, perhaps better than anyone, the misgivings that it has aroused."

[Johnson then touts the progress the United States has made in strengthening the South Vietnamese government and military, and urges Congress to pass a new tax bill to help pay for the war.]

.... I cannot promise that the initiative that I have announced tonight will be completely successful in achieving peace any more than the 30 others that we have undertaken and agreed to in recent years. But it is our fervent hope that North Vietnam, after years of fighting that have left the issue unresolved, will now cease its efforts to achieve a military victory and will join with us in moving toward the peace table. And there may come a time when South Vietnamese—on both sides—are able to work out a way to settle their own differences by free political choice rather than by war.

As Hanoi considers its course, it should be in no doubt of our intentions. It must not miscalculate the pressures within our democracy in this election year. We have no intention of widening this war. But the United States will never accept a fake solution to this long and arduous struggle and call it peace.

No one can foretell the precise terms of an eventual settlement. Our objective in South Vietnam has never been the annihilation of the enemy. It has been to bring about a recognition in Hanoi that its objective—taking over the South by force—could not be achieved. We think that peace can be based on the Geneva Accords of 1954—under political conditions that permit the South Vietnamese—all the South Vietnamese—to chart their course free of any outside domination or interference, from us or from anyone else.

So tonight I reaffirm the pledge that we made at Manila—that we are prepared to withdraw our forces from South Vietnam as the other side withdraws its forces to the north, stops the infiltration, and the level of violence thus subsides. Our goal of peace and self-determination in Vietnam is directly related to the future of all of Southeast Asia—where much has happened to inspire confidence during the past 10 years. We have done all that we knew how to do to contribute and to help build that confidence.

A number of its nations have shown what can be accomplished under conditions of security. Since 1966, Indonesia, the fifth largest nation in all the world, with a population of more than 100 million people, has had a government that is dedicated to peace with its neighbors and improved conditions for its own people. Political and economic cooperation between nations has grown rapidly.

I think every American can take a great deal of pride in the role that we have played in bringing this about in Southeast Asia. We can rightly judge—as responsible Southeast Asians themselves do—that the progress of the past 3 years would have been far less likely—if not completely impossible—if America's sons and others had not made their stand in Vietnam....

One day, my fellow citizens, there will be peace in Southeast Asia. It will come because the people of Southeast Asia want it—those whose armies are at war tonight, and those who, though threatened, have thus far been spared. Peace will come because Asians were willing to work for it—and to sacrifice for it—and to die by the thousands for it.

But let it never be forgotten: Peace will come also because America sent her sons to help secure it. It has not been easy—far from it. During the past 4 1/2 years, it has been my fate and my responsibility to be Commander in Chief. I have lived—-daily and nightly—with the cost of this war. I know the pain that it has inflicted. I know, perhaps better than anyone, the misgivings that it has aroused.

Throughout this entire, long period, I have been sustained by a single principle: that what we are doing now, in Vietnam, is vital not only to the security of Southeast Asia, but it is vital to the security of every American. Surely we have treaties which we must respect. Surely we have commitments that we are going to keep. Resolutions of the Congress testify to the need to resist aggression in the world and in Southeast Asia.

But the heart of our involvement in South Vietnam—under three different presidents, three separate administrations—has always been America's own security. And the larger purpose of our involvement has always been to help the nations of Southeast Asia become independent and stand alone, self-sustaining, as members of a great world community—at peace with themselves, and at peace with all others.

With such an Asia, our country—and the world—will be far more secure than it is tonight. I believe that a peaceful Asia is far nearer to reality because of what America has done in Vietnam. I believe that the men who endure the dangers of battle—fighting there for us tonight—are helping the entire world avoid far greater conflicts, far wider wars, far more destruction, than this one.

The peace that will bring them home someday will come. Tonight I have offered the first in what I hope will be a series of mutual moves toward peace. I pray that it will not be rejected by the leaders of North Vietnam. I pray that they will accept it as a means by which the sacrifices of their own people may be ended. And I ask your help and your support, my fellow citizens, for this effort to reach across the battlefield toward an early peace.

Finally, my fellow Americans, let me say this:

Of those to whom much is given, much is asked. I cannot say and no man could say that no more will be asked of us. Yet, I believe that now, no less than when the decade began, this generation of Americans is willing to "pay any price, bear any burden, meet any hardship, support any friend, oppose any foe to assure the survival and the success of liberty."

Since those words were spoken by John F. Kennedy, the people of America have kept that compact with mankind's noblest cause. And we shall continue to keep it. Yet, I believe that we must always be mindful of this one thing, whatever the trials and the tests ahead. The ultimate strength of our country and our cause will lie not in powerful weapons or infinite resources or boundless wealth, but will lie in the unity of our people.

This I believe very deeply.

Throughout my entire public career I have followed the personal philosophy that I am a free man, an American, a public servant, and a member of my party, in that order always and only. For 37 years in the service of our Nation, first as a Congressman, as a Senator, and as Vice President, and now as your President, I have put the unity of the people first. I have put it ahead of any divisive partisanship.

And in these times as in times before, it is true that a house divided against itself by the spirit of faction, of party, of region, of religion, of race, is a house that cannot stand.

There is division in the American house now. There is divisiveness among us all tonight. And holding the trust that is mine, as President of all the people, I cannot disregard the peril to the progress of the American people and the hope and the prospect of peace for all peoples. So, I would ask all Americans, whatever their personal interests or concern, to guard against divisiveness and all its ugly consequences.

Fifty-two months and 10 days ago, in a moment of tragedy and trauma, the duties of this office fell upon me. I asked then for your help and God's, that we might continue America on its course, binding up our wounds, healing our history, moving forward in new unity, to clear the American agenda and to keep the American commitment for all of our people.

United we have kept that commitment. United we have enlarged that commitment.

Through all time to come, I think America will be a stronger nation, a more just society, and a land of greater opportunity and fulfillment because of what we have all done together in these years of unparalleled achievement.

Our reward will come in the life of freedom, peace, and hope that our children will enjoy through ages ahead. What we won when all of our people united … must not now be lost in suspicion, distrust, selfishness, and politics among any of our people.

Believing this as I do, I have concluded that I should not permit the Presidency to become involved in the partisan divisions that are developing in this political year.

With America's sons in the fields far away, with America's future under challenge right here at home, with our hopes and the world's hopes for peace in the balance every day, I do not believe that I should devote an hour or a day of my time to any personal partisan causes or to any duties other than the awesome duties of this office—the Presidency of your country.

Accordingly, I shall not seek, and I will not accept, the nomination of my party for another term as your President.

But let men everywhere know, however, that a strong, a confident, and a vigilant America stands ready tonight to seek an honorable peace—and stands ready tonight to defend an honored cause—whatever the price, whatever the burden, whatever the sacrifice that duty may require.

Thank you for listening.

Good night and God bless all of you.

Source: Johnson, Lyndon B. Nationally televised speech of March 31, 1968. *Public Papers of the Presidents of the United States: Lyndon B. Johnson, 1968-69*. Washington, DC: Office of the Federal Register, 1970.

9.6
Flying Into and Over the War in Vietnam – 1968
Excerpt from Dispatches, *by Michael Herr*

Journalist Michael Herr covered the war in Vietnam for parts of 1967 and 1968. These years were among the most chaotic of the entire war, for they were marked by fierce antiwar demonstrations back in the United States and troubling indications in Vietnam that even after years of mounting troop and civilian casualties, an American victory was far away. During these years, a growing number of soldiers and journalists also expressed their belief that the Vietnam War was different than previous wars in which American soldiers had fought. They said that the exotic climate and ter-

rain, the vicious guerrilla attacks, and the frequent inability to tell which Vietnamese were friend and which were foe gave the conflict a surreal, nightmarish quality.

Herr shared this belief. When he set about writing Dispatches, *an account of what he had seen and heard during his months in Vietnam, he decided to discard standard reporting conventions in favor of a more impressionistic and emotional account. "Conventional journalism could no more reveal this war than conventional firepower could win it," he wrote. The final result was a book that is almost universally acclaimed as one of the best books ever written about the Vietnam War. Following is an excerpt.*

... In the months after I got back the hundreds of helicopters I'd flown in began to draw together until they'd formed a collective meta-chopper, and in my mind it was the sexiest thing going; saver-destroyer, provider-waster; right hand-left hand, nimble, fluent, canny and human; hot steel, grease, jungle-saturated canvas webbing, sweat cooling and warming up again, cassette rock and roll in one ear and door-gun fire in the other, fuel, heat, vitality and death, death itself, hardly an intruder. Men on the crews would say that once you'd carried a dead person he would always be there, riding with you. Like all combat people they were incredibly superstitious and invariably self-dramatic, but it was (I knew) unbearably true that close exposure to the dead sensitized you to the force of their presence and made for long reverberations; long. Some people were so delicate that one look was enough to wipe them away, but even bone-dumb grunts seemed to feel that something weird and extra was happening to them.

Helicopters and people jumping out of helicopters, people so in love they'd run to get on even when there wasn't any pressure. Choppers rising straight out of small cleared jungle spaces, wobbling down onto city rooftops, cartons of rations and ammunition thrown off, dead and wounded loaded on. Sometimes they were so plentiful and loose that you could touch down at five or six places in a day, look around, hear the talk, catch the next one out. There were installations as big as cities with 30,000 citizens, once we dropped in to feed supply to one man. God knows what kind of Lord Jim phoenix numbers he was doing in there, all he said to me was, "You didn't see a thing, right Chief? You weren't even here." There were posh fat air-conditioned camps like comfortable middle-class scenes with the violence tacit, "far away"; camps named for commanders' wives LZ [Landing Zone] Thelma, LZ Betty Lou; number-named hilltops in trouble where I didn't want to stay; trail, paddy, swamp, deep hairy bush, scrub, swale, village, even city, where the ground couldn't drink up what the action spilled, it made you careful where you walked.

Sometimes the chopper you were riding in would top a hill and all the ground in front of you as far as the next hill would be charred and pitted and still smoking, and something between your chest and your stomach would turn over. Frail gray smoke where they'd burned off the rice fields around a free-strike zone, brilliant white smoke from phosphorous ("Willy Peter/Make you a buh liever"), deep black smoke from 'palm, they said that if you stood at the base of a column of napalm smoke it would suck the air right out of your lungs. Once we fanned over a little ville that had just been airstruck and the words of a song by Wingy Manone that I'd heard when I was a few years old snapped into my head, "Stop the War, These Cats Is Killing Themselves." Then we dropped, hovered, settled down into purple lz smoke, dozens of children broke from their hootches to run in toward the focus of our landing, the pilot laughing and saying, "Vietnam, man. Bomb 'em and feed 'em, bomb 'em and feed 'em."

Flying over jungle was almost pure pleasure, doing it on foot was nearly all pain. I never belonged in there. Maybe it really was what its people had always called it, Beyond; at the very least it was serious, I gave up things to it I probably never got back. ("Aw, jungle's okay. If you know her you can live in her real good, if you don't she'll take you down in an hour. Under.") Once in some thick jungle corner with some grunts standing around, a correspondent said, "Gee, you must really see some beautiful sunsets in here," and they almost pissed themselves laughing. But you could fly up and into hot tropic sunsets that would change the way you thought about light forever. You could also fly out of places that were so grim they turned to black and white in your head five minutes after you'd gone.

That could be the coldest one in the world, standing at the edge of a clearing watching the chopper you'd just come in on taking off again, leaving you there to think about what it was going to be for you now: if this was a bad place, the wrong place, maybe even the last place, and whether you'd made a terrible mistake this time....

Airmobility, dig it, you weren't going anywhere. It made you feel safe, it made you feel Omni, but it was only a stunt, technology. Mobility was just mobility, it saved lives or took them all the time (saved mine I don't know how many times, maybe dozens, maybe none), what you really needed was a flexibility far greater than anything the technology could provide, some generous, spontaneous gift for accepting surprises, and I didn't have it. I got to hate surprises, control freak at the crossroads, if you were one of those people who always thought they had to know what was coming next, the war could cream you. It was the same with your ongoing attempts at getting used to the jungle or the blow-you-out climate or the saturating strangeness of the place which didn't lessen with exposure so often as it fattened and darkened in accumulating alienation. It was great if you could adapt, you had to try, but it wasn't the same as making a discipline, going into your own reserves and developing a real war metabolism, slow yourself down when your heart tried to punch its way through your chest, get swift when everything went to stop and all you could feel of your whole life was the entropy whipping through it. Unlovable terms.

The ground was always in play, always being swept. Under the ground was his, above it was ours. We had the air, we could get up in it but not disappear in *to* it, we could run but we couldn't hide, and he could do each so well that sometimes it looked like he was doing them both at once, while our finder just went limp. All the same, one place or another it was always going on, rock around the clock, we had the days and he had the nights. You could be in the most protected place in Vietnam and still know that your safety was provisional, that early death, blindness, loss of legs, arms or balls, major and lasting disfigurement—the whole rotten deal—could come in on the freakyfluky as easily as in the so-called expected ways, you heard so many of those stories it was a wonder anyone was left alive to die in firefights and mortar-rocket attacks. After a few weeks, when the nickel had jarred loose and dropped and I saw that everyone around me was carrying a gun, I also saw that any one of them could go off at any time, putting you where it wouldn't matter whether it had been an accident or not. The roads were mined, the trails booby-trapped, satchel charges and grenades blew up jeeps and movie theaters, the VC got work inside all the camps as shoeshine boys and laundresses and honey-dippers, they'd starch your fatigues and burn your shit and then go home and mortar your area. Saigon and Cholon and Danang held such hostile vibes that you felt you were being dry-sniped every time someone looked at you, and choppers fell out of the sky like fat poisoned birds a hundred times a day. After a while I couldn't get on one without thinking that I must be out of my fucking mind.

"All you could do was look around at the other people on board and see if they were as scared and numb as you were. If it looked like they weren't you thought they were insane, if it looked like they were it made you feel a lot worse."

Fear and motion, fear and standstill, no preferred cut there, no way to even be clear about which was really worse, the wait or the delivery. Combat spared far more men than it wasted, but everyone suffered the time between contact, especially when they were going out every day looking for it; bad going on foot, terrible in trucks and APCs [armored personnel carriers], awful in helicopters, the worst, traveling so fast toward something so frightening. I can remember times when I went half dead with my fear of motion, the speed and direction already fixed and pointed one way. It was painful enough just flying "safe" hops between firebases and lz's; if you were ever on a helicopter that had been hit by ground fire your deep, perpetual chopper anxiety was guaranteed. At least actual contact when it was happening would draw long raggedy strands of energy out of you, it was juicy, fast and refining, and traveling toward it was hollow, dry, cold and steady, it never let you alone. All you could do was look around at the other people on board and see if they were as scared and numb as you were. If it looked like they weren't you thought they were insane, if it looked like they were it made you feel a lot worse....

"Boy, you sure get offered some shitty choices," a Marine once said to me, and I couldn't help but feel that what he really meant was that you didn't get offered any at all. Specifically, he was just talking about a couple of C-ration cans, "dinner," but considering his young life you couldn't blame him for thinking that if he knew one thing for sure, it was that there was no one anywhere who cared less about what *he* wanted. There wasn't anybody he wanted to thank for his food, but he was grateful that he was still alive to eat it, that the motherfucker hadn't scarfed him up first. He hadn't been anything but tired and scared for six months and he'd lost a lot, mostly people, and seen far too much, but he was breathing in and breathing out, some kind of choice all by itself.

He had one of those faces, I saw that face at least a thousand times at a hundred bases and camps, all the youth sucked out of the eyes, the color drawn from the skin, cold white lips, you knew he wouldn't wait for any of it to come back. Life had made him old, he'd live it out old. All those faces, sometimes it was like looking into faces at a rock concert, locked in, the event had them; or like students who were very heavily advanced, serious beyond what you'd call their years if you didn't know yourself what the minutes and hours of those years were made up of. Not just like all the ones you saw who looked like they couldn't drag their asses through another day of it. (How do you feel when a nineteen-year-old kid tells you from the bottom of his heart that he's gotten too old for this kind of shit?) Not like the faces of the dead or wounded either, they could look more released than overtaken. These were the faces of boys whose whole lives seemed to have backed up on them, they'd be a few feet away but they'd be looking back at you over a distance you knew you'd never really cross. We'd talk, sometimes fly together, guys going out on R&R, guys escorting bodies, guys who'd flipped over into extremes of peace or violence. Once I flew with a kid who was going home, he looked back down once at the ground where he'd spent the year and spilled his whole load of tears. Sometimes you even flew with the dead.

Once I jumped on a chopper that was full of them. The kid in the op shack had said that there would be a body on board, but he'd been given some wrong information. "How bad do you want to get to Danang?" he'd asked me, and I'd said, "Bad."

When I saw what was happening I didn't want to get on, but they'd made a divert and a special landing for me, I had to go with the chopper I'd drawn, I was afraid of looking squeamish. (I remember, too, thinking that a chopper full of dead men was far less likely to get shot down than one full of living.) They weren't even in bags. They'd been on a truck near one of the firebases in the DMZ that was firing support for Khe Sanh, and the truck had hit a Command-detonated mine, then they'd been rocketed. The Marines were always running out of things, even food, ammo and medicine, it wasn't so strange that they'd run out of bags too. The men had been wrapped around in ponchos, some of them carelessly fastened with plastic straps, and loaded on board. There was a small space cleared for me between one of them and the door gunner, who looked pale and so tremendously furious that I thought he was angry with me and I couldn't look at him for a while. When we went up the wind blew through the ship and made the ponchos shake and tremble until the one next to me blew back in a fast brutal flap, uncovering the face. They hadn't even closed his eyes for him.

The gunner started hollering as loud as he could, "Fix it! Fix it!," maybe he thought the eyes were looking at him, but there wasn't anything I could do. My hand went there a couple of times and I couldn't, then I did. I pulled the poncho tight, lifted his head carefully and tucked the poncho under it, and then I couldn't believe that I'd done it. All during the ride the gunner kept trying to smile, and when we landed at Dong Ha he thanked me and ran off to get a detail. The pilots jumped down and walked away without looking back once, like they'd never seen that chopper before in their lives. I flew the rest of the way to Danang in a general's plane....

Nights were when the air and artillery strikes were heaviest, because that was when we knew that the NVA [North Vietnamese Army] was above ground and moving. At night you could lie out on some sandbags and watch the C-47's mounted with Vulcans doing their work. The C-47 was a standard prop flareship, but many of them carried .20- and .762-mm. guns on their doors, Mike-Mikes that could fire out 300 rounds per second, Gatling style, "a round in every square inch of a football field in less than a minute," as the handouts said. They used to call it Puff the Magic Dragon, but the Marines knew better: they named it Spooky. Every fifth round fired was a tracer, and when Spooky was working, everything stopped while that solid stream of violent red poured down out of the black sky. If you watched from a great distance, the stream would seem to dry up between bursts, vanishing slowly from air to ground like a comet tail, the sound of the guns disappearing too, a few seconds later. If you watched at a close range, you couldn't believe that anyone would have the courage to deal with that night after night, week after week, and you cultivated a respect for the Viet Cong and the NVA who had crouched under it every night now for months. It was awesome, worse than anything the Lord had ever put down on Egypt, and at night, you'd hear the Marines talking, watching it, yelling, "Get some!" until they grew quiet and someone would say, "Spooky understand." The nights were very beautiful. Night was when you really had the least to fear and feared the most. You could go through some very bad numbers at night.

Because, really, what a choice there was; what a prodigy of things to be afraid of! The moment that you understood this, really understood it, you lost your anxiety instantly. Anxiety was a luxury, a joke you had no room for once you knew the variety of deaths and mutilations the war offered. Some feared head wounds, some dreaded chest wounds or stomach wounds, everyone feared the wound of wounds, the Wound. Guys would pray and pray—Just you and me, God. Right?—offer anything, if only they could be spared that: Take my legs, take my hands, take my eyes, take my fucking *life*, You Bastard, but please, please, please, don't take *those*. Whenever a shell landed in a group, everyone forgot about the next rounds and skipped back to rip their pants away, to check, laughing hysterically with relief even though their legs might be shattered, their kneecaps torn away, kept upright by their relief and shock, gratitude and adrenaline.

There were choices everywhere, but they were never choices that you could hope to make. There was even some small chance for personal style in your recognition of the one thing you feared more than any other. You could die in a sudden blood-burning crunch as your chopper hit the ground like dead weight, you could fly apart so that your pieces would never be gathered, you could take one neat round in the lung and go out hearing only the bubble of the last few breaths, you could die in the last stage of malaria with that faint tapping in your ears, and that could happen to you after months of firefights and rockets and machine guns. Enough, too many, were saved for that, and you always hoped that no irony would attend your passing. You could end in a pit somewhere with a spike through you, everything stopped forever except for the one or two motions, purely involuntary, as though you could kick it all away and come back. You could fall down dead so that the medics would have to spend half an hour looking for the hole that killed you, getting more and more spooked as the search went on. You could be shot, mined, grenaded, rocketed, mortared, sniped at, blown up and away so that your leavings had to be dropped into a sagging poncho and carried to Graves Registration, that's all she wrote. It was almost marvelous.

Source: Herr, Michael. *Dispatches*. New York: Knopf, 1977.

9.7

Correspondence between Richard Nixon and Ho Chi Minh – 1969
The Text of Letters Exchanged Just Before President Ho's Death

Shortly after President Richard Nixon took office in January 1969, he began to gradually withdraw American forces from Vietnam and shift primarily responsibility for the war's prosecution to South Vietnam. Nixon harbored hopes that this tactical withdrawal would convince Ho Chi Minh and the North Vietnamese leadership to be more conciliatory at ongoing—but floundering—peace talks in Paris. To this end, Nixon sent a letter to Ho on July 15, 1969. A little over one month later, Ho replied to Nixon's letter. The

Communist leader died a few days later, on August 28, 1969, but his death did not appreciably change the dynamics of the war. Following is the text of both letters.

President Nixon's Letter
July 15, 1969

Dear Mr. President: I realize that it is difficult to communicate meaningfully across the gulf of four years of war. But precisely because of this gulf, I wanted to take this opportunity to reaffirm in all solemnity my desire to work for a just peace. I deeply believe that the war in Vietnam has gone on too long and delay in bringing it to an end can benefit no one—least of all the people of Vietnam. My speech on May 14 laid out a proposal which I believe is fair to all parties. Other proposals have been made which attempt to give the people of South Vietnam an opportunity to choose their own future. These proposals take into account the reasonable conditions of all sides. But we stand ready to discuss other programs as well, specifically the 10-point program of the NLF [National Liberation Front].

As I have said repeatedly, there is nothing to be gained by waiting. Delay can only increase the dangers and multiply the suffering.

The time has come to move forward at the conference table toward an early resolution of this tragic war. You will find us forthcoming and open-minded in a common effort to bring the blessings of peace to the brave people of Vietnam. Let history record that at this critical juncture, both sides turned their fact toward peace rather than toward conflict and war.

President Ho's Letter
August 25, 1969

Mr. President,

I have the honor to acknowledge receipt of your letters.

The war of aggression of the United States against our people, violating our fundamental national rights, still continues in South Vietnam. The United States continues to intensify military operations, the B-52 bombings and the use of toxic chemical products multiply the crimes against the Vietnamese people. The longer the war goes on, the more it accumulates the mourning and burdens of the American people. I am extremely indignant at the losses and destructions caused by the American troops to our people and our country. I am also deeply touched at the rising toll of death of young Americans who have fallen in Vietnam by reason of the policy of American governing circles.

Our Vietnamese people are deeply devoted to peace, a real peace with independence and real freedom. They are determined to fight to the end, without fearing the sacrifices and difficulties in order to defend their country and their sacred national rights. The overall solution in 10 points of the National Liberation Front of

South Vietnam and of the Provisional Revolutionary Government of the Republic of South Vietnam is a logical and reasonable basis for the settlement of the Vietnamese problem. It has earned the sympathy and support of the peoples of the world.

In your letter you have expressed the desire to act for a just peace. For this the United States must cease the war of aggression and withdraw their troops from South Vietnam, respect the right of the population of the South and of the Vietnamese nation to dispose of themselves, without foreign influence. This is the correct manner of solving the Vietnamese problem in conformity with the national rights of the Vietnamese people, the interests of the United States and the hopes for peace of the peoples of the world. This is the path that will allow the United States to get out of the war with honor.

With good will on both sides we might arrive at common efforts in view of finding a correct solution of the Vietnamese problem.

Source: Correspondence between U.S. President Richard M. Nixon and North Vietnamese President Ho Chi Minh, August 1969. *Department of State Bulletin*, November 24, 1969.

9.8
Nixon's "Silent Majority" Speech – 1969
The Text of a Nationally Televised Speech Delivered by President Richard Nixon

When Richard Nixon became president in January 1969, he inherited a war in Vietnam that seemed to be growing more controversial and unpopular with the American people with each passing day. Over the ensuing months, his administration gradually began withdrawing American troops from Vietnam and giving South Vietnam more responsibility for its defense. But he repeatedly stated his belief that the United States needed to maintain a significant military presence in Vietnam if it wanted to keep it from being conquered by the Communists. He also insisted that even though the antiwar movement had garnered a lot of attention from the media, many Americans still supported the U.S. involvement in Vietnam. He expressed these beliefs in the following speech, which was broadcast to the nation on November 3, 1969. Nixon seeks to assure both the war's opponents and it supporters—who he terms the nation's "silent majority"—about the wisdom of his policies in Vietnam.

Good evening, my fellow Americans.

Tonight I want to talk to you on a subject of deep concern to all Americans and to many people in all parts of the world—the war in Vietnam.

I believe that one of the reasons for the deep division about Vietnam is that many Americans have lost confidence in what their Government has told them about our policy. The American people cannot and should not be asked to support a policy which involves the overriding issues of war and peace unless they know the truth about that policy.

Tonight, therefore, I would like to answer some of the questions that I know are on the minds of many of you listening to me. How and why did America get involved in Vietnam in the first place? How has this administration changed the policy of the previous administration? What has really happened in the negotiations in Paris and on the battlefront in Vietnam? What choices do we have if we are to end the war? What are the prospects for peace? Now, let me begin by describing the situation I found when I was inaugurated on January 20:

The war had been going on for four years. One thousand Americans had been killed in action. The training program for the South Vietnamese was behind schedule; 540,000 Americans were in Vietnam with no plans to reduce the number. No progress had been made at the negotiations in Paris and the United States had not put forth a comprehensive peace proposal. The war was causing deep division at home and criticism from many of our friends as well as our enemies abroad.

In view of these circumstances there were some who urged that I end the war at once by ordering the immediate withdrawal of all American forces. From a political standpoint this would have been a popular and easy course to follow. After all, we became involved in the war while my predecessor was in office. I could blame the defeat which would be the result of my action on him and come out as the peacemaker. Some put it to me quite bluntly: This was the only way to avoid allowing Johnson's war to become Nixon's war.

But I had a greater obligation than to think only of the years of my administration and of the next election. I had to think of the effect of my decision on the next generation and on the future of peace and freedom in America and in the world.

Let us all understand that the question before us is not whether some Americans are for peace and some Americans are against peace. The question at issue is not whether Johnson's war becomes Nixon's war. The great question is: How can we win America's peace?

Well, let us turn now to the fundamental issue. Why and how did the United States become involved in Vietnam in the first place? Fifteen years ago North Vietnam, with the logistical support of communist China and the Soviet Union, launched a campaign to impose a communist government on South Vietnam by instigating and supporting a revolution.

In response to the request of the Government of South Vietnam, President Eisenhower sent economic aid and military equipment to assist the people of

South Vietnam in their efforts to prevent a communist takeover. Seven years ago, President Kennedy sent 16,000 military personnel to Vietnam as combat advisers. Four years ago, President Johnson sent American combat forces to South Vietnam.

Now, many believe that President Johnson's decision to send American combat forces to South Vietnam was wrong. And many others—I among them—have been strongly critical of the way the war has been conducted.

But the question facing us today is: Now that we are in the war, what is the best way to end it?

In January I could only conclude that the precipitate withdrawal of American forces from Vietnam would be a disaster not only for South Vietnam but for the United States and for the cause of peace.

For the South Vietnamese, our precipitate withdrawal would inevitably allow the Communists to repeat the massacres which followed their takeover in the North 15 years before; they then murdered more than 50,000 people and hundreds of thousands more died in slave labor camps.

We saw a prelude of what would happen in South Vietnam when the Communists entered the city of Hue last year. During their brief rule there, there was a bloody reign of terror in which 3,000 civilians were clubbed, shot to death, and buried in mass graves. With the sudden collapse of our support, these atrocities of Hue would become the nightmare of the entire nation—and particularly for the million and a half Catholic refugees who fled to South Vietnam when the Communists took over in the North.

For the United States, this first defeat in our nation's history would result in a collapse of confidence in American leadership, not only in Asia but throughout the world.

Three American presidents have recognized the great stakes involved in Vietnam and understood what had to be done.

In 1963, President Kennedy, with his characteristic eloquence and clarity, said:

'… We want to see a stable government there, carrying on a struggle to maintain its national independence. We believe strongly in that. We are not going to withdraw from that effort. In my opinion, for us to withdraw from that effort would mean a collapse not only of South Vietnam, but Southeast Asia. So we are going to stay there.'

President Eisenhower and President Johnson expressed the same conclusion during their terms of office.

For the future of peace, precipitate withdrawal would thus be a disaster of immense magnitude. A nation cannot remain great if it betrays its allies and lets down its friends. Our defeat and humiliation in South Vietnam without question would promote recklessness in the councils of those great powers who have not yet abandoned their goals of world conquest. This would spark violence wherever our commitments help maintain the peace—in the Middle East, in Berlin, eventually even in the Western Hemisphere. Ultimately, this would cost more lives. It would not bring peace; it would bring more war.

For these reasons, I rejected the recommendation that I should end the war by immediately withdrawing all of our forces. I chose instead to change American policy on both the negotiating front and battlefront. In order to end a war fought on many fronts, I initiated a pursuit for peace on many fronts. In a television speech on May 14, in a speech before the United Nations, and on a number of other occasions I set forth our peace proposals in great detail.

We have offered the complete withdrawal of all outside forces within one year.

We have proposed a cease-fire under international supervision.

We have offered free elections under international supervision with the Communists participating in the organization and conduct of the elections as an organized political force. And the Saigon Government has pledged to accept the result of the elections.

We have not put forth our proposals on a take-it-or-leave-it basis. We have indicated that we are willing to discuss the proposals that have been put forth by the other side. We have declared that anything is negotiable except the right of the people of South Vietnam to determine their own future. At the Paris peace conference, Ambassador Lodge has demonstrated our flexibility and good faith in 40 public meetings.

Hanoi has refused even to discuss our proposals. They demand our unconditional acceptance of their terms, which are that we withdraw all American forces immediately and unconditionally and that we overthrow the Government of South Vietnam as we leave.

We have not limited our peace initiatives to public forums and public statements. I recognized, in January, that a long and bitter war like this usually cannot be settled in a public forum. That is why in addition to the public statements and negotiation I have explored every possible private avenue that might lead to a settlement....

But the effect of all the public, private and secret negotiations which have been undertaken since the bombing halt a year ago and since this administration came into office on January 20 can be summed up in one sentence: No progress whatever has been made except agreement on the shape of the bargaining table.

Well now, who is at fault?

It has become clear that the obstacle in negotiating an end to the war is not the President of the United States. It is not the South Vietnamese Government. The obstacle is the other side's absolute refusal to show the least willingness to join us in seeking a just peace. And it will not do so while it is convinced that all it has to do is to wait for our next concession, and our next concession after that one, until it gets everything it wants.

There can now be no longer any question that progress in negotiation depends only on Hanoi's deciding to negotiate, to negotiate seriously.

I realize that this report on our efforts on the diplomatic front is discouraging to the American people, but the American people are entitled to know the truth—the bad news as well as the good news—where the lives of our young men are involved.

Now let me turn, however, to a more encouraging report on another front. At the time we launched our search for peace I recognized we might not succeed in bringing an end to the war through negotiation. I, therefore, put into effect another plan to bring peace—a plan which will bring the war to an end regardless of what happens on the negotiating front.

It is in line with a major shift in U.S. foreign policy which I described in my press conference at Guam on July 25. Let me briefly explain what has been described as the Nixon Doctrine—policy which not only will help end the war in Vietnam, but which is an essential element of our program to prevent future Vietnams.

We Americans are a do-it-yourself people. We are an impatient people. Instead of teaching someone else to do a job, we like to do it ourselves. And this trait has been carried over into our foreign policy. In Korea and again in Vietnam, the United States furnished most of the money, most of the arms, and most of the men to help the people of those countries defend their freedom against Communist aggression.

Before any American troops were committed to Vietnam, a leader of another Asian country expressed this opinion to me when I was traveling in Asia as a private citizen. He said: "When you are trying to assist another nation defend its freedom, U.S. policy should be to help them fight the war but not to fight the war for them."

Well, in accordance with this wise counsel, I laid down in Guam three principles as guidelines for future American policy toward Asia:

First, the United States will keep all of its treaty commitments.

Second, we shall provide a shield if a nuclear power threatens the freedom of a nation allied with us or of a nation whose survival we consider vital to our security.

Third, in cases involving other types of aggression, we shall furnish military and economic assistance when requested in accordance with our treaty commitments. But we shall look to the nation directly threatened to assume the primary responsibility of providing the manpower for its defense.

After I announced this policy, I found that the leaders of the Philippines, Thailand, Vietnam, South Korea, and other nations which might be threatened by Communist aggression welcomed this new direction in American foreign policy.

The defense of freedom is everybody's business—not just America's business. And it is particularly the responsibility of the people whose freedom is threatened. In the previous administration, we Americanized the war in Vietnam. In this administration, we are Vietnamizing the search for peace.

The policy of the previous administration not only resulted in our assuming the primary responsibility for fighting the war, but even more significantly did not adequately stress the goal of strengthening the South Vietnamese so that they could defend themselves when we left.

The Vietnamization plan was launched following Secretary Laird's visit to Vietnam in March. Under the plan, I ordered first a substantial increase in the training and equipment of South Vietnamese forces.

In July, on my visit to Vietnam, I changed General Abrams' orders so that they were consistent with the objectives of our new policies. Under the new orders, the primary mission of our troops is to enable the South Vietnamese forces to assume the full responsibility for the security of South Vietnam. Our air operations have been reduced by over 20 percent. And now we have begun to see the results of this long overdue change in American policy in Vietnam.

After five years of Americans going into Vietnam, we are finally bringing American men home. By December 15, over 60,000 men will have been withdrawn from South Vietnam, including 20 percent of all of our combat forces. The South Vietnamese have continued to gain in strength. As a result they have been able to take over combat responsibilities from our American troops.

Two other significant developments have occurred since this administration took office.

Enemy infiltration, infiltration which is essential if they are to launch a major attack, over the last three months is less than 20 percent of what it was over the same period last year. Most important—United States casualties have declined during the last two months to the lowest point in three years....

My fellow Americans, I am sure you can recognize from what I have said that we really only have two choices open to us if we want to end this war. I can order an immediate, precipitate withdrawal of all Americans from Vietnam without regard to the effects of that action. Or we can persist in our search for a just peace through a negotiated settlement if possible, or through continued implementation of our plan for Vietnamization if necessary, a plan in which we will withdraw all of our forces from Vietnam on a schedule in accordance with our program, as the South Vietnamese become strong enough to defend their own freedom.

I have chosen this second course. It is not the easy way. It is the right way. It is a plan which will end the war and serve the cause of peace—not just in Vietnam but in the Pacific and in the world.

In speaking of the consequences of a precipitate withdrawal, I mentioned that our allies would lose confidence in America. Far more dangerous, we would lose confidence in ourselves. Oh, the immediate reaction would be a sense of relief that our men were coming home. But as we saw the consequences of what we had done, inevitable remorse and divisive recrimination would scar our spirit as a people.

We have faced other crises in our history and have become stronger by rejecting the easy way out and taking the right way in meeting our challenges. Our greatness as a nation has been our capacity to do what had to be done when we knew our course was right. I recognize that some of my fellow citizens disagree with the plan for peace I have chosen. Honest and patriotic Americans have reached different conclusions as to how peace should be achieved.

"I want to end [the war] so that the energy and dedication of you, our young people, now too often directed into bitter hatred against those responsible for the war, can be turned to the great challenges of peace."

In San Francisco a few weeks ago, I saw demonstrators carrying signs reading: "Lose in Vietnam, bring the boys home." Well, one of the strengths of our free society is that any American has a right to reach that conclusion and to advocate that point of view. But as president of the United States, I would be untrue to my oath of office if I allowed the policy of this nation to be dictated by the minority who hold that point of view and who try to impose it on the nation by mounting demonstrations in the street.

For almost 200 years, the policy of this nation has been made under our Constitution by those leaders in the Congress and the White House elected by all of the people. If a vocal minority, however fervent its cause, prevails over reason and the will of the majority, this nation has no future as a free society.

And now I would like to address a word, if I may, to the young people of this nation who are particularly concerned, and I understand why they are concerned, about this war.

I respect your idealism. I share your concern for peace. I want peace as much as you do. There are powerful personal reasons I want to end this war. This week I will have to sign 83 letters to mothers, fathers, wives and loved ones of men who have given their lives for America in Vietnam. It is very little satisfaction to me that this is only one-third as many letters as I signed the first week in office. There is nothing I want more than to see the day come when I do not have to write any of those letters.

I want to end the war to save the lives of those brave young men in Vietnam.

But I want to end it in a way which will increase the chance that their younger brothers and their sons will not have to fight in some future Vietnam someplace in the world.

And I want to end the war for another reason. I want to end it so that the energy and dedication of you, our young people, now too often directed into bitter hatred against those responsible for the war, can be turned to the great challenges of peace, a better life for all Americans, a better life for all people on this Earth.

I have chosen a plan for peace. I believe it will succeed. If it does succeed, what the critics say now won't matter. If it does not succeed, anything I say then won't matter.

I know it may not be fashionable to speak of patriotism or national destiny these days. But I feel it is appropriate to do so on this occasion.

Two hundred years ago this nation was weak and poor. But even then, America was the hope of millions in the world. Today we have become the strongest and richest nation in the world. And the wheel of destiny has turned so that any hope the world has for the survival of peace and freedom will be determined by whether the American people have the moral stamina and the courage to meet the challenge of free world leadership.

Let historians not record that when America was the most powerful nation in the world we passed on the other side of the road and allowed the last hopes for peace and freedom of millions of people to be suffocated by the forces of totalitarianism.

And so tonight—to you, the great silent majority of my fellow Americans—I ask for your support. I pledged in my campaign for the presidency to end the war in a way that we could win the peace. I have initiated a plan of action which will enable me to keep that pledge. The more support I can have from the American people, the sooner that pledge can be redeemed; for the more divided we are at home, the less likely the enemy is to negotiate at Paris.

Let us be united for peace. Let us also be united against defeat. Because let us understand: North Vietnam cannot defeat or humiliate the United States. Only Americans can do that....

Source: Nixon, Richard M. *Public Papers of the Presidents of the United States: Richard M. Nixon, 1969.* Washington, DC: Office of the Federal Register, 1971.

9.9
The Fall of Saigon – 1975
"After the Crusade" by Tobias Wolff

In January 1973 the United States and North Vietnam signed the Paris peace accords, ending the direct involvement of U.S. military troops in the war. Over the next two years, America continued to provide military advice and economic aid to South Vietnam, but the actual fighting against the Communists was carried out entirely by South Vietnamese troops. In 1974 and early 1975 North Vietnamese forces launched several defensive thrusts deep into South Vietnamese territory. These attacks were clear violations of the terms of the 1973 Paris Peace Accords, but the United States remained on the sidelines.

The U.S. decision not to re-enter the war sealed South Vietnam's fate. Buoyed by the knowledge that they no longer had to worry about deadly American bombers and helicopters, Communist forces roared through South Vietnam. This offensive, which prompted a huge refugee crisis across the South, reached the outskirts of the South Vietnamese capital of Saigon in late April 1975. The United States mounted a frantic helicopter evacuation of American officials and selected South Vietnamese civilians and their families across the capital. This helicopter lift lasted from the morning of April 29 to the early morning hours of April 30, when President Gerald R. Ford ordered a halt to the evacuation. A few hours later, North Vietnamese tanks rolled into the captured city, ending the war once and for all. In the following excerpt, author—and Vietnam veteran—Tobias Wolff recalls how he felt when he heard about the fall of Saigon.

I was living in San Francisco when Saigon fell, teaching high school. I picked up the paper after work and read it during the bus ride home. So. It was over, almost seven years to the day since I finished my own tour of duty in that already ancient war. When you've served in a war, gloriously or not—not, in my case—you are bound to take an interest in the news that your side has lost. I found nothing surprising in the reports of how effortlessly Saigon had been taken. But there was this picture: a helicopter perched on a mere nub of a rooftop in the city, its crew chief reaching down to help someone up a ladder while a long line of people wait below for their own chance to escape. A joke of fate that the very machine that was supposed to guarantee our victory should prove the means of our retreat.

It didn't occur to me that this photograph would become the enduring image of our failure in Vietnam. But it worked strongly on me, and still does: that wide-open sky waiting above the helicopter like freedom itself; the dark line of people bearing their hopes of deliverance; the apparent fragility of the craft, its precarious roost, the spindliness of the rotors on which all these hopes depend; and, most eloquent, the figure of the crew chief silhouetted against the empty sky, pulling some fearful soul from one life into another, as we had set out to do by other means so many years before.

If I found nothing to be surprised at in the fall of Saigon, of Vietnam itself, it was because the war had already been lost by the time I got there in the spring of 1967. The suspicion that this was so came upon me not as a thought but as a deepening unease at the way we treated the Vietnamese and the way they treated one another. I hadn't been 10 minutes off the plane at Bienhoa before I saw one of our troops abusing the baggage handlers; the bus driver who ferried us to the transit barracks spent most of the trip screaming insults at the people on the road, and nearly made good on his threat to run down an old woman who was slow getting out of his way.

That was just the beginning. Everywhere I went I saw Americans raining contempt on Vietnamese, handling them roughly, speaking to them like badly behaved children, or dogs. In time I learned to do it myself. Fear was our teacher; it taught us some bad lessons, and taught them well.

Still, it was obvious to even the rosiest fantasts that we couldn't win this war by simple force of arms, that the real battle was for the trust and loyalty of the common man. We knew this, but our anger and fear kept getting the better of us. Why didn't they get behind us? Why didn't they care that we were dying for them? Yet every time we slapped someone around, or trashed a village, or shouted curses from a jeep, we defined ourselves as the enemy and thereby handed more power and legitimacy to the people we had to beat.

The government soldiers were worse. Their army suffered from a corruption so pervasive and timeworn that it had become institutionalized: officers didn't get paid enough money to live on because it was assumed they'd make up the rest by graft. Their soldiers had it even harder, and they passed on their sufferings, with interest, to the people they were supposed to protect. They went into the field not to fight but to oppress. There were exceptions of course. Some officers and men were honest and compassionate; some of their units fought well. Most didn't.

The war could have been won only through the most heroic moral discipline. To prevail, our side had to prove to the people that we were serving a coherent and humane vision of the future, that we cared more than our enemies did about them. But by 1967—long before then, in truth—the South Vietnamese government had suffered a catastrophic moral collapse. Same with the army. This was plain to the Americans serving there and didn't exactly stiffen our own resolve. Who wants to get killed or crippled so that bullies and thieves can go about their business in safety?

Whatever innocence we had left came to an end during the Tet offensive of 1968. The scale of the offensive surprised us and frightened us, and brought to a boil all the bitterness we felt toward the Vietnamese people—how could such a massive operation have been carried out without their knowledge and complicity? After the first shock passed, we opened the gate of hell on that country, and we didn't spend much time making distinctions between enemies and friends. Entire towns were destroyed, others devastated by our jets and artillery. Most of the dead were civilians. In this way we taught the people—and taught ourselves, once and for all—that we didn't love them and wouldn't protect them, and that we were prepared to kill them all to save ourselves.

This recognition cost us dearly. American soldiers don't go to war in the spirit of mercenaries or legionnaires; we have to think of ourselves as crusaders. It may be self-delusion, but a sense of chivalric purpose is essential to our spiritual survival when we find ourselves called upon to kill others and risk being killed. In its absence we become at worst cynical and corrupt, at best simply professional. After Tet we were legionnaires, but legionnaires couldn't win over there, as France had already learned. The war had been fought in the soul, and lost in the soul, long before the fall of Saigon.

The last battle ended 20 years ago, but if the end of a war is peace, we're still waiting for it. The communist regime in Vietnam was so harsh and vengeful in the aftermath of its victory that more than 800,000 people took flight, hundreds of thousands on the open sea rather than remain at home. We haven't finished fighting it out here either. Even in the toxic atmosphere of our political discourse, it is hard to imagine another issue that could inspire a Congressman, speaking on the House floor, to accuse his President of treason.

A few years ago, I was invited to join a group of men who were meeting every other week or so to talk about Vietnam. Three of us had served there. Of the others, one had been a conscientious objector; another had got lucky with the draft; a third had been too old for Vietnam but was active in the antiwar movement. Though our circumstances had placed us in very different, even conflicting positions, nobody was of a mind to find fault with anyone else. Indeed, the other two veterans had both become pacifists some years back.

We came together with the best will in the world, but as soon as we began to talk, it grew obvious that our experiences had opened distances between us that no amount of goodwill could bridge. One of the veterans, a former captain, had been in almost continous combat; the men under his command were shot up and killed so regularly that he couldn't keep track of them. One day he told us about sending out the body of an 18-year-old only a few hours after the boy had joined the unit. "What was I supposed to tell his parents?" he said. "I hadn't even met him." Then he added, in that tone of cold, slashing drollery soldiers use to mock their breaking hearts: "Tag 'em and bag 'em."

He is a man, as we all knew, of utmost gentleness and decency, but at that last phrase one of the nonveterans bridled a little; nothing was said, but our histories slammed down between us once again. The three of us who'd served couldn't help falling into a certain manner and language when recalling those days. "You're doing it again," one of the others said to us at such a moment, with rueful good nature. We understood him, but the old covenant was too strong to resist, and too dear.

That was the simplest of the divisions between us, but hardly the only one. My tour in Vietnam had been different from the former captain's. I could not follow him to that extremity of desolation where his memories often led; he was alone there. Nor could the lottery winner follow the conscientious objector to his outpost of remembrance. The more we talked, the farther away we seemed to be. And we weren't even arguing.

But the deepest fissures were those within us. Whether you went or not, that war put a crack in you because of the impossibility of finding an untainted response to it. If you protested the war, you couldn't help worrying about the bafflement and pain you were causing those in danger, and their families. How did you make peace with the fact that, however unintentionally, you were encouraging a hard, often murderous enemy who was doing his best to kill boys you'd grown up with? If you went, you had to notice that the government we were trying to save wasn't worth saving, and the people were generally uninterested in our brand of help. In time you might even come to see them as the enemy. Where did that leave you? And why did you go in the first place? From conviction, or from fear of being thought, and thinking yourself, a coward? How could you be sure? Only the most self-satisfied ideologues on either side of the problem could avoid questioning their own motives.

After four or five meetings, my discussion group decided to pack it in. We did so with a sense of relief, and humility. We had hoped to understand one another a little better; we hadn't expected to settle anything, to cast out any demons. But I think we were all a little chastened to find out how many demons there were, and how much power they still had to complicate even our affections and trust.

Ho Chi Minh City is filled with American capitalists now. There are nightclubs and discos and billboards. You can take a tour of the Cu Chi tunnels, squeeze off a few rounds with an AK-47, a dollar a pop. I've heard good stories from guys who've gone back. One of them visited the scene of his worst memories in the company of a former NVA officer who'd led an attack against his unit. There they were, together, walking the ground where they had tried to kill each other and where friends of theirs had died. And at the end of the day they managed to do what we at home have yet to learn to do. They shook hands.

One last look at the photograph, at the figure of the crew chief reaching down to the person on the ladder. There is such gallantry in his stance. It expresses in every line the strength and simplicity of his intent: to be of help. That's why we went there in the first place, and why this final image of our leaving touches me, in the end, with pride.

Source: Wolff, Tobias. "After the Crusade." *Time*, April 24, 1995.

10

DÉTENTE AND "THE CHINA CARD"

Soviet Premier Leonid Brezhnev (left) and U.S. President Gerald Ford
converse prior to their signing of the historic 1975 Helsinki Accords.

INTRODUCTION

Despite America's struggles in Vietnam, relations between the West and the Soviet empire actually improved somewhat during the late 1960s and early 1970s. This easing of tensions, known as *détente*, was partly due to the heavy economic burden that the nuclear arms race was placing on both sides. U.S. President Richard Nixon and his chief advisor, Henry Kissinger (who served first as Nixon's national security advisor and then from 1973-1977 as secretary of state), recognized that the United States still maintained a clear advantage in terms of its overall nuclear arsenal. But they were aware that the Soviets had definitely closed the gap between the two powers. In addition, Nixon and Kissinger recognized that the unpopular war in Vietnam had eroded American support for fighting Communism overseas. The Nixon White House thus saw détente as a way of preserving the existing world order before the West suffered any greater erosion in its position. "We were becoming like other nations in the need to recognize that our power, while vast, had limits," Kissinger later wrote in his memoir *White House Years*.

For their part, Soviet leaders believed that arms control agreements could reduce the danger of nuclear war and also free resources to strengthen struggling Soviet and Eastern bloc economies. "Détente did not mean replacing the Cold War with a structure of peace, to be sure, despite the pious rhetoric from both sides that so stated," explained historian Robert J. McMahon. "Rather, it meant managing the Cold War in a safer and more controlled manner so as to minimize the possibility either of accidental war or of a destabilizing arms spiral."

Another major factor driving the two sides toward détente was the People's Republic of China. By the late 1960s many observers in both Washington and

317

Moscow viewed China as a dangerous and unpredictable presence on the world stage. Mao Zedong and other Chinese leaders had not only launched the brutal Cultural Revolution against its own citizens, but they were also loudly denouncing Soviet leaders as betrayers of the Communist ideal. Moreover, Chinese forces were displaying an alarming willingness to clash with Russian forces along Central Asia's long Sino-Soviet border.

In Washington, the Nixon administration believed that the rising tensions between the world's two Communist giants gave the United States a number of promising diplomatic openings. Nixon and Kissinger, in particular, believed that America could exploit the turmoil in Sino-Soviet relations to diminish Soviet influence around the world and stop China's slide into international isolation.

An Overture to China

With these considerations in mind, Nixon decided to "play the China card." Kissinger began holding secret negotiations with the Chinese, even as American and Soviet diplomats held substantive arms control discussions in Moscow. As it turned out, both Communist powers were receptive to the American overtures. "To have the two Communist powers competing for good relations with us could only benefit the cause of peace," Kissinger later recalled in *White House Years*.

Over the next several years the Nixon White House achieved a number of important diplomatic victories. In July 1971 Kissinger made a secret trip to Beijing, becoming the first American official to visit the People's Republic of China since its founding in 1949. In February 1972 Nixon himself made an historic trip to China, visiting famous landmarks such as the Great Wall of China and Tiananmen Square in the company of Chairman Mao. In May 1972 Nixon continued his diplomatic offensive by visiting Moscow, where he was warmly received by Soviet leader Leonid Brezhnev. On May 26, 1972, the two leaders signed a major treaty, Strategic Arms Limitation Talks I (SALT). This treaty placed strict limits on each nation's missile systems, including antiballistic missiles (ABMs), intercontinental ballistic missiles (ICBMs), and submarine-launched ballistic missiles (SLBMs). The treaty even included an unenforceable but heartfelt pledge by the signatories to "do their utmost to avoid military confrontations and to prevent the outbreak of nuclear war."

One year later, events in the Middle East tested the commitment of the United States and the Soviet Union to "peaceful co-existence." In October 1973 Egypt and Syria attacked Israel after years of mounting tensions between the countries. Since Egypt and Syria were friendly with the Soviets, and Israel was a major ally of the United States, many observers feared that the Middle East unrest might reignite Cold War tensions. But after an initial burst of anxiety and suspicion, U.S. and Soviet negotiators helped arrange a cease-fire.

Nixon's diplomatic breakthroughs with China and the Soviet Union, though, could not save his presidency from scandal. Battered by the Watergate affair and facing impeachment, Nixon resigned the presidency on August 8, 1974. Following Nixon's resignation, the new president, Gerald R. Ford, arranged for a November 1974 summit with Brezhnev. This meeting paved the way for the historic Final Act of the Conference on Security and Cooperation in Europe. This agreement, also known as the Helsinki Accords, was signed in August 1975 by the United States, Canada, the Soviet Union, and nearly three dozen other European nations. It formally approved existing European borders; laid out principles of diplomatic, economic, technological, and environmental cooperation; and emphasized the importance of freedom of speech and other political rights to people across Europe.

Human Rights and U.S.-Soviet Relations

The Soviets staunchly opposed the human rights section, or "basket," of the accords. In fact, some conservative members of the Communist Party saw these clauses as such an intrusion on state authority that they urged Brezhnev not to sign. But Brezhnev soothed their fears, coolly noting that "We are masters in our own house; we shall decide what we implement and what we ignore."

As it turned out, however, the subject of human rights could not be dismissed so easily. In November 1976 Democratic presidential nominee Jimmy Carter narrowly defeated Ford to win the White House. When he took office in January 1977, Carter made it clear that human rights issues would be an important part of his administration's foreign policy. A few weeks after his inauguration, Carter exchanged warm correspondence with Andrei Sakharov, the leading dissident figure in the entire Soviet Union. A month later, the Carter White House signaled its support for Charter 77, a declaration of human rights issued by dissidents in the repressive Czech Republic, a satellite state of the Soviet Union.

The Soviets also watched the continued thaw in relations between China and the United States with apprehension. Relations improved after Deng Xiaoping assumed leadership of China in 1977, following the death of Mao Zedong the previous year. In January 1979, the United States and the People's Republic of China established full diplomatic relations. "If we really want to place curbs on the Russian bear, the only realistic thing is for us to unite," Deng told U.S. officials.

319

Carter did reach out to the Soviets on a number of fronts. His administration actively courted the Kremlin to seek out additional cuts in nuclear arms, for example. But the leadership of the USSR proved unable or unwilling to decipher these mixed signals, which came at a time of growing domestic unrest. By the late 1970s the Soviet empire was grappling with a host of internal challenges, including Brezhnev's growing feebleness, steady declines in the Soviet standard of living, and increasing unrest in East bloc countries.

In July 1979, American and Soviet negotiators managed to sign another arms control agreement, SALT II (Strategic Arms Limitations Talks). But the fanfare that accompanied the SALT I treaty was absent this time. In fact, SALT II was roundly condemned in America by an emerging group of conservative, deeply anti-Communist lawmakers, scholars, and opinion-makers. These experts were convinced that the United States' emphasis on arms control and human rights considerations had actually benefited Communism worldwide, and particularly in the Third World.

In 1979 momentous events in Central Asia finally put an end to the era of détente. In January, America lost its most reliable ally in the strategically important Persian Gulf region when Muslim fundamentalists overthrew the Shah of Iran. Then, ten months later, Iranian militants seized the American embassy in Tehran and took 66 Americans hostage. The Iranian hostage crisis endured for 444 days. It badly damaged the presidency of Carter, who received much of the blame for the nation's inability to bring the hostages home. In December 1979, meanwhile, the Soviet Union launched a massive invasion of Afghanistan to defend that nation's Communist regime against a fundamentalist Islamic insurgency. Carter was outraged by the Soviet action, describing it as "the most serious threat to peace since the Second World War." He promptly withdrew SALT II from Senate consideration, imposed economic sanctions on the Soviet Union, announced a U.S. boycott of the upcoming Olympics scheduled to be held in Moscow, and called for major new investments in defense spending.

These events, along with simmering crises in Latin America and Africa, made it impossible for Washington and Moscow to keep détente alive. Instead, they brought the Cold War back in all its former intensity. "All in all," admitted Soviet ambassador Anatoly Dobrynin, "one could say that détente was to a certain extent buried in the fields of Soviet-American rivalry in the Third World."

10.1
China's Cultural Revolution – 1966
The Text of a News Article Published in the Peking Review

In 1964 Communist China successfully detonated an atomic bomb, thus joining the United States, USSR, United Kingdom, and France as a nuclear power. Two years later, Communist Party Chairman Mao Zedong struck against political opponents by launching the "Cultural Revolution." The Cultural Revolution was a concerted effort to entrench his "Maoist" philosophy of socialism across all strata of Chinese society. Participants used violence in an effort to hasten revolutionary social change and to eliminate the entrenched bureaucracy of the Chinese Communist Party. Mao encouraged Chinese students and workers to attack authorities of the Chinese Communist Party and other representatives of the elite, particularly at universities. He exhorted the students to take power and return China to the path of pure socialism. Mao specifically called for the destruction of the "four olds": old ideas, old culture, old customs, and old habits.

Over the next several years, hordes of militant youth known as Red Guards carried out Mao's wishes, plunging the country into chaos. They killed or imprisoned millions of Chinese and destroyed countless cultural artifacts and artistic treasures. The Cultural Revolution finally ended in 1976 with the death of Mao and the arrest of the so-called "Gang of Four" group of Communist Party leaders. In the following article published in the Chinese newspaper the Peking Review *on September 2, 1966, in the opening months of this grim period in Chinese history, the writer glorifies the activities of the Red Guards in Beijing and other areas.*

Red Guards Destroy the Old and Establish the New

Since August 20, the young Red Guards of Peking [Beijing], detachments of students, have taken to the streets. With the revolutionary rebel spirit of the proletariat, they have launched a furious offensive to sweep away reactionary, decadent bourgeois and feudal influences, and all old ideas, culture, customs and habits. This mounting revolutionary storm is sweeping the cities of the entire nation. "Let Mao Tse-tung's thought occupy all positions; use it to transform the mental outlook of the whole of society; sweep away all ghosts and monsters; brush aside all stumbling-blocks and resolutely carry the great proletarian cultural revolution through to the end!" This is the militant aim of the young revolutionary fighters. Their revolutionary actions have everywhere received the enthusiastic support of the revolutionary masses.

In Peking. During the past week and more Red Guards have scored victory after victory as they pressed home their attack against the decadent customs and habits of the exploiting classes. Beating drums and singing revolutionary songs detachments of Red Guards are out in the streets doing propaganda work, holding aloft big portraits of Chairman Mao, extracts from Chairman Mao's works, and great banners with the words: We are the critics of the old world; we are the builders of the new world. They have held street meetings, put up big-character posters and distributed leaflets in their attack against all the old ideas and habits of the exploiting classes. As a result of the proposals of the Red Guards and with the support of the revolutionary masses, shop signs which spread odious feudal and bourgeois ideas have been removed, and the names of many streets, lanes, parks, buildings and schools tainted with feudalism, capitalism or revisionism or which had no revolutionary significance have been replaced by revolutionary names. The service trades have thrown out obsolete rules and regulations.

Support for the revolutionary actions of the Red Guards has been expressed in countless big-character posters which the masses of revolutionary workers and staff have put up in the newly renamed major thoroughfares of the capital. They have also expressed their support with street demonstrations.

Draping the many-storied front of the newly renamed Peking Department Store are gigantic banners with the words: "Resolute support for the revolutionary students' revolutionary actions!" and "Salute to the young revolutionary fighters!" Workers of the Peking Steel Plant, encouraged by the actions of the revolutionary students, have launched vigorous attacks on old ideas, styles of work, methods and systems that hamper the revolution and production in their plant. They have put forward many revolutionary proposals and already begun reforms. Workers at the Peking No. 2 Cotton Textile Mill are emulating the revolutionary rebel spirit of the Red Guards and are attacking all old influences. The workers hold that everyone has the right to sweep away the influences of the old, not only outside, in the streets, but also in the factories and all other enterprises and in government offices. In this way, by sweeping together, the great proletarian cultural revolution will be carried through to complete victory.

Commanders and fighters of the People's Liberation Army in the capital have unanimously expressed support for the revolutionary students' revolutionary actions, and the carrying of the great proletarian cultural revolution through to the end. They say that the great revolutionary actions of the revolutionary students in attacking bourgeois ideology, customs and habits is another instance of the great material strength that is generated by Mao Tse-tung's thought once it grips the revolutionary masses. Speaking at a discussion meeting of the 12th company of a garrison unit in Peking commanders and fighters said that the revolutionary actions of the young fighters are smashing the old world and building a new world. Pao Hsiming, of a P.L.A. Navy Air Force unit who won a combat citation, second class, for shooting down a U.S. made plane of the Chiang gang, told a Hsinhua correspondent that the revolutionary actions of the Red Guards were thoroughgoing revolutionary actions as the result of their following the teachings of Chairman Mao and acting according to his instructions. "They are doing right and doing fine," he said.

In Shanghai. In this huge city which has the largest concentration of capitalists in the country and which, until the liberation had long been under the rule of the imperialists and domestic reactionaries, the revolutionary students and the broad masses of workers and staff have taken up their iron brooms to sweep away all old habits and customs. The shop windows of the Wing On Co., one of the biggest department stores in the city, are plastered with big-character posters put up by the Red Guards and workers and staff of the store, proposing that "Wing On" (Eternal Peace) should be changed into "Yong Hong" (Red For Ever) or "Yong Dou" (Struggle For Ever). The posters point out that in the old society the boss of the store chose the name "Wing On" because he wanted to be left in peace for ever to exploit the working people. "For a long time now the store has been in the hands of the people and we are certainly not going to tolerate this odious name a day longer," say the posters.

In "The Great World," the biggest amusement centre of Shanghai, workers and staff together with the Red Guards took down the old name sign which was several metres long. When the last character of the sign was brought down, thousands of revolutionary people in the streets and in the windows of neighbouring buildings applauded and cheered: "Long live Chairman Mao!" and "Long live the great proletarian cultural revolution!"

The waterfront of the Whangpoo River in Shanghai was, until the liberation, the centre of imperialist plunder of the Chinese people. The buildings here have still carried many reminders of the imperialists and here the Red Guards and revolutionary workers and staff have gone in for revolutionizing in a big way. They have taken down all the imperialist signs from walls and removed the bronze lions outside one of the big buildings.

The revolutionary workers and staff of Shanghai barber shops have adopted revolutionary measures in response to the proposals of the Red Guards: they no longer cut and set hair in the grotesque fashions indulged in by a small minority of people; they cut out those services specially worked out for the bourgeoisie such as manicuring, beauty treatments and so on. In those shops which sold only goods catering to the needs of a small minority of people, workers and staff have taken the revolutionary decision to start supplying the people at large with good popular commodities at low prices.

323

In Tientsin. For the past several days there has been a new revolutionary atmosphere in the streets. Drums and gongs have been sounding around Binjiang Street, the business centre, and firecrackers have crackled all day long; many shops have discarded their old shop signs, and replaced them with new revolutionary ones. Inspired by the revolutionary spirit of the Red Guards, the revolutionary workers and staff members of "Quanyechang," one of the biggest markets in the city, smashed the name sign inlaid in its wall for the past 38 years and hung up a new sign, the "People's Market." The "Beiyang Textile Mill" which was established in the time of the Northern warlords 45 years ago is now renamed "Four-New Textile Mill," meaning a mill with new ideas, new culture, new customs and new habits. The "Golden Tripod," the factory's old trademark, has been changed for a new trademark, "Worker and Peasant."

In Hangchow. The Tungpo Theatre, Tungpo Road, and the Su Ti (Su Dike) on Hangehow's West Lake named after Su Tung-po, a feudal man of letters of eight centuries ago, have been given new names with revolutionary meanings. The scissors shops which used the former shop owner's name—Chang Hsiao-chuan—as their shop sign for the past three centuries, have now taken the new name: "Hangchow Scissors Shop."

In Sining. In the capital of Chinghai Province, western China, the broad masses of revolutionary workers and staff, revolutionary cadres and poor and lower-middle peasants are giving resolute support to the young revolutionary fighters for their revolutionary rebel spirit of defying heaven or earth. Some shops, cinemas and theatres have been given new revolutionary names. Carrying large portraits of Chairman Mao and beating drums and gongs, the workers of the Sining Transport Vehicle Plant, a model enterprise, paraded the streets, pledging their support to the young fighters. Backing up the young revolutionary fighters, the poor and lower middle peasants of the Mafang People's Commune have changed their commune's name into the "Workers, Peasants and Soldiers Commune."

In Lhasa. This city's streets have been bubbling with excitement throughout the past few days. Carrying big portraits of Chairman Mao, displaying declarations of war on the old world, and beating drums and gongs, hundreds of Red Guards and revolutionary students and teachers of the Tibetan Normal School and the Lhasa Middle School took to the streets in a vigorous offensive to destroy the "four olds"—old ideas, old culture, old customs and old habits. In their declaration, the Red Guards and revolutionary students and teachers of Lhasa Middle School proclaimed: A decade and more has rolled by since Lhasa was liberated. It was the great Communist Party of China and our great leader Chairman Mao who led us in winning our emancipation and thus we were brought to a happy life. However, the spiritual shackles put upon us by the three kinds of serf-owners were still tight around our necks. This can no longer be tolerated. It is high time for us to settle accounts with them.

Red Guards and revolutionary students and teachers in Lhasa have proposed to change the names of places, streets and houses which are tainted with feudal serfdom and superstition. They also propose that literary and art groups forbid the performance of operas and plays which reek of imperialism and feudalism. The broad masses of workers and peasants in Lhasa have unanimously pledged themselves to give strong backing to the young Red Guard fighters and battle shoulder to shoulder with them to transform the city of Lhasa into a new, highly proletarianized and revolutionized city.

Source: "Red Guards Destroy the Old and Establish the New." *Peking Review*, September 2, 1966. Available online at the Morning Sun, http://www.morningsun.org/smash/pr9_1966.html.

10.2
Andrei Gromyko Assesses Soviet-American Relations During the Vietnam Era – 1967
An Excerpt from a Foreign Policy Memorandum by the Soviet Foreign Minister

Even as the United States became mired in Vietnam, American and Soviet diplomats managed to make their first tentative steps toward détente, an easing of tensions between the two superpowers. The following excerpt is taken from a confidential memorandum prepared by Soviet Foreign Minister Andrei Gromyko on January 13, 1967. This document indicates that the Soviets were genuinely interested in improving relations with the United States, albeit for their own strategic purposes. "Those who thought at the time that the Soviet Union was embarked on an aggressive program of world conquest … would have been confounded by this secret memorandum if they could have read it at the time," wrote former Soviet diplomat Anatoly Dobrynin in his memoir In Confidence. "Although in the West and the United States in particular, North Vietnam's attacks on the South were seen as the spearhead of some communist master plan of conquest, our official analysis offered no justification for this kind of aggressive military posture. It was mainly remarkable for its confidence in the eventual triumph of our social system—confidence that history proved was utterly misplaced."

The experience of recent years shows the great complexity of the task of coexisting with the United States. On the whole, international tension does not suit the state interests of the Soviet Union and its friends. The construction of socialism and the development of economy call for the maintenance of peace. In the conditions of détente it is easier to consolidate and broaden the positions of the Soviet Union in the world.

The main foreign policy principle of Kennedy and Johnson is to preserve the status quo in the world. The American concept of "spheres of vital interest" for the United States and the Soviet Union, and of a "third sphere" generally reflects the fact that American ruling circles have to acknowledge the present correlation of forces and the achievements of socialism. However, the American government has set out to prevent communism from further spreading all over the world, which is, of course, impossible.

Accordingly, in the present situation the leaders of the socialist countries and international working movement have to take into consideration, one way or another, the real state of affairs. This concerns, in particular, their approach to the questions of European security, West Berlin, etc.

The forces of the left in the United States are still relatively weak. That is why the policy of coexistence has to be oriented more at the moderate and liberal circles in the American ruling class and also at those elements in the government who essentially favor the status quo. It is true, these circles' eagerness to preserve the status quo may sometimes lead to sharp differences and indeed crises in individual regions, as further major progressive changes in the world are historically inevitable. Besides, the very forces in the United States that champion the status quo combine their policy with the continuation of the arms race and with readiness for local armed conflicts.

In this respect, we should stress the immense importance of the October 1964 Plenum of the CPSU [Communist Party of the Soviet Union] Central Committee which put an end to the voluntarism and verbiage in the foreign policy of the Soviet Union.

If we consider relations between the Soviet Union and the United States in a broad perspective, rather than against a background of the current unfavorable state of our relations caused by the U.S. aggression against Vietnam, it can be said that in the present epoch of transition the question is, in the final analysis, just how the transition of countries and nations from capitalism to socialism will proceed: under the conditions of world peace or amidst a world war. However, the answer to the question of whether a global nuclear missile war should break out, without any doubt depends just on the status of Soviet-American relations.

This, in its turn, proves the correctness of the conclusion made in the CPSU Program that at the present historical stage a world war is not fatally inevitable. We must resolutely continue to disassociate ourselves politically and ideologically from adventurous schemes of the Chinese leaders, who have pinned their hopes on the inevitability of an armed confrontation between the socialist countries headed by the Soviet Union and the United States within 8 to 10 years. The opinion that the Americans are out for war anyway and, consequently, a war with the United States is inevitable, would reflect precisely the position of the Chinese. The concentration of our main efforts on the domestic purposes is fully in line with Lenin's statement that the final victory of socialism over capitalism will be ensured by the creation of a new, much higher level of labor productivity.

While not ruling out in principle the possibility of coordinated Soviet-American actions aimed at maintaining peace and ensuring the solution of some major international issues, we must, of course, avoid creating the impression that in recognizing the special weight of the two powers we have neglected the interests of other states.

Under certain conditions the Soviet-American dialogue, suspended in 1963, can be resumed on even a far larger scale. This possibility and appropriate arrangements must be thought out as systematically and profoundly as it was the case from 1942 throughout World War II in relation to the postwar organization of the world.

We should not cut off the possibility of diplomatic maneuver for ourselves in relations with individual Western countries, including the United States, by adhering to a one-sided view on imperialism. In certain cases it is necessary to draw a more distinct line between the activity of the Comintern and that of the foreign ministry, the difference stressed by Lenin. In order to make our policy more flexible and effective in relation to the United States, the official foreign political statements and actions of the Soviet government should be predominantly and most clearly based on the interests of relations with other countries. Inasmuch as it does not affect relations with other countries, the sociological and ideological aspects of the struggle between the two systems, and the criticism toward the policy of the United States and other Western imperialist states from the ideological point of view, should be conducted predominantly through the party, public organizations and the press.

As regards the American aggression against Vietnam and its effect on bilateral relations, we should go on rendering comprehensive assistance to the DRV [Democratic Republic of Vietnam] in consolidating its defense capacity to repulse the aggression, without getting directly involved in the war. We must get the Americans to fully understand that further escalation in the military actions against the DRV will compel the Soviet Union to render its assistance to this country in an ever-growing scale, and that the only way out of the present situation is reaching a political solution on the basis of respecting legitimate rights of the Vietnamese people. Nevertheless, putting an end to the Vietnam conflict would undoubtedly have a positive effect on Soviet-American relations and open up new possibilities for solving certain international problems.

We should not avoid agreement with the United States on questions of our interest if such agreements do not contradict our position of principle in regard to Vietnam. Needless to say, we should avoid a situation where we have to fight on two fronts, that is against China and the United States. Maintaining Soviet-American relations on a certain level is one of the factors that will help us achieve this objective.

The struggle for the unity of socialist countries is the main means of countering American efforts to split the socialist community.

As to our objective of weakening U.S. positions in Western Europe, we should consistently hold to the principle that European problems can only have "European solutions." We must tirelessly promote the idea that Europe itself can and must ensure its security and consolidate confidence in the relations between Eastern and Western Europe.

Cuba: Our main and long-term task remains rendering economic and political assistance to Cuba, as well as strengthening its defense capability. We should avoid any actions or statements putting in question the assurances of the U.S. leaders that they will not attack Cuba.

The issues of the national liberation movement. The line of the Twenty-Third Congress of the CPSU for all-round support of this movement meets our foreign policy interests in every way. Considering the shortage of our reserves, we should focus on economic cooperation with the most progressive countries that have embarked on the road of noncapitalist development, such as Egypt, Syria, Algeria, Mali, Guinea, Burma, Congo, Tanzania, and the countries of strategic importance to us (Afghanistan, Turkey, Pakistan, and Iran). We must pursue our activities in other countries of Asia and Africa in such a manner so as to build our economic and trade cooperation with them increasingly on the principle of mutual benefit and commerce.

Considering the experience of Vietnam and the Middle East, we should take timely measures to relax tension in the ganglions in the three continents where sharp conflicts are possible which, in turn, can combine to lead to an "acute situation." In this connection we should, while supporting the Arab countries in their struggle against Israel's expansionist policy, flexibly dampen the extremist trends in the policy of certain Arab states, e.g., Syria, orienting them toward the domestic consolidation.

Disarmament: We should keep our active stand on disarmament. Along with a further struggle for universal and comprehensive disarmament which is expected to take a long period of time, we must pay special attention to some limited measures, first of all, to reaching an agreement on the nonproliferation of nuclear weapons. It is necessary to complete our dialogue with the United States and seek the conclusion of such an agreement in order to prevent any access to the FRG [Federal Republic of Germany] and other nonnuclear states to nuclear arms.

Simultaneously, it is essential to continue to exert pressure on the United States in favor of the measures that the American administration has declared unacceptable, but which are met with understanding by world public opinion and help expose the imperialist course of the United States. These measures include liquidation of foreign military bases, withdrawal of armed troops from foreign territories and cutting of military budgets.

On possibilities to influence the alignment of political forces in the United States: All our ways and means should be brought into play to broaden the gap between the moderate politicians and the maniacs in the United States, to isolate the "war party" in order to prevent the aggressive forces of imperialism from unleashing a nuclear world war in the future. In this regard a replacement of President Johnson by a Republican (through elections) could hardly meet our interests, as all known Republican candidates are even more rightist than Johnson. Accordingly, when conducting our foreign policy actions involving the United States we should avoid the situations when these actions may consolidate the positions of his opponents among the ultras. Simultaneously, it is useful to keep in touch with the "loyal opposition" to Johnson (Senators Fulbright, R[obert] Kennedy, [Dick] Clark, etc.). It is also expedient to broaden, through our public organizations, our contracts with liberal and democratic forces, as well as cultural exchanges and exchanges in the sphere of art and education.

Source: Gromyko, Andrei. Confidential Memorandum, January 13, 1967. Reprinted in *In Confidence: Moscow's Ambassador to America's Six Cold War Presidents* by Anatoly Dobrynin. New York: Crown, 1995.

10.3
"War Between Russia and China: A Communist Nightmare" – 1969
An Excerpt from a State Department Memo on Rising Sino-Soviet Tensions

During the 1960s political and military tensions between China and the Soviet Union became a serious issue. At one point, the Kremlin decided to use the Australian Communist Party to deliver a particularly threatening message to the regime in Beijing. This rhetoric was apparently so belligerent that Communist organizations around the world were soon speculating about the odds of a major military clash between the two Communist giants. In the following report, dated September 23, 1969, U.S. State Department analysts study the rising Sino-Soviet tensions in Asia.

Subject: War between Russia and China: A Communist Nightmare

The recent letter from the Australian Communist Party to several fraternal parties asking them to help avert the possible "colossal disaster" of actual warfare between the Soviet Union and Communist China reflects the alarm with which some members of the world communist movement view the present course of the Sino-Soviet dispute. Whether the Australians were prompted to sound the tocsin only after getting a letter from the CPSU [Communist Part of the Soviet Union] which suggested rising Soviet impatience with the Chinese, or simply found their worst fears confirmed upon receiving such a communication is a moot question. In either case, Australian concern over Soviet arrogance, manifested by the USSR's continued insensitivity to the fortunes of other communist parties, stems from the Czech crisis of last year and was probably reinforced by the reportedly abrasive encounters of key Australian communists with senior CPSU leaders during the preparations for the world communist meeting in Moscow.

Misperceptions or Insurmountable Cleavage Although the Australian CP, along with the Italian and Spanish parties, are the only pro-Soviet parties that have thus far been both critical and horrified by the behavior of the Soviets and the Chinese, any further worsening of the crisis, particularly the onset of actual hostilities, would undoubtedly find a sizable number of other parties joining them in their condemnation. For such parties the very notion of a military attack by one communist giant on the other gnaws at the roots of their political faith. Actual war would end the long-cherished Marxist tenet that conflicts are inseparably linked to capitalism since outside parties are likely to continue to view both China and the USSR as communist states (unlike the position taken by each combatant toward the other, viz, that the rival has abandoned communism).

Neither the Soviets nor the Chinese seem to be aware that their increasingly bitter wrangling over territorial questions has evoked dismay in the rest of the communist movement. Both are consumed by their own particular interests, and they have failed to draw the proper conclusions from the fact that neither Soviet invocations of the threat of nuclear war nor Chinese charges of blatant aggression have served to rally other increasingly mortified communist parties to either side. Wittingly or not, the actions of both communist nations have only conjured up the specter of actual conflict between them in the manner characteristic of traditional great powers.

Finding itself increasingly under attack for fanning narrow national instincts against Communist China under the guise of defending "proletarian internationalism" the Soviet Union has sought vainly to buttress its position with the ideological arguments of a by-gone period, only to have those same arguments thrown back at it by Peking in equally self-serving fashion. However, neither contestant can any longer speak for its own camp, let alone for the entire communist movement. The Australian CP statement to the other parties put this very clearly, when it rejected the claims of either side to be the sole interpreter and custodian of Marxism, and thereby to assume a position of hegemony over others. In a sense, the current war scare has accelerated the transformation of the Sino-Soviet dispute from a battle between two ideological camps into a considerably more diffuse conflict where the two principal contestants may become the chief ideological target for a growing number of communist parties.

Opposition: A Deterrent or Irrelevant? The fact that a number of communist parties take seriously—and are mightily disturbed by—the possibility of war between the Soviet Union and China is not in itself evidence that war is about to break out. Nor does it imply that such outside criticism would effectively deter either side from mounting an attack, if other motivations were strongly present. At the same time, the role and position of other communist parties in the event of such a cataclysmic confrontation cannot be entirely discounted.

Even if speculation is confined to Moscow (the rival often portrayed as more likely to initiate an attack), it seems evident that the Kremlin is still the prisoner of ideological perceptions and preconceptions, as is demonstrated by the persistence over several years of the Soviet leaders in pushing to fruition, in June 1969, an international communist party conference. This alone would incline the leaders to react with major discomfiture to mounting dissent from other communist parties over Soviet handling of the China problem. What cannot be predicted, however, is how Moscow would take on its critics—whether it would move to squash them (the prospects for which, based on recent precedents, would seem poor outside of the Warsaw Pact countries); whether it would delay and temporize in an effort partially to accommodate them; or whether it would ostensibly ignore them, on the assumption that success, if it came, in a military adventure against China would cause waverers to rally to a Soviet bandwagon.

Source: U.S. State Department, Bureau of Intelligence and Research. Intelligence Note. "War Between Russia and China: A Communist Nightmare," September 23, 1969. National Archives. Available online at the National Security Archive, George Washington University, http://www.gwu.edu/~nsarchiv/NSAEBB/NSAEBB49/sino.sov.23.pdf.

10.4
Kissinger's Secret Trip to China – 1971
Excerpts from a Memorandum from Henry Kissinger to President Richard Nixon

U.S. President Richard Nixon and Secretary of State Henry Kissinger saw the strained relations between the Soviet Union and Communist China as a great diplomatic opportunity. They believed that pursuing better relations with each nation would force both the Soviets and the Chinese to take American interests into greater account when devising domestic and foreign policy.

Accordingly, Kissinger began holding secret diplomatic negotiations with the Chinese, who were receptive to his overtures. In July 1971 Kissinger made a secret trip to the capital city of Beijing (spelled Peking in the memo below; in addition, Mao Zedong is here spelled Mao-Tse-tung). There he addressed a wide range of international issues, including Taiwan, the Vietnam War, and relations with the Soviet Union. The primary representative of China in these secret meetings was Chou En-lai, the Chinese foreign minister. Kissinger's trip made him the first American official to visit the People's Republic of China since its founding in 1949. The trip was a diplomatic success, and it paved the way for Nixon's historic visit to China in February 1972.

July 14, 1971
MEMORANDUM FOR: THE PRESIDENT
FROM: HENRY A. KISSINGER
SUBJECT: My talks with Chou En-lai

Introduction

My two-day visit to Peking resulted in the most searching, sweeping and significant discussions I have ever had in government. I spent seventeen hours in meetings and informal conversation with Chou En-lai, flanked by Marshall Yeh Chien-ying, member of the Politburo and of the Military Commission; Huang Hua, the new Chinese Ambassador in Ottawa; and Chang Wen-chin, head of the West European and American Department in the Foreign Ministry. Another four hours was spent with Huang and Chang, mostly on drafting a communiqué. These meetings brought about a summit meeting between you and Mao Tse-Tung, covered all major issues between our two countries at considerable length and with great candor, and may well have marked a major new departure in international relations.

It is extremely difficult to capture in a memorandum the essence of this experience. Simply giving you a straightforward account of the highlights of our talks, potentially momentous as they were, would do violence to an event so shaped by the atmosphere and the ebb and flow of our encounter, or to the Chinese behavior so dependent on nuances and style. Thus, this memorandum will sketch the overall sequence of events and philosophic framework, as well as the substance of our exchanges. For the intangibles are crucial and we must understand them if we are to take advantage of the opportunities we now have, deal effectively with these tough, idealistic, fanatical, single-minded and remarkable people, and thus transform the very framework of global relationships.

What Happened

The Chinese treated the entire visit with elaborate correctness and courtesy. They were extremely tough on substance and ideological in their approach but their dealings were meticulous; they concentrated on essentials; they eschewed invective and haggling over details. The atmosphere on the human plane was relaxed and cordial, matter-of-factly; (one did not have the sense that they were carrying out instructions to be cordial as is often the case with Dobrynin.) ...

I gave the substance of the opening statement you had approved, considerably truncated to get to the point quickly, laying out a possible agenda which we in fact took up point-by-point in our meetings—the summit, Taiwan, Indochina, relations with major countries such as Japan and the Soviet Union, South Asia, future American-Chinese communications, arms control, and any other topics of interest to the Chinese. He immediately moved to their fundamental concern, Taiwan, and I rejoined with our position on Indochina.

We broke at 8:00 p.m. for dinner, continuing a low-keyed substantive discussion. Indochina came up again as we finished off the last few of the fifteen or so dishes.

Our resumed session from 9:30 to 11:20 p.m. was dominated by the subject of great power relations in general. Chou spoke of the Chinese fear of a remilitarized Japan, and violently and contemptuously attacked Soviet imperialism which he claimed had learned its lessons from the U.S. I explained the philosophical framework of U.S. foreign policy in the post-war period culminating in the Nixon Doctrine. Chou listened raptly, asking very probing but non-contentious questions, some based on the President's remarks in Kansas City of July 6. (It was characteristic of Chou that when I indicated that I had seen only press reports, I found Chou's own annotated copy of the text waiting for me at breakfast with a request to return it since it was the only copy he had.)

On Saturday morning, July 10, we were taken to the Forbidden City, where the entire, enormous Imperial Palace grounds had been closed off from the public for a half day so that we could take a secret tour. For two and a half hours we absorbed the magnificently simple and proportionate sweeps of the red and gold buildings, the courtyards each with its own character, and the living quarters of past emperors. The Director of all of China's archeological museums guided us past ancient relics of China that had been unearthed in recent years.

"Those forty-eight hours, and my extensive discussions with Chou in particular, had all the flavor, texture, variety and delicacy of a Chinese banquet."

We then proceeded to the Great Hall of the People where we were greeted by Chou for another four and a half hours of discussions sandwiched around a one and a half hour roast duck lunch.

Before lunch Chou made a one and a half hour presentation, as always without notes, responding to each of the seven points on my original agenda. This was an extremely tough presentation, though put forward without rhetorical flourish—the preoccupation with Taiwan; the support for the North Vietnamese; the spectre of big power collusion, specifically of being carved up by the US, USSR, and Japan; the contempt of the Indians, hatred for the Russians and apprehension over the Japanese; the disclaimer that China is, or would want to be, a superpower like the Russians and we who have "stretched out our hands too far"; and throughout, the constant view that the world must move toward peace, that there is too "much turmoil under the heavens." ...

I responded very toughly, pointing out that *they* had raised the issue of a Presidential visit and that we could not accept any conditions. I would not raise the issue again; they had to decide whether to issue an invitation. I then launched into a deliberately brusque point-by-point rebuttal of Chou's presentation. Chou stopped me after the first point, saying the duck would get cold if we did not eat first.

At lunch the mood changed and Chou's geniality returned. I gathered the impression that his speech had been largely for the record.

At the end of lunch Chou launched into a moving account of the Cultural Revolution which he continued to relate even after I noted that this was China's internal affair. One could tell that the Revolution was an anguishing period for him. He described China as torn between its fear of bureaucracy and the excesses of revolution with each side claiming to speak for Mao until the acknowledged excesses threatened to destroy the fruits of some fifty years of struggle.

After lunch I continued my comments on his remarks, having covered Taiwan and Japan before the break. On Indochina, as on Taiwan, I noted the need for time for a political evolution and I re-emphasized the link between the two questions. After moving through the other issues such as great power relations, South Asia, communication between our governments and arms control, we had laid a sound substantive framework. Chou, suddenly, matter-of-factly returned to your visit to China. He suggested the summer of 1972, indicating that they would prefer it if you met the Soviet leaders first. He said that they were not afraid of anyone but they were not looking for unnecessary trouble either. I said that a US-Soviet summit had been agreed in principle but I could make no promises and would accept no condition. I also said that a summer summit might look like a political campaign gesture. Chou then moved up your visit to the spring....

The next morning we held a final two hour meeting which wrapped up the summit, the communiqué, and final substantive comments. In the first forty minutes we reached agreement with Huang and Chang on the Communique at Tab A. This capped a drafting process that had its quota of tension but was marked by the other side's clear willingness to meet us half way. Our negotiating over the language was free of the pettiness and elbowing that we have experienced with the Russians. And once the basic bargain was struck, the rest of our business flowed comparatively easily.

Chou, who had been waiting nearby—so as to avoid a confrontation over language—suddenly appeared after the announcement was agreed, and we proceeded to settle all the major principles of your visit along the lines you wished.

After bidding farewell to Chou, we and the other Chinese officials had a final lunch. All tension was gone and Marshal Yeh's normally impassive face was finally creased by smiles. On the way to the airport he recounted some of his experiences—how over forty years ago as a division commander of Chiang, he heard of

Mao and his 2000 followers in the mountains and joined them. And as we drove up toward the waiting Pakistani plane he remarked that none of them on the Long March had ever dreamed to see victory in their lifetimes. They had thought their struggle was for future generations.

Yet, he said, "here we are and here you are."…

[*Kissinger's memorandum then engages in lengthy summaries of his discussions with the Chinese on specific issues such as Taiwan, the Vietnam War, arms control, and the terms of Nixon's proposed summit with Mao the following spring.*]

Conclusion

I am frank to say that this visit was a very moving experience. The historic aspects of the occasion; the warmth and dignity of the Chinese; the splendor of the Forbidden City, Chinese history and culture; the heroic stature of Chou En-lai; and the intensity and sweep of our talks combined to make an indelible impression on me and my colleagues.

Those forty-eight hours, and my extensive discussions with Chou in particular, had all the flavor, texture, variety and delicacy of a Chinese banquet. Prepared from the long sweep of tradition and culture, meticulously cooked by hands of experience, and served in splendidly simple surroundings, our feast consisted of many courses, some sweet and some sour, all interrelated and forming a coherent whole. It was a total experience, and one went away, as after all good Chinese meals, very satisfied but not at all satiated.

We have laid the groundwork for you and Mao to turn a page in history. But we should have no illusions about the future. Profound differences and years of isolation yawn between us and the Chinese. They will be tough before and during the summit on the question of Taiwan and other major issues. And they will prove implacable foes if our relations turn sour. My assessment of these people is that they are deeply ideological, close to fanatic in the intensity of their beliefs. At the same time they display an inward security that allows them, within the framework of their principles, to be meticulous and reliable in dealing with others.

Furthermore, the process we have no started will send enormous shock waves around the world. It may panic the Soviet Union into sharp hostility. It could shake Japan loose from its heavily American moorings. It will cause a violent upheaval in Taiwan. It will have major impact on our other Asian allies, such as Korea and Thailand. It will increase the already substantial hostility in India. Some quarters may seek to sabotage the summit over the coming months.

However, we were well aware of these risks when we embarked on this course. We were aware too that the alternative was unacceptable—continued isolation from one-quarter of the world's most talented people and a country rich in past achievements and future potential.

And even the risks can be managed and turned to our advantage if we maintain steady nerves and pursue our policies responsibly. With the Soviet Union we will have to make clear the continued priorities we attach to our concrete negotiations with them. Just as we will not collude with them against China, so we have no intention of colluding with China against them. If carefully managed, our new China policy could have a longer term beneficial impact on Moscow....

Source: Kissinger, Henry. "My talks with Chou En-lai." July 14, 1971. Nixon Presidential Materials Project, Box 1033. National Archives and Records Administration. Available online at the National Security Archive, George Washington University, http://www.gwu.edu/~nsarchiv/NSAEBB/NSAEBB66/ch-40.pdf.

10.5
The Basic Treaty – 1972
The Text of the Treaty Establishing Diplomatic Relations Between East Germany and West Germany

One of the most visible manifestations of the age of détente was the Basic Treaty, which established diplomatic relations between East Germany (German Democratic Republic) and West Germany (Federal Republic of Germany). This diplomatic triumph was largely due to the dogged efforts of West German Chancellor Willy Brandt and his "Ostpolitik" policies, which centered on finding common ground with Communist Eastern European nations in general and East Germany in particular. Following is the complete text of the treaty, signed in Berlin on December 21, 1972. Both the East and West German governments formally recognized the legitimacy of the other and pledged to cooperate with one another on trade and other issues.

The High Contracting Parties,
In consideration of their responsibility for the preservation of peace,
Anxious to contribute to détente and security in Europe,

Conscious that the inviolability of frontiers and respect for the territorial integrity and sovereignty of all States in Europe within their present frontiers are a fundamental condition for peace,

Recognizing that therefore the two German States are to refrain from the threat or use of force in their relations,

Proceeding from the historical facts and without prejudice to the differing views of the Federal Republic of Germany and the German Democratic Republic on questions of principle, including the national question,

336

Guided by the desire to create the conditions for co-operation between the Federal Republic of Germany and the German Democratic Republic for the benefit of the people in the two German States,

Have agreed as follows:

Article 1

The Federal Republic of Germany and the German Democratic Republic shall develop normal good-neighbourly relations with each other on the basis of equal rights.

Article 2

The Federal Republic of Germany and the German Democratic Republic will be guided by the purposes and principles embodied in the United Nations Charter, in particular the sovereign equality of all States, respect for independence, autonomy and territorial integrity, the right of self-determination, the preservation of human rights, and non-discrimination.

Article 3

In accordance with the United Nations Charter, the Federal Republic of Germany and the German Democratic Republic shall settle their disputes exclusively by peaceful means and refrain from the threat or use of force.

They reaffirm the inviolability now and in the future of the border existing between them and undertake fully to respect their territorial integrity.

Article 4

The Federal Republic of Germany and the German Democratic Republic proceed on the assumption that neither of the two States can represent the other internationally or act in its name.

Article 5

The Federal Republic of Germany and the German Democratic Republic will promote peaceful relations between the European States and contribute to security and co-operation in Europe.

They shall support the efforts to reduce armed forces and armaments in Europe without disadvantages being allowed to rise therefrom for the security of those concerned.

With the aim of general and complete disarmament under effective international control, the Federal Republic of Germany and the German Democratic Republic will support efforts serving international security to achieve armaments limitation and disarmament, especially with regards to nuclear weapons and other weapons of mass destruction.

Article 6

The Federal Republic of Germany and the German Democratic Republic proceed on the principle that the jurisdiction of each of the two States is confined to its own territory. They shall each respect the other's independence and autonomy in its internal and external affairs.

Article 7

The Federal Republic of Germany and the German Democratic Republic state their readiness to regulate practical and humanitarian questions in the process of the normalization of their relations. They will conclude agreements with a view to developing and promoting co-operation in the fields of economics, science and technology, traffic, judicial relations, posts and telecommunications, health, culture, sport, environmental protection, and in other fields, on the basis of the present Treaty and for their mutual benefit. The details have been agreed in the Supplementary Protocol.

Article 8

The Federal Republic of Germany and the German Democratic Republic will exchange permanent missions. They will be established at the respective seat of government.

Practical questions relating to the establishment of the missions will be dealt with separately.

Article 9

The Federal Republic of Germany and the German Democratic Republic are agreed that the present Treaty does not affect the bilateral and multilateral international treaties and agreements previously concluded by them or concerning them.

Article 10

The present Treaty is subject to ratification and shall enter into force on the day after the exchange of appropriate notes.

In witness whereof, the plenipotentiaries of the High Contracting Parties have signed this Treaty.

Done at Berlin, on 21 December 1972, in two originals in the German language.

For the Federal Republic of Germany
Egon Bahr

For the German Democratic Republic
Michael Kobl

Source: U.S. Department of State. "Treaty on the Basis of Relations between the Federal Republic of Germany and the German Democratic Republic and Supplementary Documents" ("The Basic Treaty"), December 21, 1972. *Documents on Germany, 1944-1985*. Washington, DC: Department of State, 1985. Available online at the European Navigator, Centre virtuel de la connaissance sur l'Europe, http://www.ena.lu.

10.6
The Helsinki Accords – 1975
President Gerald Ford's Address in Helsinki Before the Conference on Security and Cooperation in Europe

The Helsinki Accords are often characterized as the high point of the age of détente between the American-led West and the Soviet empire. The Helsinki agreement settled longstanding disagreements between East and West on political borders; promised greater cooperation on a wide range of economic, technological, and environmental issues between its 35 signatories; and raised the profile of human rights issues in the East. But while some American analysts continue to see the Helsinki accords as one of détente's greatest moments, citing its spirit of reconciliation and its emphasis on human rights, others are far more critical. When the Helsinki Accords were announced, some conservative analysts expressed great anger and disappointment that Western negotiators accepted the post-World War II territorial changes imposed on Eastern Europe by the Soviets. And in the years after the agreement was signed, the Soviet empire made little effort to adhere to the human rights principles outlined at Helsinki.

Following are remarks from a speech that U.S. President Gerald R. Ford delivered on August 1, 1975, the eve of the signing ceremony for the Accords.

… Our visit here, though short, has brought us a deeper appreciation of the pride, industry and friendliness which Americans always associate with the Finnish nation.

The nations assembled here have kept the general peace in Europe for 30 years. Yet there have been too many narrow escapes from major conflict. There remains, to this day, the urgent issue of how to construct a just and lasting peace for all peoples.

I have not come across the Atlantic to say what all of us already know—that nations now have the capacity to destroy civilization and, therefore, all our foreign policies must have as their one supreme objective the prevention of a thermonuclear war. Nor have I come to dwell upon the hard realities of continuing ideological differences, political rivalries, and military competition that persist among us.

I have come to Helsinki as a spokesman for a nation whose vision has always been forward, whose people have always demanded that the future be brighter than the past, and whose united will and purpose at this hour is to work diligently to promote peace and progress not only for ourselves but for all mankind.

I am simply here to say to my colleagues: We owe it to our children, to the children of all continents, not to miss any opportunity, not to malinger for one minute, not to spare ourselves or allow others to shirk in the monumental task of building a better and a safer world.

The American people, like the people of Europe, know well that mere assertions of good will, passing changes in the political mood of governments, laudable declarations of principles are not enough. But if we proceed with care, with commitment to real progress, there is now an opportunity to turn our peoples' hopes into realities.

In recent years, nations represented here have sought to ease potential conflicts. But much more remains to be done before we prematurely congratulate ourselves. Military competition must be controlled. Political competition must be restrained. Crises must not be manipulated or exploited for unilateral advantages that could lead us again to the brink of war. The process of negotiation must be sustained, not at a snail's pace, but with demonstrated enthusiasm and visible progress.

Nowhere are the challenges and the opportunities greater and more evident than in Europe. That is why this Conference brings us all together. Conflict in Europe shakes the world. Twice in this century we have paid dearly for this lesson; at other times, we have come perilously close to calamity. We dare not forget the tragedy and the terror of those times.

Peace is not a piece of paper.

But lasting peace is at least possible today because we have learned from the experiences of the last 30 years that peace is a process requiring mutual restraint and practical arrangements.

This Conference is a part of that process—a challenge, not a conclusion. We face unresolved problems of military security in Europe; we face them with very real differences in values and in aims. But if we deal with them with careful preparation, if we focus on concrete issues, if we maintain forward movement, we have the right to expect real progress.

The era of confrontation that has divided Europe since the end of the Second World War may now be ending. There is a new perception and a shared perception of a change for the better, away from confrontation and toward new possibilities for secure and mutually beneficial cooperation. That is what we all have been saying here. I welcome and I share these hopes for the future.

The postwar policy of the United States has been consistently directed toward the rebuilding of Europe and the rebirth of Europe's historic identity. The nations of the West have worked together for peace and progress throughout Europe. From the very start, we have taken the initiative by stating clear goals and areas for negotiation.

We have sought a structure of European relations, tempering rivalry with restraint, power with moderation, building upon the traditional bonds that link us with old friends and reaching out to forge new ties with former and potential adversaries.

In recent years, there have been some substantial achievements. We see the Four-Power Agreement on Berlin of 1971 as the end of a perennial crisis that on at least three occasions brought the world to the brink of doom. The agreements between the Federal Republic of Germany and the states of Eastern Europe and the related intra-German accords enable Central Europe and the world to breathe easier. The start of East-West talks on mutual and balanced force reductions demonstrate a determination to deal with military security problems of the continent.

The 1972 treaty between the United States and the Soviet Union to limit antiballistic missiles and the interim agreement limiting strategic offensive arms were the first solid breakthroughs in what must be a continuing, long-term process of limiting strategic, nuclear arsenals.

I profoundly hope that this Conference will spur further practical and concrete results. It affords a welcome opportunity to widen the circle of those countries involved in easing tensions between East and West.

Participation in the work of detente and participation in the benefits of detente must be everybody's business—in Europe and elsewhere. But detente can succeed only if everybody understands what detente actually is.

First, detente is an evolutionary process, not a static condition. Many formidable challenges yet remain. Second, the success of detente, of the process of detente, depends on new behavior patterns that give life to all our solemn declarations. The goals we are stating today are the yardstick by which our performance will be measured.

The people of all Europe and, I assure you, the people of North America are thoroughly tired of having their hopes raised and then shattered by empty words and unfulfilled pledges. We had better say what we mean and mean what we say, or we will have the anger of our citizens to answer.

While we must not expect miracles, we can and we do expect steady progress that comes in steps—steps that are related to each other that link our actions with words in various areas of our relations. Finally, there must be an acceptance of mutual obligation. Detente, as I have often said, must be a two-way street. Tensions cannot be eased by one side alone. Both sides must want detente and work to achieve it. Both sides must benefit from it.

Mr. Chairman, my colleagues, this extraordinary gathering in Helsinki proves that all our peoples share a concern for Europe's future and for a better and more peaceful world. But what else does it prove? How shall we assess the results?

Our delegations have worked long and hard to produce documents which restate noble and praiseworthy political principles. They spell out guidelines for national behavior and international cooperation.

But every signatory should know that if these are to be more than the latest chapter in a long and sorry volume of unfulfilled declarations, every party must be dedicated to making them come true.

These documents which we will sign represent another step—how long or short a step only time will tell—in the process of detente and reconciliation in Europe. Our peoples will be watching and measuring our progress. They will ask how these noble sentiments are being translated into actions that bring about a more secure and just order in the daily lives of each of our nations and its citizens.

The documents produced here represent compromises, like all international negotiations, but these principles we have agreed upon are more than the lowest common denominator of governmental positions. They affirm the most fundamental human rights: liberty of thought, conscience, and faith; the exercise of civil and political rights; the rights of minorities. They call for a freer flow of information, ideas, and people; greater scope for the press, cultural and educational exchange, family reunification, the right to travel and to marriage between nationals of different states; and for the protection of the priceless heritage of our diverse cultures. They offer wide areas for greater cooperation: trade, industrial production, science and technology, the environment, transportation, health, space, and the oceans. They reaffirm the basic principles of relations between states: nonintervention, sovereign equality, self-determination, territorial integrity, inviolability of frontiers, and the possibility of change by peaceful means.

The United States gladly subscribes to this document because we subscribe to every one of these principles. Almost 200 years ago, the United States of America was born as a free and independent nation. The descendants of Europeans who proclaimed their independence in America expressed in that declaration a decent respect for the opinions of mankind and asserted not only that all men are created equal but they are endowed with inalienable rights to life, liberty, and the pursuit of happiness.

The founders of my country did not merely say that all Americans should have these rights but all men everywhere should have these rights. And these principles have guided the United States of America throughout its two centuries of nationhood. They have given hopes to millions in Europe and on every continent....

To our fellow participants in this Conference: My presence here symbolizes my country's vital interest in Europe's future. Our future is bound with yours. Our economic well-being, as well as our security, is linked increasingly with yours. The distance of geography is bridged by our common heritage and our common destiny. The United States, therefore, intends to participate fully in the affairs of Europe and in turning the results of this Conference into a living reality.

To America's allies: We in the West must vigorously pursue the course upon which we have embarked together, reinforced by one another's strength and mutual confidence. Stability in Europe requires equilibrium in Europe. Therefore, I assure you that my country will continue to be a concerned and reliable partner. Our partnership is far more than a matter of formal agreements. It is a reflection of beliefs, traditions, and ties that are of deep significance to the American people. We are proud that these values are expressed in this document.

To the countries of the East: The United States considers that the principles on which this Conference has agreed are a part of the great heritage of European civilization, which we all hold in trust for all mankind. To my country, they are not cliches or empty phrases. We take this work and these words very seriously. We will spare no effort to ease tensions and to solve problems between us. But it is important that you recognize the deep devotion of the American people and their Government to human rights and fundamental freedoms and thus to the pledges that this Conference has made regarding the freer movement of people, ideas, information....

Our people want a better future. Their expectations have been raised by the very real steps that have already been taken—in arms control, political negotiations, and expansion of contacts and economic relations. Our presence here offers them further hope. We must not let them down.

If the Soviet Union and the United states can reach agreement so that our astronauts can fit together the most intricate scientific equipment, work together, and shake hands 137 miles out in space, we as statesmen have an obligation to do as well on Earth.

History will judge this Conference not by what we say here today, but by what we do tomorrow—not by the promises we make, but by the promises we keep.

Source: Ford, Gerald R. "Address in Helsinki Before the Conference on Security and Cooperation in Europe." *Public Papers of the Presidents of the United States: Gerald Ford, 1975.* Washington, DC: Office of the Federal Register, 1977.

10.7
The Charter 77 Manifesto – 1977
The Text of an Announcement by Czech Dissidents

In January 1977, 230 prominent Czech intellectuals signed and distributed a manifesto announcing the formation of Charter 77, a group dedicated to expanding human rights in the Eastern bloc nations. Notable signatories included playwright Vaclav Havel, a founder of Charter 77 who became the nation's first president after the collapse of the Soviet empire. Havel later admitted that many people who were asked to sign the document were "anguished" by the fear that doing so could result in harm to themselves or their family. "[But] when they finally signed it, they found themselves in a state of euphoria," he recalled. "It was a community of free people in the middle of an unfree society, and they had a feeling of harmony with themselves."

The manifesto was published in various Western newspapers on January 6, 1977. Czech authorities arrested several of the signatories the next day, denounced them and began cracking down on dissident activities. Many were imprisoned, and Havel was placed under house arrest. Following is the full text of the manifesto.

In the Czechoslovak Register of Laws No. 120 of October 13, 1976, texts were published of the International Covenant on Civil and Political Rights, and of the International Covenant on Economic, Social and Cultural Rights, which were signed on behalf of our republic in 1968, reiterated at Helsinki in 1975 and came into force in our country on March 23, 1976. From that date our citizens have enjoyed the rights, and our state the duties, ensuing from them.

The human rights and freedoms underwritten by these covenants constitute features of civilized life for which many progressive movements have striven throughout history and whose codification could greatly assist humane developments in our society. We accordingly welcome the Czechoslovak Socialist Republic's accession to those agreements.

Their publication, however, serves as a powerful reminder of the extent to which basic human rights in our country exist, regrettably, on paper alone.

The right to freedom of expression, for example, guaranteed by Article 19 of the first-mentioned covenant, is in our case purely illusory. Tens of thousands of our citizens are prevented from working in their own fields for the sole reason that they hold views differing from official ones, and are discriminated against and harassed in all kinds of ways by the authorities and public organizations. Deprived as they are of any means to defend themselves, they become victims of a virtual apartheid.

Hundreds of thousands of other citizens are denied that "freedom from fear" mentioned in the preamble to the first covenant, being condemned to the constant risk of unemployment or other penalties if they voice their own opinions.

In violation of Article 13 of the second-mentioned covenant, guaranteeing everyone the right to education, countless young people are prevented from studying because of their own views or even their parents'. Innumerable citizens live in fear of their own or their children's right to education being withdrawn if they should ever speak up in accordance with their convictions.

Any exercise of the right to "seek, receive and impart information and ideas of all kinds, regardless of frontiers, either orally, in writing or in print" or "in the form of art" specified in Article 19, Clause 2 of the first covenant is followed by extra-judicial and even judicial sanctions, often in the form of criminal charges, as in the recent trial of young musicians.

Freedom of public expression is inhibited by the centralized control of all the communication media and of publishing and cultural institutions. No philosophical, political or scientific view or artistic activity that departs ever so slightly from the narrow bounds of official ideology or aesthetics is allowed to be published; no open criticism can be made of abnormal social phenomena; no public defense is possible against false and insulting charges made in official propaganda — the legal protection against "attacks on honor and reputation" clearly guaranteed by Article 17 of the first covenant is in practice non-existent: false accusations cannot be rebutted, and any attempt to secure compensation or correction through the courts is futile; no open debate is allowed in the domain of thought and art.

Many scholars, writers, artists and others are penalized for having legally published or expressed, years ago, opinions which are condemned by those who hold political power today.

Freedom of religious confession, emphatically guaranteed by Article 18 of the first covenant, is continually curtailed by arbitrary official action; by interference with the activity of churchmen, who are constantly threatened by the refusal of the state to permit them the exercise of their functions, or by the withdrawal of such permission; by financial or other transactions against those who express their religious faith in word or action; by constraints on religious training and so forth.

One instrument for the curtailment or in many cases complete elimination of many civic rights is the system by which all national institutions and organizations are in effect subject to political directives from the machinery of the ruling party and to decisions made by powerful individuals.

The constitution of the republic, its laws and legal norms do not regulate the form or content, the issuing or application of such decisions; they are often only given out verbally, unknown to the public at large and beyond its powers to check; their originators are responsible to no one but themselves and their own hierarchy; yet they have a decisive impact on the decision-making and executive organs of government, justice, trade unions, interest groups and all other organizations, of the other political parties, enterprises, factories, institutions, offices and so on, for whom these instructions have precedence even before the law.

Where organizations or individuals, in the interpretation of their rights and duties, come into conflict with such directives, they cannot have recourse to any non-party authority, since none such exists. This constitutes, of course, a serious limitation of the right ensuing from Articles 21 and 22 of the first-mentioned covenant, which provides for freedom of association and forbids any restriction on its exercise, from Article 25 on the right to take part in the conduct of public affairs, and from Article 26 stipulating equal protection by the law without discrimination.

This state of affairs likewise prevents workers and others from exercising the unrestricted right to establish trade unions and other organizations to protect their economic and social interests, and from freely enjoying the right to strike provided for in Clause 1 of Article 8 in the second-mentioned covenant.

Further civic rights, including the explicit prohibition of "arbitrary interference with privacy, family, home or correspondence" (Article 17 of the first covenant), are seriously vitiated by the various forms of interference in the private life of citizens exercised by the Ministry of the Interior, for example by bugging telephones and houses, opening mail, following personal movements, searching homes, setting up networks of neighborhood informers (often recruited by illicit threats or promises) and in other ways.

The ministry frequently interferes in employers' decisions, instigates acts of discrimination by authorities and organizations, brings weight to bear on the organs of justice and even orchestrates propaganda campaigns in the media. This activity is governed by no law and, being clandestine, affords the citizen no chance to defend himself.

In cases of prosecution on political grounds the investigative and judicial organs violate the rights of those charged and those defending them, as guaranteed by Article 14 of the first covenant and indeed by Czechoslovak law. The prison treatment of those sentenced in such cases is an affront to their human dignity and a menace to their health, being aimed at breaking their morale.

Clause 2, Article 12 of the first covenant, guaranteeing every citizen the right to leave the country, is consistently violated, or under the pretense of "defense of national security" is subjected to various unjustifiable conditions (Clause 3). The granting of entry visas to foreigners is also treated arbitrarily, and many are unable to visit Czechoslovakia merely because of professional or personal contacts with those of our citizens who are subject to discrimination.

Some of our people — either in private, at their places of work or by the only feasible public channel, the foreign media — have drawn attention to the systematic violation of human rights and democratic freedoms and demanded amends in specific cases. But their pleas have remained largely ignored or been made grounds for police investigation.

Responsibility for the maintenance of rights in our country naturally devolves in the first place on the political and state authorities. Yet not only on them: everyone bears his share of responsibility for the conditions that prevail and accordingly also for the observance of legally enshrined agreements, binding upon all individuals as well as upon governments.

It is this sense of co-responsibility, our belief in the importance of its conscious public acceptance and the general need to give it new and more effective expression that led us to the idea of creating Charter 77, whose inception we today publicly announce.

Charter 77 is a loose, informal and open association of people of various shades of opinion, faiths and professions united by the will to strive individually and collectively for the respecting of civic and human rights in our own country and throughout the world — rights accorded to all men by the two mentioned international covenants, by the Final Act of the Helsinki conference and by numerous other international documents opposing war, violence and social or spiritual oppression, and which are comprehensively laid down in the U.N. Universal Charter of Human Rights.

Charter 77 springs from a background of friendship and solidarity among people who share our concern for those ideals that have inspired, and continue to inspire, their lives and their work.

Charter 77 is not an organization; it has no rules, permanent bodies or formal membership. It embraces everyone who agrees with its ideas and participates in its work. It does not form the basis for any oppositional political activity. Like many similar citizen initiatives in various countries, West and East, it seeks to promote the general public interest.

It does not aim, then, to set out its own platform of political or social reform or change, but within its own field of impact to conduct a constructive dialogue with the political and state authorities, particularly by drawing attention to individual cases where human and civic frights are violated, to document such grievances and suggest remedies, to make proposals of a more general character calculated to reinforce such rights and machinery for protecting them, to act as an intermediary in situations of conflict which may lead to violations of rights, and so forth.

By its symbolic name Charter 77 denotes that it has come into being at the start of a year proclaimed as Political Prisoners' Year — a year in which a conference in Belgrade is due to review the implementation of the obligations assumed at Helsinki.

As signatories, we hereby authorize Professor Dr. Jan Patocka, Dr. Vaclav Havel and Professor Dr. Jiri Hajek to act as the spokesmen for the Charter. These spokesmen are endowed with full authority to represent it vis-a-vis state and other bodies, and the public at home and abroad, and their signatures attest to the authenticity of documents issued by the Charter. They will have us and others who join us as their colleagues taking part in any needful negotiations, shouldering particular tasks and sharing every responsibility.

We believe that Charter 77 will help to enable all citizens of Czechoslovakia to work and live as free human beings.

Prague, 1 January 1977

Source: "The Charter 77 Manifesto," January 1977. *Czechoslovakia: A Country Study*, 3rd ed., by Ihor Gawdiak, Federal Research Division, Library of Congress. Washington, DC: Government Printing Office, 1989. Document available online at the Library of Congress, http://memory.loc.gov.

10.8
Anatoly Dobrynin Comments on Worsening U.S.-Soviet Relations – 1978
Excerpts from a Letter from the Soviet Ambassador to the Kremlin

By the late 1970s relations between the United States and the Soviet Union seemed to be deteriorating with each passing month. The Kremlin placed the blame for this downturn squarely on the shoulders of President Jimmy Carter and his administration, which had made human rights issues a cornerstone of American foreign policy. Anatoly Dobrynin, longtime Soviet Ambassador to the United States, clarified the Soviet perspective on Carter's policies in the following letter sent to Moscow on July 11, 1978.

Almost eighteen months ago—20 January 1977—the new, 39th President of the USA, J. Carter, stepped across the threshhold of the White House. Since that time, a definite policy has been conducted by his administration, the basic elements of which are the subject of the review in the present political letter.

1. As has already been noted by the Embassy, Soviet-American relations during the Carter Administration have been characterized by instability, major swings, which to a great extent are due to its calculations of the state of affairs in both its internal and external dimensions. In the middle of April of this year, Carter, as is well known, conducted in his country residence, Camp David, a meeting of the members of his cabinet and closest advisors, at which was taken a decision to carry out a regular reevaluation of Soviet-American relations. The initiative for this affair came from Brzezinski and several Presidential advisors on domestic affairs, who convinced Carter that he would succeed in stopping the process of worsening of his position in the country if he would openly initiate a harsher course vis a vis the Soviet Union. Africa (events on the Horn of Africa, and then in the Shaba Province of Zaire) was chosen as the pretext around which the Administration would begin earnestly to create tension in Soviet-American relations. In fact, in connection to these African events it was decided to attempt a review of the entire concept of the policy of detente, subordinating it to the needs of the Administration, not stopping even before publicly putting under threat the chances of concluding a new agreement on the limitation of offensive strategic weapons (by artificially linking it with other issues).

In the country, however, by the way pretty unexpectedly for Carter, this "harsh" course, which had been firmly and clearly rejected by the Soviet Union, caused a reaction in which was evident a clear apprehension among broad strata of the American population regarding the long-term condition and fate of Soviet-

---

Political letter of Soviet Ambassador to the United States Anatoly F. Dobrynin, July 11, 1978. Reprinted with permission from the Cold War International History Project Virtual Archive (http://www.cwihp.org).

American relations. There was expressed the depth of the American mood in support of the policy of detente, which had developed in the course of the last few years and which in the minds of the unsophisticated residents of this country is associated with a simple thesis: detente mitigates the threat of confrontation with the Soviet Union, and thus, of nuclear war with it. Characteristically, there were such apprehensions even in the Congress, the representatives of which began to demand explanations of the Administration, where anyway the matter of relations with the Soviet Union is heading and wasn't the Administration trying to bring about some sort of big changes in these relations without the consent of the Congress.

And so, Carter became convinced that detente is not a "faucet" which he can turn on and off whenever he feels so disposed. The Administration was obliged to quickly make some adjustments in its position (particularly in light of the speech of L.I. Brezhnev, and also our answer in Pravda to Carter's speech in Annapolis, which he had found to be unexpectedly firm). The President, having let [Secretary of State Cyrus] Vance go out front, decided to restrain Brzezinski a bit. Vance usually stresses the positive accomplishments in Soviet-American relations without leaving out, however, the negative things which are associated with Carter himself (for example, the notorious policy of "defense of human rights" or "dissidents").

> *"As often happens in the USA, the [anti-Soviet] rhetoric is transformed, influences policy, and sometimes itself becomes policy."*

2. Consequently, insofar as it is possible to judge on the basis of information which the Embassy has at its disposal, the Carter Administration has come to its own variety of a selective, half-hearted conception of detente (of which Brzezinski himself first accused us). Detente in its current concrete application by the White House is, as if, being partitioned. It is seen as important and necessary—in support of the national interests of the United States itself and the corresponding formation of public opinion—regarding problems associated with nuclear weapons, issues of war and peace (limitation of strategic weapons, a total ban on nuclear tests, certain other disarmament-related issues). As far as the majority of other questions is concerned, as in the past it is applied subject to the "behavior" of the Soviet Union in Africa, in the Middle East, in relation to "human rights," and so on. The reaction of the Administration to the recently-begun Shcharansky process is in this regard sufficiently instructive.

The Carter Administration variously denies that it is supporting a return to the "Cold War." It seems that it fears a decline of relations with the Soviet Union to a level when the threat of a serious, to say nothing of a military, conflict with us would be interpreted by the American people, and also in other countries of the world, as something real. Carter, evidently has come to realize that this would cause deep alarm among the population of the country and would for him be a political loss, and maybe would represent a catastrophe in the 1980 presidential elections. In this regard the choice—"cooperation or confrontation"—which he tried to pose for us in his speech in Annapolis, seemed in its essence directed in the USA itself to him personally; the heartland is expecting from Carter himself an answer to that choice, and he—thanks to the adherence to principle in our position—has turned out to have not quite as free a choice as he tried to present it.

Overall, having moved to an obvious lowering of the level of relations with the Soviet Union, the Carter Administration has shown lately a desire to smooth them out a little. This however, should so far be understood like this, that although it is not generally averse to improving them, the White House at the same time does not want to sacrifice such irritants to our relations as efforts to interfere in our internal affairs or actions like Carter's planned visit to the "Berlin Wall." In a word, the Administration itself has imposed a definite barrier to the possible improvement in our relations (which coincides with the tasks of strengthening NATO, the arms race, the game with China, and so forth).

A lot depends, of course, on how the President himself will behave in the future. His views on Soviet-American relations, as in the past, are inconsistent, they contain plenty of dribs of this and drabs of that. Flirting with the conservative moods in the country (the strength of which he at times clearly overestimates), Carter frequently resorts to anti-Soviet rhetoric in order to, as they say, win cheap applause. The danger is found in the fact that such rhetoric is picked up and amplified by the means of mass communication, in Congress, and so forth. Ultimately, as often happens in the USA, the rhetoric is transformed, influences policy, and sometimes itself becomes policy. It would be incorrect, however, to speak about some sort of hopelessness or irreconcilability in our relations with the USA and, in particular, with the current Administration, personally with Carter, although this issue is exteremely complex. In the USA other things are also going on, which, together with the noted-above general attitudes in the country, require Carter and the Administration to maintain relations with the Soviet Union at a certain level, regardless of all the vacillation of the current President. The following are included among these things:

A general recognition in the USA of the primacy of Soviet-American relations (in its early days, the Administration—this was Brzezinski's doing—tried to reduce their significance, but had to stop doing this when it collided with the realities of the international situation.)

The firm and principled line of the Soviet leadership on relations with the USA, which is finding here a growing response. In the ruling circles of the USA there is not by any means a united negative approach to relations with the Soviet Union. Influential political and business circles continue to support a search for agreement with us in various areas, understanding from experience that the paths of confrontation with us are hopeless. The Administration cannot but take into account the fact that the main Western partners of the USA—to say nothing of the majority of developing countries—speak more or less consistently in support of a policy of detente.

Carter has to realize the vulnerability of his position in the 1980 Presidential elections, if he goes into those elections as a President who caused a strategic arms agreement with the Soviet Union to fail, and who led Soviet-American relations to the edge of Cold War. Under conditions of an erosion of Carter's mass base in comparision to his standing in 1976, the issue of relations with the Soviet Union really could be decisive for Carter in the next Presidential elections.

Under conditions of the serious economic difficulties facing the USA, the possibility of decreasing military spending by limiting the arms race is proving more and more impressive to average American taxpayers. For the population of the USA (and for Carter), inflation has become problem number 1.

Among Americans, as in the past, a strong mood "not to allow another Vietnam," particularly in Africa, continues to hold. In the same way, the Administration's interference in African affairs is causing growing suspiciousness among the Negro population of the country, which is feeling a sense of solidarity with the Africans in their conflict with the racist regimes. For Carter, who defeated Ford with the support of a majority of Negro voters, the views towards him of this category of Americans subsequently may become critically important.

3. On a practical level, the Carter Administration, based on everything, intends to continue the search for an agreement with the Soviet Union on those issues which are perceived by the public to touch directly on the problem of the prevention of nuclear war. It goes without saying that it is necessary to use this in our interest. On other issues, so far no Administration desire to review its position or to cease the anti-Soviet rhetoric to which it resorts from time to time is visible. This applies particularly to the "defense of human rights" in the Soviet Union, NATO military preparations, opposition to the Soviet Union in Africa, in the Middle East, and in other regions of the world. In this regard, special attention has lately been assigned to the Administration's policy towards China, which according to all signs bears witness—if not formally, then in essence—to its yearning for a plot with China against the interests of the Soviet Union. The danger of this course to our interests is self-evident. Brzezinski, whom Gus Hall named "the Carter regime's Rasputin," continues to play a significant role in all of this.

Our firm reaction to the recent blast of anti-Soviet rhetoric by the Carter Administration forced it to noticeably soften its tone. We have to assert that this type of action will be effective in the future too. However, it would not be in our interests to pass by specific positive aspects of Carter's approach to relations with the Soviet Union—in the first place his great personal interest in a meeting with

L.I. Brezhnev, his support in principle for a treaty on SALT, and others. Appropriate positive reactions from our side, apart from anything else, would strengthen the positions of those individuals and circles which are trying to to influence the President from the perspective of the need for the development of Soviet-American relations over the long term. A.A. Gromyko's meetings with Vance and Carter, and also L.I. Brezhnev's reception of Vance, have great significance in this regard.

Source: Dobrynin, Anatoly. Letter to Moscow, July 11, 1978. Obtained and translated by the Cold War International History Project. Available online at the Cold War International History Project Virtual Archive, http://www.wilsoncenter.org.

10.9
American Reaction to the Soviet Afghan Invasion – 1979
Excerpts from a Memorandum by National Security Advisor Zbigniew Brzezinski

The Soviet invasion of Afghanistan in 1979 officially brought the détente era to a close and brought the Cold War back. In this memorandum to President Jimmy Carter dated December 26, 1979, National Security Advisor Zbigniew Brzezinski offered his assessment of appropriate American strategy toward the USSR in the post-détente era. He also speculated about the likely political fallout in the United States from the Soviet incursion in Afghanistan.

… As I mentioned to you a week or so ago, we are now facing a regional crisis. Both Iran and Afghanistan are in turmoil, and Pakistan is both unstable internally and extremely apprehensive externally. If the Soviets succeed in Afghanistan [DELETION], and the age-long dream of Moscow to have direct [Indian] Ocean [access] will have been fulfilled.

Historically, the British provided the barrier to that drive and Afghanistan was their buffer state. We assumed that role in 1945, but the Iranian crisis has led to the collapse of the balance of power in Southwest Asia, and it could produce Soviet presence right down on the edge of the Arabian and Oman Gulfs.

Accordingly, the Soviet intervention in Afghanistan poses for us an extremely grave challenge, both internationally and domestically. While it could become a Soviet Vietnam, the initial effects of the intervention are likely to be adverse for us for the following domestic and international reasons:

Domestic

A. The Soviet intervention is likely to stimulate calls for more immediate U.S. military action in Iran. Soviet 'decisiveness' will be contrasted with our restraint, which will no longer be labeled as prudent but increasingly as timid;

B. At the same time, regional instability may make a resolution of the Iranian problem more difficult for us, and it could bring us into a head to head confrontation with the Soviets;

C. SALT is likely to be damaged, perhaps irreparably, because Soviet military aggressiveness will have been so naked;

D. More generally, our handling of Soviet affairs will be attacked by both the Right and the Left.

International

A. Pakistan, unless we somehow manage to project both confidence and power into the region, [DELETION]

B. With Iran destabilized, there will be no firm bulwark in Southwest Asia against the Soviet drive to the Indian Ocean;

C. The Chinese will certainly note that Soviet assertiveness in Afghanistan and in Cambodia is not effectively restrained by the United States.

Compensating Factors

There will be, to be sure, some compensating factors:

A. World public opinion may be outraged at the Soviet intervention. Certainly, Moslem countries will be concerned, and we might be in a position to exploit this.

B. There are already 300,000 refugees from Afghanistan in Pakistan, and we will be in a position to indict the Soviets for causing massive human suffering. That figure will certainly grow, and Soviet-sponsored actions in Cambodia have already taken their toll as well.

C. There will be greater awareness among our allies for the need to do more for their own defense.

A Soviet Vietnam?

However, we should not be too sanguine about Afghanistan becoming a Soviet Vietnam:

A. The guerrillas are badly organized and poorly led;

B. They have no sanctuary, no organized army, and no central government—all of which North Vietnam had;

C. They have limited foreign support, in contrast to the enormous amount of arms that flowed to the Vietnamese from both the Soviet Union and China;

D. The Soviets are likely to act decisively, unlike the U.S., which pursued in Vietnam a policy of 'inoculating' the enemy.

As a consequence, the Soviets might be able to assert themselves effectively, and in world politics nothing succeeds like success, whatever the moral aspects....

Source: Brzezinski, Zbigniew. Memorandum to President Jimmy Carter, December 26, 1979. Carter-Brezhnev Collection. National Security Archives. Washington, DC. Reprinted in *The Cold War: A History in Documents and Eyewitness Accounts* by Jussi M. Hanhimäki and Odd Arne Westad. Oxford: Oxford University Press, 2003.

11

PROXY WARS

"Contras" move through a village in 1983. Contra forces received significant U.S. aid during the 1980s in their guerrilla war against Nicaragua's Socialist Sandinista regime.

INTRODUCTION

The Cold War between the United States and the USSR took many forms, but among the most deadly of the engagements between the two giants were so-called "proxy wars." Rather than fight each other directly, the two superpowers intervened in—or even triggered—civil wars in a number of developing nations. In these proxy wars, the U.S. and the Soviets each provided military aid or covert support to whichever side shared their basic political philosophy. Thus the U.S. actively supported anti-Communist "freedom fighters" around the world, while the Kremlin supported socialist governments and movements.

Such proxy wars took place even during the era of détente. In 1973 in Chile, for instance, the CIA helped orchestrate the downfall of the democratically elected government of socialist Salvador Allende. Chilean General Augusto Pinochet, supported by U.S. agents and policy makers, spent several months maneuvering against the Allende government; in September of that year he engineered a successful military coup. Over the next three decades the United States and Chile remained staunch allies, even as Pinochet's dictatorship became one of the most ruthless and brutal regimes on the continent.

The next victory on the Third World battlefield belonged to the Soviet Union. In Africa, Cuban troops and Soviet military aid helped Communist forces win power in Angola in 1976 after a bloody civil war. One year later, a Marxist government assumed power in Ethiopia, which had once been a reliable ally of the West. Then, in early 1978, the Soviets engineered a decisive Ethiopian victory over neighboring Somalia (a recent convert to the West) in the Horn of Africa. Little wonder, then, that the Soviet Union's December 1979 invasion of Afghanistan was

357

regarded in Washington as further proof that the Kremlin was willing to use force to advance the Communist cause throughout the Third World.

The War in Nicaragua

During the post-détente 1980s, Latin America emerged as the primary battleground in the Cold War, and the Central American nation of Nicaragua soon became the frontline in the war on Communism. U.S. President Ronald Reagan, a conservative Republican who had taken office in January 1981, was a fierce opponent of Communism who was deeply committed to containing its spread. The Reagan administration was thus deeply opposed to Nicaragua's new Sandinista government, a Marxist regime headed by President Daniel Ortega. The Reagan administration viewed the Sandinistas—who had overthrown the corrupt and repressive government of U.S. ally Anastasio Somoza in 1979—as agents of the Soviet Union who would work to advance Communism throughout Latin America. When the Nicaraguan countryside exploded into civil war in 1981, Reagan and his conservative allies in Congress were quick to lend military aid and intelligence to the right-wing "Contras" seeking to oust Ortega.

Over the next several years the CIA and the U.S. military became deeply involved in the battle over Nicaragua. Reagan repeatedly described the conflict as vital to American security interests. "If the Soviet Union can aid and abet subversion in our hemisphere, then the United States has a legal right and a moral duty to help resist it," Reagan declared in 1984. "This is not only in our strategic interest; it is morally right." This belief in Nicaragua's strategic importance eventually culminated in the 1985 Iran-Contra affair. In this scandal, Reagan administration officials secretly—and illegally—sold arms to the fundamentalist regime in Iran and then used the profits from those illegal arms sales to help support the Nicaraguan Contras.

In 1984 the Nicaraguan government sued the United States in the International Court of Justice, alleging that the United States was illegally using military force against Nicaragua and intervening in its internal affairs. In 1985 the United States announced that it would not participate in the case and that it would ignore any further proceedings of the court on the matter. On June 27, 1986, the court ruled in favor of Nicaragua. It rejected the U.S. claim of "collective self-defense," in which the U.S. argued that Nicaragua was supporting guerrilla warfare against the governments of El Salvador, Honduras, and Costa Rica. The Court also found the United States guilty of violating its treaty obligations to Nicaragua.

The United States remained opposed to the Nicaraguan government until 1990, when the Sandinistas were defeated in national elections. The new Nicaraguan president, Violeta Chamorro, who was supported by Washington, dropped all legal claims that the previous regime had made against the United States. A few weeks later, Washington forgave $260 million in loans made to Nicaragua.

The War in El Salvador

The United States also became deeply involved in El Salvador, another Central American nation roiled by political violence, during Reagan's years in office. But in this instance, the U.S. provided military assistance to the government in power—a pro-American military junta—against leftist rebels supported by Cuba. Determined to keep El Salvador out of the hands of Communists, the Reagan administration steadily increased its military aid to the ruling government despite growing evidence that government-sponsored "death squads" were terrorizing and murdering ordinary citizens. Perhaps the most infamous of the death squad assassinations was carried out in 1980 against Oscar Romero, the Catholic Archbishop of San Salvador and a strong critic of U.S. military aid to the El Salvadoran government.

The Romero assassination and numerous other incidents sparked strong condemnation of U.S. foreign policy from human rights organizations and other observers. But Reagan and his supporters defended their actions in Central America as essential to the future of the Western hemisphere. In any case, the civil war in El Salvador dragged on throughout the 1980s, claiming thousands of innocent lives. The two sides remained at war until 1992, when they signed the Chapultepec Peace Accords.

11.1

America Targets Chilean President Salvador Allende – 1970
An Excerpt from a Memorandum from Secretary of State Henry Kissinger to President Richard Nixon

Salvador Allende was an outspoken socialist leader in Chile who was elected president of the country in September 1970. An ally of the Soviets and a fierce critic of U.S. business interests in Chile, Allende was viewed with suspicion by the United States

On November 5, 1970, Secretary of State Henry Kissinger sent the following secret memorandum to President Nixon. In his memo, Kissinger describes the election of Allende as "one of the most serious challenges ever faced in this hemisphere." He also urges Nixon to adopt a policy of "covert" but unrelenting pressure and opposition against the Allende government. Nixon agreed to this approach, which became the guiding position of the U.S. government toward Chile for the next three years.

Allende was keenly aware that he had enemies maneuvering against him. In one December 1972 speech before the United Nations, for example, he charged that "external pressure has tried to cut us off from the world, to strangle our economy.... We find ourselves facing forces operating in the twilight, without a flag, with powerful weapons." In September 1973, after years of plotting by U.S. operatives and allies among Chile's economic elite, Allende's socialist government was finally brought down. Allende died during a military coup led by General Augusto Pinochet, who established a dictatorship that was a reliable ally to the United States.

A. DIMENSIONS OF THE PROBLEM

The election of Allende as President of Chile poses for us one of the most serious challenges ever faced in this hemisphere. Your decision as to what to do about it may be the most historic and difficult foreign affairs decision you will have to make this year, for what happens in Chile over the next six to twelve months will have ramifications that will go far beyond just US-Chilean relations. They will have an effect on what happens in the rest of Latin America and the developing world; on what our future position will be in the hemisphere; and on the larger world picture, including our relations with the USSR. They will even affect our own conception of what our role in the world is.

Allende is a tough, dedicated Marxist. He comes to power with a profound anti-US bias. The Communist and Socialist parties form the core of the political coalition that is his power base. Everyone agrees that Allende will purposefully seek:

- to establish a socialist, Marxist state in Chile;

- to eliminate US influence from Chile and the hemisphere;

- to establish close relations and linkages with the USSR, Cuba and other Socialist countries.

- *The consolidation of Allende in power in Chile*, therefore, *would pose some very serious threats to our interests and position in the hemisphere*, and would affect developments and our relations to them elsewhere in the world:

- US investments (totaling some one billion dollars) may be lost, at least in part; Chile may default on debts (about $1.5 billion) owed the US Government and private US banks.

- Chile would probably became a leader of opposition to us in the inter-American system, a source of disruption in the hemisphere, and a focal point of support for subversion in the rest of Latin America.

- It would become part of the Soviet/Socialist world, not only philosophically but in terms of power dynamics; and it might constitute a support base and entry point for expansion of Soviet and Cuban presence and activity in the region.

- The example of a successful elected Marxist government in Chile would surely have an impact on—and even precedent value for—other parts of the world, especially in Italy; the imitative spread of similar phenomena elsewhere would in turn significantly affect the world balance and our own position in it.

While events in Chile pose these potentially very adverse consequences for us, *they are taking a form which makes them extremely difficult for us to deal with or offset*, and which in fact poses *some very painful dilemmas for us*:

a. Allende was elected legally, the first Marxist government ever to come to power by free elections. He *has* legitimacy in the eyes of Chileans and most of the world; there is nothing we can do to deny him that legitimacy or claim he does not have it.

b. We are strongly on record in support of self-determination and respect for free election; you are firmly on record for non-intervention in the internal affairs of this hemisphere and of accepting nations "as they are." It would therefore be very costly for us to act in ways that appear to violate those principles, and Latin Americans and others in the world will view our policy as a test of the credibility of our rhetoric.

On the other hand, our failure to react to this situation risks being perceived in Latin America and in Europe as indifference or impotence in the face of clearly adverse developments in a region long considered our sphere of influence.

c. Allende's government is likely to move along lines that will make it very difficult to marshal international or hemisphere censure of him—he is most likely to appear as an "independent" socialist country rather than a Soviet satellite or "Communist government."

Yet a Titoist government in Latin America would be far more dangerous to us than it is in Europe, precisely because it can move against our policies and interests more easily and ambiguously and because its "model" effect can be insidious....

C. OUR CHOICES

There are deep and fundamental differences among the agencies on this basic issue [of how to deal with Allende]. They manifest themselves in essentially three possible approaches:

1. *The Modus Vivendi Strategy:*

This school of thought, which is essentially State's position, argues that *we really do not have the capability of preventing Allende from consolidating himself* or forcing his failure; that the main course of events in Chile will be determined primarily by the Allende government and its reactions to the internal situation; and that the best thing we can do in these circumstances is maintain our relationship and our presence in Chile so that over the long haul we may be able to foster and influencing [sic] domestic trends favorable to our interests. In this view actions to exert pressure on Allende or to isolate Chile will not only be ineffective, but will only accelerate adverse developments in Chile and limit our capacity to have any influence on the long-range trend.

In this view the risks that Allende will consolidate himself and the long-range consequences therefrom are less dangerous to us than the immediate probable reaction to attempts to oppose Allende. Its perception of Allende's long-term development is essentially optimistic and benign. Implicit is the argument that it is not certain he can overcome his internal weaknesses, that he may pragmatically limit this opposition to us, and that if he turns into another Tito that would not be bad since we deal with other governments of this kind anyway.

2. *The Hostile Approach:*

DOD [Department of Defense], CIA [Central Intelligence Agency] and some state people, on the other hand, argue that it is patent that Allende is our enemy, that he will move counter to us just as soon and as strongly as he feels he can; and that when his hostility is manifest to us it will be because he has consolidated his power and then it really will be too late to do very much—the process is irreversible. In this view, therefore, we should try to prevent him from consolidating *now* when he is at his weakest.

Implicit in this school of thought is the assumption that we *can* affect events, and that the risks of stirring up criticism to our position elsewhere are less dangerous to us than the long-term consolidation of a Marxist government in Chile.

Within this approach there are in turn two schools of thought:

a. Overt Hostility.

This view argues that we should not delay putting pressure on Allende and therefore should not wait to react to his moves with counter-punches. It considers the dangers of making our hostility public or of initiating the fight less important than making unambiguously clear what our position is and where we stand. It assumes that Allende does not really need our hostility to help consolidate himself, because if he did he would confront us now. Instead he appears to fear our hostility.

This approach therefore would call for (1) initiating punitive measures, such as terminating aid or economic embargo; (2) making every effort to rally international support of this position; and (3) declaring and publicizing our concern and hostility.

b. Non-overt Pressure, Cold, Correct Approach

This approach concurs in the view that pressure should be placed on Allende now and that we should oppose him. But it argues that *how* we package that pressure and opposition is crucial and may make the difference between effectiveness and ineffectiveness....

Implicit in this approach is the judgment that how unambiguous our public position is and making a public record are all less important in the long run than maximizing our pressure and minimizing risks to our position in the rest of the world.

This approach therefore calls for essentially the same range of pressures as the previous one, but would use them quietly and covertly; on the surface our posture would be correct, but cold. Any public manifestation or statement of hostility would be geared to his actions to avoid giving him the advantage of arguing he is the aggrieved party....

D. ASSESSMENTS

.... The great weakness in the modus vivendi approach is that:

- it gives Allende the strategic initiative;
- it plays into his game plan and almost insures that he will consolidate himself;
- if he does consolidate himself, he will have even more freedom to act against us after a period of our acceptance of him than if we had opposed him all along;

- there are no apparent reasons or available intelligence to justify a benign or optimistic view of an Allende regime over the long term. In fact, as noted, an "independent" rational socialist state linked to Cuba and the USSR can be even more dangerous for our long-term interests than a very radical regime.

There is nothing in this strategy that promises to deter or prevent adverse anti-U.S. actions when and if Chile wants to pursue them—and there are far more compelling reasons to believe that he will when he feels he is established than that he will not.

The main question with the hostile approach is whether we *can* effectively prevent Allende from consolidating his power. There is at least some prospect that we can. But the argument can be made that even if we did not succeed—provided we did not damage ourselves too severely in the process—we could hardly be worse off than letting him entrench himself; that there is in fact some virtue in posturing ourselves in a position of opposition as a means of at least containing him and improving our chances of inducing others to help us contain him later if we have to.

In my judgment the dangers of doing nothing are greater than the risks we run in trying to do something, especially since we have flexibility in tailoring our efforts to minimize those risks.

I recommend, therefore that you make a decision that we will oppose Allende as strongly as we can and do all we can to keep him from consolidating power, taking care to packing those efforts in a style that gives us the appearance of reacting to his moves....

Source: Kissinger, Henry. White House Memorandum for the President. "SUBJECT: NSC Meeting, November 6—Chile," November 5, 1970. Nixon Presidential Materials Project, National Archives and Records Administration. Available online at National Security Archive, http://www.gwu.edu/~nsarchiv.

11.2
Recalling the Overthrow of Salvador Allende – 1973
An Excerpt from Pinochet and Me: A Chilean Anti-Memoir, *by Marc Cooper*

The following is an excerpt from a memoir written by Marc Cooper, an American who worked in Chilean President Salvador Allende's socialist government as chief translator of Allende's writings and speeches. Cooper was an admirer of Allende with similar political leanings, and he was infuriated by American efforts to undermine the regime. When General Augusto Pinochet led a military coup of Allende's government in September 1973, Cooper fled for his life. He left Chile under the protection of the United Nations eight days after the coup.

I could hardly call myself a personal confidant of the President. We were separated by forty years in age and by a couple of worlds' worth of political experience. But my close contact with him only enhanced my admiration for the man, politically and personally.

Salvador Allende was a hectically complex and contradictory figure—romantic and rebel, revolutionary and parliamentarian, Socialist and mason, physician and master politician. He had few counterparts among politicians of the twentieth century. Even his most bitter detractors had to admit that few men were as politically canny. He was, indeed, the master of the felicitous maneuver. Yet at the same time he was desperately honest.

For thirty-five years he battled indefatigably for the interests of the *rotos* [members of Chile's lowest class] without ever being accused of betrayal or sellout. More than any single individual Allende could claim credit for the myriad social legislation that had made Chile, even before his election, one of the most advanced democracies in the hemisphere....

Allende nimbly straddled the ideological span of the modern Left. He was at once a dogged and tenacious defender of a human socialism, a friend and admirer of Che Guevara and a frequent visitor to Cuba. He was a founder of the Cuban-inspired Organization of Latin American Solidarity that served as a sort of coordinating committee for continental guerilla war. And yet he believed with every bone of his body that the only path to socialism in Chile would be legal, parliamentary, and peaceful. He made no such prescription for other countries. But Allende was unmovable in his conviction that Chile was different. As a young militant in the 1930s he had seen some brief, violent interruptions of his beloved Chilean democracy.

But absolutely nothing could have prepared Salvador Allende for the grueling dilemmas he faced during the third year of his presidency. By mid-1973, his Popular Unity government, his presidency, and Chile itself, stood poised at a daunting and ominous impasse.

Perhaps no single date better encapsulated Chile's predicament than July 26, 1973.

On that day, Chile was no longer honeymooning with the dream of a peaceful revolutionary transition. Since Castro's visit, now a year and a half ago, Allende's government had scored some stunning successes. But so had the opposition. Class strife had blown apart the peaceful facade of Chilean politics. In the countryside a virtual ground war had erupted between increasingly well-organized landless and peasant movements who were dedicated to seizing massive farms and the oligarchs who owned the land. The orderly three-year plan formulated by Allende to nationalize the farms and compensate the *patrones* was sabotaged by a rightist-controlled

Congress that blocked legal land reform. So farm workers simply took the revolution into their own hands.

At first Allende tried to dissuade the agrarian movement. But as hundreds and then thousands of farms were seized, Allende had no choice but to "legalize" the seizures after the fact. The agrarian sweep was encouraged by the Socialists and the MIR [Movimeiento de Izquierda Revolucionaria/Movement of the Revolutionary Left] while the more moderate Communists openly fretted about the revolution going too far too fast.

In the months leading up to July 1973, some 50 per cent of Chilean agricultural land had been expropriated, either by the state or directly by farm workers. All farms larger than 175 acres had been taken. Now the peasant groups were planning phase two: seizure down to 80 acres.

The political atmosphere was just as hot in Chile's big cities, especially Santiago. On June 29, 1973, a renegade tank battalion linked to an ultra-rightist cell staged what turned out to be a comic-opera coup attempt. Early that morning a few tanks rolled up to the Moneda and began lobbing shells and calling for a general uprising.

In those first uncertain moments, when the balance of power could have tipped in either direction, Allende, speaking through our Press Office network, called on the workers of Chile to take defensive measures by "occupying" all workplaces, farms, and factories. Within hours, the coup attempt melted away. But the factories were still in the hands of the workers. Embryonic workers' councils, which had previously been encouraged by the Socialists and bitterly denounced by the Communists, came all of a sudden into full blossom as veritable administrators and masters of the dark and dank industrial strips concentrated in four areas of the capital.

By July 26, 1973, it was abundantly clear to all that the Councils had no intention of returning any of the major workplaces to their private owners. The Allende government was caught in a bind. It could not turn its back on its own popular base and use force to dislodge the workers. And yet, Allende—and just about everyone else—had to know that this was all leading to a dangerous point of no return. Almost overnight, the worst nightmare of the Chilean elite had come to pass: in the space of a few hours they had been dispossessed of most of their productive wealth as the smoke-and-smog smudged walls of the factory gates were draped with red flags and the surrounding cramped industrial neighborhoods turned into worker-run liberated zones.

Chilean socialism, measured by the economic and political power of the workers, grew more in one day—thanks to the botched coup attempt—than it had in the previous two years of parliamentary gradualism. The dialectic of peaceful change in Chile was clearly exhausting itself. The country had become a giant powder keg engulfed in a blaze of conflicting passions. The leading intellectual journal of the Left, *Punto Final*, editorialized: "For Chile, the cards are on the table. It will either be socialism or fascism—nothing in between."

The Chilean Right was hardly standing by idly. And in its anti-Allende efforts it was getting enormous help from the Nixon administration. Since the onset of the Cuban revolution, Chile, with its active and powerful electoral Left, had always been a central focus of US hemispheric policy. During the 1960s, for example, Chile was the largest per capita recipient of American Alliance for Progress funding. There had also been substantial covert CIA funding to Chile's Christian Democratic Party during the 1964 election, precisely in order to thwart one of Allende's earlier presidential challenges.

No surprise, then, that his eventual election in September 1970 set off alarm bells in Washington. In the Nixon White House, a special "Committee of 40" was established to monitor such events. And, indeed, a full two months before Allende's election, the administration's approach was established by Nixon foreign-policy guru Henry Kissinger, who told the Committee in reference to the predicted democratic electoral victory of Allende: "I don't see why we need to stand by and watch a country go Communist due to the irresponsibility of its own people."

While some on the Left—both in Chile and in the US—naively thought that Washington would take a more benign view of Allende's democratic ascension to power, Kissinger had a radically different notion. He thought that the example of a peacefully elected Socialist government coming to power was even more threatening to US geopolitical interests than the model of armed revolution. Large Socialist and Communist parties in France and Italy were gaining electoral momentum and Kissinger was plagued with nightmares of a Chileanized Western Europe weakening the anti-Soviet NATO alliance.

Efforts to stop Allende were already well under way immediately after his election and during the sixty-day window before his inauguration. The sinister euphemism of "destabilization" was introduced into the Cold War political lexicon. In cooperation with the White House, the International Telephone and Telegraph Company (IT&T) put up a million dollars for a secret campaign against Allende and in defense of the private Chilean phone system of which it was owner.

For its part, the CIA fashioned a two-track strategy. On the one hand, centrist and conservative Chilean politicians were offered CIA bribes to consider a parliamentary maneuver to block Allende's inauguration. (Elected in a three-way race with a 38 per cent plurality, Allende required a full majority vote of Congress to formally take office.) Simultaneously, the CIA developed a second, more violent track in collaboration with a neo-fascist group. The plan was to kidnap the Commander-in-Chief of the armed forces and provoke a coup that would prevent Allende's inauguration.

Both approaches failed miserably. The bungled kidnapping of General René Schneider just two weeks before Allende's swearing-in ended with the General dying of gunshot wounds. The shock and revulsion, and the fear, that swept Chile were so great that whatever thoughts some politicians had entertained to deny Allende his due in exchange for American bribes were swept away by popular anger.

Allende was handed the presidential sash, but the US destabilization program only escalated. At the close of one White House meeting on Chile, Nixon slammed his fist down on the table and barked orders to his CIA Director to make the Chilean economy "scream." American export-import credits to Chile were cut off. After Allende nationalized the Chilean holdings of the two American copper giants, Kennecot and Anaconda, with unanimous approval of the opposition-controlled Chilean Congress, the US economic embargo was drawn tighter. Relations further worsened when the Chilean government confiscated the IT&T-owned phone company and hotels.

The CIA covert program—several million dollars in total—also continued unabated. CIA funds flowed to anti-Allende political parties and their campaign organizations, to extreme right extra-parliamentary forces, to Chile's premier conservative daily, *El Mercurio*, and to various anti-Allende business groups like the powerful Truckers' Association. During the then-current transport industry work stoppage, the influx of CIA funding had been so great that, for the first time since Allende's election, the value of the US dollar plummeted: there were just too many greenbacks flooding the black market.

But during this entire CIA destabilization drive, the US government continued to maintain normal contacts and exchanges with the Chilean military, granting it millions in funding credits while the US strangled the rest of the civilian economy.

The CIA strategy, once Allende was elected, seemed not so much to conspire to stage a coup, but rather to lay the economic, social, and political groundwork to make such a coup likely.

The Chilean Right, always a formidable force, and now with its back to the wall, was delighted to receive such foreign encouragement. It had sensed that the corner had been turned and that it was now Allende who was on the defensive....

Indeed, Chile had already pitched itself into a dizzying dance of chaos and blood. As Allende's reforms deepened, as he nationalized the American copper mines and telephone company, as large rural estates were handed over to their sharecroppers, as wages soared and unions gained a voice in national affairs, as rents were lowered and taxes on the rich increased, the political Right and eventually the Centre jettisoned their attachment to the rule of law. Opposition groups fielded chain-swinging thugs against government marches. Oil pipelines were dynamited. Industrial production was sabotaged. The wealthy hoarded food and other consumer goods and then loudly protested the resulting shortages.

Just a week previous to this morning, on September 4, the Chilean Left held its last great public gathering to commemorate the third anniversary of Allende's election. While the President stood granite-faced on a balcony from the early afternoon till late into the night, more than a half-million Chilean workers and their families marched before him, voicing the nearly unanimous chant: "We want guns! We want guns!" It was a horrible, wrenching moment, one permanently seared in my consciousness. Yes guns. But what guns? From where? And how? My friends and I walked home that evening with a dark foreboding. The end was surely near.

In the seven days that followed, the Right drew the noose tighter. Commerce and transport ground to a halt. The night before September 11, the transport stoppage had waylaid me and my girlfriend at Melvin's house. We had gone out as a foursome, wound up snacking at Melvin's, and got stranded without a way back to my downtown apartment.

My only chance of transport that morning was with my friends at RadioTaxi 33. Militant revolutionaries, the drivers there had long ago seized the company from its conservative owners and had turned the place into the most efficient cab service in Santiago. And when the drivers weren't working their shifts, they'd volunteer as drivers and messengers for the most powerful workers' council in Santiago, the Cordon Vicuña McKenna.

After a forty-five minute wait on the corner, I became concerned. I went back to the house to call the taxi company again but, inexplicably, the phone lines were now permanently busy. I walked back to the corner and eventually was able to flag down a passing cab.

The driver, pale and harried, rolled down the window. "Can you take me downtown?" I asked.

"Downtown?"

"Yeah. To the immigration office," I answered.

With classic Chilean understatement and cool diplomacy the cabbie replied: "But, sir, there are problems downtown."

"Problems?"

"Yes, problems," he said refusing to be more specific. After all, these were highly polarized times. You never knew who you were talking to. One person's problem was another person's liberation. But a sinking feeling in my gut told me the worst was upon us.

Mustering my own diplomatic skills, I asked. "Problems, you say? Problems with men in uniform you mean?"

"Yes, sir, problems with men in uniform," the cabbie said. But now, the fear of the future already imprinted on him, he took what he probably knew would be his last foray into freedom for some time and added: "Yes, the fucking fascists are overthrowing the government."

370

7:55 am, Tuesday September 11

Everyone else in the house was still asleep. I switched on the massive Grundig radio and waited impatiently for the vacuum tubes to warm up. As the audio came alive I turned the dial and confirmed the cabbie's report: virtually every station was playing the same military march.

I stopped the dial on Radio Corporación, the station of the Socialist Party. Allende was speaking, a nervous inflection in his voice. His words made material the nightmares that had haunted us for months: "This is the President of the Republic speaking from La Moneda Palace. Confirmed reports indicate that a sector of the Navy has isolated and occupied the port city of Valparaiso, which means an uprising against the government is under way … Under these circumstances, I call upon the workers of the country to occupy your workplaces … but I urge you to stay calm. At this moment, there have been no extraordinary troop movements in the capital … I am here defending the government that represents the will of the people.…" Allende assured those listening that he would be back with any further information but that for the moment we should all remain in a state of alert.

On just about every other station on the dial a stern-voiced announcer suddenly materialized. By order of the military junta, he said, all radio stations were immediately to link up to the armed forces network or "they will be bombarded." The names of the four commanders making up the junta were then read: leading the National Police—the *carabineros*—was a general Cèsar Mendoza, a little-known name. For the Air Force there was Gustavo Leigh and for the Navy, Admiral José Merino. But the most important person on the list was Army General Augusto Pinochet. Pinochet, previously the Commander of the Santiago garrison, had two weeks earlier taken over as Commander-in-Chief, swearing his loyalty to the President he was now trying to overthrow.

Some more Prussian marches. And then another announcement. An ultimatum to President Allende. I sat chilled and shaking as I strained to scribble down the text of what a steely voice called Military Communiqué Number 2: "The Moneda Palace must be evacuated before 11 am otherwise it will be attacked by the Chilean Air Force. The workers must remain in their workplaces and homes as it [is] strictly prohibited to leave them. If they disobey, they will also be attacked by air and ground forces.

I sat paralyzed. A few moments later the same dry baritone voice read out Communiqué Number 3: Again I noted it on a yellow pad. "The population is hereby warned not to let themselves be carried away by incitements to violence from either foreign or national activists. And let the foreign ones know that in this country we do not accept violent attitudes or any extreme positions. This should be remembered as means are adopted for their rapid deportation from the country. Any resistance will be met with the full rigor of military justice."

Yet another announcement proclaimed a curfew "until further notice." Anyone found on the streets "will be shot on sight." I had roused the others in the house. We sat dumbfounded in the chilly living room listening to Radio Magallanes, the Communist Party station, boldly resisting the order to broadcast the armed forces network. Over the air, workers were being urged to report to their factories and organize defense committees.

> *"I can only remember the four of us in that living room listening and sobbing for I don't know how long. The fear was palpable. To go onto the street was to risk arrest and execution."*

But this was an empty gesture. Those of us who worked in the Allende government knew the sad truth: that in spite of the right-wing chorus that Allende had formed a "parallel army," we had no such units. Allende had been scrupulous in his commitment to a constitutional, legal, and peaceful transition to socialism. The only guns in the country, he vowed, would remain in the hands of the armed forces. Yes, some Socialists and others had formed clandestine militias—but they were operationally risible.

This war was going to be a short, one-sided massacre. And the tragic irony was that those conservative and centrist political forces that for 150 years had defended a constitutional system as long as it served their interests were now rebelling against it. The last man left standing in defense of the "bourgeois" constitution would be the Marxist President, AK-47 in hand.

10 am, Tuesday September 11

Miraculously, my first attempt to phone the office where I worked in the Moneda Palace went through. Over the sound of crackling gunfire, a secretary, Ximena, told me in tears that she and the others were about to flee the building. My next call was to the US Embassy—up on the fourteenth floor of an office building diagonally opposite the Moneda. I had had virtually no contact with the Embassy and had, in fact, made every effort to steer clear of it. Even my mail was routed to the Canadian Embassy—a government that had showed more sympathy to Allende.

But I phoned the US Embassy that morning hoping that some safety provisions were being made for resident Americans. I figured it was only a matter of time before I would be swept up in the military dragnet.

The Embassy phone answered on the first ring. An accented English told me I was speaking with a Chilean employee—always more American than the Americans. When I asked if the Embassy had issued any special instructions, my respondent only laughed. "No special orders. Just stay off the streets." And then with another chuckle she added: "I'm looking out the window now with binoculars. Looks like Mr. Allende is finally going to get it." She hung up.

11 am, Tuesday September 11

The leftist Radio Corporación and Radio Portales are off the air. But Salvador Allende's metallic voice is coming live over Radio Magallanes. Via telephone, from inside the Moneda, with troops and tanks poised outside, with the Air Force Hawker-Hunter jets arming their rockets in readiness, Allende spoke:

'This is surely the last opportunity I will have to address you. The Air Force has bombed the towers of Radio Portales and Corporación. My words are not bitter but they are full of disillusionment. And they will serve as moral sanction for those who have betrayed their oath of loyalty: the soldiers of Chile, the branch commanders ... Admiral Merino who has named himself Chief of the Navy ... Mr. Mendoza, a slinking general who only yesterday swore his loyalty to the government, who has proclaimed himself head of the Police ... In the face of these events I can only say this to the workers. I will not resign ... With my life I will pay for defending the principles dear to our nation ... History cannot be stopped by repression or violence ... Surely Radio Magallanes will be silenced and with it my voice. But that's of no importance. You will continue hearing me as I will always be by your side. At least you will remember me as a man of dignity, a man who was always loyal to you .... You must know that, sooner rather than later, the grand avenues on which a free people walk will open and a better society will be at hand .... These are my last words...'

I sat stunned and devastated. I can only remember the four of us in that living room listening and sobbing for I don't know how long. The fear was palpable. To go onto the street was to risk arrest and execution. We had no access to any information except what the military broadcast over the radio. The phone lines were now dead.

Everything I had learned over the previous two years told me the Chilean Revolution had come to its end....

As I board the train to return to Argentina, I leave behind me a Chile still in the grip of a homicidal spasm. Pinochet and the military, to the applause of the Chilean Right, and with the nodding approval of the Nixon administration, staged their 1973 coup in the name of liberating Chile from Marxian socialism. But under the overthrown Socialist government of Salvador Allende, a liberal constitution was fully in force. A vibrant private sector dominated the economy. A fully functional Congress was controlled by the conservative opposition. A dozen daily newspapers, from far right to extreme left flourished free of all censorship. Not one Chilean was in jail for political crimes. Freedom of speech and assembly was fully respected. Allende's election had enriched, not atrophied democracy.

And now the junta that has overthrown him in the name of freedom is constructing a regime every bit as noxious—and in many ways worse—than the Stalinist governments of which it claims to be the antithesis. The Congress has been padlocked, the free press trashed and burned along with the courts and the political system itself, all opposition is banned, and those suspected of resistance are hunted down, tortured, beaten, dismembered, assassinated, and "disappeared." Pinochet's patrons in the White House and State Department, and those in the ideologically blinkered media establishment who were so horrified by Allende's nationalization of the US-owned copper mines, can barely bring themselves to hiccup a protest over what they call the "excesses" of the Pinochet dictatorship. He's a sonofabitch for sure. But he's "our" sonofabitch. His defenders and apologists in Washington point to his free-market policies as proof positive they have backed the right horse. But it's really the mounting body count that stands as the most fitting monument to the first two years of achievement of the military regime. And sitting atop it all, his arms crossed over his chest, his lips clamped together, his eyes hidden behind pitch-black lenses, is, indeed, the Liberator of Chile, General Augusto Pinochet Ugarte.

Source: Cooper, Marc. *Pinochet and Me: A Chilean Anti-Memoir*. New York: Verso, 2000.

11.3
The Church Committee Report on CIA Covert Action – 1975
An Excerpt from "Alleged Assassination Plots Involving Foreign Leaders"

During the early 1970s concerns mounted that U.S. government intelligence agencies were engaging in "illegal, improper, or unethical" operations in foreign countries. These concerns, combined with the Watergate scandal that had enveloped the nation, convinced the U.S. Senate to launch an investigation of U.S. intelligence operations. Chaired by Senator Frank Church of Idaho, the so-called "Church Committee" held public hearings on the activities of both the Central Intelligence Agency (CIA) and Federal Bureau of Investigation (FBI) and issued highly critical reports on both agencies.

The Church Committee's work prompted both President Gerald Ford and President Jimmy Carter to issue executive orders to increase presidential control over the CIA's covert operations. It also was directly responsible for the passage of the Intelligence Oversight Act of 1980. One year later, President Ronald Reagan issued Executive Order No. 12,333, which specifically stated that "no person employed by or acting on behalf of the U.S. government shall engage in or conspire to engage in assassination."

Alleged Assassination Plots Involving Foreign Leaders

… The Committee believes that it is still in the national interest of the United States to help nations achieve self-determination and resist Communist domination. However, it is clear that this interest cannot justify resorting to the kind of abuses covered in this report....

The evidence establishes that the United States was implicated in several assassination plots. The Committee believes that, short of war, assassination is incompatible with American principles, international order, and morality. It should be rejected as a tool of foreign policy....

The Committee believes the truth about the assassination allegations should be told because democracy depends upon a well-informed electorate. We reject any contention that the facts disclosed in this report should be kept secret because they are embarrassing to the United States. Despite the temporary injury to our national reputation, the Committee believes that foreign peoples will, upon sober reflection, respect the United States more for keeping faith with its democratic ideal than they will condemn us for the misconduct revealed....

The Committee finds that the system of executive command and control was so ambiguous that it is difficult to be certain at what levels assassination activity was known and authorized. This situation creates the disturbing prospect that Government officials might have undertaken the assassination plots without it having been uncontrovertibly clear that there was explicit authorization from the Presidents. It is also possible that there might have been a successful "plausible denial" in which Presidential authorization was issued but is now obscured. Whether or not the respective Presidents knew of or authorized the plots, as chief executive officer of the United States, each must bear the ultimate responsibility for the activities of his subordinates....

The Committee finds that officials of the United States Government initiated and participated in plots to assassinate Patrice Lumumba and Fidel Castro.

The plot to kill Lumumba was conceived in the latter half of 1960 by officials of the United States Government, and quickly advanced to the point of sending poisons to the Congo to be used for the assassination.

The effort to assassinate Castro began in 1960 and continued until 1965. The plans to assassinate Castro using poison cigars, exploding seashells, and a contaminated diving suit did not advance beyond the laboratory phase. The plot involving underworld figures reached the stage of producing poison pills, establishing the contacts necessary to send them to Cuba, procuring potential assassins within Cuba, and apparently delivering the pills to the island itself.... The poisons intended to use against Patrice Lumumba were never administered to him, and there is no evidence that the United States was in any way involved in Lumumba's death at the hands of his Congolese enemies. The efforts to assassinate Castro failed....

American officials clearly desired the overthrow of [Dominican President Rafael] Trujillo, offered both encouragement and guns to local dissidents who sought his overthrow and whose plans included assassination.... The record reveals that United States officials offered encouragement to the Chilean dissidents who plotted the kidnapping of General Rene Schneider [in 1970], but American officials did not desire or encourage Schneider's death. Certain high officials did know, however, that the dissidents planned to kidnap General Schneider....

This country was created by violent revolt against a regime believed to be tyrannous, and our founding fathers (the local dissidents of that era) received aid from foreign countries. Given that history, we should not today rule out support for dissident groups seeking to overthrow tyrants. But passing beyond that principle, there remain serious questions: for example, whether the national interest of the United States is genuinely involved; whether any such support would be overt rather than covert; what tactics should be used; and how such actions should be authorized and controlled by the coordinate branches of government....

No doubt, the CIA's general efforts against the regimes discussed in this report were authorized at the highest levels of the government. However, the record is unclear and serious doubt remains concerning whether assassination was authorized by the respective Presidents.... Whether or not the Presidents in fact knew about the assassination plots, and even if their subordinates failed in their duty of full disclosure, it still follows that the Presidents should have known about the plots. This sets a demanding standard, but one the Committee supports. The future of democracy rests upon such accountability.

The various Presidents and their senior advisors strongly opposed the regimes of Castro and Trujillo, the accession to power of Allende, and the potential influence of Patrice Lumumba. Orders concerning action against those foreign leaders were given in vigorous language. For example, President Nixon's orders to prevent Allende from assuming power left [CIA Director Richard] Helms feeling that "if I ever carried a marshall's baton in my knapsack out of the Oval Office, it was that day." Similarly, General Lansdale described the Mongoose effort against Cuba as "a combat situation," and Attorney General [Robert] Kennedy emphasized that "a solution to the Cuba problem today carries top priority." Helms testified that the pressure to "get rid of Castro and the Castro regime" was intense, and [deputy director of planning at the CIA Ted] Bissell testified that he had been ordered to "get off your ass about Cuba."

It is possible that there was a failure of communication between policymakers and the agency personnel who were experienced in secret, and often violent, action. Although policymakers testified that assassination was not intended by such words as "get rid of Castro," some of their subordinates in the Agency testified that they perceived that assassination was desired and that they should proceed without troubling their superiors....

The perception of certain Agency officials that assassination was within the range of permissible activity was reinforced by the continuing approval of violent covert actions against Cuba that were sanctioned at the Presidential level, and by the failure of the successive administrations to make clear that assassination was not permissible....

Source: U.S. Senate. Select Committee to Study Governmental Operations with Respect to Intelligence Activities. *Alleged Assassination Plots Involving Foreign Leaders: An Interim Report,* November 20, 1975, 94th Congress, 1st session. Washington, DC: U.S. Government Printing Office, 1975.

11.4

A Soviet Journalist Examines the Soviet Failure in Afghanistan – 1979-1989

Excerpts from an Interview for the PBS Series "Red Files"

In 1979 Soviet troops invaded the Central Asian nation of Afghanistan. This invasion was meant to shore up Afghanistan's repressive Communist regime, which was struggling with "Mujahideen" rebel groups to keep its grip on power. But despite its best efforts, Soviet forces were unable to crush the rebels. In fact, much of Afghanistan outside of the capital of Kabul remained under the control of Muslim guerrillas for much of the 1980s. This Afghan resistance movement, which received military aid from the United States, Pakistan, and Saudi Arabia, among others, turned the war into a bloody stalemate. By the mid-1980s, the war in Afghanistan was being described as the Soviet Union's "Vietnam"—a reference to the war that had spilled so much American blood in the 1960s and early 1970s. In February 1989 the Soviet military withdrew from the country for good after losing an estimated 15,000 soldiers. Their withdrawal paved the way for the rise of the Taliban, a nationalistic organization of Islamic fundamentalists that took control of most of the country by 1996. The Taliban was later overthrown when U.S. forces entered Afghanistan in search of Osama bin Laden after the terrorist attacks on September 11, 2001.

In the following excerpt, Soviet journalist Vladimir Pozner describes the Soviet view of the war in Afghanistan and comments on claims that it became the Soviet Union's "Vietnam."

Interviewer: Vladimir, can you talk about how the West jumped on Afghanistan and made it out to be the Soviet Union's Vietnam?

Pozner: The West jumped on Afghanistan for very good reason. It was proof positive, if you will, that Communism was on the march, and that Communism by force was going to take new territories, something that the West had consistently warned and spoken about. Of course the Soviet reason for going into Afghanistan is a whole different story that not many people have ever looked at. It was more like an attempt to say—look we've tried to get an agreement so that you will not install these medium range missiles in Europe. We've tried to get an agreement to sign SALT. You guys aren't doing it. Okay, we're going to show you a thing or two. The Soviets thought that it would be like a parade, they'd walk in, and it would be all over. Turned out to be the opposite, turned out to be the Soviet Union's Vietnam in senses more than one, not only because they lost that war like the United States lost in Vietnam, but also the morale of the fighting man. And what it did to the country psychologically speaking is also very much what Vietnam did to the United States.

Interviewer: Can you talk about the similarities between Vietnam and Afghanistan?

Pozner: Obviously, when you compare the Vietnam War and the Afghan War there are many similarities. Both countries lost, and these are countries that are not used to losing wars. Number 1, Number 2, both countries came to understand that these were not just wars. These were somehow dishonest wars and therefore, the armed forces were affected by the wars. And not just the armed forces, the people, the man in the street, so that psychologically, it was a devastating blow and that distrust, if you will, is still very much there. I think the attitude of the average Soviet and now Russian, towards the armed forces is colored by what happened in Afghanistan.

Interviewer: Can you talk about how the Soviet media portrayed it internally? I was told that at first they were just not able to report truly what was happening in the war in Afghanistan but then it was out of synch with people's thinking, because by then they were already a bit cynical and didn't believe the media.

Pozner: When the war began in Afghanistan it was portrayed as the Soviet Union doing its internationalist duty to come to the aid of the country. They asked for aid, and initially it was seen as a very quick thrust by the military that would end it all and everything would be fine. As the war dragged, it became clear that more and more people were dying. It also became clear that we were not being told how many people were dying. Mothers were not being told that their children had been killed, they were not allowed to bury them publicly. They were not allowed to do that. The truth about the war was being hidden from the population, and that gradually became public knowledge. I think that was another factor in eroding the belief system of the average Soviet. Now the Government was engaged in an unjust war and was lying to me, the average citizen, about what was going on there. And lying in the most horrendous way.

Interviewer: Did the image of America protesting Vietnam make Soviet people think they could protest?

Pozner: Soviet people never thought they could protest, because they knew that was terribly dangerous. Pictures, television pictures of protests in the United

States, which were put on for a propaganda effect to show that the people of the United States are against this terrible war, Imperialist war that is being waged against the people of Vietnam, in one sense worked. But in the other sense back-fired in that we looked at this, and said, "Yeah, they're against the war, and they're protesting, they don't seem to be afraid." Yeah, sometimes there are clashes with the police but it's not the same thing. People here knew that if you tried to demonstrate, you were dead meat. You'd be arrested and sent off to some camp—some Gulag place so that basically there were no protests. Whatever protests there were, were from a small group of dissidents who were immediately whisked off, either put in an insane asylum or in a prison, and that was the end of that.

Interviewer: Do you think propaganda became less and less effective? Just because you can only hit someone so many times?

Pozner: Propaganda became less and less effective inside the Soviet Union, because you cannot tell someone "Oh, we have a lot of meat" when there is no meat in the stores. You simply cannot do that. I mean you can do it. I think that probably what was described to Lincoln, "You can fool some of the people most of the time and most of the people some of the time, but you can't fool all the people all of the time" applies perfectly. Yes, some of the people were fooled most of the time and still are, and most of the people for some of the time. But then, eventually, when what was being said totally did not correspond to what I would see. There was a wonderful Soviet joke about a man who goes to see the doctor. He wants the eye-ear doctor. He is told there is no such thing, you can go and see the doctor who examines your eyes and the one who examines your ears, nose and throat, but the eye-ear doctor, why would you want that? He says well because I keep hearing one thing and seeing something completely different! That is the reflection of propaganda no longer working.

Source: Interview with Vladimir Pozner. "Episode 4: Soviet Propoganda," *Red Files*, PBS, 1999. Available online at http://www.pbs.org/redfiles/prop/deep/interv/p_int_vladimir_pozner.htm.

11.5
The Case for U.S. Intervention in Central America – 1984
An Excerpt from a Nationally Televised Address by Ronald Reagan

During the 1980s the administration of President Ronald Reagan labored mightily to topple the Sandinista government in the Central American nation of Nicaragua. President Reagan viewed the Sandinistas as part of a Communist conspiracy to convert all of Central America into a Soviet colony of sorts. In the following speech to the American public, Reagan explained his beliefs about the strategic importance of Central America to the future of the United States. He specifically praised the "Contras," a right-wing rebel orga-

nization that was trying to overthrow the Sandinistas. The Reagan adminis-
tration provided both financial assistance and military intelligence to the
Contras, which the president characterizes here as freedom fighters.

… Our diplomatic objectives will not be attained by good will and noble aspirations alone. In the last 15 years the growth of Soviet military power has meant a
radical change in the nature of the world we live in.
This does not mean, as some would have us believe,
that we're in imminent danger of nuclear war. We're
not.

> *"What we see in El Salvador is an attempt to destabilize the entire region and eventually move chaos and anarchy toward the American border."*

As long as we maintain the strategic balance
and make it more stable by reducing the level of
weapons on both sides, then we can count on the
basic prudence of the Soviet leaders to avoid that
kind of challenge to us. They are presently chal-
lenging us with a different kind of weapon: subversion and the use of surrogate forces—Cubans, for
example. We've seen it intensifying during the last
10 years as the Soviet Union and its surrogates
moved to establish control over Vietnam, Laos,
Kampuchea, Angola, Ethiopia, South Yemen, Afghanistan, and recently, closer to
home in Nicaragua and now El Salvador. It's the fate of this region, Central America, that I want to talk to you about tonight.

The issue is our effort to promote democracy and economic well-being in the
face of Cuban and Nicaraguan aggression, aided and abetted by the Soviet Union.
It is definitely not about plans to send American troops into combat in Central
America.…

The defense policy of the United States is based on a simple premise: we do
not start wars. We will never be the aggressor. We maintain our strength in order to
deter and defend against aggression—to preserve freedom and peace. We help our
friends defend themselves.

Central America is a region of great importance to the United States. And it is
so close—San Salvador is closer to Houston, Texas, than Houston is to Washington, D.C. Central America is America; it's at our doorstep. And it has become the
stage for a bold attempt by the Soviet Union, Cuba, and Nicaragua to install communism by force throughout the hemisphere.…

Right now in El Salvador, Cuban-supported aggression has forced more than
400,000 men, women, and children to flee their homes. And in all of Central
America, more than 800,000 have fled, many, if not most, living in unbelievable
hardship. Concerns about the prospect of hundreds of thousands of refugees fleeing communist oppression to seek entry into our country are well founded.

What we see in El Salvador is an attempt to destabilize the entire region and eventually move chaos and anarchy toward the American border.

As the National Bipartisan Commission on Central America, chaired by Henry Kissinger, agreed, if we do nothing or if we continue to provide too little help, our choice will be a communist Central America with additional communist military bases on the mainland of this hemisphere and communist subversion spreading southward and northward. This communist subversion poses the threat that 100 million people from Panama to the open border on our south could come under the control of pro-Soviet regimes.

If we come to our senses too late, when our vital interests are even more directly threatened, and after a lack of American support causes our friends to lose the ability to defend themselves, then the risks to our security and our way of life will be infinitely greater....

We can and must help Central America. It's in our national interest to do so; and, morally, it's the only right thing to do. But, helping means doing *enough*—enough to protect our security and enough to protect the lives of our neighbors so that they may live in peace and democracy without the threat of communist aggression and subversion....

If the communists can start war against the people of El Salvador, then El Salvador and its friends are surely justified in defending themselves by blocking the flow of arms. If the Soviet Union can aid and abet subversion in our hemisphere, then the United States has a legal right and a moral duty to help resist it. This is not only in our strategic interest; it is morally right. It would be profoundly immoral to let peace-loving friends depending on our help be overwhelmed by brute force if we have any capacity to prevent it.

But making this choice requires a commitment from all of us, our Administration, the American people, and the Congress. So far, we have not yet made that commitment. We've provided just enough aid to avoid outright disaster but not enough to resolve the crisis; so El Salvador is being left to slowly bleed to death.

Part of the problem, I suspect, is not that Central America isn't important, but that some people think our administration may be exaggerating the threat we face. Well, if that's true, let me put that issue to rest....

The Sandinista rule is a communist reign of terror. Many of those who fought alongside the Sandinistas saw their revolution betrayed; they were denied power in the new government; some were imprisoned, others exiled. Thousands who fought with the Sandinistas have taken up arms against them and are now called the *contras*. They are freedom fighters.

What the Sandinistas have done to Nicaragua is a tragedy. But we Americans must understand and come to grips with the fact that the Sandinistas are not content to brutalize their own land. They seek to export their terror to every other country in the region....

The role that Cuba has long performed for the Soviet Union is now also being played by the Sandinistas. They have become Cuba's Cubans. Weapons, supplies, and funds are shipped from the Soviet bloc to Cuba, from Cuba to Nicaragua, and from Nicaragua to the Salvadoran guerrillas....

The simple questions are: will we support freedom in this hemisphere or not? Will we defend our vital interests in this hemisphere or not? Will we stop the spread of communism in this hemisphere or not? Will we act while there is still time?

There are those in this country who would yield to the temptation to do nothing. They are the new isolationists, very much like the isolationists of the late 1930s, who knew what was happening in Europe but chose not to face the terrible challenge history had given them. They preferred a policy of wishful thinking that if they only gave up one more country, allowed just one more international transgression, then surely, sooner or later, the aggressor's appetite would be satisfied.

Well, they didn't stop the aggressors, they emboldened them. They didn't prevent war; they assured it.... It's up to all of us, the Administration, you as citizens, and your representatives in the Congress. The people of Central America can succeed if we provide the assistance I have proposed. We Americans should be proud of what we're trying to do in Central America, and proud of what, together with our friends, we can do in Central America, to support democracy, human rights, and economic growth, while preserving peace so close to home. Let us show the world that we want no hostile, communist colonies here in the Americas: South, Central, or North.

Source: Reagan, Ronald. "Address to the Nation on United States Policy in Central America," May 9, 1984. The Public Papers of President Ronald Reagan, Ronald Reagan Presidential Library. Available online at http://www.reagan.utexas.edu/archives/speeches/1984/50984h.htm.

11.6
Death of a Salvadoran Church Worker – 1985
The Text of an Article Published in Sojourners

During the 1980s the United States actively supported the El Salvadoran government in its war against a leftist guerrilla movement, even as evidence accumulated that government-sponsored "death squads" were terrorizing towns and farmhouses across the countryside. The following account, written by an American seminary student traveling in Central America, tells the story of one anonymous victim of those death squads.

I was seeking the pastor of a poor Catholic parish located somewhere on the outskirts of San Salvador. It had been a laborious search. Nobody in El Salvador, not even the most faithful of churchgoers, will tell you the name of their pastor. Not that they don't know. It is just that handing over a name to a stranger is treason in El Salvador.

But I did nail down the right pastor after a week of asking. And after he pulled his pick-up truck into the rectory, which was really a garage, we had some time to talk. We would never know last names. That was an unspoken rule. We agreed to a Tuesday morning meeting to discuss the work of the church in El Salvador. He promised to have church workers with him. I promised not to ask their names.

We had set our Tuesday appointment for 8 A.M., but when I arrived at the rectory, the assistant pastor was there alone, reading the book of Isaiah and chain-smoking non-filter cigarettes. His first words were an offer of breakfast. His eyes were weary and his face drawn. "Something terrible happened here last night," he began. "They killed one of our people—a catechist of the children. The cadaver is in the street. Father's gone to find someone to take the body away."

He didn't know where the body was. "I'm new here [in El Salvador]," he continued. "It isn't a good idea for me to go to the cadaver. I have got to say Mass for the Mothers of the Disappeared at 10 A.M. And now this...." His voice trailed off. He ran his fingers down his face. Then he lit another cigarette.

There was no need for him to explain further. The Committee of the Mothers of the Disappeared—a group started by Archbishop Oscar Romero—was considered subversive by the Salvadoran military. I knew that first hand. The week before I had been picked up by the National Police for carrying subversive material—documents of the Mother's Committee—in my pack.

I decided to search out the body myself. At the first street corner, I met a young boy selling newspapers. I asked him where the body was. He ignored me. I asked again, this time adding that I was a friend of the pastor. Without looking at me, he finally whispered, "Straight ahead."

I followed a dirt road. Houses lined one side, an empty lot with garbage on the other side. In the middle of the street, people were gathered around a station wagon.

She was there in the midst of them, lying in the back of the car. Her face was calm and relaxed. Her features were like those of the indigenous people, with soft, mocha-colored skin and thick black hair pulled back, much like my own hair. She had bled from a bullet wound above the right eye, and the blood had trickled down the side of her face. Her cotton pants had been torn from the knee down. Whether she had been macheted or machine-gunned in the knee was difficult to tell: I couldn't find the knee in the midst of this sea of blood. The crowd backed away quietly as, between my own heart beats, I took photos of the body. Then the station wagon drove her away.

"The Death of a Salvadoran Church Worker," by Terri Troia, Sojourners, March 1985. © 1985 Sojourners. Reprinted with permission.

Who was this young woman of 15 years? Was she a David who tried to slay Goliath and was met with machine-gun fire? Was she Judith trying to enter the enemy camp under cover of darkness, caught in her act? Yet this was not the ground of the enemy. This street was her barrio.

Back at the rectory, with the testimony of unnamed witnesses and church workers, a story begins to unfold. She taught communion class to the parish children. Last night the lights went out at 6 P.M. in this barrio. A squad of 12 members of the Civil Defense, a division of the Armed Forces, was patrolling the streets. At 7:30 P.M., a barrage of machine-gun fire was heard. A witness recounted that then the squad of soldiers turned the corner from the street where her body lay. There the body remained, unclaimed for 13 hours. No one touches the body of someone slain by the military in El Salvador.

And her name. No one would say her name. But in the rectory hung a memorial of those church workers slain by the military. Some of the names are familiar to us—Oscar Romero, Ita Ford, Maura Clarke, Dorothy Kazel, Jean Donovan. But many names were unfamiliar. And somehow I felt that this unspoken name had already taken its place among them.

That afternoon only one of the newspapers reported the death: "Idalia _____appeared dead of bullets that were fired last night at 7:30 P.M. in Barrio _____, when there were no lights. The death of the youth, it is said, was reported to the parochial church, anonymously."

Idalia never had a funeral. She was buried in secret, far away from her family and church. This is the fate of those murdered by the military: marked in death, as she was in life.

Neither President Reagan, nor the members of Congress who voted to continue this madness, will ever meet her. But I met Idalia in the back of a station wagon. And I know the truth that her death tells. A broken candle in the night, she was. And what in God's name are we?

Source: Troia, Terry. "Death of a Salvadoran Church Worker." *Sojourners*, March 1985.

11.7

President Reagan Assesses the Sandinistas – 1985
Excerpts from a Speech Delivered at a Fundraising Dinner for the Nicaragua Refugee Fund

One of the bedrock principles of President Ronald Reagan's foreign policy toward Central America was that the Sandinista regime in Nicaragua posed a potentially serious threat to the long-term security of the United States. As part of his efforts to bolster support for this position, Reagan and other members of his administration alleged that the Sandinistas had created a repressive police state that was contemptuous of basic human rights. Following are excerpts from a Reagan speech that focuses on these issues from April 15, 1985.

As you know, the Sandinista dictatorship has taken absolute control of the government and the armed forces. It is a Communist dictatorship. It has done what Communist dictatorships do: created a repressive state security and secret police organization assisted by Soviet, East German, and Cuban advisers; harassed, and in many cases expunged, the political opposition; and rendered the democratic freedoms of speech, press, and assembly punishable by officially sanctioned harassment and imprisonment or death.

But the Communists are not unopposed. They are facing great resistance from the people of Nicaragua, resistance from the patriots who fight for freedom and their unarmed allies from the prodemocracy movement.

There is growing evidence of Sandinista brutality. We've recently learned that ten or eleven members of the Social Christian Party have been rounded up and jailed. The Sandinistas are trying to get them to confess to being counterrevolutionaries. And you might be interested in knowing one way the Communists are coercing these confessions. They have also arrested more than a hundred relatives of the political prisoners. And according to our most recent information, the Social Christian Party members are being held in the dark in small, overheated cells. Prisoners are served meals at irregular intervals—after twelve hours, for instance, and then the next in another two. The purpose is to disorient them and wear them down. Where do they get that idea? This same method has been used against political prisoners in Cuba.

Now, we do not know the exact number of political prisoners in Nicaragua today, but we get an indication from the testimony of José Gonzalez, a former vice-president of the Social Democratic Party. Gonzalez told Pope John Paul II there were about 8,000 political prisoners in 1981. He also told the Pope the Sandinistas practice repression and torture. Gonzalez, as you know, was arrested when he returned from Rome. He left Nicaragua and now lives in exile.

But the most compelling evidence of Sandinista brutality and of why people are fleeing is the Sandinistas' scorched-earth policy. We know the Sandinistas have ordered and are carrying out the forced relocation of tens of thousands of peasants. We have reports that 20,000 peasants have been moved in the past two months from their homes to relocation camps. Peasants who have escaped call themselves hostages and call the relocation camps concentration camps. The Communists themselves had admitted they're engaged in the forced resettlement of an estimated 65,000 people. Peasants and journalists tell of entire villages, homes, stores, and churches being burnt to the ground. They tell of animals slaughtered, crops burned, and villagers taken away at gunpoint in government trucks.

Why are the Communists doing this? Massed forced relocations are a common feature of modern Communist tyrannies, but there are other purposes here. For the people of many villages are actively supporting the freedom fighters, and so the Communists have decided to put more and more of the people of Nicaragua into closely guarded pens, and that way it will be easier for the regime to stalk the freedom fighters in the countryside. A Sandinista security chief has explained, "Anyone still in the hills is a guerilla."

While all this is terrible, it can hardly come as a surprise to those who know what was done to the Miskito Indians. As you know, the Miskitos supported the Sandinistas against Somoza. But shortly after taking power, the Sandinistas attempted to indoctrinate the Miskitos in Marxist dogma, and the Indians resisted. The Sandinistas tried to put their own people in as leaders of the Miskito community, and the Indians resisted, so much that the Sandinistas labeled them "bourgeois" and, therefore, enemies of the people. They began to arrest Indian leaders. Some were murdered; some were tortured. One Miskito leader told our AFL-CIO that Tomás Borge and other leaders of the Sandinistas "came to my cell and warned me that Sandinismo would be established on the Atlantic coast even if every single Miskito Indian had to be eliminated."

Well, the Sandinistas came close. There were massacres. Eyewitnesses said some Miskitos were buried alive. Ten thousand Indians were force-marched to relocation camps. Miskito villages were burned down; they're still being burned down. Miskito villages were bombed and shelled, and they are still being bombed and shelled. In the name of humanity, these atrocities must be stopped....

Unfortunately, it's widely believed outside Nicaragua that the Sandinistas enjoy the support of the people inside, but you know this is completely untrue. We know this from many sources, even recently the American press.

A few months ago, the *New Republic* carried a report by Robert Leiken, who had long been sympathetic to the Sandinistas and who had formerly testified in Congress against aid to the *contras*. He wrote, "One of the most common means of sustaining the myth of popular support is the Sandinistas' use of the rationing system as a lever—ration cards are confiscated for nonattendance at Sandinista meetings." And talk of inflation is branded as "counterrevolutionary plot." Sympathy with the *contras*, he said, is more and more pervasive. In fact, the peasants now call them *Los Muchachos*, the affectionate term they once used exclusively for the Sandinistas. And what do they call the Sandinistas? Well, the latest worker's chant is "the Sandinistas and Somoza are the same thing."

In spite of all this, the Sandinista government retains its defenders in this country and in the West. They look at all the evidence that the Sandinistas have instituted a Communist regime: all the pictures of dictator Ortega embracing Castro and visiting Moscow, all the Soviet-bloc advisers, and all the Sandinista votes in the UN, such as their decision in line with the Soviet bloc to refuse the credentials of Israel. They look at this, and they say: "The Sandinistas aren't Communists, or aren't real Communists. Why, they're only nationalists, only socialists."

But these defenders admit there is a problem in Nicaragua. The problem they say, is the freedom fighters. Well, just a few weeks ago, the whole world was treated to a so-called independent investigation of charges that the freedom fighters have committed atrocities. It spoke of these so-called atrocities in a rather riveting manner. And the report received great attention on television and in leading newspapers and publications. The report

> *"This cruelty [of the Sandinistas] is the natural expression of a Communist government, a cruelty that flows naturally from the heart of totalitarianism."*

ignored Communist brutality, the murder of the Indians, and the arrest, torture, and murder of political dissidents. But we really shouldn't be surprised by that because, as our State Department discovered and *Time* magazine reported, this so-called independent investigation was the work of one of dictator Ortega's supporters, a sympathizer who has openly embraced Sandinismo and who was shepherded through Nicaragua by Sandinista operatives.

The truth is, there are atrocities going on in Nicaragua, but they're largely the work of the institutionalized cruelty of the Sandinista government. This cruelty is the natural expression of a Communist government, a cruelty that flows naturally from the heart of totalitarianism. The truth is Somoza was bad, but so many of the people of Nicaragua know the Sandinistas are infinitely worse.

We have here this evening many individuals who know these truths firsthand. Some of you may know of Bayardo Santaeliz. He is a twenty-nine-year-old Nicaraguan refugee and a former lay preacher of the Pentecostal Missionary Church in Nicaragua. And this is his story, a story told in sworn testimony before a Honduran civil rights commission. A few years ago, the Sandinistas began pressuring Bayardo to stop preaching and start fighting for the revolution. And one night after holding a prayer session in a home on the slopes of the Momotombo Volcano, Bayardo went to bed. He was awakened by Sandinista soldiers who asked if he was an evangelical preacher. Bayardo said yes. The Sandinistas arrested him, accused him of counterrevolutionary activity, verbally abused him, and then tied him and two others to a pillar. Then the Sandinistas doused the house with gasoline and threw in a match. The room went up in flames, but they burned the rope that bound Bayardo, and he escaped with his clothes in flames and his body burned. He hid in the countryside and was rescued by *campesinos* who got him to a hospital, where he lied about the causes of his injuries. And not long after, he left Nicaragua....

Some people say this isn't America's problem. Why should we care if Nicaragua is a democracy or not? Well, we should care for a whole host of reasons.

Democracy has its own moral imperatives, as you well know, but it also has advantages that are profoundly practical. Democratic states do not attack their neighbors and destabilize regions. Democratic states do not find it easy to declare and carry out war. Democratic states are not by their nature militaristic. Democracies are traditionally reluctant to spend a great deal of money on arms. Democratic states have built-in controls on aggressive, expansionist behavior because democratic states must first marshal wide popular support before they move.

None of these characteristics applies to totalitarian states, however. And so, totalitarian Nicaragua poses a threat to us all.

The Sandinistas have been engaged for some time in spreading their Communist revolution beyond their borders. They're providing arms, training, and a headquarters to the Communist guerillas who are attempting to overthrow the democratically elected Duarte government of El Salvador. The Sandinistas have been caught supporting similar antidemocratic movements in Honduras and Costa Rica; Guatemala, too, is threatened. If these governments fall, as Nicaragua has fallen, it will send millions of refugees north, as country after country collapses. Already, the refugee situation is building to unacceptable levels. More than a quarter of a million refugees have fled Nicaragua since the Sandinistas took control. Some weeks, a hundred Nicaraguans a day stream into Costa Rica alone. It must be noted here that many of these refugees carry no papers, register in no official camps, and wind up on no one's official list of those who've fled. They simply cross the border of one country or another and settle where they can.

And let me emphasize a very important point: These refugees are not simply people caught in the middle of a war. They're people fleeing for their lives from the Sandinista police state. They are fleeing from people who are burning down their villages, forcing them into concentration camps, and forcing their children into military service....

Some claim that the freedom fighters are simply former *Somocistas* who want to reimpose a dictatorship. That is simply not true. Listen to the roll call of their leaders: Adolpho Calero, a Nicaraguan businessman who was imprisoned by Somoza; Alfonso Robelo, a member of the original Sandinista government, now leading freedom fighters in the south; Arturo Cruz, another former member of the Sandinista government who is supporting the freedom fighters; Edén Pastora, the famed Commander Zero, a hero of the anti-Somoza revolution.

These men are not putting their lives on the line to restore a dictatorship of the past; these men are fighting for freedom. Already they control large sections of the countryside. And as for their level of support, there are now three times as many freedom fighters fighting the Sandinistas as there were Sandinistas fighting Somoza.

There are those who say America's attempt to encourage freedom in Nicaragua interferes with the right of self-determination of the Nicaraguan people. Self-determination—you wonder what the ghosts of the Miskito Indians would say to that; you wonder what the journalists who cannot print the truth and the political prisoners who cannot speak it would say about self-determination and the Sandinistas. I think they would say that when a small Communist clique seizes a country, there is no self-determination and no chance of it.

I truly believe the history of this century forces me to believe that to do nothing in Central America is to give the first Communist stronghold on the North American continent a green light to spread its poison throughout this free and increasingly democratic hemisphere.

No evil is inevitable unless we make it so. We cannot have the United States walk away from one of the greatest moral challenges in postwar history. I pledge to you that we will do everything we can to win this great struggle.

And so, we're hopeful. We will fight on. We'll win this struggle for peace. Thank you for inviting me.

Viva Nicaragua libre. Thank you, and God bless you.

Source: Reagan, Ronald. "Remarks at a Fundraising Dinner for the Nicaragua Refugee Fund," April 15, 1985. The Public Papers of President Ronald Reagan, Ronald Reagan Presidential Library. Available online at http://www.reagan.utexas.edu/archives/speeches/1985/41585f.htm.

11.8
Americas Watch Condemns U.S. Policies in Nicaragua – 1985
An Excerpt from Human Rights in Nicaragua: Reagan, Rhetoric, and Reality

In early 1985 President Ronald Reagan urged the U.S. Congress to support his administration's policies in Nicaragua. He was so adamant, in fact, that he compared the contras waging war against Nicaragua's Sandinista government to America's own founding fathers. His comparison of the contras to such American icons as Thomas Jefferson and George Washington was embraced by other supporters of the contras in the United States. But it was sharply criticized by others, including the editors of The New Yorker. *"How are the contras the moral equal of our Founding Fathers?" the editors asked in the March 25, 1985, issue of the magazine. "In days to come, when we find ourselves thinking of those men, the framers of our democracy, might we now find ourselves free-associating to images of torture and indiscrimi-*

nate murder? It's as if the president had carelessly dumped toxic waste in the very wellspring of our nation's heritage. Already the poison is leaching into the stream, irretrievably contaminating the very waters that we need to drink every day."

This negative view stemmed in large part from claims made by journalists, aid workers, and other observers operating in Nicaragua that some contra groups engaged in brutal and murderous treatment of innocents caught in the civil war. One of the world's foremost human rights organizations, Americas Watch, was one of the strongest critics. The roots of this organization were formed in 1978, when the group Helsinki Watch was established to monitor compliance with the 1975 Helsinki Accords. Over the next several years, the organization formed a number of other "watch committees"— including Americas Watch—to monitor human rights developments in other regions of the world (in 1988 these committees were combined into one group under the banner Human Rights Watch).

Americas Watch issued two reports on Nicaragua in 1985. The first, Viola-tions of the Laws of War by Both Sides in Nicaragua, 1981-1985, document-ed human rights violations by both contra and Sandinista forces. The report condemned the Sandinista government for some "major abuses," but was even more critical of contra forces that "have systematically violated the applicable laws of war throughout the conflict. They have attacked civilians indiscriminately; they have tortured and mutilated prisoners; they have murdered those placed hors de combat by their wounds; they have taken hostages; and they have committed outrages against personal dignity."

In July 1985 Americas Watch published a second report on Nicaragua that focused on Reagan Administration rhetoric attacking the Sandinista govern-ment and supporting the contras. Following is an excerpt from that report, which was titled Human Rights in Nicaragua: Reagan, Rhetoric, and Reality.

…The Reagan administration, since its inception, has characterized Nicaragua's revolutionary government as a menace to the Americas and to the Nicaraguan people. Many of its arguments to this effect are derived from human rights "data," which the administration has used in turn to justify its support for the *contra* rebels. The Americas Watch does not take a position on the U.S. geopo-litical strategy in Central America. But where human rights are concerned we find the administration's approach to Nicaragua deceptive and harmful.…

The administration has disregarded the norms of impartial human rights reporting when it deals with Nicaragua. The administration's accusations against

---

Nicaragua rest upon a core of fact; the Sandinistas have committed serious abuses, especially in 1981 and 1982, including arbitrary arrests and the summary relocation of thousands of Miskito Indians. Around the core of fact, however, U.S. officials have built an edifice of innuendo and exaggeration. The misuse of human rights data has become pervasive in officials' statements to the press, in White House handouts on Nicaragua, in the annual *Country Report* on Nicaraguan human rights prepared by the State Department, and most notably, in the president's own remarks. When inconvenient, findings of the U.S. embassy in Managua have been ignored; the same is true of data gathered by independent sources.

> *"The contras have systematically engaged in the killing of prisoners and the unarmed; ... selective attacks on civilians and indiscriminate attacks; [and] torture and other outrages against personal dignity."*

In Nicaragua there is no systematic practice of forced disappearances, extrajudicial killings, or torture—as has been the case with the "friendly" armed forces in El Salvador. While prior censorship has been imposed by emergency legislation, debate on major social and political questions is robust, outspoken, even often strident. The November 1984 elections, though deficient, were a democratic advance over the past five decades of Nicaraguan history and compare favorably with those of El Salvador and Guatemala and do not suffer significantly in comparison with those of Honduras, Mexico, or Panama. The Sandinista Party obtained a popular mandate, while the opposition parties that chose to participate secured some 30 percent of the seats in the Constituent Assembly. Nor has the government practiced elimination of cultural or ethnic groups, as the administration frequently claims; indeed in this respect, as in most others, Nicaragua's record is by no means so bad as that of Guatemala, whose government the administration consistently defends. Moreover, some notable reductions in abuses have occurred in 1982, despite the pressure caused by escalating external attacks.

The Nicaraguan government must be held to account for the abuses which continue to take place, like restrictions on press freedom and due process. But unless those abuses are fairly described, the debate on Nicaragua ceases to have meaning.

Inflammatory terms, loosely used, are of particular concern. President Reagan has described Nicaragua's elected president, Daniel Ortega, as "a little dictator" and has termed the Nicaraguan government's recent relocations of civilians a "Stalinist" tactic. Such epithets seek to prejudice public debate through distortion. Perhaps most harmful in this respect is the term most frequently used by President Reagan and administration officials to denounce the Nicaraguan government—that is, "totalitarian." This is a misuse of the term and it misrepresents the situation in Nicaragua.

… The Catholic Church and several Protestant denominations not only operate independently in Nicaragua but they are outspoken in expressing their views on religious matters and also on every conceivable secular issue; similarly, business and professional associations and labor unions are not only independent but are unhesitatingly critical of the government and its leaders. Political parties representing a wide spectrum of views not only operate, but have elected representatives who debate issues in the Constituent Assembly. The parties that chose to participate in the 1984 national elections—from which no party was banned—were free to be as strident as they chose in attacking the Sandinista Party and its leaders, and frequently exercised this right on television and radio time provided to them without cost to conduct this campaign. An independent human rights commission maintains professionally staffed offices in Managua, prints and distributes—both nationally and internationally—detailed monthly reports on human rights abuses by the government, and does not seem to circumscribe itself in denouncing those abuses. A newer human rights group operates without restraint in seeking redress for Miskito Indians who have been victims of human rights abuses.

Any Nicaraguan and any visitor to Nicaragua can walk into a score or more of offices in the country's capital and encounter the officers and employees of various independent institutions who will not only voice their opinions freely in criticism of the government and its leaders, and even challenge the legitimacy of the state, but will also do so for attribution. Some will hand out literature expressing those opinions. This is inconceivable in any state appropriately described as totalitarian. Moreover, it is inconceivable in many of the countries vigorously supported by the United States. While a visitor to nearby El Salvador, Guatemala, or Haiti, for example, may encounter criticism of the government, if it is criticism that is as strong as one regularly encounters in Nicaragua, the speaker will ordinarily request anonymity. Similarly, it is impossible to find independent institutions speaking so freely in more distant allies of the United States such as Turkey, Saudi Arabia, Indonesia, Zaire, Morocco—to name just a few.

To point out that dissent is expressed openly and robustly in Nicaragua is not to deny that many of those expressing dissent have legitimate grievances. We believe that the abuses that led to those grievances should be carefully documented and condemned vigorously.…

With respect to the human rights practices of the *contras*, we have examined the administration's claims for the moral character of these insurgents and find, to the contrary, that the *contras* have systematically engaged in the killing of prisoners and the unarmed, including medical and relief personnel; selective attacks on civilians and indiscriminate attacks; torture and other outrages against personal dignity; and the kidnappings and harassment of refugees. We find that the most violent abuses of human rights in Nicaragua today are being committed by the *contras*, and that the Reagan administration's policy of support for the *contra* is, therefore, a policy clearly inimical to human rights.

Source: Americas Watch Committee. *Human Rights in Nicaragua: Reagan, Rhetoric, and Reality*. Washington, DC: Americas Watch Committee, 1985.

11.9

Aldrich Ames, American Spy for the Soviets – 1985-1994
The Text of CIA Director John Deutch's Statement to the Senate Select Committee on Intelligence

Throughout the Cold War, espionage agents for East and West continually maneuvered for advantage. These spies engaged in a wide range of activities over this forty-year period, including assassination of enemy targets, surveillance and blackmail of political leaders and scientists, propaganda campaigns, and relentless efforts to obtain state secrets, either by outright theft or by convincing individuals to betray their country—usually for money. This long secret war, fought mainly between the KGB in the Soviet Union and the CIA in the United States, "helped make the spy thriller into the distinctive cultural genre of the period," wrote historian Martin Walker in The Cold War: A History.

One of the most infamous American citizens to engage in treasonous behavior for profit was Aldrich Ames, a longtime CIA official. Ames began passing state secrets to KGB agents in 1985, and over the next decade he revealed more than 100 secret CIA operations to his Soviet contacts. In addition, the CIA estimates that he betrayed at least 30 undercover American agents, including 10 who were later executed by the Soviet Union. Finally discovered and arrested in 1994, Ames was convicted of treason and sentenced to life in prison without parole. Following are excerpts from CIA Director John Deutch's testimony to the Senate Select Committee on Intelligence on December 7, 1995. In his testimony, Deutch offers a grim assessment of the impact of Ames's actions on American intelligence during the last years of the Cold War.

From the earliest days of the Republic, the United States has recognized the compelling need to collect intelligence by clandestine means. For much of our history, this collection could only be done by human agents. Recent technological developments have, of course, vastly increased our ability to collect intelligence. The capacity of these technical systems is awesome and our achievements are astonishing. However, these technical means can never eliminate the need for human sources of information. Often, the more difficult the target is, the greater is the need for human agents.

Throughout our history, the contribution of the clandestine service of the United States has frequently been the difference between victory and defeat, success and failure. It has saved countless American lives.

In recent years, human agents have provided vital information on military and political developments in the Soviet Union, terrorist groups, narcotics trafficking, development of weapons of mass destruction and other grave threats to the United States. These agents often provided the key piece of information that formed the United States' understanding of a critical international situation.

For decades, information from human agents inside the Soviet Union gave us vital insights into the intentions and capabilities of the Soviets. Ames clearly dealt a crushing blow to those efforts. Nonetheless, I am convinced that when the full history of the Cold War is written, American intelligence—and human intelligence in particular—will be recognized as having played an important role in winning that war.

It must be remembered that for over forty years the United States faced a hostile state with enormous nuclear power. A misstep by either side could have destroyed the world. That nuclear war did not occur and that the Soviet Union ultimately collapsed is in no small part attributable to the brave, tireless and too often thankless efforts of the clandestine intelligence service of the United States. The DCI [Department of Counter Intelligence] has a great responsibility to preserve and nurture this vital capability.

That said, it must be pointed out that while human agent operations have the potential for high gain, they also entail high risk. Human agent operations are almost always in violation of another country's laws. It is therefore imperative that they be subject to tight policy control and carried out within the scope of American law. These operations must be carried out in secret, for secrecy is vital to success.

The American public is often troubled by activities that are done in secret. This is a natural and healthy instinct. It has served our democracy extremely well for over two hundred years. However, I believe the American people understand the need for secrecy in human agent operations. They agree with a letter written by George Washington when he was Commander-in-Chief of the Continental Army in the summer of 1777:

The necessity of procuring good Intelligence is apparent & need not be further urged—All that remains for me to add is, that you keep the whole matter as secret as possible, For upon Secrecy, Success depends in Most Enterprizes of the kind, and for want of it, they are generally defeated, however well planned & promising a favorable issue.

The American people will accept secret intelligence activity only if four conditions are met. First, the acts must be consistent with announced policy goals.

Second, they must be carefully controlled under U.S. law. Third, the operations should be consistent with basic American values and beliefs. And fourth, when American intelligence services make mistakes—as we have and will surely do again—we learn from those mistakes.

Because much of what the intelligence services do is secret, Congressional oversight is the key to providing the American people the confidence that their intelligence services are meeting these four conditions. Indeed Congressional oversight is the best way this confidence can be assured.

We must not quit simply because we have made errors, even serious ones. The need for effective intelligence is too important. We must constantly learn from our mistakes, make the necessary changes, and continue to take the risks necessary to collect vital intelligence so urgently needed by the President, the Congress, and other senior policymakers....

On the 31st of October, I appeared before the House and Senate Intelligence Committees in closed sessions to describe the results of the Ames damage assessment commissioned by my predecessor, Jim Woolsey. Following that testimony, we have continued to review the report of the Damage Assessment Team (DAT) and to consult with both Committees, the Department of Defense, the Department of State and other interested agencies. Accordingly, I believe it is appropriate to report to you on our continuing review and our consultations with other agencies. I also believe it is important that additional information be made available to the American public so that they can understand the nature and extent of the damage caused by Ames.

I have attached a copy of the public statement that I issued on the 31st of October. Let me add some details on the scope of the damage.

Aldrich Ames' espionage on behalf of the Soviet Union and Russia from April 1985 through February 1994 caused severe, wide-ranging and continuing damage to US national security interests. In addition to the points that I made in my public statement on 31 October, Ames did the following:

- In June 1985, he disclosed the identity of numerous U.S. clandestine agents in the Soviet Union, at least nine of whom were executed. These agents were at the heart of our effort to collect intelligence and counterintelligence against the Soviet Union. As a result, we lost opportunities to better understand what was going on in the Soviet Union at a crucial time in history.

- He disclosed, over the next decade, the identity of many US agents run against the Soviets, and later the Russians.

- He disclosed the techniques and methods of double agent operations, details of our clandestine trade craft, communication techniques and agent validation methods. He went to extraordinary length to learn about U.S. double agent operations and pass information on them to the Soviets.

- He disclosed details about US counterintelligence activities that not only devastated our efforts at the time, but also made us more vulnerable to KGB operations against us.

- He identified CIA and other intelligence community personnel. Ames contends that he disclosed personal information on, or the identities of, only a few American intelligence officials. We do not believe that assertion.

- He provided details of US intelligence technical collection activities and analytic techniques.

- He provided finished intelligence reports, current intelligence reporting, arms control papers, and selected Department of State and Department of Defense cables. For example, during one assignment, he gave the KGB a stack of documents estimated to be 15 to 20 feet high.

Taken as a whole, Ames' activities also facilitated the Soviet, and later the Russian, effort to engage in "perception management operations" by feeding carefully selected information to the United States through agents whom they were controlling without our knowledge. Although the extent and success of this effort cannot now be determined with certainty, we know that some of this information did reach senior decisionmakers of the United States....

The combination of the loss of key human sources compromised by Ames, plus the directed information the KGB and SVR provided to the U.S. through controlled sources, had a serious impact on our ability to collect and analyze intelligence information. The DAT concluded that Ames' actions diminished our ability to understand:

- Internal Soviet development, particularly the views and actions of the hard liners with the respect to Gorbachev in the late 1980s.

- Soviet, and later Russian, foreign policy particularly Yeltsin's policies on nonproliferation and Russian involvement in the former CIS [Commonwealth of Independent States].

- The extent of the decline of Soviet and Russian military technology and procurement programs.

....I regret that I cannot discuss in public more detail about the actual damage done by Aldridge Ames. To do so would compound that damage by confirming to the Russians the extent of the damage and permit them to evaluate the success and failures of their activities. That I cannot do.

However, it is extremely important that we not underestimate the terrible damage done by Ames' treachery. It is impossible to describe the anger and sense of betrayal felt by the Intelligence Community. It reverberates to this day and has given all of us renewed motivation to do our jobs. Across the board, in all areas of intelligence activities—from collection, to counterintelligence, to security, to analysis and production, to the administrative activities that support the Community effort—we must renew our efforts to ensure that our activities are conducted with integrity, honesty, and the highest standards of professionalism. To do less is to fail.

I believe that the most important value the Intelligence Community must embrace is integrity—both personal and professional. We operate in a world of deception. It is our job to keep this nation's secrets safe and to obtain the secrets of other nations. We engage in deception to do our job and we confront deception undertaken by other nations.

But we must never let deception become a way of life. We must never deceive ourselves. Perhaps more than any other government agency, we in the CIA must have the highest standards of personal and professional integrity. We must be capable of engaging in deceptive activities directed toward other nations and groups while maintaining scrupulous honesty among ourselves and with our customers. We must not let the need for secrecy obscure the honest and accurate presentation of the intelligence we have collected or the analyses we have produced.

I believe we have approached the damage caused by Ames with honesty and integrity. We have made the hard calls. We may have to make more. We have taken the steps necessary to discipline those responsible, to reduce the likelihood of such damage recurring and to begin to restore the confidence of our customers and the American people.

As I said at the beginning of this report, clandestine human operations remain vital to this country's security. They are often the most dangerous and difficult intelligence operations to conduct. But I want to assure the Congress and the American people that the American clandestine service will continue to conduct these operations and do so in the highest tradition of integrity, courage, independence and ingenuity that have made our service the best in the world.

Source: Deutch, John. "Statement of the Director of Central Intelligence on the Clandestine Services and the Damage Caused by Aldrich Ames." *CI Reader: American Revolution into the New Millennium: A Counterintelligence Reader.* Vol. 3. Available online at http://www.ncix.gov/history/CIReaderPlain/Vol3Chap4.pdf.

12

REAGAN AND GORBACHEV:
FROM STAR WARS
TO PERESTROIKA

Soviet President Mikhail Gorbachev (left) and U.S. President Ronald Reagan
chat during their historic November 1985 summit in Geneva, Switzerland.

INTRODUCTION

Throughout his early political career and his presidency, Ronald Reagan demonstrated a deep and unswerving view of Communism as an immoral and dangerous governing philosophy. Determined to win the Cold War, he openly criticized SALT II and other arms agreements that he saw as too advantageous to the Soviets. When he entered the White House in January 1981, he was armed with a deep conviction that American military strength and preparedness had weakened over the previous decade. With that in mind, he pushed through major increases in defense spending in his first term of office. This self-described mission to revitalize the American military resulted in massive budget deficits, despite significant cutbacks in some domestic spending areas.

Reagan's rhetoric toward the Kremlin, meanwhile, was unmistakably hostile. In 1982 he told the British Parliament of his certainty that Marxism was destined for "the ash heap of history." Early the next year, he told an American evangelical group that the USSR was an "evil empire," and he described the ongoing conflict between democracy and Communism as a moral struggle between "right and wrong." Meanwhile, Reagan and his allies described the Sandinastas in Nicaragua and other leftist groups or governments around the world as agents of Moscow who were willing to "commit any crime" to advance "a one-world Socialist or Communist state."

These anti-Soviet statements greatly alarmed the USSR, which was experiencing its greatest upheaval in leadership since the 1964 ouster of Nikita Khrushchev. In November 1982 Soviet leader Leonid Brezhnev finally passed away after years of illness. He was replaced by veteran KGB spymaster Yuri Andropov. American analysts expected Andropov to adopt a hard-line approach toward the West, but instead he reached out to the United States in a number of areas. He called for new arms reduction negotiations and bans on arms sales in the Third World. He even floated the idea of developing a formal peace agreement between the Warsaw Pact nations and those of NATO. And in the domestic sphere, Andropov expressed genuine disgust with the rising level of corruption within the Communist party—and hence, the Soviet state—during the Brezhnev years.

"Star Wars"

These gestures did not sway Reagan, however. In March 1983 he rejected the principle of mutual deterrence that had long guided relations between the U.S. and the USSR. Instead, he called for billions in funding to build the Strategic Defense Initiative (SDI), an anti-missile defense network. SDI—widely known as "Star Wars"—was envisioned as a space-based defensive system capable of intercepting any nuclear missiles launched against American targets. Shrugging off questions about the cost and technical feasibility of such a system, the Reagan administration instead emphasized the benefits of such a defensive shield. It claimed that the deployment of such a satellite system would render the United States invulnerable to a Soviet nuclear attack. "What if free people could live secure in the knowledge that their security did not rest upon the threat of instant U.S. retaliation to deter a Soviet attack, that we could intercept and destroy strategic ballistic missiles before they reached our own soil or that of our allies?" said Reagan.

The proposed SDI project was controversial in the United States. Supporters praised it as bold and visionary, while detractors ridiculed it as a foolish and colossal waste of taxpayer money. Reaction in other parts of the world, meanwhile, was largely negative. America's European allies worried that if such a defensive shield were ever erected, Europe would become the primary target of Communist attacks by the Soviet Union or China. Leaders such as British Prime Minister Margaret Thatcher subsequently scrambled to convince Reagan to include all of NATO under the proposed SDI umbrella. Many critics saw this new policy as a departure from the long-time strategy of deterrence through fear of retaliation, and some viewed it as an escalation of the arms race.

Meanwhile, Moscow reacted to Reagan's SDI proposal with a mixture of fear and disbelief. Soviet leaders wondered aloud how they could possibly protect themselves from American missiles if the threat of mutually assured destruction was removed. "Engaging in this [pursuit of SDI] is not just irresponsible, it is insane," stated Andropov. "Washington's actions are putting the entire world in jeopardy."

Relations between the United States and Soviet Union reached a new low in August 1983, when a Soviet fighter plane shot down a Korean commercial airliner that had strayed deep into Soviet airspace. The incident claimed the lives of 269 passengers and crew, including 61 Americans, and it generated a firestorm of criticism from around the world. Reagan himself called it "an act of barbarism, born of a society which wantonly disregards individual rights and the value of human life." The Soviets responded defensively, falsely claiming that the plane was on a spy mission.

In the fall of 1983 the level of hostility and distrust between nations in the East and West became even more acute. Soviet negotiators walked out of arms-limitation talks after the United States planted an array of Pershing and cruise missiles in Western Europe—despite massive protests from nuclear freeze advocates in the host nations. And in early November, NATO engaged in such extensive military exercises that Soviet observers became half-convinced that the United States was planning an actual nuclear attack on the USSR. Fighter jet squadrons and missile bases were put on heightened alert in the Soviet Union and East Germany, and Kremlin officials spent several tense days awaiting word as to whether World War Three had begun. Some officials even argued for a pre-emptive nuclear strike against the United States.

Moscow gradually recognized that the NATO exercises were not a prelude to nuclear attack. But when word of the Soviet reaction to the exercises reached Washington, it forced policymakers to take a hard look at the image America was conveying to the USSR. Clearly, the Soviet Union had become rattled by Washington's hostile rhetoric. At the same time, political strategists in the Reagan White House warned that public doubts about the administration's foreign policy and military priorities posed a potential threat to the president's re-election prospects.

From this point forward, the Reagan administration used more conciliatory language toward Moscow. This new tone endured even after Reagan defeated Democratic nominee Walter Mondale for another four-year term in November 1984. Less than two weeks after the election, Reagan stated in a nationally televised speech that "if Soviet youth could attend American schools and universities, they could learn firsthand ... that we do not wish the Soviet people any harm.... They would learn that we're all God's children, with much in common."

Washington's shift toward a more diplomatic, conciliatory tone coincided with an historic changing of the guard at the Kremlin. On February 9, 1984, Andropov died after only fifteen months at the Soviet helm. He was replaced four days later as general secretary by Konstantin Chernenko, a conservative bureaucrat in the Brezhnev mold. Hampered by old age and illness from the moment he took office, Chernenko's reign was brief. His death on March 10, 1985, paved the way for another Soviet leader to stride into the global spotlight. But this new general secretary, Mikhail Gorbachev, was unlike any of the men who had ruled the USSR in decades past.

Gorbachev Takes the Stage

Dynamic, sophisticated, and self-assured, Gorbachev was at the forefront of a legion of reform-minded party officials who had blossomed within the vast Communist party machinery over the previous quarter-century. The sensibilities of this new generation of leaders had been forged during the "thaw" years of the Khrushchev era. Their views had been further sharpened during the Brezhnev era, when the Kremlin leadership seemed oblivious to the economic stagnation, government corruption, and social dislocation afflicting the Soviet state.

When Gorbachev took power in 1985, he acted immediately on his deep conviction that the future of the Communist Soviet Union depended on the successful introduction of major and wide-reaching economic and political reforms. At first he proceeded carefully. He knew that the Communist Party was still full of conservative hard-liners who opposed any attempts to change the corrupt system that had enabled them to lead privileged lives. With this in mind, Gorbachev cloaked his calls for reform in reassuring and patriotic terms.

Even so, Gorbachev made it clear that a new era was at hand. Flanked by allies such as foreign minister Eduard Shevardnadze, Boris Yeltsin, and Alexander Yakovlev, he unveiled the concepts that would become the centerpieces of his governing vision: *glasnost* (openness) and *perestroika* (societal reconstruction or restructuring). Over the ensuing months, Gorbachev initiated a series of modest economic reforms, orchestrated high-profile prosecutions of corrupt party officials (including Brezhnev's son-in-law), and allocated money for new social services. In addition, he gave reformers the cover they needed to throw light on some of the darkest days of Soviet history. "With each week another taboo fell to the floor," wrote David Remnick in *Lenin's Tomb*. "One day it was all right to know that Stalin was 'rude,' as Lenin put it in his last testament; then it was all right to know he had slaughtered millions during the collectivization of Ukraine."

The twin forces of glasnost and perestroika had an intoxicating effect on people throughout the Soviet empire. Books and articles demanding new political freedoms and economic reforms appeared all across the Soviet Union and the Eastern bloc. And for the first time in their lives, people of the East found themselves able to engage in honest discussions about the essence and character of the Communist system under which they lived.

The United States watched all of these developments with undisguised fascination. The Reagan administration was still not quite sure what to make of Gorbachev, but when the Soviet leader proposed new arms control talks, Reagan accepted the offer. Gorbachev made this overture because he recognized that the arms race with the West was crippling the Soviet empire. Spending on defense consumed as much as half of the Soviet Union's annual gross national product every year, and the state was starving itself of the funds it needed to modernize its economy and improve its citizens' standard of living. Ending the military rivalry with the United States, then, was one of Gorbachev's top priorities.

The Reagan-Gorbachev Summits

The first meeting between Reagan and Gorbachev took place in Geneva in November 1985. This encounter got off to a chilly start, but by the time the parties left for their respective homes the two men had established a certain comfort level with each other. Over the next few months, Gorbachev proposed a variety of schemes to reduce U.S. and Soviet nuclear stockpiles and missile bases. The United States was noncommittal on these proposals.

In October 1986 Reagan and Gorbachev met again, this time at Reykjavik, Iceland. During this remarkable summit, Gorbachev stunned Reagan and his staff by proposing massive reductions in virtually every area of strategic arms. Once the Americans adjusted to the magnitude of what the Soviet leader was proposing, they warmed to the task. As the summit continued, Reagan and Secretary of State George Schultz reached agreement with Gorbachev on a host of major issues, from a complete withdrawal of intermediate-range missiles from Europe to total elimination of all ballistic missiles over a ten-year period. Gorbachev then pledged dramatic cuts in Soviet conventional forces in exchange for meaningful cuts in nuclear delivery systems and tactical nuclear weapons. "For a day and a half, Gorbachev and I made progress on arms reduction that even now seems breathtaking," recalled Reagan. "George [Schultz] and I couldn't believe what was happening. We were getting amazing agreements. As the day went on, I felt something momentous was occurring."

The Reykjavik summit ended in disappointing fashion when the two sides failed to find common ground on SDI. Gorbachev wanted the United States to scrap the program—or at least dramatically curtail the scope of the research—but Reagan refused to yield on this point. The impasse over SDI made it impossible for negotiators to finalize the other agreements that had been discussed. Nevertheless, neither leader was willing to describe the summit as a failure. Reagan asserted that "the significance of that meeting in Reykjavik is not that we didn't sign agreements in the end; the significance is that we got as close as we did." And years later, Gorbachev wrote in *Perestroika* that "Reykjavik marked a turning point in world history. It tangibly demonstrated that the world could be improved."

405

Gorbachev and Reagan returned to the bargaining table in 1987. By this time, the U.S. Congress had made deep cuts in funding for SDI and prohibited any tests of the system in space. With SDI out of the way as a bargaining issue, the two sides resurrected the arms control agreements that had been discussed at Reykjavik. In December 1987 Reagan and Gorbachev signed the Intermediate Nuclear Forces Treaty, which called for both nations to remove all medium and short-range nuclear missiles from Europe. Both men expressed great pride in the historic treaty, which marked the first time in the atomic era that an entire class of nuclear weapons had been eliminated. Gorbachev, for example, described the treaty as a "sapling" that he hoped would "one day grow into a mighty tree of peace."

In the spring of 1988 the intriguing relationship that had developed between Reagan and Gorbachev took yet another turn. After the Soviet Union announced that it intended to withdraw its troops from Afghanistan, Reagan led an American delegation to a superpower summit in Moscow. The summit did not produce any significant arms control agreements—despite a flurry of wide-reaching proposals from the Soviet leader—but Gorbachev and Reagan exchanged warm and seemingly heartfelt declarations of friendship and mutual respect. At one point Reagan even said that the USSR was no longer an evil empire, explaining that "I was talking about another time and another era."

Reaction to Gorbachev's Reforms

From 1985 to 1988, Gorbachev's efforts to reform and revitalize the Soviet state made him a star in the West. Most Western media outlets gave him rapturous reviews, and *Time* magazine even named him its "Man of the Year" for 1987. Back at home, though, Gorbachev was operating in a turbulent political environment that he later compared to a "lake of gasoline."

By mid-1987 Gorbachev's domestic reforms and arms control initiatives had aroused the anger of a large cross-section of the Soviet and party bureaucracy. Some opponents viewed Gorbachev's reforms as a betrayal of Communist principles, while others knew that the changes threatened their privileged position in the Soviet empire. The growing opposition to his policies led Gorbachev to slow the pace of change. This, in turn, brought angry rebukes from maverick reformers like Boris Yeltsin, who wanted to accelerate the implementation of glasnost and perestroika.

Gorbachev's high-wire political balancing act was made even more complicated by the forces that he had helped unleash. "The more Gorbachev reformed the system, the more he destabilized it," wrote scholar Martin Walker in *The Cold War:*

A History. "The more he convinced the West that the Soviet Union was genuinely ready to accept perestroika in the Eastern European empire, the less he was able to control events there. Gorbachev's hesitant efforts to reform the Soviet economy, which were easily nullified by an entrenched, baffled and suspicious bureaucracy, led to a growing imbalance between the soaring political hopes in the Soviet Union, and the creeping despair about the economy."

Ultimately, however, Gorbachev's belief that his nation's troubled Communist system could only be saved through major surgery led him to forge ahead. On December 7, 1988, the Soviet leader delivered an historic speech to the United Nations General Assembly in New York City. Proclaiming that "freedom of choice is a universal principle to which there should be no exceptions," he urged all nations to forsake military confrontation in favor of a new era of international cooperation. He then backed up this call by announcing drastic cuts to the Soviet military, including the removal of most Soviet troops and arms from Eastern Europe. Gorbachev's UN speech—judged by the *Washington Post* to be "as remarkable as any ever delivered at the United Nations"—set the stage for 1989, the so-called "Year of Miracles" in Eastern Europe.

DOCUMENTS

12.1
President Reagan Describes the Soviet Union as an "Evil Empire" – 1983
Excerpts from a Speech to the National Association of Evangelicals

Throughout Ronald Reagan's political career, he voiced deep distrust of Soviet leaders and international Communism. These feelings remained one of the pillars of his foreign policy views when he moved into the White House in Washington, D.C. in January 1981. During Reagan's first term as president, he continued to speak of Communism in general and the Soviet Union in particular in harshly negative terms. One particularly noteworthy example of this rhetoric came on March 8, 1983, when Reagan delivered a speech at the Annual Convention of the National Association of Evangelicals in Orlando, Florida. Reagan spent much of the speech discussing his religious faith and his opposition to legalized abortion. But the latter part of his address was devoted to the Soviet empire, which he bluntly condemned as "evil."

.… During my first press conference as President, in answer to a direct question, I pointed out that, as good Marxist-Leninists, the Soviet leaders have openly and publicly declared that the only morality they recognize is that which will further their cause, which is world revolution. I think I should point out I was only quoting Lenin, their guiding spirit, who said in 1920 that they repudiate all morality that proceeds from supernatural ideas—that's their name for religion—or ideas that are outside class conceptions. Morality is entirely subordinate to the interests of class war. And everything is moral that is necessary for the annihilation of the old, exploiting social order and for uniting the proletariat.

Well, I think the refusal of many influential people to accept this elementary fact of Soviet doctrine illustrates an historical reluctance to see totalitarian powers for what they are. We saw this phenomenon in the 1930s. We see it too often today.

This doesn't mean that we should isolate ourselves and refuse to seek an understanding with them. I intend to do everything I can to persuade them of our peaceful intent, to remind them that it was the West that refused to use its nuclear monopoly in the forties and fifties for territorial gain and which now proposes 50-percent cuts in strategic ballistic missiles and the elimination of an entire class of land-based, intermediate-range nuclear missiles.

At the same time, however, they must be made to understand we will never compromise our principles and standards. We will never give away our freedom. We will never abandon our belief in God. And we will never step searching for a genuine peace. But we can assure none of these things America stands for through the so-called nuclear freeze solutions proposed by some. The truth is that a freeze now would be a very dangerous fraud, for that is merely the illusion of peace. The reality is that we must find peace through strength....

A freeze would reward the Soviet Union for its enormous and unparalleled military buildup. It would prevent the essential and long overdue modernization of United States and allied defenses and would leave our aging forces increasingly vulnerable. And an honest freeze would require extensive prior negotiations on the systems and numbers to be limited and on the measures to ensure effective verification and compliance. And the kind of a freeze that has been suggested would be virtually impossible to verify. Such a major effort would divert us completely from our current negotiations on achieving substantial reductions.

A number of years ago, I heard a young father, a very prominent young man in the entertainment world, addressing a tremendous gathering in California. It was during the time of the cold war, and communism and our own way of life were very much on people's minds. And he was speaking to that subject. And suddenly, though, I heard him saying, "I love my little girls more than anything –" And I said to myself, "Oh, no, don't. You can't—don't say that." But I had underestimated him. He went on: "I would rather see my little girls die now, still believing in God, than have them grow up under communism and one day die no longer believing in God."

There were thousands of young people in that audience. They came to their feet with shouts of joy. They had instantly recognized the profound truth in what he had said, with regard to the physical and the soul and what was truly important.

Yes, let us pray for the salvation of all of those who live in that totalitarian darkness—pray that they will discover the joy of knowing God. But until they do, let us be aware that while they preach the supremacy of the state, declare its omnipotence over individual man, and predict its eventual domination of all people's on the Earth, they are the focus of evil in the modern world....

So, I urge you to speak out against those who would place the United States in a position of military and moral inferiority.... In your discussions of the nuclear freeze proposals, I urge you to beware the temptation of pride—the temptation of blithely declaring yourselves above it all and label both sides equally at fault, to ignore the facts of history and the aggressive impulses of an evil empire, to simply call the arms race a giant misunderstanding and thereby remove yourself from the struggle between right and wrong and good and evil....

Source: Reagan, Ronald. "Remarks at the Annual Convention of the National Association of Evangelicals in Orlando, Florida" March 8, 1983. The Public Papers of President Ronald Reagan, Ronald Reagan Presidential Library. Available online at http://www.reagan.utexas.edu/archives/speeches/1983/30883b.htm.

12.2
Kremlin Fears of an American Nuclear Strike – 1983
Excerpts from In Confidence, *by Anatoly Dobrynin*

During Ronald Reagan's first term as president of the United States, he urged huge investments in new missile systems and bomber programs. He also made a series of threatening and condemnatory statements about the Soviet Union, including his famous remark that the USSR was an "evil empire." This rhetoric, combined with the dramatic upswing in U.S. defense spending, led many Kremlin politicians and analysts to wonder whether Reagan might be capable of launching an unprovoked nuclear attack on the Soviet Union. In the following excerpt from his memoir In Confidence, *Soviet ambassador Anatoly Dobrynin confirms that Soviet fears of an American nuclear attack increased dramatically during Reagan's first years in office.*

One of the elements of Reagan's rhetoric was his air of injured innocence about whether the United States posed a military threat to the Soviet Union. Could anyone even imagine that the United States could launch a nuclear attack on the Soviet Union? ...

I can testify that the possibility of a nuclear war with the United States was considered seriously indeed by Khrushchev, Brezhnev, Andropov, and Konstantin Chernenko, who was the last leader of the old school. All these leaders and their associates proceeded from the assumption that the United States did pose a real military threat to our country's security in the long term. Hence our military planning was keyed to an overwhelming strategy of defense based on the possibility of retaliating by inflicting unacceptable damage. But with the probable exception of Andropov, they did not believe an attack could take place unexpectedly at any moment, like Hitler's attack on the Soviet Union or the Japanese attack on Pearl Harbor in 1941. Such apprehensions were minor on our side, because we knew that the existing political and social structure of the United States was the best guarantee against an unprovoked first strike against us. We knew that the two superpowers had no history of confrontations that led to military clashes, with the possible exception of the Cuban crisis of 1962, and that crisis itself helped define the limits that actually prevented open warfare. In any case I personally never believed that any president was ever planning a nuclear attack on the Soviet Union; this conviction settled in me as I lived for years in the United States.

Moscow's apprehension of military confrontation grew less out of the fear of sneak attack that seems to sit in the American historic consciousness and more from what happened in Cuba—some tense political conflict that might develop and escalate unpredictably at some unforeseen time in the future. Considering the continuous political and military rivalry and tension between the two superpowers, and an adventurous president such as Reagan, there was no lack of concern in Moscow that American bellicosity and simple human miscalculation could combine with fatal results. Andropov once said to me in a very private conversation: "Reagan is unpredictable. You should expect anything from him." All in all, the Kremlin leaders took Reagan seriously—perhaps far more so than he took his own antics—and they therefore watched him with increasing vigilance. Our intelligence services were also more on alert than during other presidencies to pick up any advance signals of U.S. military action.

> *"If you had been able to poll the Soviet populace at that time and asked who they thought was more likely to push the nuclear button first—Brezhnev and Andropov or Reagan, the answer would probably have been practically unanimous—Reagan."*

While still head of the KGB, Andropov did believe that the Reagan administration was actively preparing for war, and he was joined in this belief by Ustinov, the defense minister. They persuaded the Politburo to approve the largest peacetime military intelligence operation in Soviet history, known by its code name of Operation Ryon, an acronym of the Russian words *Raketno-Yadernoye Napadenie*—Nuclear Missile Attack. In 1983 all KGB residents received urgent and detailed instructions to collect any evidence of plans for an American first strike. Only in the following year, when Reagan's policy began to turn, did Moscow give a less paranoid interpretation to the evil empire, Star Wars, and the like. The Foreign Ministry did not inform our ambassadors about this operation, leaving it to the KGB. I learned about it from the KGB resident in Washington. We both remained skeptical but he forwarded what he could get (mostly rumors and guesses) to Moscow.

The Soviet political leadership and military high command felt they had no choice but to reckon with the possibility of a nuclear war because they were certain that a serious military conflict between the Soviet Union and the United States, if it ever were to happen, would inevitably lead to the use of nuclear weapons. For all their patriotic propaganda, they did not really believe that a nuclear war might be winnable, and they profoundly hoped that the supreme military leadership in Washington believed as they did. But they were by no means confident that their potential opponents really felt the same way, and the incessant American attempts to attain strategic superiority made them fear otherwise. Hence our determination to make irreversible the nuclear parity we had achieved.

The American public reacted to the threat of nuclear war somewhat more strongly than the Soviet people; Americans were continuously reminded of it by the mass media and Hollywood reveling in the horrors of nuclear war. But the Soviet people experienced a deeper and persistent feeling of danger, having personally endured terrible suffering during World War II. If you had been able to poll the Soviet populace at that time and asked who they thought was more likely to push the nuclear button first—Brezhnev and Andropov or Reagan, the answer would probably have been practically unanimous—Reagan. If you asked the same question of the American people, most would have said Brezhnev—but more than a few would have been just as apprehensive about their own president. That certainly was my impression, and although I never took any poll I talked to plenty of Americans.

A prime and literally strategic example of this anxiety was provided by Marshall Sergei Akhromeyev, the chief of the General Staff of the Soviet Army during the 1980s. He was one of the most intelligent and knowledgeable military leaders I knew, and impressed his opposite numbers in the Pentagon when he later visited the United States. During one of my visits to Moscow ... I asked the marshall to give me a short summary of our military situation vis-à-vis the United States. He ran his pointer along our borders, particularly in the West where the Soviet Union was close to the NATO countries. In this sector, he said as he pointed, we had enough forces, but in another we needed three or four divisions for reinforcements and additional fortifications would have to be built. At some points our forces ought to be reinforced with tanks, aircraft, mechanized infantry, and so forth. "You can't do that overnight," he said, "and we are short of funds. We'll have to ask the Politburo again. The General Staff believes we should be prepared along all our lines."

I asked him straight out, "Do you indeed believe the United States and NATO could attack us some day?"

"It's not my mission to believe, or not to believe," he replied emphatically. "I can't depend on you diplomats and all your conferences or whatever you call them. You seem to agree with Washington on some point today, but a new outbreak of hostility in the world or in Soviet-American relations tomorrow can put the clock back to the time of the Cold War or even cause a military conflict. Suffice it to remember the Arab-Israeli conflict of 1973, when the United States put its armed forces on high combat alert against us. Incidentally, that happened in the period of détente under Nixon. Now, does President Reagan inspire more confidence? That is why my motto as chief of General Staff is 'National military security along all azimuths.' We proceed from the worst conceivable scenario of having to fight the United States, its West European allies, and probably Japan. We must be prepared for any kind of war with any kind of weapon. Soviet military doctrine can be summed up as follows: 1941 shall never be repeated."

... I have no doubt that our marshall's American counterparts in the Pentagon also proceeded from "the worst conceivable scenario." One can hardly imagine what would have happened to humanity if these scenarios had actually been played out, although Thomas Watson, who served as U.S. Ambassador to Moscow, confided to me that he once looked into the American military mind and found it similarly bleak.

When Watson headed IBM, President Carter asked him to serve on a panel of American industrialists studying American preparedness for nuclear war. They studied all aspects of the U.S. nuclear triad and the command structure of the Pentagon. At the final meeting with the Pentagon generals, he asked them to tell his group how they would wage a nuclear war against the Soviet Union. With huge maps and lighted charts lining the walls, they showed him more than a thousand targets on Soviet territory marked for destruction during the first hours of war. Soviet casualties would be more than one hundred million.

"And what about our casualties?" Watson asked.

They replied that about eighty million Americans and many major industries would be destroyed, just as in the Soviet Union.

"And what would you do after almost everything was destroyed?" Watson persisted.

The generals looked at each other and did not have much to say.

Several days later Watson presented his report to the president with the principal conclusion that questions of nuclear war should not be left to generals. They could wage such a war, he explained, but they do not consider it their business to be concerned about what humanity—or what would be left of it—would do afterward.

Source: Dobrynin, Anatoly. *In Confidence: Moscow's Ambassador to America's Six Cold War Presidents.* New York: Crown, 1995.

12.3

President Reagan Condemns the Soviet Attack on a Korean Jetliner – 1983
Reagan's Remarks to Reporters

Relations between the leadership of the Soviet Union and the administration of U.S. President Ronald Reagan deteriorated badly during Reagan's first term in office. One of the causes for their strained relations was Reagan's proposed Strategic Defense Initiative (SDI), a defensive missile shield that would make the United States invulnerable to Soviet nuclear missiles. Another factor was an incident that occurred on September 1, 1983. A Soviet fighter plane shot down a Korean commercial airliner—Korean Air Lines flight 007—that had accidentally slipped into Soviet airspace during a flight from

Anchorage, Alaska. The incident claimed the lives of 269 passengers and crew, including 61 Americans. By all accounts, Reagan saw the tragedy as clear evidence that the Soviet system and leadership were morally bankrupt.

Reagan was vacationing at his ranch outside Santa Barbara, California, when the shooting took place. During his return to Washington, DC, on September 2, 1983, he made the following statement to reporters at Point Mugu Naval Air Station in California.

… Now, in the wake of the barbaric act committed yesterday by the Soviet regime against a commercial jetliner [Korean Air Lines flight 007], the United States and many other countries of the world made clear and compelling statements that expressed not only our outrage but also our demand for a truthful accounting of the facts.

Our first emotions are anger, disbelief, and profound sadness. While events in Afghanistan and elsewhere have left few illusions about the willingness of the Soviet Union to advance its interests through violence and intimidation, all of us had hoped that certain irreducible standards of civilized behavior, nonetheless, obtained. But this event shocks the sensibilities of people everywhere. The tradition in a civilized world has always been to offer help to mariners and pilots who are lost or in distress on the sea or in the air. Where human life is valued, extraordinary efforts are extended to preserve and protect it, and it's essential that as civilized societies, we ask searching questions about the nature of regimes where such standards do not apply.

Beyond these emotions the world notes that stark contrast that exists between Soviet words and deeds. What can we think of a regime that so broadly trumpets its vision of peace and global disarmament and yet so callously and quickly commits a terrorist act to sacrifice the lives of innocent human beings? What could be said about Soviet credibility when they so flagrantly lie about such a heinous act? What can be the scope of legitimate and mutual discourse with a state whose values permit such atrocities? And what are we to make of a regime which establishes one set of standards for itself and another for the rest of humankind?

We've joined in the call for an urgent United Nations Security Council meeting today. The brutality of this act should not be compounded through silence or the cynical distortion of the evidence now at hand. And tonight I shall be meeting with my advisors to conduct a formal review of this matter, and this weekend I shall be meeting with the congressional leadership.

To the families of all those on the ill-fated aircraft, we send our deepest sympathy, and I hope they know our prayers are with them all.

Source: Reagan, Ronald. "Remarks to Reporters on the Soviet Attack on a Korean Civilian Airliner," September 2, 1983. The Public Papers of Ronald Reagan, Ronald Reagan Presidential Library. Available online at http://www.reagan.utexas.edu/archives/speeches/1983/90283c.htm.

12.4

Reagan Assesses the Geneva Summit with Gorbachev – 1985
The Text of Nationally Televised Address Before a Joint Session of Congress

The first of the historic summit meetings between U.S. President Ronald Reagan and Soviet Premier Mikhail Gorbachev took place in November 1985 in Geneva, Switzerland. This meeting did not produce any significant arms control agreements, but it was an important step in helping to develop the relationship, for it planted seeds of mutual trust and respect that would flourish in subsequent meetings. After returning to Washington after the Geneva meeting, Reagan offered the following assessment of the trip in a nationally televised speech before a joint session of Congress on November 21, 1985.

.… I guess you know that I have just come from Geneva and talks with General Secretary Gorbachev.… I can't claim that we had a meeting of the minds on such fundamentals as ideology or national purpose, but we understand each other better, and that's a key to peace. I gained a better perspective; I feel he did, too. It was a constructive meeting; so constructive, in fact, that I look forward to welcoming Mr. Gorbachev to the United States next year. And I have accepted his invitation to go to Moscow the following year. We arranged that out in the parking lot. I found Mr. Gorbachev to be an energetic defender of Soviet policy. He was an eloquent speaker and a good listener.

Our subject matter was shaped by the facts of this century. These past 40 years have not been an easy time for the West or for the world. You know the facts; there is no need to recite the historical record. Suffice it to say that the United States cannot afford illusions about the nature of the U.S.S.R. We cannot assume that their ideology and purpose will change; this implies enduring competition. Our task is to assure that this competition remains peaceful. With all that divides us, we cannot afford to let confusion complicate things further. We must be clear with each other and direct. We must pay each other the tribute of candor.

When I took the oath of office for the first time, we began dealing with the Soviet Union in a way that was more realistic than in, say, the recent past. And so, in a very real sense, preparations for the summit started not months ago, but 5 years ago when, with the help of Congress, we began strengthening our economy, restoring our national will, and rebuilding our defenses and alliances. America is once again strong, and our strength has given us the ability to speak with confidence and see that no true opportunity to advance freedom and peace is lost. We must not now abandon policies that work. I need your continued support to keep America strong.

That is the history behind the Geneva summit, and that is the context in which it occurred. And may I add that we were especially eager that our meetings give a push to important talks already underway on reducing nuclear weapons. On this subject it would be foolish not to go the extra mile or, in this case, the extra 4,000 miles. We discussed the great issues of our time. I made clear before the first meeting that no question would be swept aside, no issue buried, just because either side found it uncomfortable or inconvenient. I brought these questions to the summit and put them before Mr. Gorbachev.

We discussed nuclear arms and how to reduce them. I explained our proposals for equitable, verifiable, and deep reductions. I outlined my conviction that our proposals would make not just for a world that feels safer, but one that really is safer. I am pleased to report tonight that General Secretary Gorbachev and I did make a measure of progress here. We have a long way to go, but we're still heading in the right direction. We moved arms control forward from where we were last January, when the Soviets returned to the table. We are both instructing our negotiators to hasten their vital work. The world is waiting for results.

Specifically, we agreed in Geneva that each side should move to cut offensive nuclear arms by 50 percent in appropriate categories. In our joint statement we called for early progress on this, turning the talks toward our chief goal—offensive reductions. We called for an interim accord on intermediate-range nuclear forces, leading, I hope, to the complete elimination of this class of missiles—and all of this with tough verification. We also made progress in combating, together, the spread of nuclear weapons, an arms control area in which we've cooperated effectively over the years.

We are also opening a dialog on combating the spread and use of chemical weapons, while moving to ban them altogether. Other arms control dialogs—in Vienna on conventional forces and in Stockholm on lessening the chances for surprise attack in Europe—also received a boost. And finally, we agreed to begin work on risk reduction centers, a decision that should give special satisfaction to Senators Nunn and Warner who so ably promoted this idea.

I described our Strategic Defense Initiative, our research effort, that envisions the possibility of defensive systems which could ultimately protect all nations against the danger of nuclear war. This discussion produced a very direct exchange of views. Mr. Gorbachev insisted that we might use a strategic defense system to put offensive weapons into space and establish nuclear superiority. I made it clear that SDI has nothing to do with offensive weapons; that, instead, we are investigating nonnuclear defense systems that would only threaten offensive missiles, not people. If our research succeeds, it will bring much closer the safer, more stable world that we seek. Nations could defend themselves against missile attack and mankind, at long last, [could] escape the prison of mutual terror. And this is my dream.

So, I welcomed the chance to tell Mr. Gorbachev that we are a nation that defends, rather than attacks; that our alliances are defensive, not offensive. We don't seek nuclear superiority. We do not seek a first-strike advantage over the

417

Soviet Union. Indeed, one of my fundamental arms control objectives is to get rid of first-strike weapons altogether. This is why we've proposed a 50-percent reduction in the most threatening nuclear weapons, especially those that could carry out a first strike.

I went further in expressing our peaceful intentions. I described our proposal in the Geneva negotiations for a reciprocal program of open laboratories in strategic defense research. We're offering to permit Soviet experts to see firsthand that SDI does not involve offensive weapons. American scientists would be allowed to visit comparable facilities of the Soviet strategic defense program, which, in fact, has involved much more than research for many years. Finally, I reassured Mr. Gorbachev on another point. I promised that if our research reveals that a defense against nuclear missiles is possible, we would sit down with our allies and the Soviet Union to see how together we could replace all strategic ballistic missiles with such a defense, which threatens no one.

We discussed threats to the peace in several regions of the world. I explained my proposals for a peace process to stop the wars in Afghanistan, Nicaragua, Ethiopia, Angola, and Cambodia—those places where insurgencies that speak for the people are pitted against regimes which obviously do not represent the will or the approval of the people. I tried to be very clear about where our sympathies lie; I believe I succeeded. We discussed human rights. We Americans believe that history teaches no clearer lesson than this: Those countries which respect the rights of their own people tend, inevitably, to respect the rights of their neighbors. Human rights, therefore, is not an abstract moral issue; it is a peace issue. Finally, we discussed the barriers to communication between our societies, and I elaborated on my proposals for real people-to-people contacts on a wide scale. Americans should know the people of the Soviet Union—their hopes and fears and the facts of their lives. And citizens of the Soviet Union need to know of America's deep desire for peace and our unwavering attachment to freedom.

As you can see, our talks were wide ranging. And let me at this point tell you what we agreed upon and what we didn't. We remain far apart on a number of issues, as had to be expected. However, we reached agreement on a number of matters, and as I mentioned, we agreed to continue meeting, and this is important and very good. There's always room for movement, action, and progress when people are talking to each other instead of about each other.

We've concluded a new agreement designed to bring the best of America's artists and academics to the Soviet Union. The exhibits that will be included in this exchange are one of the most effective ways for the average Soviet citizen to learn about our way of life. This agreement will also expand the opportunities for Americans to experience the Soviet people's rich cultural heritage, because their artists and academics will be coming here. We've also decided to go forward with a number of people-to-people initiatives that will go beyond greater contact, not only between the political leaders of our two countries but our respective students, teachers, and others as well. We have emphasized youth exchanges. And this will help break down stereotypes, build friendships, and, frankly, provide an alternative to propaganda....

All of these steps are part of a long-term effort to build a more stable relationship with the Soviet Union. No one ever said it could be easy, but we've come a long way. As for Soviet expansionism in a number of regions of the world—while there is little chance of immediate change, we will continue to support the heroic efforts of those who fight for freedom. But we have also agreed to continue, and to intensify, our meetings with the Soviets on this and other regional conflicts and to work toward political solutions.

We know the limits as well as the promise of summit meetings. This is, after all, the 11th summit of the postwar era and still the differences endure. But we believe continued meetings between the leaders of the United States and the Soviet Union can help bridge those differences. The fact is, every new day begins with possibilities; it's up to us to fill it with the things that move us toward progress and peace. Hope, therefore, is a realistic attitude and despair an uninteresting little vice.

And so, was our journey worthwhile? Well, 30 years ago, when Ike, President Eisenhower, had just returned from a summit in Geneva, he said, " ... the wide gulf that separates so far East and West is wide and deep." Well, today, three decades later, that is still true. But, yes, this meeting was worthwhile for both sides. A new realism spawned the summit. The summit itself was a good start, and now our byword must be: steady as we go. I am, as you are, impatient for results. But good will and good hopes do not always yield lasting results, and quick fixes don't fix big problems. Just as we must avoid illusions on our side, so we must dispel them on the Soviet side. I have made it clear to Mr. Gorbachev that we must reduce the mistrust and suspicions between us if we are to do such things as reduce arms, and this will take deeds, not words alone. And I believe he is in agreement.

Where do we go from here? Well, our desire for improved relations is strong. We're ready and eager for step-by-step progress. We know that peace is not just the absence of war. We don't want a phony peace or a frail peace. We didn't go in pursuit of some kind of illusory detente. We can't be satisfied with cosmetic improvements that won't stand the test of time. We want real peace.

As I flew back this evening, I had many thoughts. In just a few days families across America will gather to celebrate Thanksgiving. And again, as our forefathers who voyaged to America, we traveled to Geneva with peace as our goal and freedom as our guide. For there can be no greater good than the quest for peace and no finer purpose than the preservation of freedom. It is 350 years since the first Thanksgiving, when Pilgrims and Indians huddled together on the edge of an unknown continent. And now here we are gathered together on the edge of an unknown future, but, like our forefathers, really not so much afraid, but full of hope and trusting in God, as ever.

Thank you for allowing me to talk to you this evening, and God bless you all.

Source: Reagan, Ronald. "Address Before a Joint Session of Congress Following the Soviet-United States Summit Meeting in Geneva," November 21, 1985. The Public Papers of President Ronald Reagan, Ronald Reagan Presidential Library. Available online at www.reagan.utexas.edu/archives/speeches/1985/112185c.htm.

12.5
Searching for a Way Out of Afghanistan - 1986
Excerpts from the Transcript of a Soviet Politburo Meeting

After Mikhail Gorbachev took the reins of power in the Soviet Union in 1985, one of his first priorities was to find a way to get the Red Army out of Afghanistan. Soviet forces had entered Afghanistan back in December 1979 in order to defend the nation's Communist government against a fundamentalist Islamic insurgency. But the war became such a bloody stalemate that analysts began to refer to it as the USSR's "Vietnam." In addition, the war in Afghanistan was consuming government resources and eating away at national confidence at a time when Gorbachev was preparing to roll out his "perestroika" and "glasnost" reforms. He knew that those reforms had a much greater chance of success if Soviet soldiers were no longer dying in Afghanistan.

In the following transcript excerpt from a November 13, 1986, meeting of Gorbachev and his top aides, Gorbachev flatly declares that the USSR needs to withdraw from Afghanistan within two years. Other speakers from this excerpt are Politburo members Andrei Gromyko, Mikhail Solomentsev, and Viktor Chebrikov. Soviet forces did leave Afghanistan—without obtaining victory—on February 15, 1989, 27 months after this meeting took place. Their departure paved the way for the fundamentalist Islamic Taliban regime to take power in Afghanistan.

.... **Gorbachev:** We have been fighting in Afghanistan for nearly six years. If the approach is not changed, we will continue to fight for another 20-30 years. This would cast a shadow on our abilities to affect the evolution of the situation. Our military should be told that they are learning badly from this war.... In general, we have not selected the keys to resolving this problem. What, are we going to fight endlessly, as a testimony that our troops are not able to deal with the situation? We need to finish this process as soon as possible.

Gromyko: It is necessary to establish a strategic target. Too long ago we spoke on the fact that it is necessary to close off the border of Afghanistan with Pakistan and Iran. Experience has shown that we were unable to do this in view of the diffi-

CPSU CC Politburo transcript, November 13, 1986. Reprinted with permission from the Cold War International History Project Virtual Archive (http://www.cwihp.org).

cult terrain of the area and the existence of hundreds of passes in the mountains. Today it is necessary to precisely say that the strategic assignment concludes with the carrying of the problem towards ending the war.

Gorbachev: It is necessary to include in the resolution the importance of ending the war in the course of one year—at maximum two years.

Gromyko: It should be concluded so Afghanistan becomes a neutral country. Apparently, on our part there was an underestimation of difficulties, when we agreed with the Afghan government to give them our military support. The social conditions in Afghanistan made the resolution of the problem in a short amount of time impossible. We did not receive domestic support there. In the Afghan army the number of conscripts equals the number of deserters.... Concerning the Americans, they are not interested in the settlement of the situation in Afghanistan. On the contrary, it is to their advantage for the war to drag out.

Gorbachev: That's right.

Gromyko: It should be considered how to link India into the settlement. A delay in the resolution of these problems does not increase our opportunities for settlement. Right now the situation is worse than half a year ago. In one word, it is necessary to more actively pursue a political settlement. Our people will breathe a deep sigh if we undertake steps in that direction.

Our strategic goal is to make Afghanistan neutral, not to allow it to go over to the enemy camp. Of course it is important to also preserve that which is possible in the social arena. But most important—to stop the war. I would agree that it is necessary to limit this to a period of one-two years.

Solomentsev: It would be good to complete a political settlement for the 70th anniversary of [the 1917] October [Revolution].

Gromyko: It would be difficult to talk about such a period of time.

Chebrikov: On this question many decisions have been made. Much energy has been put in. But, unfortunately, the situation, both in Afghanistan and around it, continues to remain difficult. I support the proposal of Mikhail Serge'evich [Gorbachev] that it is necessary to liven up and push the problem towards a logical conclusion. Indeed, we posed the question of closing the border. Andrei Andre'e-vich [Gromyko] is partly right, speaking about the difficulties of such a closing, due to the geographic and other conditions. But partly the failure in the closing is also tied to the fact that not everything was done that could have been. Right now the enemy is changing its tactics. He is going underground. It is necessary to look for the means to a political solution of the problem. The military path for the past six years has not given us a solution....

Source: CPSU CC Politburo transcript, November 13, 1986. Obtained and translated by the Cold War International History Project. Available online at the Cold War International History Project Virtual Archive, http://www.wilsoncenter.org/index.cfm?topic_id=1409&fuseaction=va2.browse&sort=Collection.

12.6

"Mr. Gorbachev, Tear Down This Wall!" – 1987
Excerpts from Ronald Reagan's Speech at the Brandenburg Gate in West Berlin

> *On June 12, 1987, President Ronald Reagan gave a speech at Germany's historic Brandenburg Gate, which straddles West and East Berlin. This address was delivered to a crowd of West Berliners, but it was broadcast worldwide—and it was reportedly audible to listeners on the East side of the Berlin Wall. In his remarks, Reagan spoke at length about the dark symbolism of the Berlin Wall, and he delivered a blunt challenge to Soviet leader Mikhail Gorbachev to bring the wall down.*

… We come to Berlin, we American presidents, because it's our duty to speak, in this place, of freedom. But I must confess, we're drawn here by other things as well: by the feeling of history in this city, more than 500 years older than our own nation; by the beauty of the Grunewald and the Tiergarten; most of all, by your courage and determination. Perhaps the composer Paul Lincke understood something about American presidents. You see, like so many presidents before me, I come here today because wherever I go, whatever I do: Ich hab noch einen Koffer in Berlin [I still have a suitcase in Berlin].

Our gathering today is being broadcast throughout Western Europe and North America. I understand that it is being seen and heard as well in the East. To those listening throughout Eastern Europe, a special word: Although I cannot be with you, I address my remarks to you just as surely as to those standing here before me. For I join you, as I join your fellow countrymen in the West, in this firm, this unalterable belief: Es gibt nur ein Berlin. [There is only one Berlin.]

Behind me stands a wall that encircles the free sectors of this city, part of a vast system of barriers that divides the entire continent of Europe. From the Baltic, south, those barriers cut across Germany in a gash of barbed wire, concrete, dog runs, and guard towers. Farther south, there may be no visible, no obvious wall. But there remain armed guards and checkpoints all the same—still a restriction on the right to travel, still an instrument to impose upon ordinary men and women the will of a totalitarian state. Yet it is here in Berlin where the wall emerges most clearly; here, cutting across your city, where the news photo and the television screen have imprinted this brutal division of a continent upon the mind of the world. Standing before the Brandenburg Gate, every man is a German, separated from his fellow men. Every man is a Berliner, forced to look upon a scar.

President von Weizsacker has said, "The German question is open as long as the Brandenburg Gate is closed." Today I say: As long as the gate is closed, as long as this scar of a wall is permitted to stand, it is not the German question alone that remains open, but the question of freedom for all mankind. Yet I do not come here to lament. For I find in Berlin a message of hope, even in the shadow of this wall, a message of triumph.

In this season of spring in 1945, the people of Berlin emerged from their air-raid shelters to find devastation. Thousands of miles away, the people of the United States reached out to help. And in 1947 Secretary of State—as you've been told—George Marshall announced the creation of what would become known as the Marshall Plan. Speaking precisely 40 years ago this month, he said: "Our policy is directed not against any country or doctrine, but against hunger, poverty, desperation, and chaos."

In the Reichstag a few moments ago, I saw a display commemorating this 40th anniversary of the Marshall Plan. I was struck by the sign on a burnt-out, gutted structure that was being rebuilt. I understand that Berliners of my own generation can remember seeing signs like it dotted throughout the western sectors of the city. The sign read simply: "The Marshall Plan is helping here to strengthen the free world." A strong, free world in the West, that dream became real. Japan rose from ruin to become an economic giant. Italy, France, Belgium—virtually every nation in Western Europe saw political and economic rebirth; the European Community was founded.

In West Germany and here in Berlin, there took place an economic miracle, the Wirtschaftswunder. Adenauer, Erhard, Reuter, and other leaders understood the practical importance of liberty—that just as truth can flourish only when the journalist is given freedom of speech, so prosperity can come about only when the farmer and businessman enjoy economic freedom. The German leaders reduced tariffs, expanded free trade, lowered taxes. From 1950 to 1960 alone, the standard of living in West Germany and Berlin doubled.

Where four decades ago there was rubble, today in West Berlin there is the greatest industrial output of any city in Germany—busy office blocks, fine homes and apartments, proud avenues, and the spreading lawns of parkland. Where a city's culture seemed to have been destroyed, today there are two great universities, orchestras and an opera, countless theaters, and museums. Where there was want, today there's abundance—food, clothing, automobiles—the wonderful goods of the Ku'damm. From devastation, from utter ruin, you Berliners have, in freedom, rebuilt a city that once again ranks as one of the greatest on earth. The Soviets may have had other plans. But my friends, there were a few things the Soviets didn't count on—Berliner Herz, Berliner Humor, ja, und Berliner Schnauze. [Berliner heart, Berliner humor, yes, and a Berliner Schnauze.]

In the 1950s, Khrushchev predicted: "We will bury you." But in the West today, we see a free world that has achieved a level of prosperity and well-being unprecedented in all human history. In the Communist world, we see failure, technological backwardness, declining standards of health, even want of the most basic kind—too little food. Even today, the Soviet Union still cannot feed itself. After these four decades, then, there stands before the entire world one great and inescapable conclusion: Freedom leads to prosperity. Freedom replaces the ancient hatreds among the nations with comity and peace. Freedom is the victor.

And now the Soviets themselves may, in a limited way, be coming to understand the importance of freedom. We hear much from Moscow about a new policy of reform and openness. Some political prisoners have been released. Certain foreign news broadcasts are no longer being jammed. Some economic enterprises have been permitted to operate with greater freedom from state control.

> *"Are these the beginnings of profound changes in the Soviet state? Or are they token gestures, intended to raise false hopes in the West?"*

Are these the beginnings of profound changes in the Soviet state? Or are they token gestures, intended to raise false hopes in the West, or to strengthen the Soviet system without changing it? We welcome change and openness; for we believe that freedom and security go together, that the advance of human liberty can only strengthen the cause of world peace. There is one sign the Soviets can make that would be unmistakable, that would advance dramatically the cause of freedom and peace.

General Secretary Gorbachev, if you seek peace, if you seek prosperity for the Soviet Union and Eastern Europe, if you seek liberalization: Come here to this gate! Mr. Gorbachev, open this gate! Mr. Gorbachev, tear down this wall!

I understand the fear of war and the pain of division that afflict this continent—and I pledge to you my country's efforts to help overcome these burdens. To be sure, we in the West must resist Soviet expansion. So we must maintain defenses of unassailable strength. Yet we seek peace; so we must strive to reduce arms on both sides.

Beginning 10 years ago, the Soviets challenged the Western alliance with a grave new threat, hundreds of new and more deadly SS-20 nuclear missiles, capable of striking every capital in Europe. The Western alliance responded by committing itself to a counter-deployment unless the Soviets agreed to negotiate a better solution; namely, the elimination of such weapons on both sides. For many months, the Soviets refused to bargain in earnestness. As the alliance, in turn, prepared to go forward with its counter-deployment, there were difficult days—days of protests like those during my 1982 visit to this city—and the Soviets later walked away from the table.

But through it all, the alliance held firm. And I invite those who protested then—I invite those who protest today—to mark this fact: Because we remained strong, the Soviets came back to the table. And because we remained strong, today we have within reach the possibility, not merely of limiting the growth of arms, but of eliminating, for the first time, an entire class of nuclear weapons from the face of the earth.

As I speak, NATO ministers are meeting in Iceland to review the progress of our proposals for eliminating these weapons. At the talks in Geneva, we have also proposed deep cuts in strategic offensive weapons. And the Western allies have likewise made far-reaching proposals to reduce the danger of conventional war and to place a total ban on chemical weapons.

While we pursue these arms reductions, I pledge to you that we will maintain the capacity to deter Soviet aggression at any level at which it might occur. And in cooperation with many of our allies, the United States is pursuing the Strategic Defense Initiative—research to base deterrence not on the threat of offensive retaliation, but on defenses that truly defend; on systems, in short, that will not target populations, but shield them. By these means we seek to increase the safety of Europe and all the world. But we must remember a crucial fact: East and West do not mistrust each other because we are armed; we are armed because we mistrust each other. And our differences are not about weapons but about liberty. When President Kennedy spoke at the City Hall those 24 years ago, freedom was encircled, Berlin was under siege. And today, despite all the pressures upon this city, Berlin stands secure in its liberty. And freedom itself is transforming the globe.

In the Philippines, in South and Central America, democracy has been given a rebirth. Throughout the Pacific, free markets are working miracle after miracle of economic growth. In the industrialized nations, a technological revolution is taking place—a revolution marked by rapid, dramatic advances in computers and telecommunications.

In Europe, only one nation and those it controls refuse to join the community of freedom. Yet in this age of redoubled economic growth, of information and innovation, the Soviet Union faces a choice: It must make fundamental changes, or it will become obsolete.

Today thus represents a moment of hope. We in the West stand ready to cooperate with the East to promote true openness, to break down barriers that separate people, to create a safe, freer world. And surely there is no better place than Berlin, the meeting place of East and West, to make a start. Free people of Berlin: Today, as in the past, the United States stands for the strict observance and full implementation of all parts of the Four Power Agreement of 1971. Let us use this occasion, the 750th anniversary of this city, to usher in a new era, to seek a still fuller, richer life for the Berlin of the future. Together, let us maintain and develop the ties between the Federal Republic and the Western sectors of Berlin, which is permitted by the 1971 agreement.

And I invite Mr. Gorbachev: Let us work to bring the Eastern and Western parts of the city closer together, so that all the inhabitants of all Berlin can enjoy the benefits that come with life in one of the great cities of the world.

To open Berlin still further to all Europe, East and West, let us expand the vital air access to this city, finding ways of making commercial air service to Berlin more convenient, more comfortable, and more economical. We look to the day when West Berlin can become one of the chief aviation hubs in all central Europe.

With our French and British partners, the United States is prepared to help bring international meetings to Berlin. It would be only fitting for Berlin to serve as the site of United Nations meetings, or world conferences on human rights and arms control or other issues that call for international cooperation.

There is no better way to establish hope for the future than to enlighten young minds, and we would be honored to sponsor summer youth exchanges, cultural events, and other programs for young Berliners from the East. Our French and British friends, I'm certain, will do the same. And it's my hope that an authority can be found in East Berlin to sponsor visits from young people of the Western sectors.

One final proposal, one close to my heart: Sport represents a source of enjoyment and ennoblement, and you may have noted that the Republic of Korea—South Korea—has offered to permit certain events of the 1988 Olympics to take place in the North. International sports competitions of all kinds could take place in both parts of this city. And what better way to demonstrate to the world the openness of this city than to offer in some future year to hold the Olympic games here in Berlin, East and West? In these four decades, as I have said, you Berliners have built a great city. You've done so in spite of threats—the Soviet attempts to impose the East-mark, the blockade. Today the city thrives in spite of the challenges implicit in the very presence of this wall. What keeps you here? Certainly there's a great deal to be said for your fortitude, for your defiant courage. But I believe there's something deeper, something that involves Berlin's whole look and feel and way of life—not mere sentiment. No one could live long in Berlin without being completely dis-abused of illusions. Something instead, that has seen the difficulties of life in Berlin but chose to accept them, that continues to build this good and proud city in contrast to a surrounding totalitarian presence that refuses to release human energies or aspirations. Something that speaks with a powerful voice of affirmation, that says yes to this city, yes to the future, yes to freedom. In a word, I would submit that what keeps you in Berlin is love—love both profound and abiding.

Perhaps this gets to the root of the matter, to the most fundamental distinction of all between East and West. The totalitarian world produces backwardness because it does such violence to the spirit, thwarting the human impulse to create, to enjoy, to worship. The totalitarian world finds even symbols of love and of worship an affront. Years ago, before the East Germans began rebuilding their churches, they erected a secular structure: the television tower at Alexander Platz. Virtually ever since, the authorities have been working to correct what they view as the tower's one major flaw, treating the glass sphere at the top with paints and chemicals of every kind. Yet even today when the sun strikes that sphere—that sphere that towers over all Berlin—the light makes the sign of the cross. There in Berlin, like the city itself, symbols of love, symbols of worship, cannot be suppressed.

As I looked out a moment ago from the Reichstag, that embodiment of German unity, I noticed words crudely spray-painted upon the wall, perhaps by a young Berliner: "This wall will fall. Beliefs become reality." Yes, across Europe, this wall will fall. For it cannot withstand faith; it cannot withstand truth. The wall cannot withstand freedom.

And I would like, before I close, to say one word. I have read, and I have been questioned since I've been here about certain demonstrations against my coming. And I would like to say just one thing, and to those who demonstrate so. I wonder if they have ever asked themselves that if they should have the kind of government they apparently seek, no one would ever be able to do what they're doing again.

Source: Reagan, Ronald. "Remarks on East-West Relations at the Brandenburg Gate in West Berlin," June 12, 1987. The Public Papers of President Ronald Reagan, Ronald Reagan Presidential Library. Available online at www.reagan.utexas.edu/archives/speeches/1987/061287d.htm.

12.7
Mikhail Gorbachev Describes a New Soviet World Vision – 1988
Excerpt from Gorbachev's Speech to the United Nations General Assembly

On December 7, 1988, Soviet General Secretary Mikhail Gorbachev addressed the United Nations General Assembly. After speaking about the recent changes in the Soviet Union, Gorbachev amazed the global community when he announced drastic cuts in the Soviet military presence in Eastern Europe and along the Chinese border. He also issued an urgent appeal for member nations to restructure international politics to better address stated goals of economic and political freedom.

Gorbachev's idealistic speech was widely praised in the West. The New York Times, for example, issued an editorial claiming that "perhaps not since Woodrow Wilson presented his Fourteen Points in 1918 or since Franklin Roosevelt and Winston Churchill promulgated the Atlantic Charter in 1941 has a world figure demonstrated the vision of Mikhail Gorbachev, displayed yesterday at the United Nations.… Breathtaking. Risky. Bold. Naïve. Diversionary. Heroic. All fit. So sweeping is his agenda that it will require weeks to sort out. But whatever Mr. Gorbachev's motives, his ideas merit—indeed compel—the most serious response from President-elect Bush and other lead-ers." Following are excerpts from Gorbachev's famous UN address.

What will mankind be like when it enters the twenty-first century? People are already fascinated by this not-too-distant future. We are looking ahead to it with hopes for the best, and yet with a feeling of concern.

The world in which we live today is radically different from what it was at the beginning, or even in the middle, of this century, and it continues to change, as do all its components.

The advent of nuclear weapons was just another tragic reminder of the funda-mental nature of that change. A material symbol and expression of absolute mili-tary power, nuclear weapons at the same time revealed the absolute limits of that power. The problem of mankind's survival and self-preservation came to the fore.

We are witnessing most profound social change. Whether in the East or the South, the West or the North, hundreds of millions of people, new nations and States, new public movements and ideologies have moved to the forefront of histo-ry. Broad-based and frequently turbulent popular movements have given expres-sion, in a multidimensional and contradictory way, to a longing for independence, democracy, and social justice. The idea of democratizing the entire world order has become a powerful socio-political force....

Today, we have entered an era when progress will be shaped by universal human interests. Awareness of that dictates that world politics, too, should be guided by the primacy of universal human values.

The history of past centuries and millennia was a history of wars that raged almost everywhere, of frequent desperate battles to the point of mutual annihila-tion. They grew out of clashes of social and political interests, national enmity, ide-ological or religious incompatibility. All that did happen. And even today, many would want those vestiges of the past to be accepted as immutable law.

However, concurrently with wars, animosities and divisions among peoples and countries, another trend, with equally objective causes, was gaining momen-tum: the process of the emergence of a mutually interrelated and integral world. Today, further world progress is possible only through a search for universal human consensus as we move forward to a new world order.

We have come to a point where the disorderly play of elemental forces leads to an impasse. The international community must learn how it can shape and guide developments in such a way as to preserve our civilization and to make it safe for all and conducive to normal life.

Mikhail Gorbachev, Address to the United Nations General Assembly, December 7, 1988. Reprinted with permission from the United Nations, and The Gorbachev Foundation – Moscow.

We are speaking of co-operation, which could be more accurately termed co-creation and co-development. The formula of development at the expense of others is on the way out. In the light of existing realities, no genuine progress is possible at the expense of the rights and freedoms of individuals and nations or at the expense of nature.

Efforts to solve global problems require a new scope and quality of interaction of States and socio-political currents, regardless of ideological or other differences.

Of course, radical changes and revolutionary transformations will continue to occur within individual countries and social structures. This is how it was and this is how it will be. But here, too, our time marks a change. Internal transformations can no longer advance their national goals if they develop only along parallel courses with others without making use of the achievements of the outside world and of the potential inherent in equitable co-operation....

It is also quite clear to us that the principle of freedom of choice is mandatory. Its non-recognition is fraught with extremely grave consequences for world peace. Denying that right to peoples, under whatever pretext or rhetorical guise, jeopardizes even the fragile balance that has been attained. Freedom of choice is a universal principle that should allow of no exceptions.

It was not simply out of good intentions that we came to the conclusion that that principle was absolute. We were driven to it by an unbiased analysis of the objective trends of today. More and more characteristic of them is the increasingly multi-optional nature of social development in different countries. This applies both to the capitalist and to the socialist systems. The diversity of the socio-political structures that have grown out of national liberation movements over the past decades also attests to this.

This objective fact calls for respect for the views and positions of others, tolerance, a willingness to perceive something different as not necessarily bad or hostile, and an ability to learn to live side by side with others, while remaining different and not always agreeing with each other....

The new phase also requires de-ideologizing relations among States. We are not abandoning our convictions, our philosophy or traditions, nor do we urge anyone to abandon theirs. However, neither do we have any intention of being hemmed in by our values, which would result in intellectual impoverishment, for it would mean rejecting a powerful source of development—the exchange of everything original that each nation has independently created.

In the course of such exchange, let everyone show the advantages of their social systems, their way of life and their values, not just by words or propaganda, but by real deeds. That would be a fair rivalry of ideologies. But it should not be extended to relations among States, otherwise we should simply be unable to solve any of the world's problems, such as developing wide-ranging, mutually beneficial and equitable co-operation among nations; making efficient use of the achievements of scientific and technological revolution; restructuring the world economy and protecting the environment; and overcoming backwardness and eliminating hunger, disease, illiteracy and other global scourges. Similarly, we would not be able to eliminate the nuclear threat and militarism.

These are our reflections on the patterns of world development on the threshold of the twenty-first century.

Of course, we are far from claiming to be in possession of the ultimate truth, but, on the basis of a thorough analysis of the past and newly-emerging realities, we have concluded that it is on these lines that we should jointly seek the way to the supremacy of the universal human idea over the endless multitude of centrifugal forces, and to preserve the vitality of this civilization, which is possibly the only one in the entire universe.

Could this view be a little too romantic? Are we not overestimating the potential and maturity of the world's social consciousness? We have heard such doubts and such questions, both in our country and from some of our Western partners.

I am convinced that we are not floating above reality. Forces have already emerged in the world that in one way or another stimulate the arrival of a period of peace. The peoples and large sectors of the public do, indeed, ardently wish for an improvement in the situation. They want to learn to co-operate. It is sometimes amazing how powerful this trend is. It is also important that it is beginning to shape policies....

Our country is going through a period of truly revolutionary uplifting.

The process of *perestroika* is gaining momentum. We began with formulation of the theoretical concept of *perestroika*. We had to evaluate the nature and the magnitude of problems, to understand the lessons of the past and express that in the form of political conclusions and programs. That was done.

The theoretical work, a reassessment of what is happening, the finalization, enrichment and readjustment of political positions have not been completed. They are continuing.

But it was essential to begin with an overall concept, which, as now confirmed by the experience of these past years, has generally proved to be correct and has no alternative.

For our society to participate in efforts to implement the plans of *perestroika*, it had to be democratized in practice. Under the sign of democratization, *perestroika* has now spread to politics, the economy, intellectual life and ideology.

We have initiated a radical economic reform. We have gained experience. At the start of the next year, the entire national economy will be redirected to new forms and methods of operation. That also means profoundly reorganizing relations of production and releasing the tremendous potential inherent in socialist property.

Undertaking such bold revolutionary transformations, we realized that there would be mistakes, and also opposition, that new approaches would generate new problems. We also foresaw the possibility of slow-downs in some areas.

But the guarantee that the overall process of *perestroika* will steadily move forward and gain strength lies in a profound democratic reform of the entire system of power and administration.

With the recent decisions by the USSR Supreme Soviet on amendments to the Constitution and the adoption of the Law on Elections, we have completed the first stage of the process of political reform.

Without pausing, we have begun the second stage of this process with the main task of improving the relationship between the center and the republics, harmonizing inter-ethnic relations on the principles of Leninist internationalism that we inherited from the Great Revolution, and at the same time reorganizing the local system of Soviet power.

A great deal of work lies ahead. Major tasks will have to be dealt with concurrently.

We are full of confidence. We have a theory and a policy, and also the vanguard force of *perestroika*—the Party, which is also restructuring itself in accordance with new tasks and fundamental changes in society as a whole.

What is most important is that all our peoples and all generations of citizens of our great country support *perestroika*.

We have become deeply involved in building a socialist State based on the rule of law. Work on a series of new laws has been completed or is nearing completion.

Many of them will enter into force as early as 1989, and we expect them to meet the highest standards from the standpoint of ensuring the rights of the individual.

Soviet democracy will be placed on a solid normative base. I am referring, in particular, to laws on the freedom of conscience, *glasnost*, public associations, organizations, and many others.

In places of confinement there are no persons convicted for their political or religious beliefs.

Additional guarantees are to be included in the new draft laws that rule out any form of persecution on those grounds.

Naturally this does not apply to those who have committed actual criminal offences or State crimes, such as espionage, sabotage, terrorism and so on, whatever their political or ideological beliefs. Draft amendments to the penal code have been prepared and are awaiting their turn. Among the articles being revised are those relating to capital punishment.

The problem of exit from and entry to our country, including the question of leaving it for family reunification, is being dealt with in a humane spirit. As the Assembly will know, one of the reasons for refusal of permission to leave is a person's knowledge of secrets. Strictly warranted time limitations on the secrecy rule will now be applied. Every person seeking employment at certain agencies or enterprises will be informed of this rule. In case of disputes there is a right of appeal under the law. This removes from the agenda the problem of the so-called refuseniks.

We intend to expand the Soviet Union's participation in the human rights monitoring arrangements of the United Nations and the Conference on Security and Co-operation in Europe (CS CE). We believe that the jurisdiction of the International Court of Justice at The Hague as regards the interpretation and implementation of agreements on human rights should be binding on all States. We regard as part of the Helsinki process the cessation of jamming of all foreign radio broadcasts beamed at the Soviet Union.

Overall, this is our credo: political problems must be solved by political means only; human problems in a humane way only.

Let me now turn to the main issue without which none of the problems of the coming century can be solved: disarmament.

International development and communications have been distorted by the arms race and the militarization of thinking. As the Assembly will know, on 15 January 1986 the Soviet Union put forward a program for building a nuclear-weapon-free world. Translated into actual negotiating positions, it has already produced material results. Tomorrow marks the first anniversary of the signing of the Treaty between the United States of America and the Union of Soviet Socialist Republics on the Elimination of Their Intermediate-Range and Shorter-Range Missiles-INF Treaty. I am therefore particularly pleased to note that the implementation of the Treaty—the elimination of missiles—is proceeding normally in an atmosphere of trust and businesslike work. A large breach has thus been made in a seemingly unbreakable wall of suspicion and animosity. We are witnessing the emergence of a new, historic reality; a turning away from the principle of super-armament to the principle of reasonable defense sufficiency.

We are present at the birth of a new model of ensuring security, not through the build-up of arms, as was almost always the case in the past, but on the contrary through their reduction on the basis of compromise. The Soviet leadership has decided to demonstrate once again its readiness to reinforce this healthy process, not only by worlds but also by deeds.

Today I can report to the General Assembly that the Soviet Union has taken a decision to reduce its armed forces. Within the next two years their numerical strength will be reduced by 500,000 men. The numbers of conventional armaments will also be substantially reduced. This will be done unilaterally, without relation to the talks on the mandate of the Vienna meeting.

By agreement with our Warsaw Treaty allies we have decided to withdraw, by 1991, six tank divisions from the German Democratic Republic, Czechoslovakia and Hungary and to disband them. Assault landing troops and several other formations and units, including assault crossing units with their weapons and combat equipment, will also be withdrawn from the groups of Soviet forces stationed in those countries. Soviet forces stationed in those countries will be reduced by 50,000 men and their armaments by 5,000 tanks.

All Soviet divisions remaining for the time being on the territories of our allies are being reorganized. Their structure will be different from what it is now; after a major cutback in their tanks it will become clearly defensive.

At the same time we shall reduce the numerical strength of the armed forces and the numbers of armaments stationed in the European part of the Soviet Union. In total, Soviet armed forces in this part of our country and in the territories of our European allies will be reduced by 10,000 tanks, 8,500 artillery systems and 800 combat aircraft.

Over these two years we intend to reduce significantly our armed forces in the Asian part of our country too. By agreement with the Government of the Mongolian People's Republic a major portion of Soviet troops temporarily stationed there will return home.

In taking this fundamental decision the Soviet leadership is expressing the will of the people, who have undertaken a profound renewal of their entire socialist society. We shall maintain our country's defense capability at a level of reasonable and reliable sufficiency so that no one will be tempted to encroach on the security of the Soviet Union and our allies.

By all our activities in favor of demilitarizing international relations we wish to draw the attention of the international community to yet another pressing problem: the problem of transition from the economy of armaments to an economy of disarmament. Is conversion of military production a realistic idea? I have already had occasion to speak about this. We think that it is indeed realistic.

For its part the Soviet Union is prepared to take the following steps: within the framework of our economic reform to draw up and make public our internal conversion plan; in the course of 1989 to draw up, as an experiment, conversion plans for two or three defense plants; and to make public our experience in providing employment for specialists from military industry and in using its equipment, buildings and structures in civilian production.

It is desirable that all States, and in the first place the major military Powers, should submit their national conversion plans to the United Nations. It would be useful also to set up a group of scientists to undertake a thorough analysis of the problem of conversion as a whole and as applied to individual countries and regions and report to the Secretary-General of the United Nations, and subsequently for this matter to be considered at a session of the General Assembly.

Finally, since I am here on American soil, and also for other obvious reasons, I have to turn to the subject of our relations with this great country. I had a chance to appreciate the full measure of its hospitality during my memorable visit to Washington exactly a year ago. Relations been the Soviet Union and the United States of America have a history of five and a half decades. As the world has changed, so have the nature, role and place of those relations in world politics. For too long they developed along the lines of confrontation and sometimes animosity, either overt or covert. But in the last few years the entire world has been able to breathe a sigh of relief, thanks to the changes for the better in the substance and the atmosphere of the relationship between Moscow and Washington.

> *"In the last few years the entire world has been able to breathe a sigh of relief, thanks to the changes for the better in the substance and the atmosphere of the relationship between Moscow and Washington."*

No one intends to underestimate the seriousness of our differences and the toughness of our outstanding problems. We have, however, already graduated from the primary school of learning to understand each other and seek solutions in both our own and the common interest.

The USSR and the United States have built the largest nuclear and missile arsenals; but it is those two counties that, having become specifically aware of their responsibility, have been the first to conclude a treaty on the reduction and physical elimination of a portion of their armaments which posed a threat to both of them and to all other countries. Both countries possess the greatest and most sophisticated military secrets; but it is those two counties that have laid a basis for and are further developing a system of mutual verification both of the elimination of armaments and of the reduction and prohibition of their production. It is those two countries that are accumulating experience for future bilateral and multilateral agreements.

We value this. We acknowledge and appreciate the contributions made by President Ronald Reagan and by the members of his Administration, particularly Mr. George Shultz.

All this is our joint investment in a venture of historic importance. We must not lose that investment, or leave it idle.

The next United States administration, headed by President-elect George Bush, will find us a partner who is ready—without long pauses or backtracking—to continue the dialogue in a spirit of realism, openness and goodwill, with a willingness to achieve concrete results working on the agenda which covers the main issues of Soviet/United States relations and world politics.

I have in mind, above all, consistent movement towards a treaty on 50-percent reductions in strategic offensive arms while preserving the Treaty on the Limitation of Anti-Ballistic Missile Systems (ABM Treaty); working out a convention on the elimination of chemical weapons—here, as we see it, prerequisites exist to make 1989 a decisive year; and negotiations on the reduction of conventional arms and armed forces in Europe.

I also have in mind economic, environmental and humanistic problems in their broadest sense....

We are not inclined to simplify the situation in the world.

Yes, the trend towards disarmament has been given a powerful impetus, and the process is gaining a momentum of its own. But it has not yet become irreversible.

Yes, the willingness to give up confrontation in favor of dialogue and co-operation is being felt strongly. But it is still far from becoming a permanent feature in the practice of international relations.

Yes, movement towards a nuclear-weapon-free and non-violent world is capable of radically transforming the political and intellectual identity of our planet. But only the first steps have been taken, and even they have been met with mistrust in certain influential quarters and face resistance.

The legacy and the inertia of the past continue to be felt. Profound contradictions and the roots of many conflicts have not disappeared. And there remains another fundamental fact, which is that a peaceful period will be taking shape in the context of the existence and rivalry of different socio-economic and political systems.

However, the thrust of our international efforts and one of the key elements of the new thinking is that this rivalry should be given a quality of reasonable competition with due regard for freedom of choice and balance of interests. Then it would even become useful and productive from the standpoint of global development.

Otherwise, if as in the past the arms race remains its basic component, this rivalry would be deadly. More and more people throughout the world—leaders as well as ordinary people—are beginning to understand that.

I conclude my first address to the United Nations with the same feeling that I had when I began it—a feeling of responsibility to my own people and to the world community.

We are meeting at the end of a year which has meant so much for the United Nations and on the eve of a year from which we all expect so much.

I should like to believe that our hopes will be matched by our joint efforts to put an end to an era of wars, confrontation and regional conflicts, to aggressions against nature, to the terror of hunger and poverty as well as to political terrorism.

That is our common goal and we can only reach it together.

Source: Gorbachev, Mikhail. "Address to the United Nations General Assembly, December 7, 1988." Official Records of the General Assembly, Forty-Third Session, Provisional Verbatim Record of the 72nd Meeting.

13

THE COLLAPSE
OF THE SOVIET EMPIRE

In November 1989 the Berlin Wall fell, sparking euphoric celebrations
across the long-divided capital and all of Germany.

INTRODUCTION

In the late 1980s, Soviet leader Mikhail Gorbachev charted a path of *glasnost* (openness) and *perestroika* (societal reconstruction or restructuring) for the Soviet empire. As this campaign continued, however, the forces that Gorbachev had unleashed began to erode the political foundations of the Soviet Union and reveal long-festering problems within the empire. Gorbachev watched these developments with mounting concern. He had never intended for glasnost to become an instrument responsible for the dismantling of the Soviet Union, but with each passing month the cries for independence from Soviet rule grew louder.

The spirit of reform even drifted over to China, where the Communists had long kept a tight grip on power. In the spring of 1989, students organized a series of pro-democracy protests in Beijing and other cities. Shortly after Gorbachev visited the country on a diplomatic mission to normalize relations between the two Communist powers, millions of Chinese students poured into the streets of Beijing demanding greater political freedom. As soon as Gorbachev returned to Moscow, however, the Chinese government rolled tanks into Tiananmen Square to crush the uprising.

1989—The Year of Miracles

But the Tiananmen Square crackdown failed to slow the momentum of glasnost in Russia and other parts of the Soviet empire. In the spring of 1989—in what became known as the "year of miracles"—the Soviet Union held its freest elections in nearly a century. Communists won the vast majority of seats, but several leading party leaders were defeated and the dissident Boris Yeltsin became mayor of Moscow. Two months later, Soviet citizens were stunned to hear newly elected representatives give speeches condemning the KGB and party leaders for cruelty, corruption, or incompetence. "No newspaper, no film, book, or play had ever had such an immediate political effect on the people of the Soviet Union," wrote David Remnick in *Lenin's Tomb*. "The sessions were broadcast live for two weeks, and factories and collective farms reported that no work was getting done. Everyone was gathered around television sets and transistor radios. People simply could not believe what they were hearing."

In the Eastern bloc, meanwhile, an equally stunning transformation was occurring in country after country. Democratic protests and reform movements roared to life all across the region, energized by the knowledge that the repressive regimes that had ruled their lives for so long could no longer count on the support of Soviet tanks and troops. In June 1987, Pope John Paul II's historic trip to Poland gave Lech Walesa's Solidarity Movement the momentum it needed to end Communist rule two years later. In September 1989 the ruling Communist Party in Hungary formally cast off its Soviet chains, announcing its independence and its intention to pursue a course of democratic socialism. Two months later, in November 1989, the Berlin Wall fell in dramatic fashion after weeks of massive rallies against the repressive East German regime. The demolishment of this icon of Cold War hostilities reunited families and countrymen that had been separated for decades, and it further fanned the flames of revolution across Eastern Europe.

In December 1989 Communist governments fell in Bulgaria, Romania, and Czechoslovakia. These dictatorships had been among the most cruel and tyrannical in the world, and their passing was marked by several indelible images. In Czechoslovakia, where the peaceful "Velvet Revolution" brought down the Communist government, delirious crowds welcomed back Alexander Dubček, the Czech leader who had been chased into exile by Soviet tanks back in the Prague Spring of 1968. In Romania, meanwhile, citizens were mesmerized by television footage that showed the crumpled bodies of dictator Nicolae Ceaușescu and his wife Elena after their execution on Christmas Day.

The Right Pushes Back

In 1990 it became clear that the forces that Gorbachev had set in motion were no longer under his control. He and other Kremlin leaders worked feverishly to prevent the unification of Germany, which had wreaked so much destruction on the Russian people over the years. They also labored to dissuade restless Baltic republics from leaving the Soviet empire. But they failed in both endeavors.

Gorbachev also worked desperately to prevent the dissolution of the USSR itself. Until this point, only satellite nations that were part of the Soviet bloc in

Eastern Europe had openly rejected Soviet Communist control. But now the individual republics of the USSR—parts of the actual country itself—began to break away. In March 1990 Lithuania announced its independence, and both Russia and Ukraine declared their sovereignty from Soviet laws a few months later. Meanwhile, the German people rejoiced—and the Kremlin despaired—when Germany was formally reunified on October 3, 1990. This event, and Germany's subsequent alliance with the West, has often been cited as the closing chapter in the Cold War.

As the Soviet empire unraveled, a desperate Gorbachev pondered various military and political options to regain control of events. During 1990, for example, the relentless momentum of reform led Gorbachev to approve an end to one-party rule and a whole new slate of economic and political reforms. But when these steps failed to stop the crumbling of the Soviet empire, he increasingly resorted to hard-line policies favored by anti-reform party leaders and state officials. "[Gorbachev's] maneuvering, his attempt to erode the power of the Party and slowly build up democratic institutions, was the political feat of an age," Remnick wrote. "No czar or general secretary had ever put himself and his power in such jeopardy. And now it had all gone wrong.... The reality of a new psychology, independent and defiant, confused him, sent him running to the reliable bases of traditional power. He ignored those who told him what he did not want to hear. The only men who would flatter him were precisely those who would one day betray him. His tragedy had begun."

In the fall of 1990 Gorbachev gave ominous signals that he was prepared to keep the rebellious republics in the Soviet fold by force if necessary. In both Azerbaijan and Lithuania, Soviet troops killed rebellious citizens. He also withdrew his support for the so-called "500 Days Plan," a daring economic reform program, under pressure from conservative party officials and KGB and military leaders. Reformers throughout the Soviet Union and Eastern Europe viewed this decision as an unmistakable sign that the empire's traditional powers would not surrender control without a fight. On December 20, 1990, foreign minister Eduard Shevardnadze submitted his resignation, warning that the Soviet Union was in danger of sliding into a dictatorship.

Buffeted by critics on both the right and left, Gorbachev in late 1990 proposed to save the USSR by granting increased independence to each republic in a new Union Treaty. At the same time, Gorbachev lobbied Western powers for economic aid to help him usher in his economic reforms. But Georgia rejected the proposed Union Treaty and declared its independence from the USSR in April 1991. Meanwhile, the West decided against an aid package despite growing concerns that Gorbachev's reign was in peril from right-wing plotters in the Kremlin.

The August Coup

In June 1991 Gorbachev's enemies in the Communist Party made an unsuccessful bid to dislodge him from power through parliamentary means. Two months later, they joined with a handful of veteran Soviet military commanders in a plot to remove him from office by force. When Gorbachev and his wife went to their villa on the Black Sea for a holiday in mid-August, the coup plotters made their move. On August 18 conspirators trapped Gorbachev in his own villa and ordered him to relinquish power. When he refused, they cut off all communications links to the outside world and put him under arrest. Meanwhile, the conspirators announced that Gorbachev was ill and that Vice President Gennady Yanayev, one of the conspirators, was assuming the powers of the presidency. But Yeltsin angrily denounced the plotters and organized massive protests against the coup, and the conspirators never secured the full support of the Soviet army. Within 24 hours the coup had fizzled.

Gorbachev returned to Moscow a few days later, only to find that the failed coup had, in its own strange way, succeeded in stripping him of his power. When he appeared before the Russian parliament, Yeltsin forced him to read documents implicating his own officials in the coup against him. This public humiliation spelled the end of Gorbachev's rule and solidified Yeltsin's new status as the most powerful political figure in the disintegrating Soviet empire.

In August 1991 the Soviet Union slowly fell apart as a succession of republics declared their independence, becoming individual and separate nations. In December Yeltsin engineered the creation of the Commonwealth of Independent States (CIS), a loose confederation of the former Soviet republics. On December 25, 1991, the Union of Soviet Socialist Republics formally ceased to exist. Faced with the surreal prospect of being the president of a now-nonexistent USSR, Gorbachev resigned from office.

Winners and Losers of the Cold War

In the years since the end of the Cold War and the crumbling of the Soviet empire, historians and politicians have offered starkly different assessments of those earth-shaking events of the late 1980s and early 1990s. Some observers say that Ronald Reagan's SDI initiative and his other military policies enabled the West to "win" the Cold War, while others insist that the Cold War ended in relatively peaceful fashion despite American "warmongering" during the 1980s.

Gorbachev's role has been debated as well. Virtually all scholars echo Robert McMahon's contention that "the astonishing changes of the 1985-1990 period become nearly inconceivable" were it not for "this remarkable individual." But scholars also offer dramatically different assessments of the Soviet leader's performance during his tenure.

For his part, Gorbachev has stated his belief that such debates are meaningless. "For several years people have argued about who won and who lost the Cold War," he wrote in *On My Country and the World*. "In our view, the very question does nothing more than pay tribute to the past and to the old confrontational way of thinking. From the standpoint of reason it is obvious that all of humankind—every country, every human being—won. The threat of a nuclear holocaust became history—unless, of course, we backslide."

13.1
Solidarity and the Pope's Visit to Poland – 1987
An Excerpt from The Struggle and the Triumph: An Autobiography, *by Lech Walesa*

The 1980s were a decade of turmoil and hope in Poland, a Communist satellite of the Soviet empire. After years of repression and economic stagnation, an independent labor union called "Solidarity" had coalesced into a formidable new political force in the country. As the decade unfolded, Solidarity and its leadership, most notably Lech Walesa, made steady progress in undercutting the Communist Party's longtime status as the dominant political voice in Poland. Walesa and his allies were greatly aided in these efforts by the perestroika programs that were being instituted at that time by Soviet leader Mikhail Gorbachev.

In 1987 Poland's Communist leadership was still clinging to power, but the momentum was clearly with Walesa and the Solidarity movement. This shift was underscored by Pope John Paul II's visit to the country that year. Indeed, in the following excerpt from Walesa's memoir The Struggle and the Triumph, *the labor leader described the Pope's 1987 visit as "the turning point" in the struggle for Poland's political future. In 1989 parliamentary elections lifted the Solidarity movement to power, and the following year Lech Walesa won the presidency of Poland.*

The most important event of 1987 for Solidarity, and for all of Poland, was the pope's third visit. While some people might want to interpret the history of Solidarity differently–and emphasize its autonomy from any external influence—the pope's visit was undeniably a turning point in the national mood. For the first time, John Paul II, so beloved by the Poles, was permitted to travel to the forbidden city of Gdansk—and, better yet, to the new community of Zaspa, former site of an airfield, where I was then living. His itinerary was the subject of lengthy negotiations, for in Poland at the time everything was still considered symbolically charged, as well as potentially subversive. Every participant, every building, every ceremony might suddenly assume political dimensions that could endanger the "normalization process," meaning the old order.

The Communist government was acting as though it was less and less sure that its policies were guided by any coherent principles. Only two years later did we become fully aware of the doubts that assailed it. But at the time local and regional authorities behaved arrogantly, overcompensating for their fears that the era of their power was ending. Stanislaw Bejger, first secretary of the Polish United Workers' Party, told the bishop of Gdansk, "The pope's visit to the Monument for the Shipyard Dead will not be possible; however, we do agree to his visiting the Monument to the Defenders of Westerplatte." [The Polish naval base at Westerplatte was heavily bombarded by German forces before being taken in the first days of World War II.]

A war of monuments had been going on for some time. Whoever could erect the most, endow them with the greatest significance, and make them the most visible, would prevail. So at night and on the sly, a monument to the victims of Katyn Forest was erected by one faction; by day, the government built one to the noble agents of the Security Service who had fallen during the postwar struggle to consolidate the new order. The people put up plaques commemorating the heroic leadership of the Home Army; the authorities put up similar plaques to the memory of various fallen Communists.

In the end, the pope paid his respects to both monuments—to the shipyard dead as well as to the defenders of Westerplatte. As for comrade Bejger, his name is all but forgotten now.

Perestroika had not yet reached Poland by the spring of 1987 (and in the Soviet Union its future was still uncertain), but its effects were already beginning to be felt, and one of those effects was to offer us new alternatives. Deep-seated prejudices against the Russians kept the public from taking any real interest in news from our giant eastern neighbor. Mikhail Gorbachev was regarded as simply a new and more skillful deceiver. I admit to thinking the same myself, initially. Then I realized that he had embarked on a perilous journey, mounted on a horse, that might at any moment run away with him; once on, he had no choice but to ride it out. His enemies were waiting for him to fall....

Preparing for John Paul II's arrival was a major effort. When he came to Gdansk, the pope would recognize our achievements, I told the editor of the Catholic paper *W Drodze [On the Way]*, and his visit would affect our destiny—whatever that destiny was. I went on to say, "We inhabit a country that over the centuries has been overrun and [with] the Holy Father's visit in 1987, he underscored a simple fact: Without a free Poland, a free Europe is not possible." We were aware that the pope would not solve our problems, but he would tell the world about the will of the majority of the Polish people, and about what millions of Poles prayed for. He would be the instigator of changes outside Poland whose effects would eventually reach us and push Poland in the right direction—toward an era of faith, honesty, and social reform.

In my own neighborhood I could witness the effects that the mere expectation of his visit was having. From a clump of gray apartment blocks—they looked something like huge dormitories—my residential development was transformed into a living organism, a community of people with distinct personalities and angles of vision. Unexpected qualities began to appear in Falowce, home to several thousand people who had patronizingly been nicknamed "the Kolkhozians" [collective farmers] or "the Ants," and allusion to their sheer numbers and to Pharaoh's "swarming ants" in the Bible. Each floor, each balcony, became a shrine loudly proclaiming its residents' attachment to the Faith. I knew that the people weren't as religious as their very gaudy decorations seemed to indicate, but the important thing was that, if only for a moment, for a single day, they wished to be religious. Their souls were stirred.

> *"I realized that [Gorbachev] had embarked on a perilous journey, mounted on a horse, that might at any moment run away with him; once on, he had no choice but to ride it out."*

In the middle of the leftover airstrip at the heart of the suburbs a huge altar was constructed, an ancient ship onto whose bridge the Pilot of the Church was to ascend. Marian Kolodziej, the set designer of the Gdansk Theater (prisoner number 432 at Auschwitz), had drawn the design for this ship; it rose over 130 feet high into the air and had a great billowing sail visible from everywhere in the community. Hundreds of people donated their labor to the construction of this altar, whose beauty almost redeemed the ugliness of the socialist planned community that surrounded it. For days, the pounding of innumerable hammers was heard late into the evening. Residents strolled around as if it were a fair, commenting on the progress of the work, imagining what it would look like when finished, hoping that it would be left standing when everything was over.

A week before the pope's arrival, the central administrative authorities abruptly ordered work on the altar to halt. The masts formed three crosses that echoed the symbolism of the Gdansk shipyard monument; that upset them. It took great powers of persuasion to convince them that *these* three crosses were not *those* three crosses! And so, just three days before the pope's arrival, the ban was lifted, and the altar was completed in the nick of time. In Poland, struggle against the cross has always proven futile....

During the fall of 1980, in a record time of three months, a 140-foot monument had been erected near the gates of the Gdansk Shipyards to honor its dead: three anchors were affixed to three giant crosses. The monument was unveiled on the tenth anniversary of the December 1970 demonstrations, when the Militia had killed forty-eight workers protesting price hikes. During the ceremony, which was held in frigid weather, three hundred thousand people listened to *Lacrymosa*, a meditation on death composed for the occasion by Krzysztof Penderecki. No one would have suspected that exactly a year later, in this same place, battalions of

ZOMO would attack the shipyards and force their way through gates already flattened by tanks.

Now, in June 1987, the pope's voice rang out from beneath the very same monument. Though some had tried to convince the secretariat of the Vatican that the pope should avoid visiting it, John Paul II himself made clear his desire to pay his respects to those it memorialized, knowing full well the significance the monument had assumed. It was eventually agreed that the Holy Father's visit to Solidarity Square would be "unofficial"—a term that of course meant nothing to the Poles, who followed him everywhere. The Security Service cleared the square of people, trying to minimize the impact of his visit. But that only had the negative effect of making the square look sinister.

So then the government created its own crowd, calling on Party loyalists and young people from state-run enterprises to turn out and welcome the pope. Some of them regarded this as a privilege—many agreed without realizing that the whole thing was being staged—and in some districts tickets to the monument were in such demand they were issued by lottery. Party members who knew what was really going on tried to wriggle out of the trip, but a bit of persuasion brought obedience: "Comrades! It is every member's duty! You must greet the pope with dignity!" Despite all this, there still weren't enough people to fill the square, so buses were driven to the state-owned farms and loaded up with people the government hoped would be ignorant of the complicated issues involved—and hence would most reliably represent the interests of the state. Those chosen gathered at the shipyards (which were closed for the day), and they stood around smoking and waiting for instructions. They were told to react neither too coldly nor too enthusiastically to the pope, and of course there were to be no upraised hands, no V-for-victory signs, no cheering. Each of them was handed a small flag and assigned a place to stand. Solidarity Square was at last ready to greet the guest from the Vatican.

The line of vehicles passed quickly through the silent crowd. There was no clamoring, no emotion, only small flags waving mechanically back and forth. The figure in white approached the monument, followed close behind by Cardinal Glemp and Archbishops Casaroli, Colasuonno, and Martínez. The pope knelt, prayed, and gazed thoughtfully at the three anchors. "Divine Providence could not do better," he said. "In this place, silence is a cry!"

A moment later, he returned to his car and was driven toward the jubilant crowds decked out in traditional costumes. Meanwhile "the guardians of society" stayed behind to protect the monument from the common people who had gathered five hundred yards away; those who had been designated to stand closer went off to get the hot meal the government had prepared for them.

For me, the image of these puppets around the monument remains a nightmarish one. On one side of the monument, a few hundred yards away, was a joyous throng of men and women singing songs and children holding flowers, while on the other stood a morose crew sullenly waving little flags and then waiting in line between the endless rows of police dogs and the silent ZOMO agents for their ration of pea soup.

That afternoon, I was able to receive Holy Communion from the hands of John Paul II, with his ringing words echoing in my ears:

'One of the state's most important tasks is to create a space in which everyone, through his work, can grow and develop. Individual development in this created space is the precondition of the common good. If it does not exist, if life becomes too constricting and too narrow for human initiative—even if in the name of some collective good—that will work against society and against the common good.... Shoulder each other's burdens!'

These words, spoken not far from my gray apartment complex, touched a million hearts along with my own. Seeing the hundreds of banners, and feeling the enthusiasm of a crowd no longer cowed by the police, I became sure all at once that the era of intimidation was over. General Jaruzelski's program of "entente and struggle" was coming to an end. Without a legalized Solidarity, there would be no social stability and no reform.

Alas, two more years were to pass before it all came true.

Source: Walesa, Lech, with Arkadiusz Rybicki. *The Struggle and the Triumph: An Autobiography*. Translated by Franklin Philip and Helen Mahut. New York: Arcade, 1992.

13.2
At President Gorbachev's Side – 1988-1989
Excerpts from the Diary of Gorbachev Aide Anatoly Chernyaev

Anatoly Chernyaev was an aide to Soviet leader Mikhail Gorbachev, who launched major economic and political reforms in the Soviet Union during the late 1980s. In this first excerpt from the diary that Chernyaev kept during this time, he expresses deep admiration for Gorbachev's political daring and world vision. In the second excerpt written less than seven months later, however, Chernyaev despairs that Gorbachev's reformist agenda is degenerating into chaos.

[October 28, 1988]

[West German Chancellor Helmut] Kohl met one-on-one with Gorbachev (plus me and Horst Teltschik, assistant to the Chancellor). And when I saw this

Excerpt from *Anatoly Chernyaev 1991: The Diary of an Assistant to the President of the USSR*. Reprinted with permission from the Cold War International History Project Virtual Archive (http://www.cwihp.org).

striving at the highest level to speak as one human being to another human being (mutually), I felt physically that we were entering a new world, where class struggle, ideology, and, in general, polarity and enmity are no longer decisive. And something all-human is taking the upper hand. And then I came to realize how brave and farsighted M.S. [Gorbachev] is. He declared a "new thinking" "without any theoretical preparation" and began to act according to common sense. His ideas are: freedom of choice, mutual respect for each other's values, balance of interest, renunciation of force in politics, all-European house, liquidation of nuclear armaments, etc. All this, each by itself, is not original or new. What is new is that a person—who came out of Soviet Marxism-Leninism, Soviet society conditioned from top to bottom by Stalinism—began to carry out these ideas with all earnestness and sincerity when he became the head of state. No wonder that the world is stunned and full of admiration. And our public still cannot appreciate that he has already transferred all of them from one state to another....

[May 2, 1989]

Inside me, depression and alarm are growing, the sense of crisis in the Gorbachevian idea. He is prepared to go far. But what does it mean. His favorite catchword is "unpredictability." And most likely we will come to a collapse of the state and something like chaos. He feels that he is losing the levers of power irreversibly, and this realization prevents him from "going far." For this reason he holds to conventional methods but acts with "velvet gloves." He has no concept of where we are going. His declaration about socialist values, the ideals of October, as he begins to tick them off, sound like irony to the cognoscenti. Behind them—emptiness.

Source: Chernyaev, Anatoly. *Anatoly Chernyaev 1991: The Diary of an Assistant to the President of the USSR.* Moscow: TERRA, 1997. Translated from Russian by Vladislav Zubok. Obtained by the Cold War International History Project. Available online at the Cold War International History Project Virtual Archive, http://www.wilsoncenter.org/index.cfm?topic_id=1409&fuseaction=va2.browse&sort=Collection.

13.3
America Monitors Events in China's Tiananmen Square – 1989
Excerpts from a U.S. State Department Intelligence Summary

In 1989 Eastern Europe was convulsed by a wave of powerful independence movements. As a result, numerous states that had long been faithful members of the Soviet empire severed their ties with Communism and charted new and independent courses. Rebellion against state authority also reared its head in Communist China. But in this case, ruthless political leaders successfully squashed the rebellion. The most visible steps taken by China's Communist leadership to maintain their iron grip on power unfolded in Bei-

*jing's Tiananmen Square. In the spring of 1989, Chinese students organized
a series of pro-democracy protests there. The Chinese government countered
by rolling tanks into Tiananmen Square to crush the uprising, and government troops massacred hundreds of protesting students. The following summary of events in Tiananmen Square was prepared by the U.S. State Department's Bureau of Intelligence and Research on June 5, 1989.*

Secretary's Morning Summary for June 5, 1989

1. China

A. After the Bloodbath

Yesterday and this morning troops continued to fire indiscriminately at citizens in the area near Tiananmen Square. Citizens tried to block streets and burned
armored vehicles and army trucks. Hundreds of military vehicles including at least
34 tanks and numerous armored personnel carriers have been destroyed over the
last two days, according [excised] and press reports. Secured a university campus
where students had captured an armored personnel carrier, and issued a warning
that executions of students will begin tonight according to [excised]. Units are
poised outside several other colleges, and the military said troops will move against
the campuses if resistance does not cease. Some students have seized weapons and
are vowing to resist. Non-violent protests have occurred in half a dozen other cities;
[excised] press have reported that more than 1,000 soldiers and police were killed
or wounded and that some civilians were killed. Foreign estimates range from hundreds to as many as 2,600 civilians killed and thousands injured. But the severity of
the assault on Tiananmen Square is clear. Troops shot indiscriminately into crowds
of unarmed civilians, including women and children, often with automatic
weapons. In one case, students attempting to parlay with troops were gunned
down. Foreign journalists report seeing fleeing protestors shot in the back. Enraged
protesters burned personnel carriers and killed some security personnel.

Source: "Secretary's Summary for June 5, 1989." National Security Archive, George Washington University.
    Available online at http://www.gwu.edu/~nsarchiv/NSAEBB/NSAEBB16/documents/17-01.htm.

13.4
The Fall of the Berlin Wall – 1989
The Text of "Deutschland, Deutschland," by CNN Journalist Bettina Lüscher

*In 1989 the political reforms that were rocking the Soviet Union extended deep
into Eastern Europe. Reformers throughout the Eastern bloc became convinced
that the suffocating Soviet grip on the region was finally loosening, and popu-*

lar democratic movements burst into life in nation after nation. By the end of 1989 these revolutionary movements had swept out of power every Communist regime in Eastern Europe. Even East Germany, architect of the Berlin Wall and home to one of the Eastern bloc's most repressive governments, was swept along by this tide of change. On November 9, 1989, the Berlin Wall was breached and overrun by celebrating crowds that had gathered on both sides of the barrier. The peaceful fall of the Wall—perhaps the best-known symbol of the Cold War divide between East and West—made it clear to all that the world really was undergoing momentous changes.

One of the witnesses to the remarkable turn of events in Berlin was journalist Bettina Lüscher, a native West German who covered European affairs for CNN from its Frankfurt bureau. Lüscher recalled her memories of the fall of the Berlin Wall for CNN's "Cold War" online exhibition.

It's easy to say you saw it coming, the fall of the Wall. But if you are honest, you'd have to admit you had no clue. None. The Wall coming down? German unification?

It seemed unthinkable.

Yes, we knew Gorbachev had warned his East German counterparts with an old verse: "Those who arrive late will be punished by life."

Yes, there was perestroika and glasnost in the former evil empire.

Yes, the East Germans were getting daring in their demands for change. But that ugly Wall, cutting through Berlin's neighborhoods, seemed invincible.

Maybe in a few years, a few decades—but not now.

On the late afternoon of Thursday, November 9, 1989, East German government official Guenter Schabowski read from a small piece of paper in a news conference and announced that travel documents were no longer necessary for East Germans wanting to travel West.

We journalists looked at each other in disbelief. Is that what we think it is? Can everyone leave? Is the Wall open?

One colleague from German television uttered, "They can't do that to me…. There goes the rundown for my show."

And then we ran—to telephones, to computer terminals, to the Wall. And there they came—the East Berliners.

It didn't feel like a new phase of Ostpolitik. It didn't feel like a new phase of the Cold War. It was much more immediate. Much more intense. Joy. Laughter. Happiness. Curiosity. Confusion. Uncertainty. Fear.

Bettina Lüscher, "Deutschland, Deutschland: Reflections on the Wall." Reprinted courtesy of CNN.

During the previous weeks and months, a growing movement of discontent had become much more visible in East Germany. It started in small dissident groups, was nurtured by the churches, and exploded in that hot summer of '89 with the flight of hundreds of East Germans into West German embassies in the Eastern bloc.

If the world had not realized that change was in the air in the East, it could now watch it on television.

Hof, a city on the Western side of the German-German border, would be remembered as one of the first stops we journalists made on our whistle-stop tour of crumbling socialist empires, of blossoming new democracies.

The trains full of East German refugees arrived in the drab train station in Hof—tired faces peering out of the windows, wiping away tears, waving towards reporters, shouting "Deutschland, Deutschland."

It sounded awkward to many of us West Germans on that platform.

Deutschland, Deutschland? It was a new sound, an unusual chant, maybe sometimes heard at international soccer games, but not like this! We were not quite sure what it meant: Freedom? One country instead of two? Hope? Promise? Or a new nationalism? We wondered.

A few weeks later, Leipzig was the place that shook the East Berlin government to its core. First hundreds, then thousands, finally tens of thousands of East Germans marched for reform, for change.

Armed with hidden video cameras, the Western TV networks descended on that city every Monday, taping those moments of civil discontent. The protesters were amazing. They stood in front of those feared men in gray and blue windbreakers—the uniform of the Stasi, the East German state security. The protesters stared them down, refused to be intimidated any more, shouted: "Stasi down, Stasi down.... Stasi into the coal mines."

It was daring, rebellious, inspiring.

It was great TV. We rushed back to Berlin and crossed the border checkpoints with our small video cassettes to feed the pictures via satellite to the world.

By early November we didn't worry about smuggling those tapes back to West Berlin. East German state TV broadcast those Leipzig "Monday demos" live. Erich Honecker had stepped down. East Berlin was a city full of rumor.

On the 4th, hundreds of thousands marched toward Alexanderplatz. They wanted a different government. They poked fun at the new man in charge. Egon Krenz, famous for his big toothed-grin, was depicted as the wolf from the fairy tale "Little Red Riding Hood." A banner asked, "Why is this man smiling?"

Dissidents spoke, authors spoke. And a spy, too. Markus Wolf addressed the masses. The infamous master spy—once nicknamed "the Man Without a Face" by frustrated Western spy agencies—wanted to see if there was a spot for him in this movement. But the people didn't want those men anymore. They wanted something new. But what? And how?

The atmosphere was different from that in Leipzig. Here it was somber, more organized, more orderly. One could sense that people were worried about their future. It wasn't as joyful as in Leipzig. It was heavy with concern over whether the situation could get out of control—along with an awareness that it was easier to oppose a regime than to try to change it. And change it to what?

There was no united movement. Different factions were demanding a variety of contradictory things: New socialism. Unification with the West. A separate East German state for now. No unification under any circumstance.

Five days later it was over. The Wall was open. Berliners were dancing on the Wall, hammering away at the Wall, kissing strangers on the Wall, driving their "Trabi" cars through the opened Wall. It was over.

The TV networks built platforms overlooking the Wall, showed the scenes live around the world around the clock, anchored special after special in languages from every corner of the world.

It was the story of a lifetime. Having worked for 30 hours straight in front of the Brandenburg Gate, I sat on our TV platform at 5 in the morning, sorting through notes, cables and videotapes.

A man in his mid-30s walked up to me.

"Hello," he said. He looked at all the expensive high-tech gear the modern media circus travels with. He looked at all the telephones we had organized within hours after the fall of the Wall.

"Hmm," he said, "we sometimes had to wait 10 years for a phone."

I looked at him with that West German expression full of guilt for having been wealthier, luckier, better off somehow.

He started smiling and said, "Have a wonderful day."

"Danke, you too!" I replied. He waved and walked away. Westward.

Source: Lüscher, Bettina. "Deutschland, Deutschland: Reflections on the Wall." *CNN: The Cold War*. Available online at CNN, http://www.cnn.com/SPECIALS/cold.war/episodes/23/reflections.

13.5

Vaclev Havel Leads the Velvet Revolution – 1989
The Text of the Declaration of the Civic Forum

The political tumult that rocked Eastern Europe in the late 1980s affected Czechoslovakia as well. The resistance movement in that country started out small, but by 1989 the resistance had grown well beyond the original small group of writers and other intellectuals. Sensing that a new age of political freedom was within their grasp, large numbers of students and workers declared their support for playwright Vaclav Havel and other resistance leaders. "The emergence of the playwright Vaclav Havel as a heroic and pivotal figure for the opposition was an important turning point," wrote former President George H.W. Bush and National Security Advisor Brent Scowcroft in their book A World Transformed. *"When, as a result of disturbances in January [1989], the government decided to make an example of him through arrest, trial, and imprisonment, it instead revealed Havel as a charismatic leader. In a way, he became the Czech Lech Walesa, symbolizing—and vocalizing in unparalleled fashion—the hopes of his people. This peaceable and quiet man soon became a rallying figure for the entire population."*

Havel's imprisonment was brief, and in November 1989 his leadership of the so-called "Velvet Revolution" sweeping across Czechoslovakia culminated with a public declaration of political goals by the Civic Forum, a coalition of pacifist forces that were nonetheless determined to bring about a new age of political freedom in the country. Following is the full text of the declaration, dated November 23, 1989. On December 29, 1989, Havel was elected president by the Czech Federal Assembly, and he retained the presidency one year later after free and open elections were held.

The Declaration of The Civic Forum

After twenty years Czechoslovakia once again finds itself at a historical intersection thanks to the people's movement, to which all generations and segments of the population and the majority of the still existing social organizations are quickly adding themselves. This movement is a movement of both of our nations. Its mouthpiece has spontaneously become the Civic Forum, which today is the real representative of the will of the people. Its natural component has become the well-organized student movement, which, through its protest demonstration, gave us the impulse for dramatic social movement. Within it work all the current independent initiatives, artistic unions headed by the theater—the first to be in solidarity with the students—and the renewed currents in the National Front, including many former and current members of the CPCz [Czechoslovak Communist Party]. The Catholic Church supported the Civic Forum through the words of the cardinal, and other churches in Czechoslovakia. Anyone who agrees with its demands is joining, and may join, the Civic Forum.

The Civic Forum is prepared to secure a dialogue between the public and the present leadership immediately and has at its disposal qualified forces [from] all areas of society, capable of carrying out a free and objective dialogue about real paths toward a change in the political and economic conditions in our country.

The situation is open now, there are many opportunities before us, and we have only two certainties.

The first is the certainty that there is no return to the previous totalitarian system of government, which led our country to the brink of an absolute spiritual, moral, political, economic and ecological crisis.

Our second certainty is that we want to live in a free, democratic, and prosperous Czechoslovakia, which must return to Europe, and that we will never abandon this ideal, no matter what transpires in these next few days.

The Civic Forum calls on all citizens of Czechoslovakia to support its fundamental demands by the demonstration of a general strike declared for Monday, 27 November 1989, at noon. Whether our country sets out in a peaceful way on the road to a democratic social order, or whether an isolated group of Stalinists, who want at any price to preserve their power and their privileges disguised as empty phrases about reconstruction will conquer, may depend upon the success of this strike.

We challenge the leadership of this country to grasp the gravity of this situation, rid themselves of compromised individuals and prevent all eventual efforts for a violent revolution.

We call on all the members of the ruling party to join the citizenry and respect its will.

We challenge all members of the People's Militias to not come out violently against their comrade workers and thus spit upon all the traditions of worker solidarity.

We challenge all the members of the Police to realize that they are first and foremost human beings and citizens of this country and only second subordinate to their superiors.

We challenge the Czechoslovak People's Army to stand on the side of the people and, if necessary, to come out in its defense for the first time.

We call on the public and the governments of all countries to realize that our homeland is from time immemorial the place where European and world confrontations have begun and ended, and that in our country it is not only its fate which is at stake, but the future of all of Europe. We therefore demand that they support in every way the people's movement and the Civic Forum.

We are opponents of violence; we do not want revenge; we want to live as dignified and free people, who have the right to speak for the fate of their homeland and who also think of future generations.

The Civic Forum
23 November 1989

Source: "The Declaration of Civic Forum Representative Václav Havel on Wenceslas Square, Prague, 23 November 1989." *Cold War International History Project Bulletin*, Issue 12/13, Fall/Winter 2001. Available online at the Woodrow Wilson International Center for Scholars, http://www.wilsoncenter. org/topics/pubs/ACF35.pdf.

13.6

Romania After the Fall of the Ceaușescu Regime – 1989
An Excerpt from The Hole in the Flag *by Andrei Codrescu*

Journalist and poet Andrei Codrescu endured a quarter-century period of exile before returning to Romania in late December 1989. Arriving mere days after President Nicolae Ceaușescu and his wife Elena had been executed in retribution for decades of tyrannical rule, Codrescu roamed the streets of Bucharest and the nation's mountainous countryside. He recounted these experiences in The Hole in the Flag, *a memoir that mixed memories of his childhood during the dark Ceaușescu years with impressions of the changes sweeping across Eastern Europe after the collapse of the Soviet empire.*

Moments before the end of the decade I stood in the cold, ice-covered center of University Square in Bucharest, Romania, and said a brief prayer of thanks. The only light came from the small sea of candles burning in the snow at the martyrs' shrine before me. Bits of paper taped to a Christmas tree at the center of the shrine fluttered in the bitter wind. Penciled awkwardly on them: "Thank you, children, for dying so that we could be free!" "Your young lives ended here for us!" "You brought us Christmas!" "Good-bye, my child, you died for your country!" A few days before, dozens of young people had died here, murdered by machine-gun pistols firing point-blank into the unarmed crowd. There was still blood under the layers of ice and snow under my feet.

"I remember listening to Radio Free Europe in my childhood with the shades drawn, the lights off. If I walked down any darkened street of my hometown at that hour, I would have seen the lowered shades and the furtive dark in which glowed the soft dial of the radio."

They had also died so that I could stand here for the first time, twenty-five years after leaving my homeland. This magical city of my youth, which I had once thought to conquer with my poetry, was both different and the same. The dome of the Athenaeum and some of the snow-covered church cupolas near the venerable music academy were just the way I'd kept them in memory. But other landmarks, including many churches, had fallen to the dictator's bulldozers. In their stead rose a forest of uniformly depressing apartment buildings. Beyond them, etched against the frozen sky, was a steel gray forest of cranes that would have built yet another layer of these ordered hives that had been Ceaușescu's vision of his gridded, controlled world.

The dictator's architects had been poised to erase the country's past in order to transform it into a single cube of square cement in homage to their boss.

Over the two decades and a half of my exile I had nursed countless fantasies of return, all of them triumphant, involving Bucharest in late summer or fall. I saw myself at a sidewalk café, drinking the new wine, in animated conversation with the friends of my youth. Now and then a spray of linden flowers would descend gently from the tress above us to land in the wine and in our hair. The girls had deep black eyes and long raven black hair. We were, all of us, exactly the way I left us, in that faraway autumn of 1965 when I took the airplane to another world....

I stood in the fierce December cold, feeling happily warm. My personal triumph now did not involve only my person; it was the triumph of an entire people. I silently thanked the student martyrs of Bucharest, invoking a deity I rarely appealed to, because I, like the young people who died here, had been raised under communism to believe only in the material world. But the events of December that transformed Romania in the course of a few days were a miracle. The only appropriate response before a miracle is prayer. And the small tree blazing in the square was a Christmas tree, not a New Year's tree, as it had been euphemistically called for forty-five years. When I was six years old, my nanny, Kiva, taught me the Christians' Lord's Prayer, the words of which, in Romanian, I used only in cases of extreme emergency. After I left Romania and came to live in America, I spoke less and less Romanian, and after many years my world was almost entirely in English. But there remained at the core of myself a little island of Romanian, at the center of which there lived this small prayer. These words surged out of me now like a bright shaft of childhood spanning two languages and two worlds....

As I stood holding on to the nearly empty bottle of champagne before the martyrs' candles, I felt both euphoria and estrangement well up inside me. The dream motifs of magic and folklore have never lost their power here. "We are a dream in the mind of a madman," people said of the Ceauşescu years. The evil dreamer was gone, but journeying from his dream to the shores of reality was a dreamlike journey itself....

Looming in monolithic ugliness behind us was the Hotel InterContinental, where our small news team from National Public Radio was quartered. The thirteenth floor of the hotel, which the elevator skipped entirely, had belonged to Securitate [the Romanian secret police]. Two days after Ceauşescu's downfall, in full view of the world's cameras, men came and carted away two trucks full of consoles, wires, headphones, and other, more obscure electronics. According to the former head of Romania's secret police, Ion Mihai Pacepa, there had been ten million microphones in a country of twenty-three million people. That would mean that nearly everyone had been listened to and then blackmailed into listening and reporting on others. A maze of psychic tunnels led from one person to another. The immediate effect of such perceived attention to the minutiae of everyone's life had been a dreadful intimacy, a lack of privacy equal to the shared living quarters in the block buildings of the cities. A feeling of claustrophobic oppression held everyone as if he or she were already living underground, in a place without heat and light, which was also actually true. Heat and electricity had been withheld for most of the 1980s so that Romania's foreign debt could be paid. People had been living in an increasingly cold darkness. But the dread and secrecy did not begin with Ceaușescu. I remember listening to Radio Free Europe in my childhood with the shades drawn, the lights off. If I walked down any darkened street of my hometown at that hour, I would have seen the lowered shades and the furtive dark in which glowed the soft dial of the radio. Everyone hid the obvious from everyone else. In the light of day we were forced to obscure ourselves. Thus, daylight was the time of the lie, while night held the truth. Everything had been thus twisted, reversed, made to stand on its head in the world the Communists made. This revolution, like all the others in Communist Europe, had to come in order to restore a sense of reality. But in Romania, unlike the other countries of Central and East Europe, this necessary change was made with the blood of children....

"The Antichrist died on Christmas Day!" With these words the Romanian radio announcers let the nation and the world know that Nicolae and Elena Ceaușescu, the rulers of Romania for a quarter of a century, had been put to death by a firing squad after a summary trial by a military court.

On television Romanians saw the two crumpled bodies fallen away from each other on the frozen ground of a small, dingy courtyard. The two corpses filled the living rooms of billions of people all over the world, via satellite. Thousands of miles away, in New Orleans, I watched, fascinated and repelled. Few images conveyed as starkly the end of an era. I remembered seeing Ceaușescu on TV less than a week before, standing woodenly on the balcony of his palace with his arms extended, speaking to an obedient crowd of hundreds of thousands. When the sea of people began suddenly booing him, he stood there, his mouth open, his arms frozen in a useless gesture. His face white, he turned and was gone—forever. At that moment he had looked already dead. Paradoxically, in death Ceaușescu looked more alive than he had on his balcony, making that last speech....

It was later reported that at the very last moment, when it became apparent that they would indeed be executed—a job for which the entire unit volunteered, though only three were chosen—the Ceaușescus tried to run. Certainly, whether they tried to run or not, at the moment of their deaths the Ceaușescus must have tried desperately to find the entrance to their tunnels. But the ground didn't open, the gate stayed elusive. They were cut down in childish flight, recipients of some thirty bullets each. Soldiers, who are only people, kill with guns, but the spirit kills with irony. The spirits of those who perished in the regime's jails and undergrounds made sure the smallest possible death would tend their murderer. And yet the faces of the crumpled bodies on the ground are still disbelieving. We are not

459

dead, they seem to say, because we cannot possibly die in such a tiny, dirty place. This expression is perhaps what makes them seem more alive than they were at the stone-faced apex of their power. Ceaușescu had been one of the last of his kind. I remembered the grim parade of Communist leaders standing woodenly on rostrums at official parades. Some of them, like Leonid Brezhnev, may have been actually dead up there. No one could tell the difference. By the end of 1989 these leaders and the ossified societies they managed crumbled like mummies exposed to sudden daylight. How long had the people of these countries been ruled by the dead? And how long will it take them to shake off the chill of the grave?

Source: Codrescu, Andrei. *The Hole in the Flag: A Romanian Exile's Story of Return and Revolution.* New York: William Morrow, 1991.

13.7
Ten Minutes to Midnight – 1990
The Text of an Editorial Published by the Board of Directors of the Bulletin of the Atomic Scientists

The Bulletin of the Atomic Scientists *was founded by a group of scientists who worked on the Manhattan Project during World War II. The Manhattan Project was the code name for the group that built the first atomic bomb. Since 1947, the Board of Directors of the Bulletin of the Atomic Scientists has maintained a "Doomsday Clock," a symbol of nuclear danger in which "midnight" is meant to represent nuclear armageddon. In the aftermath of the end of the Cold War, the Board moved the clock back from six minutes to midnight to ten minutes to midnight. This decision reflected their belief that the world had made progress in avoiding nuclear war. Following is the text of an editorial published by the Board in April 1990 to explain their reasoning in moving the clock back.*

The end of the Cold War has not ended fears of nuclear disaster, however. In 1998 the Board of the Bulletin of the Atomic Scientists changed the Doomsday Clock to nine minutes to midnight after India and Pakistan both announced nuclear testing. In 2002 the Board moved the hand forward to seven minutes to midnight, citing the September 11, 2001, terrorist attacks in America, security problems with Russia's nuclear stockpiles, troubled relations between India and Pakistan, and continued nuclear proliferation.

Ten Minutes to Midnight

A solitary Chinese man standing in the path of a column of tanks. Demonstrating South African women being attacked by police dogs. A playwright named

460

president of Czechoslovakia. The bodies of six Salvadoran priests. All are faces of human courage in the struggle for freedom and dignity.

While aware that the struggle continues around the world, we rejoice in humanity's momentous victory in Eastern Europe. People revolted against the communist leaders whose power, exercise through rigid bureaucracies and brutal police apparatuses, ultimately rested on the Soviet army. This time, in contrast to 1956 and 1968, the Soviets did not intervene.

Now, 44 years after Winston Churchill's "Iron Curtain" speech, the myth of monolithic communism has been shattered for all to see, the ideological conflict known as the Cold War is over, and the risk of global nuclear war being ignited in Europe is significantly diminished. Although success is in no way guaranteed, this is the greatest opportunity in four decades to create a safe, sustainable world. In response, we turn back the hands of the Bulletin clock four minutes, to stand at 10 minutes to midnight.

The Cold War mindset interpreted world events through the distorting prism of East-West conflict. The competition was labeled "cold" to distinguish it from World War II, a hot war where guns were fired, bombs exploded, tens of millions of people killed. Yet, during the past 45 years approximately 125 wars were fought, more than 20 million people killed.

The conflict was cold only in that World War III did not happen. Aside from the close call in Cuba in 1962, U.S. and Soviet leaders didn't square off in a direct fight that could have led to nuclear disaster. Instead, they grudgingly respected each other's right to police their respective empires, demonstrated restrained opposition to each other's bloody interventions in Vietnam and Afghanistan, fought proxy wars, and profited by becoming the world's largest arms suppliers. They popularized language that segregated most people on earth into a separate "Third World."

Through it all, the people of the United States and Soviet Union put the world at greater risk than at any time in history. Mesmerized by Cold War rhetoric, they allowed, even urged, their governments to build massive nuclear arsenals, amounting today to one million times the explosive power of the Hiroshima bomb. Until those arsenals are eliminated, the danger persists that an accident, a miscalculation, or irrational act will cause nuclear holocaust. We urge speedy conclusion of a U.S. Soviet Strategic Arms Reduction Treaty (START) as a next step.

Rapid progress toward nuclear disarmament by the superpowers and other nuclear-armed nations has become urgent for other reasons. Domestic strife in a nation with nuclear weapons stockpiles opens the possibility that weapons could fall into the hand of unstable groups. Furthermore, deep reductions would strengthen the case for stopping the proliferation of weapons of mass destruction and minimize the risk that they will be used in regional wars. All nuclear weapons tests should be halted.

Due to Cold War rationales, the two military superpowers are organized as national security states upheld by vast military and intelligence bureaucracies and shielded from public scrutiny by layers of secrecy. These powerful infrastructures must now be dismantled and sensible defense policies established. "National security" should no longer justify bankrupt policies and conceal misdeeds. American and Soviet citizens are just beginning to reassess their countries' genuine defense needs, a prerequisite for drastic reduction in military spending and the reallocation of resources. People must work more vigorously to demilitarize their societies and effectively address fundamental issues of poverty, hunger, and environmental damage.

The transition into the post-Cold War era will not be painless. Along with the joy and promise, the demise of the old order, as witnessed in Eastern Europe and the Soviet Union, can unleash previously suppressed ethnic and religious rivalries. The quest throughout the world for economic structures that avoid the unjust extremes of monopoly communism and laissez-faire capitalism will produce instability and conflict. That this is now less likely to trigger global war offers no solace to the victims.

The difficulties in creating a better world should not be underestimated, but we believe that the overall trend is positive. We are encouraged, for example, by the impressive United Nations efforts to resolve international conflicts in Namibia, Iran and Iraq, and elsewhere. The actual dismantling of U.S. and Soviet intermediate-range ballistic missiles under the INF Treaty and the unilateral Soviet withdrawals of thousands of tanks and troops from central Europe are significant deeds.

Much remains to be done before the greatest short-term threat to the planet—the risk of nuclear war—is eliminated. Additional concrete actions that disarm the relations among nations are needed before the hands of the clock can be turned back further. Still, the termination of the Cold War has lifted a grim weight from the human psyche. It has returned to humanity its hope for a future, and the chance to create one.

Source: "Ten Minutes to Midnight." *Bulletin of the Atomic Scientists*, April 1990. Available online at http://www.thebulletin.org/pdf/046_003_005.pdf.

13.8
Gorbachev's Farewell Address to the Soviet Citizens – 1991
The Text of a Nationally Televised Address

By the end of 1991 Mikhail Gorbachev had become a powerless figurehead. On December 21-22, 1991, eleven of the fifteen former Soviet republics confirmed their independence at a conference of former Soviet states in Alma Ata, Kazakhstan. Their stand brought the already teetering USSR crashing to the ground. With no unified union to preside over, President Gorbachev no longer had any official functions to fulfill. Accepting this reality, Gorbachev delivered a nationally televised farewell address to the people of Russia and the other former Soviet republics on December 25, 1991. The full text of this address is reprinted below.

Dear fellow countrymen! Compatriots!

Given the current situation and the formation of the Commonwealth of Independent States, I am ceasing my activities as President of the USSR. I have arrived at this decision for reasons of principle.

I have always spoken out in favour of autonomy and the independence of nations and sovereignty of the republics. But at the same time, I support the preservation of a Union state and the integrity of the country.

Events have taken a different course. A trend towards dismembering the country and the disintegration of the state has prevailed, which I cannot accept. My position on this issue has not changed after the Alma Ata meeting and the decisions made there.

Furthermore, I am convinced that decisions of such importance should have been made by popular will. However, I will do everything within my power to ensure that the Alma Ata agreements bring real unity to our society and pave the way out of the crisis, facilitating a sustained reform process.

Addressing you for the last time as President of the USSR, I find it necessary to state my position with regard to the path we have embarked upon since 1985—especially since controversial, superficial and biased judgements abound.

Fate had decided that, when I became head of state, it was already obvious that there was something wrong in this country. We had plenty of everything: land, oil, gas and other natural resources, and God has also endowed us with intellect and talent—yet we lived much worse than people in other industrialized countries and the gap was constantly widening.

The reason was apparent even then—our society was stifled in the grip of a bureaucratic command system. Doomed to serve ideology and bear the heavy burden of the arms race, it was strained to the utmost.

All attempts at implementing half-hearted reforms—and there have been many—failed, one after the other. The country was losing hope. We could not go on living like this. We had to change everything radically.

For this reason, I never regretted that I did not use my position as General Secretary merely to 'reign' for a few years. This would have been irresponsible and immoral.

Mikhail Gorbachev, Address to the Soviet Citizens, 25 December 1991. Reprinted with permission from the Gorbachev Foundation.

I understood that initiating reforms on such a large scale in a society like ours was a most difficult and risky undertaking. But even now, I am convinced that the democratic reforms started in the spring of 1985 were historically justified.

The process of renovating this country and bringing about fundamental changes in the international community proved to be much more complex than originally anticipated. However, let us acknowledge what has been achieved so far.

Society has acquired freedom; it has been freed politically and spiritually. And this is the most important achievement, which we have not fully come to grips with, in part because we still have not learned how to use our freedom. However, a historic task has been accomplished.

- The totalitarian system, which prevented this country from becoming wealthy and prosperous a long time ago, has been dismantled.

- A breakthrough has been made on the road to democratic reforms. Free elections, freedom of the press, freedom of worship, representative legislatures, and a multi-party system have all become realities.

- We have set out to introduce a pluralistic economy, and the equality of all forms of ownership is being established. In the course of the land reform, the peasantry is reviving, individual farmers have appeared, and millions of hectares of land have been allocated to the urban and rural population. Laws were passed on the economic freedom of producers, and free enterprise, shareholding and privatization are under way.

- Shifting the course of our economy towards a free market, we must not forget that this is being done for the benefit of the individual. In these times of hardship, everything must be done to ensure the social protection of the individual—particularly old people and children.

We live in a new world:

- An end has been put to the 'Cold War,' the arms race and the insane militarization of our country, which crippled our economy, distorted our thinking and undermined our morals. The threat of a world war is no more.

Once again, I should like to stress that I have done everything in my power during the transition period to ensure safe control over nuclear weapons.

- We opened ourselves up to the rest of the world, renounced interference in the affairs of others and the use of troops beyond our borders. In response, we have gained trust, solidarity, and respect.

- We have become a major stronghold for the reorganization of modern civilization on the basis of peaceful, democratic principles.

- The peoples and nations of this country have acquired genuine freedom to choose their own way toward self-determination. The quest for a democratic reform of our multinational state has led us to the point where we were about to sign a new Union treaty.

All these changes demanded utmost exertion and were carried through under conditions of an unrelenting struggle against the growing resistance from the old, obsolete and reactionary forces—the former Party and state structures and the economic management apparatus—as well as our patterns, our ideological prejudices, our egalitarian and parasitic psychology. The change ran up against our intolerance, a low level of political culture, and a fear of change. That is why we have wasted so much time. The old system tumbled down before the new one could begin functioning. And our society slid into an even deeper crisis.

I am aware of the dissatisfaction with today's grave situation, the harsh criticism of the authorities at all levels and of my personal role. But I would like to stress once again: in so vast a country, given its heritage, fundamental changes cannot be carried out without difficulties and pain.

The August coup brought the overall crisis to a breaking point. The most disastrous aspect of this crisis is the collapse of statehood. And today I watch apprehensively the loss of the citizenship of a great country by our citizens—the consequences of this could be grave, for all of us.

I consider it vitally important to sustain the democratic achievements of the last few years. We have earned them through the suffering of our entire history and our tragic experience. We must not abandon them under any circumstances, under any pretext. Otherwise, all our hopes for a better future will be buried.

I am speaking of this frankly and honestly. It is my moral duty.

Today I want to express my gratitude to all those citizens who have given their support to the policy of renovating this country and who participated in the democratic reforms.

I am thankful to statesmen, political and public leaders, and millions of ordinary people in other countries—to all those who understood our objectives and gave us their support, meeting us halfway and offering genuine cooperation.

I leave my post with concern—but also with hope, with faith in you, your wisdom and spiritual strength. We are the heirs of a great civilization, and its revival and transformation to a modern and dignified life depend on all and everyone.

I would like to express my heartfelt thanks to those who stood by my side, defending the right and good cause over all these years. We certainly could have avoided certain errors and done better in many ways. But I am convinced that, sooner or later, our common efforts will bear fruit and our peoples will live in a prosperous and democratic society.

I wish all the best to everyone.

Source: Gorbachev, Mikhail. Address to the Soviet Citizens, December 25, 1991. Reprinted in *Memoirs*, English translation by Wolf Jobst Siedler Verlag. New York: Doubleday, 1995.

13.9
Gorbachev Exits the Kremlin – 1991
Excerpts from Memoirs, *by Mikhail Gorbachev*

After the dissolution of the USSR, former President Mikhail Gorbachev returned to private life. According to this excerpt from his Memoirs, his final days in the Kremlin were both disillusioning and humiliating. He blamed much of this on Russian President Boris Yeltsin, a one-time ally who had become a fierce political foe in the late 1980s. Their rivalry began after Yeltsin, a political maverick, decided that Gorbachev was not sufficiently dedicated to instituting major economic and political reforms.

Goodbye to the Kremlin

In Alma Ata the council of leaders of the Commonwealth of Independent States [CIS] made a decision concerning my status after I ceased to be President of the USSR.

At my request, the Russian President signed a decree providing premises for the political and socio-economic research fund I had decided to create and direct in order to continue my activities under the new conditions. (Yeltsin retracted this decision only a few months later.)

There were no farewells. None of the leaders of the states of the CIS telephoned me, neither on the day of my departure nor since—in over four years.

The transfer of Supreme Command to the Russian President was scheduled for the evening of 25 December. We had agreed that the ceremony should take place in my Kremlin office. Defence minister Shaposhnikov, with a group of generals and the officers who were continually keeping guard over the famous presidential "briefcases" with the control system for nuclear arms, was already waiting for us. A few minutes passed—the Russian President was apparently late. Then I was told that he had refused to come, in spite of our agreement. It turned out that Yeltsin, together with his entourage, had listened to my televised speech [a goodbye address to the Soviet citizenry, delivered on December 25, 1991] and flown into a rage.

After a while, I was told that the Russian President proposed to meet on 'neutral territory'—in the Catherine Hall, i.e. the part of the Kremlin where talks with foreign leaders were usually held. Yeltsin and his team apparently saw this as a symbolic gesture. However, their action looked rather comical, not to say stupid. I therefore decided to send immediately a package to Yeltsin containing the decree of the USSR President on the transfer of Supreme Command over the armed forces to the President of Russia. I handed the briefcase to Shaposhnikov, asking him to take it to its new owner as quickly as possible and report back to me. The entire procedure took only a few minutes.

Thus even in the first minutes after stepping down I was faced with impudence and a lack of courtesy. Ensuing events proved that this action, rather than an isolated backlash of Yeltsin's feelings of revenge, was part of the policy he had adopted towards me.

Yeltsin put off his presidential duties to supervise personally my 'expulsion' from the Kremlin. He gave instructions for the lowering of the Soviet flag and the hoisting of the flag of the Russian Federation, and personally saw to it that the procedure should be completed according to schedule and filmed by television cameras. We had initially agreed that I should vacate my Kremlin office by 30 December. An interview with journalists from the Japanese newspaper *Yomiuri* was scheduled for 27 December. However, on the morning of the 27th, I received a telephone call from the Kremlin reception-room: I was informed that Yeltsin, Khasbulatov and Burbolis had occupied my office at 8:30 a.m. and held a party there, emptying a bottle of whiskey.... This was the triumph of plunderers—I can find no other word for it.

I was told to vacate both the country residence and the presidential apartment within three days. On 25 December, even before my television address, a group of people appeared at the house in Kosygin Street to seal the presidential apartment. Everything had to be done in a rush; we were forced to move to different lodgings within twenty-four hours. I saw the results in the morning—heaps of clothes, books, dishes, folders, newspapers, letters and God knows what lying strewn on the floor.

Following this 'exodus,' we settled into our new apartment. I busied myself with my personal belongings (the library, all sorts of papers that had accumulated over the years—notes, letters, telegrams, photographs, documents...). Waves of recollection swept over me, pictures of both remote and recent events. These caused me to meditate on the past.

I was under the spell of painful reflections. Time and again I reached the same conclusion: we were still only at the beginning of the road we had chosen in March 1985. Let people talk about the end of the Gorbachev era as much as they want— the main act was only just about to begin....

Meanwhile developments in the country took an alarming turn. The so-called 'shock therapy'—a 'cavalry attack' on our economy—brought enormous hardships for the people of Russia. Power was in the hands of irresponsible, incompetent people, who were both ambitious and ruthless. With every passing day, it becomes more and more obvious that what the country needs is a new balance of political forces and a new policy. Not only Russia, but all the other states of the CIS, the former republics of the USSR, are in this difficult situation.

All of this is to a great extent an aftermath of the December coup, a black page in the history of Russia and the Union. However, it is obviously not the last page. Life continues and the peoples of the republics, once they have 'mastered' the newly gained freedom, will find new paths towards reunification and the renewal of their lives. This is my hope and my belief.

Source: Gorbachev, Mikhail. *Memoirs*, English translation by Wolf Jobst Siedler Verlag. New York: Doubleday, 1995.

14

RUSSIA AND THE WORLD IN THE POST-COLD WAR ERA

In this St. Petersburg street scene, an elderly Russian woman begs for money as office workers bustle past.

INTRODUCTION

As the Soviet Union dissolved in 1991, fifteen independent republics were formed. These former republics, as well as the nations of Eastern Europe that once lived under Communist rule, have struggled mightily to adjust to the post-Cold War world. Economic hardship is profound across much of the former Soviet empire. For millions of people, the quality of health care, education, and daily existence has declined. In fact, nostalgia for the old Soviet state and the old Communist system is evident in many struggling cities and villages. Opinion polls taken in the early 2000s even suggest that a majority of Russians would welcome a return of the old USSR. Russian President Vladimir Putin, who succeeded Boris Yeltsin as president in 1999, has acknowledged this unhappiness. In his 2005 State of the Nation address, he declared that "the collapse of the Soviet Union was a major geopolitical disaster of the [twentieth] century."

Putin's stewardship of Russia, by far the largest of the former Soviet republics, has been controversial. Western powers have encouraged his efforts to revive the Russian economy through foreign investment and other means. They note that while poverty, crime, and corruption are persistent problems, some Russians are thriving in the country's evolving social and business environment. Russia also signaled its resolve to stand with the United States against international terrorism after the attacks of September 11, 2001.

But other trends in Russia have been troubling. Under Putin, Russia has repeatedly tried to unduly influence events in other former Soviet states. In fact, many analysts believe that Putin's description of the collapse of the Soviet empire as a "disaster" is due to mounting frustration about Russia's diminished stature and capabilities. Russia also remains mired in a long and bloody campaign to wipe out

471

rebels in the breakaway republic of Chechnya. Long a part of Russia, Chechnya declared its independence in 1991. But the Russian government has refused to recognize it, and heavy fighting continues in the region. In addition, arms control advocates have complained that Russia's still-sizable nuclear arsenal is vulnerable to terrorists. Finally, many observers believe that Russia is slipping away from democratic ideals and moving back in the direction of authoritarian rule. These critics note that Putin has eliminated most political opposition, and that he has taken firm control of virtually all significant media outlets in the country.

Other states that were once part of the Soviet Union seem—after brief experiments with democratic reforms in the 1990s—to be sliding back into political repression and autocracy as well. Former Soviet states like Uzbekistan, Belarus, and Kazakhstan all feature increasingly totalitarian regimes that have moved to stamp out democratic reform movements. These and other former parts of the Soviet bloc also are grappling with the empire's dark legacy of environmental devastation, ranging from the nuclear horror of Chernobyl to the destruction of the Aral Sea.

Meanwhile, former Warsaw Pact countries like Poland, Hungary, and the Czech Republic have been accepted into NATO. In these and other nations such as Germany, however, the transition to more capitalist and democratic systems has been painful and disorienting for many citizens. In the Balkan state of Yugoslavia, the post-Cold War years were particularly devastating. Here, nationalism and bigotry led to years of civil war and "ethnic cleansing." This nightmare ended only after military intervention by U.S. and UN troops and the subsequent break-up of the troubled country into numerous states.

The end of the Cold War, then, has not ushered in a new era of global peace and democracy. Still, the collapse of the Soviet empire has brought new levels of political liberty and economic prosperity to many people throughout Eastern Europe and Central Asia. In the "revolution" countries of Kyrgyzstan, Georgia, and Ukraine, for example, democratic reforms have transformed the culture of these former Soviet states. Freedom of the press, freedom of religion, and freedom of thought are now realities for millions of people in these and other regions of the old Soviet empire. And as these people forge ahead to create a better world for their own children, they do so without the shadow of the Cold War darkening their every step.

14.1

Ronald Reagan Reflects on the End of the Cold War – 1990
Text of a Speech Delivered at Westminster College in Fulton, Missouri

On November 9, 1990, former president Ronald Reagan delivered a speech at Westminster College in Fulton, Missouri, the same school where British Prime Minister Winston Churchill had delivered his famous "Sinews of Peace" address in 1946. Reagan's remarks were part of the dedication ceremonies for the "Breakthrough" monument, a memorial to the end of the Cold War. Sculpted by Churchill's granddaughter Edwina Sandys out of eight huge sections of the fallen Berlin Wall, the monument was designed to symbolize both the dissolution of the Soviet empire and the beginning of a new era of freedom. Reagan's address explored both of these themes, while also paying tribute to Churchill's prescient speech.

I can hardly visit this magnificent setting, so rich in memory and symbolism, without recalling the comment Sir Winston Churchill made when he was congratulated on the size of an audience gathered to hear him speak. Any other politician would have been flattered. Not Churchill. It was no great achievement to draw a crowd, he said. Twice as many would have turned out for a public hanging.

Maybe so, but I am deeply grateful to each of you for your warm welcome. What an honor it is for me to come to Fulton—indelibly stamped with the name and eloquence of Churchill. What a privilege to be on hand to help dedicate Edwina Sandys' sculpture celebrating the triumph of her grandfather's principles. And what a source of pride to receive an honorary degree from this distinguished college, whose illustrious past is equaled only by its future promise.

Today we rejoice in the demise of the Berlin Wall that was permanently breached just one year ago.

We remember brave men and women on both sides of the iron curtain who devoted their lives—and sometimes sacrificed them—so that we might inhabit a world without barriers. And we recall with the intensity born of shared struggles the greatest Briton of them all, a child of parliamentary democracy who boasted of an American mother and who therefore claimed to be an English-speaking union all by himself.

Who standing here beside this magnificent 12th Century church that commemorated Sir Winston's 1946 visit can ever forget the indomitable figure with the bulldog expression and the upthrust "V" for victory?

Ronald Reagan, "Remarks at the Dedication of the Cold War Memorial at Westminster College," November 9, 1990. Reprinted with permission from The Ronald Reagan Presidential Foundation.

As the greatest communicator of our time, Sir Winston enlisted the English language itself in the battle against Hitler and his hateful doctrines. When the Nazi might have prevailed from Warsaw to the Channel Islands and from Egypt to the Arctic Ocean, at a time when the whole cause of human liberty stood trembling and imperiled, he breathed defiance in phrases that will ring down through centuries to come.

And when the guns at last fell silent in the Spring of 1945, no man on earth had done more to preserve civilization during the hour of its greatest trial.

Near the end of World War II, but before the election that everyone knew must follow V-E Day, *The Times* of London prepared an editorial suggesting that Prime Minister Churchill run as a non-partisan figure, above the fray of parliamentary politics, and that he gracefully retire soon after to rest on his laurels and bask in the glow of yesterday's triumph. The editor informed Sir Winston of both points he intended to make. Churchill had a ready reply. As for the first suggestion, "Mr. Editor," he said, "I fight for my corner." And as for the second, "Mr. Editor, I leave when the pub closes."

For a while in the Summer of 1945 it looked as if perhaps the pub *had* closed. We all know that democracy can be a fickle employer. But that does little to ease the pain. It's hard to be philosophical on the day after an election slips through your fingers. Clementine, trying to think of anything to say that might console her husband, looked at the returns and concluded that it might well be a blessing in disguise. The old lion turned to his wife and said, "At the moment it seems quite effectively disguised."

"I have no regrets," Churchill told visitors in the aftermath of his death. "I leave my name to history." But Winston Churchill rarely did the easy thing. He could not rest so long as tyranny threatened any part of the globe. So when Harry Truman invited him to speak at Westminster College in the Spring of 1946, Churchill leapt at the chance. He hoped that by traveling to the heartland of America he might reach the heart of America. He would do so in an address whose timeless eloquence would be matched by its indisputable logic. Churchill addressed a nation at the pinnacle of world power—but a nation unaccustomed to wielding such authority and historically reluctant to intrude in the affairs of Europe.

In the exhausted aftermath of World War II, few were prepared to listen to warnings of fresh danger. But Churchill was undaunted. Once before his had been a voice crying out in the wilderness against the suicidal dogmas of appeasement. Once before he had sounded an alarm against those deluded souls who thought they could go on feeding the crocodile with bits and pieces of other countries and somehow avoid his jaws themselves. His warnings had been ignored by a world more in love with temporary ease than long-term security. Yet time had proven him tragically correct.

His Fulton speech was a firebell in the night, a Paul Revere warning that tyranny was once more on the march. "From Stettin in the Baltic to Trieste in the Adriatic, an iron curtain has descended across the continent," he said.

Churchill titled his speech "The Sinews of Peace," but the reaction it provoked was anything but peaceful. Newspaper editors on both sides of the Atlantic rushed to brand its author a warmonger. Labor MP's asked Prime Minister Attlee to formally repudiate his predecessor's remarks. From Moscow came a blast of rhetoric labeling Stalin's former wartime ally "false and hypocritical" and claiming that having lost an election in his homeland he had decided to try his luck in the United States. Harry Truman knew better. The people of Missouri were highly pleased by Churchill's visit, and had enjoyed what their distinguished visitor had to say.

And for those trapped behind the iron curtain, spied on and lied to by their corrupt governments, denied their freedoms, their bread, even their faith in a power greater than that of the state—for them Churchill was no warmonger and the western alliance no enemy. For the victims of communist oppression, the iron curtain was made all too real in a concrete wall, surrounded by barbed wire and attack dogs and guards with orders to shoot on sight anyone trying to escape the so-called worker's paradise of East Germany.

"In the churches and the school, in the factories and on the farms, a once silent people found their voice and with it a battering ram to knock down walls, real and imagined."

Today we come full circle from those anxious times. Ours is a more peaceful planet because of men like Churchill and Truman and countless others who shared their dream of a world where no one wields a sword and no one drags a chain. This is their monument. Here, on a grassy slope between the Church of St. Mary the Virgin and Champ Auditorium, a man and a woman break through the wall and symbolically demolish whatever remaining barriers stand in the way of international peace and the brotherhood of nations.

Out of one man's speech was born a new Western resolve. Not warlike, not bellicose, not expansionist—but firm and principled in resisting those who would devour territory and put the soul itself into bondage. The road to a free Europe that began there in Fulton led to the Truman Doctrine and The Marshall Plan, to N.A.T.O. and the Berlin Airlift, through nine American presidencies and more than four decades of military preparedness.

By the time I came to the White House, a new challenge had arisen. Moscow had decided to deploy intermediate-range nuclear missiles like the SS-20 that would threaten every city in Western Europe.

It never launched those missiles, but fired plenty of trial balloons into the air, and it rained propaganda on the United States and the Federal Republic of Germany in an effort to prevent the modernization of N.A.T.O.'s forces on West German soil.

But the Government in Bonn was not deterred. Neither was the rest of Western Europe deceived. At the same time, we in the United States announced our own intention to develop S.D.I.—the Strategic Defense Initiative, to hasten the day when the nuclear nightmare was ended forever and our children's dreams were no longer marred by the specter of instant annihilation.

Of course, not everyone agreed with such a course. For years it had been suggested by some opinion-makers that all would be well in the world if only the United States lowered its profile. Some of them would not only have us lower our profile—they would also lower our flag. I disagreed. I thought that the 1980s were a time to stop apologizing for America's legitimate national interest, and start asserting them.

I was by no means alone. Principled leaders like Helmut Kohl and Margaret Thatcher reinforced our message that the West would not be blackmailed and that the only rational course was to return to the bargaining table in Geneva and work out real and lasting arms reductions fair to both sides.

A new Soviet leader appeared on the scene, untainted by the past, unwilling to be shackled by crumbling orthodoxies. With the rise of Mikhail Gorbachev came the end of numbing oppression. Glasnost introduced openness to the world's most closed society. Perestroika held out the promise of a better life, achieved through democratic institutions and a market economy. And real arms control came to pass, as an entire class of weapons was eliminated for the first time in the atomic age.

Within months the Soviet Empire began to melt like a snowbank in May.

One country after another overthrew the privileged cliques that had bled their economies and curbed their freedoms. Last month Germany itself was reunited, in the shadow of The Brandenburg Gate and under the democratic umbrella of N.A.T.O. I know something about that neighborhood. Back in June 1987 I stood in the free city of West Berlin and asked Mr. Gorbachev to tear down the wall.

Was he listening? Whether he was, or not, neither he nor the rulers of Eastern Europe could ignore the much louder chants of demonstrators in the streets of Leipzig and Dresden and dozens of other German cities.

In the churches and the school, in the factories and on the farms, a once silent people found their voice and with it a battering ram to knock down walls, real and imagined.

Because of them, the political map of Europe has been rewritten. The future has been redefined, even as the veil has been lifted on a cruel and bloody past. Just last week, thousands of Soviet citizens, many of them clutching photographs of relatives who died in Stalin's labor camps, marched to the Moscow headquarters of the K.G.B. to unveil a monument to the victims of Stalinist repression. An aging woman named Alla Krichevskaya held up a photograph of a young man in an old fashioned high collar. She wept softly. "This was my father," she said. "I never knew him. He was sent to Sologetsky [labor camp] in 1932, a few months before I was born, and they shot him in 1937."

In dedicating this memorial, may we pause and reflect on the heroism and the sacrifice of Alla's father and so many, many others like him. Fifty years after Winston Churchill rallied his people in the Battle of Britain, the world is a very different place. Soviet Russia is coming out of the dark to join the family of nations. Central and Eastern Europe struggle to create both freedom and prosperity through market economies. How pleased Sir Winston would be!

Let me conclude with a special word to the student of Westminster College, the empire builders of the 21st century. Before you leave this place, do not forget why you came. You came to Westminster to explore the diversity of ideas and experience what we call civilization. Here you discover that so long as books are kept open, then minds can never be closed. Here you develop a sense of self, along with the realization that self alone is never enough for a truly satisfying life. For while we make a living by what we get, we make a life by what we give.

Tragically, many walls still remain to endanger our families and our communities. Later today the Fulton Optimist Club will join with others in recognizing winners of an essay contest called "Why should I say no to drugs?" Obviously Fulton cares about its future as well as its past—above all, it cares about the children who represent that future.

In Fulton, Missouri, as in London, Berlin, or Los Angeles, the future is what you make it.

Certainly, it was unreasonable for a sixty-five-year-old parliamentarian, his counsel rejected until the emergency was at hand, to believe that he could defy the world's most lethal fighting force and crush Hitler in his Berlin lair. It was unreasonable to suggest that an ancient church, all but destroyed by enemy bombs, could be reconstructed five thousand miles away as a permanent tribute to the man of the century. It was unreasonable to hope that oppressed men and women behind the iron curtain could one day break through to the sunlight of freedom—and that the Soviet Politburo itself would yield to people in the streets.

All this was unreasonable. But it all came true. My fondest wish is that each of you will be similarly unreasonable in pursuing Churchill's objectives—justice, opportunity, and an end to walls wherever they divide the human race.

Shortly before he died, Sir Winston received a letter from his daughter Mary. "In addition to all the feelings a daughter has for a loving, generous father," she wrote. "I owe you what every Englishman, woman and child does—liberty itself." We owe him nothing less.

In dedicating this magnificent sculpture, may we dedicate ourselves to hastening the day when all God's children live in a world without walls. That would be the greatest empire of all.

And now, let me speak directly to the young people and the students here. I wonder yet if you've appreciated how unusual—terribly unusual—this country of ours is?

I received a letter just before I left office from a man. I don't know why he chose to write it, but I'm glad he did. He wrote that you can go to live in France, but you can't become a Frenchman. You can go to live in Germany or Italy, but you can't become a German, an Italian. He went through Turkey, Greece, Japan, and other countries. But he said anyone, from any corner of the world, can come to live in the United States and become an American.

Some may call it mysticism if they will, but I cannot help but feel that there was some divine plan that placed this continent here between the two great oceans to be found by people from any corner of the earth—people who had an extra ounce of desire for freedom and some extra courage to rise up and lead their families, their relatives, their friends, their nations and come here to eventually make this country.

The truth of the matter is, if we take this crowd and if we could go through and ask the heritage, the background of every family represented here, we would probably come up with the names of every country on earth, every corner of the world, and every race. Here, is the one spot on earth where we have the brotherhood of man. And maybe as we continue with this proudly, this brotherhood of man made up from people representative of every corner of the earth, maybe one day boundaries all over the earth will disappear as people cross boundaries and find that, yes, there is a brotherhood of man in every corner.

Thank you all and God bless you all.

Source: Reagan, Ronald. "Brotherhood of Man." Speech at the Westminster College Cold War Memorial, November 9, 1990. Available online at Westminster College website, http://www.westminster-mo.edu/News/speeches/Reagan.asp.

14.2
Gorbachev Reflects on the End of the Cold War – 2002
An Excerpt from Conversations with Gorbachev, *by Mikhail Gorbachev and Zdenek Mlynar*

Several years after the collapse of the Soviet empire, former Soviet President Mikhail Gorbachev sat down for a series of interviews with Zdenek Mlynar, a Czech politician who had been a reformer during the Prague Spring of 1968 and who later helped found the Charter 77 dissident group. In the following exchange, the two politicians comment on their respective legacies.

Zdenek Mlynar: After 1968 I was tormented for a long time by the knowledge that, regardless of my intentions, after the suppression of the Prague Spring that situation, not just for Czechs and Slovaks, but for all democratic socialist politics in general, became much worse than it had been previously. And there's no getting around it; even though military intervention was the result of someone else's decision, not mine—even though Brezhnev bore the responsibility, not I—nevertheless, intervention happened precisely because I, along with others, tried to carry through policies that Moscow reacted against in just that way.

The question of assigning blame in such cases is not the only question because, as is well known, you can be "at fault" without being entirely "to blame." For that reason for several years I kept asking myself over and over again: Wouldn't it have been better, strictly speaking, not to have undertaken any such experiments at all? Just to have waited, as others did, conducting oneself as Kádár did in Hungary? These questions remained open, although I did find answers to other ones. For example, could we or could we not have done things in a more cautious way, running less risk? Or on the other hand, would it perhaps have been worthwhile to offer military resistance to military intervention? To these and similar questions I answered in the negative, but the main question remained unanswered: Was it worthwhile to have begun this process at all? And should I myself have taken personal responsibility for it?

In the end, on my own, I came to the following answer to my questions: I must always live in such a way as to feel myself to be a person who shares the responsibility for what happens. One cannot avoid responsibility by reference to good intentions, for as Dante long ago observed, the road to hell is paved with them. In spite of that, I think I simply could not have avoided taking part in the attempt to carry through the Prague Spring. Because if out of fear of defeat I had done nothing, I could not have justified myself to my own conscience, neither as the confirmed Marxist I was at the time nor as the person I was with the life story I had. Today I can justify myself to my conscience, but I must of course admit that everyone else who did not have the possibility of choosing, nevertheless, had to pay for that experiment and has the right to judge me differently than I do myself.

Today one often hears or reads unambiguous condemnations of you, Misha. Not just in Western publications, where such things are usually limited assertions that Gorbachev failed or achieved the opposite of what he wanted. In your own country, in Russia, this takes the form more usually of rude insults, tactless and one-sided allegations that social, political, and governmental decline—and everything bad in general—"began under Gorbachev."

On the one hand, this is the "voice of the people" being expressed in an unjust way, the voice of people whose hopes were disappointed. On the other

---

hand, it is the continuation of an earlier campaign against you and your policies by a number of your opponents. All of this is common enough in history, and I don't really want to talk about that aspect. My question is: How do you personally regard your own actions at the time when you were the chief representative and initiator of new Soviet policies domestically and internationally?

Mikhail Gorbachev: To begin with, I'd like to say a few words about your problem in relation to 1968. I think you're quite right to draw the conclusion that despite its defeat the Prague Spring had it own meaning and significance. Because that defeat represented not just a new wave of repression against all attempts at democracy under "actually existing socialism," but from a dialectical point of view it also represented nothing less than the beginning of the end for the totalitarian system. So I think you should have a clear conscience on that score.

Naturally I feel troubled by the fact that I did not succeed in keeping the entire process of perestroika within the framework of my intentions, primarily within the framework of gradual but profound democratic change. I probably feel even more troubled than you did [over the Prague Spring] because my responsibility was greater, both on the scale of the Soviet Union and of world politics, and this responsibility increased the longer I remained at the head of the political leadership. Especially now, when I see that everything has been distorted and the reforms are heading in quite a different direction, it causes me great distress. But I suffer precisely over that, not because I actually began the struggle for democracy and fundamental change of the Soviet system. I do not regret that I began that struggle. It had to be done.

Now, with a certain distance from those events, I of course see many things differently, but in my fundamental positions nothing has changed: I would do it all over, and I would begin again with the struggle for "more democracy, more socialism." However, my understanding of socialism would now be different, and therefore I would approach the task in a more mature way. Because in 1985, and for some time after that, our desire was to improve, to make more socialist, a system that was not truly socialist. And the whole drama of our situation lay in that.

Today I would know that the goal had to be the removal of the totalitarian system, that reforms in all spheres of life—from monopoly ownership up to and including the ideological monopoly—would have to be more radical, more profound, more directed toward fundamental principles. But I would not abandon the basic choice I made—seeking to change what existed—and today I still think that was correct. Not only because it was necessary for the USSR, but because the rest of the world also needed it. And in that sense my conscience is also clear.

Source: Gorbachev, Mikhail, and Zdenek Mlynar. *Conversations with Gorbachev: On Perestroika, the Prague Spring, and the Crossroads of Socialism.* New York: Columbia University Press, 2002.

14.3
The Legacy of Soviet Rule in Uzbekistan – 2001
An Excerpt from Chasing the Sea *by Tom Bissell*

Official policies of the Soviet Union throughout the twentieth century placed a much greater emphasis on industrialization and security than they did on environmental stewardship. The full extent to which this was true, however, was not revealed until the collapse of the Soviet empire in 1989. When the Iron Curtain was lifted, the ecological damage that riddled large parts of Eastern Europe and the Soviet states finally became clear to all.

The stories of ecological destruction in the former Soviet empire are legion, but one of the most famous concerns the Aral Sea, a sea in Central Asia that in 1960 was the fourth-largest inland body of water in the world. In the space of three decades, though, Soviet irrigation policies shrank the Aral to a fraction of its former size, and many scientists believe that it will disappear entirely over the course of the next three decades. In the following excerpt, journalist Tom Bissell recounts his experiences in Moynaq, a town that was once a prosperous fishing community on the banks of the sea.

One of the most puzzling aspects of the Aral Sea disaster was how it was able to deteriorate so rapidly while so little attention was paid to it. But in the end, not even the Soviets could hide a vanishing sea. In the comparatively permissive year of 1987 the Uzbek writer Maruf Jalil published an eyewitness article entitled, "The Sea That Is Fleeing Its Shores." A number of Central Asian celebrities, including the Kyrgyz novelist Chinghiz Aitmatov, mobilized to fund a Save the Aral committee. The outcry grew, until the Politburo in Moscow was prepared to divert two Siberian rivers, the Ob and the Irtysh, toward the Aral Sea in order to restore it. This unbelievably bad idea was well under way when Mikhail Gorbachev canceled the scheme, having bowed to sensible pressure from Russian environmental groups and what many viewed as nakedly racist pressure from Slavic supremacists.... While Moscow did scale back its demands for Central Asian cotton, it persisted in blaming the Uzbeks and Karakalpaks for "wasting" water. By 1990 the Save the Aral committee, after reviewing its three years of work, concluded that all had been for naught. Less than naught. The Aral Sea was still shrinking, despite the fact that forty organizations were now at work on the crisis. Amazingly, this had been the zenith of hope for Karakalpakistan....

[Bissell enters a Moynaq museum in the company of a Kazakh teenager]. We found a wall of black-and-white photos hung on a mid-room partition. Saghitjan and I looked at water in photo after photo. In this place it was easy to forget that water, as a bulk phenomenon, still existed. Even black-and-white water seemed exquisite, primally wet. The fishermen in these photos smilingly held aloft nets bulging with their haul. Some photos seemed almost pornographic in their abundance of fish. Slowly, the photos seemed less sad than hubristic. Overfishing the Aral Sea was a problem long before the amphetamine of Soviet industrialization arrived. The Aral Sea was not a deep body of water. It was a desert sea, fragile by definition, as disastrously susceptible to heavy fishing as the League of Nations was to global war. What had these people expected? ...

> *"Growing from the seabed were hundreds of shrubby plants and small, evil-looking trees that looked conjured up from a terrifying children's book.... Revenge plants, these were, the helpless counterstrike of a devastated ecosystem."*

The road out of Moynaq and into the nonexistent sea was, like everything, covered with thick salty dust.... My feet came down on hard, crunchy soil that was, by far, the most chemically transmuted I had yet encountered in Karakalpakistan. My boots left no footprints. This was interesting, but not nearly as interesting as the huge beached trawler to my left. About the size of a baleen whale, this vessel had once been part of Moynaq's considerable armada of fishing boats. At their peak the Aral Sea's fishermen provided a tenth of the entire Soviet catch. In the 1920s their heroism and resolve helped save Russia from widespread famine. In Moynaq alone 10,000 fishermen plied their trade, a number more than triple its current population. Even if the Aral Sea were not more than an hour's drive away, the most determined angler would have found it impossible to eke out a merely miserable existence. Not a single fish, not even the fish that had been reintroduced into the sea as recently as last summer, survived. I studied the boat, its strangeness tearing through successive veils of disbelief. It was sun-blistered, gutted, encased in a shell of baked, flaky rust. The rust came in six different hues, the whole spectrum of oxidation. The boat was atop a high dune, its bow pushed out over the dune's edge as though recalling the weightlessness with which it once breached the Aral Sea's crests. Mote-speckled sunlight poured through the slots of its missing ribs.

I turned to see half a dozen other boats thirty yards away. From a distance they looked like alien technology, a desert-roaming flotilla of skiffs piloted by pirate mutants. I walked toward them atop a dirty white crystallized glaze of salt. Despite the condition of the soil, life, of a sort, had carried on. Growing from the seabed were hundreds of shrubby plants and small, evil-looking trees that looked conjured up from a terrifying children's book. One walked near them at one's peril, their grayish branches covered with long white hook-tipped thorns. Revenge plants, these were, the helpless counterstrike of a devastated ecosystem....

It was a peculiar thing to stand here in one of the most obscure corners of the former Soviet empire. Socialism was not supposed to work like this. Never had a systematic way of thinking been nobler in theory and more destructive in practice. In 1918 Lenin used an Ovid quote, of all things, to inspire the Russian masses: "The golden age is coming; people will live without laws or punishment, doing of their own free will what is good and just." Gazing around, as close to Jerusalem as I was to Moscow, I wondered, suddenly, how anyone could have believed that any other result but this was possible. It was simply infeasible for decades of central planning to have succeeded in a nation as vast as the Soviet Union. As though one Gordian gnarl of Moscow bureaucrats might have ever been able to simultaneously provide for the Yakuts of the high arctic, the *flâneurs* of St. Petersburg, the Muslim tribal elders of Merv. And they knew it. They knew it. Everyone did. How did this happen? Why did anyone allow it? As far as I knew, no one had ever explained why the reddest sort of Communism seemed able to beguile (with the exception of Cuba) only gigantic nations of huge topographical, philosophical, and ethnic variances such as the Soviet Union or China. Perhaps it thrived on the confusion such societies created....

The landscape surrounding this road was huge, yellow, vacant as sky. It looked somehow microwaved. The farther we got from Moynaq, the more Blakean the terrain became. A stanza from "Holy Thursday" filled my suddenly cavernous mind: "And their sun does never shine./ And their fields are bleak & bare./ And their ways are fill'd with thorns./ It is eternal winter there." After a few miles' journey, we jackknifed off the road and jumped along an uneven tire-trenched path. The ships soon appeared. Five of them lay in a careless cluster among erosion-planed dunes. Another half-dozen ships were visible in the heat-distorted distance.

There were several separate batches of ships scattered around the former seabed. This batch had the sad distinction of being the farthest from Moynaq. For years after the sea abandoned Moynaq's shoreline, some of the town's more desperate fishermen dug numerous canals out to meet it. Each morning they patiently steered their ships down the narrow, brackish passageways. "Chasing the sea," they called it. In 1986, commonly regarded as the year in which the last of the Aral Sea's native fish expired, the ships were left more or less where they lay. I found I did not want to contemplate the long, difficult walk back to town these brave, deluded men had the day they realized everything was over....

A mile out of town, atop a small hill overlooking the cliffs of Moynaq's former seashore, stands a small war memorial honoring the dead of World War Two, which is known in the former Soviet Union as the Great Patriotic War Against Fascism. The people of the former Soviet Union take their war memorials very seriously, as they should. Uzbekistan alone sacrificed around a million soldiers to defeat the man they know as Gitler. The dead this memorial honors gave their lives to end a war that only gave rise to another, colder struggle. Discounting its half-dozen proxy conflicts, its secret agents garroted in East Berlin basements, and its handful of obliterated spy-plane pilots, the Cold War's balance of terror is commonly thought to have ensured a confrontation without casualties. But cotton was grown to outfit the Soviet army in socks and trousers and T-shirts, to perpetuate the Cold War, to *win* the Cold War. And as with Afghanistan, another of the Cold War's hidden, long-quiet casualties, the full ramifications of the Aral Sea's destruction might not be apparent for years, perhaps decades. I look out over the cliffs, past the homes of people who have little worldly stake but that of their own well-being. What once must have been a lovely vista of foam-etched sea is now an empty yellow wilderness broken only by an occasional salt marsh. But it, too, is beautiful, terribly so. The wind sounds like waves. Everyone who came here remarked on that. But it does. A few seagulls circle overhead, altogether confused. Socks, I think. *Trousers.* In a few hours a party will begin at Ian Small's rented house. In a few days I will return to Tashkent. I do not want to leave. What is to be done? Listen to the wind blow.

Source: Bissell, Tom. *Chasing the Sea.* New York: Vintage Departures, 2003.

14.4
Post-Cold War Life in Reunified Germany – 2002
An Excerpt from After the Wall *by Jana Hensel*

> *In 2002 a young German woman named Jana Hensel published a memoir about her childhood in East Germany and her adolescent years in the reunited Federal Republic of Germany. "Many books about the difficulty of negotiating the East-West divide have followed," commented Jefferson Chase, who later translated the book for English-speaking audiences. "But Hensel's stands as the first to define a cultural phenomenon–the alienation and loss felt by the last generation of East German youth after the fall of the Wall."*

> *Hensel's* Zonenkinder *became a bestseller in Germany. It was particularly popular among younger Germans—both from the former East and former West—who had directly experienced the turmoil and uncertainty that came with the reunification of Germany back in October 1990. In 2004 Hensel's memoir was published in the United States as* After the Wall: Confessions from an East German Childhood and the Life that Came Next. *The following is an excerpt from the book.*

The fall of the Wall had transformed each of us into something akin to a child prodigy, upon whom great expectations were placed. There was not much for older

East Germans to be proud of. The GDR [German Democratic Republic] had lost to the West, and not all East Germans were expected to assimilate into West German society. That, in turn, was viewed as a kind of collective upward social mobility, and we, the children of the first "immigrants," were expected to achieve that goal. We had come from nowhere, and now everyone expected great things. At least, that's what people whispered in our ears. To achieve this greatness, our gazes had to be directed ahead and not behind. It was crucial for us to forget our roots as quickly as possible. We had to become flexible, adaptable. It made no difference whether we came from a family of painters, plumbers, photographers, dentists, or teachers. We were the sons and daughters of history's losers—mocked by the victors as proletarians, people to whom totalitarian conformity and the reputation for laziness clung like a bad odor.

The real truth about East Germany was to be kept to ourselves. We never admitted to our parents that the ugliness and banality of the East depressed us; or that we found it absurdly pompous for Dresden or Leipzig to behave as though they were major world metropolises. We never said that we found the new cadre of politicians in the East, by turns, ridiculous, self-righteous, odious, suspect, or simply unbelievably bland. We never told them how sick we were of our countrymen—the stupid skinheads on the Baltic coast who lined up in pseudo-military rows outside their tents; the old men in the supermarket who ordered us to get a shopping basket, if we wanted to buy something; the old ladies who complained that our cars were blocking the entrance to the Laundromat. If we rode our bikes on the sidewalk, cane-brandishing retirees would leap out in front of us, sending us flying over the handlebars when we jammed on the brakes. It was all so provincial, so small-minded.

Our parents knew nothing of this. Conversations with them weren't exactly the best forum for us to come out of the closet as East-West hermaphrodites. At home we spoke with Eastern accents, relearning them, if necessary, for the occasion. No matter how much effort we had exerted trying to speak like everybody else, the East wasn't going to let our generation off easy. And talking back wasn't an option.

Jonathan, of course, couldn't understand why we couldn't discuss things with our parents. Occasionally he would suggest that Jenny simply try to have a constructive chat with her folks about her problems at university and the way she wanted to live her life. Jenny's face would go pale, and she'd briefly consider whether to admit that she wasn't really certain whether her parents even knew what she was studying. But then, she would look into her boyfriend's eyes and decide that it was probably better to say nothing at all.

Jonathan was of the opinion that our problems with our parents were a typical generational conflict, part and parcel of the changing times, which could be solved if all concerned agreed to compromise. He said that everyone, sooner or later, had to leave the nest. He'd been through it himself when he moved from Hamburg to Berlin.

> *"Who were we to say that, in their places, we would have done things any differently [than our parents]—that we wouldn't have collaborated with the Secret Police or joined the Party?"*

Jenny wasn't sure whether he really understood what we were talking about, and it irritated her that Jonathan would always look at her out of the corner of his eye when giving this advice, as though realizing for the first time that his girlfriend was from the GDR. As though he were wondering whether she might not be exactly like her parents.

I tried to picture Jonathan at home—having constructive discussions with his parents—and every time I did so I'd mentally stretch out the word "constructive" as though pulling it apart from both ends in my fingers. Jonathan's family probably solved the newspaper crossword puzzle together before sitting down to eat. Then they'd debate the problems in the Third World and the federal budget deficit, and argue, democratically, about who would drive out on the weekend and buy next week's non-pasteurized cheese from the farmers in Schleswig-Holstein.

We East Germans couldn't afford to engage in "constructive" generational conflict. We didn't have the luxury of rebelling against our parents. Their generation was depressed and defeated enough as it was, and we, who had been lucky enough to have been born relatively late in the life of the GDR, didn't want to kick people who were already down.

The fall of the Wall had already destroyed all our parents' illusions. They had nothing important left for us to undermine.

And who were we to say that, in their places, we would have done things any differently—that we wouldn't have collaborated with the Secret Police or joined the Party? Would we really have distributed political flyers, published an underground newspaper, or absconded to the West? The German Democratic Republic already had consigned itself to the ashcan of history before we even had to face such questions.

It would be presumptuous of us to pass judgment on our parents. So we had no option other than to join them in a pact of mutual aggression. God knows, there'd been enough distance between us and our parents in the past, and there was sure to be more in the future.

Our common history ended the day the Wall came down. After that, they'd spent their time worrying about their jobs, while we memorized the organizational structures of the West German parliament, the lyrics to the national anthem, and the facts surrounding the 1953 popular uprising against the Communist regime. Their marriages failed, while we tried to decide whether to spend our year abroad in the United States during high school or to wait until after we had started university. They cursed their new West German bosses while we flirted in lecture halls with our peers from Lübeck or Ingolstadt. Now, we had nothing in common. They said very little about their lives, and we said nothing at all about ours. Their experience had become obsolete—at least for us. There was no advice they could give us.

And that's why none of us even dreamed of inviting West German friends to go out with us and our parents. Our family bonds were too tenuous—they consisted of some sympathy and a large quantity of pity. We didn't attack our parents. We didn't ask what they had done in the past. We tried to defend them, the way you do when your little brother is teased by bullies at school....

The normal parent-child relationship has been inverted. We long for the days when we'll earn our own money, not because we want to free ourselves from our parents' expectations, but because that's how our parents measure success in what they describe as "today's day and age." It's embarrassing to see how they, a few years short of normal retirement age, earn just enough money every month to cover the basic costs of living—like young adults just starting out in their careers. The demise of the GDR has set them back more than twenty years in their working lives.

It's painful to watch them struggle with their new situation. They're like hamsters running around in wheels. Unaware that they can drive themselves as fast or as slow as they like, they spin themselves round and round in circles for fear that the wheel could come to a permanent halt. They purchase a computer so they can surf the Web from home. They enroll in English lessons. What for? Nobody knows. They just think that's what everybody is supposed to do in "today's day and age." We wish they could have the comfort—the stasis—that characterizes the part of Germany we're not from. We pine for the timeless tedium that settles over people's lives in the West like a fog, enveloping everything, leaving no ruptures or open seams.

Our parents are just too old and tired for these times. They're the demoted pupils of another epoch—lost, confused, angry, and frustrated. While we don't pass judgment on them, can anyone blame us for feeling superior? After all, we know more than they do.

We have no other option than to be successful. We want to earn money and show everyone how well we've learned to play the game in the West. If we each make our way and get good jobs in the next ten years, then our parents will have the retrospective satisfaction of not having done everything wrong. If we fail, we'll be one more piece of evidence that the Western system is impenetrable—that no one ever gets ahead without connections. But that possibility is one more thing we don't talk about.

Source: Hensel, Jana. *After the Wall: Confessions from an East German Childhood and the Life that Came Next.* New York: Public Affairs, 2004.

14.5

President Vladimir Putin Assesses the State of Russia – 2005
An Excerpt from the Text of a Speech to the Russian Federal Assembly

> *On April 25, 2005, Russian President Vladimir Putin delivered his annual "state of the nation" address to the Russian Federal Assembly and the citizens of Russia. In this address, he stated that he recognized the many economic, political, and social challenges facing both the government and the average Russian citizen, from attracting business investment to high rates of alcoholism and drug addiction. To the deep disappointment of many Westerners, Putin also implied in his speech that things would not be so bad were it not for the demise of the Communist system. "Above all," he said at one point, "we should acknowledge that the collapse of the Soviet Union was a major geopolitical disaster of the century." But he also used the speech to address mounting concerns of both Western and Russian observers that he seemed to be steering Russia away from the path of democracy and toward a more totalitarian state. His top priorities, he stated, were to introduce a slate of pro-business reforms and to further develop Russia into a "free and democratic state." Following are excerpts from Putin's speech.*

… I consider the development of Russia as a free and democratic state to be our main political and ideological goal. We use these words fairly frequently, but rarely care to reveal how the deeper meaning of such values as freedom and democracy, justice and legality is translated into life.

Meanwhile, there is a need for such an analysis. The objectively difficult processes going on in Russia are increasingly becoming the subject of heated ideological discussions. And they are all connected with talk about freedom and democracy. Sometimes you can hear that since the Russian people have been silent for centuries, they are not used to or do not need freedom. And for that reason, it is claimed our citizens need constant supervision.

I would like to bring those who think this way back to reality, to the facts. To do so, I will recall once more Russia's most recent history.

Above all, we should acknowledge that the collapse of the Soviet Union was a major geopolitical disaster of the century. As for the Russian nation, it became a genuine drama. Tens of millions of our co-citizens and compatriots found themselves outside Russian territory. Moreover, the epidemic of disintegration infected Russia itself.

Individual savings were depreciated, and old ideals destroyed. Many institutions were disbanded or reformed carelessly. Terrorist intervention and the

Khasavyurt capitulation that followed damaged the country's integrity. Oligarchic groups—possessing absolute control over information channels—served exclusively their own corporate interests. Mass poverty began to be seen as the norm. And all this was happening against the backdrop of a dramatic economic downturn, unstable finances, and the paralysis of the social sphere.

Many thought or seemed to think at the time that our young democracy was not a continuation of Russian statehood, but its ultimate collapse, the prolonged agony of the Soviet system. But they were mistaken.

That was precisely the period when the significant developments took place in Russia. Our society was generating not only the energy of self-preservation, but also the will for a new and free life. In those difficult years, the people of Russia had to both uphold their state sovereignty and make an unerring choice in selecting a new vector of development in the thousand years of their history. They had to accomplish the most difficult task: how to safeguard their own values, not to squander undeniable achievements, and confirm the viability of Russian democracy. We had to find our own path in order to build a democratic, free and just society and state.

When speaking of justice, I am not of course referring to the notorious "take away and divide by all" formula, but extensive and equal opportunities for everybody to develop. Success for everyone. A better life for all.

In the ultimate analysis, by affirming these principles, we should become a free society of free people. But in this context it would be appropriate to remember how Russian society formed an aspiration for freedom and justice, how this aspiration matured in the public mind.

Above all else Russia was, is and will, of course, be a major European power. Achieved through much suffering by European culture, the ideals of freedom, human rights, justice and democracy have for many centuries been our society's determining values.

For three centuries, we—together with the other European nations—passed hand in hand through reforms of Enlightenment, the difficulties of emerging parliamentarism, municipal and judiciary branches, and the establishment of similar legal systems. Step by step, we moved together toward recognizing and extending human rights, toward universal and equal suffrage, toward understanding the need to look after the weak and the impoverished, toward women's emancipation, and other social gains. I repeat we did this together, sometimes behind and sometimes ahead of European standards.

It is my firm belief that for present-day Russia democratic values are no less important than economic success or people's social welfare. First, every law-abiding citizen is only entitled to firm legal guarantees and state protection in a free and just society. And, no doubt, safeguarding rights and freedoms is crucial both to Russia's economic development and its social and political life....

You know that in the last five years we have had to tackle difficult tasks to prevent the degradation of state and public institutions in our country. At the same time, we had to create the foundation for development in the next few years and decades. We cleared the debris together and gradually moved ahead. In that sense, the stabilization policy was practically a policy of reaction to the accumulated problems. This policy was, in general, successful. However, it has reached the limit of its effectiveness.

It must be replaced with a policy oriented towards the future. And for that, we must have an efficient state. However, despite many positive changes, this key problem has not been solved so far.

Our bureaucratic apparatus is still largely an exclusive and often arrogant caste regarding state service as an alternative form of business. Therefore, our priority remains making state management more effective, ensuring that officials strictly obey the law, and quality public services are provided to the population.

A specific feature of recent times has been that the dishonest part of our bureaucracy (at the federal and local levels alike) has been particularly keen on using the achieved stability in its own mercenary interests. It started using the favorable conditions and emerging opportunities to achieve its own selfish goals rather than to increase the prosperity of society.

It is worth mentioning that in this respect the party and corporate elites behave no better than the state bureaucracy.

Today, when we have created the necessary preconditions for serious and large-scale work, if the state falls into the trap of finding simplified solutions, the bureaucratic reaction will only benefit from it. Instead of a breakthrough, we will face stagnation. The potential of civil society will not be used effectively, while the level of corruption, irresponsibility and lack of professionalism will rocket, throwing us back on the way of economic and intellectual degradation and creating a growing rift between the authorities and public interests, with state apparatus refusing to heed public requests.

I repeat: we cannot be satisfied with the current situation in the country. While freeing major mass media from the oligarchs' censorship, we failed to protect them from the unhealthy zeal of certain officials. Focusing the efforts of law enforcement bodies on the fight against crime, including tax evasion, we encountered frequent violations of the rights of our business community, and sometimes a blatant racket on the part of state officials.

Many bureaucrats believe this situation will never be changed, and such violations are the inevitable result of past and current polices. I must disappoint them. Our plans do not include handing over the country to the inefficient rule of a corrupted bureaucracy.

We proceed from the idea that it is both essential and economically advantageous to have developed democratic procedures in the country; that it is politically prudent to maintain a responsible dialogue with society. Therefore, a modern Russian official must learn to speak with the public using the modern language of cooperation, the language of common public interest, dialogue and real democracy, rather than the jargon of military orders. This is our fundamental approach and we will strictly follow it....

In my opinion a third important task is to pursue vigorous policy in promoting liberalization in private enterprise. I'd like to focus on measures to stabilize civil law relations and to achieve a dramatic increase in opportunities for free enterprise and capital investment....

Stability of the right to private property is the alpha and omega of any business. The rules to which the state adheres in this sphere should be clear to everyone, and, importantly, these rules should be stable. This enables people developing their business to plan normally both this business and their own lives. This allows citizens to feel comfortable and conclude, without any apprehensions, contracts on such vital issues as the acquisition of housing or its privatization, which has already been almost completed in our country. In general, this encourages people to buy property and expand production....

> *"Russia is a country that has chosen democracy through the will of its own people.... As a sovereign nation, Russia can and will decide for itself the time frame and conditions for its progress along this road."*

Dear Colleagues,

The creation of an effective legal and political system is an essential condition for developing democracy in our country. But developing democratic procedures should not come at the cost of law and order, the stability that we worked so hard to achieve, or the continued pursuit of our chosen economic course.

The democratic road we have chosen is independent in nature, a road along which we move ahead, all the while taking into account our own specific internal circumstances. But we must and we shall move forward, basing our action on the laws and on the guarantees our constitution provides.

Of course, the state authorities must refrain from any abuse of the administrative levers they have at their disposal, and must work continually to open up new opportunities for building up the institutions of a genuine democracy in our country.

To deny our people, to deny ourselves the ability to live according to democratic laws is to have no respect either for ourselves or for our fellow citizens and would signify that we neither understand the past nor see the future.

"State power," wrote the great Russian philosopher Ivan Ilyin, "has its own limits defined by the fact that it is authority that reaches people from outside.... State power cannot oversee and dictate the creative states of the soul and mind, the inner states of love, freedom and goodwill. The state cannot demand from its citizens faith, prayer, love, goodness and conviction. It cannot regulate scientific, religious and artistic creation.... It should not intervene in moral, family and daily private life, and only when extremely necessary should it impinge on people's economic initiative and creativity." Let us not forget this.

Russia is a country that has chosen democracy through the will of its own people. It chose this road of its own accord and it will decide itself how best to ensure that the principles of freedom and democracy are realised here, taking into account our historic, geopolitical and other particularities and respecting all fundamental democratic norms. As a sovereign nation, Russia can and will decide for itself the time frame and conditions for its progress along this road....

But consistent development of democracy in Russia is possible only through legal means. All methods of fighting for national, religious and other interests that are outside the law contradict the very principles of democracy and the state will react to such methods firmly but within the law.

We want all our law-abiding citizens to be able to be proud of the work of our law enforcement agencies and not to cross the street when they see someone in uniform. There can be no place in our law enforcement agencies for people whose primary aim is to fill their own pockets rather than uphold the law. The motivation for our law enforcement officers should be above all about providing quality protection of our citizens' rights and freedoms.

Finally, if part of Russian society continues to see the court system as corrupt, there can be no speaking of an effective justice system in our country.

Overall, I want to note that we need principally new approaches to fighting crime in our country. The relevant decisions will be prepared.

Eradicating the sources of terrorist aggression on Russian territory is an integral part of ensuring law and order in our country. We have taken many serious steps in the fight against terrorism over recent years. But we cannot allow ourselves to have any illusions—the threat is still very real, we still find ourselves being dealt serious blows and criminals are still committing terrible crimes in the aim of frightening society. We need to summon our courage and continue our work to eradicate terrorism. The moment we show signs of weakness, lack of firmness, the losses would become immeasurably greater and could result in a national disaster.

I hope for energetic work to strengthen security in the southern part of Russia and firmly establish the values of freedom and justice there. Developing the economy, creating new jobs and building social and production infrastructure are prerequisites for this work.

I support the idea of holding parliamentary elections in the Republic of Chechnya this year. These elections should lay the foundation for stability and for developing democracy in this region.

I want to note that the North Caucasus region already has good conditions for achieving rapid economic growth. The region has one of Russia's best-developed transport infrastructures, a qualified labour force, and surveys show that the number of people in this region wanting to start up their own business is higher than the national average. At the same time, however, the shadow economy accounts for a bigger share in this region and there is criminalisation of economic relations in general. In this respect, the authorities should not only work on strengthening the law enforcement and court systems in the region, but should also help develop business activity among the population.

We should be paying no less attention to other strategically important regions of the Russian Federation. Here, I am referring to the Far East, Kaliningrad Region and other border areas. In these areas we should be concentrating state resources on expanding the transport, telecommunications and energy infrastructure, including through the creation of cross-continent corridors. These regions should become key bases for our cooperation with our neighbours.

Esteemed Assembly,

Very soon, on May 9, we shall celebrate the 60th anniversary of victory. This day can be justly called the day of civilisation's triumph over fascism. Our common victory enabled us to defend the principles of freedom, independence and equality between all peoples and nations.

It is clear for us that this victory was not achieved through arms alone but was won also through the strong spirit of all the peoples who were united at that time within a single state. Their unity emerged victorious over inhumanity, genocide and the ambitions of one nation to impose its will on others.

But the terrible lessons of the past also define imperatives for the present. And Russia, bound to the former Soviet republics—now independent countries—through a common history, and through the Russian language and the great culture that we share, cannot stay away from the common desire for freedom.

Today, with independent countries now formed and developing in the post-Soviet area, we want to work together to correspond to humanistic values, open up broad possibilities for personal and collective success, achieve for ourselves the standards of civilisation we have worked hard for—standards that would emerge as a result of common economic, humanitarian and legal space.

While standing up for Russia's foreign political interests, we also want our closest neighbours to develop their economies and strengthen their international authority. We would like to achieve synchronisation of the pace and parameters of reform processes underway in Russia and the other members of the Commonwealth of Independent States. We are ready to draw on the genuinely useful experience of our neighbours and also to share with them our own ideas and the results of our work....

In speaking of our values, I would like to raise another issue I think is very important, that of the level of public morals and culture. It is well known that a good business reputation has always been a prerequisite for concluding deals, and human decency has been a necessary condition for taking part in state and public life. Russian society has always condemned immorality, and indecent behaviour has always been publicly reprimanded.

Law and morals, politics and morality have traditionally been considered close and related concepts in Russia, at least, such was always the declared ideal and aim. Despite the problems we all know, the level of morality in tsarist Russia and during the Soviet years was always a very meaningful scale and criteria for people's reputation, at work, in society and in private life. No one can deny that values such as close friendship, mutual assistance, trust, comradeship and reliability have flourished in Russia over the course of centuries, becoming enduring and immutable values here....

We should remember that corruption among state officials and rising crime are also consequences of the lack of trust and moral strength in our society. Russia will begin to prosper only when the success of each individual depends not only on his level of wealth but also on his decency and level of culture....

Our country is about to celebrate the anniversary of our great victory, a victory that came at the terrible cost of countless lives and sacrifices. The soldiers of the Great Patriotic War are justly called the soldiers of freedom. They saved the world from an ideology of hatred and tyranny. They defended our country's sovereignty and independence. We will always remember this. Our people fought against slavery. They fought for the right to live on their own land, to speak their native language and have their own statehood, culture and traditions. They fought for justice and for freedom. They stood up for their right to independent development and they gave our Motherland a future. Just what kind of future this will be now depends on us, on today's generation.

Thank you for your attention.

Source: Putin, Vladimir. "Annual Address to the Federal Assembly, The Kremlin, Moscow, April 25, 2005." Available online at Official Website of the President of Russia, http://www.kremlin.ru/eng/speeches/2005/04/25/2031_type70029_87086.shtml.

14.6
Russia's Status in the New Millennium: An American Perspective – 2005
An Excerpt from "Russia," a Congressional Research Service Issue Brief for Congress

In 2005 the nonpartisan Congressional Research Service (CRS) issued a report on recent political, military, and economic developments in Russia. The report echoed concerns expressed by many American analysts and journalists over the previous few years about the course that Russian President Vladimir Putin was charting in his efforts to restore Russia to its former status as one of the leading economic, military, and political powers in the world. According to the CRS, many of Putin's policies have placed Russia's fragile political freedoms and democratic institutions in jeopardy. They have also placed Russia at greater risk of sliding into the same sort of single-party, totalitarian state that ruled the country during the Cold War. Following are excerpts from the CRS report.

Summary

Vladimir Putin won reelection as Russian President in March 2004, in an exercise in "managed democracy" in which he took 71% of the vote and faced no serious competition. The pro-Putin Unified Russia party similarly swept the parliamentary election in December 2003 and controls more than two-thirds of the seats in the Duma. Also in March, Putin replaced long-serving Premier Kasyanov with a little-known bureaucrat, Mikhail Fradkov, indicating Putin's intent to take the reins of government even more completely into his own hands. Putin's twin priorities remain to revive the economy and strengthen the state. He has brought TV and radio under tight state control and virtually eliminated effective political opposition. Federal forces have suppressed large-scale military resistance in Chechnya but face the prospect of prolonged guerrilla warfare and terrorist style attacks.

The economic upturn that began in 1999 is continuing. The GDP [Gross Domestic Product] and domestic investment are growing impressively after a long decline, inflation is contained, the budget is balanced, and the ruble is stable. Major problems remain: 18% of the population live below the poverty line, foreign investment is low, and crime, corruption, capital flight, and unemployment remain high. Putin apparently seeks simultaneously to tighten political control and accelerate economic reform.

Russian foreign policy has grown more assertive, fueled in part by frustration over the gap between Russia's self-image as a world power and its greatly diminished capabilities. Russia's drive to reassert dominance in and integration of the former Soviet states is most successful with Belarus and Armenia but arouses opposition in Georgia, Ukraine, Azerbaijan, and Moldova. The Commonwealth of Independent States (CIS) as an institution is failing. Washington and Moscow continue to disagree over Russian nuclear reactor sales to Iran, among other issues. After the September 11, 2001, attacks, however, Russia adopted a generally more cooperative attitude on many issues.

The military is in turmoil after years of severe force reductions and budget cuts. The armed forces now number about one million, down from 4.3 million Soviet troops in 1986. Weapons procurement is down sharply. Readiness, training, morale, and discipline have suffered. Putin's government has increased defense spending sharply but there is conflict between the military and the government and within the military over resource allocation, restructuring, and reform.

> *"[Putin] has brought TV and radio under tight state control and virtually eliminated effective political opposition."*

After the collapse of the Soviet Union, the United States sought a cooperative relationship with Moscow and supplied over $4 billion in grant aid to encourage democracy, market reform, and WMD [weapons of mass destruction] threat reduction in Russia. Early hopes for a close partnership waned however, due to mutual disillusionment. Direct U.S. foreign aid to Russia, under congressional pressure, fell over the past decade. Indirect U.S. assistance, however, through institutions such as the IMF [International Monetary Fund], was substantial. The United States has imposed economic sanctions on Russian organizations for exporting military technology and equipment to Iran and Syria. There are more restrictions on aid to Russia in the FY2005 foreign aid bill. In the spirit of cooperation after September 11, however, the two sides agreed on a strategic nuclear force reduction treaty and a strategic framework for bilateral relations, signed at the Bush-Putin summit in May 2002....

Political Developments

The ongoing political struggle in Russia has many aspects, including contests over political ideology, the character of government, and the pace and character of economic reform; institutional clashes between the central government and the regions; and rivalries among competing political-economic cliques. Some argue that what has appeared on the surface to be "normal" competition among politicians and parties of varying ideological hues masked a deeper underlying contest—an ongoing venal competition among elites to seize ownership of vast, previously state-owned assets.

Former President Boris Yeltsin's surprise resignation (December 31, 1999) propelled Vladimir Putin (whom Yeltsin had plucked from obscurity in August 1999 to be his fifth Premier in three years) into the Kremlin as Acting President.

Putin's meteoric rise in popularity was due to a number of factors: his tough policy toward Chechnya; his image as a youthful, vigorous, sober, and plain-talking leader; and massive support from state-owned TV and other mass media. In March 2000, Putin was elected president in his own right with 52.5% of the vote. His closest rival, Communist Party leader Gennady Zyuganov, got just under 30%. All other candidates were in single digits.

Putin, who was a Soviet KGB foreign intelligence officer for 16 years and later headed Russia's Federal Security Service (domestic component of the former KGB), is an intelligent, disciplined statist. His priorities appear to be strengthening the central government, reviving the economy, and restoring Russia's status as a great power.

On the domestic political scene, Putin early on won major victories over regional leaders, reclaiming authority for the central government that Yeltsin had allowed to slip away. First, Putin created seven super-regional districts overseen by presidential appointees. Then he pushed legislation to change the composition of the Federation Council, the upper chamber of parliament (a body that was comprised of the heads of the regional governments and regional legislatures), giving those leaders exclusive control of that chamber and also parliamentary immunity from criminal prosecution. With Putin's changes, Federation Council Deputies are appointed by the regional leaders and legislatures, but once appointed, they are somewhat independent. A related bill gives the president the right to remove popularly elected regional leaders who violate federal law.

The Putin regime has been steadily working to gain control of the broadcast media. A key target was the media empire of Vladimir Gusinsky, which included Russia's only independent television network, NTV, which had been critical of Putin. Gusinsky, one of the so-called oligarchs who rose to economic and political prominence under Yeltsin, was arrested in June 2000 on corruption charges and was later released and allowed to leave the country. Many viewed this as an act of political repression by the Putin regime. In April 2001, the state-controlled gas monopoly Gazprom took over NTV and appointed Kremlin loyalists to run it. A few days later, Gusinsky's flagship newspaper, *Segodnya*, was shut down and the editorial staff of his respected newsweekly, *Itogi*, was fired. The government then forced the prominent oligarch Boris Berezovsky to give up ownership of his controlling share of the ORT TV network. In January 2002, TV-6, the last significant independent Moscow TV station, was shut down, the victim, many believe, of government pressure. The government has also moved against the independent radio network, Echo Moskvuy, and other electronic media.

A law on political parties, introduced by the government and explicitly aimed at reducing the number of parties, gives the government the authority to register, or deny registration to, political parties. In April 2001, Putin proposed that the Duma be stripped of its power to debate or vote on specific components of the budget and instead either approve or reject the government's proposed budget as a whole. In April 2002, the pro-Putin bloc in the Duma staged a political coup against the Communist Party faction, depriving it of most of its committee chairmanships and other leadership posts. Putin's September 2004 political changes will further reduce the number of parties in the Duma by raising the threshold for representation from 5% to 7% of the total vote and banning parliamentary blocs (coalitions of several parties).

In the summer of 2003, the Russian government launched a campaign against Mikhail Khodorkovski, CEO of Yukos, the world's fourth largest oil company. After numerous searches and seizures of Yukos records and the arrest of several senior Yukos officials, Federal Security Service police arrested Khodorkovski on October 25. Five days later prosecutors froze Yukos stock worth some $12 billion. Khodorkovski, the wealthiest man in Russia, became a multi-billionaire in the 1990s in the course of the often corrupt privatization of state-owned assets under former president Yeltsin. Khodorkovski, however, subsequently won respect in the West by adopting open and "transparent" business practices while transforming Yukos into a major global energy company. Khodorkovski criticized some of President Putin's actions, financed anti-Putin political parties, and hinted that he might enter politics in the future. Khodorkovski's arrest is seen by many as politically motivated, aimed at eliminating a political enemy and making an example of him to other Russian oligarches. Many observers also see this episode as the denouement of a long power struggle between two Kremlin factions: a business-oriented group of former Yeltsin loyalists and a rising group of Putin loyalists drawn mainly from the security services and Putin's home town of St. Petersburg. A few days after Khodorkovski's arrest, Presidential Chief of Staff Aleksandr Voloshin, reputed head of the Kremlin-era group, resigned, as did several of his close associates, leaving the Kremlin in the hands of the "policemen." Khodorkovski went on trial in June 2004 on multiple criminal charges of tax evasion and fraud. The trial is coming to an end in May 2005, with a guilty verdict virtually a foregone conclusion.

Yukos is being broken up and its principal assets sold off to satisfy tax debts alleged totaling $28 billion. On December 19, 2004, Yuganskneftegaz, the main oil production subsidiary of Yukos, was sold at a state-run auction, ostensibly to satisfy tax debts. The winning, and sole, bidder, Baikalfinansgrup, paid $9.7 billion, about half of its market value, according to western industry specialists. It was subsequently revealed that the previously unheard-of Baikalfinansgrup is a group of Kremlin insiders headed by Igor Sechin, Deputy head of the Presidential Administration and a close associate of President Putin. On December 22, Baikalfinansgrup was purchased by Rosneft, a wholly state-owned Russian oil company. Sechin has been Chairman of Rosneft's Board of Directors since July 2004. The de-facto nationalization of Yuganskneftegaz was denounced by Andrei Illarionov, a senior Putin economic advisor, as "the scam of the year."

In parliamentary elections on December 7, 2003, the big winners were the Unified Russia Party, identified with President Putin, and the newly created pro-Kremlin populist/nationalist party, Motherland. When the new Duma convened on December 29, Unified Russia had 300 of the 450 seats. With its two-thirds majority and the added support of the Motherland Party and Vladimir Zhirinovsky's right-wing Liberal Democratic Party, the Kremlin's control of the Duma is absolute, sufficient to pass any legislation and to amend the Constitution. The big losers were the Communist Party, which lost half its seats, and the two liberal, pro-western parties, Yabloko and Union of Rightist, which failed to reach the 5% threshold and were virtually eliminated from the Duma. The Communist Party now holds 52 seats; Motherland and the Zhirinovsky's LDP hold 36 seats each. These are the only four parties with meaningful representation in the Duma.

The pro-Kremlin sweep in the Duma election foretold the results of the presidential election three months later. Demonstrating what some of Putin's own advisors call "managed democracy," the Kremlin team used levels of power and influence to affect the electoral process, including determining the opposition candidates. So-called "administrative resources" (financial, bureaucratic, and judicial) were mobilized at the federal, regional, and local level in support of Putin's campaign. The state-controlled national broadcast media lionized Putin and generally ignored and/or denigrated his opponents. On March 14, 2004, Putin, as expected, won reelection to a second term with a reported 71 percent of the vote, and no serious opposition. Community Party leader Zyuganov declined to run, as did Zhirinovsky, both of whom designated surrogates to put up a show of contesting the election. In the event, the Kremlin's biggest campaign challenge turned out to be maintaining the appearance of a politically meaningful contest. Most objective observers, Russian and international, concluded that in this the Putin team failed....

On September 13, 2004, in the aftermath of the bloody Beslan school hostage crisis ... President Putin proposed a number of changes to the political system that would further concentrate power in his hands, necessitated, he said, by Russia's intensified war against international terrorism. He proposed, *inter alia*, that regional governors no longer be popularly elected, but instead that regional legislatures confirm the president's appointees as governors and that all Duma Deputies be elected on the basis of national party lists, based on the proportion of votes each party gets nationwide. The first proposal would make regional governors wholly dependent on, and subservient to, the president, undermining much of what remains of Russia's nominally federal system. The second proposal would eliminate independent deputies and further strengthen the pro-presidential parties that already control an absolute majority in the Duma. Putin and his supporters argue that these measures will help reduce corruption in the regions and "unify" the country, the better to fight against terrorism. Critics see the proposals as further, major encroachments on the fragile democratic reforms of the 1980s and 1990s that have already suffered serious setbacks under Putin. They warn of Putin's growing authoritarianism. President Bush, Secretary of State Powell, and many members of Congress voiced concern that Putin's September 13 proposals threaten Russian democracy.

In January 2005, the Russian government monetized many previously in-kind social benefits for retirees, military personnel, and state employees. The cash payments, however, only partly compensated for the lost benefits. At the same time, another government "reform" substantially raised housing and public utility costs. This led to massive, prolonged anti-government demonstrations bringing hundreds of thousands of protestors into the streets in what many have called the most serious challenge to Putin's five-year rule. These widespread protests, following the September 2004 Beslan school hostage disaster and Putin's public humiliation in the Ukrainian presidential election in December [in which independent candidate Viktor Yushchenko defeated the openly pro-Moscow Prime Minister, Viktor Yanukovych], brought Putin's public approval rating down to 41% in March 2005, from the high 70s a year earlier.

Source: Goldman, Stuart D. Congressional Research Service. CRS Issue Brief for Congress. "Russia." Updated May 24, 2005. Washington, DC: Library of Congress. Available online at the U.S. State Department, Foreign Press Centers, http://fpc.state.gov/documents/organization/48589.pdf.

GLOSSARY

Leading Figures of the Cold War

Allende, Salvador (1908-1973) – President of Chile from 1970 to 1973, when he was killed during a military coup.

Andropov, Yuri (1914-1984) – Soviet KGB official who served as general secretary of the Soviet Communist Party for sixteen months, from 1982 to early 1984, before his death.

Batista, Fulgencio (1901-1973) – Long-time leader of Cuba who was overthrown in 1959 in the Cuban Revolution by Fidel Castro and his followers.

Brezhnev, Leonid (1906-1982) – Soviet politician who served as General Secretary of the Soviet Communist Party from 1964 to 1982.

Bush, George H.W. (1924-) – President of the United States from January 1989 to January 1993; it was during his presidency that the Soviet empire dissolved and the Cold War ended.

Carter, Jimmy (1924-) – President of the United States from January 1977 to January 1981.

Castro, Fidel (1927-) – Communist leader of Cuba since 1959, when he led a successful uprising against the regime of Fulgencia Batista.

Ceauşescu, Nicolae (1918-1989) – Dictatorial leader of Communist Romania from 1965 until December 25, 1989, when he and his wife Elena were executed after his regime was overthrown.

Chernenko, Konstantin (1911-1985) – Soviet politician who led the USSR for thirteen months, from February 1984 to March 1985, before his death.

Chiang Kai-shek (1887-1975) – Ruler of China from 1928 to 1949, when Communist Chinese opponents forced him to retreat to Taiwan and establish a government-in-exile.

Churchill, Winston (1874-1965) – Prime minister of England from 1940 to 1945 and again from 1951 to 1955.

Deng Xiaoping (1904-1997) – Leader of the People's Republic of China from the late 1970s to 1992; relations with the West improved markedly during his tenure.

Dobrynin, Anatoly (1919-) – Soviet diplomat who served as ambassador to the United States from 1962 to 1986.

Dubček, Alexander (1921-1992) – Secretary of the Czech Communist Party from January 1968 to April 1969; his reforms led the Soviets to invade Czechoslovakia in August 1968.

Dulles, John Foster (1888-1959) – U.S. Secretary of State from 1953 to 1959, during which time he helped shape major elements of American Cold War foreign policy.

Eisenhower, Dwight D. (1890-1969) – President of the United States from January 1953 to January 1961, an era of high Cold War tensions.

Ford, Gerald R. (1913-) – President of the United States from August 1974 to January 1977.

Gorbachev, Mikhail (1931-) – General secretary of the Soviet Communist Party from March 1985 to December 1991, when the Soviet Union formally dissolved; his reformist policies of *perestroika* and *glasnost* are frequently cited as the chief catalysts in the collapse of the Soviet Union and the end of the Cold War.

Havel, Vaclev (1936-) – Dissident playwright who played a leading role in Czechoslovakia's "Velvet Revolution" in 1989; he served as the first elected president of Czechoslovakia from 1989 to 1992, then served two terms as the first president of the Czech Republic from 1993 to 2003.

Hiss, Alger (1904-1996) – U.S. State Department official who became embroiled in the most famous espionage trial in Cold War history; accused of being a Communist spy in 1948, he was convicted of perjury in 1950.

Ho Chi Minh (1890-1969) – Vietnamese Communist leader who served as president of North Vietnam from 1955 to 1969.

Hoover, J. Edgar (1895-1972) – Director of the U.S. Federal Bureau of Investigation from 1924 until his death in 1972.

Johnson, Lyndon B. (1908-1973) – President of the United States from November 1963 to January 1969, during which time America became heavily involved in the Vietnam War.

Kennan, George F. (1904-2005) – American diplomat and political advisor who became a leading architect of U.S. foreign policy during the early years of the Cold War.

Kennedy, John F. (1917-1963) – President of the United States during the Cuban Missile Crisis; his presidency began in January 1961 but was cut short when he was assassinated in November 1963.

Khrushchev, Nikita (1894-1971) – General Secretary of the Soviet Communist Party from 1953 to 1964, when he was ousted from power by Kremlin hardliners.

Kim Il-Sung (1912-1994) – Leader of Communist North Korea from its 1948 founding until his death in 1994.

Kissinger, Henry (1923-) – American diplomat who helped usher in the *Détente* era as secretary of state in the 1970s in the administrations of President Richard M. Nixon and Gerald R. Ford,

Lenin, Vladimir (1870-1924) – Russian revolutionary leader who became the first premier of the Soviet Union.

Mao Zedong (1893-1976) – Chairman of the Chinese Communist Party from 1943 until his death; Mao unified mainland China under Communist rule and helped transform it into a world power, but he also launched the nation's self-destructive "Cultural Revolution" program in the late 1960s.

Marshall, George C. (1880-1959) – American general and statesman whose "Marshall Plan" is credited with reviving Europe after World War II.

McCarthy, Joseph (1908-1957) – American senator from Wisconsin who charged that Communist agents had deeply infiltrated vital U.S. institutions; his accusations intensified American paranoia and suspicions about Communist activities in the United States and around the world.

Nagy, Imre (1896-1958) – Prime minister of Hungary who was executed in 1958, two years after Soviet-led Warsaw Pact forces put down a national rebellion aimed at severing ties with Moscow.

Nasser, Gamal Abdel (1918-1970) – Egyptian soldier and statesman who served as president of Egypt from 1956 to 1970.

Nixon, Richard M. (1913-1994) – President of the United States from January 1969 to August 1974, when he resigned because of the Watergate scandal.

Ortega, Daniel (1945-) – Longtime Sandinista leader who was president of Nicaragua from 1985 to 1990.

Putin, Vladimir (1952-) – Former KGB official who succeeded Boris Yeltsin as President of the Russian Federation on December 31, 1999; in March 2004 he was elected to a second term as president.

Reagan, Ronald (1911-2004) – President of the United States from January 1981 to January 1989; a pivotal figure in the closing years of the Cold War.

Roosevelt, Franklin D. (1882-1945) – President of the United States from January 1933 until his death in April 1945, by which time the Allies were poised for victory in World War II.

Rosenberg, Julius (1918-1953) and **Ethel** (1915-1953) – American citizens who were convicted of being Soviet spies and executed in 1953.

Stalin, Joseph (1878-1953) – Tyrannical leader of the Union of Soviet Socialist Republics (USSR) from the mid-1920s until his sudden death in 1953.

Tito, Josep (1892-1980) – Communist leader of Yugoslavia from 1945 until his death in 1980.

Truman, Harry S. (1884-1972) – President of the United States from April 1945 to January 1953, the opening years of the Cold War.

Walesa, Lech (1943-) – A co-founder of the Solidarity trade union movement, Walesa served as president of Poland from 1990 to 1995.

Yeltsin, Boris (1931-) – A leading reformist politician in the Soviet Union in the 1980s, Yeltsin served from 1991 to 1999 as the first popularly-elected president of Russia.

Cold War Terms

Antiballistic missiles (ABMs) – Missiles designed to intercept and neutralize ballistic missiles, including those carrying nuclear warheads.

Ballistic missiles – Rocket-propelled military missiles that take a set prescribed course to reach their destination after launch.

Bourgeoisie – A derogatory Communist term that refers to members of the wealthy social class in capitalist societies who unfairly prosper from the labor of the working class.

Capitalism – An economic system, dominant in the United States and other Western nations, based on private or corporate ownership—rather than government ownership—of goods and resources.

Cold War – The political, military, and economic rivalry that endured between the United States and the Soviet Union—and their respective allies—from the end of World War II to the dissolution of the USSR in 1991.

Colonialism – Economic and political control exerted by one country over another region or people, usually for the purposes of improving its own financial or strategic standing in the world.

Cominform – Abbreviated name for the Communist Information Bureau, a USSR-led organization of world Communist parties.

Communism – A political system in which the state controls all resources and means of producing wealth and all citizens share equally in that wealth, according to their relative needs.

Contras – A U.S.-supported rebel group that fought against Nicaragua's socialist Sandinista government during the 1980s.

Cultural Revolution – Tumultous decade (1966-1976) of Chinese history in which Chinese Communist leader Mao Zedong carried out a campaign to neutralize political opponents and institute "Maoism" as the state's dominant ideology; Mao's actions ushered in a decade of political repression and terrorism that cost millions of Chinese citizens their lives.

Glasnost – Russian term for "openness," this word was appropriated by Soviet leader Mikhail Gorbachev to describe his policies of increased freedom of speech and government transparency.

House Un-American Activities Committee (HUAC) –A committee of the U.S. House of Representatives that became a leading investigator of alleged domestic Communist activity during the Cold War.

Intercontinental ballistic missiles (ICBMs) – Ballistic missiles with a range greater than 2,000 miles; typically designed to carry nuclear warheads, since their payload is too limited for the efficient delivery of conventional explosives.

KGB – The Russian-language acronym for the Soviet Union's State Security Committee, the primary police/security/intelligence agency of the USSR from 1954 to 1991.

Kremlin – The Russian word for "citadel" or "fortress"; during the Cold War this became a shorthand term for the Soviet central government, which was based in Moscow's heavily fortified complex of building known as the Moscow Kremlin.

Marxism – A social, economic, and political philosophy based on the works of Karl Marx, a nineteenth-century German philosopher and revolutionary; its emphasis on class struggle as a driving force in the growth of Socialism became a central tenet of twentieth-century Communism.

McCarthyism – Named after anti-Communist Senator Joe McCarthy, this word refers to the feverish pursuit—or hysterical "witch hunts," in the view of users of this derogatory term—of alleged Communist spies and sympathizers in the United States during the 1950s.

Mutual Assured Destruction (MAD) – Doctrine of nuclear military strategy that holds that if either of two nuclear powers launches a full-scale attack on the other, the destruction of both sides is assured.

NATO (North Atlantic Treaty Organization) – Mutual defense organization formed in 1949, when the United States, Canada, and ten Western European governments signed the North Atlantic Treaty, a mutual defense pact.

NKVD (Narodnyi Komissariat Vnutrennikh Del) – Soviet state agency that was responsible for state security and police functions during the Stalin era.

Perestroika – The Russian word for the policies of economic reform introduced by Soviet leader Mikhail Gorbachev in the late 1980s; its literal meaning is "restructuring."

Politburo – An abbreviated version of the term "political bureau," this was the executive organization of the Communist Party in the Soviet Union and several other Communist states during the Cold War.

Proletariat – Lower economic or social classes in a society; in Marxist thought, this term referred generally to the working class, seen as the heart and soul of society.

Proxy wars – Armed struggles in developing nations between forces that allied themselves with the United States or the USSR.

SALT – Strategic Arms Limitation Talks. The historic SALT I agreement between the U.S. and USSR was signed in 1972; the SALT II talks, which continued through the remainder of the 1970s, did not produce a ratified agreement, but its terms were generally honored by both superpowers.

Sandinistas – Members of the Sandinista National Liberation Front, the Socialist political party that ruled Nicaragua from 1979 to 1990.

Socialism – A social and economic system based on collective ownership of societal resources and abolition of concepts of private ownership.

Soviet Union – The Union of Soviet Socialist Republics (USSR), a confederation of 15 republics, of which Russia was the largest and most prominent.

Star Wars – The nickname given to the Reagan administration's proposed Strategic Defense Initiative (SDI) in the 1980s.

Strategic Defense Initiative (SDI) – A satellite-based anti-missile defense system proposed by the Reagan administration in the 1980s.

Warsaw Pact – Mutual defense alliance organized by the Soviet Union in 1955 that included the Communist nations of East Germany, Albania, Bulgaria, Hungary, Poland, Romania, and Czechoslovakia.

CHRONOLOGY

Note: This Chronology of Cold War events includes a see reference feature. Under this arrangement, many events listed in the chronology include page references to relevant primary documents featured in the book.

1945

February 4-11   Soviet, British, and American leaders gather at the Yalta Summit. *See p. 9.*

April 12   U.S. President Franklin D. Roosevelt dies and Harry S. Truman is sworn in as president.

May 7   Germany surrenders, ending World War II in Europe.

June 26   Fifty-one nations sign the founding charter for the United Nations.

July 17   American, British, and Soviet leaders begin postwar negotiations at the historic Potsdam Conference. *See p. 16.*

August 6   The United States drops an atomic bomb on the Japanese city of Hiroshima; three days later, a U.S. airplane drops a second atomic bomb on Nagasaki.

August 14   Japan surrenders, bringing an end to World War II.

1946

February   American analyst George Kennan delivers his "Long Telegram" on Soviet ambitions. *See p. 22.*

March 5   Winston Churchill delivers his "Sinews of Peace" address, in which he warns that an "iron curtain" of Communism is being drawn down across Europe by the USSR. *See p. 27.*

1947

March 12   President Truman outlines the "Truman Doctrine" before a joint session of Congress. *See p. 47.*

June 5	Secretary of State George Marshall announces the "Marshall Plan" of aid to Europe. *See p. 52.*
September	Soviet Union establishes the Communist Information Bureau (Cominform) to consolidate control over Eastern Europe.
October 19	The House Un-American Activities Committee (HUAC) opens hearings to investigate "alleged Communist infiltration" of the American motion picture industry.

1948

February	Communist forces complete takeover of Czechoslovakia.
June 24	The Berlin Blockade begins.
June 25	The United States and Great Britain begin the Berlin Airlift. *See p. 57.*

1949

April 4	The North Atlantic Treaty Organization (NATO) is formed. *See p. 63.*
May 12	Stalin calls a halt to the Berlin Blockade.
September 23	The Soviet Union successfully detonates its first atomic bomb.
September 30	The United States and Great Britain end their airlift shipments into Berlin.
October 1	Communist Mao Zedong takes formal leadership of the People's Republic of China after two decades of civil war.

1950

February	Mao Zedong and Joseph Stalin negotiate a Sino-Soviet Treaty of Friendship, Alliance and Mutual Assistance.
February 9	Wisconsin Senator Joseph McCarthy declares that he has evidence of Communist infiltration of the State Department; his announcement marks the beginning of the "McCarthyism" era in America. *See p. 103.*
April	The National Security Council delivers its influential "NSC-68" memorandum on Soviet military capabilities and goals. *See p. 201.*
May	The United States begins providing military and economic aid to French forces fighting Communist guerrillas in Vietnam.
June 25	North Korea launches a surprise invasion of South Korea.
June 27	President Truman sends American military forces into Korea. *See p. 73.*
September 15	U.S. forces seize the momentum in the Korean War with the Inchon landing. *See p. 80.*

September 23   Congress overrides Truman's veto to pass the anti-Communist Internal Security Act.

October   China enters the Korean War on the side of Communist North Korea. *See p. 83.*

1952

October 3   Great Britain conducts its first atomic bomb test.

November 1   The United States successfully detonates its first hydrogen bomb; the Soviets announce their first hydrogen bomb tests less than a year later.

November 4   Republican Dwight D. Eisenhower defeats Democrat Adlai Stevenson in the 1952 U.S. presidential election; Eisenhower takes office two months later.

1953

March 5   Joseph Stalin dies.

June 19   Julius and Ethel Rosenberg are executed in the United States after their convictions on charges that they passed atomic secrets to the Soviets. *See p. 112.*

July 27   Armistice ending the Korean War is signed, leaving the border between South Korea and North Korea in virtually the same place as it was before the war began.

September 12   Nikita Khrushchev becomes the chairman of the Soviet Communist Party, ensuring his place as Stalin's successor.

1954

April 22-June 17   American television networks broadcast live coverage of the "Army-McCarthy" hearings. *See p. 119.*

May 7   Vietnamese Communists led by Ho Chi Minh defeat French colonial forces in the pivotal battle at Dien Bien Phu.

July   The Geneva Accords divide Vietnam into a northern half controlled by Ho Chi Minh and his Communist followers and a southern half led by a U.S.-supported government under Ngo Dinh Diem.

December 2   The U.S. Senate censures Joseph McCarthy for dishonorable conduct. *See p. 127.*

1955

January 12   U.S. Secretary of State John Foster Dulles announces the doctrine of "massive retaliation."

May 9   West Germany is admitted into the North Atlantic Treaty Organization (NATO).

May 14   The Warsaw Pact, an alliance of states under the Soviet sphere of influence, is announced. *See p. 135.*

July   United States and Soviet Union hold their first diplomatic summit since the end of World War II.

1956

February 25   Khrushchev denounces Stalinism. *See p. 140.*

October   British, French, and Israeli forces seize the Suez Canal. *See p. 157.*

November 1   Hungarian Prime Minister Imre Nagy announces withdrawal of Hungary from Warsaw Pact and declares neutrality in the Cold War.

November 3   Soviet forces roll into Hungary and crush the rebellion. *See p. 143.*

1957

January 5   President Eisenhower unveils his "Eisenhower Doctrine" in a speech before a Joint Session of Congress. *See p. 159.*

April   The Suez Canal is reopened under the authority of the United Nations.

October 4   The Soviets successfully launch Sputnik, the first satellite to orbit the Earth; this triumph marks the beginning of the "space race" between the United States and the USSR. *See p. 165.*

1958

November 10   Khrushchev demands the withdrawal of all foreign troops from Berlin; two weeks later, the Kremlin issues a six-month deadline for complete withdrawal, warning of forcible eviction of troops that remain.

1959

January 1   A guerrilla insurgency led by Fidel Castro succeeds in overthrowing the regime of Fulgencio Batista in Cuba. Castro becomes prime minister of Cuba six weeks later.

September 15   Khrushchev begins a historic tour of the United States.

1960

February 13   France conducts its first atomic bomb test.

May 1   Soviet forces shoot down a U.S. U2 spy plane over Soviet territory, triggering higher U.S.-Soviet tensions. *See p. 210.*

November 8   Democratic candidate John F. Kennedy narrowly defeats Republican nominee Richard M. Nixon to win the White House; Kennedy is inaugurated two months later.

1961

January 17   Outgoing President Eisenhower publicly warns U.S. citizens about the undue influence of the nation's "military-industrial complex." *See p. 218.*

April 17   The United States launches its failed Bay of Pigs invasion of Cuba. *See p. 237.*

August 13   The East German border in Berlin is sealed, and construction of the Berlin Wall begins four days later. *See p. 188.*

1962

June   President Kennedy and Premier Khrushchev hold a diplomatic summit in Vienna.

October 14   American reconnaissance flights over Cuba reveal that Soviet missile sites are being built on the island.

October 22   President Kennedy informs a national television audience about the escalating Cuban missile crisis. *See p. 246.*

October 26   Khrushchev offers to remove the missiles from Cuba in exchange for assurances that the United States will not invade the island; a short time later he sends a second letter explicitly linking the removal of missiles from Cuba with the withdrawal of NATO missiles from Turkey. *See p. 253.*

October 27   Kennedy agrees to the terms of the first letter from Khrushchev, essentially ignoring the existence of the second letter. *See p. 253.*

October 28   Radio Moscow announces that the Soviet Union is removing all missiles from Cuba, an announcement that brings the Cuban Missile Crisis to a close. *See p. 265.*

1963

June 20   The United States and the Soviet Union agree to install a "hot line" so that leaders of the two nations can directly communicate with each other in the case of another dangerous incident like the Cuban Missile Crisis.

June 26   Kennedy visits West Berlin.

July 25   The Nuclear Test Ban Treaty is ratified.

November 22   Kennedy is assassinated and Lyndon B. Johnson takes office.

1964

August 7   Congress passes the Tonkin Gulf Resolution, paving the way for U.S. military involvement in Vietnam. *See p. 284.*

October 10   Khruschev is ousted from leadership by political opponents in the Kremlin.

October 16   China successfully detonates its first atomic bomb.

November 3   Johnson wins a full term as president in fall elections.

1965

March   First U.S. combat troops are deployed in Vietnam; the American bombing campaign known as Operation Rolling Thunder begins.

1966

Mao Zedong launches the Cultural Revolution in China, a convulsive event that claims the lives of millions of Chinese citizens. *See p. 321.*

1967

January 27   The United States, United Kingdom, and USSR sign an aerial nuclear test ban treaty.

June 5   The Six Day War begins in the Middle East.

1968

January   Communist leader Alexander Dubček assumes power in Czechoslovakia and promptly begins implementing significant economic and political reforms.

January 30   Communist forces launch the Tet Offensive in Vietnam. *See p. 288.*

March 31   U.S. President Lyndon B. Johnson announces that he will not seek re-election. *See p. 290.*

May   The United States and North Vietnam open peace negotiations in Paris.

August 20   Soviet-led troops march into Czechoslovakia and crush the nation's fledgling reformist movement. *See p. 227.*

November 5   Republican Richard M. Nixon narrowly wins the American presidency over Democratic candidate Hubert Humphrey.

November 13   Soviet leader Leonid Brezhnev lays out his "Brezhnev Doctrine" in a speech in Poland.

1969

March 2   Military skirmishes erupt along the Soviet-Chinese border. *See p. 329.*

November 3   Nixon delivers his "Silent Majority" speech to a national television audience. *See p. 303.*

November 17   SALT negotiations between the United States and the Soviet Union open in Helsinki.

1970

March 5   One hundred and thirty-five nations sign the Treaty on the Non-Proliferation of Nuclear Weapons.

April   Nixon's decision to extend the Vietnam War into neighboring Cambodia sparks campus unrest across the United States; the most famous demonstrations occur at Ohio's Kent State University, where four unarmed students are slain by National Guardsmen.

June 26   Congress repeals the Tonkin Gulf Resolution.

November 3   Salvador Allende elected president of Chile. *See p. 361.*

1971

July   U.S. Secretary of State Henry Kissinger becomes the first American official to visit China since the founding of the People's Republic of China in 1949. *See p. 331.*

1972

February   President Nixon Visits China.

May 22   Nixon begins diplomatic visit to the Soviet Union.

May 26   The United States and the Soviet Union sign the SALT I arms limitations treaty.

December 21   East and West Germany sign the Basic Treaty, establishing diplomatic relations between the two countries. *See p. 336.*

1973

January   The United States and North Vietnam sign a cease fire agreement at the Paris Peace Accords; it becomes valid on January 27.

July   U.S. Congress passes the Case-Church Amendment banning further American military involvement in Vietnam.

September   Chilean General Augusto Pinochet engineers the overthrow of Socialist President Salvador Allende. *See p. 365.*

1974

August 8   Nixon resigns over the Watergate scandal; he is replaced by Gerald R. Ford.

November   Ford and Brezhnev agree on the basic framework for a SALT II treaty.

1975

April 30   Communist forces cap an extended offensive into South Vietnam by capturing the capital city of Saigon; this victory brings an end to the war and reunifies Vietnam under a single Communist government. *See p. 311.*

August   The historic Helsinki Accords are signed by the United States, Canada, the Soviet Union, and nearly three dozen European nations. *See p. 339.*

1976

November 2 Democratic nominee Jimmy Carter defeats incumbent Gerald Ford for the presidency of the United States.

1977

January   Jimmy Carter assumes the presidency and immediately announces that human rights will be a centerpiece of his administration's foreign policy.

February   Czech dissidents issue the Charter 77 declaration of human rights. *See p. 343.*

1979

January   The United States and the People's Republic of China establish full diplomatic relations.

January   The Shah of Iran, a longtime U.S. ally, is overthrown and replaced by an anti-American fundamentalist Islamic regime.

June 18   Carter and Brezhnev sign SALT II agreement.

December 25 Soviet troops invade Afghanistan, prompting Carter to remove SALT II from Senate consideration and boycott the 1980 Olympic Games in Moscow. *See p. 352.*

1980

August 14   Labor leader Lech Walesa spearheads worker strikes at shipyards in Gdansk, Poland; the strikes quickly spread across the country, forming the nucleus of the Solidarity Movement.

November 4 Republican candidate Ronald Reagan defeats incumbent Jimmy Carter for the presidency.

1981

November   The United States begins providing covert assistance to rebel forces operating against Nicaragua's Sandinista government.

December 13 Martial law is declared in Poland.

1982

November 10 Soviet leader Leonid Brezhnev dies after years of illness; he is succeeded by Yuri Andropov.

1983

March 23 President Reagan unveils his Strategic Defense Initiative (SDI), a proposed space defense network that subsequently becomes known as "Star Wars."

September 1 A Soviet military plane shoots down a Korean commercial airliner that had strayed into Soviet airspace, killing 269. *See p.414.*

1984

February 9 Soviet leader Yuri Andropov dies; he is replaced by Konstantin Chernenko.

May 9 Reagan gives a nationally televised address to explain his administration's anti-Communist foreign policy in Central America. *See p. 379.*

November 6 Reagan defeats Democratic candidate Walter Mondale to win a second term as president of the United States.

1985

March 10 Chernenko dies, paving the way for the ascension of Mikhail Gorbachev to leadership of the Soviet Union.

November 21 Reagan and Gorbachev hold their first diplomatic summit in Geneva. *See p. 416.*

1986

October Reagan and Gorbachev hold a summit at Reykjavik, Iceland, during which the two leaders nearly reach agreement on dramatic cuts to all manner of military programs.

November The Iran-Contra affair, in which Reagan administration officials illegally sold arms to Iran to provide money to Nicaraguan Contras, is publicly revealed.

1987

June Pope John Paul II visits Poland. *See p. 445.*

June 12 At a speech at West Berlin's historic Brandenburg Gate, Reagan issues a challenge to Gorbachev to "tear down" the Berlin Wall. *See p. 422.*

December 8   Reagan and Gorbachev sign the Intermediate Nuclear Forces Treaty calling for both sides to remove all medium- and short-range missiles from Europe.

1988

November 8   Republican nominee (and incumbent vice president) George H. W. Bush defeats Democratic candidate Michael Dukakis in the U.S. presidential election.

December 7   Gorbachev announces sweeping changes in Soviet military and diplomatic policies in a speech to the United Nations General Assembly. *See p. 427.*

1989

February   The Soviet Union withdraws from Afghanistan after losing an estimated 15,000 troops; the fanatical Islamic group known as the Taliban subsequently assumes control over most of the country. *See p. 420.*

June 4   After weeks of pro-democracy protests led by students, the Chinese government crushes the protest movement in the Tiananmen Square Massacre, a military action that resulted in the deaths of 400-800 civilians. *See p. 450.*

June 4   Poland's once-outlawed Solidarity Movement wins control of the federal government in national elections.

September   Hungary's Communist government publicly cuts all ties with the Soviet Union and announces its intention to pursue policies of democratic socialism.

November 9   The Berlin Wall falls after weeks of massive rallies against the East German government. *See p. 451.*

December   Communist governments in Bulgaria, Romania, and Czechoslovakia all are toppled. The only violent turnover in power occurs in Romania, where despised dictator Nicolae Ceaușescu and his wife Elena are executed by firing squad on December 25. *See p. 457.*

1990

February   Leaders of the U.S.-backed National Opposition Union take the reins in Nicaragua after defeating the incumbent Sandinista government. These election results bring an end to the decade-long U.S. campaign against the Sandinistas.

March   Lithuania becomes the first of numerous Soviet republics to declare its independence from the USSR.

March 18   East Germany holds free elections.

October 3   West and East Germany are formally united as the Federal Republic of Germany.

December 20   Soviet Foreign Minister Edward Zhevardnadze submits his resignation, warning that the USSR is on the brink of sliding into a dictatorship.

1991

August 18   Communist conspirators launch a failed coup to remove Gorbachev from power and reestablish the Communist Party as the director of all Soviet affairs.

December 12   Eleven of fifteen former Soviet republics confirm their independence from the USSR at a conference in Alma Ata, Kazakhstan; Boris Yeltsin engineers the creation of the Commonwealth of Independent States (CIS), a loose confederation of the former Soviet republics.

December 25   The Union of Soviet Socialist Republics (USSR) is formally dissolved; Gorbachev submits his resignation from the presidency of the USSR. *See p. 462.*

PHOTO CREDITS

FURTHER READING

General/Overview

Chang, Gordon H. *Friends and Enemies: The United States, China, and the Soviet Union, 1948-1972*. Stanford, CA: Stanford University Press, 1990.

Cohen, Warren I. *America in the Age of Soviet Power, 1945-1991*. New York: Cambridge University Press, 1993.

Gaddis, John Lewis. *Strategies of Containment: A Critical Appraisal of Postwar American National Security Policy*. New York: Oxford University Press, 1982.

Gaddis, John Lewis. *We Now Know: Rethinking Cold War History*. New York: Oxford University Press, 1997.

Isaacs, Jeremy, and Taylor Downing. *Cold War: An Illustrated History, 1945-1991*. Boston: Little, Brown, 1998.

McMahon, Robert J. *The Cold War: A Very Short Introduction*. New York: Oxford University Press, 2003.

Volkogonov, Dmitri. *Autopsy for an Empire: The Seven Leaders Who Built the Soviet Regime*. New York: Free Press, 1998.

Walker, Martin. *The Cold War: A History*. London: Fourth Estate, 1993.

The End of World War II and the Descent of the Iron Curtain

McMahon, Robert J., and Thomas G. Patterson, eds. *The Origins of the Cold War*. Lexington, MA: Heath, 1991.

Mee, Charles L. *Meeting at Potsdam*. New York: Evans, 1975.

Thomas, Hugh. *Armed Truce: The Beginnings of the Cold War, 1945-46*. London: H. Hamilton, 1986.

Yergin, Daniel. *Shattered Peace: The Origins of the Cold War*. New York: Penguin, 1990.

The Marshall Plan and the Berlin Airlift

Acheson, Dean. *Present at the Creation: My Years at the State Department*. New York: Norton, 1969.

McCullough, David. *Truman*. New York: Simon and Schuster, 1993.

Mee, Charles L., Jr. *The Marshall Plan*. New York: Simon and Schuster, 1984.

Miller, Roger G. *To Save a City: The Berlin Airlift, 1948-1949*. College Station, TX: Texas A&M University Press, 2000.

Milward, Alan. *The Reconstruction of Western Europe, 1945-1951*. Berkeley: University of California Press, 1984.

Tusa, Ann, and John Tusa. *The Berlin Blockade*. London: Hodder and Stoughton, 1988.

The Korean War

Blair, Clay. *The Forgotten War: America in Korea, 1950-1953*. Annapolis, MD: Naval Institute Press, 1987.

Chen Jian. *China's Road to the Korean War: The Making of the Sino-American Confrontation*. New York: Columbia University Press, 1994.

Goldstein, Donald M., and Harry J. Maihafer. *The Korean War*. Washington, DC: Brassey's, 2000.

"Korea+50: No Longer Forgotten." Truman Presidential Museum and Library. 2003. Online at www.trumanlibrary.org/korea/index.html.

Ridgway, Matthew B. *The Korean War*. Garden City, NY: Doubleday, 1967.

Tomedi, Rudi. *No Bugles, No Drums: An Oral History of the Korean War*. New York: Viking, 1976.

Truman, Harry S. *Memoirs*. 2 vols. Garden City, NY: Doubleday, 1955-1956.

McCarthyism and the "Red Menace"

Fariello, Griffin. *Red Scare: Memories of the American Inquisition: An Oral History*. New York: Norton, 1995.

Fried, Albert. *McCarthyism: The Great American Scare: A Documentary History*. New York: Oxford University Press, 1996.

Fried, Richard M. *Nightmare in Red: The McCarthy Era in Perspective*. New York: Oxford University Press, 1991.

Herman, Arthur. *Joseph McCarthy: Reexamining the Life and Legacy of America's Most Hated Senator*. New York: Free Press, 1999.

Morgan, Ted. *Reds: McCarthyism in Twentieth-Century America*. New York: Random House, 2003.

Radosh, Ronald, and Joyce Milton. *The Rosenberg File*. 2d ed. Yale University Press, 1997.

Schrecker, Ellen. *Many are the Crimes: McCarthyism in America*. Boston: Little, Brown, 1998.

Whitfield, Stephen J. *The Culture of the Cold War*. Baltimore: Johns Hopkins University Press, 1990.

Behind the Curtain

Keep, John L. *Last of the Empires: A History of the Soviet Union, 1945-1991*. New York: Oxford University Press, 1995.

Khrushchev, Nikita. *Khrushchev Remembers*. Edited and translated by Strobe Talbott. Boston: Little, Brown, 1970.

Service, Robert. *A History of Twentieth-Century Russia*. Cambridge, MA: Harvard University Press, 1998.

Smith, Hedrick. *The Russians*. New York: Quadrangle/New York Times Books, 1976.

Solzhenitsyn, Aleksandr I. *The Gulag Archipelago, 1918-1956*. New York: Harper & Row, 1985.

Taubman, William. *Khrushchev: The Man and His Era*. New York: Norton, 2003.

Zubok, Vladislav, and Constantine Pleshakov. *Inside the Kremlin's Cold War: From Stalin to Khrushchev*. Harvard University Press, 1996.

The Cold War Heats Up

Ambrose, Stephen E. *Eisenhower*. 2 vols. New York: Simon and Schuster, 1983-84.

Andrew, Christopher, and Oleg Gordievsky. *KGB: The Inside Story of Its Foreign Operations from Lenin to Gorbachev*. New York: HarperCollins, 1990.

Divine, Robert A. *Eisenhower and the Cold War*. New York: Oxford University Press, 1981.

Divine, Robert A. *The Sputnik Challenge: Eisenhower's Response to the Soviet Satellite*. New York: Oxford University Press, 1993.

Gelb, Norman. *The Berlin Wall: Kennedy, Khrushchev and a Showdown in the Heart of Europe*. New York: Simon and Schuster, 1986.

Karabell, Zachary. *Architects of Intervention: The United States, the Third World, and the Cold War, 1946-1962*. Lousiana State University Press, 1999.

Kennan, George F. *Memoirs: 1925-50*. Boston: Little, Brown, 1967.

Taubman, William. *Khrushchev: The Man and His Era*. New York: Norton, 2003.

Whitfield, Stephen J. *The Culture of the Cold War*. Baltimore: Johns Hopkins, 1996.

Wyden, Peter. *Wall: The Inside Story of Divided Berlin*. New York: Simon and Schuster, 1989.

Mutual Assured Destruction

Beschloss, Michael R. *The Crisis Years: Kennedy and Khrushchev, 1960-1963*. New York: HarperCollins, 1991.

Freedman, Lawrence. *Kennedy's Wars: Berlin, Cuba, Laos, and Vietnam*. New York: Oxford University Press, 2000.

Laird, Robbin F. *The Soviet Union, the West, and the Nuclear Arms Race*. New York: New York University Press, 1986.

Powaski, Ronald E. *March to Armageddon: The United States and the Nuclear Arms Race, 1939 to the Present*. New York: Oxford University Press, 1987.

Rhodes, Richard. *Dark Sun: The Making of the Hydrogen Bomb*. New York: Simon and Schuster, 1995.

The Bay of Pigs and the Cuban Missile Crisis

Acheson, Dean. "Homage to Plain Dumb Luck." *Esquire*, February 1969.

Frankel, Max. *High Noon in the Cold War: Kennedy, Khrushchev, and the Cuban Missile Crisis*. Presidio, 2004.

Fursenko, Aleksandr, and Timothy Naftali. *"One Hell of a Gamble": Khrushchev, Castro, and Kennedy, 1958-1964*. New York: Norton, 1997.

Kennedy, Robert F. *Thirteen Days: A Memoir of the Cuban Missile Crisis*. New York: Norton, 1971.

Sorensen, Theodore. *Kennedy*. New York: Harper and Row, 1965.

The Vietnam War

Appy, Christian G. *Patriots: The Vietnam War Remembered from All Sides*. New York: Viking, 2003.

FitzGerald, Frances. *Fire in the Lake: The Vietnamese and the Americans in Vietnam*. Boston: Little, Brown, 1972.

Gardner, Lloyd C. *Pay any Price: Lyndon Johnson and the Wars of Vietnam*. Ivan R. Dee, 1995.

Halberstam, David. *The Best and the Brightest*. New York: Random House, 1972.

Hendrickson, Paul. *The Living and the Dead: Robert McNamara and Five Lives of a Lost War*. New York: Alfred A. Knopf, 1996.

Karnow, Stanley. *Vietnam: A History*. New York: Viking Press, 1983.

Maclear, Michael. *The Ten Thousand Day War: Vietnam, 1945-1975*. New York: St. Martin's Press, 1981.

McNamara, Robert. *In Retrospect: The Tragedy and Lessons of Vietnam*. New York: Random House, 1995.

Sheehan, Neil. *A Bright, Shining Lie: John Paul Vann and America in Vietnam*. New York: Random House, 1988.

Wells, Tom. *The War Within: America's Battle over Vietnam*. Berkeley: University of California Press, 1994.

Détente and "The China Card"

Jian, Chen. *Mao's China and the Cold War*. Chapel Hill, NC: University of North Carolina Press, 2001.

Garthoff, Raymond L. *Détente and Confrontation: American-Soviet Relations from Nixon to Reagan*. Washington, DC: Brookings Institution, 1994.

Kissinger, Henry. *White House Years*. Boston: Little, Brown, 1979.

Mann, James. *About Face: A History of America's Curious Relationship with China, from Nixon to Clinton*. New York: Knopf, 1998.

Proxy Wars

Buckley, Tom. *Violent Neighbors: El Salvador, Central America, and the United States*. New York: Times Books, 1984.

Cockburn, Leslie. *Out of Control: The Story of the Reagan Administration's Secret War in Nicaragua, the Illegal Arms Pipeline, and the Contra Drug Connection*. New York: Atlantic Monthly Press, 1987.

Gettleman, Marvin E. *El Salvador: Central America in the Cold War*. New York: Grove, 1987.

Kornbluh, Peter. *Nicaragua: The Price of Intervention: Reagan's War Against the Sandinistas*. Washington, DC: Institute for Policy Studies, 1987.

Kornbluh, Peter, ed. *The Pinochet File*. New York: New Press, 2003.

Rodman, Peter. *More Precious than Peace: Fighting and Winning the Cold War in the Third World*. New York: Scribner, 1994.

Reagan and Gorbachev: From Star Wars to Perestroika

Cannon, Lou. *President Reagan: The Role of a Lifetime*. New York: Simon and Schuster, 1991.

Cordovez, Diego, and Selig S. Harrison. *Out of Afghanistan: The Inside Story of the Soviet Withdrawal*. New York: Oxford University Press, 1995.

FitzGerald, Frances. *Way Out There in the Blue: Reagan, Star Wars, and the End of the Cold War*. New York: Simon and Schuster, 2000.

Gorbachev, Mikhail. *Memoirs*. New York: Doubleday, 1996.

Gorbachev, Mikhail. *Perestroika*. London, 1987.

Matlock, Jack F., Jr. *Reagan and Gorbachev: How the Cold War Ended*. New York: Random House, 2004.

National Review. *Tear Down This Wall: The Reagan Revolution*. Washington, DC: National Review, 2004.

Oberdorfer, Don. *From the Cold War to a New Era: The United States and the Soviet Union, 1983-1991*. Baltimore: Johns Hopkins University Press, 1998.

Schultz, George. *Turmoil and Triumph: My Years as Secretary of State*. New York: Scribner, 1993.

The Collapse of the Soviet Empire

Ash, Timothy Garton. *The Magic Lantern: The Revolution of '89 Witnessed in Warsaw, Budapest, Berlin, and Prague*. New York: Random House, 1990.

Beschloss, Michael R., and Strobe Talbott. *At the Highest Levels: The Inside Story of the End of the Cold War*. Boston: Little, Brown, 1993.

Brown, Archie. *The Gorbachev Factor*. New York: Oxford University Press, 1996.

Jones, David-Pryce. *The Strange Death of the Soviet Empire*. New York: Henry Holt, 1995.

Remnick, David. *Lenin's Tomb: The Last Days of the Soviet Empire*. Random House, 1993.

Schultz, George P. *Turmoil and Triumph: My Years as Secretary of State*. New York: Scribner, 1993.

Russia and the World in the Post-Cold War Era

Baker, Peter, and Susan Glasser. *Kremlin Rising: Vladimir Putin's Russia and the End of Revolution*. New York: Scribner, 2005.

Bissell, Tom. *Chasing the Sea*. New York: Vintage Departures, 2003.

Brown, Archie, and Lillia Shevtosa, eds. *Gorbachev, Yeltsin, and Putin: Political Leadership in Russia's Transition*. New York: Carnegie Endowment for International Peace, 2001.

Gorbachev, Mikhail. *On My Country and the World*. New York: Columbia University Press, 2000.

Hoffman, Eva. *Exit into History: A Journey Through the New Eastern Europe*. New York: Viking, 1994.

Shevtosa, Lilia. *Yeltsin's Russia: Myths and Reality*. New York: Carnegie Endowment for International Peace, 1998.

INDEX